1,001 BEST

LOW-FAT

RECIPES

EDITED BY

SUE SPITLER

WITH LINDA R. YOAKAM, R.D.,M.S.

SURREY BOOKS

CHICAGO

Surrey Books is an imprint of Agate Publishing, Inc.
Art direction, book design, and typesetting: Joan Sommers Design, Chicago
Nutritional analyses: Linda R. Yoakam, R.D., M.S.

Printed in Canada.

Library of Congress Cataloging-in-Publication Data
    1,001 best low-fat recipes : the quickest, easiest, healthiest, tastiest, best low-fat collection ever edited by / Sue Spitler, with Linda R. Yoakam.
    p. cm.
    Summary: "Over 1,000 low-fat recipes, from appetizers to desserts. Includes nutritional data and exchanges for all recipes, a menu-planner, and designation of quickly-prepared dishes"—Provided by publisher.
    Includes index.
    ISBN-13: 978-1-57284-087-4 (pbk.)
    ISBN-10: 1-57284-087-0 (pbk.)
    1. Low-fat diet—Recipes. I. Spitler, Sue. II. Yoakam, Linda R. III. Title: One thousand one best low-fat recipes. IV. Title: One thousand and one best low-fat recipes.
    RM237.7.A1834 2007
    641.5'6384—dc22

                                                                                      2007008537

12 11 10 09 08 07

10 9 8 7 6 5 4 3 2 1

Agate and Surrey books are available in bulk at discount prices. For more information, go to agatepublishing.com.

CONTENTS

ACKNOWLEDGMENTS

Many thanks to Perrin Davis, editor, for her dedication and amazing skill in editing and indexing this new book, and to Caroline Olson, editorial assistant, for handling all the behind-the-scenes details that are so important. Also a big thanks to art director Joan Sommers and Linda Yoakam, R.D., M.S. for their invaluable contributions. Publisher Doug Seibold's enthusiasm for this collection of the very best recipes is greatly appreciated.

INTRODUCTION

H EALTHFUL EATING IS NO LONGER just a trend; it's become a delicious lifestyle that everyone can enjoy. We all realize that a nutritious, low-fat diet does make a difference in how we feel and is important in maintaining optimum health. *1,001 Best Low-Fat Recipes* provides more than 1,001 of our very best low-fat, low-calorie recipes, flavorfully prepared with fresh and healthy ingredients, creatively seasoned, and presented in 15 chapters for your eating pleasure.

Recipes are easy to prepare, using readily available ingredients and requiring no special cooking skills or techniques. Keeping convenience in mind, many recipes can be prepared in advance and refrigerated or frozen. Every delicious recipe is appropriate for family dining or for casual entertaining.

Delicious snack munchies and party hors d' oeuvres found in this book include Garden Patch Pizza and Black Bean Hummus.

Fabulous soups like Bean Gazpacho and Hot Sour Soup can begin a meal or can be a satisfying main course.

Family favorites include Swedish Meatballs with Noodles, Crisp Oven-Fried Chicken, and Beef Stroganoff.

Beef Bourguignon, Steak au Poivre, and Tandoori Chicken with Orange Cilantro Rice are perfect recipes for festive entertaining.

For breakfast or brunch, Breakfast Burritos, Sweet Potato Hash with Poached Eggs, and Eggs Benedict are unbeatable.

Mediterranean Torta, Sausage Lasagne, Tamale Pie, and Autumn Pot Pie are some of the many casserole selections.

Wilted Spinach Salad, German Potato Salad, and Wheat Berry Waldorf are a few of the many tempting salads you and your family will enjoy.

Corn Pudding, Creamy Potato and Bean Mashers, and Green Bean Casserole are a few of the side dishes that will round out any menu.

Freshly baked and fragrant Focaccia, Garlic Bread, and Multigrain Batter Bread will complement any meal.

Delicious, rich-tasting desserts, such as Flourless Chocolate Cake, Carrot Cake with Cream Cheese Frosting, Pecan Crunch Tart, and Sugared Lemon Squares, will satisfy every sweet craving.

Recipe preparation has been designed to be as streamlined as possible to accommodate busy lifestyles. In fact, more than 520 of the recipes can be prepared in 45 minutes or less! For easy identification, these recipes will have this symbol: **45** If the recipe requires baking, refrigeration, or freezing in addition to the preparation time, the symbols and will also appear. To prepare the designated recipes in 45 minutes, you'll want to assemble ingredients and equipment and read through the recipe to plan your preparation strategy. For example, you'll want to begin cooking pasta first and prepare other ingredients while pasta is cooking. Or, you'll start a pizza dough and proceed with the rest of the pizza's recipe while the dough is rising. To aid in strategy planning, many recipes include a 45 Minute Preparation Tip, located at the end of the recipe.

As many people are vegetarian or are choosing to include meatless meals in their lifestyle, recipes are coded as follows so you can quickly tell which are vegan, lacto-ovo vegetarian, lacto vegetarian, or ovo vegetarian.

V (vegan)—Recipes contain only plant-based food, with no dairy products or eggs.

LO (lacto-ovo vegetarian)—Recipes contain dairy products and eggs.

L (lacto vegetarian)—Recipes contain dairy products, but no eggs.

O (ovo vegetarian)—Recipes contain eggs, but no dairy products.

NUTRITIONAL INFORMATION

These healthful recipes were created by using the high-quality, low-fat food products available today. Low-fat chicken breast, beef eye of round, and pork tenderloin are used instead of higher-fat cuts of meat and poultry. The many excellent fat-free and reduced-fat dairy products such as fat-free and low-fat milk, cheese, yogurt, sour cream, and whipped topping are substituted for their full-fat counterparts. Egg whites and egg substitute often replace whole eggs. Fat-free, reduced sodium broths are used. Herbs and spices enhance flavors without adding fat. Also, foods are cooked using healthful cooking methods such as baking, broiling, and poaching.

In accordance with American Heart Association guidelines, very few recipes in this book exceed 30 percent calories from fat, and almost all adhere to the following nutritional criteria:

Type of Recipe Maximum Amounts per Serving

	Calories	Cholesterol (mg)	Sodium (mg)
Soups, First Courses	200	50	600
Main-Dish Soups, Entrées, Salads, Sandwiches	400	100	800
Main-Dish Meals (including pasta, rice, grains)	500	125	800
Main-Dish Eggs, Cheese	400	450	800
Side-Dish Salads, Pasta, Grains, Vegetables	200	50	600
Sauces, Condiments	200	25	600
Breads	200	50	600
Desserts	350	90	600

Specific nutritional information is provided for each recipe (not including variations) in this book, but remember that nutritional data are not always infallible. The nutritional analyses are derived with computer software that is highly regarded by nutritionists and dietitians, but they intended as guidelines only. The figures are based on actual laboratory values of ingredients, so results may vary slightly depending upon the brand or manufacturer of an ingredient that are used.

Ingredients noted as "optional," "to taste," or "as garnish" are not included in the nutritional analyses. When alternate choices or amounts of ingredients are given, the ingredient and amount listed first are used for analysis. Similarly, where a range is given, data is based on the first number of servings shown. Nutritional analyses are also based on the reduced-fat cooking methods used; the addition of margarine, oil, or other ingredients to the recipes will invalidate the data.

Other factors that can affect the accuracy of nutritional data include variability in sizes, weights, and measures of fruits, vegetables, and other foods. There is also a possible 20 percent error factor in the nutritional labeling of prepared foods.

If you have any health problems that require strict dietary require-
ments, it is important to consult a physician, dietitian, or nutritionist
before using recipes in this or any other cookbook. Also, if you are a
diabetic or require a diet that restricts calories, fat, or sodium, remember
that the nutritional data may be accurate for the recipe as written, but not
for the food you cooked due to the variables explained above.

INGREDIENT INFORMATION

ALL THE INGREDIENTS in this book are readily available in supermarkets and health food stores. Following is helpful information on some of the ingredients we've used, with explanations of those you may not be very familiar with.

Bead Molasses — Used mostly in Asian recipes, bead molasses is very dark and thick with an intense flavor. Like other molasses products, it is refined from the concentrated juice of sun-ripened sugar cane. It is readily available in Asian sections of supermarkets; other molasses products can be substituted.

Butter — Butter is suggested as an alternate for margarine, except in vegan recipes, for its lower trans-fat content and improved flavor.

Chili Oil — As the name implies, this oil is *hot!* Use sparingly. The oil is found in the Asian section of supermarkets; store it at room temperature.

Cream Cheese — The block-type of reduced-fat and fat-free cream cheese is used in the recipes; the tub-type is much softer in texture and does not always work the same in recipes. If substituting fat-free cream cheese in your favorite recipes for dips, use the block type and add any liquid ingredients gradually, as the cream cheese thins much more quickly than full-fat or reduced-fat cream cheese. Fat-free cream cheese can be used to make cake glaze but not frosting, as it thins with the addition of powdered sugar and cannot be thickened.

Cooking sprays — Vegetable and olive oil cooking sprays are used to greatly reduce the amounts of oil or fat needed in recipes. When a recipe calls for "sautéing in a lightly greased skillet", spray the skillet lightly with cooking spray or wipe the pan with a lightly oiled paper towel.

Fillo Pastry — These paper-thin pastry sheets are found in the freezer section of supermarkets or in Mediterranean groceries; store them in the freezer. Before using, thaw the entire package of fillo overnight in the refrigerator, or for several hours at room temperature. After removing fillo from the package, always cover the unused sheets with a damp cloth to keep them soft, as they become dry and brittle very quickly. Unused fillo can be rolled or folded, sealed in plastic wrap, and refrozen.

Herbs and Spices — In most recipes, dried herbs are called for. Fresh herbs may be substituted by using two to three times as much as indicated for the dried version.

Margarine — Use an all-vegetable product. Use regular rather than diet margarine and be sure to shop for one of the new trans-fat free varieties.

Olive Oil — As we have kept the use of oil to a minimum, we prefer using virgin olive oil to take advantage of its more intense flavor. Canola oil can be substituted, if desired.

Pasta and Rice — When dried and uncooked pasta or rice are called for, the ingredient will read: "8 ounces spaghetti (or rice), cooked." When a cooked pasta or rice is called for, the ingredient will read: "12 ounces cooked spaghetti (or rice)." When dry pasta is called for, it is always egg-free and can be used in vegan dishes. Fresh or refrigerated pasta such as ravioli, tortellini, wontons, and some flat noodles do contain eggs.

Roasted Garlic — See Roasted Garlic and Three-Cheese Spread, Step 1 (p. 5) for directions on roasting garlic. We suggest roasting several heads at a time to keep extra on hand for your favorite recipes. Roasted garlic can be refrigerated, wrapped in plastic wrap, up to 2 weeks. Purchased chopped roasted garlic can be used for convenience, but the flavor is less robust.

Sesame Oil — We prefer Asian sesame oil in recipes, as this dark oil has an intense sesame flavor; it can be purchased in ethnic sections of supermarkets. There is also a light-colored sesame oil that can be found in the vegetable oil section of the supermarket; it can be substituted, but the sesame flavor is extremely subtle. Store at room temperature.

Shortening — The manufacturing process of shortening usually creates trans-fats; shop carefully for one of the new trans-fat free brands.

Tahini Paste — This flavorful paste is made with ground toasted sesame seeds and is used in Greek hummus and other Mediterranean dishes. See our recipes for Black Bean Hummus and Sun-Dried Tomato Hummus (pp. 5, 4). Store in the refrigerator.

Tamari Soy Sauce — This highly flavored soy sauce is naturally brewed and is made without sugar. It is available in regular or low-sodium brands in Asian sections of supermarkets. Other soy sauce products can be substituted. Store in the refrigerator.

Check your local grocery periodically for new convenience food items. Literally hundreds of fresh, frozen, canned, and packaged new food products find their way to grocery shelves each year. An occasional visit to a gourmet store may garner specialty items to keep in your pantry or freezer for interesting menu additions.

ONE

Appetizers, Snacks,
and
Beverages

BAKED ARTICHOKE DIP

LO *Everyone's favorite, modified for healthful, low-fat goodness.*

45 **16 servings** (about 3 tablespoons each)

1 can (15 ounces) artichoke hearts, rinsed, drained
4 ounces fat-free cream cheese, room temperature
½ cup each: grated fat-free Parmesan cheese, fat-free
   mayonnaise, fat-free sour cream
1–2 teaspoons lemon juice
1 green onion, thinly sliced
2 teaspoons minced garlic
2–3 drops red pepper sauce
Salt and cayenne pepper, to taste
Dippers: assorted vegetables, bread sticks, or crackers

Per Serving:
Calories: 39
% of calories from fat: 2
Fat (gm): 0.1
Saturated fat (gm): 0
Cholesterol (mg): 0
Sodium (mg): 190
Protein (gm): 3.5
Carbohydrate (gm): 6.8

Exchanges:
Milk: 0.0
Vegetable: 1.5
Fruit: 0.0
Bread: 0.0
Meat: 0.0
Fat: 0.0

1. Process artichoke hearts, cream cheese, Parmesan cheese,
mayonnaise, sour cream, and lemon juice in food processor until
smooth. Stir in green onion, garlic, and red pepper sauce. Season
to taste with salt and cayenne pepper. Bake in small casserole,
uncovered, at 350 degrees until lightly browned, 20 to 25 minutes.
Serve warm with dippers (not included in nutritional data).

CURRY DIP

LO *Raw sweet potato slices and broccoli florets are particularly good with this dip.*

45 **12 servings** (about 2 tablespoons each)

1½ cups fat-free mayonnaise
½ cup fat-free sour cream
¼ cup thinly sliced green onions
1½–2 teaspoons each: prepared horseradish,
   curry powder
2–3 teaspoons sugar
2–4 teaspoons lemon juice
Salt and white pepper, to taste
Dippers: assorted vegetable relishes, Pita Chips
   (see p. 496)

Per Serving:
Calories: 34
% of calories from fat: 1
Fat (gm): 0
Saturated fat (gm): 0
Cholesterol (mg): 0
Sodium (mg): 393
Protein (gm): 0.7
Carbohydrate (gm): 8

Exchanges:
Milk: 0.0
Vegetable: 0.0
Fruit: 0.0
Bread: 0.5
Meat: 0.0
Fat: 0.0

1. Mix mayonnaise, sour cream, green onions, horseradish, curry powder, and sugar. Season to taste with lemon juice, salt, and white pepper. Refrigerate several hours for flavors to blend. Serve with dippers (not included in nutritional data).

TOASTED ONION DIP

45 *This dip brings back memories of the popular dip made with onion soup mix! Toasting the dried onion flakes is the flavor secret.*

12 servings (about 2 tablespoons each)

3–4 tablespoons dried onion flakes

8 ounces fat-free cream cheese, room temperature

⅓ cup each: reduced-fat plain yogurt, fat-free
  mayonnaise

2 small green onions, chopped

2 cloves garlic, minced

¼ teaspoon crushed vegetable bouillon cube

2–3 tablespoons fat-free milk

½–1 teaspoon lemon juice

2–3 drops red pepper sauce

Salt and white pepper, to taste

Dippers: assorted vegetable relishes and bread sticks

Per Serving:
Calories: 32
% of calories from fat: 4
Fat (gm): 0.1
Saturated fat (gm): 0.1
Cholesterol (mg): 0.4
Sodium (mg): 223
Protein (gm): 3.3
Carbohydrate (gm): 3.9

Exchanges:
Milk: 0.0
Vegetable: 0.0
Fruit: 0.0
Bread: 0.0
Meat: 0.5
Fat: 0.0

1. Cook onion flakes in small skillet over medium to medium-low heat until toasted, 3 to 4 minutes, stirring frequently; remove from heat. Mix cream cheese, yogurt, mayonnaise, green onions, garlic, and bouillon in medium bowl until smooth, adding enough milk to make desired dipping consistency. Stir in onions; season to taste with lemon juice, pepper sauce, salt, and white pepper. Serve with dippers (not included in nutritional data).

SUN-DRIED TOMATO HUMMUS

L

Sun-dried tomatoes and herbs embellish this Mediterranean favorite.

45
❄

8 servings (about ¼ cup each)

1 can (15 ounces) chick peas, rinsed, drained
⅓ cup fat-free yogurt
2–3 tablespoons tahini (sesame seed paste)
3 cloves garlic
4 sun-dried tomato halves (not in oil), softened,
   finely chopped
1 teaspoon each: dried oregano and mint leaves
2–3 teaspoons lemon juice
Salt and white pepper, to taste
Dippers: pita breads, cut into wedges, or Pita Chips
   (see p. 496)

Per Serving:
Calories: 73
% of calories from fat: 21
Fat (gm): 1.7
Saturated fat (gm): 0.2
Cholesterol (mg): 0.2
Sodium (mg): 256
Protein (gm): 3.6
Carbohydrate (gm): 11.4

Exchanges:
Milk: 0.0
Vegetable: 0.0
Fruit: 0.0
Bread: 1.0
Meat: 0.0
Fat: 0.0

1. Process chick peas, yogurt, tahini, and garlic in food processor until smooth. Stir in sun-dried tomatoes and herbs; season to taste with lemon juice, salt, and white pepper. Refrigerate 1 to 2 hours for flavors to blend. Serve with dippers (not included in nutritional data).

VARIATION

Parthenon Platter — Make hummus as above and spoon into a 6-inch flattened mound on serving platter. Combine 4 chopped canned artichoke hearts, ⅓ cup each halved grape tomatoes, crumbled fat-free feta cheese, and julienned sliced salami, 6 sliced Greek olives, 2 tablespoons olive oil, and ¾ teaspoon dried Italian seasoning; toss and spoon over hummus. Garnish plate with pepperoncini and serve with Pita Chips (see p. 496).

BLACK BEAN HUMMUS

Tahini (ground sesame paste) and soy sauce season this unusual bean dip.

6 servings (about ¼ cup each)

1 can (15 ounces) black beans, rinsed, drained
¼ cup reduced-sodium vegetable broth or water
2–3 tablespoons tahini
3 cloves garlic
2–2½ tablespoons lemon juice
1½ tablespoons soy sauce
Salt and cayenne pepper, to taste
Pita Chips (recipe follows) or pita breads, cut
    into wedges

Per Serving:
Calories: 178
% of calories from fat: 17
Fat (gm): 3.5
Saturated fat (gm): 0.5
Cholesterol (mg): 0
Sodium (mg): 668
Protein (gm): 7.8
Carbohydrate (gm): 30.2

Exchanges:
Milk: 0.0
Vegetable: 0.0
Fruit: 0.0
Bread: 2.0
Meat: 0.0
Fat: 0.5

1. Process beans, broth, tahini, garlic, lemon juice, and soy sauce in food processor until smooth; season to taste with salt and cayenne pepper. Refrigerate 1 to 2 hours for flavors to blend. Serve with Pita Chips (see p. 496).

ROASTED GARLIC AND HERB CANNELLINI DIP

Another good-for-you dip that tastes terrific! Italian cannellini beans are white kidney beans that are similar in flavor and appearance to navy or Great Northern beans.

6 servings (about ¼ cup each)

1 can (15 ounces) cannellini or Great Northern
    beans, rinsed, drained
1 teaspoon minced roasted garlic
1 tablespoon each: olive oil, prepared horseradish
2 tablespoons minced chives
½ teaspoon each: dried oregano and basil leaves
2–3 drops hot pepper sauce
2–3 teaspoons lemon juice
Salt and white pepper, to taste
Dippers: Pita Chips (see p. 496) and
    assorted vegetables

Per Serving:
Calories: 75
% of calories from fat: 25
Fat (gm): 2.8
Saturated fat (gm): 0.3
Cholesterol (mg): 0
Sodium (mg): 167
Protein (gm): 5.3
Carbohydrate (gm): 13.1

Exchanges:
Milk: 0.0
Vegetable: 0.0
Fruit: 0.0
Bread: 1.0
Meat: 0.0
Fat: 0.5

1. Process beans, garlic, olive oil, and horseradish in food processor until smooth. Mix in chives, herbs, and hot pepper sauce. Season to taste with lemon juice, salt, and white pepper. Refrigerate 1 to 2 hours for flavors to blend. Serve with dippers (not included in nutritional data).

BLACK BEAN DIP WITH BAKED TORTILLA CHIPS

L

Nutritious black beans are a great source of folate.

45   **12 servings** (about 2 tablespoons each)

½ cup thinly sliced green onions

1–2 cloves garlic, minced

1 can (15 ounces) black beans, rinsed, drained

¾ cup (3 ounces) shredded reduced-fat
    Cheddar cheese

¼ teaspoon salt

⅓ cup vegetable broth or water

1–2 tablespoons finely chopped cilantro

Baked Tortilla Chips (recipe follows)

Per Serving:
Calories: 48
% of calories from fat: 21
Fat (gm): 3.8
Saturated fat (gm): 0.5
Cholesterol (mg): 3.8
Sodium (mg): 254
Protein (gm): 4.5
Carbohydrate (gm): 7

Exchanges:
Milk: 0.0
Vegetable: 0.0
Fruit: 0.0
Bread: 0.5
Meat: 0.0
Fat: 0.5

1. Sauté onions and garlic in lightly greased skillet until tender, about 3 minutes.

2. Process black beans, cheese, and salt in food processor or blender until almost smooth, adding enough broth to make desired dipping consistency. Mix in onion mixture and cilantro. Serve with Baked Tortilla Chips.

Baked Tortilla Chips

6 flour or corn tortillas (6-inch), each cut into 8 wedges
Vegetable cooking spray
Salt, to taste

1. Arrange tortilla strips on cookie sheet; spray lightly with cooking spray and toss. Bake at 375 degrees until browned, about 10 minutes, stirring occasionally.

PINTO BEAN AND AVOCADO DIP

Avocado and tomato brighten this well-flavored bean dip. Increase the amount of jalapeño chili if you dare!

12 servings (about 2 tablespoons each)

1 can (15 ounces) pinto beans, rinsed, drained
¾ cup finely chopped onion
2 cloves garlic, minced
½ jalapeño chili, minced
3 tablespoons finely chopped cilantro
1 large tomato, chopped
½ medium avocado, chopped
Salt and pepper, to taste
Baked tortilla chips

Per Serving:
Calories: 50
% of calories from fat: 25
Fat (gm): 1.4
Saturated fat (gm): 0.2
Cholesterol (mg): 0.0
Sodium (mg): 114
Protein (gm): 2.1
Carbohydrate (gm): 7.7

Exchanges:
Milk: 0.0
Vegetable: 0.0
Fruit: 0.0
Bread: 0.5
Meat: 0.0
Fat: 0.5

1. Process beans in food processor or blender until smooth; add onion, garlic, jalapeño chili, and cilantro and process until blended. Mix in tomato and avocado; season to taste with salt and pepper. Refrigerate 1 to 2 hours for flavors to blend. Serve with tortilla chips (not included in nutritional data).

CHILI CON QUESO

Our health-conscious version of this popular dip is made with reduced-fat pasteurized processed cheese for creamy texture and fat-free Cheddar cheese for accented flavor.

12 servings (about 2 tablespoons each)

5 medium anaheim or 2 medium poblano chilies, seeds and veins discarded, halved
⅓ cup each: chopped onion, tomato
½ teaspoon dried oregano leaves
2 cups (8 ounces) shredded reduced-fat pasteurized processed cheese
1 cup (4 ounces) shredded fat-free Cheddar cheese
2–4 tablespoons fat-free milk
Baked tortilla chips

Per Serving:
Calories: 72
% of calories from fat: 26
Fat (gm): 2.8
Saturated fat (gm): 1.8
Cholesterol (mg): 9.1
Sodium (mg): 412
Protein (gm): 7.4
Carbohydrate (gm): 5.7

Exchanges:
Milk: 0.0
Vegetable: 0.0
Fruit: 0.0;
Bread: 0.5
Meat: 1.0
Fat: 0.0

1. Place chilies, skin sides up, on baking pan. Broil 6 inches from heat source until chilies are browned and soft, 5 to 8 minutes. Cool and cut into strips.

2. Sauté onion, tomato, and oregano in lightly greased skillet until onion is tender, about 5 minutes. Add cheeses and chili strips; cook over low heat until cheeses are melted, stirring in milk for desired consistency. Serve warm with tortilla chips (not included in nutritional data).

QUESO FUNDIDO

The flavorful Chorizo recipe can be used to inspire many of your Mexican dishes. Any extra can be frozen for later use.

8 servings

¼ cup chopped red bell pepper

¾ cup (3 ounces) shredded fat-free Cheddar cheese

½ cup (2 ounces) cubed reduced-fat pasteurized
   processed cheese

¼–⅓ cup fat-free milk

8 corn tortillas (6-inch), warm

½ cup cooked, crumbled Chorizo (¼ recipe)
   (see p. 154)

2 tablespoons each: finely chopped green onion,
   finely chopped cilantro

Per Serving:
Calories: 112
% of calories from fat: 15
Fat (gm): 1.9
Saturated fat (gm): 0.7
Cholesterol (mg): 12.8
Sodium (mg): 274
Protein (gm): 8.7
Carbohydrate (gm): 15.2

Exchanges:
Milk: 0.0
Vegetable: 0.0
Fruit: 0.0
Bread: 1.0
Meat: 1.0
Fat: 0.0

1. Sauté bell pepper until tender in lightly greased skillet, 2 to 3 minutes. Add cheeses; cook over low heat until melted, stirring in milk for desired consistency. Spoon about 2 tablespoons cheese mixture in the center of each tortilla. Sprinkle with Chorizo, green onion, and cilantro, and roll up.

EGGPLANT CAVIAR

L

Middle Eastern flavors will tempt you to second helpings!

45

6 servings (about 2 tablespoons each)

1 large eggplant (1½ pounds)
½ cup chopped tomato
¼ cup finely chopped onion
3 cloves garlic, minced
¼ cup fat-free yogurt
2 teaspoons extra-virgin olive oil
½ teaspoon dried oregano leaves
1–2 tablespoons lemon juice
Salt and pepper, to taste
4 pitted ripe olives, chopped
Dippers: lavosh or pita bread wedges

Per Serving:
Calories: 59
% of calories from fat: 28
Fat (gm): 2.1
Saturated fat (gm): 0.3
Cholesterol (mg): 0.2
Sodium (mg): 19.1
Protein (gm): 1.8
Carbohydrate (gm): 10.1

Exchanges:
Milk: 0.0
Vegetable: 1.5
Fruit: 0.0
Bread: 0.0
Meat: 0.0
Fat: 0.5

1. Pierce eggplant in several places with fork; place in baking pan. Bake at 350 degrees until eggplant is soft, 45 to 50 minutes; cool. Cut eggplant in half; scoop out pulp with spoon. Mash eggplant and mix with tomato, onion, garlic, yogurt, olive oil, and oregano in bowl; season to taste with lemon juice, salt, and pepper. Garnish with olives. Refrigerate 3 to 4 hours for flavors to blend. Serve with dippers (not included in nutritional data).

EGGPLANT MARMALADE

V

A quick kitchen tip—gingerroot does not have to be peeled before using!

45

12 servings (about 3 tablespoons each)

2 medium eggplant (1¼ pounds each),
   unpeeled, cubed
⅓ cup coarsely chopped onion
2 tablespoons minced roasted garlic
3 tablespoons each: minced gingerroot, light
   brown sugar
1½ teaspoons fennel seeds, crushed
2 tablespoons red wine vinegar
2 teaspoons Asian sesame oil
⅓ cup golden raisins
⅓ cup reduced-sodium vegetable broth
2–3 tablespoons toasted pine nuts or slivered almonds
Whole wheat lavosh, or crackers

Per Serving:
Calories: 75
% of calories from fat: 21
Fat (gm): 1.9
Saturated fat (gm): 0.3
Cholesterol (mg): 0
Sodium (mg): 6
Protein (gm): 1.6
Carbohydrate (gm): 14.9

Exchanges:
Milk: 0.0
Vegetable: 2.0
Fruit: 0.5
Bread: 0.0
Meat: 0.0
Fat: 0.0

1. Combine eggplant, onion, garlic, gingerroot, brown sugar, and
fennel; toss with vinegar and oil and arrange in single layer on
greased, foil-lined jelly roll pan. Bake at 425 degrees until eggplant
is browned and wrinkled, about 1½ hours, stirring every 30 minutes.
Stir raisins and broth into mixture; bake until broth is absorbed, 10
to 15 minutes. Stir in pine nuts and cool. Refrigerate overnight for
flavors to blend. Serve with lavosh (not included in nutritional data).

CHUTNEY CHEESE SPREAD

L

*Enjoy these flavors inspired by India. Ginger contributes "heat" as well as
flavor to the spread, so adjust according to your taste. Make Pita Chips with
curry powder or ground cumin.*

45

8 servings (about 2 tablespoons each)

8 ounces fat-free cream cheese, room temperature
1 cup (4 ounces) shredded reduced-fat Cheddar cheese
½ cup chopped mango chutney, divided
¼ cup finely chopped onion

2 tablespoons raisins, chopped

1–2 teaspoons each: finely chopped gingerroot, garlic

½–1 teaspoon curry powder

1–2 tablespoons chopped dry-roasted cashews

Thinly sliced green onion tops, as garnish

Pita Chips (see p. 496) or assorted vegetables

Per Serving:
Calories: 116
% of calories from fat: 21
Fat (gm): 2.6
Saturated fat (gm): 1.1
Cholesterol (mg): 7.6
Sodium (mg): 367
Protein (gm): 7.4
Carbohydrate (gm): 14.6

Exchanges:
Milk: 0.0
Vegetable: 0.0
Fruit: 1.0
Bread: 0.0
Meat: 0.5
Fat: 0.5

1. Mix cheeses, 2 tablespoons chutney, onion, raisins, gingerroot, garlic, and curry powder until blended (do not beat, or fat-free cream cheese will become thin in texture). Refrigerate 1 to 2 hours for flavors to blend.

2. Mound spread on plate; spoon remaining 6 tablespoons chutney over or around spread. Sprinkle with cashews and onion tops; serve with Pita Chips (see p. 496) (not included in nutritional data).

ROASTED GARLIC AND THREE-CHEESE SPREAD

L

For best flavor, make this dip a day in advance.

45
❄

12 servings (about 2 tablespoons each)

1 small bulb garlic

Olive oil cooking spray

8 ounces fat-free cream cheese, room temperature

1½–2 ounces goat cheese

¼ cup (2 ounces) grated fat-free Parmesan cheese

⅛ teaspoon white pepper

2–4 tablespoons fat-free milk

Vegetable relishes and assorted crackers

Per Serving:
Calories: 43
% of calories from fat: 28
Fat (gm): 1.3
Saturated fat (gm): 0.9
Cholesterol (mg): 3.8
Sodium (mg): 142
Protein (gm): 4.7
Carbohydrate (gm): 2.5

Exchanges:
Milk: 0.0
Vegetable: 0.0
Fruit: 0.0
Bread: 0.0
Meat: 0.5
Fat: 0.5

1. Cut off top of garlic bulb to expose cloves. Spray garlic lightly with cooking spray and wrap in aluminum foil; bake at 400 degrees until very tender, 35 to 40 minutes. Cool; gently press cloves to remove from skins. Mash cloves with fork.

2. Mix cheeses, garlic, and white pepper in bowl, adding enough milk to make desired spreading consistency. Refrigerate 2 to 3 hours for flavors to blend. Serve with relishes and crackers (not included in nutritional data).

PEPPER-ONION RELISH AND CREAM CHEESE

L

Pepper-Onion Relish can be made and refrigerated 4 to 5 days in advance.

45

6 servings

1 cup each: thinly sliced red and yellow bell pepper, onion
2 teaspoons minced jalapeño chili
1½ tablespoons olive oil
¼ cup packed light brown sugar
¼ cup each: cider vinegar, water
8 ounces fat-free cream cheese, room temperature
Assorted crackers

Per Serving:
Calories: 129
% of calories from fat: 27
Fat (gm): 4.1
Saturated fat (gm): 0.8
Cholesterol (mg): 3
Sodium (mg): 212
Protein (gm): 6.3
Carbohydrate (gm): 18

Exchanges:
Milk: 0.0
Vegetable: 0.0
Fruit: 0.0
Bread: 1.0
Meat: 0.0
Fat: 1.0

1. Sauté bell pepper, onion and jalapeño chili in oil in large skillet until softened, 6 to 8 minutes. Stir in brown sugar, vinegar, and water and simmer, covered, over medium heat until very tender, about 5 minutes. Simmer, uncovered, until mixture is glazed and thickened, about 5 minutes; cool. Place cream cheese on serving plate and spoon pepper mixture over. Serve with crackers (not included in nutritional data).

CRANBERRY-PISTACHIO CREAM CHEESE

Substitute dried cherries or blueberries for the cranberries, or combine all three!

6 servings

¼ cup thinly sliced onion
⅓ cup each: dried cranberries, chopped pistachios, apricot preserves, orange juice
8 ounces fat-free cream cheese, room temperature
Crusty bread or assorted crackers

Per Serving:
Calories: 145
% of calories from fat: 22
Fat (gm): 3.6
Saturated fat (gm): 0.8
Cholesterol (mg): 3
Sodium (mg): 271
Protein (gm): 7.2
Carbohydrate (gm): 22

Exchanges:
Milk: 0.0
Vegetable: 0.0
Fruit: 0.0
Bread: 1.5
Meat: 0.0
Fat: 1.0

1. Sauté onion in lightly greased medium skillet until tender, 3 to 4 minutes. Add cranberries, pistachios, preserves, and orange juice; cook over medium heat until mixture is thickened, but spoonable. Cool. Place cream cheese on serving plate and spoon cranberry mixture over. Serve with bread or crackers(not included in nutritional data).

VARIATION

Raisin-Marmalade Cream Cheese — Make recipe above, substituting green onion for the onion, and raisins, pecans and orange marmalade for the cranberries, pistachios, and apricot preserves.

PINE NUT SPINACH PÂTÉ

L

Toasted pine nuts provide flavor and texture accents in this unique dip.

45

12 servings (about 2 tablespoons each)

1 package (10 ounces) frozen chopped spinach, thawed, well drained

¼ cup each: coarsely chopped onion, celery

1 clove garlic

2–3 teaspoons lemon juice

1 teaspoon dried dill weed

1–2 tablespoons toasted pine nuts or slivered almonds

4 ounces fat-free cream cheese, room temperature

Salt and pepper, to taste

Bruschetta (see p. 495)

Per Serving:
Calories: 19
% of calories from fat: 21
Fat (gm): 0.5
Saturated fat (gm): 0.1
Cholesterol (mg): 0
Sodium (mg): 73
Protein (gm): 2.1
Carbohydrate (gm): 1.9

Exchanges:
Milk: 0.0
Vegetable: 0.5
Fruit: 0.0
Bread: 0.0
Meat: 0.0
Fat: 0.0

1. Process spinach, onion, celery, garlic, lemon juice, and dill weed in food processor until almost smooth; add pine nuts and process until coarsely chopped. Stir in cream cheese; season to taste with salt and pepper. Refrigerate several hours for flavors to blend. Serve with Bruschetta (not included in nutritional data).

WILD MUSHROOM PÂTÉ

L

This pâté is most flavorful when made with wild mushrooms, though any type of mushrooms can be used.

45

8 servings (about 2 tablespoons each)

12 ounces coarsely chopped shiitake or portobello
   mushrooms

½ cup chopped onion

2–4 cloves garlic, minced

¼ cup dry sherry or water

2 tablespoons grated fat-free Parmesan cheese

2–3 teaspoons lemon juice

Salt and pepper, to taste

Crusty bread or crackers

Per Serving:
Calories: 42
% of calories from fat: 2
Fat (gm): 0.1
Saturated fat (gm): 0
Cholesterol (mg): 0
Sodium (mg): 14
Protein (gm): 1.4
Carbohydrate (gm): 8.4

Exchanges:
Milk: 0.0
Vegetable: 1.5
Fruit: 0.0
Bread: 0.0
Meat: 0.0
Fat: 0.0

1. Cook mushrooms, onion, garlic, and sherry in lightly greased skillet, covered, over medium heat until mushrooms are wilted, about 5 minutes. Cook, uncovered, over medium heat until vegetables are very tender and all liquid is gone, 8 to 10 minutes. Cool.

2. Process mushroom mixture and Parmesan cheese in food processor until smooth. Season to taste with lemon juice, salt, and pepper. Refrigerate 2 to 3 hours for flavors to blend. Serve in crock with bread or crackers (not included in nutritional data).

EDAMAME SNACKERS

V

What snack could be healthier or easier!?

45   8 servings

1 pound fresh or frozen edamame in the shell
Kosher salt, to taste

1. Simmer edamame in 2 quarts water in large saucepan, covered, until tender, 5 to 8 minutes; drain. Serve edamame warm or at room temperature, sprinkled lightly with salt.

Per Serving:
Calories: 38
% of calories from fat: 28
Fat (gm): 1.1
Saturated fat (gm): 0.2
Cholesterol (mg): 0.0
Sodium (mg): 5.7
Protein (gm): 3
Carbohydrate (gm): 3.4

Exchanges:
Milk: 0.0
Vegetable: 0.0
Fruit: 0.0
Bread: 0.5
Meat: 0.0
Fat: 0.0

JICAMA WITH LIME AND CILANTRO

V *Very simple, and incredibly tasty!*

45   4 servings

1 medium jicama, peeled, thinly sliced
Salt and lime juice, to taste
1–2 tablespoons finely chopped cilantro

1. Arrange jicama slices on large serving plate and sprinkle lightly with salt, lime juice, and cilantro.

Per Serving:
Calories: 17
% of calories from fat: 2
Fat (gm): 0
Saturated fat (gm): 0
Cholesterol (mg): 0
Sodium (mg): 0
Protein (gm): 0.5
Carbohydrate (gm): 3.8

Exchanges:
Milk: 0.0
Vegetable: 1.0
Fruit: 0.0
Bread: 0.0
Meat: 0.0
Fat: 0.0

SPINACH AND CHEESE MINI-QUICHES

L *The tiny fillo shells, delicious and wonderfully crisp, are available in the frozen food section of supermarkets. You can also make small pastries in mini-muffin cups using a favorite pie pastry.*

45

1½ dozen (1 per serving)

1¼ cups fat-free cottage cheese
¼ cup (1 ounce) grated fat-free Parmesan cheese
2 tablespoons each: fat-free milk, flour
½ cup finely chopped fresh spinach
½ teaspoon each: dried oregano and thyme leaves
Salt and white pepper, to taste
2 eggs
1½ dozen frozen mini-fillo shells, thawed

Per Mini-Quiche:
Calories: 48
% of calories from fat: 30
Fat (gm): 1.6
Saturated fat (gm): 0.2
Cholesterol (mg): 23.7
Sodium (mg): 61
Protein (gm): 3.9
Carbohydrate (gm): 4.3

Exchanges:
Milk: 0.0
Vegetable: 0.0
Fruit: 0.0
Bread: 0.5
Meat: 0.0
Fat: 0.5

1. Mix cheeses, milk, flour, spinach, and herbs; season to taste with salt and pepper. Stir in eggs. Spoon mixture into fillo shells on cookie sheet or in mini-muffin tins. Bake at 325 degrees until puffed and beginning to brown on the tops, about 20 minutes.

BAKED SPINACH BALLS

L

These savory baked treats are rich in flavor.

45

12 servings (2 each)

2 cups herb-seasoned bread stuffing cubes
¼ cup each: grated fat-free Parmesan cheese,
    chopped green onions
2 cloves garlic, minced
⅛ teaspoon ground nutmeg
1 package (10 ounces) frozen chopped spinach,
    thawed, well drained
¼–⅓ cup reduced-sodium vegetable broth
2 tablespoons margarine or butter, melted
Salt and pepper, to taste
1 egg, lightly beaten

Per Serving:
Calories: 86
% of calories from fat: 24
Fat (gm): 2.4
Saturated fat (gm): 0.4
Cholesterol (mg): 0
Sodium (mg): 271
Protein (gm): 4.2
Carbohydrate (gm): 13

Exchanges:
Milk: 0.0
Vegetable: 1.0
Fruit: 0.0
Bread: 0.5
Meat: 0.0
Fat: 0.5

1. Combine stuffing cubes, Parmesan cheese, green onions, garlic, and nutmeg in medium bowl. Mix in spinach, broth, and margarine; season to taste with salt and pepper. Mix in egg. Shape mixture into 24 balls. Bake at 350 degrees on greased jelly roll pan until spinach balls are browned, about 15 minutes.

CURRIED ONION CROUSTADES

L

The Croustades can be filled with the onion mixture and refrigerated several hours before baking.

8 servings (2 each)

2 cups chopped onions
2 cloves garlic, minced
1 teaspoon curry powder
½ teaspoon ground cumin
2 tablespoons flour
1 cup fat-free half-and-half or fat-free milk
2 tablespoons dried fruit bits
1 tablespoon minced cilantro
Salt, cayenne, and black pepper, to taste

Per Serving:
Calories: 125
% of calories from fat: 13
Fat (gm): 1.8
Saturated fat (gm): 0.3
Cholesterol (mg): 0
Sodium (mg): 167
Protein (gm): 4.2
Carbohydrate (gm): 22.3

Exchanges:
Milk: 0.0
Vegetable: 1.0
Fruit: 0.0
Bread: 1.0
Meat: 0.0
Fat: 0.5

Croustades (see p. 496)
4 teaspoons chopped almonds

1. Sauté onions and garlic in lightly greased skillet 5 minutes; add spices and cook, covered, over low heat until onions are very soft, about 20 minutes. Stir in flour; cook 1 minute longer. Stir half-and-half and dried fruit into onion mixture; heat to boiling. Reduce heat and simmer, stirring, until thickened. Stir in cilantro; season to taste with salt, cayenne, and black pepper.

2. Place Croustades in baking pan and fill each with slightly rounded tablespoon of onion mixture; sprinkle with almonds. Bake, uncovered, at 425 degrees 10 minutes.

NACHOS

A favorite Mexican appetizer, without the guilt. Cooked, crumbled Chorizo (see p. 154) can be added to make these nachos "grandes"!

6 servings

Baked tortilla chips
1 can (15½ ounces) pinto beans, rinsed, drained, coarsely mashed
Red Tomato Salsa (recipe follows), divided
¾ teaspoon each: chili powder, dried oregano leaves
2–3 cloves garlic, minced
¼ teaspoon salt
½ cup (2 ounces) shredded reduced-fat Cheddar or Monterey Jack cheese
1 medium tomato, chopped
½ small avocado, chopped
2 green onions, sliced
6 pitted ripe olives, sliced
¼ cup fat-free sour cream

Per Serving:
Calories: 182
% of calories from fat: 24
Fat (gm): 5.2
Saturated fat (gm): 1.2
Cholesterol (mg): 6.3
Sodium (mg): 376
Protein (gm): 7.7
Carbohydrate (gm): 28.8

Exchanges:
Milk: 0.0
Vegetable: 0.0
Fruit: 0.0
Bread: 2.0
Meat: 0.0
Fat: 1.0

1. Spread tortilla chips in single layer in jelly roll pan. Spoon combined beans, ¼ cup salsa, herbs, garlic, and salt over tortilla chips; sprinkle with cheese. Bake at 350 degrees until beans are hot and cheese melted, about 10 minutes. Sprinkle with tomato, avocado, onions, and olives; garnish with dollops of sour cream. Serve with remaining ¾ cup salsa.

Red Tomato Salsa
Makes about 1 cup

1 cup chopped tomato
3 tablespoons each: chopped onion, poblano chili or green bell pepper
¼ jalapeño chili, minced
1 clove garlic, minced
¼ cup loosely packed cilantro, chopped
Salt, to taste

1. Mix all ingredients, except salt. Season to taste with salt.

BEEF EMPANADAS

Pork tenderloin or chicken breast can be substituted for the beef in this recipe. The raisins and spices lend a sweet flavor to this traditional Mexican meat filling.

10 servings (3 each)

12 ounces boneless beef eye of round steak, fat trimmed
¼ cup finely chopped onion
3 cloves garlic, minced
2 small tomatoes, finely chopped
⅓ cup raisins
2 tablespoons slivered almonds
1 tablespoon cider vinegar
½ teaspoon ground cinnamon
⅛ teaspoon ground cloves
3 tablespoons finely chopped cilantro
Salt and pepper, to taste
Empanada Pastry (recipe follows)
2 tablespoons fat-free milk

Per Serving:
Calories: 159
% of calories from fat: 29
Fat (gm): 5.1
Saturated fat (gm): 1.5
Cholesterol (mg): 16.5
Sodium (mg): 57
Protein (gm): 8.7
Carbohydrate (gm): 19.5

Exchanges:
Milk: 0.0
Vegetable: 0.0
Fruit: 0.0
Bread: 0.5
Meat: 0.5
Fat: 0.0

1. Cut beef into 2-inch cubes and place in saucepan with 2 inches water; heat to boiling. Reduce heat and simmer, covered, until beef is tender, about 15 minutes. Drain, reserving beef and ½ cup broth. Shred beef finely.

2. Sauté onion and garlic in lightly greased medium skillet until tender, about 5 minutes. Add reserved beef and ½ cup broth, tomatoes, raisins, almonds, vinegar, cinnamon, and cloves; cook over medium heat until broth has evaporated but mixture is still moist, about 10 minutes. Stir in cilantro; season to taste with salt and pepper.

3. Roll ½ of the Empanada Pastry on floured surface to ⅛ inch thickness; cut into 3-inch rounds with cookie cutter. Place scant tablespoon meat mixture on each piece pastry. Brush edges of pastry with water; fold in half and crimp edges firmly by hand or with tines of fork. Make cut in top of each pastry with sharp knife. Repeat with remaining pastry and meat mixture. Brush tops of pastries lightly with milk. Bake on greased cookie sheets at 400 degrees until golden, 15 to 20 minutes.

Empanada Pastry

1¼ cups all-purpose flour
1 tablespoon sugar
¼ teaspoon baking powder
⅛ teaspoon salt
3 tablespoons vegetable shortening
1 teaspoon lemon juice or distilled white vinegar
4 tablespoons fat-free milk or water

1. Combine flour, sugar, baking powder, and salt in small bowl; cut in shortening until mixture resembles coarse crumbs. Mix in lemon juice and milk, a tablespoon at a time, to form soft dough. Refrigerate until ready to use.

FIVE-SPICE VEGETABLE POTSTICKERS

o *Purchased wonton wrappers make this recipe simple to prepare. Wonton wrappers can be cut into circles with a 2½-inch cutter, if you like. Assemble wontons up to 1 day in advance; dust lightly with flour and refrigerate, covered, in a single layer on a plate.*

12 servings (4 each)

2 cups sliced Chinese or napa cabbage

½ cup shredded carrot

¼ cup each: thinly sliced green onions, celery

1–2 teaspoons minced gingerroot

1 clove garlic, minced

1 tablespoon reduced-sodium tamari soy sauce

¼–½ teaspoon each: hot chili paste, five-spice powder

48 wonton or gyoza wrappers

1 egg white, beaten

Vegetable cooking spray

Tamari Dipping Sauce (recipe follows)

Per Serving:
Calories: 130
% of calories from fat: 4
Fat (gm): 0.6
Saturated fat (gm): 0.1
Cholesterol (mg): 4
Sodium (mg): 431
Protein (gm): 5.2
Carbohydrate (gm): 25.9

Exchanges:
Milk: 0.0
Vegetable: 2.0
Fruit: 0.0
Bread: 1.0
Meat: 0.0
Fat: 0.0

1. Stir-fry cabbage, carrot, green onions, celery, gingerroot, and garlic in lightly greased wok or large skillet over medium to medium-high heat until cabbage is wilted, 2 to 3 minutes. Remove from heat; stir in soy sauce, chili paste, and five-spice powder and cool.

2. Spoon ½ tablespoon filling on wonton wrapper; brush edges of wrapper with egg white. Fold wrapper in half and press edges to seal. Repeat with remaining filling, wrappers, and egg white. Add 6 or 8 wontons to large saucepan of boiling water; simmer, uncovered, until wontons rise to the surface, 2 to 3 minutes. Remove with slotted spoon and drain. Repeat with remaining wontons.

3. Add single layer of wontons to lightly greased wok or large skillet and cook over medium heat until browned on the bottom, 2 to 3 minutes. Spray tops of wontons lightly with cooking spray; turn and cook until browned. Repeat with remaining wontons. Serve hot with Tamari Dipping Sauce.

Tamari Dipping Sauce

12 servings (1 tablespoon each)

½ cup reduced-sodium tamari or soy sauce
2 tablespoons rice wine vinegar
4 teaspoons lemon juice
2 teaspoons honey

1. Mix all ingredients.

CRANBERRY-CHEESE WONTONS

LO *Dried cranberries and gingerroot add a lively accent to these unusual cheese wontons.*

12 servings (2 each)

6 ounces fat-free cream cheese, room temperature
3 tablespoons chopped dried cranberries
2 tablespoons each: finely chopped chives, parsley
½–¾ teaspoon minced gingerroot
Salt and white pepper, to taste
24 wonton wrappers
1 egg white, beaten
Canola or peanut oil, for frying
⅓ cup jalapeño jelly, heated, or Tamari Dipping
   Sauce (see p. 21)

Per Serving:
Calories: 91
% of calories from fat: 10
Fat (gm): 1
Saturated fat (gm): 0.1
Cholesterol (mg): 2
Sodium (mg): 184
Protein (gm): 3.9
Carbohydrate (gm): 15.8

Exchanges:
Milk: 0.0
Vegetable: 0.0
Fruit: 0.5
Bread: 0.5
Meat: 0.5
Fat: 0.0

1. Mix cream cheese, cranberries, chives, parsley, and gingerroot in small bowl; season to taste with salt and white pepper. Spoon ½ tablespoon filling on wonton wrapper; brush edges of wrapper with egg white. Fold wrapper in half and press edges to seal. Repeat with remaining filling, wrappers, and egg white.

2. Heat 2 inches of oil to 375 degrees in large saucepan. Fry wontons, 6 to 8 at a time, until golden, 1 to 2 minutes. Drain on paper toweling. Serve with jalapeño jelly or Tamari Dipping Sauce.

SESAME WONTON CUPS

| o |

These delicious snacks can also be served as a novel accompaniment to soups.

| 45 |

8 servings (2 each)

24 wonton wrappers
2 teaspoons Asian sesame oil
1 cup thinly sliced napa cabbage
½ cup each: broccoli sprouts, thinly sliced snow peas, shredded carrots
1 green onion, thinly sliced
Sweet Sesame Dressing (recipe follows)
Wasabi peas and toasted sesame seeds, as garnish

Per Serving:
Calories: 125
% of calories from fat: 27
Fat (gm): 4
Saturated fat (gm): 0.6
Cholesterol (mg): 1.5
Sodium (mg): 116
Protein (gm): 2.5
Carbohydrate (gm): 21.6

Exchanges:
Milk: 0.0
Vegetable: 0.0
Fruit: 0.5
Bread: 1.0
Meat: 0.0
Fat: 0.5

1. Lightly brush edges of wonton wrappers with Asian sesame oil. Press wontons, oil side up, in miniature muffin cups to form shells, using every other cup in muffin tin so that edges do not touch. Bake at 350 degrees until lightly browned, 6 to 7 minutes. Cool on wire racks.

2. Combine cabbage, broccoli sprouts, snow peas, carrots, and green onion in bowl; pour Sweet Sesame Dressing over and toss. Spoon mixture into wonton cups and garnish each with 2 or 3 wasabi peas and a sprinkling of sesame seeds.

Sweet Sesame Dressing

Makes about ½ cup

1 tablespoon Asian sesame oil
2–3 tablespoons rice wine vinegar
⅓ cup apricot preserves
1 teaspoon each: soy sauce, minced gingerroot
2–3 teaspoons peanut butter

1. Mix all ingredients.

MIXED VEGETABLE EGG ROLLS

o *The Asian sesame oil in this recipe has a more distinctive sesame flavor than the light-colored domestic brands. Nutritious spinach, alfalfa sprouts, and black beans add a new dimension to these egg rolls.*

12 servings (1 each)

1 tablespoon sesame seeds

2–3 teaspoons Asian sesame oil

2 green onions, sliced

1 tablespoon minced gingerroot

2 cloves garlic, minced

2 cups sliced spinach

½ cup each: chopped water chestnuts, shredded carrot, sliced small mushrooms

1 can (15½ ounces) black beans, rinsed, drained

1–1½ teaspoons reduced-sodium tamari soy sauce

Salt and pepper, to taste

2 egg whites

1 cup alfalfa sprouts

12 egg roll wrappers

Peanut or vegetable oil

Plum Sauce (recipe follows)

Per Egg Roll:
Calories: 101
% of calories from fat: 12
Fat (gm): 1.6
Saturated fat (gm): 0.2
Cholesterol (mg): 0
Sodium (mg): 342
Protein (gm): 5.8
Carbohydrate (gm): 19

Exchanges:
Milk: 0.0
Vegetable: 1.5
Fruit: 0.0
Bread: 1.0
Meat: 0.0
Fat: 0.0

1. Sauté sesame seeds in sesame oil in large skillet until beginning to brown, 1 to 2 minutes. Add green onions, gingerroot, and garlic; sauté until onions are tender, 1 to 2 minutes. Add spinach, water chestnuts, carrot, and mushrooms; cook, covered, over medium heat until spinach and mushrooms are wilted. Stir in beans and tamari sauce; season to taste with salt and pepper. Cool 5 to 10 minutes; stir in egg whites and alfalfa sprouts.

2. Spoon about ⅓ cup vegetable mixture near corner of 1 egg roll wrapper. Brush edges of wrapper with water. Fold bottom corner of egg roll wrapper up over filling; fold sides in and roll up. Repeat with remaining filling and wrappers.

3. Heat about 2 inches of oil to 375 degrees in deep skillet or large saucepan. Fry egg rolls until golden, 4 to 5 minutes. Drain on paper toweling. Serve hot with Plum Sauce.

Plum Sauce

Makes about 1 cup

¾ cup Oriental plum sauce

2–3 tablespoons each: reduced-sodium tamari soy sauce, rice wine vinegar
   or cider vinegar

1 tablespoon each: grated gingerroot, sliced green onion

1–2 teaspoons light brown sugar, minced garlic

1. Mix all ingredients; refrigerate until ready to serve.

WASABI POTATO SLICES

LO

45

*If you prefer, use 12 tiny red potatoes for this recipe, cutting them into
halves and scooping a small amount of potato from the center of each half.*

12 servings (2 each)

4 small red potatoes, cooked, chilled

Butter-flavor cooking spray

Salt and pepper, to taste

½ cup fat-free sour cream

½ teaspoon wasabi paste

Thinly sliced green onion tops and chopped
   hard-cooked egg, as garnish

Per Serving:
Calories: 37
% of calories from fat: 1.3
Fat (gm): .1
Saturated fat (gm): 0
Cholesterol (mg): 1.7
Sodium (mg): 10.6
Protein (gm): 1.4
Carbohydrate (gm): 7.7

Exchanges:
Milk: 0.0
Vegetable: 0.0
Fruit: 0.0
Bread: 0.5
Meat: 0.0
Fat: 0.0

1. Cut each potato into 3 scant ½-inch slices, reserving ends for
another use; scoop small amount of potato from center of each
with melon baller. Spray tops of slices with cooking spray and
sprinkle with salt and pepper; broil 4 inches from heat source in
baking pan until lightly browned, 3 to 4 minutes. Cool.

2. Mix sour cream and wasabi paste; spoon into centers of potato
slices and sprinkle with green onion tops and egg.

ARTICHOKE-STUFFED APPETIZER BREAD

45

For easy entertaining, assemble this appetizer a day or two in advance. Bread pieces removed from the loaf can be used to make fresh bread crumbs or croutons.

8 servings (2 each)

8 ounces fat-free cream cheese, room temperature

1 can (14 ounces) artichoke hearts, drained, chopped

½ cup each: chopped red bell pepper, celery

¼ cup chopped pitted green or black, olives

2 teaspoons each: drained capers, minced garlic

½ teaspoon each: dried basil and oregano leaves

1–2 teaspoons white wine vinegar or lemon juice

Salt and white pepper, to taste

1 loaf French bread (8 ounces) (about 15 inches long)

Per Serving:
Calories: 151
% of calories from fat: 29
Fat (gm): 5.1
Saturated fat (gm): 0.3
Cholesterol (mg): 0
Sodium (mg): 600
Protein (gm): 6.9
Carbohydrate (gm): 20.9

Exchanges:
Milk: 0.0
Vegetable: 1.0
Fruit: 0.0
Bread: 1.0
Meat: 0.0
Fat: 1.0

1. Mix cream cheese, artichoke hearts, bell pepper, celery, olives, capers, garlic, and herbs; season to taste with vinegar, salt, and white pepper.

2. Slice bread lengthwise in half. Remove bread from centers of bread halves, using a paring knife or serrated grapefruit spoon, leaving ¾-inch shell of bread. Spoon filling into each bread half; press halves together firmly and wrap in plastic wrap. Refrigerate 2 hours or until serving time. Cut into 16 pieces.

APPLE-CABBAGE STRUDELS

The strudels can be assembled several hours in advance; refrigerate, tightly covered. Spray tops of strudels with cooking spray before baking.

12 servings (2 each)

½ cup thinly sliced onion

2 cloves garlic, minced

3 cups thinly sliced cabbage

⅓ cup apple cider or apple juice

1½ cups peeled, chopped, tart apples

¼ cup dark raisins

1–1½ teaspoons curry powder

Salt and pepper, to taste

8 sheets frozen fillo pastry, thawed

Butter-flavored cooking spray

Per Serving:
Calories: 34
% of calories from fat: 5
Fat (gm): 0.2
Saturated fat (gm): 0
Cholesterol (mg): 0
Sodium (mg): 8
Protein (gm): 0.6
Carbohydrate (gm): 8.5

Exchanges:
Milk: 0.0
Vegetable: 0.0
Fruit: 0.5
Bread: 0.0
Meat: 0.0
Fat: 0.0

1. Sauté onion and garlic in lightly greased skillet until tender, about 5 minutes. Add cabbage and apple cider; cook, covered, over medium heat until cabbage is wilted, about 5 minutes. Stir in apples, raisins, and curry powder; cook, uncovered, until apples are crisp-tender and mixture is almost dry, 5 to 8 minutes. Season to taste with salt and pepper. Cool.

2. Place 1 sheet fillo on clean surface. Cover remaining fillo with damp towel to keep from drying. Spray fillo lightly with butter-flavored cooking spray; top with second sheet of fillo and spray. Repeat with 3 more sheets of fillo. Spoon half the cabbage mixture evenly along short edge of fillo, leaving a 1-inch space from the edge. Roll up from short edge, tucking ends under. Place seam side down on greased cookie sheet. Repeat with remaining fillo, cooking spray, and cabbage mixture. Spray tops of strudels with cooking spray. Bake at 400 degrees until golden, about 15 minutes. Cool slightly; cut diagonally into 1-inch pieces with serrated knife. Serve warm or at room temperature.

ONION AND BLUE CHEESE FOCACCIA

L

Serve larger portions as a bread with entrée salads.

45

8 servings

2 cups thinly sliced onions
4 cloves garlic, minced
½ teaspoon dried rosemary leaves
Salt and pepper, to taste
1 focaccia (10 ounces)
¼ cup chopped softened sun-dried tomatoes
  (not in oil)
2–3 ounces crumbled blue cheese
2 tablespoons grated fat-free Parmesan cheese

Per Serving:
Calories: 146
% of calories from fat: 21
Fat (gm): 3.5
Saturated fat (gm): 1.6
Cholesterol (mg): 5.2
Sodium (mg): 354
Protein (gm): 5.9
Carbohydrate (gm): 23.3

Exchanges:
Milk: 0.0
Vegetable: 2.0
Fruit: 0.0
Bread: 1.0
Meat: 0.0
Fat: 0.5

1. Cook onions and garlic in lightly greased skillet, covered, over medium heat until wilted, about 5 minutes. Cook, uncovered, over low heat until tender and lightly browned, 10 to 15 minutes; stir in rosemary and season with salt and pepper. Arrange onions on focaccia; sprinkle with sun-dried tomatoes and cheeses. Bake at 350 degrees until bread is hot and cheese melted, about 15 minutes. Cut into 8 wedges.

SWEET ONION TARTE TATIN

V

You'll win raves when you serve this beautiful upside-down tart! For best flavor, use a sweet onion, such as Vidalia.

6–8 servings

1 tablespoon sugar
2½ pounds small sweet onions, peeled,
  halved crosswise
Salt and pepper, to taste
⅓ cup dark or light raisins
1 teaspoon dried thyme leaves
¼ teaspoon ground allspice
1½ cups reduced-sodium vegetable broth
2 teaspoons balsamic vinegar
Tarte Tatin Crust (recipe follows)

Per Serving:
Calories: 291
% of calories from fat: 25
Fat (gm): 8.3
Saturated fat (gm): 1.6
Cholesterol (mg): 0
Sodium (mg): 126
Protein (gm): 5.9
Carbohydrate (gm): 49.8

Exchanges:
Milk: 0.0
Vegetable: 3.0
Fruit: 0.5
Bread: 1.5
Meat: 0.0
Fat: 1.5

1. Heat lightly greased 12-inch skillet with ovenproof handle over medium heat until hot; sprinkle bottom evenly with sugar. Place onion halves, cut sides down, in skillet, fitting in as many as possible. Cut remaining onion halves into pieces, or chop coarsely, and fill in any spaces between onion halves. Sprinkle lightly with salt and pepper; sprinkle with raisins, thyme, and allspice. Cook, uncovered, over medium heat until onions begin to brown on the bottoms, 8 to 10 minutes.

2. Add broth and vinegar to skillet; heat to boiling. Reduce heat and simmer, covered, until onions are tender, 20 to 25 minutes. Heat to boiling; reduce heat and simmer rapidly, uncovered, until liquid is almost gone.

3. Roll pastry for Tarte Tatin Crust on floured surface into 13-inch circle. Ease pastry over onions in skillet, tucking in edges to fit. Bake at 375 degrees until pastry is browned and juices are bubbly, 30 to 35 minutes. Cool in pan on wire rack 10 minutes; place large serving plate over skillet and invert onto plate. Serve warm or at room temperature.

Tarte Tatin Crust

1½ cups all-purpose flour
½ teaspoon baking powder
½ teaspoon dried thyme leaves
Pinch salt
4 tablespoons cold margarine or butter, cut into pieces
5–6 tablespoons ice water

1. Combine flour, baking powder, thyme, and salt in medium bowl; cut in margarine until mixture resembles coarse crumbs. Add water a tablespoon at a time, mixing lightly with a fork after each addition, until dough just holds together. Refrigerate, covered, at least 30 minutes.

CURRIED ONION BAKLAVA

v *A unique baklava that is not a dessert! Serve in small pieces as an appetizer, or in larger pieces for an entrée or side dish.*

8 servings

2 pounds onions, thinly sliced

3 tablespoons curry powder

¼ cup all-purpose flour

½ cup orange juice

¼ cup each: chopped mango chutney, dried apricots

Salt and pepper, to taste

¼ cup ground almonds

½ cup ground ginger snaps

½ teaspoon ground cinnamon

Butter-flavored vegetable cooking spray

10 sheets frozen fillo, thawed

½ cup water

3 tablespoons each: sugar and honey

Per Serving:
Calories: 198
% of calories from fat: 15
Fat (gm): 3.4
Saturated fat (gm): 0.4
Cholesterol (mg): 0
Sodium (mg): 57
Protein (gm): 3.6
Carbohydrate (gm): 40.8

Exchanges:
Milk: 0.0
Vegetable: 3.0
Fruit: 0.5
Bread: 1.0
Meat: 0.0
Fat: 0.5

1. Sauté onions in lightly greased large skillet 5 minutes; cook, covered, over medium-low heat until onions are very tender, 15 to 20 minutes. Sprinkle with curry powder and flour and cook, stirring, 1 minute. Stir in orange juice, chutney, and apricots; heat to boiling. Reduce heat and simmer, uncovered, until apricots are softened and mixture thickened, about 5 minutes. Season to taste with salt and pepper; cool.

2. Combine almonds, ginger snaps, and cinnamon. Spray bottom of 13 x 9-inch baking pan with cooking spray. Fold 1 sheet of fillo in half crosswise and place in pan; spray with cooking spray and sprinkle with 4 teaspoons almond mixture. Repeat with fillo and almond mixture four times, ending with fillo.

3. Spread onion mixture over fillo. Add remaining fillo and almond mixture in layers, as in Step 2, ending with fillo. Spray fillo with cooking spray and score with sharp knife into serving pieces. Bake at 350 degrees 45 minutes, covering loosely with foil if becoming too brown. Cut into pieces while hot.

4. Heat water, sugar, and honey to boiling in small saucepan, stirring to dissolve sugar. Pour mixture over hot baklava. Cool 10 to 15 minutes before serving, or cool completely and serve at room temperature.

SQUASH AND MUSHROOM GALETTE

LO   *The Galette Pastry Dough, made with yeast, is quite special.*

4–6 servings

½ cup each: thinly sliced leek, chopped onion, red
    bell pepper

2 medium portobello mushrooms, sliced

8 cloves garlic, minced

1½ teaspoons dried sage leaves

1 tablespoon olive oil

1½ cups cooked mashed acorn or butternut squash

Salt and pepper, to taste

Galette Pastry Dough (recipe follows)

½ cup (2 ounces) shredded fat-free Cheddar cheese

2 tablespoons grated Parmesan cheese

1 egg white, beaten

Per Serving:
Calories: 339
% of calories from fat: 18
Fat (gm): 7.1
Saturated fat (gm): 1.7
Cholesterol (mg): 58.3
Sodium (mg): 338
Protein (gm): 16.5
Carbohydrate (gm): 54

Exchanges:
Milk: 0.0
Vegetable: 1.0
Fruit: 0.0
Bread: 3.0
Meat: 1.0
Fat: 1.0

1. Sauté leek, onion, bell pepper, mushrooms, garlic, and sage in oil in large skillet until tender, about 5 minutes. Mix in squash; season to taste with salt and pepper.

2. Roll Galette Pastry Dough on lightly floured surface to 14-inch circle; transfer to greased cookie sheet or large pizza pan. Spoon vegetable mixture evenly on dough, leaving 2-inch border around edge. Sprinkle with cheeses. Fold edge of dough over edge of vegetable mixture, pleating to fit; brush dough with egg white. Bake at 400 degrees until crust is golden, about 25 minutes. Cut into wedges; serve warm.

Galette Pastry Dough

1 teaspoon active dry yeast
⅓ cup warm water (115 degrees)
1 egg, beaten
3 tablespoons fat-free sour cream
1½ cups all-purpose flour
¼ teaspoon salt

1. Stir yeast into warm water in medium bowl; let stand 5 minutes. Add egg and sour cream, mixing until smooth. Stir in flour and salt, making a soft dough. Knead dough on lightly floured surface until smooth, about 10 minutes.

VARIATION

Peperonata Galette — Make Peperonata (see p. 433). Roll Galette Pastry Dough as directed in Step 2 above. Spoon peperonata mixture evenly on dough, leaving a 2-inch border around edge; sprinkle with ½ cup (2 ounces) shredded fat-free mozzarella cheese and 1 tablespoon shredded Parmesan cheese. Fold edge of dough over edge of vegetable mixture, pleating to fit. Brush dough with egg white. Bake as above.

CURRIED PINWHEELS

LO

45
❄

Make these easy appetizers up to 2 days in advance and refrigerate until ready to serve.

12 servings (3 each)

6 pieces small lavosh (5-inch)
12 ounces fat-free cream cheese, room temperature
2 tablespoons fat-free mayonnaise
1–2 teaspoons spicy brown mustard
1 clove garlic, minced
1–1½ teaspoons curry powder
½ cup finely chopped apple
¼ cup each: finely chopped celery, green onions, dry-roasted peanuts
¾ cup chopped chutney

Per Pinwheel:
Calories: 38
% of calories from fat: 14
Fat (gm): 0.6
Saturated fat (gm): 0.1
Cholesterol (mg): 0
Sodium (mg): 79
Protein (gm): 1.9
Carbohydrate (gm): 6.2

Exchanges:
Milk: 0.0
Vegetable: 0.0
Fruit: 0.5
Bread: 0.0
Meat: 0.0
Fat: 0.0

1. Brush lavosh lightly with water and place between damp kitchen towels until softened enough to roll, about 20 minutes.

2. Mix cream cheese, mayonnaise, mustard, garlic, and curry powder in bowl; spread about 3 tablespoons mixture on each lavosh. Combine remaining ingredients, except chutney, and sprinkle over cheese mixture. Roll lavosh tightly; wrap each roll in plastic wrap and refrigerate at least 4 hours. Cut each roll into 6 pieces; serve with chutney.

SWISS CHEESE AND SPINACH PINWHEELS

These fabulous sandwiches can be made in advance and refrigerated up to 2 days—always ready for hungry appetites!

8 servings (2 slices each)

1 large whole wheat lavosh (16 inches diameter)
8 ounces fat-free cream cheese, room temperature
1 tablespoon fat-free sour cream
2 tablespoons minced onion
1 teaspoon fennel seeds, crushed
10 slices (7½ ounces) fat-free Swiss cheese
4 cups loosely packed spinach leaves
2 medium tomatoes, thinly sliced
⅓ cup drained, sliced olives

Per Serving:
Calories: 177
% of calories from fat: 29
Fat (gm): 5.8
Saturated fat (gm): 0.9
Cholesterol (mg): 0
Sodium (mg): 782
Protein (gm): 13.4
Carbohydrate (gm): 18.4

Exchanges:
Milk: 0.0
Vegetable: 1.0
Fruit: 0.0
Bread: 1.0
Meat: 1.0
Fat: 0.5

1. Place lavosh between 2 damp clean kitchen towels; let stand until lavosh is softened enough to roll, about 20 minutes.

2. Mix cream cheese, sour cream, onion, and fennel seeds in small bowl; spread on lavosh. Arrange Swiss cheese, spinach, tomatoes, and olives on top. Roll lavosh tightly; wrap in plastic wrap and refrigerate at least 4 hours, but no longer than 2 days. Trim ends and cut into 1-inch slices.

SLICED MUSHROOM PINWHEELS

L

45
❄

Easy to make and carry, lavosh sandwiches are great for picnics, as well as home dining.

8 servings (2 slices each)

1 large whole wheat lavosh (16 inches diameter)
4 ounces mushrooms
8 ounces fat-free cream cheese, room temperature
1 tablespoon fat-free sour cream
1 teaspoon minced garlic
1–2 teaspoons Dijon mustard
1 medium onion, thinly sliced
⅓ cup red bell pepper, thinly sliced
3 tablespoons fat-free Italian salad dressing

Per Serving:
Calories: 122
% of calories from fat: 27
Fat (gm): 3.7
Saturated fat (gm): 0.7
Cholesterol (mg): 0
Sodium (mg): 309
Protein (gm): 6.5
Carbohydrate (gm): 16

Exchanges:
Milk: 0.0
Vegetable: 1.0
Fruit: 0.0
Bread: 1.0
Meat: 0.0
Fat: 0.5

1. Place lavosh between 2 damp clean kitchen towels; let stand until lavosh is softened enough to roll, about 20 minutes.

2. Remove mushroom stems and chop; slice mushroom caps. Mix cream cheese, chopped mushroom stems, sour cream, garlic, and mustard in small bowl; spread mixture on lavosh. Toss sliced mushrooms, onion, and bell pepper with salad dressing; arrange over cheese mixture. Roll lavosh tightly; wrap in plastic wrap and refrigerate at least 4 hours, but no longer than 2 days. Trim ends and cut into 1-inch slices.

GOAT CHEESE QUESADILLAS WITH TROPICAL FRUIT SALSA

L *Goat cheese and tropical fruits combine for a new flavor in quesadillas.*

45   **8 servings**

4 ounces fat-free cream cheese, room temperature

2 ounces goat cheese

½ small jalapeño chili, minced

½ teaspoon each: dried marjoram and thyme leaves

⅛ teaspoon white pepper

8 whole wheat or white flour tortillas (6-inch)

Butter-flavored cooking spray

Tropical Fruit Salsa (see p. 317)

Per Serving:
Calories: 186
% of calories from fat: 25
Fat (gm): 5.2
Saturated fat (gm): 2.2
Cholesterol (mg): 7.5
Sodium (mg): 285
Protein (gm): 8
Carbohydrate (gm): 26.3

Exchanges:
Milk: 0.0
Vegetable: 1.0
Fruit: 0.5
Bread: 1.0
Meat: 0.5
Fat: 0.5

1. Combine cream cheese, goat cheese, jalapeño chili, herbs, and white pepper; spread about 3 tablespoons mixture on each of 4 tortillas. Top with remaining tortillas.

2. Cook 1 quesadilla in lightly greased skillet on medium to medium-low heat until browned on the bottom, 2 to 3 minutes. Spray top of quesadilla with cooking spray; turn and cook until browned on the bottom. Repeat with remaining quesadillas. Cut quesadillas into wedges; serve warm with Tropical Fruit Salsa.

BLACK BEAN QUESADILLAS

Substitute pinto beans for the black beans if you like, and vary the amount of jalapeño chili to taste.

12 servings

1 can (15 ounces) black beans, rinsed, drained

1 cup mild or hot chili salsa, divided

¼ cup thinly sliced green onions

3 tablespoons finely chopped cilantro

2–3 teaspoons minced jalapeño chili

12 whole wheat or white flour tortillas (6-inch)

¾ cup (3 ounces) each: shredded reduced-fat Monterey Jack
  cheese, fat-free Cheddar cheese

Butter-flavored cooking spray

1. Mash beans slightly; mix in ¼ cup salsa, green onions, cilantro, and jalapeño chili. Divide mixture on 6 tortillas, spreading almost to edges. Sprinkle with cheeses and top with remaining tortillas.

2. Cook 1 quesadilla on medium to medium-low heat in lightly greased skillet until browned on the bottom, 2 to 3 minutes. Spray top of quesadilla with cooking spray; turn and cook until browned on the bottom. Repeat with remaining quesadillas. Cut into wedges; serve warm with remaining ¾ cup salsa.

Per Serving:
Calories: 169
% of calories from fat: 21
Fat (gm): 3.9
Saturated fat (gm): 1.2
Cholesterol (mg): 5.1
Sodium (mg): 427
Protein (gm): 9
Carbohydrate (gm): 24.2

Exchanges:
Milk: 0.0
Vegetable: 0.0
Fruit: 0.0
Bread: 1.5
Meat: 0.5
Fat: 0.5

TORTILLA WEDGES

Our Mexican version of a pizza! Lean ground beef can replace the Chorizo, if you prefer.

12 servings

Chorizo (see p. 154)
½ cup each: chopped green bell pepper, onion
4 large flour tortillas (10-inch)
1 cup (4 ounces) each: shredded reduced-fat
   Monterey Jack cheese, shredded fat-free
   Cheddar cheese
Red Tomato Salsa (see p. 18) or prepared salsa
¾ cup fat-free sour cream

Per Serving:
Calories: 135
% of calories from fat: 24
Fat (gm): 3.7
Saturated fat (gm): 1.5
Cholesterol (mg): 24.8
Sodium (mg): 313
Protein (gm): 14.4
Carbohydrate (gm): 11.4

Exchanges:
Milk: 0.0
Vegetable: 0.5
Fruit: 0.0
Bread: 0.5
Meat: 1.5
Fat: 0.0

1. Cook Chorizo, bell pepper, and onion in lightly greased medium skillet over medium heat until onion is tender and Chorizo is browned, crumbling with fork.

2. Place tortillas on baking sheets; sprinkle evenly with Monterey Jack cheese. Sprinkle with Chorizo mixture and top with Cheddar cheese. Bake at 450 degrees until edges of tortillas are browned and cheese is melted, 6 to 8 minutes. Top with Red Tomato Salsa and sour cream. Cut each tortilla into 6 wedges.

SAUSAGE AND EGG PIZZA

45

Tempting for healthy snacking or for lunch.

6 servings

2 large poblano chilies, sliced
1 cup chopped onion
1 clove garlic, minced
8 eggs, lightly beaten
¼ cup fat-free milk
4 ounces Italian-style turkey sausage, cooked, crumbled
Salt and pepper, to taste
Potato Pizza Crust (recipe follows)
½–1 cup (2–4 ounces) shredded fat-free
    mozzarella cheese

Per Serving:
Calories: 294
% of calories from fat: 25
Fat (gm): 8.1
Saturated fat (gm): 2.4
Cholesterol (mg): 257.6
Sodium (mg): 449
Protein (gm): 20.2
Carbohydrate (gm): 35.8

Exchanges:
Milk: 0.0
Vegetable: 1.0
Fruit: 0.0
Bread: 2.0
Meat: 2.0
Fat: 0.5

1. Cook chilies, onion, and garlic in lightly greased large skillet over medium to medium-low heat until chilies are very soft, 20 to 30 minutes. Remove from skillet. Add combined eggs and milk to skillet; cook until eggs are just set, stirring occasionally. Stir in sausage and chili mixture; season to taste with salt and pepper. Spoon mixture onto Potato Pizza Crust and sprinkle with cheese; bake at 400 degrees until cheese is melted, about 5 minutes.

Potato Pizza Crust

Makes 1 crust

1 package (1¼ pounds) refrigerated shredded potatoes
    for hash browns
⅓ cup finely chopped onion
1 egg
¼ teaspoon each: salt, pepper
Vegetable cooking spray

1. Mix all ingredients, except vegetable cooking spray; press mixture evenly on bottom and 1 inch up side of lightly greased 12 inch ovenproof skillet. Spray potatoes with cooking spray. Bake at 400 degrees until browned, about 20 minutes.

45-MINUTE PREPARATION TIP: Make Potato Pizza Crust while preparing the rest of the recipe.

PIZZA WITH CARAMELIZED ONIONS AND SMOKED TURKEY

45

Caramelized onions and smoked turkey make a flavorful pizza topping.

4 servings

2 cups thinly sliced onions

2 teaspoons sugar

1½ tablespoons margarine

3 ounces deli reduced-fat smoked turkey, cut into thin strips

1 large unbaked pizza crust

⅔ cup pizza sauce

½–1 cup (2–4 ounces) shredded reduced-fat mozzarella cheese

Per Serving:
Calories: 332
% of calories from fat: 26
Fat (gm): 9.7
Saturated fat (gm): 2.9
Cholesterol (mg): 7.5
Sodium (mg): 719
Protein (gm): 16.7
Carbohydrate (gm): 45.3

Exchanges:
Milk: 0.0
Vegetable: 3.0
Fruit: 0.0
Bread: 2.0
Meat: 2.0
Fat: 0.0

1. Sauté onions and sugar in margarine in large skillet over medium heat, stirring frequently, until very tender and well browned, about 15 minutes. Add turkey and cook 2 to 3 minutes.

2. Place crust on large cookie sheet; spread with pizza sauce and sprinkle with cheese. Spoon onion mixture over cheese. Bake at 450 degrees until edges and bottom of crust are browned, about 12 minutes.

TOMATO FILLO PIZZA

45

Use summer's ripest tomatoes for this gourmet pizza.

8 slices

Olive oil cooking spray

8 sheets frozen fillo pastry, thawed

2 cups (8 ounces) shredded fat-free mozzarella cheese

½ cup thinly sliced onion

1 pound tomatoes, thinly sliced

Salt and pepper, to taste

¼ cup (1 ounce) grated Parmesan cheese

¾ teaspoon each: dried dill weed, basil leaves

Per Slice:
Calories: 79
% of calories from fat: 14
Fat (gm): 1.2
Saturated fat (gm): 0.6
Cholesterol (mg): 2.5
Sodium (mg): 270
Protein (gm): 12
Carbohydrate (gm): 5.4

Exchanges:
Milk: 0.0
Vegetable: 0.0
Fruit: 0.0
Bread: 0.5
Meat: 1.0
Fat: 0.0

1. Spray jelly roll pan with cooking spray; place sheet of fillo on pan and spray generously with spray. Repeat with remaining fillo. Sprinkle mozzarella cheese and onion over fillo; arrange tomato slices on top. Sprinkle with salt and pepper, Parmesan cheese, and herbs. Bake at 375 degrees until fillo is browned and cheese melted, about 15 minutes.

GAZPACHO PIZZA

45

Gazpacho, chilled and refreshing, served on a crust!

LO

8 slices

8 ounces fat-free cream cheese, room temperature
2 tablespoons fat-free mayonnaise
½ teaspoon dry mustard
1 tablespoon chopped chives
1 large whole wheat lavosh (16 inches)
1 cup each: chopped seeded tomato, cucumber
½ cup each: chopped onion, yellow and green bell pepper, avocado
1 teaspoon each: minced garlic, jalapeño chili
¼ cup fat-free Italian salad dressing

Per Slice:
Calories: 153
% of calories from fat: 29
Fat (gm): 5.1
Saturated fat (gm): 0.4
Cholesterol (mg): 0
Sodium (mg): 415
Protein (gm): 7.4
Carbohydrate (gm): 19.9

Exchanges:
Milk: 0.0
Vegetable: 1.5
Fruit: 0.0
Bread: 1.0
Meat: 0.0
Fat: 1.0

1. Mix cream cheese, mayonnaise, dry mustard, and chives; spread on lavosh. Combine remaining ingredients and spoon evenly onto lavosh; serve immediately.

GARDEN PATCH PIZZA

L

45

This great snack can be prepared without the salad dressing and refrigerated up to 1 hour; drizzle with dressing just before serving.

8 slices

8 ounces fat-free cream cheese, room temperature
2 tablespoons fat-free sour cream
1 teaspoon dried Italian seasoning
1 large whole wheat lavosh (16 inches)

1 cup each: broccoli florets, chopped, seeded cucumber

2–3 marinated artichoke hearts, drained, sliced

¼ cup each: sliced carrot, sliced green onion

1–2 tablespoons sliced ripe olives

½ cup (2 ounces) shredded reduced-fat Havarti cheese

¼ cup French or other fat-free salad dressing

Per Slice:
Calories: 149
% of calories from fat: 28
Fat (gm): 4.6
Saturated fat (gm): 0.8
Cholesterol (mg): 5.1
Sodium (mg): 419
Protein (gm): 9.3
Carbohydrate (gm): 17.2

Exchanges:
Milk: 0.0
Vegetable: 2.0
Fruit: 0.0
Bread: 0.5
Meat: 0.5
Fat: 0.5

1. Mix cream cheese, sour cream, and Italian seasoning; spread on lavosh. Arrange vegetables and cheese on top and drizzle with salad dressing.

SPINACH SALAD PIZZA

LO

45

This salad on a pizza is made with a large, crisp lavosh. Serve with any salad dressing you like.

8 slices

12 ounces fat-free cream cheese, room temperature

5 tablespoons fat-free sweet-sour salad
   dressing, divided

1 large whole wheat lavosh (16 inches)

2 cups packed torn spinach leaves

1 cup sliced mushrooms

½ cup thinly sliced red onion

2 hard-cooked eggs, sliced

2 slices bacon, cooked crisp, crumbled

Per Serving:
Calories: 178
% of calories from fat: 30
Fat (gm): 6.1
Saturated fat (gm): 1.6
Cholesterol (mg): 57.7
Sodium (mg): 450
Protein (gm): 10.6
Carbohydrate (gm): 21.4

Exchanges:
Milk: 0.0
Vegetable: 1.0
Fruit: 0.0
Bread: 1.0
Meat: 1.0
Fat: 0.5

1. Mix cream cheese and 2 tablespoons sweet-sour dressing; spread on lavosh. Top with spinach, mushrooms, onion, eggs, and bacon. Serve immediately, or refrigerate no longer than 1 hour, drizzling with remaining 3 tablespoons sweet-sour dressing before serving.

FRUIT NUGGETS

V

Bite-sized and perfect for a snack with a favorite beverage.

45   3 dozen

2 cups finely ground low-fat graham crackers

½ cup finely ground ginger snaps or low-fat graham crackers

½ teaspoon each: ground cinnamon, nutmeg, ginger

½ cup each: finely chopped dried apples, dried apricots, dates, golden raisins

½ cup orange juice

2–3 tablespoons honey

3 tablespoons sugar

Per Nugget:
Calories: 57
% of calories from fat: 8
Fat (gm): 0.5
Saturated fat (gm): 0.1
Cholesterol (mg): 0
Sodium (mg): 29
Protein (gm): 0.8
Carbohydrate (gm): 12.8

Exchanges:
Milk: 0.0
Vegetable: 0.0
Fruit: 0.5
Bread: 0.5
Meat: 0.0
Fat: 0.0

1. Combine all ingredients, except sugar, in bowl, stirring until mixture holds together. Roll into 36 balls, each about 1 inch in diameter. Roll in sugar to coat; store in covered container at room temperature.

SWEET CINNAMON COFFEE

V

This spiced coffee is also refreshing served chilled and over ice.

45   **8 servings** (about ½ cup each)

4 cups water

⅓–½ cup packed light brown sugar

1 small cinnamon stick

4 whole cloves

¼ cup dark roast regular grind coffee

Per Serving:
Calories: 37
% of calories from fat: 0
Fat (gm): 0
Saturated fat (gm): 0
Cholesterol (mg): 0
Sodium (mg): 6
Protein (gm): 0.1
Carbohydrate (gm): 9.4

Exchanges:
Milk: 0.0
Vegetable: 0.0
Fruit: 0.0
Bread: 0.5
Meat: 0.0
Fat: 0.0

1. Heat water, brown sugar, and spices to boiling in medium saucepan; stir in coffee. Reduce heat and simmer, covered, 2 to 3 minutes. Remove from heat and let stand 2 to 3 minutes for grounds to settle. Strain coffee; serve in small mugs.

HOT MULLED CIDER

Great for cold fall evenings, this punch can be made in a slow cooker and kept warm during a party; cook on low heat for 2 to 3 hours.

16 servings (about ½ cup each)

2 quarts apple cider
½ cup packed light brown sugar
1½ teaspoons whole cloves
1 teaspoon whole allspice
2 whole cinnamon sticks
1 medium orange, sliced

Per Serving:
Calories: 93
% of calories from fat: 2
Fat (gm): 0.2
Saturated fat (gm): 0
Cholesterol (mg): 0
Sodium (mg): 7
Protein (gm): 0.2
Carbohydrate (gm): 25

Exchanges:
Milk: 0.0
Vegetable: 0.0
Fruit: 1.5
Bread: 0.0
Meat: 0.0
Fat: 0.0

1. Heat all ingredients in large saucepan to boiling; reduce heat and simmer, covered, 30 minutes. Strain and discard spices; serve warm.

VARIATIONS

Ginger-Spiced Cider — Make recipe as above deleting brown sugar, cloves, allspice, and orange slices. Add eight ¼-inch slices gingerroot to cider and simmer, covered, 30 minutes. Strain and discard ginger and cinnamon sticks; serve warm or chilled.

Hot Spiced Wine — Make recipe as above, substituting 8 cups sweet red wine or sweet sherry for the apple cider.

MARGARITAS

Our favorite Mexican libation! For best flavor, use fresh lime juice.

2 servings (about ½ cup each)

1 lime wedge
Coarse salt (optional)
½ cup tequila
¼ cup fresh lime juice
2 tablespoons orange liqueur
Ice cubes

1. Rub rims of 2 margarita or stemmed glasses with lime wedge; dip rims in salt. Pour combined tequila, lime juice, and orange liqueur over ice cubes in margarita or stemmed glasses.

VARIATION

Strawberry Margaritas — Make recipe as above, processing tequila, lime juice, orange liqueur, and 12 to 14 fresh or frozen strawberries in food processor or blender until smooth; pour over ice cubes in margarita glasses.

Per Serving:
Calories: 185
% of calories from fat: 0
Fat (gm): 0
Saturated fat (gm): 0
Cholesterol (mg): 0
Sodium (mg): 1
Protein (gm): 0.2
Carbohydrate (gm): 8.6

Exchanges:
Milk: 0.0
Vegetable: 0.0
Fruit: 0.5
Bread: 0.0
Meat: 0.0
Fat: 3.5

SANGRIA

America has adopted this famous Spanish wine punch; it also can be made with the addition of sparkling water. Serve well chilled.

6 servings (about 1 cup each)

4 cups dry red wine, chilled
2 cups orange juice, chilled
¼ cup lime juice
¾–1 cup sugar
½ each: thinly sliced lime, orange
Ice cubes

1. Mix all ingredients, except ice, in large pitcher; pour over ice cubes in tall glasses.

Per Serving:
Calories: 88
% of calories from fat: 1
Fat (gm): 0.1
Saturated fat (gm): 0
Cholesterol (mg): 0
Sodium (mg): 6
Protein (gm): 0.6
Carbohydrate (gm): 9

Exchanges:
Milk: 0.0
Vegetable: 0.0
Fruit: 0.5
Bread: 0.0
Meat: 0.0
Fat: 1.5

TROPICAL FRUIT SHAKE

L

45

Use any desired ripe fruit—vary flavors with honey, lemon juice, or even rum!

4 servings (about 1 cup each)

3 cups cubed fresh fruit (pineapple, banana, melon, strawberries, etc.)
1 cup fat-free frozen yogurt
½ cup fat-free milk
3–4 tablespoons honey

Ice cubes
Freshly grated nutmeg, as garnish

1. Process fruit, yogurt, milk, and honey in blender until smooth. Pour over ice cubes in tall glasses; sprinkle with nutmeg.

Per Serving:
Calories: 172
% of calories from fat: 3
Fat (gm): 0.6
Saturated fat (gm): 0.1
Cholesterol (mg): 0.5
Sodium (mg): 45
Protein (gm): 3
Carbohydrate (gm): 40.6

Exchanges:
Milk: 0.0
Vegetable: 0.0
Fruit: 2.0
Bread: 0.5
Meat: 0.0
Fat: 0.0

POMEGRANATE PASSION

V

Heart healthy pomegranate juice is an excellent source of antioxidants.

45

4 servings (about 1 cup each)

1 cup pomegranate juice
½ cup orange juice
1½ cups halved strawberries
1 large banana, sliced
Honey, to taste

1. Process all ingredients, except honey, in blender or food processor until smooth; sweeten to taste with honey.

Per Serving:
Calories: 95
% of calories from fat: 3
Fat (gm): 0.3
Saturated fat (gm): 0.1
Cholesterol (mg): 0.0
Sodium (mg): 3.6
Protein (gm): 1
Carbohydrate (gm): 23.4

Exchanges:
Milk: 0.0
Vegetable: 0.0
Fruit: 1.5
Bread: 0.0
Meat: 0.0
Fat: 0.0

VARIATION

Blueberry Breeze — Make recipe as above, substituting blueberries for the strawberries and apple cider for the orange juice.

ORANGE JULIA

L

Our version of the ever-popular Orange Julius—delicious and refreshing!

45 **4 servings** (about 1 cup each)

1 can (6 ounces) frozen orange juice concentrate
1 cup each: fat-free milk, water
2 tablespoons sugar
1 teaspoon vanilla
12 ice cubes

1. Process all ingredients, except ice cubes, in blender 10 seconds; add ice cubes, several at a time, processing until smooth.

Per Serving:
Calories: 117
% of calories from fat: 2
Fat (gm): 0.2
Saturated fat (gm): 0.1
Cholesterol (mg): 1
Sodium (mg): 33
Protein (gm): 3.1
Carbohydrate (gm): 25.8

Exchanges:
Milk: 0.0
Vegetable: 0.0
Fruit: 2.0
Bread: 0.0
Meat: 0.0
Fat: 0.0

EGGNOG WITH RUM

LO

A holiday favorite—thick, rich, and creamy!

45 **12 servings** (about ½ cup each)

½ cup sugar
2 tablespoons cornstarch
1 quart fat-free milk, divided
2 eggs, lightly beaten
1–1½ cups light rum
1 cup light whipped topping
Ground cinnamon or nutmeg, as garnish

Per Serving:
Calories: 106
% of calories from fat: 14
Fat (gm): 1.6
Saturated fat (gm): 1
Cholesterol (mg): 36.8
Sodium (mg): 57
Protein (gm): 3.8
Carbohydrate (gm): 7.6

Exchanges:
Milk: 0.5
Vegetable: 0.0
Fruit: 0.0
Bread: 0.0
Meat: 0.0
Fat: 1.5

1. Mix sugar, cornstarch, and 3 cups milk in medium saucepan; heat to boiling, whisking frequently. Boil, whisking until thickened, about 1 minute. Stir about half the milk mixture into the eggs; stir egg mixture back into saucepan. Cook over low heat, whisking, 1 minute. Cool; refrigerate until chilled, 3 to 4 hours.

2. Stir remaining 1 cup milk and rum into eggnog; stir in whipped topping. Serve in small glasses or mugs; sprinkle with cinnamon.

SPARKLING GREEN PUNCH

V *Remember this punch for St. Patrick's Day and winter holidays!*

45 **20 servings** (about ½ cup each)

2 cans (6 ounces each) frozen limeade
concentrate, thawed

1 can (6 ounces) frozen lemonade
concentrate, thawed

2 cups cold water

Few drops green food color

2 bottles (28 ounces each) diet ginger ale, chilled

Ice cubes

Per Serving:
Calories: 59
% of calories from fat: 1
Fat (gm): 0
Saturated fat (gm): 0
Cholesterol (mg): 0
Sodium (mg): 16
Protein (gm): 0.1
Carbohydrate (gm): 15.6

Exchanges:
Milk: 0.0
Vegetable: 0.0
Fruit: 1.0
Bread: 0.0
Meat: 0.0
Fat: 0.0

1. Mix concentrates, water, and food color in large pitcher; pour into punch bowl; stir in ginger ale and ice.

TWO

Soups

CREAM OF ARTICHOKE AND MUSHROOM SOUP

L

45

Shiitake or cremini mushrooms can be substituted for the portobello mushrooms.

4 first-course servings (about 1 cup each)

¾ cup chopped portobello mushrooms

2 tablespoons chopped onion

1 tablespoon each: margarine or butter, flour

3 cups fat-free milk

1 vegetable bouillon cube

1 package (9 ounces) frozen artichoke hearts, thawed, finely chopped

Salt and white pepper, to taste

Paprika, as garnish

Per Serving:
Calories: 135
% of calories from fat: 22
Fat (gm): 3.6
Saturated fat (gm): 0.8
Cholesterol (mg): 3
Sodium (mg): 422
Protein (gm): 9.2
Carbohydrate (gm): 18.9

Exchanges:
Milk: 1.0
Vegetable: 1.0
Fruit: 0.0
Bread: 0.0
Meat: 0.0
Fat: 0.5

1. Sauté mushrooms and onion in margarine in medium saucepan until tender, about 5 minutes. Stir in flour; cook 1 minute. Stir in milk and bouillon cube; heat to boiling. Add artichoke hearts and simmer, uncovered, 5 minutes. Season to taste with salt and white pepper. Sprinkle with paprika.

FLORIDA AVOCADO AND TOMATO CHOWDER

In this easy recipe, colorful ingredients create a kaleidoscope of fresh colors and flavors.

4 entrée servings (about 1½ cups each)

3 cups cubed, peeled potatoes

1 can (14 ounces) reduced-sodium fat-free chicken broth

1 teaspoon dried thyme leaves

8 ounces smoked turkey breast, cubed

1 cup each: whole kernel corn, chopped plum tomatoes, cubed avocado

Juice of 1 lime

3 slices bacon, cooked, crumbled

Salt and pepper, to taste

Per Serving:
Calories: 333
% of calories from fat: 26
Fat (gm): 10.2
Saturated fat (gm): 2.4
Cholesterol (mg): 51.1
Sodium (mg): 765
Protein (gm): 21
Carbohydrate (gm): 44.7

Exchanges:
Milk: 0.0
Vegetable: 2.0
Fruit: 0.0
Bread: 2.0
Meat: 2.0
Fat: 1.5

1. Heat potatoes, broth, and thyme to boiling in medium saucepan; reduce heat and simmer, covered, until potatoes are tender, about 10 minutes. Using slotted spoon, transfer ½ the potatoes to a medium bowl. Process remaining mixture in food processor or blender until smooth; return to saucepan. Add turkey, corn, and reserved potatoes; heat to boiling. Reduce heat and simmer 5 minutes. Stir in tomatoes, avocado, lime juice, and bacon. Season to taste with salt and pepper.

FRESH HERB AND POTATO SOUP

L

45

For flavor variation, make the soup with another favorite garden herb, such as rosemary, oregano, lemon thyme, or marjoram.

6 first-course servings (about 1 cup each)

4 cups reduced-sodium vegetable broth

1 cup each: firmly packed basil and parsley

½ cup chopped onion

1 teaspoon sugar

2 cups potatoes, peeled, cubed

1 cup fat-free milk

¼ cup all-purpose flour

1 tablespoon margarine or butter

Salt and white pepper, to taste

Chopped parsley, as garnish

Per Serving:
Calories: 128
% of calories from fat: 17
Fat (gm): 2.5
Saturated fat (gm): 0.5
Cholesterol (mg): 0.8
Sodium (mg): 355
Protein (gm): 4
Carbohydrate (gm): 22.7

Exchanges:
Milk: 0.0
Vegetable: 0.0
Fruit: 0.0
Bread: 1.5
Meat: 0.0
Fat: 0.5

1. Heat broth, basil, parsley, onion, and sugar to boiling in medium saucepan. Simmer, covered, 30 minutes. Strain; return broth to saucepan. Add potatoes and heat to boiling; reduce heat and simmer, covered, until potatoes are tender, about 15 minutes. Mix milk and flour; stir into saucepan and heat to boiling, stirring, until thickened, about 1 minute; stir in margarine. Season to taste with salt and white pepper; sprinkle each bowl of soup with parsley.

DILLED BEET SOUP

It's not necessary to peel beets, as the skins slip off easily after cooking.

8 first-course servings (about 1¼ cups each)

12 medium beets, tops trimmed (about 3 pounds)
3 cups water
2–3 chicken bouillon cubes
Water
¾–1 cup dry red wine or chicken broth
1½–2 teaspoons dried dill weed
2–3 tablespoons red wine vinegar
Salt and pepper, to taste
Thin lemon slices, as garnish

Per Serving:
Calories: 63
% of calories from fat: 3
Fat (gm): 0.3
Saturated fat (gm): 0
Cholesterol (mg): 0
Sodium (mg): 318
Protein (gm): 1.8
Carbohydrate (gm): 10.6

Exchanges:
Milk: 0.0
Vegetable: 2.0
Fruit: 0.0
Bread: 0.0
Meat: 0.0
Fat: 0.0

1. Heat beets, 3 cups water, and bouillon cubes to boiling in large saucepan; reduce heat and simmer, covered, until beets are tender, 30 to 40 minutes. Drain, reserving cooking liquid. Slip skins off beets and cut into quarters.

2. Add enough water to reserved cooking liquid to make 6 cups. Process beets, wine, reserved cooking liquid, and dill weed in food processor or blender until smooth. Season to taste with vinegar, salt, and pepper. Serve warm or chilled; garnish each bowl of soup with a lemon slice.

BEET BORSCHT

45

This delicious soup is flavored in the traditional way with Polish sausage.

8 first-course servings (about 1¼ cups each)

8 ounces low-fat smoked Polish sausage, sliced (½-inch)
2 teaspoons margarine or butter
6 cups reduced-sodium fat-free beef broth
1 small head red cabbage, thinly sliced
4 medium beets, peeled, julienned
2 carrots, julienned
1 clove garlic, minced

1 bay leaf

2–3 teaspoons sugar

2 tablespoons cider vinegar

Salt and pepper, to taste

Chopped dill weed, as garnish

Per Serving:
Calories: 120
% of calories from fat: 25
Fat (gm): 0.4
Saturated fat (gm): 0.6
Cholesterol (mg): 17.2
Sodium (mg): 437
Protein (gm): 10.9
Carbohydrate (gm): 13.1

1. Sauté sausage in margarine in Dutch oven until browned, about 5 minutes. Add remaining ingredients, except salt, pepper, and dill weed; heat to boiling. Reduce heat and simmer, covered, until vegetables are tender, about 15 minutes. Season to taste with salt and pepper; sprinkle each bowl of soup with dill weed.

Exchanges:
Milk: 0.0
Vegetable: 3.0
Fruit: 0.0
Bread: 0.0
Meat: 1.0
Fat: 0.0

CREAM OF BROCCOLI SOUP

45 *Eat broccoli often—it's high in antioxidants and packed with nutrients. Serve this soup warm or chilled.*

6 first-course servings (about 1 cup each)

1 cup chopped onion

3 cloves garlic, minced

2 pounds broccoli, cut into pieces (2-inch)

½ teaspoon dried thyme leaves

⅛ teaspoon ground nutmeg

3½ cups reduced-sodium fat-free chicken broth

½ cup fat-free half-and-half or fat-free milk

Salt and white pepper, to taste

6 tablespoons fat-free sour cream

1½ cups Croutons (½ recipe, see p. 498)

Per Serving:
Calories: 99
% of calories from fat: 9
Fat (gm): 1.1
Saturated fat (gm): 0.2
Cholesterol (mg): 0
Sodium (mg): 110
Protein (gm): 6.8
Carbohydrate (gm): 17.6

Exchanges:
Milk: 0.0
Vegetable: 2.0
Fruit: 0.0
Bread: 0.5
Meat: 0.0
Fat: 0.0

1. Sauté onion and garlic in lightly greased saucepan until tender, 3 to 5 minutes. Stir in broccoli, thyme, and nutmeg; cook 2 minutes longer. Add broth to saucepan and heat to boiling; reduce heat and simmer, covered, until broccoli is tender, about 10 minutes. Stir in half-and-half.

2. Process soup in food processor or blender until smooth; season to taste with salt and white pepper. Stir 1 tablespoon sour cream into each bowl of soup; sprinkle with Croutons.

VARIATIONS

Dilled Broccoli Soup — Make recipe as above, deleting thyme, nutmeg, and Croutons (see p. 498). Add ⅔ cup loosely packed fresh dill weed to soup when pureeing.

Broccoli-Kale Soup — Make recipe as above, increasing broth to 5 cups and deleting the half-and-half, Croutons, and nutmeg. Stir 2 cups lightly packed kale into the soup during the last 5 minutes of cooking time. Process as above, adding more broth if needed for desired consistency.

HERBED BROCCOLI AND PASTA SOUP

45 *A versatile soup, as any vegetable in season and favorite herb can be substituted for the broccoli and thyme.*

6 first-course servings (about 1 cup each)

3 cans (14½ ounces each) reduced-sodium
   fat-free chicken broth
4 cloves garlic, minced
2 teaspoons dried thyme leaves
3 cups small broccoli florets
1 cup uncooked fusilli (spirals)
2–3 tablespoons lemon juice
Salt and pepper, to taste

Per Serving:
Calories: 151
% of calories from fat: 7.8
Fat (gm): 1.3
Saturated fat (gm): 0.1
Cholesterol (mg): 0.0
Sodium (mg): 801
Protein (gm): 6.4
Carbohydrate (gm): 29

Exchanges:
Milk: 0.0
Vegetable: 3.0
Fruit: 0.0
Bread: 1.0
Meat: 0.0
Fat: 0.0

1. Heat broth, garlic, and thyme to boiling in medium saucepan. Stir in broccoli and fusilli. Reduce heat and simmer, uncovered, until broccoli is tender and pasta is al dente, about 10 minutes. Season to taste with lemon juice, salt, and pepper.

RUSSIAN CABBAGE SOUP

Use red or green cabbage, fresh or canned beets in this savory soup.

8 first-course servings (about 1½ cups each)

2 medium onions, sliced

1 tablespoon margarine or butter

7 cups reduced-sodium fat-free beef broth

1 can (16 ounces) reduced-sodium whole tomatoes, undrained, coarsely chopped

6 cups thinly sliced red cabbage

4 large beets, peeled, cubed

1 cup each: sliced carrots, cubed turnip, potato

1 tablespoon cider vinegar

Salt and pepper, to taste

8 tablespoons fat-free sour cream

Per Serving:
Calories: 109
% of calories from fat: 17
Fat (gm): 2.2
Saturated fat (gm): 0.4
Cholesterol (mg): 0
Sodium (mg): 91
Protein (gm): 4
Carbohydrate (gm): 20.7

Exchanges:
Milk: 0.0
Vegetable: 3.0
Fruit: 0.0
Bread: 0.5
Meat: 0.0
Fat: 0.0

1. Sauté onions in margarine in Dutch oven until tender, about 5 minutes. Add broth, vegetables, and vinegar; heat to boiling. Reduce heat and simmer, uncovered, 20 to 30 minutes; season to taste with salt and pepper. Top each bowl of soup with a tablespoon of sour cream.

LIGHT MINESTRONE

Minestrone does not always contain pasta, nor is it always a heavy, hearty soup. Enjoy this light version of an old favorite, selecting vegetables that are freshest and most plentiful.

8 first-course servings (about 1¼ cups each)

1 cup sliced carrots
½ cup each: chopped onion, celery, fennel bulb
2 cloves garlic, minced
1 tablespoon olive oil
5 cups reduced-sodium fat-free beef broth
1 can (19 ounces) garbanzo beans, rinsed, drained
1 cup each: snap peas, broccoli florets, zucchini, sliced
¾–1 teaspoon each: dried basil and oregano leaves
1 cup halved cherry tomatoes
¼ cup finely chopped parsley
Salt and pepper, to taste
1½ cups Parmesan Croutons (½ recipe) (see p. 498)

Per Serving:
Calories: 146
% of calories from fat: 21
Fat (gm): 3.5
Saturated fat (gm): 0.6
Cholesterol (mg): 0.5
Sodium (mg): 447
Protein (gm): 8.6
Carbohydrate (gm): 21.3

Exchanges:
Milk: 0.0
Vegetable: 1.0
Fruit: 0.0
Bread: 1.0
Meat: 0.0
Fat: 0.5

1. Sauté carrots, onion, celery, fennel, and garlic in oil in Dutch oven until onion is tender, 5 to 8 minutes. Add broth, beans, peas, broccoli, zucchini, and herbs; heat to boiling. Reduce heat and simmer, covered, until vegetables are tender, 10 to 15 minutes, adding tomatoes and parsley during last 5 minutes of cooking time. Season to taste with salt and pepper. Sprinkle each bowl of soup with Parmesan Croutons.

SUMMER MINESTRONE

Thick and savory, this traditional Italian soup is always a favorite.

8 first-course servings (about 1 cup each)

2 cups each: cubed potatoes, sliced carrots
1 small zucchini, cubed
1 cup each: halved green beans, sliced zucchini, carrots,
    cabbage, chopped onion
½ cup sliced celery

3–4 cloves garlic, minced

2 teaspoons dried Italian seasoning

1 teaspoon dried oregano leaves

4 cups reduced-sodium chicken broth

1 can (15 ounces) each rinsed, drained kidney beans, and reduced-sodium stewed tomatoes

2 cups water

1½ cups uncooked mostaccioli

½ teaspoon pepper

2 tablespoons grated Parmesan or Romano cheese

Per Serving:
Calories: 177
% of calories from fat: 9
Fat (gm): 1.8
Saturated fat (gm): 0.6
Cholesterol (mg): 1.2
Sodium (mg): 256
Protein (gm): 8.1
Carbohydrate (gm): 33.7

Exchanges:
Milk: 0.0
Vegetable: 2.0
Fruit: 0.0
Bread: 1.5
Meat: 0.5
Fat: 0.0

1. Sauté fresh vegetables and garlic in lightly greased large saucepan until crisp-tender, 10 to 12 minutes. Stir in Italian seasoning and oregano; cook 1 minute longer. Add broth, beans, tomatoes, and water; heat to boiling. Reduce heat and simmer, covered, 10 minutes. Heat soup to boiling and add pasta. Reduce heat and simmer, uncovered, until pasta is al dente, 10 to 12 minutes. Stir in pepper; sprinkle each bowl of soup with cheese.

BEAN-THICKENED SOUP

V *Pureed beans contribute a hearty texture and subtle flavor to this soup.*

45 **4 first-course servings** (about 1⅓ cups each)

2 carrots, sliced

1 small onion, chopped

2 large cloves garlic, minced

1¾ cups vegetable broth

1 can (16 ounces) whole tomatoes, undrained, coarsely chopped

1 can (15 ounces) Great Northern beans, rinsed, drained, pureed

½ teaspoon each: dried thyme and sage leaves

Salt and pepper, to taste

Per Serving:
Calories: 176
% of calories from fat: 5
Fat (gm): 1
Saturated fat (gm): 0.2
Cholesterol (mg): 0
Sodium (mg): 208
Protein (gm): 9.8
Carbohydrate (gm): 34

Exchanges:
Milk: 0.0
Vegetable: 2.0
Fruit: 0.0
Bread: 1.5
Meat: 0.5
Fat: 0.0

1. Sauté carrots, onion, and garlic in lightly greased large saucepan until onion is tender, about 5 minutes. Stir in broth, tomatoes with liquid, pureed beans, and herbs. Heat to boiling; reduce heat and simmer, covered, until carrots are tender, about 10 minutes. Season to taste with salt and pepper.

DILLED CARROT SOUP

45 | *Carrots team with dill for a fresh, clean flavor.*

6 first-course servings (about 1½ cups each)

1½ cups chopped onions
2 cloves garlic, minced
6 cups reduced-sodium fat-free chicken broth
1 can (16 ounces) reduced-sodium diced
  tomatoes, undrained
2 pounds carrots, cut into 2-inch pieces
1 medium Idaho potato, peeled, cubed
2–3 tablespoons lemon juice
1–1½ teaspoons dried dill weed
Salt and white pepper, to taste
6 tablespoons fat-free plain yogurt
Dill sprigs, as garnish

Per Serving:
Calories: 139
% of calories from fat: 6
Fat (gm): 1
Saturated fat (gm): 0.1
Cholesterol (mg): 0.3
Sodium (mg): 88
Protein (gm): 4.4
Carbohydrate (gm): 30.5

Exchanges:
Milk: 0.0
Vegetable: 6.0
Fruit: 0.0
Bread: 0.0
Meat: 0.0
Fat: 0.0

1. Sauté onions and garlic in lightly greased saucepan until tender, about 5 minutes. Add broth, tomatoes and liquid, carrots, and potato; heat to boiling. Reduce heat and simmer, covered, until vegetables are tender, about 15 minutes.

2. Process soup in food processor or blender until smooth. Add lemon juice and dill weed; season to taste with salt and white pepper. Serve soup warm or chilled. Top each bowl of soup with a tablespoon of yogurt; garnish with dill sprigs.

CREAM OF CAULIFLOWER SOUP WITH CHEESE

45 | *Fat-free half-and-half adds a rich creaminess to the soup.*

6 first-course servings (about 1 cup each)

½ cup chopped onion
2 cloves garlic, minced
2 tablespoons flour
3½ cups reduced-sodium fat-free chicken broth
12 ounces cauliflower, cut into florets

1 large Idaho potato, peeled, cubed
¼–½ cup fat-free half-and-half or fat-free milk
¾ cup (3 ounces) reduced-fat Cheddar cheese
Salt and white pepper, to taste
Ground mace or nutmeg, as garnish

Per Serving:
Calories: 98
% of calories from fat: 22
Fat (gm): 2.4
Saturated fat (gm): 1.1
Cholesterol (mg): 7.6
Sodium (mg): 214
Protein (gm): 5.5
Carbohydrate (gm): 13.6

Exchanges:
Milk: 0.0
Vegetable: 1.0
Fruit: 0.0
Bread: 0.5
Meat: 0.5
Fat: 0.0

1. Sauté onion and garlic in lightly greased saucepan until tender, about 10 minutes. Stir in flour; cook about 1 minute longer. Add broth, cauliflower, and potato and heat to boiling; reduce heat and simmer, covered, until vegetables are tender, 10 to 15 minutes. Remove about half the vegetables from the soup with a slotted spoon and reserve. Puree remaining soup in food processor or blender until smooth.

2. Return soup to saucepan; stir in reserved vegetables, half-and-half, and cheese. Cook over low heat, stirring, until cheese is melted, 3 to 4 minutes. Season to taste with salt and white pepper; sprinkle each bowl of soup with mace.

HEARTY CORN AND POTATO CHOWDER

45 *If a thicker soup is desired, mix 2 tablespoons flour with ¼ cup water; stir into boiling soup. Boil, stirring until thickened, about 1 minute.*

4 entrée servings (about 1⅓ cups each)

2 cups whole kernel corn
1 medium onion, chopped
1 tablespoon canola oil
2 cups each: reduced-sodium chicken broth,
    cubed potatoes
½ cup sliced celery
½ teaspoon dried thyme leaves
1¾ cups fat-free half-and-half or fat-free milk
Salt and pepper, to taste

Per Serving:
Calories: 248
% of calories from fat: 19
Fat (gm): 5.6
Saturated fat (gm): 1.5
Cholesterol (mg): 5.3
Sodium (mg): 447
Protein (gm): 8.2
Carbohydrate (gm): 44.7

Exchanges:
Milk: 0.0
Vegetable: 0.0
Fruit: 0.0
Bread: 3.0
Meat: 0.0
Fat: 1.0

1. Sauté corn and onion in oil in large saucepan until onion is tender, 5 to 8 minutes. Process ½ the vegetable mixture and the broth in food processor or blender until finely chopped; return to saucepan. Add potatoes, celery, and thyme; heat to boiling. Reduce heat and simmer, covered, until vegetables are tender, 10 to 15 minutes. Stir in half-and-half and cook 2 to 3 minutes; season to taste with salt and pepper.

CUCUMBER AND SORREL SOUP

45

Spinach or kale can be substituted for the sorrel.

6 first-course servings (about 1¼ cups each)

¼ cup sliced green onions

1 clove garlic, minced

3 cups peeled, seeded, chopped cucumbers

1 cup coarsely chopped sorrel

2 cups each: fat-free milk, reduced-sodium fat-free chicken broth

1 tablespoon cornstarch

2 tablespoons water

Salt and white pepper, to taste

1½ cups Herb Croutons (½ recipe) (see p. 498)

Per Serving:
Calories: 70
% of calories from fat: 10
Fat (gm): 0.8
Saturated fat (gm): 0.2
Cholesterol (mg): 1.3
Sodium (mg): 94
Protein (gm): 4.5
Carbohydrate (gm): 11.7

Exchanges:
Milk: 0.0
Vegetable: 2.5
Fruit: 0.0
Bread: 0.0
Meat: 0.0
Fat: 0.0

1. Sauté ¼ cup green onions and garlic in lightly greased saucepan until tender, 3 to 4 minutes. Add cucumbers and sorrel, and cook over medium heat 5 minutes. Add milk and broth; heat to boiling. Reduce heat and simmer, covered, until cucumbers are tender, 5 to 10 minutes.

2. Process soup in food processor or blender until smooth; return to saucepan and heat to boiling. Whisk in combined cornstarch and water, whisking until thickened, about 1 minute. Season to taste with salt and white pepper. Serve chilled; top each bowl of soup with Herb Croutons.

45-MINUTE PREPARATION TIP: Make Herb Croutons and bake while preparing soup.

EGGPLANT SOUP WITH ROASTED RED PEPPER SAUCE

45 *Grilling gives eggplant a distinctive smoky flavor. For indoor cooking, eggplant can be oven roasted. Pierce the eggplant in several places with a fork and place in a baking pan. Bake at 350 degrees until soft, 45 to 50 minutes.*

4 first-course servings (about 1 cup each)

2 medium eggplants (about 2½ pounds)
¾ cup chopped onion
¼ cup chopped green bell pepper
2 cloves garlic, minced
1 tablespoon olive oil
4–5 cups reduced-sodium fat-free chicken broth
Salt and white pepper, to taste
Roasted Red Pepper Sauce (recipe follows)

Per Serving:
Calories: 250
% of calories from fat: 19
Fat (gm): 6
Saturated fat (gm): 0.7
Cholesterol (mg): 0
Sodium (mg): 25
Protein (gm): 6.8
Carbohydrate (gm): 44.8

Exchanges:
Milk: 0.0
Vegetable: 2.0
Fruit: 0.0
Bread: 2.0
Meat: 0.0
Fat: 1.0

1. Pierce eggplant in several places with fork. Grill over medium hot coals, turning frequently, until eggplant is very soft, about 30 minutes; cool slightly. Cut eggplant in half, scoop out pulp, and chop coarsely.

2. Sauté onion, pepper, and garlic in oil in large saucepan until tender, 5 to 8 minutes. Add broth and eggplant and heat to boiling. Reduce heat and simmer, covered, 10 minutes. Process soup in food processor or blender until smooth. Season to taste with salt and white pepper. Serve warm or chilled; swirl about ¼ cup Roasted Red Pepper Sauce into each bowl of soup.

Roasted Red Pepper Sauce
Makes about ¾ cup

2 large red bell peppers, halved
1 teaspoon sugar

1. Place peppers, skin sides up, on broiler pan. Broil 4 to 6 inches from heat source until skins are blistered and blackened. Place peppers in plastic bag for 5 minutes; remove and peel off skins.

2. Process peppers and sugar in food processor or blender until smooth. Refrigerate until ready to use.

NOTE: 1 jar (12 ounces) roasted red peppers, drained, can be substituted for the peppers in the recipe.

CREAM OF MUSHROOM SOUP

45   *For a richer soup, use fat-free half-and-half instead of fat-free milk.*

4 first-course servings (about 1¼ cups each)

1 pound mushrooms
2 tablespoons margarine or butter, divided
1 cup chopped onion
2½ cups reduced-sodium chicken broth
2½ cups fat-free milk, divided
2 tablespoons plus 2 teaspoons cornstarch
Salt and pepper, to taste

Per Serving:
Calories: 207
% of calories from fat: 29
Fat (gm): 7
Saturated fat (gm): 1.4
Cholesterol (mg): 2.5
Sodium (mg): 185
Protein (gm): 8.6
Carbohydrate (gm): 25.3

Exchanges:
Milk: 0.5
Vegetable: 2.5
Fruit: 0.0
Bread: 0.5
Meat: 0.0
Fat: 1.5

1. Slice enough mushroom caps to make 2 cups; finely chop stems and remaining mushrooms. Sauté sliced mushrooms in 1 tablespoon margarine in large saucepan until browned, about 5 minutes; remove and reserve.

2. Sauté onion and chopped mushrooms in remaining 1 tablespoon margarine in saucepan until onion is tender, about 5 minutes. Add broth and 2 cups milk and heat to boiling. Mix remaining ½ cup milk and cornstarch and stir into boiling mixture until thickened, about 1 minute. Stir in reserved sliced mushrooms. Season to taste with salt and pepper.

SAVORY MUSHROOM AND BARLEY SOUP

45

V

Use of quick-cooking barley speeds preparation. Other grains, such as wild rice or oat groats, can be substituted for the barley; cook before adding to the soup.

4 first-course servings (about 1½ cups each)

1 cup each: chopped onion, celery, carrots

1 teaspoon dried savory leaves

¾ teaspoon fennel seeds, crushed

1 quart water

1 can (16 ounces) reduced-sodium whole tomatoes, undrained, coarsely chopped

½ cup quick-cooking barley

2 cups sliced cremini or white mushrooms

¼ cup chopped parsley

Salt and pepper, to taste

Per Serving:
Calories: 151
% of calories from fat: 8
Fat (gm): 1.4
Saturated fat (gm): 0.1
Cholesterol (mg): 0
Sodium (mg): 53
Protein (gm): 5.6
Carbohydrate (gm): 32.1

Exchanges:
Milk: 0.0
Vegetable: 2.0
Fruit: 0.0
Bread: 1.5
Meat: 0.0
Fat: 0.0

1. Sauté onion, celery, and carrots in lightly greased saucepan until onion is tender, about 5 minutes. Stir in herbs; cook about 1 minute longer. Add water, tomatoes with liquid, barley, and mushrooms to saucepan; heat to boiling. Cook, covered, until barley is tender, 10 to 15 minutes. Stir in parsley; season to taste with salt and pepper.

BLACK MUSHROOM SOUP

45

Chinese black mushrooms (dried shiitake mushrooms) add a fragrant, woodsy flavor to this soup.

6 first-course servings (about 1¼ cups each)

1½ ounces dried Chinese black mushrooms

1 ounce dried cloud ear mushrooms

2 cups boiling water

¼ cup each: chopped onion, green onions

5 cups reduced-sodium fat-free chicken broth

3 cups sliced cremini mushrooms

Salt and white pepper, to taste

1. Place dried mushrooms in bowl; add boiling water. Let stand until mushrooms are softened, about 15 minutes. Drain, reserving liquid. Slice mushrooms, discarding tough stems from black mushrooms.

2. Sauté onions until tender in lightly greased saucepan, about 5 minutes. Add dried mushrooms, reserved liquid and broth; heat to boiling. Reduce heat and simmer, covered, 20 minutes, adding cremini mushrooms during last 10 minutes. Season to taste with salt and white pepper.

Per Serving:
Calories: 72
% of calories from fat: 16
Fat (gm): 1.4
Saturated fat (gm): 0.1
Cholesterol (mg): 0
Sodium (mg): 10
Protein (gm): 2.9
Carbohydrate (gm): 11.1

Exchanges:
Milk: 0.0
Vegetable: 3.0
Fruit: 0.0
Bread: 0.0
Meat: 0.0
Fat: 0.0

SHIITAKE-PORTOBELLO CHOWDER

L

Celebrate the rich mushroom, cheese and wine flavors in this chowder.

45   **4 first-course servings** (about 1½ cups each)

4 shallots, thinly sliced
2 teaspoons margarine or butter, divided
2 large potatoes, cubed (¼-inch)
3 cups reduced-sodium vegetable broth
2 cups each: sliced shiitake mushroom caps, cubed
  portobello mushrooms
¼ cup (1 ounce) shredded Gruyère or Swiss cheese
2 tablespoons Marsala wine (optional)
Salt and white pepper, to taste

Per Serving:
Calories: 162
% of calories from fat: 26
Fat (gm): 5
Saturated fat (gm): 1.8
Cholesterol (mg): 7.8
Sodium (mg): 114
Protein (gm): 5.6
Carbohydrate (gm): 24.7

Exchanges:
Milk: 0.0
Vegetable: 2.0
Fruit: 0.0
Bread: 1.0
Meat: 0.0
Fat: 1.0

1. Sauté shallots in 1 teaspoon margarine in large saucepan 2 to 3 minutes; add potatoes and broth and heat to boiling. Reduce heat and simmer, covered, until potatoes are tender, about 15 minutes. Process mixture in blender or food processor until smooth; return to saucepan.

2. Sauté mushrooms in remaining 1 teaspoon margarine in large skillet until lightly browned, about 8 minutes; stir into potato mixture. Cook, uncovered, over medium heat until hot, about 5 minutes. Remove from heat; add cheese and wine, stirring until cheese is melted. Season to taste with salt and white pepper.

GARLIC SOUP WITH TOASTED BREAD

45 *Often a beaten egg is slowly stirred into this Mexican soup before serving.*

4 first-course servings (about 1 cup each)

4 slices firm bread (French or sourdough)
Vegetable cooking spray
6–8 cloves garlic, finely chopped
½ teaspoon each: ground cumin, dried oregano leaves
1 tablespoon olive oil
2 cans (14½ ounces each) reduced-sodium fat-free
   chicken broth
Salt and cayenne pepper, to taste
Chopped cilantro, as garnish

Per Serving:
Calories: 162
% of calories from fat: 28
Fat (gm): 5
Saturated fat (gm): 0.7
Cholesterol (mg): 0
Sodium (mg): 202
Protein (gm): 3.2
Carbohydrate (gm): 20.6

Exchanges:
Milk: 0.0
Vegetable: 1.0
Fruit: 0.0
Bread: 1.5
Meat: 0.0
Fat: 0.5

1. Spray both sides of bread slices generously with cooking spray; cook in large skillet, over medium heat, until golden, about 2 minutes on each side.

2. Sauté garlic and herbs in oil in medium saucepan until lightly browned, about 3 minutes. Add broth and heat to boiling; reduce heat and simmer, covered, 5 minutes. Season to taste with salt and cayenne pepper. Place slices of bread in bottoms of shallow bowls; ladle soup over and sprinkle with cilantro.

FRENCH ONION SOUP

This classic soup is topped with Bruschetta and fat-free cheese for healthful, delicious dining.

8 first-course servings (about 1¼ cups each)

6 cups (1½ pounds) thinly sliced Spanish onions
2 cloves garlic, minced
1 teaspoon sugar
6 cups reduced-sodium fat-free beef broth
2 bay leaves
Salt and white pepper, to taste
8 Bruschetta (⅓ recipe) (see p. 495)
8 tablespoons (2 ounces) shredded fat-free Swiss cheese

1. Add onions and garlic to lightly greased Dutch oven and cook, covered, over medium-low heat until wilted, 8 to 10 minutes. Stir in sugar and continue cooking, uncovered, until onions are lightly browned, about 10 minutes. Stir in broth and bay leaves; heat to boiling. Reduce heat and simmer, covered, 30 minutes. Discard bay leaves; season to taste with salt and white pepper.

2. Top each Bruschetta with 1 tablespoon cheese; broil 6 inches from heat source until cheese is melted. Top each bowl of soup with a Bruschetta.

Per Serving:
Calories: 126
% of calories from fat: 7
Fat (gm): 1
Saturated fat (gm): 0.1
Cholesterol (mg): 0.0
Sodium (mg): 542
Protein (gm): 4.9
Carbohydrate (gm): 25

Exchanges:
Milk: 0.0
Vegetable: 0.0
Fruit: 0.0
Bread: 1.5
Meat: 0.0
Fat: 0.0

VIDALIA ONION SOUP

The mild sweetness of Vidalia onions makes this soup special, but try it with other flavorful onion varieties too.

8 first-course servings (about 1¼ cups each)

6 cups (1½ pounds) thinly sliced Vidalia onions
2 cloves garlic, minced
1 teaspoon sugar
⅓ cup all-purpose flour
6 cups reduced-sodium fat-free chicken or
　　vegetable broth
1½ teaspoons dried sage leaves
2 bay leaves
Salt, cayenne, and white pepper, to taste
Snipped chives, as garnish

Per Serving:
Calories: 88
% of calories from fat: 3
Fat (gm): 0.3
Saturated fat (gm): 0.1
Cholesterol (mg): 0
Sodium (mg): 13
Protein (gm): 2.2
Carbohydrate (gm): 16.4

Exchanges:
Milk: 0.0
Vegetable: 2.0
Fruit: 0.0
Bread: 0.5
Meat: 0.0
Fat: 0.0

1. Add onions and garlic to lightly greased saucepan and cook, covered, over medium-low heat until wilted, 8 to 10 minutes. Stir in sugar and continue cooking, uncovered, until onions are lightly browned, about 10 minutes. Stir in flour; cook 1 minute. Add broth and herbs; heat to boiling. Reduce heat and simmer, covered, 30 minutes. Discard bay leaves.

2. Process half the soup in food processor or blender until smooth; return to saucepan and season to taste with salt, cayenne, and white pepper. Serve warm or chilled; sprinkle each bowl of soup with chives.

THREE-ONION SOUP WITH MUSHROOMS

Mushrooms are a flavorful addition to this onion soup. Substitute canned reduced-sodium vegetable broth to speed preparation.

6 first-course servings (about 1½ cups each)

3 cups thinly sliced onions
1½ cups thinly sliced leeks
½ cup chopped shallots or green onions
1 tablespoon margarine or butter
1 teaspoon sugar
2 cups sliced mushrooms
6½ cups reduced-sodium fat-free chicken broth
Salt and pepper, to taste

Per Serving:
Calories: 119
% of calories from fat: 21
Fat (gm): 3
Saturated fat (gm): 0.5
Cholesterol (mg): 0
Sodium (mg): 218
Protein (gm): 2.7
Carbohydrate (gm): 18.5

Exchanges:
Milk: 0.0
Vegetable: 3.0
Fruit: 0.0
Bread: 0.0
Meat: 0.0
Fat: 0.5

1. Cook onions, leeks, and shallots in margarine in large saucepan, covered, over medium-low heat 15 minutes. Stir in sugar; cook, uncovered, until onion mixture is golden, about 15 minutes. Stir in mushrooms; cook over medium heat until tender, about 5 minutes. Add broth and heat to boiling; reduce heat and simmer, uncovered, 15 minutes. Season to taste with salt and pepper.

ONION AND LEEK SOUP WITH MUSHROOMS

Mushrooms add flavor and texture interest to this soup.

6 first-course servings (about 1½ cups each)

3 cups sliced onions
1½ cups sliced leeks
½ cup chopped shallots or green onions
1 tablespoon margarine or butter
1 teaspoon sugar
4 ounces mushrooms, sliced
6½ cups reduced-sodium chicken broth
Salt and pepper, to taste

Per Serving:
Calories: 211
% of calories from fat: 3
Fat (gm): 0.8
Saturated fat (gm): 0.1
Cholesterol (mg): 0
Sodium (mg): 234
Protein (gm): 12.9
Carbohydrate (gm): 37.1

Exchanges:
Milk: 0.0
Vegetable: 2.0
Fruit: 0.0
Bread: 2.0
Meat: 0.0
Fat: 0.0

1. Cook onions, leeks, and shallots in margarine in large saucepan, covered, over medium heat until wilted, 5 to 8 minutes. Stir in sugar and mushrooms; cook, uncovered, over medium-low heat until onion mixture is golden, 10 to 15 minutes. Add broth and heat to boiling; reduce heat and simmer, uncovered, 15 minutes. Season to taste with salt and pepper.

POBLANO CHILI SOUP

45 *Poblano chilies give this soup extraordinary flavor. Taste the peppers, as they can vary in flavor from mild to very hot; if they are too hot for your taste, substitute some green bell peppers.*

8 first-course servings (about 1 cup each)

2 medium onions, chopped

4 medium poblano chilies, seeded, chopped

½–1 small jalapeño chili, seeded, finely chopped

2 cans (14½ ounces each) reduced-sodium fat-free chicken broth

3 cups tomato juice

½ teaspoon ground cumin

Salt and pepper, to taste

Chopped cilantro, as garnish

Per Serving:
Calories: 88
% of calories from fat: 3
Fat (gm): 0.4
Saturated fat (gm): 0
Cholesterol (mg): 0
Sodium (mg): 498
Protein (gm): 6.4
Carbohydrate (gm): 18.2

Exchanges:
Milk: 0.0
Vegetable: 3.5
Fruit: 0.0
Bread: 0.0
Meat: 0.0
Fat: 0.0

1. Sauté onions and chilies in lightly greased skillet until onions are tender, about 5 minutes. Add broth, tomato juice, and cumin and heat to boiling; reduce heat and simmer, covered, until chilies are very tender, about 10 minutes. Process in food processor or blender until smooth; season to taste with salt and pepper. Serve warm or chilled; sprinkle each bowl of soup with cilantro.

CHILLED PEA SOUP

45

A refreshing soup for hot sultry days; serve with a ripe tomato salad and crusty bread or rolls.

6 entrée servings (about 1 cup each)

½ cup chopped onion

½ teaspoon each: dried marjoram and thyme leaves

2 cups reduced-sodium fat-free chicken broth

2 packages (20 ounces each) frozen peas

2 cups sliced romaine lettuce

Salt and white pepper, to taste

½ cup fat-free sour cream

Paprika, as garnish

Per Serving:
Calories: 257
% of calories from fat: 4
Fat (gm): 1.1
Saturated fat (gm): 0.2
Cholesterol (mg): 0
Sodium (mg): 274
Protein (gm): 17.4
Carbohydrate (gm): 46.6

Exchanges:
Milk: 0.0
Vegetable: 0.0
Fruit: 0.0
Bread: 3.0
Meat: 0.5
Fat: 0.0

1. Sauté onion and herbs in lightly greased large saucepan until onion is tender, about 5 minutes. Stir in broth, peas, and lettuce; heat to boiling. Reduce heat and simmer, covered, until peas are tender, 5 to 8 minutes. Process soup in food processor or blender until smooth; season to taste with salt and pepper. Serve chilled; stir in sour cream before serving and sprinkle with paprika.

SNOW PEA SOUP

45

Make this soup a day in advance so that flavors can blend.

6 first-course servings (about 1¼ cups each)

½ cup each: chopped green onions, yellow onion

1 tablespoon margarine or butter

1 pound snow peas, trimmed

4 cups coarsely chopped romaine lettuce

4 cups reduced-sodium fat-free chicken broth

½ teaspoon each: dried tarragon and mint leaves

Salt and white pepper, to taste

6 tablespoons plain fat-free yogurt

Fresh mint or tarragon sprigs

Per Serving:
Calories: 76
% of calories from fat: 28
Fat (gm): 2.5
Saturated fat (gm): 0.5
Cholesterol (mg): 0.3
Sodium (mg): 47
Protein (gm): 4.3
Carbohydrate (gm): 9.8

Exchanges:
Milk: 0.0
Vegetable: 2.0
Fruit: 0.0
Bread: 0.0
Meat: 0.0
Fat: 0.5

1. Sauté onions in margarine in large saucepan until tender, about 5 minutes. Add snow peas and lettuce; sauté 3 to 4 minutes longer. Add broth, tarragon, and mint; heat to boiling. Reduce heat and simmer, covered, 15 minutes or until snow peas are very tender.

2. Process soup in food processor or blender until smooth; strain and discard solids. Season to taste with salt and white pepper. Serve warm or chilled; garnish each bowl of soup with yogurt and fresh mint.

SWEET RED PEPPER SOUP

45

L

Use jarred roasted peppers for this soup, or roast 3 medium red bell peppers. (See Roasted Red Pepper Sauce, p. 59, for roasting directions).

4 first-course servings (about 1 cup each)

1 medium onion, chopped

½ small jalapeño chili, seeded, minced

1 clove garlic, minced

1 jar (15 ounces) roasted red bell peppers, drained

1 cup reduced-sodium tomato juice

1 can (14½ ounces) vegetable broth

½ teaspoon dried marjoram leaves

Salt and pepper, to taste

¼ cup fat-free sour cream

Sliced green onion, as garnish

Per Serving:
Calories: 77
% of calories from fat: 5
Fat (gm): 0.4
Saturated fat (gm): 0.1
Cholesterol (mg): 0
Sodium (mg): 264
Protein (gm): 2.9
Carbohydrate (gm): 13.4

Exchanges:
Milk: 0.0
Vegetable: 3.0
Fruit: 0.0
Bread: 0.0
Meat: 0.0
Fat: 0.0

1. Sauté onion, jalapeño chili, and garlic in lightly greased saucepan until tender, about 5 minutes. Process onion mixture, bell peppers, and tomato juice in food processor or blender until smooth. Return mixture to saucepan and add broth and marjoram; heat to boiling. Reduce heat and simmer, covered, 15 minutes. Season to taste with salt and pepper. Serve warm or chilled; top each bowl of soup with a dollop of sour cream and sprinkle with green onion.

POTATO CHOWDER

45 *A basic soup that is versatile: substitute any desired vegetables, such as carrots, zucchini, green beans, or corn, for part of the potatoes for a delectable vegetable chowder.*

6 entrée servings (about 1 cup each)

1 cup chopped onion
¼ cup thinly sliced celery
2 tablespoons margarine or butter
3 tablespoons flour
2 cups reduced-sodium chicken broth
3½ cups peeled, cubed Idaho potatoes
¼–½ teaspoon celery seeds
2 cups fat-free milk
Salt and pepper, to taste

Per Serving:
Calories: 212
% of calories from fat: 17
Fat (gm): 4.2
Saturated fat (gm): 0.9
Cholesterol (mg): 1.3
Sodium (mg): 210
Protein (gm): 7.5
Carbohydrate (gm): 37.1

Exchanges:
Milk: 0.0
Vegetable: 1.0
Fruit: 0.0
Bread: 2.0
Meat: 0.0
Fat: 1.0

1. Sauté onion and celery in margarine in large saucepan until tender, 5 to 8 minutes; stir in flour and cook 1 minute longer. Add broth, potatoes, and celery seeds to saucepan; heat to boiling. Reduce heat and simmer, covered, until potatoes are tender, 10 to 15 minutes. Stir in milk and cook until hot, 2 to 3 minutes. Season to taste with salt and pepper.

HOT CHILI VICHYSSOISE

45 *Potato soup will never be boring if served Tex-Mex style. This version, prepared with peppers, packs a punch!*

6 entrée servings (about 1 cup each)

1 each: medium leek (white part only), poblano and jalapeño chili
1 pound new red potatoes, unpeeled, halved
6 cloves garlic, peeled
Vegetable cooking spray
1½ teaspoons ground cumin
½ teaspoon each: chili powder, dried oregano leaves
4 cups reduced-sodium fat-free chicken broth, divided
½–¾ cup fat-free half-and-half or fat-free milk
¼ cup chopped cilantro
Salt, to taste

1. Cut leek and chilies into ¾-inch pieces. Arrange vegetables and garlic in single layer greased foil-lined jelly roll pan; spray with cooking spray and sprinkle with herbs. Roast at 425 degrees until browned and tender, about 40 minutes, removing garlic when tender, after about 30 minutes.

2. Process vegetables and 1 to 2 cups broth in food processor or blender until smooth. Heat vegetable mixture and remaining broth to boiling in large saucepan; reduce heat to medium. Stir in half-and-half and cook until hot, 3 to 4 minutes. Stir in cilantro; season with salt. Serve warm or chilled.

Per Serving:
Calories: 113
% of calories from fat: 2
Fat (gm): 0.3
Saturated fat (gm): 0
Cholesterol (mg): 0
Sodium (mg): 169
Protein (gm): 6.6
Carbohydrate (gm): 20.9

Exchanges:
Milk: 0.0
Vegetable: 1.0
Fruit: 0.0
Bread: 1.0
Meat: 0.0
Fat: 0.0

CINNAMON-SPICED PUMPKIN SOUP

45

L

For convenience, 2 cans (16 ounces each) pumpkin can be substituted for the fresh pumpkin. Any yellow winter squash such as butternut, Hubbard, or acorn can also be used.

4 first-course servings (about 1¼ cups each)

4 cups cubed, seeded, peeled pumpkin
2 cups fat-free half-and-half or fat-free milk
1–2 tablespoons light brown sugar
½ teaspoon ground cinnamon
¼–½ teaspoon ground nutmeg
Snipped chives, as garnish

Per Serving:
Calories: 125
% of calories from fat: 1
Fat (gm): 0.2
Saturated fat (gm): 0.1
Cholesterol (mg): 0
Sodium (mg): 122
Protein (gm): 5.2
Carbohydrate (gm): 23.2

Exchanges:
Milk: 1.0
Vegetable: 0.0
Fruit: 0.0
Bread: 0.5
Meat: 0.0
Fat: 0.0

1. Cook pumpkin in medium saucepan, covered, in 1 inch simmering water until tender, about 15 minutes; drain. Process pumpkin and half-and-half in food processor or blender; return to saucepan. Stir in brown sugar and spices and heat to boiling; reduce heat and simmer, uncovered, 5 minutes. Sprinkle each bowl of soup with chives.

ORANGE-SCENTED SQUASH SOUP

L

Subtly seasoned with orange and spices, this delicious soup can be served warm or chilled.

6 first-course servings (about 1⅓ cups each)

¾ cup chopped onion

1 teaspoon ground cinnamon

¼ teaspoon each: ground nutmeg, cloves

1½ cups water

3 pounds winter yellow squash (Hubbard, butternut, or acorn), peeled, cubed

1 large, tart cooking apple, peeled, cored, cubed

1 strip orange zest (3 x ½ inch)

¼–½ cup orange juice

1½–2 cups fat-free half-and-half or fat-free milk

Salt and white pepper, to taste

6 thin orange slices

Snipped chives, as garnish

Per Serving:
Calories: 144
% of calories from fat: 8
Fat (gm): 1.4
Saturated fat (gm): 0.3
Cholesterol (mg): 0
Sodium (mg): 64
Protein (gm): 4.1
Carbohydrate (gm): 30.2

Exchanges:
Milk: 0.0
Vegetable: 0.0
Fruit: 0.0
Bread: 2.0
Meat: 0.0
Fat: 0.0

1. Sauté onion in lightly greased saucepan until tender, about 5 minutes. Stir in spices; cook 1 minute longer. Add water, squash, apple, and orange zest to saucepan; heat to boiling. Reduce heat and simmer, covered, until squash is tender, 10 to 15 minutes.

2. Process soup and orange juice in food processor or blender until smooth; add half-and-half. Season to taste with salt and white pepper. Serve warm or chilled. Garnish each bowl of soup with an orange slice and chives.

VARIATION

Winter Squash Soup — Make recipe as above, deleting cloves, orange zest, and orange juice. Add ¼ teaspoon each ground ginger and cumin, and 1 cup apple cider; reduce fat-free half-and-half to ½–1 cup.

SUMMER SQUASH SOUP

Use any summer squash in this soup.

6 first-course servings (about 1¼ cups each)

4 medium zucchini, chopped
1 cup peeled, cubed Idaho potato
½ cup chopped shallots
¼ cup sliced green onions
2 cloves garlic, minced
4 cups reduced-sodium fat-free chicken broth
1 cup chopped kale or spinach leaves
1–½ teaspoons dried tarragon leaves
¼–½ cup fat-free half-and-half or fat-free milk
Salt and white pepper, to taste
Cayenne pepper, as garnish
1½ cups Sourdough Croutons (½ recipe) (see p. 498)

Per Serving:
Calories: 100
% of calories from fat: 7
Fat (gm): 0.8
Saturated fat (gm): 0.1
Cholesterol (mg): 0
Sodium (mg): 65
Protein (gm): 3.8
Carbohydrate (gm): 20.6

Exchanges:
Milk: 0.0
Vegetable: 1.0
Fruit: 0.0
Bread: 1.0
Meat: 0.0
Fat: 0.0

1. Sauté zucchini, potato, shallots, green onions, and garlic in lightly greased saucepan until lightly browned, about 8 minutes. Add broth, kale, and tarragon. Heat to boiling; reduce heat and simmer, covered, until vegetables are tender, 10 to 15 minutes.

2. Process soup in food processor or blender until smooth; stir in half-and-half and season to taste with salt and white pepper. Serve warm or chilled; sprinkle each of bowl soup with cayenne pepper and top with Sourdough Croutons.

CREAM OF TOMATO SOUP

45 *A soup similar to the favorite-brand canned tomato soup we all remember eating as kids! Canned tomatoes are necessary for the flavor, so don't substitute fresh.*

4 first-course servings (about 1¼ cups each)

2 cans (14½ ounces each) reduced-sodium whole tomatoes, undrained
1–3 teaspoons beef bouillon crystals
2 cups fat-free milk

3 tablespoons cornstarch

⅛ teaspoon baking soda

2 teaspoons sugar

1–2 tablespoons margarine or butter

Salt and pepper, to taste

Per Serving:
Calories: 142
% of calories from fat: 22
Fat (gm): 3.7
Saturated fat (gm): 0.8
Cholesterol (mg): 2
Sodium (mg): 395
Protein (gm): 6.3
Carbohydrate (gm): 22.6

1. Process tomatoes with liquid in food processor or blender until smooth; heat tomatoes and bouillon crystals to boiling in large saucepan. Stir in combined milk and cornstarch, stirring until thickened, about 1 minute. Add baking soda, sugar, and margarine, stirring until margarine is melted. Season to taste with salt and pepper.

Exchanges:
Milk: 0.5
Vegetable: 2.0
Fruit: 0.0
Bread: 0.5
Meat: 0.0
Fat: 0.5

SUN-DRIED TOMATO AND LINGUINE SOUP

45 *Great soup in less than 45 minutes! One-half cup uncooked orzo can be substituted for the linguine, if preferred.*

4 first-course servings (about 1 cup each)

½ cup thinly sliced celery

2 tablespoons thinly sliced green onions

2 cloves garlic, minced

2 cans (14½ ounces each) reduced-sodium chicken broth

2 ounces uncooked linguine, broken into pieces (3-inch)

2 sun-dried tomatoes (not in oil), softened, chopped

1–2 teaspoons lemon juice

Salt and pepper, to taste

Per Serving:
Calories: 111
% of calories from fat: 10
Fat (gm): 1.3
Saturated fat (gm): 0.1
Cholesterol (mg): 0
Sodium (mg): 155
Protein (gm): 3.3
Carbohydrate (gm): 16.8

Exchanges:
Milk: 0.0
Vegetable: 1.0
Fruit: 0.0
Bread: 1.0
Meat: 0.0
Fat: 0.0

1. Sauté celery, onions, and garlic in lightly greased medium saucepan until tender, 5 to 7 minutes. Stir in broth and heat to boiling; add linguine and sun-dried tomatoes. Reduce heat and simmer, uncovered, until pasta is al dente, about 10 minutes. Season with lemon juice, salt and pepper.

TWO-TOMATO SOUP

45 | *The concentrated flavor of sun-dried tomatoes enhances the taste of garden-ripe tomato soup.*

6 first-course servings (about 1¼ cups each)

1 cup chopped onion
½ cup each: chopped celery, carrot
2 teaspoons minced roasted garlic
4 cups reduced-sodium fat-free chicken broth
4 cups chopped ripe tomatoes or 2 cans (16 ounces
   each) reduced-sodium whole tomatoes, undrained,
   coarsely chopped
1 large Idaho potato, peeled, cubed
½ cup sun-dried tomatoes (not in oil)
½ teaspoons dried basil leaves
½ cup fat-free half-and-half or fat-free milk
2–3 teaspoons sugar
Salt and pepper, to taste

Per Serving:
Calories: 117
% of calories from fat: 5
Fat (gm): 0.8
Saturated fat (gm): 0.1
Cholesterol (mg): 0
Sodium (mg): 150
Protein (gm): 3.7
Carbohydrate (gm): 22.6

Exchanges:
Milk: 0.0
Vegetable: 2.0
Fruit: 0.0
Bread: 1.0
Meat: 0.0
Fat: 0.0

1. Sauté onion, celery, carrot, and garlic in lightly greased large saucepan until lightly browned, 5 to 8 minutes. Add broth, tomatoes with liquid, potato, sun-dried tomatoes, and basil; heat to boiling. Reduce heat and simmer, covered, until vegetables are tender, 10 to 15 minutes.

2. Process soup in food processor or blender until smooth; return to saucepan. Stir in half-and-half and heat until hot, 3 to 5 minutes; season to taste with sugar, salt, and pepper.

GAZPACHO

 L

 45

Easy to make and served cold, Gazpacho is a wonderful soup to keep on hand in summer months.

6 first-course servings (about 1¼ cups each)

5 large tomatoes, halved, seeded
2 cups reduced-sodium tomato juice

2 cloves garlic

2 tablespoons lime juice

1 teaspoon dried oregano leaves

1 cup each: chopped yellow bell pepper, celery, cucumber

6 green onions, thinly sliced

2 tablespoons finely chopped cilantro

Salt and pepper, to taste

Avocado Sour Cream (recipe follows)

Hot pepper sauce

Per Serving:
Calories: 76
% of calories from fat: 17
Fat (gm): 1.6
Saturated fat (gm): 0.3
Cholesterol (mg): 0.1
Sodium (mg): 46
Protein (gm): 3.3
Carbohydrate (gm): 15.1

Exchanges:
Milk: 0.0
Vegetable: 2.0
Fruit: 0.0
Bread: 0.0
Meat: 0.0
Fat: 0.5

1. Chop tomatoes, reserving 1 cup. Process remaining tomatoes, tomato juice, garlic, lime juice, and oregano in food processor or blender until smooth. Mix tomato mixture, reserved tomatoes, bell pepper, celery, cucumber, green onions, and cilantro in large bowl; season to taste with salt and pepper. Serve chilled; top each bowl of soup with a dollop of Avocado Sour Cream. Serve with hot pepper sauce.

Avocado Sour Cream

Makes about ⅔ cup

½ medium avocado, chopped

¼ cup fat-free sour cream

2 tablespoons fat-free milk

Salt and white pepper, to taste

1. Process all ingredients in food processor until smooth; season to taste with salt and white pepper.

BEAN GAZPACHO

Pureed beans contribute nutritional value, plus a velvety texture, to this delicious gazpacho.

8 entrée servings (about 1⅓ cups each)

2 cans (15 ounces each) pinto beans, rinsed, drained
1 quart reduced-sodium tomato juice
3–4 tablespoons lime juice
2 teaspoons each: reduced-sodium Worcestershire sauce, minced roasted garlic
1 cup each: thick and chunky salsa, peeled, seeded, chopped cucumber, sliced celery
½ cup each: sliced green onions, chopped green bell pepper
½ cup each: chopped avocado, fat-free sour cream
1½ cups Herb Croutons (½ recipe) (see p. 498)

Per Serving:
Calories: 260
% of calories from fat: 13
Fat (gm): 3.8
Saturated fat (gm): 0.2
Cholesterol (mg): 0
Sodium (mg): 642
Protein (gm): 12.9
Carbohydrate (gm): 47.1

Exchanges:
Milk: 0.5
Vegetable: 2.0
Fruit: 0.0
Bread: 2.5
Meat: 0.5
Fat: 0.0

1. Process beans, tomato juice, lime juice, Worcestershire sauce, and garlic in food processor or blender until smooth; pour into large bowl. Mix in remaining ingredients, except avocado, sour cream, and Herb Croutons. Refrigerate until chilled, 3 to 4 hours.

2. Mix avocado into soup; garnish each bowl of soup with a dollop of sour cream and sprinkle with croutons.

45-MINUTE PREPARATION TIP: Make Herb Croutons and bake while preparing the soup.

WHITE GAZPACHO

Something different that is sure to please!

4 first-course servings (about 1 cup each)

1 large onion, sliced
4 cloves garlic, minced
2 cups fat-free milk
1 vegetable or chicken bouillon cube
1–1½ cups plain fat-free yogurt

2 teaspoons lemon juice

2 dashes hot pepper sauce

Salt and white pepper, to taste

⅓ cup each: chopped seeded cucumber, yellow
tomato, avocado

Finely chopped cilantro, as garnish

Per Serving:
Calories: 109
% of calories from fat: 27
Fat (gm): 3.4
Saturated fat (gm): 0.6
Cholesterol (mg): 2
Sodium (mg): 196
Protein (gm): 6.7
Carbohydrate (gm): 14.3

Exchanges:
Milk: 0.5
Vegetable: 2.0
Fruit: 0.0
Bread: 0.0
Meat: 0.0
Fat: 0.5

1. Sauté onion and garlic in lightly greased
skillet over medium-low heat until very tender,
about 15 minutes. Add milk and bouillon cube;
cook over medium-high heat, stirring frequently,
until mixture is hot and bouillon cube is
dissolved. Process soup, yogurt, lemon juice,
and hot pepper sauce in food processor or
blender until smooth. Season to taste with salt
and white pepper. Serve chilled; stir cucumber,
tomato, and avocado into soup and sprinkle with
cilantro.

ORIENTAL WATERCRESS SOUP

45 *Spinach can be substituted for the watercress in this fragrant
Cantonese offering.*

6 first-course servings (about 1 cup each)

6 cups reduced-sodium fat-free chicken broth

3 slices gingerroot (¼-inch)

2 cups loosely packed torn watercress

Salt and white pepper, to taste

2 sliced green onions

2 tablespoons shredded carrot

Per Serving:
Calories: 11
% of calories from fat: 9
Fat (gm): 0.1
Saturated fat (gm): 0
Cholesterol (mg): 0
Sodium (mg): 116
Protein (gm): 0.9
Carbohydrate (gm): 1.8

Exchanges:
Milk: 0.0
Vegetable: 0.0
Fruit: 0.0
Bread: 0.0
Meat: 0.0
Fat: 0.0

1. Heat broth and gingerroot to boiling in large
saucepan; reduce heat and simmer, covered, 5
minutes. Remove gingerroot with slotted spoon
and discard. Add watercress and simmer, uncovered, 10 to 15 minutes. Season to taste with salt
and white pepper. Sprinkle each bowl of soup
with green onions and carrot.

GREEK LEMON-RICE SOUP

45 *Nicely tart; use fresh lemon juice for the best flavor. If making this soup in advance, do not add egg until reheating for serving.*

4 first-course servings (about 1 cup each)

3½ cups reduced-sodium fat-free chicken broth
¼ cup long-grain rice
2 large cloves garlic, minced
¼–⅓ cup lemon juice
1 egg, lightly beaten
2 tablespoons chopped parsley
Salt and white pepper, to taste

Per Serving:
Calories: 106
% of calories from fat: 20
Fat (gm): 2.4
Saturated fat (gm): 0.5
Cholesterol (mg): 53.3
Sodium (mg): 31
Protein (gm): 3
Carbohydrate (gm): 14.4

Exchanges:
Milk: 0.0
Vegetable: 0.0
Fruit: 0.0
Bread: 1.0
Meat: 0.0
Fat: 0.5

1. Heat broth to boiling in medium saucepan; stir in rice and garlic. Reduce heat and simmer, covered, until rice is tender, about 25 minutes; reduce heat to low; Mix lemon juice and egg; slowly stir mixture into soup. Stir in parsley; season to taste with salt and white pepper.

TORTILLA SOUP

Cubed chicken can be added to the soup, if desired, to make this a more substantial dish.

6 first-course servings (about 1½ cups each)

2 corn or flour tortillas, cut into strips (2 x ¼-inch)
Vegetable cooking spray
¾ cup each: chopped onion, celery, tomato
½ teaspoon each: dried basil leaves, ground cumin
5 cups reduced-sodium fat-free chicken broth
1 can (15 ounces) pinto beans, rinsed, drained
6 ounces cooked chicken breast, shredded or cubed
2 tablespoons finely chopped cilantro
1–2 teaspoons lime juice
Salt and cayenne pepper, to taste

Per Serving:
Calories: 176
% of calories from fat: 10
Fat (gm): 2
Saturated fat (gm): 0.3
Cholesterol (mg): 24.1
Sodium (mg): 386
Protein (gm): 19.1
Carbohydrate (gm): 22.6

Exchanges:
Milk: 0.0
Vegetable: 1.0
Fruit: 0.0
Bread: 1.0
Meat: 2.0
Fat: 0.0

1. Spray tortillas lightly with cooking spray and toss; cook in lightly greased medium skillet over medium heat until browned and crisp, about 5 minutes; reserve.

2. Sauté onion, celery, tomato, basil, and cumin in lightly greased saucepan until onion is tender, 3 to 5 minutes. Add broth, beans, and chicken and heat to boiling; reduce heat and simmer, uncovered, 5 minutes. Stir in cilantro; season to taste with lime juice, salt and cayenne pepper. Add tortilla strips to soup bowls; ladle soup over.

HOT SOUR SOUP

The contrast in hot and sour flavors makes this Mandarin soup a unique offering. The hot chili sesame oil and Sour Sauce are intensely flavored, so use sparingly.

6 first-course servings (about 1 cup each)

1 ounce dried Chinese black mushrooms (shiitake)

¾ cup boiling water

1 quart reduced-sodium fat-free chicken broth

1½ cups cubed tempeh or light extra-firm tofu

½ cup bamboo shoots

¼ cup distilled white vinegar

2 tablespoons reduced-sodium tamari soy sauce

1 tablespoon each: finely chopped gingerroot, brown
    sugar, cornstarch

3 tablespoons water

Salt, cayenne, and black pepper, to taste

1 egg, lightly beaten

1 teaspoon Asian sesame oil

12–18 drops hot chili sesame oil or Szechwan chili sauce

Sour Sauce (recipe follows)

Per Serving:
Calories: 176
% of calories from fat: 28
Fat (gm): 6
Saturated fat (gm): 0.8
Cholesterol (mg): 35
Sodium (mg): 630
Protein (gm): 11
Carbohydrate (gm): 21

Exchanges:
Milk: 0.0
Vegetable: 0.0
Fruit: 0.0
Bread: 1.5
Meat: 1.5
Fat: 0.0

1. Combine mushrooms and boiling water in small bowl; let stand until mushrooms are softened, 15 to 20 minutes. Drain, reserving liquid. Slice mushrooms, discarding tough stems.

2. Heat broth, mushrooms and reserved liquid, tempeh, bamboo shoots, vinegar, soy sauce, gingerroot, and brown sugar to boiling in large saucepan. Reduce heat and simmer, uncovered, 10 minutes. Heat soup to boiling; stir in combined cornstarch and water, stirring until thickened, about 1 minute. Season to taste with salt, cayenne, and black pepper. Stir egg slowly into soup; stir in Asian sesame oil. Serve with hot chili oil and Sour Sauce.

Sour Sauce

Makes about ⅓ cup

3 tablespoons distilled white vinegar
1 tablespoon reduced-sodium tamari soy sauce
2 tablespoons packed light brown sugar

1. Mix all ingredients.

ALSATIAN PEASANT SOUP

L

45

Root vegetables, cabbage, and beans combine for a robust soup that is almost a stew. Serve with a crusty rye bread and a good beer.

6 entrée servings (about 1½ cups each)

½ cup each: chopped onion, celery
1 tablespoon olive oil
1 cup each: cubed, unpeeled potato and parsnip, sliced carrots
1 teaspoon dried thyme leaves
½ teaspoon crushed caraway seeds
1 bay leaf
3 cups reduced-sodium vegetable broth
2 cups thinly sliced cabbage
2 cans (15 ounces each) Great Northern beans, rinsed, drained
Salt and pepper, to taste
¾ cup (3 ounces) shredded reduced-fat Swiss cheese
1½ cups Rye Caraway Croutons (½ recipe, see p. 498)

Per Serving:
Calories: 300
% of calories from fat: 13
Fat (gm): 4.3
Saturated fat (gm): 1
Cholesterol (mg): 5
Sodium (mg): 352
Protein (gm): 17
Carbohydrate (gm): 50

Exchanges:
Milk: 0.0
Vegetable: 1.0
Fruit: 0.0
Bread: 3.0
Meat: 1.0
Fat: 0.0

1. Sauté onion and celery in oil in large saucepan until tender, about 5 minutes. Add potato, parsnip, carrots, and herbs; cook over medium heat 5 minutes. Add broth, cabbage, and beans to saucepan; heat to boiling. Reduce heat and simmer, covered, until vegetables are tender, 10 to 15 minutes. Discard bay leaf; season to taste with salt and pepper. Sprinkle each bowl of soup with 2 tablespoons shredded cheese and Rye Caraway Croutons.

CHICKEN VEGETABLE SOUP WITH ORZO

45 *Escarole lends a unique taste to this hearty soup; kale or spinach can also be used.*

4 entrée servings (about 2 cups each)

12 ounces boneless, skinless chicken breast, cubed (½-inch)1 cup each: chopped onion, sliced carrots, celery

3 cloves garlic, minced

2 medium zucchini or summer yellow squash, sliced

1 cup sliced mushrooms

½ teaspoon each: dried thyme and oregano leaves

5 cups reduced-sodium fat-free chicken broth

½ cup (4 ounces) uncooked orzo

½ cup frozen peas

6 medium leaves escarole, sliced or coarsely chopped

Salt and pepper, to taste

2 tablespoons grated Romano cheese

Per Serving:
Calories: 265
% of calories from fat: 10
Fat (gm): 2.9
Saturated fat (gm): 0.9
Cholesterol (mg): 3.6
Sodium (mg): 298
Protein (gm): 9.1
Carbohydrate (gm): 44.3

Exchanges:
Milk: 0.0
Vegetable: 3.0
Fruit: 0.0
Bread: 2.0
Meat: 0.0
Fat: 1.0

1. Sauté chicken in lightly greased saucepan until no longer pink in the center, about 8 minutes; remove from saucepan. Add onion, carrots, celery, and garlic in lightly greased large saucepan until onion is tender, about 5 minutes. Add zucchini, mushrooms, and herbs; cook, covered, 2 to 3 minutes. Add broth and heat to boiling. Stir in orzo, peas, and escarole; reduce heat and simmer, uncovered, until orzo is al dente, about 7 minutes. Season with salt and pepper. Sprinkle each bowl of soup with cheese.

LIGHTLY CREAMED VEGETABLE SOUP

45 *Fat-free milk, whipped with an immersion blender, lends a wonderful rich texture to this fragrant creamed soup. Or, if desired, just stir the milk into the soup near the end of the cooking time.*

6 first-course servings (about 1⅓ cups each)

1 cup each: sliced onion, carrots, yellow
   summer squash
⅔ cup each: chopped green and red bell
   pepper, celery
1 clove garlic, minced
1½ tablespoons margarine or butter
4 cups reduced-sodium fat-free chicken broth
4 peppercorns
3 whole cloves
1 bay leaf
⅓ cup all-purpose flour
⅔ cup water
Salt and pepper, to taste
½ cup fat-free milk
Ground nutmeg, as garnish

Per Serving:
Calories: 112
% of calories from fat: 27
Fat (gm): 3.6
Saturated fat (gm): 0.7
Cholesterol (mg): 0.3
Sodium (mg): 73
Protein (gm): 3.4
Carbohydrate (gm): 18

Exchanges:
Milk: 0.0
Vegetable: 2.0
Fruit: 0.0
Bread: 0.5
Meat: 0.0
Fat: 0.5

1. Sauté vegetables in margarine in large saucepan until onion is tender, 8 to 10 minutes. Add broth and herbs, tied in a cheesecloth bag; heat to boiling. Reduce heat and simmer, covered, until vegetables are tender, 10 to 15 minutes; discard herb bag. Heat soup to boiling; stir in combined flour and water until thickened, about 1 minute. Season to taste with salt and pepper.

2. Just before serving, whip fat-free milk with an immersion blender, or process in blender at high speed 30 seconds; stir into soup. Sprinkle each bowl of soup with nutmeg.

LIME-SCENTED VEGETABLE SOUP

A soup with a fresh flavor, accented with lime and cilantro.

6 first-course servings (about 1¼ cups each)

2 cups sliced carrots
¾ cup each: chopped red bell pepper, sliced celery
½ cup sliced green onions
6 cloves garlic, minced
1 small jalapeño chili, finely chopped
6 cups reduced-sodium fat-free chicken broth
½–¾ cup lime juice
½ teaspoon ground cumin
1 cup chopped tomato
½ cup each: chopped cucumber, avocado
3–4 tablespoons finely chopped cilantro
1½ cups Herb Croutons (½ recipe) (see p. 498)

Per Serving:
Calories: 106
% of calories from fat: 29
Fat (gm): 3.9
Saturated fat (gm): 0.1
Cholesterol (mg): 0
Sodium (mg): 100
Protein (gm): 3.3
Carbohydrate (gm): 17.6

Exchanges:
Milk: 0.0
Vegetable: 2.0
Fruit: 0.0
Bread: 0.5
Meat: 0.0
Fat: 0.5

1. Sauté carrots, bell pepper, celery, green onions, garlic, and jalapeño chili in lightly greased saucepan 5 minutes. Add broth, lime juice, and cumin to saucepan; heat to boiling. Reduce heat and simmer, covered, until vegetables are tender, 10 to 15 minutes. Add tomato, cucumber, and avocado to each bowl of soup; sprinkle with cilantro and Herb Croutons.

GARDEN HARVEST SOUP

Vary the vegetables according to your garden's or greengrocer's bounty.

6 first-course servings (about 1½ cups each)

2 small onions, sliced

2 cloves garlic, minced

1 tablespoon olive oil

¾ cup each: sliced carrots, red and yellow bell pepper

½ cup whole kernel corn

5 cups reduced-sodium fat-free chicken broth

1 cup each: cut green beans, sliced zucchini, yellow summer squash

½ teaspoon each: dried basil and oregano leaves

⅓ cup fat-free half-and-half or fat-free milk

Salt and pepper, to taste

Per Serving:
Calories: 136
% of calories from fat: 17
Fat (gm): 2.8
Saturated fat (gm): 0.4
Cholesterol (mg): 0
Sodium (mg): 161
Protein (gm): 8.4
Carbohydrate (gm): 21.3

Exchanges:
Milk: 0.0
Vegetable: 4.0
Fruit: 0.0
Bread: 0.0
Meat: 0.0
Fat: 0.5

1. Sauté onions and garlic in oil in large saucepan until tender, about 5 minutes. Add carrots, bell peppers, and corn and sauté 5 minutes. Add broth, remaining vegetables, and herbs; heat to boiling. Reduce heat and simmer, covered, until vegetables are tender, about 15 minutes; stir in half-and-half and simmer 2 minutes. Season to taste with salt and pepper.

SPINACH AND TORTELLINI SOUP

Soups can be made 2 to 3 days in advance, enhancing flavors. If the soup contains pasta, cook it separately and add to the soup when reheating so it's fresh and perfectly cooked.

6 entrée servings (about 1 cup each)

2 cups sliced carrots

¼ cup sliced green onions

2 cloves garlic, minced

1 teaspoon dried basil leaves

2 cans (14½ ounces) reduced-sodium chicken broth

1½ cups water

1 package (9 ounces) fresh tomato-cheese tortellini

3 cups torn spinach leaves

2–3 teaspoons lemon juice

⅛–¼ teaspoon ground nutmeg

⅛ teaspoon pepper

Per Serving:
Calories: 290
% of calories from fat: 9
Fat (gm): 2.8
Saturated fat (gm): 1
Cholesterol (mg): 3.8
Sodium (mg): 395
Protein (gm): 12.1
Carbohydrate (gm): 48

Exchanges:
Milk: 0.0
Vegetable: 2.0
Fruit: 0.0
Bread: 2.5
Meat: 1.0
Fat: 0.0

1. Sauté carrots, green onions, garlic, and basil in lightly greased large saucepan until onions are tender, about 5 minutes. Add broth and water and heat to boiling; reduce heat and simmer, covered, 10 minutes. Heat soup to boiling; stir in tortellini and spinach; reduce heat and simmer, uncovered, until tortellini are al dente, about 5 minutes. Season with lemon juice, nutmeg, and pepper.

TORTELLINI AND MUSHROOM SOUP

45

Porcini mushrooms, a Tuscan delicacy found fresh in the fall, are available in dried form year round. Porcini impart a wonderful earthy flavor to recipes. Other dried mushrooms can be substituted for a similar flavor.

6 first-course servings (about 1 cup each)

2 ounces dried porcini mushrooms

Hot water

8 ounces fresh white mushrooms, sliced

2 tablespoons finely chopped shallots or green onions

2 cloves garlic, minced

½ teaspoon dried tarragon leaves

2 cans (14½ ounces each) reduced-sodium beef broth

¼ cup dry sherry (optional)

1 package (9 ounces) fresh tomato-and-cheese tortellini

Salt and pepper, to taste

Per Serving:
Calories: 110
% of calories from fat: 16
Fat (gm): 2
Saturated fat (gm): 0.4
Cholesterol (mg): 4.2
Sodium (mg): 184
Protein (gm): 5
Carbohydrate (gm): 17.1

Exchanges:
Milk: 0.0
Vegetable: 1.0
Fruit: 0.0
Bread: 1.0
Meat: 0.0
Fat: 0.5

1. Place dried mushrooms in bowl; pour hot water over to cover. Let stand until mushrooms are soft, about 15 minutes; drain. Slice mushrooms, discarding any tough parts.

2. Sauté dried and white mushrooms, shallots, garlic, and tarragon in lightly greased saucepan until mushrooms are tender, about 5 minutes. Add broth and sherry and heat to boiling; add tortellini, salt, and pepper. Reduce heat and simmer, uncovered, until tortellini are al dente, about 5 minutes; season to taste with salt and pepper.

SPLIT PEA SOUP WITH HAM

A perfect entrée soup for hearty appetites on a crisp autumn or winter day. Serve with thick slices of Garlic Bread (see p. 497).

6 entrée servings (about 1⅓ cups each)

1½ cups each: chopped onions, cubed lean
  smoked ham
1 cup chopped carrots
½ cup sliced celery
1 tablespoon canola oil
6 cups water
1 can (14½ ounces) reduced-sodium fat-free
  chicken broth
1 pound dried split peas
1 teaspoon dried marjoram leaves
Salt and pepper, to taste

Per Serving:
Calories: 264
% of calories from fat: 11
Fat (gm): 3.4
Saturated fat (gm): 0.6
Cholesterol (mg): 16.2
Sodium (mg): 513
Protein (gm): 21.6
Carbohydrate (gm): 39.9

Exchanges:
Milk: 0.0
Vegetable: 1.0
Fruit: 0.0
Bread: 2.0
Meat: 2.0
Fat: 0.0

1. Sauté onions, ham, carrots, and celery in oil in large saucepan until tender, 8 to 10 minutes. Add water, chicken broth, split peas, and marjoram; heat to boiling. Reduce heat and simmer, covered, until peas are tender, 1 to 1¼ hours. Season to taste with salt and pepper.

COUNTRY LENTIL SOUP

L

A light soup that is wholesome in flavor and texture. This soup freezes well, so make extra.

6 entrée servings (about 1½ cups each)

1½ cups chopped onions
1 cup each: sliced celery, carrots

2 teaspoons minced garlic

1 tablespoon olive oil

3 cups vegetable broth

2 cups water

1 cup dried lentils

1 can (14½ ounces) reduced-sodium diced tomatoes, undrained

2 tablespoons chopped parsley

1 teaspoon dried marjoram leaves

½ teaspoon each: dried oregano and thyme leaves

Salt and pepper, to taste

4 tablespoons grated fat-free Parmesan cheese

Per Serving:
Calories: 275
% of calories from fat: 14
Fat (gm): 4.4
Saturated fat (gm): 0.6
Cholesterol (mg): 0
Sodium (mg): 109
Protein (gm): 15.8
Carbohydrate (gm): 42.8

Exchanges:
Milk: 0.0
Vegetable: 3.0
Fruit: 0.0
Bread: 2.0
Meat: 0.5
Fat: 0.5

1. Sauté onions, celery, carrots, and garlic in oil in large saucepan 5 to 8 minutes. Add broth, water, lentils, tomatoes with liquid, and herbs; heat to boiling. Reduce heat and simmer, covered, until lentils are tender, about 30 minutes. Season to taste with salt and pepper. Sprinkle each bowl of soup with 1 tablespoon cheese.

INDIAN LENTIL SOUP

45 *This soup (Dal Shorba) from India is flavored with curry powder and sweet coriander. Red, green, or brown lentils can be used.*

8 first-course servings (about 1 cup each)

½ cup chopped onion

1 clove garlic, minced

2 teaspoons curry powder

1 teaspoon each: crushed coriander and cumin seeds

½ teaspoon ground turmeric

¼ teaspoon crushed red pepper flakes

1 tablespoon olive oil

5 cups reduced-sodium fat-free chicken broth

4 cups water

2 cups dried red or brown lentils

Salt and pepper, to taste

6 tablespoons fat-free plain yogurt

Per Serving:
Calories: 193
% of calories from fat: 11
Fat (gm): 2.4
Saturated fat (gm): 0.3
Cholesterol (mg): 0.3
Sodium (mg): 121
Protein (gm): 16
Carbohydrate (gm): 27.6

Exchanges:
Milk: 0.0
Vegetable: 0.0
Fruit: 0.0
Bread: 2.0
Meat: 1.0
Fat: 0.0

1. Sauté onion, garlic, curry powder, herbs, and red pepper in oil in large saucepan until onion is tender, about 5 minutes. Add broth, water, and lentils; heat to boiling. Reduce heat and simmer, covered, until lentils are tender, about 30 minutes. Season to taste with salt and pepper. Top each bowl of soup with a tablespoon of yogurt.

BLACK BEAN SOUP

L *Dried beans can also be "quick cooked" rather than soaked overnight; see directions in Navy Bean Soup with Ham (p. 96). Or, substitute three cans (15 ounces each) rinsed, drained canned black beans.*

4 first-course servings (about 1¼ cups each)

1½ cups dried black beans
1 large onion, chopped
4 cloves garlic, minced
1 teaspoon dried oregano leaves
½ teaspoon dried thyme leaves
1 large tomato, chopped
Salt and pepper, to taste
6 tablespoons fat-free sour cream
Finely chopped oregano or parsley, as garnish

Per Serving:
Calories: 200
% of calories from fat: 4
Fat (gm): 0.9
Saturated fat (gm): 0.2
Cholesterol (mg): 0
Sodium (mg): 20
Protein (gm): 13.8
Carbohydrate (gm): 39

Exchanges:
Milk: 0.0
Vegetable: 1.0
Fruit: 0.0
Bread: 2.0
Meat: 0.5
Fat: 0.0

1. Cover beans with 4 inches water in large saucepan; soak overnight and drain.

2. Sauté onion, garlic and herbs in lightly greased large saucepan until softened, about 4 minutes. Add beans; cover with 2 inches water and heat to boiling. Reduce heat and simmer, covered, until beans are very tender, 1½ to 2 hours, adding tomato during last ½ hour.

3. Process soup in food processor or blender until smooth. Return soup to saucepan; heat over medium heat until hot through, 3 to 4 minutes. Season to taste with salt and pepper. Top each bowl of soup with dollop of sour cream and sprinkle with oregano.

BLACK BEAN AND OKRA GUMBO

45 *The gumbo is delicious served over warm Green Chili Corn Bread (see p. 639).*

8 entrée servings (about 1 cup each)

8–12 ounces reduced-sodium smoked turkey
  sausage, sliced
2 cups small mushrooms
1 cup each: chopped onion, sliced carrots
¾ cup each: chopped red and green bell peppers
1 tablespoon olive oil
2 cups vegetable broth
1 can (16 ounces) tomatoes with chilies, undrained
2 cans (15 ounces each) black beans, rinsed, drained
2 cups cut okra
1 tablespoon chili powder
1 teaspoon gumbo file
Salt and pepper, to taste

Per Serving:
Calories: 376
% of calories from fat: 8
Fat (gm): 2.9
Saturated fat (gm): 0.7
Cholesterol (mg): 18.3
Sodium (mg): 832
Protein (gm): 16.7
Carbohydrate (gm): 18.3

Exchanges:
Milk: 0.0
Vegetable: 2.0
Fruit: 0.0
Bread: 4.0
Meat: 1.0
Fat: 0.0

1. Sauté sausage, mushrooms, onion, carrots, and bell peppers in oil in Dutch oven or large saucepan until sausage is lightly browned, 5 to 8 minutes. Add remaining ingredients, except salt and pepper; heat to boiling. Reduce heat and simmer, covered, until vegetables are tender, about 10 minutes. Simmer, uncovered, until thickened to desired consistency, 5 to 10 minutes. Season to taste with salt and pepper.

GARBANZO BEAN SOUP

45 *Cumin adds a Mexican flavor to this soup; curry powder can be substituted to give an Indian flavor.*

4 entrée servings (about 1⅓ cups each)

2 each: finely chopped medium onions, garlic cloves

2 cans (15 ounces each) garbanzo beans,
rinsed, drained

2 cans (14½ ounces each) reduced-sodium fat-free
chicken broth

1 teaspoon ground cumin

½–¾ teaspoon dried thyme leaves

Salt and pepper, to taste

¼ cup fat-free sour cream

Paprika or chili powder, as garnish

Per Serving:
Calories: 267
% of calories from fat: 15
Fat (gm): 4.6
Saturated fat (gm): 0.6
Cholesterol (mg): 0
Sodium (mg): 627
Protein (gm): 12.4
Carbohydrate (gm): 46.4

Exchanges:
Milk: 0.0
Vegetable: 1.0
Fruit: 0.0
Bread: 3.0
Meat: 0.0
Fat: 0.0

1. Sauté onions and garlic in lightly greased large saucepan until tender, about 5 minutes. Add beans, broth, cumin, and thyme and heat to boiling; reduce heat and simmer, covered, 10 minutes. Process soup in food processor or blender until smooth; season to taste with salt and pepper. Top each bowl of soup with a dollop of sour cream and sprinkle with paprika.

CHICK PEA AND PASTA SOUP

45 *You can use any fresh vegetables you want for the zucchini and celery in this soup – carrots, cauliflower or broccoli florets, mushrooms, peas, and green beans are possible choices.*

4 entrée servings (about 1¾ cups each)

¾ cup each: chopped onion, cubed zucchini,
sliced celery

3–4 cloves garlic, minced

1 teaspoon each: dried rosemary and thyme leaves

⅛ teaspoon crushed red pepper

1 can (15 ounces) each: reduced-sodium chicken broth, reduced-sodium
stewed tomatoes, chick peas, rinsed, drained

1 cup uncooked farfalle (bow ties)

Salt, to taste

2–3 teaspoons lemon juice

1. Sauté onion, zucchini, celery, garlic, herbs, and red pepper in lightly greased large saucepan until onion is tender, about 5 minutes; add broth, tomatoes, and chick peas and heat to boiling. Reduce heat and simmer, covered, 10 minutes. Heat soup to boiling and add pasta; reduce heat and simmer, uncovered, until pasta is al dente, about 8 minutes; season to taste with salt and lemon juice.

Per Serving:
Calories: 322
% of calories from fat: 10
Fat (gm): 3.7
Saturated fat (gm): 0.5
Cholesterol (mg): 0
Sodium (mg): 514
Protein (gm): 11.5
Carbohydrate (gm): 56.4

Exchanges:
Milk: 0.0
Vegetable: 3.0
Fruit: 0.0
Bread: 3.0
Meat: 0.0
Fat: 0.5

WHITE BEAN AND SWEET POTATO SOUP WITH CRANBERRY COULIS

V *A most pleasing combination of colors and flavors!*

6 entrée servings (about 1¼ cups each)

1 cup chopped onion

1 pound sweet potatoes, peeled, cubed

1 large tart cooking apple, peeled, cored, chopped

1½ teaspoons minced gingerroot

2 cans (15 ounces each) navy or Great Northern beans rinsed, drained

3 cups reduced-sodium vegetable broth

½ teaspoon dried marjoram leaves

Salt, cayenne and white pepper, to taste

Cranberry Coulis (recipe follows)

Per Serving:
Calories: 310
% of calories from fat: 3
Fat (gm): 1.2
Saturated fat (gm): 0.3
Cholesterol (mg): 0
Sodium (mg): 650
Protein (gm): 12.6
Carbohydrate (gm): 64.6

Exchanges:
Milk: 0.0
Vegetable: 1.0
Fruit: 1.0
Bread: 3.0
Meat: 0.0
Fat: 0.0

1. Sauté onion, sweet potatoes, apple, and gingerroot in lightly greased large saucepan 5 minutes. Add beans, broth, and marjoram and heat to boiling; reduce heat and simmer, covered, until vegetables are tender, 10 to 15 minutes.

2. Process soup in food processor or blender until smooth; season to taste with salt, cayenne, and white pepper. Swirl 2 tablespoons Cranberry Coulis into each bowl of soup.

Cranberry Coulis

6 servings (about 3 tablespoons each)

1½ cups fresh or frozen cranberries
1 cup orange juice
2–3 tablespoons sugar
1–2 tablespoons honey

1. Heat cranberries and orange juice to boiling in small saucepan; reduce heat and simmer, covered, until cranberries are tender, 5 to 8 minutes. Process with sugar and honey in food processor or blender until almost smooth. Serve warm or room temperature.

FOUR-BEAN AND VEGETABLE SOUP

45

V

Any kind of dried beans can be used in the soup, or use prepackaged mixed dried beans.

12 entrée servings (about 1½ cups each)

8 ounces each: dried black, navy, pinto, and
    garbanzo beans
Water
2 cups chopped green bell pepper
1 cup chopped onion
6–8 cloves garlic, minced
2 tablespoons olive oil
6 cups reduced-sodium vegetable broth
2–3 teaspoons dried thyme leaves
3 bay leaves
2 cans (16 ounces each) reduced-sodium diced
    tomatoes, undrained
2 cups each: sliced carrots, cut green beans
Salt, cayenne, and black pepper, to taste

Per Serving:
Calories: 342
% of calories from fat: 11
Fat (gm): 4.3
Saturated fat (gm): 0.5
Cholesterol (mg): 0
Sodium (mg): 35
Protein (gm): 18.1
Carbohydrate (gm): 58.5

Exchanges:
Milk: 0.0
Vegetable: 3.0
Fruit: 0.0
Bread: 3.0
Meat: 1.0
Fat: 0.0

1. Cover dried beans with water in large saucepan; heat to boiling. Remove pan from heat; let stand 1 hour. Drain.

2. Sauté bell pepper, onion, and garlic in oil in Dutch oven until tender, 4 to 5 minutes. Add beans, broth, and herbs and heat to boiling; reduce heat and simmer, covered, until beans are tender, adding water if necessary, 1 to 1½ hours. Add tomatoes with liquid, carrots, and green beans during last 15 to 20 minutes of cooking time. Discard bay leaves; season to taste with salt, cayenne, and black pepper.

CANNELLINI AND CABBAGE SOUP

45 *Any white bean, such as Great Northern or navy, may be substituted for the cannellini.*

8 first-course servings (about 1 cup each)

3 cups thinly sliced or chopped cabbage

1 small onion, coarsely chopped

3 cloves garlic, minced

1 teaspoon crushed caraway seeds

2 cans (14½ ounces each) reduced-sodium
  chicken broth

1 cup water

1 can (15 ounces) cannellini or Great Northern
  beans, rinsed, drained

½ cup (4 ounces) mostaccioli (penne), uncooked

Salt and pepper, to taste

Per Serving:
Calories: 107
% of calories from fat: 7
Fat (gm): 1
Saturated fat (gm): 0.1
Cholesterol (mg): 0
Sodium (mg): 175
Protein (gm): 6.9
Carbohydrate (gm): 21.9

Exchanges:
Milk: 0.0
Vegetable: 1.0
Fruit: 0.0
Bread: 1.0
Meat: 0.5
Fat: 0.0

1. Sauté cabbage, onion, garlic, and caraway seeds in lightly greased medium skillet until cabbage begins to wilt, 8 to 10 minutes. Add chicken broth, water, and beans to saucepan; heat to boiling. Stir in pasta; reduce heat and simmer, uncovered, until pasta is al dente, about 15 minutes. Season to taste with salt and pepper.

TUSCAN BEAN SOUP

A hearty well-seasoned bean soup that is sure to please.

8 entrée servings (about 1½ cups each)

1 cup chopped onion
½ cup each: chopped celery, green bell pepper
2 teaspoons minced roasted garlic
2 tablespoons olive oil
1 tablespoon flour
1½ teaspoons dried Italian seasoning
2 bay leaves
7 cups reduced-sodium fat-free beef broth
2 cans (15 ounces each) cannellini or Great Northern
  beans, rinsed, drained
2 tablespoons reduced-sodium tomato paste
½ cup quick-cooking barley
1 cup each: cubed unpeeled potato, sliced carrots,
  packed baby spinach leaves
Salt and pepper, to taste

Per Serving:
Calories: 233
% of calories from fat: 18
Fat (gm): 5.6
Saturated fat (gm): 0.7
Cholesterol (mg): 0
Sodium (mg): 245
Protein (gm): 10.7
Carbohydrate (gm): 40.8

Exchanges:
Milk: 0.0
Vegetable: 2.0
Fruit: 0.0
Bread: 2.0
Meat: 0.0
Fat: 1.0

1. Sauté onion, celery, bell pepper, and garlic in oil in Dutch oven until tender, about 5 minutes. Add flour and herbs; cook 1 minute. Add broth, beans, and tomato paste and heat to boiling; reduce heat and simmer, covered, 15 minutes. Add barley, potato, carrots, and spinach; simmer until vegetables are tender, about 10 minutes. Discard bay leaves. Season to taste with salt and pepper.

BEAN AND BARLEY SOUP

 A soup that can be easily increased to serve a crowd; make it a day ahead of time for best flavor.

6 entrée servings (about 2 cups each)

¾ cup each: chopped onion, red bell pepper
2 teaspoons minced garlic
2 tablespoons olive oil
1 tablespoon flour

1½ teaspoons dried Italian seasoning

7 cups low-sodium vegetable broth

2 cans (15 ounces) cannellini or Great Northern beans, rinsed, drained

2 tablespoons reduced-sodium tomato paste

½ cup quick-cooking barley

1 cup each: cubed unpeeled Idaho potato, sliced carrots, packed baby spinach leaves

Salt and pepper, to taste

Per Serving:
Calories: 297
% of calories from fat: 17
Fat (gm): 5.6
Saturated fat (gm): 0.7
Cholesterol (mg): 0
Sodium (mg): 325
Protein (gm): 10
Carbohydrate (gm): 52.1

Exchanges:
Milk: 0.0
Vegetable: 1.0
Fruit: 0.0
Bread: 3.0
Meat: 0.0
Fat: 1.0

1. Sauté onion, bell pepper, and garlic in oil in Dutch oven 5 minutes. Add flour and Italian seasoning; cook 1 to 2 minutes longer. Add remaining ingredients, except spinach, salt, and pepper; heat to boiling. Reduce heat and simmer, uncovered, 20 to 25 minutes, adding spinach during last 5 minutes of cooking time. Season to taste with salt and pepper.

CURRIED BEAN SOUP

45

L

Use any white bean, such as cannellini, navy, soy, lima, or garbanzo in this creamy, rich soup.

6 entrée servings (about 1¼ cups each)

1 cup each: chopped onion, sliced leek (white part only)

1 tablespoon each: minced garlic, curry powder

2 tablespoons olive oil

2 cans (15½ ounces each) Great Northern beans, rinsed, drained

3½ cups reduced-sodium vegetable broth

½ cup fat-free half-and-half or fat-free milk

Salt and pepper, to taste

6 tablespoons fat-free sour cream or plain yogurt

3 tablespoons each: chopped cilantro, red bell pepper

Per Serving:
Calories: 263
% of calories from fat: 16
Fat (gm): 4.9
Saturated fat (gm): 1
Cholesterol (mg): 0
Sodium (mg): 393
Protein (gm): 13.7
Carbohydrate (gm): 42.5

Exchanges:
Milk: 0.0
Vegetable: 1.5
Fruit: 0.0
Bread: 2.5
Meat: 0.5
Fat: 0.5

1. Sauté onion, leek, garlic, and curry powder in oil in large saucepan until onion is tender, 5 to 8 minutes. Add beans and broth and heat to boiling. Reduce heat and simmer, covered, 5 minutes. Process mixture in food processor or blender until smooth; return to saucepan. Stir in half-and-half; cook over medium heat 2 to 3 minutes. Season to taste with salt and pepper. Top each bowl of soup with a tablespoon of sour cream; sprinkle with cilantro and bell pepper.

NAVY BEAN SOUP WITH HAM

45 *A quick-soak method is used for the beans. If you prefer soaking the beans overnight, omit step 1 and proceed with step 2 in the recipe, using the soaked beans.*

6 entrée servings (about 1¾ cups each)

8 ounces dried navy or Great Northern beans
Water
1½ cups cubed lean smoked ham
⅔ cup each: chopped onion, carrot, celery
2 cloves garlic, minced
1 tablespoon each: canola oil, flour
4 cups reduced-sodium chicken broth
1 cup water
¼ teaspoon dried thyme leaves
1 bay leaf
Salt and pepper, to taste

Per Serving:
Calories: 223
% of calories from fat: 16
Fat (gm): 4.0
Saturated fat (gm): 0.9
Cholesterol (mg): 21.6
Sodium (mg): 639
Protein (gm): 20.1
Carbohydrate (gm): 29.5

Exchanges:
Milk: 0.0
Vegetable: 0.0
Fruit: 0.0
Bread: 2.0
Meat: 2.0
Fat: 0.0

1. Cover beans with 2 inches of water in large saucepan; heat to boiling; boil, uncovered, 2 minutes. Remove from heat and let stand, covered, 1 hour; drain.

2. Sauté ham, onion, carrot, celery, and garlic in oil in large saucepan until vegetables are tender, 5 to 8 minutes. Stir in flour; cook 1 minute. Add beans, broth, water, and herbs to saucepan; heat to boiling. Reduce heat and simmer, covered, until beans are tender, 1 to 1¼ hours. Discard bay leaf; season to taste with salt and pepper.

TWO-BEAN AND PASTA SOUP

45 *This substantial soup thickens upon standing; thin with additional broth or water, if necessary.*

6 entrée servings (about 2 cups each)

1½ cups cubed carrots

½ cup each: chopped green bell pepper,
   sliced green onions

3 cloves garlic, minced

2 teaspoons each: dried basil and oregano leaves

2 cans (15 ounces each) reduced-sodium
   chicken broth

1 cup water

1 can (16 ounces) reduced-sodium stewed tomatoes

1 can (15 ounces) each: cannellini and pinto beans,
   rinsed, drained

1½ cups uncooked rigatoni

2–3 teaspoons lemon juice

Salt and pepper, to taste

Per Serving:
Calories: 225
% of calories from fat: 7
Fat (gm): 2
Saturated fat (gm): 0
Cholesterol (mg): 0
Sodium (mg): 522
Protein (gm): 13.6
Carbohydrate (gm): 45.7

Exchanges:
Milk: 0.0
Vegetable: 2.0
Fruit: 0.0
Bread: 2.5
Meat: 0.0
Fat: 0.0

1. Sauté carrots, bell pepper, green onions, garlic and herbs in lightly greased large saucepan until vegetables are tender, about 7 minutes. Add broth, water, tomatoes, and beans to saucepan; heat to boiling. Reduce heat and simmer, covered, 10 minutes. Heat soup to boiling and add pasta; reduce heat and simmer, uncovered, until pasta is al dente, 12 to 15 minutes. Season with lemon juice, salt, and pepper.

MONTEREY CHILI ACINI DE PEPE

L

45

Bulgur or cracked wheat can be substituted for the acini de pepe, in this flavorful chili.

4 entrée servings (about 1 cup each)

½ cup each: chopped onion, green bell pepper

1 teaspoon olive oil

1 can (15 ounces) pinto beans, rinsed drained

1 can (14 ounces) reduced-sodium diced
  tomatoes, undrained

1 tablespoon chili powder

1 teaspoon each: dried oregano leaves,
  unsweetened cocoa

½ cup acini de pepe, cooked

¼ cup chopped cilantro

Salt and pepper, to taste

¾ cup (3 ounces) shredded Monterey Jack cheese

Per Serving:
Calories: 275
% of calories from fat: 29
Fat (gm): 9.2
Saturated fat (gm): 4.5
Cholesterol (mg): 18.9
Sodium (mg): 461
Protein (gm): 14
Carbohydrate (gm): 36

Exchanges:
Milk: 0.0
Vegetable: 1.0
Fruit: 0.0
Bread: 2.0
Meat: 1.0
Fat: 1.0

1. Sauté onion and bell pepper in oil in large saucepan until tender, 3 to 4 minutes. Add beans, tomatoes with liquid, chili powder, oregano, and cocoa. Heat to boiling; reduce heat and simmer, covered, 10 minutes. Stir in acini de pepe and cilantro; season to taste with salt and pepper. Sprinkle each bowl of chili with cheese.

SWEET POTATO CHIPOTLE CHILI

45

V

Chipotle chilies are dried, smoked jalapeño chilies. When canned, they are in adobo sauce, which is made with ground chilies and spices. The chilies add a distinctive smoky flavor to this robust dish; taste before adding more, as they can be fiercely hot!

4 entrée servings (about 1½ cups each)

1 cup each: chopped onion, green bell pepper

2 teaspoons minced gingerroot

1 teaspoon each: minced garlic, crushed cumin seeds

1 tablespoons peanut or canola oil

3 cups cubed, peeled sweet potatoes

2 cans (15 ounces each) black beans, rinsed, drained

1 can (14½ ounces) chili-style chunky tomatoes, undrained

½–1 chipotle chili in adobo sauce, chopped

1 cup water or vegetable broth

Salt, to taste

Per Serving:
Calories: 213
% of calories from fat: 14
Fat (gm): 3.9
Saturated fat (gm): 0.6
Cholesterol (mg): 0
Sodium (mg): 452
Protein (gm): 8.6
Carbohydrate (gm): 44.8

1. Sauté onion, bell pepper, gingerroot, garlic, and cumin seeds in oil in large saucepan until tender, about 5 minutes. Add remaining ingredients, except salt, and heat to boiling. Reduce heat and simmer, covered, until sweet potatoes are tender, about 15 minutes. Season to taste with salt.

Exchanges:
Milk: 0.0
Vegetable: 0.0
Fruit: 0.0
Bread: 3.0
Meat: 0.0
Fat: 0.5

SPICED BEAN CHILI WITH FUSILLI

45 *Use your favorite beans and any shaped pasta in this versatile chili.*

8 entrée servings (about 1¼ cups each)

1 pound lean ground beef

2 cups chopped onions

1 cup sliced cremini or white mushrooms

½ cup sliced celery

2 cans (14½ ounces each) diced tomatoes with roasted garlic, undrained

1 can (15 ounces) each: garbanzo and dark red kidney beans, rinsed, drained

½ cup dry white wine or water

1–2 tablespoons each: chili powder, ground cumin

½ teaspoon each: dried oregano and thyme leaves

8 ounces fusilli, cooked

Salt and pepper, to taste

3–4 tablespoons sliced green or ripe olives

Per Serving:
Calories: 367
% of calories from fat: 26
Fat (gm): 10.6
Saturated fat (gm): 3.2
Cholesterol (mg): 35.2
Sodium (mg): 759
Protein (gm): 21.3
Carbohydrate (gm): 47.3

Exchanges:
Milk: 0.0
Vegetable: 1.0
Fruit: 0.0
Bread: 3.0
Meat: 1.0
Fat: 1.5

1. Sauté ground beef, onions, mushrooms, and celery in lightly greased large saucepan until beef is browned, 8 to 10 minutes. Add tomatoes with liquid, beans, wine, and herbs to saucepan; heat to boiling. Reduce heat and simmer, covered, 10 minutes. Add pasta and cook until hot, 2 to 3 minutes. Season to taste with salt and pepper; sprinkle with olives.

CHILI CON CARNE

A flavorful chili that will satisfy the heartiest of appetites!

8 entrée servings (about 1 cup each)

1 pound very lean ground beef

1½ cups chopped onions

1 cup chopped green bell pepper

2 cloves garlic, minced

1–2 tablespoons chili powder

2 teaspoons each: ground cumin, dried
    oregano leaves

¼ teaspoon ground cloves

2 cans (14½ ounces each) reduced-sodium whole
    tomatoes, undrained, coarsely chopped

1 can (15 ounces) red kidney beans, rinsed, drained

1 can (6 ounces) reduced-sodium tomato paste

¾ cup beer or reduced-sodium beef broth

1 tablespoon each: packed light brown sugar,
    unsweetened cocoa

Salt and pepper, to taste

½ cup each: shredded fat-free or reduced-fat Cheddar
    cheese (2 ounces), sliced green onions, fat-free sour cream

Per Serving:
Calories: 220
% of calories from fat: 13
Fat (gm): 3.6
Saturated fat (gm): 1
Cholesterol (mg): 32.5
Sodium (mg): 224
Protein (gm): 21.9
Carbohydrate (gm): 28.7

Exchanges:
Milk: 0.0
Vegetable: 2.0
Fruit: 0.0
Bread: 1.0
Meat: 2.0
Fat: 0.0

1. Sauté ground beef, onions, bell pepper, garlic, herbs, and spices in lightly greased large saucepan until meat is brown and vegetables are tender, 5 to 8 minutes. Add tomatoes and liquid, beans, tomato paste, beer, brown sugar, and cocoa; heat to boiling. Reduce heat and simmer, covered, 30 to 45 minutes. Uncover and simmer to thicken, if desired. Season to taste with salt and pepper. Sprinkle each serving of chili with cheese, green onions, and sour cream.

VARIATIONS

Chili Mac — Make chili as above, adding 1 cup uncooked elbow macaroni or chili mac pasta and ½ cup water to chili during last 15 minutes of cooking time.

Southwest Chili — Make recipe as above, substituting black or pinto beans for the red kidney, and adding 1 minced jalapeño chili. Garnish each serving with a generous sprinkling of chopped cilantro.

VEAL CHILI POBLANO

45 *Ground veal, poblano chili, and purchased seasoning mix make this fast-track chili an almost-instant favorite.*

4 entrée servings (about 1¼ cups each)

1 pound ground lean veal or turkey

1 each: chopped large onion, small poblano chili, rib celery

1 can (15 ounces) each: reduced-sodium crushed tomatoes, rinsed drained Great Northern beans

½–1 package (1¼ ounce-size) chili seasoning mix

1. Cook veal in lightly greased large saucepan until browned and crumbly, about 8 minutes; add onion, poblano chili, and celery, and sauté until tender, about 5 minutes. Stir in tomatoes, beans, and seasoning mix; heat to boiling. Reduce heat and simmer, uncovered, 15 minutes.

Per Serving:
Calories: 282
% of calories from fat: 18
Fat (gm): 6.1
Saturated fat (gm): 1.6
Cholesterol (mg): 99.5
Sodium (mg): 659
Protein (gm): 34.2
Carbohydrate (gm): 26.4

Exchanges:
Milk: 0.0
Vegetable: 0.0
Fruit: 0.0
Bread: 2.0
Meat: 3.0
Fat: 0.0

YELLOW SQUASH AND WHITE BEAN CHILI

For convenience, drained, rinsed beans can be substituted for the
cooked dried beans.

6 entrée servings (about 1¼ cups each)

1 pound lean ground pork

1 cup each: chopped onion, thinly sliced leek
(white part only), yellow bell pepper

1 jalapeño chili, finely chopped

2 teaspoons each: minced garlic, cumin seeds

1 tablespoon olive oil

¾ cup each: cubed yellow summer squash, peeled
red potatoes

2 cups each: cooked, dried Great Northern and
garbanzo beans

1 can (14½ ounces) reduced-sodium chicken broth

½ cup dry white wine or reduced-sodium chicken broth

1 teaspoon each: dried oregano leaves, chili powder

½ teaspoon each: ground coriander, cinnamon

1 bay leaf

Salt and pepper, to taste

1 small tomato, finely chopped

2 green onions, thinly sliced

3 tablespoons finely chopped cilantro

Per Serving:
Calories: 350
% of calories from fat: 23
Fat (gm): 10
Saturated fat (gm): 2.7
Cholesterol (mg): 49.3
Sodium (mg): 719
Protein (gm): 32.7
Carbohydrate (gm): 41.2

Exchanges:
Milk: 0.0
Vegetable: 2.0
Fruit: 0.0
Bread: 2.0
Meat: 3.0
Fat: 0.0

1. Sauté pork, onion, leek, bell pepper, jalapeño chili, garlic, and
cumin seeds in oil in large saucepan until pork is browned and
vegetables tender, about 10 minutes.

2. Add squash, potatoes, beans, broth, wine, herbs, and spices and
heat to boiling. Reduce heat and simmer, covered, until vegetables
are tender, about 10 minutes. Simmer, uncovered, until thickened, 5
to 10 minutes. Season to taste with salt and pepper; discard bay leaf.
Sprinkle each bowl of soup with tomato, green onions, and cilantro.

CINCINNATI CHILI

5-Way Cincinnati Chili gained fame in the chili parlors of Cincinnati. The sauce is seasoned with sweet spices and generally has a hint of dark chocolate. The chili is served alone, 1 way; 2 ways, over spaghetti; 3 ways, with added beans; 4 ways, with chopped onions; and 5 ways, with shredded cheese!

8 entrée servings (about 1 cup each)

12 ounces lean ground turkey or beef

½ cup chopped onion

4 cloves garlic, minced

1 can (28 ounces) reduced-sodium crushed tomatoes, undrained

1 can (8 ounces) reduced-sodium tomato sauce

½ cup water

2–3 tablespoons chili powder

1 tablespoon cocoa

2 teaspoons dried oregano leaves

1 teaspoon each: ground cinnamon, allspice

½ teaspoon each: paprika, salt, pepper

16 ounces spaghetti, cooked, warm

Canned, drained pinto beans, chopped onions, shredded reduced-fat Cheddar cheese (not included in nutritional data)

Per Serving:
Calories: 381
% of calories from fat: 13
Fat (gm): 5.7
Saturated fat (gm): 1.3
Cholesterol (mg): 31.6
Sodium (mg): 454
Protein (gm): 19.6
Carbohydrate (gm): 62

Exchanges:
Milk: 0.0
Vegetable: 3.0
Fruit: 0.0
Bread: 3.0
Meat: 1.0
Fat: 0.5

1. Sauté ground turkey in large saucepan over medium heat until beginning to brown, about 5 minutes. Add onion and garlic and sauté until onion is tender, about 5 minutes. Stir in remaining ingredients except spaghetti and garnishes; heat to boiling. Reduce heat and simmer, covered, 15 minutes; simmer, uncovered, until sauce is thickened, about 15 minutes more. Serve over spaghetti; add beans, onions, and shredded cheese, as desired.

CALIFORNIA CHILI

45 | *This zesty chili sports familiar West Coast ingredients.*

6 entrée servings (about 1¼ cups each)

1 pound boneless, skinless chicken breast,
  cubed (1-inch)
1 teaspoon crushed mixed peppercorns
4 cups sliced plum tomatoes
1 cup diced sun-dried tomatoes (not in oil)
½ cup zinfandel or other dry red wine
2 dried California chilies, chopped
1–2 tablespoons chili powder
1 avocado, chopped
2 tablespoons sunflower seeds, toasted
Salt, to taste
6 tablespoons chopped basil

Per Serving:
Calories: 258
% of calories from fat: 30
Fat (gm): 9.2
Saturated fat (gm): 1.8
Cholesterol (mg): 46
Sodium (mg): 272
Protein (gm): 21.5
Carbohydrate (gm): 19.7

Exchanges:
Milk: 0.0
Vegetable: 4.0
Fruit: 0.0
Bread: 0.0
Meat: 2.0
Fat: 1.0

1. Sauté chicken and peppercorns in lightly greased large saucepan until browned, 8 to 10 minutes. Add plum and sun-dried tomatoes, wine, chilies, and chili powder; heat to boiling. Reduce heat and simmer, covered, 10 minutes; simmer, uncovered, until thickened to desired consistency, 5 to 10 minutes. Stir in avocado and sunflower seeds; season to taste with salt. Sprinkle each bowl of chili with basil.

MESQUITE CHICKEN CHILI

45 | *A differently delicious Tex-Mex dish that will appeal to the adventurous and not-so-adventurous alike.*

4 entrée servings (about 1¾ cups each)

12 ounces boneless, skinless chicken breast, cubed
¾ cup each: chopped onion, poblano chili
1 teaspoon olive oil
1 can (28 ounces) reduced-sodium crushed tomatoes
½ pound tomatillos, husked, coarsely chopped
1 can (15 ounces) red beans, rinsed, drained

2 tablespoons chili powder

2 teaspoons minced garlic

1 teaspoon mesquite smoke flavoring

Salt and pepper, to taste

Per Serving:
Calories: 293
% of calories from fat: 15
Fat (gm): 5.3
Saturated fat (gm): 1.1
Cholesterol (mg): 51.7
Sodium (mg): 469
Protein (gm): 28.1
Carbohydrate (gm): 36.3

1. Sauté chicken, onion, and poblano chili in oil in large saucepan until chicken is browned, about 8 minutes; add remaining ingredients, except salt and pepper. Heat to boiling; reduce heat and simmer, covered, 10 minutes. Season to taste with salt and pepper.

Exchanges:
Milk: 0.0
Vegetable: 2.0
Fruit: 0.0
Bread: 2.0
Meat: 2.0
Fat: 0.0

BEEF, BARLEY AND VEGETABLE SOUP

This hearty, rib-sticking soup is even better if made a day or so in advance. Leftover soup will thicken, so thin with beef broth or water.

8 entrée servings (about 1¼ cups each)

1 pound lean beef stew meat, fat trimmed, cubed

1 cup each: chopped onion, celery, carrots

1 clove garlic, minced

1 tablespoon flour

4 cups water

1 can (14½ ounces) each: reduced-sodium beef broth, undrained diced tomatoes

½ teaspoon each: dried marjoram and thyme leaves

1 bay leaf

1 cup each: cut green beans, cubed parsnips or potatoes

½ cup each: frozen peas, quick-cooking barley

Salt and pepper, to taste

Per Serving:
Calories: 187
% of calories from fat: 16
Fat (gm): 3.3
Saturated fat (gm): 1.1
Cholesterol (mg): 35.4
Sodium (mg): 153
Protein (gm): 18.8
Carbohydrate (gm): 21.1

Exchanges:
Milk: 0.0
Vegetable: 2.0
Fruit: 0.0
Bread: 0.5
Meat: 2.0
Fat: 0.0

1. Sauté beef in lightly greased Dutch oven until browned, 8 to 10 minutes. Add onion, celery, carrots, and garlic; cook 5 minutes. Stir in flour; cook 1 minute. Add water, broth, tomatoes and liquid, and herbs; heat to boiling. Reduce heat and simmer, covered, until beef is very tender, 1 to 1½ hours, adding remaining vegetables and barley during last 15 minutes. Discard bay leaf; season to taste with salt and pepper.

MEXICAN MEATBALL SOUP

A great favorite in Mexico, this soup is traditionally seasoned with mint; we've offered oregano as an addition or alternative, if you like.

4 entrée servings (about 1½ cups each)

¼ cup chopped onion

2 cloves garlic, minced

1 small jalapeño chili, seeds and veins discarded, minced

1 tablespoon flour

2 cups each: reduced-sodium tomato juice, water

2 cans (14½ ounces each) reduced-sodium fat-free chicken broth

2 each: sliced medium carrots, zucchini

1–2 teaspoons dried oregano leaves (optional)

1 teaspoon dried mint leaves

Meatballs (recipe follows)

Salt and pepper, to taste

Per Serving:
Calories: 227
% of calories from fat: 16
Fat (gm): 4.1
Saturated fat (gm): 1.4
Cholesterol (mg): 54.7
Sodium (mg): 426
Protein (gm): 28
Carbohydrate (gm): 20.2

Exchanges:
Milk: 0.0
Vegetable: 3.0
Fruit: 0.0
Bread: 0.0
Meat: 3.0
Fat: 0.0

1. Sauté onion, garlic, and jalapeño chili in lightly greased large saucepan until tender, about 5 minutes. Stir in flour; cook over medium heat 1 minute.

Add remaining ingredients, except Meatballs, salt, and pepper; heat to boiling. Add Meatballs; reduce heat and simmer, covered, until vegetables are tender and Meatballs are cooked, 10 to 15 minutes. Season to taste with salt and pepper.

Meatballs
Makes 24

1 pound very lean ground beef

¼ cup cooked rice

⅓ cup finely chopped onion

1 clove garlic, minced

½ teaspoon each: dried mint and oregano leaves, ground cumin, salt, pepper

1. Mix all ingredients; shape into 24 meatballs.

ITALIAN MEATBALL SOUP

Substitute other pastas for the spaghetti, if you like, such as orrechiette (little ears) or conchiglie (shells).

8 entrée servings (about 2 cups each)

4 cans (14½ ounces each) reduced-sodium chicken broth

3 cups water

2 cups each: cut green beans, sliced carrots, chopped onions

1 medium plum tomatoes, coarsely chopped

2 cloves garlic, minced

1–2 teaspoons dried Italian seasoning

Turkey Meatballs (recipe follows)

8 ounces thin spaghetti, uncooked, broken into pieces (3-inch)

Salt and pepper, to taste

Per Serving:
Calories: 270
% of calories from fat: 28
Fat (gm): 8.7
Saturated fat (gm): 2
Cholesterol (mg): 31.7
Sodium (mg): 174
Protein (gm): 19
Carbohydrate (gm): 30.2

Exchanges:
Milk: 0.0
Vegetable: 1.0
Fruit: 0.0
Bread: 1.5
Meat: 2.0
Fat: 0.5

1. Heat all ingredients, except Turkey Meatballs, spaghetti, salt, and pepper to boiling in large saucepan; reduce heat and simmer, covered, until vegetables are crisp-tender, about 8 minutes. Heat soup to boiling; add Turkey Meatballs and pasta; reduce heat and simmer, uncovered, until pasta is al dente, about 7 minutes. Season to taste with salt and pepper.

Turkey Meatballs
Makes 32

1½ pounds ground turkey

1 egg

¼ cup seasoned dry bread crumbs

2 cloves garlic, minced, divided

1 tablespoon dried Italian seasoning, divided

¾ teaspoon salt

½ teaspoon pepper

1. Mix all ingredients; shape into 32 meatballs. Sauté in lightly greased large skillet until browned, 5 to 7 minutes.

CHICKEN NOODLE SOUP

Comfort food at its best!

4 entrée servings (about 1¼ cups each)

4 ounces each: boneless, skinless chicken breast
    and thighs, fat trimmed, cubed (¾-inch)
2 cups sliced celery, including some leaves
1 cup each: sliced carrots, chopped onion
2 cans (14½ ounces each) reduced-sodium
    chicken broth
1 teaspoon dried marjoram leaves
1 bay leaf
1 cup uncooked wide noodles
Salt and pepper, to taste

Per Serving:
Calories: 307
% of calories from fat: 14
Fat (gm): 5
Saturated fat (gm): 0.8
Cholesterol (mg): 32.9
Sodium (mg): 409
Protein (gm): 22.8
Carbohydrate (gm): 44.3

Exchanges:
Milk: 0.0
Vegetable: 1.0
Fruit: 0.0
Bread: 2.5
Meat: 2.0
Fat: 0.0

1. Sauté chicken, celery, carrots, and onion in lightly greased large saucepan until lightly browned, about 7 minutes. Add chicken broth and herbs; heat to boiling. Reduce heat and simmer, covered, until chicken and vegetables are tender, 15 to 20 minutes. Add noodles. Cook, uncovered, until noodles are tender, 7 to 10 minutes. Discard bay leaf; season to taste with salt and pepper.

CHICKEN CHOWDER HISPANIOLA

45 *This enticing chowder boasts sofrito, a popular Cuban seasoning found in the ethnic section of many supermarkets.*

4 entrée servings (about 1¼ cups each)

12 ounces boneless, skinless chicken breast,
    cubed (¾-inch)
1 medium onion, chopped
1 teaspoon olive oil
1 can (15 ounces) each: rinsed drained garbanzo
    beans, undrained reduced-sodium diced tomatoes
1 can (14½ ounces) reduced-sodium fat-free
    chicken broth
2 cups packed spinach leaves

Per Serving:
Calories: 346
% of calories from fat: 29
Fat (gm): 10.5
Saturated fat (gm): 1.9
Cholesterol (mg): 54.3
Sodium (mg): 639
Protein (gm): 30.5
Carbohydrate (gm): 28.2

Exchanges:
Milk: 0.0
Vegetable: 3.0
Fruit: 0.0
Bread: 1.0
Meat: 3.0
Fat: 1.0

2 tablespoons sofrito sauce (optional)

Salt and pepper, to taste

¼ cup slivered almonds, toasted

1. Sauté chicken and onion in oil in large sauce pan until chicken is lightly browned, about 8 minutes. Add beans, tomatoes with liquid, and broth and heat to boiling; reduce heat and simmer, covered, 10 minutes. Stir in spinach and sofrito; simmer until spinach is wilted, 5 minutes. Season to taste with salt and pepper. Sprinkle each bowl of stew with almonds.

POZOLE

This Mexican soup is traditionally made with a pig's head or pork hocks; our version contains lean pork tenderloin and chicken breast instead. The soup always contains hominy and is served with a variety of crisp vegetable garnishes.

4 first-course servings (about 1⅓ cups each)

2 ancho chilies, stems, seeds, and veins discarded

1 cup each: boiling water, chopped onion

1 clove garlic, minced

2 cans (14½ ounces each) reduced-sodium fat-free chicken broth

8 ounces each: cubed pork tenderloin and boneless, skinless chicken breast (1-inch)

1 can (15 ounces) each: hominy, reduced-sodium tomatoes, drained, coarsely chopped

½ teaspoon each: dried oregano and thyme leaves

Salt and pepper, to taste

6 lime wedges

¼ cup each: thinly sliced lettuce, cabbage, green onion, radish, shredded carrot

Per Serving:
Calories: 181
% of calories from fat: 16
Fat (gm): 3.2
Saturated fat (gm): 0.9
Cholesterol (mg): 44.8
Sodium (mg): 244
Protein (gm): 21.2
Carbohydrate (gm): 16.7

Exchanges:
Milk: 0.0
Vegetable: 1.0
Fruit: 0.0
Bread: 1.0
Meat: 2.5
Fat: 0.0

1. Cover chilies with boiling water in small bowl; let stand until softened, about 10 minutes. Process chilies and water in food processor or blender until smooth; reserve.

2. Sauté onion and garlic in lightly greased saucepan until tender; add broth and meats and heat to boiling. Reduce heat and simmer, covered, until meats are tender, 10 to 15 minutes; strain, returning broth to saucepan. Shred meats with fork. Add meats, reserved chili mixture, hominy, tomatoes, and herbs to saucepan; cook, covered, over low heat 10 to 15 minutes. Season to taste with salt and pepper. Serve with lime wedges and fresh vegetables for each person to add to soup.

WONTON SOUP

Your menu need not be Asian to begin with this soup; it goes well with any simple entrée.

6 first-course servings (about 1 cup each)

24 Five-Spice Potstickers (½ recipe) (see p. 20)
6 cups reduced-sodium fat-free chicken broth
1 cup sliced spinach
Reduced-sodium tamari soy sauce
Pepper, to taste

1. Make Five-Spice Potstickers through Step 2 in recipe.

2. Heat chicken broth to boiling in large saucepan; add potstickers and simmer, uncovered, until potstickers rise to the surface, 2 to 3 minutes. Stir in spinach and green onion; simmer 2 to 3 minutes longer. Season to taste with soy sauce and pepper.

Per Serving:
Calories: 139
% of calories from fat: 5
Fat (gm): 0.8
Saturated fat (gm): 0.1
Cholesterol (mg): 2.9
Sodium (mg): 426
Protein (gm): 10.7
Carbohydrate (gm): 20.3

Exchanges:
Milk: 0.0
Vegetable: 1.0
Fruit: 0.0
Bread: 1.0
Meat: 1.0
Fat: 0.0

ORIENTAL SOUP WITH NOODLES AND CHICKEN

The dried chow mein noodles in this soup are not the fried ones we have used with chop suey for many years. Be sure the correct noodles are used.

4 first-course servings (about ¾ cup each)

1 ounce dried cloud ear or shiitake mushrooms
½ cup sliced white mushrooms
½ cup julienned carrots

2 cans (14½ ounces each) reduced-sodium chicken broth

2 tablespoons dry sherry (optional)

1½ teaspoons light soy sauce

¼ teaspoon five-spice powder

8 ounces boneless, skinless chicken breast, cooked, shredded

2 ounces snow peas, trimmed

½ package (5-ounce size) dried chow mein noodles

Salt and pepper, to taste

Per Serving:
Calories: 213
% of calories from fat: 30
Fat (gm): 7.6
Saturated fat (gm): 1.2
Cholesterol (mg): 29.2
Sodium (mg): 259
Protein (gm): 16.4
Carbohydrate (gm): 19.7

Exchanges:
Milk: 0.0
Vegetable: 0.5
Fruit: 0.0
Bread: 1.0
Meat: 1.5
Fat: 1.0

1. Place dried mushrooms in bowl; pour hot water over to cover. Let stand until mushrooms are soft, about 15 minutes; drain. Slice mushrooms, discarding any tough parts.

2. Sauté dried and white mushrooms, and carrots in lightly greased medium skillet 3 to 4 minutes. Add chicken broth, sherry, soy sauce, and five-spice powder. Heat to boiling; reduce heat and simmer, covered, 10 minutes. Stir in chicken, snow peas, and noodles; cook until noodles are just tender, about 10 minutes. Season to taste with salt and pepper.

SESAME NOODLE SOUP WITH VEGETABLES

45 *The fresh Chinese-style noodles are sometimes called soup noodles, chow mein noodles, or spaghetti. Caution—fresh noodles cook very quickly.*

4 entrée servings (about 2 cups each)

½ cup sliced green onions

4 cloves garlic, minced

1 tablespoon Asian sesame oil

2 cups thinly sliced napa cabbage

1 cup chopped red bell pepper

½ cup julienned carrots

3 cans (14½ ounces each) reduced-sodium chicken broth

12 ounces boneless, skinless chicken breast, cooked, shredded

1 package (12 ounces) fresh Chinese-style noodles

Salt and pepper, to taste

Per Serving:
Calories: 302
% of calories from fat: 19
Fat (gm): 6.5
Saturated fat (gm): 1
Cholesterol (mg): 43.5
Sodium (mg): 144
Protein (gm): 23
Carbohydrate (gm): 37.8

Exchanges:
Milk: 0.0
Vegetable: 1.5
Fruit: 0.0
Bread: 2.0
Meat: 2.0
Fat: 0.0

1. Sauté green onions and garlic in sesame oil in large saucepan until tender, about 5 minutes. Add cabbage, bell pepper, and carrots; sauté until vegetables are tender, about 5 minutes. Add chicken broth and heat to boiling. Stir in chicken and noodles; reduce heat and simmer, uncovered, until noodles are tender, 2 to 3 minutes. Season to taste with salt and pepper.

CHICKEN CORN CHOWDER WITH SWEET PEPPERS

45 *Red bell peppers and picante sauce transform an ordinary corn chowder into an extra special dish.*

6 entrée servings (about 1½ cups each)

1 pound boneless, skinless chicken breast, cubed

1 teaspoon olive oil

½ cup each: chopped onion, red bell pepper

2 teaspoons minced garlic

2 cups cubed, peeled potatoes

½ cup reduced-sodium fat-free chicken broth

2 cans (15 ounces each) cream-style corn

⅓ cup picante sauce

Salt and pepper, to taste

Chopped black olives, as garnish

Per Serving:
Calories: 291
% of calories from fat: 17
Fat (gm): 3.9
Saturated fat (gm): 0.7
Cholesterol (mg): 46
Sodium (mg): 536
Protein (gm): 22
Carbohydrate (gm): 45.6

Exchanges:
Milk: 0.0
Vegetable: 0.0
Fruit: 0.0
Bread: 2.5
Meat: 2.0
Fat: 0.0

1. Sauté chicken in oil in large saucepan until browned, 8 to 10 minutes; add onion, bell pepper, and garlic and sauté 5 minutes. Stir in potatoes and broth; heat to boiling. Reduce heat and simmer, covered, until potatoes are tender, about 10 minutes. Stir in corn and picante sauce; simmer, uncovered, until slightly thickened, about 5 minutes. Season to taste with salt and pepper. Sprinkle each bowl of chowder with olives.

QUICK GNOCCHI CHOWDER WITH SMOKED TURKEY

45 *Gnocchi are often topped with butter and Parmesan cheese and served as a side dish. Here, they're the main attraction in a chowder!*

4 entrée servings (about 2 cups each)

1 cup reduced-sodium fat-free chicken broth

1 can (15 ounces) reduced-sodium crushed tomatoes, undrained

10 ounces smoked turkey breast, cubed

1 package (12 ounces) potato gnocchi

1 teaspoon poultry seasoning

2 cups each: broccoli and cauliflower florets

½ cup chopped fresh or 2 tablespoons dried basil leaves

¼ cup (1 ounce) shredded provolone cheese

Salt and pepper, to taste

Per Serving:
Calories: 221
% of calories from fat: 17
Fat (gm): 4.2
Saturated fat (gm): 2.1
Cholesterol (mg): 24.3
Sodium (mg): 7
Protein (gm): 16.8
Carbohydrate (gm): 30

Exchanges:
Milk: 0.0
Vegetable: 1.0
Fruit: 0.0
Bread: 1.5
Meat: 2.0
Fat: 0.0

1. Heat chicken broth, tomatoes and liquid, turkey, gnocchi, and poultry seasoning to boiling in large saucepan; reduce heat and simmer, covered, 5 minutes. Stir in broccoli and cauliflower; simmer until tender, 5 to 8 minutes. Add basil and cheese, stirring until cheese is melted. Season to taste with salt and pepper.

SEAFOOD SAMPLER

45 *This sensibly seasoned chowder is great with Herb Croutons (see p. 498).*

4 entrée servings (about 1½ cups each)

½ cup each: chopped yellow bell pepper,
   chopped onion
1 teaspoon olive oil
1 can (15 ounces) reduced-sodium diced
   tomatoes, undrained
2 medium potatoes, cubed
½ cup dry white wine or water
½ teaspoon celery seeds
1 teaspoon herbes de Provence or dried
   Italian seasoning
8 ounces haddock or halibut, cubed (1-inch)
4 ounces each: bay scallops, peeled deveined shrimp
½ teaspoon hot pepper sauce
Salt, to taste

Per Serving:
Calories: 231
% of calories from fat: 10
Fat (gm): 2.5
Saturated fat (gm): 0.4
Cholesterol (mg): 88
Sodium (mg): 172
Protein (gm): 23.7
Carbohydrate (gm): 24.7

Exchanges:
Milk: 0.0
Vegetable: 1.0
Fruit: 0.0
Bread: 1.0
Meat: 3.0
Fat: 0.0

1. Sauté pepper and onion in oil in large saucepan until lightly browned, about 5 minutes. Add tomatoes with liquid, potatoes, wine, and herbs; heat to boiling. Reduce heat and simmer, covered, until potatoes are tender, about 10 minutes. Add seafood; simmer until haddock is tender and flakes with a fork, about 5 minutes. Stir in hot pepper sauce; season to taste with salt.

CIOPPINO

Our version of this classic Italian soup is made with shellfish. Clams in their shells are traditionally used, but canned whole clams may be substituted, if you prefer.

6 entrée servings (about 1½ cups each)

1 cup each: thinly sliced onion, green onions, green bell pepper
1 tablespoon each: minced garlic, olive oil
1 can (14½ ounces) reduced-sodium diced tomatoes, undrained
1 cup each: clam juice, water

½ cup dry white wine or clam juice

1 teaspoon each: dried tarragon and thyme leaves

¼ teaspoon dried rosemary leaves, crushed

1 bay leaf

1 pound crabmeat or firm white fish, cubed

8–12 ounces shrimp, peeled, deveined

18 clams in shells, scrubbed

Salt and pepper, to taste

Per Serving:
Calories: 210
% of calories from fat: 19
Fat (gm): 4.3
Saturated fat (gm): 0.6
Cholesterol (mg): 130.6
Sodium (mg): 276
Protein (gm): 24.1
Carbohydrate (gm): 10.2

Exchanges:
Milk: 0.0
Vegetable: 2.0
Fruit: 0.0
Bread: 0.0
Meat: 3.0
Fat: 0.0

1. Sauté onion, green onions, bell pepper, and garlic in oil in large saucepan, over low heat, until tender, 5 to 8 minutes. Add tomatoes with liquid, clam juice, water, wine, and herbs. Heat to boiling; reduce heat and simmer, covered, 20 minutes. Add crabmeat, shrimp, and clams; heat to boiling. Reduce heat and simmer until shrimp are cooked, and clams have opened, about 8 minutes. Discard bay leaf and any clams that have not opened. Season to taste with salt and pepper.

EASY ITALIAN FISH SOUP

45 *A surprisingly simple combination of ingredients yields savory results in this healthful, hurry-up meal.*

4 entrée servings (about 1¼ cups each)

1 each: chopped large onion, rib celery

½ teaspoon minced garlic

1 tablespoon olive oil

1 can (14½ ounces) reduced-sodium diced tomatoes, undrained

1 bottle (8 ounces) clam juice

¼ cup dry white wine or clam juice

¼ teaspoon dried marjoram leaves

1 pound halibut or other lean, firm fish, cubed (1-inch)

¼ cup chopped parsley

Salt and pepper, to taste

Per Serving:
Calories: 206
% of calories from fat: 27
Fat (gm): 6.3
Saturated fat (gm): 0.9
Cholesterol (mg): 36.1
Sodium (mg): 242
Protein (gm): 25.4
Carbohydrate (gm): 9.7

Exchanges:
Milk: 0.0
Vegetable: 2.0
Fruit: 0.0
Bread: 0.0
Meat: 3.0
Fat: 0.0

1. Sauté onion, celery, and garlic in oil in large saucepan over medium heat until lightly browned, about 5 minutes. Stir in tomatoes with liquid, clam juice, wine, and marjoram; heat to boiling. Reduce heat and simmer, covered, 20 minutes; add halibut and simmer until fish is tender and flakes with a fork, about 5 minutes. Stir in parsley; season to taste with salt and pepper.

MEDITERRANEAN-STYLE SHRIMP AND VEGETABLE SOUP

45 *A fragrant vegetable soup with a citrus accent.*

6 first-course servings (about 1½ cups each)

2 cups sliced mushrooms

½ cup each: chopped onion, green bell pepper

3 cloves garlic, minced

1 can (16 ounces) reduced-sodium whole tomatoes, undrained, coarsely chopped,

1 can (8 ounces) reduced-sodium tomato sauce

1 pound peeled, deveined shrimp

1–2 cups vegetable broth

½ cup dry white wine or orange juice

½–1 cup clam juice

2 strips orange zest (3 x ½ inches)

2 bay leaves

¾ teaspoon each: dried marjoram and savory leaves

¼ teaspoon crushed fennel seeds

Salt and pepper, to taste

Per Serving:
Calories: 121
% of calories from fat: 8
Fat (gm): 1.1
Saturated fat (gm): 0.2
Cholesterol (mg): 115.6
Sodium (mg): 211
Protein (gm): 14.8
Carbohydrate (gm): 10.7

Exchanges:
Milk: 0.0
Vegetable: 2.0
Fruit: 0.0
Bread: 0.0
Meat: 1.0
Fat: 0.0

1. Sauté mushrooms, onion, bell pepper, and garlic in lightly greased large saucepan, covered, until vegetables are tender, 8 to 10 minutes. Add remaining ingredients, except salt and pepper, and heat to boiling; reduce heat and simmer, covered, 10 to 15 minutes. Remove bay leaves; season to taste with salt and pepper.

SHRIMP AND BLACK BEAN SOUP

45 *In Mexico, leaves from the avocado tree are used for seasoning in this favorite Oaxacan soup. We've substituted a bay leaf, which is somewhat stronger in flavor.*

6 entrée servings (about 1½ cups each)

2 medium onions, chopped

4 cloves garlic, minced

2 medium tomatoes, cut into wedges

3 cans (14½ ounces each) reduced-sodium fat-free chicken broth, divided

½ cup water

3 cups cooked dried black beans or 2 cans (15 ounces each) black beans, rinsed, drained

1 teaspoon each: dried oregano and thyme leaves, ground cumin

1 bay leaf

8 ounces peeled, deveined shrimp

Salt and pepper, to taste

Finely chopped cilantro, as garnish

Per Serving:
Calories: 190
% of calories from fat: 5
Fat (gm): 1.1
Saturated fat (gm): 0.3
Cholesterol (mg): 58.3
Sodium (mg): 136
Protein (gm): 19.1
Carbohydrate (gm): 27

Exchanges:
Milk: 0.0
Vegetable: 1.0
Fruit: 0.0
Bread: 1.5
Meat: 1.5
Fat: 0.0

1. Sauté onions and garlic in lightly greased medium saucepan until tender, about 5 minutes. Process onion mixture, tomatoes, and 1 can chicken broth in food processor or blender until smooth; return to saucepan. Add remaining 2 cans broth, water, beans, and herbs; heat to boiling. Reduce heat and simmer, uncovered, 10 minutes, adding shrimp during last 5 minutes. Discard bay leaf. Season to taste with salt and pepper; sprinkle with cilantro.

SHRIMP AND SAUSAGE GUMBO

45 *Okra plays a dual role in this speedy version of the bayou favorite—it thickens the gumbo while giving it a characteristic Creole flavor.*

4 entrée servings (about 1½ cups each)

4 ounces smoked turkey sausage, halved, thinly sliced

1 red bell pepper, chopped

1 clove garlic, minced

1 teaspoon margarine or butter

2 cans (14 ounces each) reduced-sodium
   stewed tomatoes

8 ounces each: fresh or frozen sliced okra, peeled
   deveined shrimp

½ teaspoon crushed red pepper

Salt, to taste

3 cups cooked rice, warm

Per Serving:
Calories: 316
% of calories from fat: 14
Fat (gm): 5
Saturated fat (gm): 1.2
Cholesterol (mg): 104.4
Sodium (mg): 395
Protein (gm): 19.9
Carbohydrate (gm): 48.9

Exchanges:
Milk: 0.0
Vegetable: 3.0
Fruit: 0.0
Bread: 2.0
Meat: 2.0
Fat: 0.0

1. Sauté sausage, bell pepper, and garlic in margarine in large saucepan until browned, about 5 minute. Stir in tomatoes, okra, shrimp, and crushed red pepper; heat to boiling. Reduce heat and simmer, covered, until shrimp are cooked, about 5 minutes. Season to taste with salt. Serve over rice in bowls.

LOBSTER AND SHRIMP CHOWDER

45 *For easiest preparation, purchase cooked lobster and shrimp in the seafood department of your supermarket.*

4 entrée servings (about 1½ cups each)

2 large Yukon gold potatoes, peeled, cubed

1 medium onion, chopped

1 can (15 ounces) reduced-sodium diced tomatoes,
   undrained

1½ cups clam juice

8 ounces cooked lobster, cut into small chunks

4 ounces cooked peeled, deveined small shrimp

1 teaspoon dried tarragon leaves

Per Serving:
Calories: 210
% of calories from fat: 9
Fat (gm): 2.1
Saturated fat (gm): 0.9
Cholesterol (mg): 100.7
Sodium (mg): 519
Protein (gm): 22.4
Carbohydrate (gm): 25.7

Exchanges:
Milk: 0.0
Vegetable: 1.0
Fruit: 0.0
Bread: 1.0
Meat: 2.0
Fat: 0.0

1 cup 1% low-fat milk

¼ cup chopped parsley

Salt and pepper, to taste

1. Combine potatoes, onion, tomatoes with liquid, and clam juice in large saucepan. Heat to boiling; reduce heat and simmer, covered, until potatoes are tender, about 10 minutes. Add remaining ingredients, except salt and pepper, and simmer, uncovered, until hot, about 5 minutes. Season to taste with salt and pepper.

SPICY CRAB AND SCALLOP CHOWDER

45 *The flavor kick in this seafood chowder comes from pickling spice!*

4 first-course servings (about 1 cup each)

1 medium onion, chopped

1 rib celery, chopped

1 tablespoon margarine or butter

1½ cups clam juice

1 can (14 ounces) reduced-sodium stewed tomatoes

2 teaspoons pickling spice

1 can (4 ounces) lump crabmeat, drained

8 ounces bay scallops

¼–½ cup 2% reduced-fat milk

Salt and pepper, to taste

Per Serving:
Calories: 144
% of calories from fat: 26
Fat (gm): 4.3
Saturated fat (gm): 0.8
Cholesterol (mg): 50.4
Sodium (mg): 485
Protein (gm): 18.2
Carbohydrate (gm): 8.9

Exchanges:
Milk: 0.0
Vegetable: 1.0
Fruit: 0.0
Bread: 0.0
Meat: 2.0
Fat: 0.0

1. Sauté onion and celery in margarine in large saucepan until softened. Add clam juice, tomatoes, and pickling spice tied in a cheesecloth bag. Heat to boiling; stir in crabmeat, scallops, and milk. Simmer, covered, until scallops are cooked and opaque, about 5 minutes. Discard pickling spice. Season to taste with salt and pepper.

CURRIED SCALLOP AND POTATO CHOWDER

45 *This chowder has a lively curry flavor and a bright yellow color!*

4 entrée servings (about 1½ cups each)

1 bottle (11 ounces) clam juice
½ cup dry white wine or water
1 pound potatoes, peeled, cubed
1 teaspoon curry powder
½ teaspoon minced garlic
1 pound sea scallops
1 cup frozen peas
¼–½ cup 1% low-fat milk
Salt and pepper, to taste

Per Serving:
Calories: 251
% of calories from fat: 7
Fat (gm): 1.8
Saturated fat (gm): 0.2
Cholesterol (mg): 49.3
Sodium (mg): 482
Protein (gm): 25.6
Carbohydrate (gm): 29.4

Exchanges:
Milk: 0.0
Vegetable: 0.0
Fruit: 0.0
Bread: 2.0
Meat: 3.0
Fat: 0.0

1. Heat clam juice, wine, potatoes, curry powder, and garlic to boiling in large saucepan; reduce heat and simmer, covered, until potatoes are tender, about 10 minutes. Process about half the mixture in food processor or blender until smooth; return to pan. Stir in scallops, peas and milk; cook over medium heat until scallops are cooked, about 5 minutes. Season to taste with salt and pepper.

EASY MANHATTAN CLAM CHOWDER

45 *Enjoy this quick version of the popular clam chowder.*

4 first-course servings (about 1½ cups each)

4 slices bacon, diced
1 cup each: chopped onion, cubed peeled potatoes
¾ cup sliced carrots
2 tablespoons flour
1 cup clam juice
1 can (15 ounces) reduced-sodium diced
   tomatoes, undrained
½ teaspoon dried thyme leaves
2 cans (6 ounces each) minced clams, undrained
Salt and pepper, to taste

Per Serving:
Calories: 187
% of calories from fat: 11
Fat (gm): 2.4
Saturated fat (gm): 0.4
Cholesterol (mg): 33.4
Sodium (mg): 305
Protein (gm): 14.9
Carbohydrate (gm): 27.5

Exchanges:
Milk: 0.0
Vegetable: 2.0
Fruit: 0.0
Bread: 1.0
Meat: 1.0
Fat: 0.0

1. Cook bacon and onion in lightly greased large saucepan over medium heat until bacon is crisp and onion tender, about 5 minutes. Add potatoes and carrots and cook 5 minutes; add flour and cook 1 minute. Add remaining ingredients, except salt and pepper, and heat to boiling; reduce heat and simmer, covered, until vegetables are tender, about 15 minutes. Season to taste with salt and pepper.

CRAB CHOWDER WITH SNOW PEAS

45 *This aromatic chowder gets its flavor essence from jasmine rice, gingerroot, and sorrel.*

4 first-course servings (about 2 cups each)

2 cups clam juice

2½ cups water

½ cup jasmine or basmati rice

2 green onions, sliced

1 tablespoon minced gingerroot

2 cans (4 ounces each) lump crabmeat

2 cups each: snow peas, halved crosswise, torn sorrel or kale leaves

1 tablespoon dry sherry (optional)

½ cup 2% reduced-fat milk

Salt and pepper, to taste

Per Serving:
Calories: 209
% of calories from fat: 8
Fat (gm): 1.9
Saturated fat (gm): 0.5
Cholesterol (mg): 52.7
Sodium (mg): 491
Protein (gm): 17.6
Carbohydrate (gm): 28.8

Exchanges:
Milk: 0.0
Vegetable: 1.0
Fruit: 0.0
Bread: 1.0
Meat: 2.0
Fat: 0.0

1. Heat clam juice and water to boiling in large saucepan. Stir in rice, green onions, and gingerroot; reduce heat and simmer, covered, until rice is tender, about 25 minutes. Stir in remaining ingredients, except salt and pepper; simmer until snow peas are crisp-tender, 3 to 4 minutes. Season to taste with salt and pepper.

HALIBUT AND POTATO CHOWDER

45 *This chunky chowder has a thick, flavorful base of pureed vegetables.*

4 entrée servings (about 2 cups each)

1 each: chopped large onion, rib celery
1½ cups clam juice
4 cups cubed, peeled potatoes
1 pound halibut, cubed (¾-inch)
1 carrot, shredded
1 cup 1% low-fat milk
1 teaspoon dried savory leaves
½–1 teaspoons hot pepper sauce
Salt, to taste
2 slices bacon, cooked crisp, crumbled

Per Serving:
Calories: 394
% of calories from fat: 12
Fat (gm): 5.4
Saturated fat (gm): 1.4
Cholesterol (mg): 45.7
Sodium (mg): 430
Protein (gm): 31.4
Carbohydrate (gm): 55.4

Exchanges:
Milk: 0.0
Vegetable: 1.0
Fruit: 0.0
Bread: 3.0
Meat: 3.0
Fat: 0.0

1. Sauté onion and celery in lightly greased large saucepan until light browned, about 5 minutes. Stir in clam juice and potatoes and heat to boiling; reduce heat and simmer, covered, until potatoes are tender, about 10 minutes. Process about half the mixture in food processor or blender until smooth; return to saucepan. Heat to boiling; add remaining ingredients, except salt and bacon. Reduce heat and simmer, covered, until halibut is tender and flakes with a fork, about 5 minutes. Season to taste with salt; sprinkle each bowl of soup with bacon.

MONKFISH-CHEDDAR CHOWDER

45 *Use any favorite firm-textured fish in this creamy, cheesy chowder.*

4 entrée servings (about 2 cups each)

½ cup each: chopped onion, sliced carrots
2 teaspoons margarine or butter
1 pound potatoes, peeled, cubed
1 can (14 ounces) reduced-sodium fat-free
   chicken broth
1 pound monkfish, cubed (¾-inch)
½ cup each: fat-free milk, shredded reduced-fat
   Cheddar cheese (2 ounces)

½–1 teaspoon hot pepper sauce

Salt, to taste

Chopped chives, as garnish

Per Serving:
Calories: 274
% of calories from fat: 19
Fat (gm): 5.9
Saturated fat (gm): 1.8
Cholesterol (mg): 35.4
Sodium (mg): 344
Protein (gm): 24.9
Carbohydrate (gm): 29.5

Exchanges:
Milk: 0.0
Vegetable: 0.0
Fruit: 0.0
Bread: 1.5
Meat: 3.0
Fat: 0.0

1. Sauté onion and carrots in margarine in large saucepan until tender, 3 to 4 minutes; add potatoes and broth. Heat to boiling; reduce heat and simmer, covered, until potatoes are tender, about 10 minutes. Process about ½ the mixture in food processor or blender until smooth; return to saucepan and heat to boiling. Add fish and milk; reduce heat and simmer, covered, until fish is tender and flakes with a fork, about 5 minutes. Stir in cheese and hot pepper sauce; stir over low heat until cheese is melted. Season to taste with salt; sprinkle each bowl of soup with chives.

SALMON AND ROASTED PEPPER CHOWDER

45 *Salmon is paired with corn and seasoned with jalapeño chilies, cumin, and oregano for a fast and fabulous feast.*

4 entrée servings (about 1¾ cups each)

Per Serving:
Calories: 259
% of calories from fat: 12
Fat (gm): 3.4
Saturated fat (gm): 0.5
Cholesterol (mg): 42.8
Sodium (mg): 197
Protein (gm): 20.5
Carbohydrate (gm): 36.4

Exchanges:
Milk: 0.0
Vegetable: 0.0
Fruit: 0.0
Bread: 2.0
Meat: 2.0
Fat: 0.0

2 cups each: whole kernel corn, reduced-sodium vegetable broth

2 medium potatoes, peeled, cubed

1 cup chopped roasted red pepper

½–1 jalapeño chili, minced

2 teaspoons minced garlic

1 teaspoon each: cumin seeds, dried oregano leaves

12 ounces salmon steaks, cubed (1-inch)

Salt and pepper, to taste

1. Combine all ingredients, except salmon, salt, and pepper in large saucepan. Heat to boiling; reduce heat and simmer, covered, until potatoes are tender, about 10 minutes. Add salmon; simmer until salmon is tender and flakes with a fork, about 5 minutes. Season to taste with salt and pepper.

THREE

Meats

OLD-FASHIONED POT ROAST

45

Cabbage, turnips, and sweet potatoes are other vegetable choices that can be used in this recipe.

6 servings

2¾ pounds beef chuck pot roast, fat trimmed

Salt and pepper, to taste

3 medium onions, cut into wedges

6 cloves garlic, minced

1 cup reduced-sodium beef broth

1 bay leaf

1 pound potatoes, unpeeled, cut into pieces (1½-inch)

8 ounces each: peeled carrots, rutabaga or parsnip, cut into pieces (1½ inch)

¼ cup all-purpose flour

½ cup water

Per Serving:
Calories: 377
% of calories from fat: 15
Fat (gm): 6.4
Saturated fat (gm): 2.2
Cholesterol (mg): 95.6
Sodium (mg): 110
Protein (gm): 37
Carbohydrate (gm): 42.6

Exchanges:
Milk: 0.0
Vegetable: 2.0
Fruit: 0.0
Bread: 1.5
Meat: 4.0
Fat: 0.0

1. Cook beef in lightly greased Dutch oven over medium heat until browned, 2 to 3 minutes on each side. Remove from pan; sprinkle lightly with salt and pepper. Add onions and garlic to pan; sauté 2 to 3 minutes. Return meat to pan; add broth and bay leaf, and heat to boiling. Transfer to oven and bake, covered, at 325 degrees until beef is fork-tender, 2¾ to 3 hours, adding remaining vegetables to pan during last 45 minutes.

2. Place meat and vegetables on serving platter; discard bay leaf. Pour meat juices into glass measure; spoon off and discard fat. Add water to juices, if necessary, to make 2 cups; heat to boiling in small saucepan. Stir in combined flour and water, stirring until thickened, about 1 minute; season to taste with salt and pepper. Serve gravy with pot roast and vegetables.

VARIATIONS

Bourbon Pot Roast — Make recipe as above, omitting rutabaga, and substituting ⅔ cup tomato juice and ⅓ cup bourbon for the beef broth. Add 1 teaspoon dry mustard and ½ teaspoon beef bouillon crystals with the tomato juice in Step 1.

Italian Pot Roast — Make recipe as above, omitting potatoes, carrots, rutabagas, and flour. Substitute 1 cup dry red wine for the beef broth. Add 1 can (15 ounces) roasted garlic diced tomatoes, 1 can (6 ounces) reduced-sodium tomato paste, and 1 teaspoon dried Italian seasoning in Step 1. Add ½ cup each chopped carrot and celery, and 1 cup sliced mushrooms during last 45 minutes of baking time. Serve with Herbed Polenta (see p. 364).

MUSTARD ROAST BEEF

45

The spicy coating makes this roast beef extra juicy and flavorful.

6 servings

¼ cup apricot preserves

2–4 tablespoons spicy brown mustard

2–3 teaspoons reduced-sodium Worcestershire sauce

1 tablespoon each: light brown sugar, prepared horseradish

1 teaspoon each: crushed caraway seeds, black peppercorns

¼ teaspoon ground allspice

1 boneless beef sirloin tip roast, fat trimmed (about 2 pounds)

Per Serving:
Calories: 264
% of calories from fat: 26
Fat (gm): 7.3
Saturated fat (gm): 2.5
Cholesterol (mg): 71.8
Sodium (mg): 185
Protein (gm): 33.9
Carbohydrate (gm): 12.5

Exchanges:
Milk: 0.0
Vegetable: 0.0
Fruit: 0.5
Bread: 0.0
Meat: 4.0
Fat: 0.0

1. Mix all ingredients, except beef; spread on all surfaces of beef. Place beef on rack in roasting pan; roast at 325 degrees to desired doneness, 160 degrees for medium, 45 to 60 minutes. Let stand 10 minutes before slicing.

VARIATION

Crumb-Crusted Roast Beef — Make recipe as above omitting brown sugar, horseradish, caraway seeds, and allspice. Combine 1 cup fresh bread crumbs, 2 teaspoons minced garlic, ¾ teaspoon each dried basil and oregano leaves with the apricot preserves, mustard, and Worcestershire sauce; pat onto beef. Roast as above.

VEGETABLE-STUFFED FLANK STEAK

45

Serve with oven-roasted potatoes and a salad for a delicious meal.

4 servings

1 pound beef flank steak
1 cup fat-free Italian salad dressing
Vegetable Stuffing (recipe follows)
1 cup reduced-sodium fat-free beef broth

Per Serving:
Calories: 281
% of calories from fat: 29
Fat (gm): 8.8
Saturated fat (gm): 3.6
Cholesterol (mg): 49.8
Sodium (mg): 744
Protein (gm): 33.6
Carbohydrate (gm): 14.4

Exchanges:
Milk: 0.0
Vegetable: 0.0
Fruit: 0.0
Bread: 1.0
Meat: 4.0
Fat: 0.0

1. Pound flank steak with meat mallet until even in thickness; score steak diagonally in diamond pattern on both sides. Pour dressing over steak in glass baking dish; refrigerate, covered, 1½ to 2 hours, turning occasionally. Drain; reserve marinade. Spread Vegetable Stuffing on steak, leaving 2-inch margin along sides. Roll up lengthwise; secure edge with wooden picks or tie with kitchen string.

2. Brown beef on all sides in lightly greased large ovenproof skillet; add broth and reserved marinade. Bake, covered, at 325 degrees to medium doneness (160 degrees) about 45 minutes.

Vegetable Stuffing

Makes about 1¼ cups

8 ounces sliced mushrooms
¼ cup each: chopped carrot, thinly sliced celery, green onions
1 clove garlic, minced
¼ cup unseasoned dry bread crumbs
1½ teaspoons dried Italian seasoning
Salt and pepper, to taste

1. Sauté mushrooms, carrot, celery, green onions, and garlic in lightly greased large skillet until tender, about 5 minutes. Add bread crumbs and Italian seasoning and cook until browned, 2 to 3 minutes; season to taste with salt and pepper.

TOURNEDOS BÉARNAISE

45 *Enjoy this healthy, low-fat version of the classic.*

4 servings

4 slices Italian bread (¾-inch)
Vegetable cooking spray
1 clove garlic, halved
4 beef tenderloin steaks (4 ounces each), fat trimmed
Salt and pepper, to taste
Mock Béarnaise Sauce (recipe follows)

Per Serving:
Calories: 335
% of calories from fat: 29
Fat (gm): 10.4
Saturated fat (gm): 3.9
Cholesterol (mg): 76.1
Sodium (mg): 488
Protein (gm): 35.1
Carbohydrate (gm): 22.7

Exchanges:
Milk: 0.0
Vegetable: 0.0
Fruit: 0.0
Bread: 1.5
Meat: 4.0
Fat: 0.0

1. Spray bread slices with cooking spray; broil 6 inches from heat source until browned, 2 to 3 minutes on each side. Rub bread slices with cut sides of garlic.

2. Sauté steaks in lightly greased medium skillet to desired degree of doneness, 3 to 4 minutes on each side for medium; season to taste with salt and pepper. Arrange steaks on bread slices; spoon Mock Béarnaise Sauce over.

Mock Béarnaise Sauce
Makes about 1½ cups

6 ounces fat-free cream cheese
⅓ cup fat-free sour cream
3–4 tablespoons fat-free milk
2 teaspoons each: minced shallot, lemon juice
½–1 teaspoon Dijon mustard
1½ teaspoons dried tarragon leaves
Salt and white pepper, to taste

1. Heat all ingredients, except salt and pepper, in small saucepan over medium-low heat until melted and smooth, stirring constantly; season to taste with salt and pepper. Serve immediately.

STEAK AU POIVRE

45 *Instead of black peppercorns, a mixture of white, pink, green, and black peppercorns can be used.*

4 servings

4 teaspoons coarsely crushed black peppercorns

4 beef eye of round or tenderloin steaks (4 ounces each), fat trimmed

Salt, to taste

⅓ cup brandy or beef broth

¼ cup fat-free sour cream

Per Serving:
Calories: 212
% of calories from fat: 20
Fat (gm): 4.5
Saturated fat (gm): 1.6
Cholesterol (mg): 64
Sodium (mg): 68
Protein (gm): 27.7
Carbohydrate (gm): 2.1

Exchanges:
Milk: 0.0
Vegetable: 0.0
Fruit: 0.0
Bread: 0.0
Meat: 3.5
Fat: 0.0

1. Press peppercorns onto both sides of steaks; sprinkle lightly with salt. Sauté in lightly greased medium skillet over medium heat to desired degree of doneness, 3 to 4 minutes on each side for medium. Remove steaks and keep warm.

2. Add brandy to skillet; heat to boiling. Boil, scraping bottom of skillet to loosen cooked particles, until reduced to about 2 tablespoons, 2 to 3 minutes. Stir in sour cream and cook over low heat 1 to 2 minutes. Spoon over steaks.

CHICKEN-FRIED STEAK

45 *The beef steaks are pounded until thin for faster cooking and tenderness.*

4 servings

4 beef eye of round steaks (4 ounces each), fat trimmed

2 tablespoons flour

1 egg, lightly beaten

¼ cup each: fat-free milk, seasoned dry bread crumbs

Salt and pepper, to taste

Cream Gravy (recipe follows)

Per Serving:
Calories: 349
% of calories from fat: 29
Fat (gm): 11
Saturated fat (gm): 3
Cholesterol (mg): 66.2
Sodium (mg): 309
Protein (gm): 36.5
Carbohydrate (gm): 23.8

Exchanges:
Milk: 0.5
Vegetable: 0.0
Fruit: 0.0
Bread: 1.5
Meat: 3.5
Fat: 0.0

1. Pound steaks with flat side of mallet to ¼ inch thickness. Coat steaks lightly with flour; dip in combined egg and milk and coat with bread crumbs. Cook steaks in lightly greased large skillet over medium heat until browned, about 5 minutes on each side. Cook, covered, over low heat until steaks are tender, turning occasionally, 20 to 25 minutes. Season to taste with salt and pepper. Serve with Cream Gravy.

Cream Gravy
Makes about 2 cups

2 tablespoons margarine or butter
¼ cup all-purpose flour
2 cups fat-free half-and-half or milk
½ teaspoon beef bouillon crystals
¼ cup fat-free sour cream
Salt and pepper, to taste

1. Melt margarine in medium saucepan; stir in flour and cook 1 minute. Whisk in half-and-half and bouillon crystals; heat to boiling, stirring until thickened, about 1 minute. Stir in sour cream and cook over low heat 1 to 2 minutes; season to taste with salt and pepper.

BEEF STEAK WITH RED AND GREEN STIR-FRY

Beef eye of round steak is a healthy choice for this entree, as it has less than 30% calories from fat.

4 servings

2 cups sliced red onions
1 cup sliced celery
2 teaspoons each: minced garlic, gingerroot
6 cups sliced Swiss chard or spinach
2 cups each: sliced red bell pepper, reduced-sodium fat-free beef broth
2 tablespoons cornstarch
1 tablespoon reduced-sodium tamari soy sauce, divided
½–¾ teaspoon hot chili paste
Salt and pepper, to taste
4 beef eye of round steaks (4 ounces each), fat trimmed

Per Serving:
Calories: 210
% of calories from fat: 17
Fat (gm): 4.1
Saturated fat (gm): 1.4
Cholesterol (mg): 54.9
Sodium (mg): 494
Protein (gm): 26.3
Carbohydrate (gm): 17.1

Exchanges:
Milk: 0.0
Vegetable: 2.0
Fruit: 0.0
Bread: 0.0
Meat: 3.0
Fat: 0.0

1. Stir-fry onions, celery, garlic, and gingerroot in lightly greased large skillet 2 to 3 minutes. Add Swiss chard and bell pepper; stir-fry until vegetables are crisp-tender, 2 to 3 minutes. Stir in combined broth, cornstarch, soy sauce, and chili paste; heat to boiling, stirring until thickened, about 1 minute. Season to taste with salt and pepper.

2. Cook steaks in lightly greased medium skillet over medium heat to desired degree of doneness, 3 to 4 minutes on each side for medium. Spoon vegetable mixture over steaks.

SICILIAN BEEF AND RICE

45 *Using frozen pepper and onion blend minimizes kitchen prep time in this easy recipe.*

4 servings

1 package (16 ounces) frozen pepper and onion blend

1 teaspoon minced garlic

12 ounces lean ground beef

2 cans (15 ounces each) reduced-sodium tomato sauce

2–3 teaspoons dried Italian seasoning

Salt and pepper, to taste

3 cups cooked long-grain rice or pasta, warm

3 tablespoons grated Parmesan cheese

Per Serving:
Calories: 422
% of calories from fat: 11
Fat (gm): 5
Saturated fat (gm): 2.2
Cholesterol (mg): 44.9
Sodium (mg): 186
Protein (gm): 29.3
Carbohydrate (gm): 61.7

Exchanges:
Milk: 0.0
Vegetable: 3.0
Fruit: 0.0
Bread: 3.0
Meat: 2.0
Fat: 0.0

1. Cook pepper and onion blend, garlic, and ground beef in lightly greased large skillet over medium heat until beef is browned and vegetables are tender, about 6 minutes. Stir in tomato sauce and Italian seasoning; simmer, uncovered, until thickened, about 20 minutes. Season to taste with salt and pepper. Serve with rice; sprinkle with Parmesan cheese.

45-MINUTE PREPARATION TIP: Begin cooking rice before preparing the rest of the recipe.

ROUND STEAK PIZZAIOLA

For variation, add 2 cups sliced or cubed vegetables to the meat and sauce during the last 20 minutes of cooking.

4 servings

1–1¼ pounds boneless beef round steak, fat trimmed, cut into thin strips

⅛ teaspoon ground black pepper

1 large onion, chopped

1 tablespoon olive oil

2 cans (15 ounces each) reduced-sodium crushed tomatoes

2–3 teaspoons dried Italian seasoning

12 ounces penne or other pasta, cooked, warm

¼ cup (1 ounce) grated Parmesan cheese

Per Serving:
Calories: 576
% of calories from fat: 18
Fat (gm): 11.4
Saturated fat (gm): 3.5
Cholesterol (mg): 59.8
Sodium (mg): 170
Protein (gm): 41
Carbohydrate (gm): 76.5

Exchanges:
Milk: 0.0
Vegetable: 4.0
Fruit: 0.0
Bread: 4.0
Meat: 3.0
Fat: 0.5

1. Sprinkle round steak with pepper; cook over medium heat in lightly greased large skillet until browned, 3 to 4 minutes on each side. Remove from skillet. Add onion and oil to skillet and sauté until tender, about 5 minutes. Return beef to skillet; add tomatoes and Italian seasoning and heat to boiling. Reduce heat and simmer, covered, until beef is tender, about 35 minutes. Serve over penne; sprinkle with cheese.

PEPPER STEAK

Always popular for buffet-style entertaining.

6 servings

3 cups thickly sliced green, red, and yellow
   bell peppers
2 cups sliced onions
4 cloves garlic, minced
1 pound beef eye of round or sirloin, fat trimmed,
   cut into strips (3 x ¼-inch)
3 tablespoons flour
2 cups reduced-sodium beef broth, divided
1 tablespoon tomato paste
½ teaspoon dried Italian seasoning
1½ cups halved cherry tomatoes
1–2 tablespoons Worcestershire sauce
Salt and pepper, to taste
4 cups cooked noodles, warm

Per Serving:
Calories: 383
% of calories from fat: 13
Fat (gm): 5.8
Saturated fat (gm): 1.2
Cholesterol (mg): 42.6
Sodium (mg): 127
Protein (gm): 28.7
Carbohydrate (gm): 56.2

Exchanges:
Milk: 0.0
Vegetable: 3.0
Fruit: 0.0
Bread: 2.5
Meat: 2.5
Fat: 0.0

1. Sauté bell peppers in lightly greased Dutch oven until tender,
about 5 minutes; remove from pan. Add onions, garlic, and beef
to skillet; cook over medium heat until beef is browned, 5 to 8
minutes. Stir in flour and cook 1 minute.

Add broth, tomato paste, and Italian seasoning; heat to boiling.
Reduce heat and simmer, covered, until beef is tender, about 45
minutes, adding tomatoes and cooked bell peppers during last 10
minutes. Season to taste with Worcestershire sauce, salt, and
pepper. Serve with noodles.

VARIATION

Sweet-Sour Pepper Steak — Make recipe as above, substituting 1½
cups snow peas for half the bell peppers and reduced-sodium soy
sauce for the Worcestershire sauce. Stir in ¼ cup apricot preserves,
½ cup sliced water chestnuts, and 2 to 3 teaspoons cider vinegar at
the end of cooking time. Serve over rice.

BEEF AND VEGETABLE LO MEIN

Fresh Chinese egg noodles are in the produce section of the supermarket.

4 servings

4 dried Chinese black (shiitake) mushrooms

1 tablespoon each: minced gingerroot, garlic, Asian sesame oil

12–16 ounces beef eye of round, fat trimmed, cut into strips (1 x ½-inch)

2 cups broccoli florets

1 cup sliced carrots

⅓ cup water

2 tablespoons dry sherry or water

1 tablespoon each: black bean paste, soy sauce

2 teaspoons cornstarch

1 package (12 ounces) fresh Chinese egg noodles, cooked

Per Serving:
Calories: 300
% of calories from fat: 18
Fat (gm): 6
Saturated fat (gm): 1.4
Cholesterol (mg): 41.2
Sodium (mg): 153
Protein (gm): 22.1
Carbohydrate (gm): 37.9

Exchanges:
Milk: 0.0
Vegetable: 1.0
Fruit: 0.0
Bread: 2.0
Meat: 2.5
Fat: 0.0

1. Cover dried mushrooms with boiling water in bowl. Let stand until mushrooms are softened, about 15 minutes; drain. Slice mushrooms, discarding tough stems.

2. Stir-fry mushrooms, gingerroot, and garlic in oil in wok or large skillet 2 minutes. Add beef and stir-fry until cooked, about 5 minutes; remove from wok. Add broccoli and carrots to wok; stir-fry until crisp-tender, 5 to 8 minutes. Return beef to wok; stir in combined water, sherry, black bean paste, soy sauce, and cornstarch. Heat to boiling, stirring until thickened, about 1 minute; stir in noodles. Cook until hot, 2 to 3 minutes.

SZECHUAN BEEF AND VEGETABLE STIR-FRY

The chili oil and crushed red pepper are hot, so begin with less, adding more to taste. Asian sesame oil can be substituted for the hot chili oil.

4 servings

1 cup reduced-sodium beef broth, divided

¼ cup each: orange juice, reduced-sodium soy sauce

1–2 teaspoons hot chili oil

1–2 pinches crushed red pepper

12–16 ounces beef flank steak, fat trimmed, thinly sliced

1 cup each: thickly sliced asparagus, carrots, red bell pepper, snow peas

½ cup each: sliced green onions, shiitake or cremini mushrooms

2–3 teaspoons minced gingerroot

4 cloves garlic, minced

2 tablespoons cornstarch

Salt and pepper, to taste

4 cups cooked brown rice, warm

¼ cup peanuts (optional)

Per Serving:
Calories: 455
% of calories from fat: 15
Fat (gm): 8.0
Saturated fat (gm): 1.3
Cholesterol (mg): 0
Sodium (mg): 663
Protein (gm): 23.3
Carbohydrate (gm): 75.8

Exchanges:
Milk: 0.0
Vegetable: 3.0
Fruit: 0.0
Bread: 4.0
Meat: 1.0
Fat: 1.0

1. Combine ½ cup broth, orange juice, soy sauce, hot chili oil, and red pepper; pour over beef in shallow glass dish and let stand 30 minutes. Drain, reserving marinade.

2. Stir-fry beef in lightly greased wok or large skillet until browned, 4 to 5 minutes. Add vegetables, gingerroot, and garlic; stir-fry until crisp-tender, 8 to 10 minutes. Add reserved marinade and heat to boiling; stir in combined cornstarch and remaining ½ cup broth, stirring, until thickened, about 1 minute. Season to taste with salt and pepper. Serve over rice; sprinkle with peanuts.

ROAST BEEF HASH

45 *Any leftover lean beef or pork can be used in this recipe.*

4 servings

½ cup each: chopped onion, green bell pepper

2 cloves garlic, minced

2 cups each: shredded cooked lean beef, cooked, cubed potatoes (½-inch)

½ teaspoon each: dried marjoram and thyme leaves

Salt and pepper, to taste

Per Serving:
Calories: 244
% of calories from fat: 22
Fat (gm): 6
Saturated fat (gm): 2.3
Cholesterol (mg): 50.7
Sodium (mg): 44
Protein (gm): 19.9
Carbohydrate (gm): 27.5

Exchanges:
Milk: 0.0
Vegetable: 1.0
Fruit: 0.0
Bread: 1.5
Meat: 2.0
Fat: 0.0

1. Sauté onion, bell pepper, and garlic in lightly greased large skillet until tender, about 5 minutes. Add beef, potatoes, and herbs; cook over medium heat until meat and potatoes are browned, about 10 minutes. Season to taste with salt and pepper.

VARIATION

Corned Beef Hash — Make recipe as above, substituting lean corned beef for the roast beef.

MEXICAN HASH

Leftover meat or poultry can be used in this dish. Serve with fried eggs for a heartier meal.

4 servings

1 pound beef eye of round, fat trimmed, cubed

1 cup each: chopped tomato, onion

2 large poblano chilies, sliced

1 pound Idaho potatoes, unpeeled, cooked, cubed

Chili powder, to taste

Salt and pepper, to taste

Per Serving:
Calories: 242
% of calories from fat: 15
Fat (gm): 4
Saturated fat (gm): 1.3
Cholesterol (mg): 54.7
Sodium (mg): 55
Protein (gm): 23.4
Carbohydrate (gm): 27.90

Exchanges:
Milk: 0.0
Vegetable: 1.5
Fruit: 0.0
Bread: 1.0
Meat: 2.5
Fat: 0.0

1. Cook beef in 2 inches simmering water in large saucepan, covered, until beef is tender, 20 to 25 minutes; drain. Cool slightly and shred. Sauté beef in lightly greased large skillet over until beginning to brown and crisp, about 5 minutes. Add tomato; cook over medium heat 5 minutes. Remove from skillet.

2. Add onion and poblano chilies to skillet; cook until tender, 5 to 8 minutes. Add potatoes and cook until browned, about 5 minutes. Add reserved meat mixture to skillet and cook until hot, 3 to 4 minutes. Season to taste with chili powder, salt, and pepper.

BEEF STEAKS WITH TOMATILLO AND AVOCADO SAUCE

45 *The Tomatillo and Avocado Sauce is also excellent with grilled or roasted poultry or pork.*

6 servings

1 medium onion, thinly sliced
6 beef eye of round or tenderloin steaks (4 ounces each), fat trimmed
Salt and pepper, to taste
1 cup Tomatillo Sauce (½ recipe) (see p. 184)
¼ cup each: mashed avocado, fat-free sour cream
6 flour or corn tortillas (6-inch), warm

Per Serving:
Calories: 271
% of calories from fat: 30
Fat (gm): 8.9
Saturated fat (gm): 3.1
Cholesterol (mg): 56.3
Sodium (mg): 101
Protein (gm): 28.2
Carbohydrate (gm): 19.2

Exchanges:
Milk: 0.0
Vegetable: 1.0
Fruit: 0.0
Bread: 1.0
Meat: 3.0
Fat: 0.0

1. Sauté onion in lightly greased large skillet 2 to 3 minutes; reduce heat to medium-low and cook until onion is very soft, 5 to 8 minutes. Remove from skillet; keep warm. Add steaks to skillet; cook over medium heat to desired degree of doneness, 3 to 4 minutes on each side for medium. Season to taste with salt and pepper.

2. Heat Tomatillo Sauce in small saucepan until hot. Stir in avocado and sour cream; cook 2 minutes. Top steaks with onions and sauce. Serve with tortillas.

BEEF AND ROASTED PEPPER FAJITAS

The beef in these fajitas is cooked with the flavorful pasilla chili for great flavor.

4 servings

1 dried pasilla chili, stem, seeds, and veins discarded

1 cup each: thickly sliced red, green and yellow bell pepper

Vegetable cooking spray

1 teaspoon ground cumin

1 pound beef eye of round, fat trimmed, cut into strips (1½ x ½-inch)

3 cloves garlic, minced

¼ small jalapeño chili, minced

¼ cup finely chopped cilantro

Salt, to taste

8 flour or corn tortillas (6-inch), warm

½ cup fat-free sour cream

Per Serving:
Calories: 365
% of calories from fat: 19
Fat (gm): 7.8
Saturated fat (gm): 1.9
Cholesterol (mg): 54.7
Sodium (mg): 355
Protein (gm): 28.9
Carbohydrate (gm): 45

Exchanges:
Milk: 0.0
Vegetable: 2.0
Fruit: 0.0
Bread: 2.0
Meat: 3.0
Fat: 0.0

1. Cover pasilla chili with hot water in small bowl; let stand until softened, about 15 minutes. Drain and chop. Arrange bell peppers in single layer on greased aluminum foil-lined jelly roll pan; spray with cooking spray. Bake at 425 degrees until tender and browned, 20 to 25 minutes. Toss with cumin and cloves.

2. Cook beef, garlic, and jalapeño and pasilla chilies in lightly greased large skillet over medium heat until beef is desired doneness, about 5 minutes for medium; stir in bell peppers and cilantro. Season to taste with salt. Spoon onto tortillas. Top with sour cream, and roll up, folding one end up to prevent filling from leaking out.

BEEF PINTO BEAN TAMALES

For variation, lean pork can be substituted for the beef, and black beans for the pintos.

6 servings (2 each)

1 medium onion, chopped
3 cloves garlic, minced
1 teaspoon dried marjoram leaves
½ teaspoon cayenne pepper
½ can (15-ounce size) pinto beans, rinsed, drained, coarsely mashed
12 ounces boneless beef eye of round, cubed, cooked, shredded
Tamale Dough (recipe follows)
½ cup reduced-sodium beef broth or water
Salt, to taste
12 corn husks, softened in boiling water, drained

Per Serving:
Calories: 204
% of calories from fat: 25
Fat (gm): 5.7
Saturated fat (gm): 1.3
Cholesterol (mg): 27.3
Sodium (mg): 328
Protein (gm): 15.8
Carbohydrate (gm): 23.6

Exchanges:
Milk: 0.0
Vegetable: 0.5
Fruit: 0.0
Bread: 1.0
Meat: 1.0
Fat: 0.5

1. Sauté onion, garlic, marjoram, and cayenne pepper in lightly greased medium skillet until onion is tender, about 5 minutes. Stir in beans and beef and cook 2 to 3 minutes; mix in Tamale Dough and broth. Season to taste with salt.

2. Spoon about ¼ cup tamale mixture onto center of each corn husk. Fold sides of husks over filling; fold top and bottom of husks toward center and tie in the center with string. Place tamales on steamer rack in saucepan with 2 inches water; steam, covered, 2 hours, adding more water to saucepan if necessary.

Tamale Dough
Makes about 1 cup

1 cup masa harina
¾ teaspoon baking powder
1½ tablespoons margarine or butter, softened
¼–½ teaspoon salt
1 cup reduced-sodium vegetable broth

1. Combine masa harina, baking powder, margarine, and salt in bowl; gradually stir in broth (mixture will be soft).

BLACK BEAN AND BEEF BURRITOS

Another favorite that's a Tex-Mex adaptation of Mexican cooking.

4 servings (1 each)

½ cup each: chopped poblano chili, onion

1 clove garlic, minced

1 can (15 ounces) black beans, rinsed, drained

1 can (8 ounces) reduced-sodium tomato sauce

Salt and pepper, to taste

Beef Filling (recipe follows)

4 large flour tortillas (10-inch), warm

½ cup each: shredded fat-free Cheddar cheese
   (2 ounces), fat-free sour cream

2 tablespoons finely chopped cilantro

Per Serving:
Calories: 379
% of calories from fat: 14
Fat (gm): 6.5
Saturated fat (gm): 1.4
Cholesterol (mg): 43.6
Sodium (mg): 677
Protein (gm): 35.5
Carbohydrate (gm): 51.8

Exchanges:
Milk: 0.0
Vegetable: 2.0
Fruit: 0.0
Bread: 2.5
Meat: 2.5
Fat: 0.0

1. Sauté poblano chili, onion, and garlic in lightly greased large skillet until onion is tender, about 5 minutes. Add beans and tomato sauce; heat to boiling. Reduce heat and simmer, covered, 5 minutes; season to taste with salt and pepper. Spoon bean mixture and Beef Filling onto tortillas; top with cheese, sour cream, and cilantro. Roll up, folding one end up to prevent filling from leaking out.

Beef Filling

Makes about 2 cups

12 ounces beef eye of round, fat trimmed, cubed (2-inch)

2 medium tomatoes, coarsely chopped

½ teaspoon ground cinnamon

Salt and pepper, to taste

1. Cook beef in 2 inches simmering water in medium saucepan, covered, until tender, 15 to 20 minutes; drain. Cool slightly; shred finely. Sauté beef in lightly greased medium skillet until beginning to brown, 3 to 4 minutes. Add tomatoes and cinnamon; cook until tomatoes are wilted. Season to taste with salt and pepper.

BEEF AND VEGETABLE ENCHILADAS

Vary these healthful enchiladas by substituting shredded chicken or pork tenderloin for the beef.

6 servings (2 each)

1½ cups each: chopped zucchini, tomatoes

¾ cup chopped carrots

¼ cup each: sliced green onions, chopped poblano chili or green bell pepper

4 cloves garlic, minced

1 teaspoon each: minced jalapeño chili, dried oregano leaves, ground cumin

1½ pounds beef eye of round, fat trimmed, cooked, shredded

Salt and pepper, to taste

12 corn or flour tortillas (6-inch)

Tomatillo Sauce (see p. 184)

¾ cup (3 ounces) shredded fat-free Cheddar cheese

3 tablespoons finely chopped cilantro

Per Serving:
Calories: 305
% of calories from fat: 16
Fat (gm): 5.5
Saturated fat (gm): 1.5
Cholesterol (mg): 57.2
Sodium (mg): 244
Protein (gm): 30.2
Carbohydrate (gm): 34.8

Exchanges:
Milk: 0.0
Vegetable: 2.0
Fruit: 0.0
Bread: 1.5
Meat: 3.0
Fat: 0.0

1. Sauté vegetables and herbs in lightly greased large skillet until tender, about 10 minutes. Add beef; cook over medium heat until hot, 5 to 8 minutes. Season to taste with salt and pepper.

2. Dip tortillas in Tomatillo Sauce to coat lightly and fill each with about ⅓ cup beef mixture; roll up and place, seam sides down, in large baking pan. Spoon remaining Tomatillo Sauce over enchiladas; sprinkle with cheese. Bake, uncovered, at 350 degrees until hot 15 to 20 minutes. Sprinkle with cilantro.

MEATBALLS IN TOMATO CHILI SAUCE

The meatballs can be made in advance and frozen; thaw before using.
Pasilla chilies are picante—use 2 only if you enjoy a truly hot sauce!

4 servings

1–2 pasilla chilies
1 can (28 ounces) reduced-sodium diced
  tomatoes, undrained
Jalapeño Meatballs (recipe follows)
Salt and pepper, to taste

Per Serving:
Calories: 240
% of calories from fat: 24
Fat (gm): 6.5
Saturated fat (gm): 2.3
Cholesterol (mg): 60.9
Sodium (mg): 435
Protein (gm): 29.3
Carbohydrate (gm): 15.9

Exchanges:
Milk: 0.0
Vegetable: 3.0
Fruit: 0.0
Bread: 0.0
Meat: 3.0
Fat: 0.0

1. Cook pasilla chilies in large lightly greased saucepan over medium heat until softened; discard stems, seeds, and veins. Process chilies and tomatoes with liquid in blender until smooth; heat to boiling in large saucepan. Add Jalapeño Meatballs; reduce heat and simmer, covered, until meatballs are cooked, about 10 minutes. Season to taste with salt and pepper.

Jalapeño Meatballs
Makes 16

8 ounces each: ground pork tenderloin, lean beef
1 egg
¼ cup each: unseasoned dry bread crumbs, finely chopped onion
½ cup shredded zucchini
2 cloves garlic, minced
1 teaspoon minced jalapeño chili
½ teaspoon each: dried oregano and thyme leaves, salt

1. Mix all ingredients; shape into 16 meatballs.

SWEDISH MEATBALLS WITH NOODLES

he meatballs and gravy can be served as an appetizer to serve 8–12 people.

4 servings

1 pound very lean ground beef
½ cup each: finely chopped onion, unseasoned
   dry bread crumbs
⅓ cup fat-free milk
1 egg
1 teaspoon dried dill weed
½ teaspoon ground allspice
½ teaspoon salt
⅛ teaspoon pepper
Cream Gravy (see p. 131)
3 cups cooked noodles, warm
Chopped fresh dill weed or parsley, as garnish

Per Serving:
Calories: 497
% of calories from fat: 24
Fat (gm): 13
Saturated fat (gm): 3.6
Cholesterol (mg): 67.3
Sodium (mg): 814
Protein (gm): 37.9
Carbohydrate (gm): 56.6

Exchanges:
Milk: 0.5
Vegetable: 0.0
Fruit: 0.0
Bread: 3.5
Meat: 3.5
Fat: 0.0

1. Combine ground beef, onion, bread crumbs, milk, egg, and seasonings; shape into 24 meatballs. Bake in baking pan at 425 degrees until meatballs are cooked and browned, 15 to 20 minutes. Combine meatballs and Cream Gravy. Spoon over noodles, and sprinkle with dill weed.

JUST PLAIN MEAT LOAF

Moist, the way meatloaf should be, with plenty of leftovers for sandwiches, too! Serve with Real Mashed Potatoes (see p. 628).

6 servings

1½ pounds very lean ground beef
1 cup quick-cooking oats
½ cup fat-free milk
1 egg
¼ cup catsup or chili sauce
½ cup each: chopped onion, green bell pepper
1 teaspoon each: minced garlic, dried Italian seasoning
¾ teaspoon salt
½ teaspoon pepper

Per Serving:
Calories: 241
% of calories from fat: 21
Fat (gm): 5.5
Saturated fat (gm): 1.8
Cholesterol (mg): 64.3
Sodium (mg): 489
Protein (gm): 31.2
Carbohydrate (gm): 15.3

Exchanges:
Milk: 0.0
Vegetable: 0.0
Fruit: 0.0
Bread: 1.0
Meat: 3.0
Fat: 0.0

1. Mix all ingredients until blended. Pat mixture into ungreased loaf pan, 9 x 5 inches, or shape into a loaf in baking pan. Bake at 350 degrees until juices run clear and meat thermometer registers 170 degrees, about 1 hour. Let stand in pan 10 minutes; invert onto serving plate.

VARIATIONS

Stuffed Green Peppers — Cut 6 medium green bell peppers lengthwise into halves; discard seeds. Cook peppers in simmering water 3 minutes; drain. Make recipe above, substituting 1 cup cooked rice for the oats. Fill peppers with mixture and place in baking pan. Bake, covered, at 350 degrees until beef mixture is cooked, about 45 minutes.

Italian Meat Loaf — Make recipe above, adding ¼ cup (1 ounce) grated fat-free Parmesan cheese, ½ cup (2 ounces) shredded reduced-fat mozzarella cheese, and 2 tablespoons chopped pitted ripe olives. After baking, spread meat loaf with 2 tablespoons seasoned tomato sauce and sprinkle with 2 tablespoons each grated Parmesan and shredded reduced-fat mozzarella cheeses. Let stand, loosely covered, 10 minutes.

Savory Cheese Meat Loaf — Make recipe above, substituting ½ pound ground lean pork for ½ pound of the beef, and adding 4 ounces fat-free cream cheese, ½ cup (2 ounces) shredded reduced-fat Cheddar cheese, and 2 tablespoons Worcestershire sauce. Spread top of loaf with ¼ cup of catsup before baking. Sprinkle ¼ cup (1 ounce) shredded reduced-fat Cheddar cheese on top of meat loaf after baking. Let stand, loosely covered, 10 minutes.

Chutney-Peanut Meat Loaf — Make recipe above, substituting ½ cup chopped chutney for the catsup, and adding ⅓ cup chopped peanuts, 1 teaspoon curry powder, and ½ teaspoon ground ginger.

LEMON MEAT LOAF

45

Meat loaf takes on a new dimension with a lemon accent and a smooth Egg Lemon Sauce.

6 servings

1½ pounds very lean ground beef

1 cup fresh bread crumbs

1 egg

⅓ cup each: chopped onion, green bell pepper

1 clove garlic, minced

1 tablespoon each: lemon juice, grated lemon zest

1 teaspoon Dijon mustard

½ teaspoon each: dried savory leaves, pepper

¾ teaspoon salt

Egg Lemon Sauce (recipe follows)

Per Serving:
Calories: 228
% of calories from fat: 29
Fat (gm): 7.2
Saturated fat (gm): 2.2
Cholesterol (mg): 94.4
Sodium (mg): 463
Protein (gm): 29.4
Carbohydrate (gm): 10.2

Exchanges:
Milk: 0.0
Vegetable: 0.0
Fruit: 0.0
Bread: 1.0
Meat: 3.0
Fat: 0.0

1. Mix all ingredients except Egg Lemon Sauce; pat mixture into ungreased loaf pan, 9 x 5 inches, or shape into a loaf in baking pan. Bake at 350 degrees until juices run clear and meat thermometer registers 170 degrees, about 1 hour. Let stand in pan 5 minutes; invert onto serving plate. Serve with Egg Lemon Sauce.

Egg Lemon Sauce

Makes about 1¼ cups

1 tablespoon margarine or butter

2 tablespoons flour

½ cup each: reduced-sodium fat-free chicken broth, fat-free milk

1 egg, lightly beaten

3–4 tablespoons lemon juice

1 teaspoon grated lemon zest

Salt and white pepper, to taste

1. Melt margarine in medium saucepan; whisk in flour and cook 1 minute. Whisk in broth and milk; heat to boiling, whisking until thickened, about 1 minute. Whisk about ½ the broth mixture into the egg; whisk mixture back into saucepan. Whisk over medium heat 1 minute. Add lemon juice and zest; season to taste with salt and white pepper.

VARIATION

Sweet-Sour Ham Loaf — Make recipe as above, substituting ½ pound ground smoked ham for ½ pound of the ground beef, and omitting lemon juice and zest, savory, and Egg Lemon Sauce. Add 2 chopped sweet pickles, ⅓ cup each coarsely chopped almonds, mixed dried fruit, apricot preserves, 1 tablespoon cider vinegar, and 2 teaspoons soy sauce.

PORCUPINE PEPPERS

45

An old favorite—the rice pokes out of the meat, resembling porcupine quills!

4 servings

1 pound very lean ground beef

1 egg, lightly beaten

¼ cup uncooked rice

1 teaspoon Worcestershire sauce, minced garlic

4 large green bell peppers, halved lengthwise, seeded

1 can (14 ounces) diced tomatoes with chilies, undrained

Per Serving:
Calories: 283
% of calories from fat: 30
Fat (gm): 9.3
Saturated fat (gm): 3.5
Cholesterol (mg): 95.1
Sodium (mg): 469
Protein (gm): 29.2
Carbohydrate (gm): 19.9

Exchanges:
Milk: 0.0
Vegetable: 1.0
Fruit: 0.0
Bread: 1.0
Meat: 3.0
Fat: 0.0

1. Mix beef, egg, rice, Worcestershire sauce, and garlic. Spoon meat mixture into peppers and place in lightly greased baking dish; pour tomatoes with liquid over. Bake, covered, at 350 degrees until beef is cooked and peppers are tender, about 1 hour.

GYROS BURGERS

45 *These delicious burgers combine ground lamb and beef.*

4 servings

8 ounces each: lean ground beef, ground lamb
2 tablespoons chopped onion
2 cloves garlic, minced
½ teaspoon each: dried oregano leaves, dill weed
1 teaspoon salt
4 pita breads
Gyros Relish (recipe follows)

Per Serving:
Calories: 435
% of calories from fat: 29
Fat (gm): 13.9
Saturated fat (gm): 5
Cholesterol (mg): 87.8
Sodium (mg): 1011
Protein (gm): 34.6
Carbohydrate (gm): 41.2

Exchanges:
Milk: 0.0
Vegetable: 0.0
Fruit: 0.0
Bread: 3.0
Meat: 3.0
Fat: 1.0

1. Combine ground meats, onion, garlic, herbs, and salt; shape into 4 patties. Cook in large skillet over medium heat to desired degree of doneness, about 5 minutes on each side for medium. Serve in pitas with Gyros Relish.

Gyros Relish
Makes about 2 cups

½ cup each: sliced green onion, seeded, chopped cucumber and tomato
⅔ cup plain fat-free yogurt
1 teaspoon each: dried mint and oregano leaves

1. Mix all ingredients.

PORK TENDERLOIN WITH APRICOT STUFFING

An elegant dish that is very easy to prepare.

4 servings

1 pound pork tenderloin
1 can (8½ ounces) apricot halves, undrained, juice reserved
⅓ cup each: finely chopped celery and onion
2 cups seasoned croutons
⅔ cup chicken or vegetable broth

3 cups cooked rice, warm

1½ tablespoons cornstarch

¼–½ teaspoon ground cinnamon

Per Serving:
Calories: 422
% of calories from fat: 17
Fat (gm): 7.8
Saturated fat (gm): 2.4
Cholesterol (mg): 78.7
Sodium (mg): 374
Protein (gm): 30
Carbohydrate (gm): 55

Exchanges:
Milk: 0.0
Vegetable: 0.0
Fruit: 1.0
Bread: 2.5
Meat: 3.0
Fat: 0.0

1. Slice tenderloin lengthwise, cutting to, but not through, opposite side. Pound meat lightly with flat side of meat mallet to rectangle about 10 x 6 inches.

2. Cut apricots into ½-inch pieces and combine with celery, onion, and croutons in large bowl; pour broth over and toss. Spread mixture evenly over tenderloin; roll up jelly-roll style, starting from short side. Secure meat roll with kitchen string, tying at 1-inch intervals. Cut meat roll into six slices; arrange over rice in 12 x 8-inch baking dish. Bake at 325 degrees, covered, until pork is slightly pink, 45 to 60 minutes.

3. Add water to apricot juice to make 1 cup; whisk with cornstarch and cinnamon in small saucepan. Heat to boiling, whisking until thickened, about 1 minute. Drizzle over pork and rice during last 10 minutes of baking time.

PORK MEDALLIONS WITH SPINACH PASTA AND YOGURT SAUCE

45

Pork baked with apples and yogurt makes a light and amazingly easy dinner.

4 servings

1 pound pork tenderloin, sliced (½-inch)

8 ounces spinach fettuccine or linguine, cooked

2 medium apples, sliced (½-inch)

½ cup apple juice

1 small onion, finely chopped

¼ teaspoon salt

½ teaspoon dried sage leaves

2 tablespoons flour

1 cup plain low-fat yogurt

1 tablespoon chopped chives or parsley

Per Serving:
Calories: 425
% of calories from fat: 14
Fat (gm): 6.3
Saturated fat (gm): 2.5
Cholesterol (mg): 126.5
Sodium (mg): 235
Protein (gm): 35.9
Carbohydrate (gm): 54.7

Exchanges:
Milk: 0.0
Vegetable: 0.0
Fruit: 1.0
Bread: 2.5
Meat: 3.0
Fat: 0.0

1. Arrange pork slices over pasta in greased baking dish, overlapping slices if necessary; arrange apples on top. Heat apple juice, onion, salt, and sage to boiling in small skillet; reduce heat and simmer, covered, until onion is tender, about 5 minutes. Whisk in combined flour and yogurt, whisking until thickened, about 1 minute. Spoon sauce over pork and apples; sprinkle with chives and bake at 325 degrees, covered, until pork is slightly pink, 45 to 60 minutes.

PORK TENDERLOIN WITH GREEN PEANUT SAUCE

Although the Mexican version of Green Peanut Sauce uses a much larger quantity of peanuts, this lower-fat version is very flavorful with a pleasing crunchy texture.

6 servings

1½ pounds pork tenderloin, sliced (¼-inch)
Salt and pepper, to taste
1 cup Tomatillo Sauce (½ recipe) (see p. 184)
⅓ cup chopped dry-roasted peanuts
4 cups cooked rice, warm

1. Sauté pork in lightly greased large skillet until cooked, 3 to 4 minutes on each side. Sprinkle lightly with salt and pepper. Add Tomatillo Sauce and peanuts to skillet; heat until hot. Serve over rice.

Per Serving:
Calories: 347
% of calories from fat: 23
Fat (gm): 8.9
Saturated fat (gm): 2
Cholesterol (mg): 65.4
Sodium (mg): 115
Protein (gm): 28.9
Carbohydrate (gm): 36.6

Exchanges:
Milk: 0.0
Vegetable: 1.0
Fruit: 0.0
Bread: 2.0
Meat: 3.0
Fat: 0.0

PORK WITH PEPPERS AND ONIONS

45   *This dish can also be made with boneless loin of pork instead of tenderloin.*

4 servings

1 pound pork tenderloin, cut into strips (1½ x ½-inch)
1 tablespoon olive oil
1 can (15 ounces) reduced-sodium tomato sauce
1 package (16 ounces) frozen pepper and onion blend

2 tablespoons dry sherry (optional)

1 teaspoon each: minced garlic, dried basil and
thyme leaves

Salt and pepper, to taste

8 ounces tricolor rotini, cooked, warm

Per Serving:
Calories: 464
% of calories from fat: 17
Fat (gm): 8.4
Saturated fat (gm): 2
Cholesterol (mg): 65.7
Sodium (mg): 99
Protein (gm): 33.9
Carbohydrate (gm): 58.6

Exchanges:
Milk: 0.0
Vegetable: 3.0
Fruit: 0.0
Bread: 3.0
Meat: 3.0
Fat: 0.0

1. Sauté pork in oil in large skillet until browned, about 5 minutes; add tomato sauce, pepper and onion blend, sherry, garlic, and herbs. Heat to boiling; reduce heat and simmer, covered, until pork is tender, about 10 minutes. Simmer, uncovered, until thickened, 2 to 3 minutes. Season to taste with salt and pepper. Serve over pasta.

45-MINUTE PREPARATION TIP: Begin cooking the rotini before preparing rest of the recipe.

FETTUCCINE WITH PORK, GREENS, AND CARAMELIZED ONIONS

Cooked chicken breast or shrimp can be used as delicious alternatives to the pork in this recipe.

4 servings

4 medium onions, sliced

1 tablespoon olive oil

1 teaspoon sugar

2 cans (14½ ounces each) reduced-sodium fat-free
chicken broth

4 cups thinly sliced greens (kale, Swiss chard, curly
endive or spinach)

¼ teaspoon each: salt, pepper

8 ounces fettuccine, cooked, warm

1 pound pork tenderloin, sliced (scant ½-inch)

Per Serving:
Calories: 408
% of calories from fat: 19
Fat (gm): 8.6
Saturated fat (gm): 2.4
Cholesterol (mg): 109.8
Sodium (mg): 702
Protein (gm): 35.7
Carbohydrate (gm): 47.2

Exchanges:
Milk: 0.0
Vegetable: 1.0
Fruit: 0.0
Bread: 3.0
Meat: 3.0
Fat: 0.0

1. Sauté onions in oil in large skillet 5 minutes; reduce heat to low and stir in sugar. Cook over medium-low heat until onions are golden and very soft, about 20 minutes. Stir in chicken broth and heat to boiling; reduce heat and simmer, uncovered, until broth is reduced by ⅓, about 10 minutes. Add greens; simmer, covered, until wilted, about 5minutes. Simmer, uncovered, until broth is almost evaporated, about 5 minutes. Stir in salt and pepper. Toss with pasta.

2. Sauté pork slices in lightly greased large skillet until cooked and browned, about 5 minutes. Serve with pasta.

CHOP SUEY

Chop Suey can also be served over crisp chow mein noodles or Chinese egg noodles.

4 servings

1 pound pork tenderloin, fat trimmed, cubed (1-inch)

1 tablespoon vegetable oil

2 cups thinly sliced Chinese cabbage

1 cup each: sliced mushrooms, chopped onion, chopped red or green bell pepper

2 cloves garlic, minced

½ cup reduced-sodium chicken broth

2 tablespoons cornstarch

½–1 tablespoon bead molasses

1½ cups fresh or canned bean sprouts, rinsed

1 can (4 ounces) each: rinsed, drained bamboo shoots and water chestnuts

Reduced-sodium soy sauce, to taste

Salt and pepper, to taste

3 cups cooked rice, warm

Per Serving:
Calories: 428
% of calories from fat: 18
Fat (gm): 8.4
Saturated fat (gm): 2
Cholesterol (mg): 65.4
Sodium (mg): 467
Protein (gm): 31.8
Carbohydrate (gm): 56.8

Exchanges:
Milk: 0.0
Vegetable: 3.0
Fruit: 0.0
Bread: 2.5
Meat: 3.0
Fat: 0.0

1. Stir-fry pork in oil in wok or large skillet until browned, about 5 minutes. Add cabbage, mushrooms, onion, bell pepper, and garlic; stir-fry until crisp-tender, 3 to 5 minutes. Stir combined broth, cornstarch, and molasses into wok and heat to boiling, stirring until thickened, about 1 minute. Stir in bean sprouts, bamboo shoots, and water chestnuts; cook until hot, 1 to 2 minutes. Season to taste with soy sauce, salt, and pepper. Serve over rice.

MOO SHU PORK

Mandarin Pancakes are delicious and can be made in advance. If you are short on time, flour tortillas can be substituted.

6 servings (2 each)

1½ ounces dried Chinese mushrooms

2–3 tablespoons reduced-sodium tamari soy sauce

2 teaspoons each: Asian sesame oil, minced
   gingerroot, sugar

1 pound pork tenderloin, cut into strips (1½ x ½-inch)

2 eggs, lightly beaten

½ cup julienned bamboo shoots

2 sliced green onions

½ cup water

2 teaspoons cornstarch

Mandarin Pancakes (recipe follows)

½–¾ cup Oriental plum sauce

12 medium green onions

Per Serving:
Calories: 278
% of calories from fat: 20
Fat (gm): 6.2
Saturated fat (gm): 1.7
Cholesterol (mg): 114.5
Sodium (mg): 266
Protein (gm): 21.7
Carbohydrate (gm): 33

Exchanges:
Milk: 0.0
Vegetable: 4.0
Fruit: 0.0
Bread: 1.0
Meat: 2.0
Fat: 0.0

1. Cover mushrooms with boiling water in bowl; let stand until softened, about 15 minutes; drain. Slice mushrooms, discarding tough centers.

2. Pour combined soy sauce, Asian sesame oil, gingerroot, and sugar over pork in bowl. Let stand 30 minutes, stirring occasionally. Scramble eggs in lightly greased wok or large skillet, breaking into small pieces with a fork; remove from wok and reserve.

3. Add pork mixture, mushrooms, bamboo shoots and sliced green onions to wok; cook over medium heat until pork is browned, 3 to 4 minutes. Stir in combined water and cornstarch; heat to boiling, stirring until thickened, about 1 minute. Stir in reserved egg.

4. Spread 1 Mandarin Pancake with 2 to 3 teaspoons plum sauce; spoon about ⅓ cup pork mixture onto pancake. Top with a green onion and roll up. Repeat with remaining ingredients.

Mandarin Pancakes
Makes 12 pancakes

⅓ cup boiling water
1 cup all-purpose flour
Vegetable cooking spray

1. Stir water into flour in small bowl until crumbly; shape into a ball. Knead on lightly floured surface until smooth and satiny, about 10 minutes. Let stand, covered, 30 minutes. Divide dough into 12 equal pieces; shape into 12 balls.

2. Roll 2 balls into 3-inch circles with lightly floured rolling pin; spray 1 circle lightly with cooking spray and cover with remaining circle. Roll both circles together into a 6-inch circle being careful not to wrinkle dough. Cook dough circle in lightly greased skillet over medium to medium-high heat until it blisters and is the color of parchment paper, turning frequently with chop sticks or tongs. Remove from skillet; separate into 2 pancakes with pointed knife. Repeat process with remaining dough, making only 1 or 2 dough circles at a time.

NOTES: As pancakes are cooked and separated, they can be covered and kept warm in a 200 degree oven. Pancakes can be cooled, stacked with plastic wrap, and frozen in a freezer bag or aluminum foil for up to 2 months.

CHORIZO

45
Serve Chorizo as patties, or cook and crumble to serve in quesadillas, enchiladas, and other dishes.

4 servings

¼ teaspoon crushed coriander and cumin seeds
1 dried ancho chili
12 ounces pork tenderloin, finely chopped or ground
1 tablespoon each: paprika, minced garlic, cider vinegar, water
½ teaspoon each: dried oregano leaves, salt

1. Cook herb seeds in lightly greased small skillet, stirring frequently, until toasted. Remove from skillet. Add ancho chili to skillet; cook over medium heat until softened, about 1 minute on each side, turning so chili does not burn. Remove and discard stem, veins, and seeds. Chop chili finely.

2. Combine pork and all ingredients in small bowl, mixing well. Refrigerate, covered, at least 4 hours or overnight for flavors to blend. Shape mixture into 4 patties; cook in small lightly greased skillet over medium heat until cooked, 4 to 5 minutes on each side.

Per Serving:
Calories: 112
% of calories from fat: 27
Fat (gm): 3.3
Saturated fat (gm): 1.1
Cholesterol (mg): 49.1
Sodium (mg): 308
Protein (gm): 17.9
Carbohydrate (gm): 2.1

Exchanges:
Milk: 0.0
Vegetable: 0.0
Fruit: 0.0
Bread: 0.0
Meat: 2.0
Fat: 0.0

TACOS PICADILLO

Picadillo, a favorite Mexican pork dish, is seasoned with raisins, almonds, sweet spices, and jalapeño chili.

12 servings (1 each)

1½ pounds pork tenderloin, cubed (1-inch)
½ cup chopped onion
2 teaspoons each: minced garlic, jalapeño chili
1 cup chopped tomato
½ cup each: dark raisins, toasted slivered almonds
1–2 teaspoons cider vinegar
2 teaspoons ground cinnamon
½ teaspoon each: dried oregano leaves, ground allspice
Salt and pepper, to taste
12 flour or corn tortillas (6-inch)
Tomato Poblano Salsa (recipe follows)

Per Serving:
Calories: 176
% of calories from fat: 23
Fat (gm): 4.5
Saturated fat (gm): 1.0
Cholesterol (mg): 327
Sodium (mg): 151
Protein (gm): 14.6
Carbohydrate (gm): 18.9

Exchanges:
Milk: 0.0
Vegetable: 1.0
Fruit: 0.0
Bread: 1.0
Meat: 1.5
Fat: 0.0

1. Cover pork with water in medium saucepan; heat to boiling. Reduce heat and simmer, covered, until pork is tender, about 10 minutes. Drain; shred into small pieces.

2. Sauté onion, garlic, and jalapeño chili in oil in medium skillet until tender, about 5 minutes. Add pork and remaining ingredients, except salt, pepper, tortillas, and Tomato Poblano Salsa. Cook over medium heat until mixture is hot, about 5 minutes; season to taste with salt and pepper. Spoon about ⅓ cup mixture on each tortilla and roll up. Serve with Tomato Poblano Salsa.

Tomato Poblano Salsa
Makes about 1 cup

¾ cup chopped tomato
¼ cup each: chopped poblano chili, cilantro
2 tablespoons finely chopped onion
1 teaspoon finely chopped jalapeño chili
1 clove garlic, minced
Salt, to taste

1. Mix all ingredients, except salt; season to taste with salt.

VEAL PROVENÇAL

Veal chops are enhanced with a sauce flavored with mushrooms, herbs, and black olives.

4 servings

4 lean veal chops (about 4 ounces each), fat trimmed
1–3 teaspoons margarine or butter
2 medium onions, chopped
8 ounces mushrooms, sliced
1 tablespoon each: flour, tomato paste
¾ cup reduced-sodium fat-free chicken broth
½ cup dry white wine or reduced-sodium fat-free chicken broth
1 teaspoon herbes de Provence or dried Italian seasoning
1 small bay leaf
¼–½ cup sliced black olives
Salt and pepper, to taste

Per Serving:
Calories: 302
% of calories from fat: 30
Fat (gm): 10.2
Saturated fat (gm): 2.2
Cholesterol (mg): 100.1
Sodium (mg): 439
Protein (gm): 32
Carbohydrate (gm): 14.5

Exchanges:
Milk: 0.0
Vegetable: 3.0
Fruit: 0.0
Bread: 0.0
Meat: 3.0
Fat: 1.0

1. Cook veal chops in margarine in large ovenproof skillet over medium heat until browned, 3 to 4 minutes on each side; remove from skillet. Add onions and mushrooms to skillet and sauté until tender, 8 to 10 minutes; sprinkle with flour and cook l minute. Add remaining ingredients, except salt and pepper and heat to boiling. Return veal chops to skillet; transfer to oven, and bake, covered, at 325 degrees until veal is tender, about 45 minutes. Season to taste with salt and pepper.

FOUR

Poultry

GLAZED CORNISH HENS WITH WILD RICE

45

Cornish hens are marmalade-glazed and served with fruited wild rice for company fare.

4 servings

2 Rock Cornish game hens (1 to 1¼ pounds each)

Vegetable cooking spray

Paprika

½ cup no-sugar-added orange marmalade, warm

¼ cup each: sliced green onions, celery

1 package (6.25 ounces) quick-cooking long-grain white and wild rice, (spice packet discarded)

1 can (14½ ounces) reduced-sodium chicken broth

1 can (11 ounces) unsweetened Mandarin orange segments, drained

2 tablespoons each: raisins, finely chopped mint or parsley, toasted pecan halves

Salt and pepper, to taste

Per Serving:
Calories: 473
% of calories from fat: 21
Fat (gm): 11.1
Saturated fat (gm): 0.8
Cholesterol (mg): 40.1
Sodium (mg): 217
Protein (gm): 31.4
Carbohydrate (gm): 63.5

Exchanges:
Milk: 0.0
Vegetable: 0.0
Fruit: 0.5
Bread: 3.5
Meat: 3.0
Fat: 0.5

1. Cut Cornish hens into halves with poultry shears and place, cut sides down, on rack in roasting pan. Spray with cooking spray and sprinkle with paprika. Roast at 350 degrees until drumstick meat feels soft when pressed and juices run clear, 1 to 1¼ hours; baste with marmalade during last 30 minutes of roasting time.

2. Sauté green onions and celery in lightly greased medium saucepan until tender, about 5 minutes. Add remaining ingredients, except salt and pepper, and simmer, covered, until rice is tender, about 5 minutes. Season to taste with salt and pepper. Serve with Cornish hens.

ROAST CHICKEN WITH CORN BREAD DRESSING

45

We've baked the dressing in a casserole; if baked in the chicken, it would absorb unwanted fat from the chicken juices.

6 servings

1 roasting chicken (about 3 pounds)
Vegetable cooking spray
1 teaspoon dried rosemary leaves
Corn Bread Dressing (recipe follows)

Per Serving:
Calories: 258
% of calories from fat: 22
Fat (gm): 6.1
Saturated fat (gm): 1.6
Cholesterol (mg): 57.9
Sodium (mg): 548
Protein (gm): 24.4
Carbohydrate (gm): 25.3

Exchanges:
Milk: 0.0
Vegetable: 0.5
Fruit: 0.0
Bread: 1.5
Meat: 2.5
Fat: 0.0

1. Spray chicken with cooking spray; sprinkle with rosemary. Roast chicken on rack in roasting pan at 375 degrees until meat thermometer inserted in thickest part of thigh registers 170 degrees (chicken leg will move freely and juices will run clear), about 1½ hours. Let chicken stand 10 minutes before carving. Serve with Corn Bread Dressing.

Corn Bread Dressing

Makes about 3 cups

¾ cup each: chopped onion, sliced celery
¼ cup coarsely chopped pecans
½ teaspoon each: dried sage, rosemary, and thyme leaves
Salt and pepper, to taste
3 cups corn bread stuffing mix
1½ cups reduced-sodium chicken broth
1 egg, lightly beaten

1. Sauté onion, celery, pecans, and herbs in lightly greased large skillet until vegetables are tender, about 5 minutes; season to taste with salt and pepper. Combine with stuffing mix in large bowl; add chicken broth and egg and toss. Spoon into greased 2-quart casserole. Bake, covered, at 375 degrees until hot, about 45 minutes.

VARIATION

Pork Chops with Bread Stuffing — Make stuffing as above, substituting white or whole wheat stuffing mix for the corn bread mix. Trim fat from 6 loin pork chops (about 5 ounces each); cook in lightly greased skillet until well browned, about 5 minutes on each side. Arrange pork chops on top of stuffing in casserole; bake, covered, at 350 degrees until pork chops are tender, 30 to 40 minutes.

45-MINUTE PREPARATION TIP: Place Corn Bread Dressing in oven with chicken during last 45 minutes of roasting time.

TANDOORI CHICKEN WITH ORANGE CILANTRO RICE

Chicken pieces are marinated in a seasoned yogurt mixture, then grilled or roasted.

4 servings

1 pound chicken pieces
Tandoori Marinade (recipe follows)
2½ cups Orange Cilantro Rice (⅔ recipe) (see p. 352)

Per Serving:
Calories: 272
% of calories from fat: 12
Fat (gm): 3.6
Saturated fat (gm): 0.9
Cholesterol (mg): 69.3
Sodium (mg): 80
Protein (gm): 29.3
Carbohydrate (gm): 28.7

Exchanges:
Milk: 0.0
Vegetable: 2.0
Fruit: 0.0
Bread: 1.0
Meat: 3.0
Fat: 0.0

1. Spread chicken with Tandoori Marinade; place in shallow glass baking dish and refrigerate 3 to 4 hours, or overnight.

2. Grill chicken over medium hot coals, covered, until browned and cooked, 10 to 15 minutes on each side. Or, roast in greased, aluminum foil-lined baking pan, covered, at 350 degrees until juices run clear, 25 to 35 minutes. Serve with Orange Cilantro Rice.

Tandoori Marinade
Makes about ½ cup

⅓ cup plain fat-free yogurt

1 small jalapeño chili, minced

2 teaspoons each: finely chopped cilantro, garlic,
   gingerroot, lime zest, paprika

1 teaspoon each: ground cumin and coriander

1. Combine all ingredients.

CHICKEN BREASTS WITH ROSEMARY

45 *Easy, yet elegant, this healthful entrée is good served with a risotto (see
Index) and a simple vegetable or salad.*

4 servings

1 tablespoon olive oil

1½ teaspoons balsamic vinegar

1 teaspoon minced garlic

1 tablespoon finely grated lemon zest

¼ teaspoon each: salt, pepper

4 boneless, skinless chicken breast halves
   (4 ounces each)

½–¾ cup dry white wine or reduced-sodium
   chicken broth

½ cup chopped tomato

1 teaspoon finely chopped fresh or ½ teaspoon
   dried rosemary leaves

Per Serving:
Calories: 188
% of calories from fat: 31
Fat (gm): 6.4
Saturated fat (gm): 1.3
Cholesterol (mg): 69
Sodium (mg): 209
Protein (gm): 25.6
Carbohydrate (gm): 2.6

Exchanges:
Milk: 0.0
Vegetable: 0.5
Fruit: 0.0
Bread: 0.0
Meat: 3.0
Fat: 0.0

1. Brush combined olive oil, vinegar, garlic, lemon zest, salt, and
pepper over chicken; let stand 10 minutes. Cook chicken in lightly
greased large skillet over medium heat until browned, about 5
minutes on each side. Add wine, tomato, and rosemary to skillet
and heat to boiling; reduce heat and simmer, covered, until chicken
is cooked, about 15 minutes.

CAJUN CHICKEN

Cajun seasoning can be purchased, but we particularly like our homemade blend—try it with beef and pork too!

4 servings

4 boneless, skinless chicken breast halves
   (4 ounces each)
Butter-flavored vegetable cooking spray
Cajun Seasoning (recipe follows)

Per Serving:
Calories: 144
% of calories from fat: 20
Fat (gm): 3.1
Saturated fat (gm): 0.9
Cholesterol (mg): 69
Sodium (mg): 206
Protein (gm): 25.7
Carbohydrate (gm): 2

Exchanges:
Milk: 0.0
Vegetable: 0.0
Fruit: 0.0
Bread: 0.0
Meat: 3.0
Fat: 0.0

1. Spray both sides of chicken pieces with cooking spray; sprinkle with Cajun Seasoning. Grill chicken over medium-hot coals, or broil 6 inches from heat source, until chicken is cooked and juices run clear, about 5 to 8 minutes on each side.

Cajun Seasoning

Makes about 2 tablespoons

2 teaspoons paprika
1 teaspoon each: onion and garlic powder
½ teaspoon each: dried thyme and oregano leaves,
   cayenne and black pepper
¼ teaspoon salt

1. Mix all ingredients; store in airtight container.

CHICKEN AND RICE ROLL-UPS

45

Colorful rice fills these moist baked chicken rolls.

4 servings

4 boneless, skinless chicken breast halves (4 ounces each)
3 cups cooked rice
1 cup each: whole kernel corn, finely chopped green bell peppers
¼ cup diced pimientos
½ cup (2 ounces) shredded Monterey Jack cheese
Paprika, salt and pepper, to taste

1. Pound chicken breasts with flat side of meat mallet to about ¼ inch thickness. Combine rice, corn, bell peppers, pimientos, and cheese in medium bowl. Spoon about ⅓ cup rice mixture on each breast; roll up and secure with toothpicks. Spoon remaining rice mixture in greased 11 x 7-inch baking dish; place chicken, seam sides down, on rice. Sprinkle lightly with paprika, salt, and pepper. Bake, covered, at 325 degrees 30 minutes; uncover and bake until cooked, 15 to 20 minutes.

Per Serving:
Calories: 391
% of calories from fat: 18
Fat (gm): 7.8
Saturated fat (gm): 3.7
Cholesterol (mg): 81.6
Sodium (mg): 142
Protein (gm): 33.6
Carbohydrate (gm): 45.6

Exchanges:
Milk: 0.0
Vegetable: 0.0
Fruit: 0.0
Bread: 3.0
Meat: 3.0
Fat: 0.0

CHICKEN OSCAR

45

Easy to make company-fare that will win raves!

6 servings

2 cups seasoned stuffing mix
½ cup reduced-sodium fat-free chicken broth
6 boneless, skinless chicken breast halves
  (4 ounces each)
24 asparagus spears, cooked crisp-tender
6 slices (½ ounce each) provolone cheese

1. Combine stuffing mix and broth; spoon stuffing into 6 mounds in greased baking pan. Top with chicken breasts. Bake, covered, at 350 degrees until chicken is cooked about 30 minutes. Uncover and top with asparagus and cheese slices; bake, uncovered, until cheese is melted, about 5 minutes.

Per Serving:
Calories: 238
% of calories from fat: 29
Fat (gm): 7.3
Saturated fat (gm): 2.8
Cholesterol (mg): 75.5
Sodium (mg): 352
Protein (gm): 32.9
Carbohydrate (gm): 8.6

Exchanges:
Milk: 0.0
Vegetable: 0.0
Fruit: 0.0
Bread: 0.5
Meat: 4.0
Fat: 0.0

CHICKEN AND PASTA VALENCIA

45

The orange-scented sauce, subtly seasoned with herbs and wine, benefits from day-ahead preparation, giving flavors an opportunity to meld.

6 servings

6 small boneless, skinless chicken breast halves
   (3 ounces each)
Flour
1 tablespoon olive oil
1 small onion, chopped
3 cloves garlic, minced
1 can (14½ ounces) reduced-sodium chicken broth
½ cup dry white wine or reduced-sodium
   chicken broth
3 tablespoons each: tomato paste, grated orange zest
1 teaspoon each: dried tarragon and thyme leaves
2 cups sliced mushrooms
¼ teaspoon each: salt, pepper
12 ounces pappardelle or fettucine, cooked, warm

Per Serving:
Calories: 343
% of calories from fat: 16
Fat (gm): 6.1
Saturated fat (gm): 1.1
Cholesterol (mg): 43.5
Sodium (mg): 133
Protein (gm): 25.4
Carbohydrate (gm): 42.7

Exchanges:
Milk: 0.0
Vegetable: 1.0
Fruit: 0.0
Bread: 2.5
Meat: 2.5
Fat: 0.0

1. Coat chicken breasts lightly with flour. Sauté in oil in Dutch oven until browned, about 4 minutes each side. Remove chicken. Add onion and garlic to pan; sauté until tender, 3 to 4 minutes. Add chicken broth, wine, tomato paste, orange zest, and herbs to pan; heat to boiling. Transfer to oven and bake at 350 degrees until chicken is tender, 45 to 60 minutes, adding mushrooms during last 15 to 20 minutes. Season to taste with salt and pepper. Serve over pasta.

SPAGHETTI SQUASH STUFFED WITH CHICKEN AND VEGETABLES

45

Jerusalem artichokes, or sun chokes, add extra crunch to the sautéed vegetables.

4 servings

2 medium spaghetti squash (about 2 pounds each), halved lengthwise, seeded

12 ounces boneless, skinless chicken breast, cubed

8 ounces cubed peeled Jerusalem artichokes

1½ cups quartered mushrooms

½ cup each: sliced celery, carrot, chopped onion

2 cloves garlic, minced

2 teaspoons flour

2 medium tomatoes, coarsely chopped

½ cup reduced-sodium fat-free chicken broth

1 teaspoon dried marjoram leaves

Salt and pepper, to taste

2 green onions, thinly sliced

Per Serving:
Calories: 243
% of calories from fat: 12
Fat (gm): 3.3
Saturated fat (gm): 0.8
Cholesterol (mg): 51.7
Sodium (mg): 104
Protein (gm): 24.8
Carbohydrate (gm): 30.8

Exchanges:
Milk: 0.0
Vegetable: 6.0
Fruit: 0.0
Bread: 0.0
Meat: 2.0
Fat: 0.0

1. Place squash halves, cut sides down, in large baking pan; add ½ inch water. Bake, covered, at 350 degrees until squash is tender, 30 to 40 minutes. Scrape pulp into large bowl, separating strands with fork; reserve shells.

2. Sauté chicken, Jerusalem artichokes, mushrooms, celery, carrot, onion, and garlic in lightly greased large skillet until chicken is light brown, about 8 minutes. Stir in flour and cook 1 minute. Add tomatoes, broth, and marjoram; heat to boiling. Cook, covered, until vegetables are tender, about 10 minutes. Season to taste with salt and pepper. Toss mixture with squash; spoon into reserved squash shells. Sprinkle with green onions.

CHICKEN WITH ONIONS AND PEPPERS

45 *Serve this Italian-inspired dish over rice or your favorite pasta.*

4 servings

1 pound boneless, skinless chicken breast, cubed
½ teaspoon minced garlic
1 tablespoon olive oil
1 cup each: sliced red bell pepper, onion
1 can (15 ounces) chunky Italian-seasoned tomato sauce
Salt and pepper, to taste
2 tablespoons grated Parmesan cheese

1. Sauté chicken and garlic in oil in large skillet until lightly browned, about 8 minutes. Move chicken to side of pan; add bell pepper and onion and cook until tender, 3 to 4 minutes. Stir in tomato sauce; heat to boiling. Reduce heat and simmer, covered, until chicken is cooked, about 10 minutes. Season to taste with salt and pepper; sprinkle with Parmesan cheese.

Per Serving:
Calories: 215
% of calories from fat: 29
Fat (gm): 7
Saturated fat (gm): 1.8
Cholesterol (mg): 71
Sodium (mg): 674
Protein (gm): 28.5
Carbohydrate (gm): 9.7

Exchanges:
Milk: 0.0
Vegetable: 2.0
Fruit: 0.0
Bread: 0.0
Meat: 3.0
Fat: 0.0

CHICKEN À LA KING IN TOAST CUPS

Great served over baked potatoes too!

4 servings

1½ cups sliced mushrooms
½ cup chopped green bell pepper
2½ tablespoons margarine or butter
⅓ cup all-purpose flour
1¼ cups each: reduced-sodium chicken broth, fat-free milk
2 tablespoons dry sherry (optional)
2 cups cubed cooked chicken breast
½ cup frozen peas, thawed
1 jar (2 ounces) chopped pimiento, drained
Salt and pepper, to taste
Toast Cups (recipe follows)

Per Serving:
Calories: 386
% of calories from fat: 24
Fat (gm): 11.7
Saturated fat (gm): 2.3
Cholesterol (mg): 55.7
Sodium (mg): 578
Protein (gm): 32.1
Carbohydrate (gm): 39.1

Exchanges:
Milk: 0.0
Vegetable: 1.0
Fruit: 0.0
Bread: 2.5
Meat: 3.0
Fat: 0.5

1. Sauté mushrooms and bell pepper in margarine in large saucepan until tender, 5 to 8 minutes. Stir in flour and cook 1 minute; stir in broth, milk, and sherry and heat to boiling, stirring until thickened, about 1 minute. Stir in chicken, peas, and pimiento; cook until hot, 3 to 4 minutes. Season to taste with salt and pepper; spoon into Toast Cups.

Toast Cups

Makes 8 (2 per serving)

Vegetable cooking spray
8 slices whole wheat or white bread, crusts trimmed

1. Spray 1 side of bread slices with cooking spray. Press bread slices in greased muffin cups with 4 corners sticking up. Bake, uncovered, at 350 degrees until browned, 10 to 15 minutes.

VARIATION

Ham and Eggs à la King — Make recipe as above, substituting smoked ham for the chicken and adding 2 chopped hard-cooked eggs. Serve over biscuits or squares of corn bread.

CHICKEN AND VEGETABLE CREPES

Enjoy Mock Hollandaise Sauce also with Eggs Benedict and Artichokes with Mock Hollandaise (see pp. 264, 416).

4 servings (2 each)

1 pound boneless, skinless chicken breast, cubed
1½ cups thinly sliced cabbage
½ cup each: thinly sliced celery, green pepper, mushrooms, green onions
2 tablespoons water
2–3 teaspoons each: sugar, lemon juice
Salt and pepper, to taste
Crepes (recipe follows), warm
Mock Hollandaise Sauce (recipe follows)

Per Serving:
Calories: 348
% of calories from fat: 21
Fat (gm): 8
Saturated fat (gm): 2.3
Cholesterol (mg): 126.2
Sodium (mg): 581
Protein (gm): 40
Carbohydrate (gm): 26.8

Exchanges:
Milk: 0.0
Vegetable: 2.0
Fruit: 0.0
Bread: 1.0
Meat: 4.0
Fat: 0.0

1. Cook chicken in lightly greased large skillet until browned, 5 to 8 minutes; add vegetables and water. Cook, covered, over medium heat until cabbage and mushrooms are wilted, about 5 minutes. Cook, uncovered, until vegetables are tender, about 5 minutes longer.

Season to taste with sugar, lemon juice, salt, and pepper. Spoon mixture along centers of crepes; roll up and arrange, seam sides down, on serving plates. Serve with Mock Hollandaise Sauce.

Mock Hollandaise Sauce
Makes about 1½ cups

6 ounces fat-free cream cheese
⅓ cup fat-free sour cream
3–4 tablespoons fat-free milk
1–2 teaspoons lemon juice
½–1 teaspoon Dijon mustard
⅛ teaspoon ground turmeric

1. Heat all ingredients in small saucepan over low heat, stirring until melted and smooth.

Crepes
Makes 4

½ cup each: all-purpose flour, fat-free milk
2 eggs
1 tablespoon melted margarine or canola oil
¼ teaspoon salt

1. Beat all ingredients in small bowl until smooth (batter will be thin). Pour scant ¼ cup batter into lightly greased 8-inch crepe pan or small skillet, tilting pan to coat bottom evenly with batter. Cook over medium heat until browned on the bottom, 2 to 3 minutes. Turn crepe and cook until browned on either side, 2 to 3 minutes. Repeat with remaining batter.

CHICKEN AND CABBAGE STRUDEL

If fresh fennel is not available, substitute sliced celery and add ½ teaspoon crushed fennel seeds with the anise and caraway seeds.

6 servings

1 pound boneless, skinless chicken breast, cubed
½ cup each: chopped onion, thinly sliced leek (white part only), and thinly sliced fennel
3 cloves garlic, minced

3 cups thinly sliced cabbage

1 cup sliced mushrooms, reduced-sodium chicken broth

½ cup dry white wine or reduced-sodium chicken broth

1 teaspoon anise seeds, crushed

½ teaspoon caraway seeds, crushed

¾ cup cooked brown rice

¼ cup raisins

Salt and pepper, to taste

6 sheets frozen fillo pastry, thawed

Anise or caraway seeds, as garnish

Fresh Tomato and Herb Sauce (recipe follows)

Per Serving:
Calories: 318
% of calories from fat: 12
Fat (gm): 4.3
Saturated fat (gm): 0.9
Cholesterol (mg): 46
Sodium (mg): 432
Protein (gm): 23.6
Carbohydrate (gm): 41.9

Exchanges:
Milk: 0.0
Vegetable: 4.0
Fruit: 0.0
Bread: 1.5
Meat: 2.0
Fat: 0.0

1. Cook chicken in lightly greased large skillet until browned, about 5 minutes; add onion, leek, fennel, and garlic and sauté 3 to 5 minutes. Add cabbage, mushrooms, broth, wine, and anise and caraway seeds; cook, covered, until cabbage wilts, 5 to 10 minutes. Cook, uncovered, over medium heat until cabbage begins to brown, about 10 minutes. Stir in rice and raisins; season to taste with salt and pepper. Cool.

2. Lay 1 sheet fillo on clean surface; cover remaining fillo with damp towel to keep from drying. Spray fillo with cooking spray; top with 2 more sheets fillo, spraying each with cooking spray. Spoon ½ the cabbage mixture across dough, 2 inches from short edge; roll up and place, seam-side down, on greased cookie sheet. Flatten roll slightly; spray with cooking spray and sprinkle with anise seeds. Repeat with remaining fillo and cabbage mixture.

3. Bake at 375 degrees until strudels are golden, 35 to 45 minutes. Cool 5 to 10 minutes before cutting. Trim ends of strudels, cutting diagonally. Cut strudels diagonally into serving pieces. Serve with Fresh Tomato and Herb Sauce.

Fresh Tomato and Herb Sauce
Makes about 4 cups

5 cups chopped tomatoes
½ cup each: chopped onion, dry red wine or water
2 tablespoons each: tomato paste, minced garlic, finely
    chopped fresh or 1½ teaspoons dried thyme leaves
1 tablespoon sugar
2 bay leaves
⅛ teaspoon each: crushed red pepper, ground black pepper
½ teaspoon salt
3–4 tablespoons finely chopped fresh or 2 teaspoons dried basil leaves

1. Combine all ingredients, except basil, in large saucepan; heat
to boiling. Reduce heat and simmer, covered, 5 minutes. Simmer,
uncovered, until sauce is reduced to medium consistency, about 30
minutes, adding basil during last 5 minutes. Discard bay leaves.

FETTUCCINE WITH CHICKEN LIVER SAUCE

45 *Enjoy the counterpoints of flavor and texture in this savory pasta dish.*

6 servings

4 ounces chicken livers
Flour
2 teaspoons olive oil
1 cup each: sliced onion, carrots
3 cloves garlic, minced
2 teaspoons dried sage leaves
1½ cups reduced-sodium fat-free chicken broth
½ cup dry white wine or chicken broth
2 medium apples, peeled, thinly sliced
1 tablespoon tomato paste
¼ teaspoon salt
⅛ teaspoon pepper
12 ounces fettuccine, cooked, warm

Per Serving:
Calories: 311
% of calories from fat: 11
Fat (gm): 3.6
Saturated fat (gm): 0.5
Cholesterol (mg): 65.2
Sodium (mg): 286
Protein (gm): 11.7
Carbohydrate (gm): 54.2

Exchanges:
Milk: 0.0
Vegetable: 0.0
Fruit: 0.0
Bread: 3.5
Meat: 1.0
Fat: 0.0

1. Coat chicken livers lightly with flour; sauté in oil in large skillet
until no longer pink in center, about 8 minutes. Remove livers

from skillet. Add onion, carrots, garlic, and sage to skillet; sauté until lightly browned, about 5 minutes. Add livers, chicken broth, and wine. Heat to boiling; reduce heat and simmer, uncovered, until vegetables are tender, about 10 minutes. Stir in apples, tomato paste, salt, and pepper; cook until apples are tender, 2 to 3 minutes. Serve over pasta.

45-MINUTE PREPARATION TIP: Begin cooking fettuccine before preparing the rest of the recipe.

CHICKEN PICCATA WITH FETTUCCINE

45 *This low fat version of the classic piccata is sure to please.*

6 servings

6 small boneless, skinless chicken breast halves
  (3 ounces each)
Flour
1 tablespoon margarine or butter
2 tablespoons flour
1 can (14½ ounces) reduced-sodium chicken broth
½ cup dry white wine or chicken broth
2 tablespoons lemon juice
1 tablespoon each: finely chopped parsley, capers
12 ounces fettuccine, cooked, warm

Per Serving:
Calories: 301
% of calories from fat: 18
Fat (gm): 6
Saturated fat (gm): 0.9
Cholesterol (mg): 43.4
Sodium (mg): 175
Protein (gm): 24.3
Carbohydrate (gm): 35

Exchanges:
Milk: 0.0
Vegetable: 0.0
Fruit: 0.0
Bread: 2.5
Meat: 2.0
Fat: 0.0

1. Pound chicken with flat side of meat mallet to ¼ inch thickness; coat lightly with flour. Cook chicken in lightly greased large skillet over medium to medium-high heat until browned and cooked, 3 to 5 minutes. Remove chicken from skillet.

2. Melt margarine in skillet; stir in 2 tablespoons flour and cook over medium heat 1 to 2 minutes. Whisk in chicken broth, wine, and lemon juice; heat to boiling. Reduce heat and simmer, uncovered, until thickened to a medium consistency, about 15 minutes. Add chicken, parsley and capers; simmer until chicken is hot, 2 to 3 minutes. Serve over pasta.

45-MINUTE PREPARATION TIP: Cook fettuccine while sauce is simmering.

CHICKEN AND FETTUCCINE ALFREDO

45

An old favorite, updated the low-fat way.

6 servings

6 boneless, skinless chicken breast halves
    (3 ounces each)
2 cloves garlic, minced
Paprika
Alfredo Sauce (recipe follows)
12 ounces fettuccine, cooked, warm

Per Serving:
Calories: 380
% of calories from fat: 26
Fat (gm): 11
Saturated fat (gm): 2.6
Cholesterol (mg): 48.4
Sodium (mg): 506
Protein (gm): 29.2
Carbohydrate (gm): 41.4

Exchanges:
Milk: 0.5
Vegetable: 0.0
Fruit: 0.0
Bread: 2.5
Meat: 2.0
Fat: 1.0

1. Place chicken in roasting pan; rub with garlic and sprinkle generously with paprika. Bake, uncovered, at 350 degrees until chicken is cooked, about 20 minutes. Toss Alfredo Sauce with fettuccine; serve with chicken breasts.

Alfredo Sauce

Makes about 2 cups

3 tablespoons margarine or butter
¼ cup all-purpose flour
2½ cups fat-free milk
¼ cup (1 ounce) grated Parmesan cheese
⅛ teaspoon ground nutmeg
½ teaspoon salt
¼ teaspoon pepper

1. Melt margarine in medium saucepan; stir in flour over medium heat 1 minute. Whisk in milk; heat to boiling, whisking until thickened, about 1 minute. Reduce heat to low and stir in remaining ingredients; cook 1 to 2 minutes.

CHICKEN-PASTA SKILLET WITH SUN-DRIED TOMATOES AND OLIVES

45

Sun-dried tomatoes and black olives lend a rich, earthy flavor to this colorful dish.

4 servings

½ cup each: chopped onion, green bell pepper

1 tablespoon olive oil

1 pound boneless, skinless chicken breast, cubed (1-inch)

1 large zucchini, cubed

1 can (15½ ounces) Italian-seasoned diced tomatoes, undrained

1 teaspoon dried marjoram leaves

3 tablespoons each: chopped sun-dried tomatoes, pitted black or Greek olives

Salt and pepper, to taste

4 ounces rigatoni, cooked, warm

Per Serving:
Calories: 330
% of calories from fat: 25
Fat (gm): 9.1
Saturated fat (gm): 1.6
Cholesterol (mg): 69
Sodium (mg): 761
Protein (gm): 30.9
Carbohydrate (gm): 30.7

Exchanges:
Milk: 0.0
Vegetable: 1.0
Fruit: 0.0
Bread: 2.0
Meat: 3.0
Fat: 0.0

1. Sauté onion and bell pepper in olive oil in large skillet until tender, about 5 minutes; add chicken and sauté 5 minutes. Stir in zucchini, tomatoes with liquid, marjoram, sun-dried tomatoes, and olives; heat to boiling. Reduce heat and simmer, uncovered, until chicken is cooked and sauce is thickened, about 10 minutes; season to taste with salt and pepper. Serve over pasta.

45-MINUTE PREPARATION TIP: Begin cooking pasta before preparing the rest of the recipe.

CHICKEN RISOTTO

45 *Microwave Risotto requires very little stirring or attention; adding chicken makes it a hearty meal.*

4 servings

Microwave Risotto (see p. 360)
12 ounces boneless, skinless chicken breast, cubed
1 tablespoon olive oil
2 cups frozen stir-fry pepper blend
¼ cup each: reduced-sodium fat-free chicken broth,
   dry white wine or dry sherry
½ teaspoon each: dried thyme and oregano leaves
Salt and pepper, to taste

Per Serving:
Calories: 391
% of calories from fat: 19
Fat (gm): 7.9
Saturated fat (gm): 2.4
Cholesterol (mg): 57
Sodium (mg): 330
Protein (gm): 30.9
Carbohydrate (gm): 42.8

Exchanges:
Milk: 0.0
Vegetable: 3.0
Fruit: 0.0
Bread: 2.0
Meat: 3.0
Fat: 0.0

1. Make Microwave Risotto, omitting Parmesan cheese.

2. Sauté chicken in oil in large skillet until lightly browned, about 5 minutes; add remaining ingredients, except salt and pepper. Heat to boiling; reduce heat and simmer, covered, until chicken is cooked, about 10 minutes. Stir chicken mixture into risotto; season to taste with salt and pepper.

CHICKEN AND VEGETABLE CURRY

45 *A variety of spices and herbs combine to make the fragrant curry that seasons this dish.*

4 servings

12–16 ounces boneless, skinless chicken breast, cubed
½ cup chopped onion
2 cloves garlic
1 tablespoon flour
1 small head cauliflower, cut into florets
1 cup each: cubed peeled potatoes, chopped tomato,
   thickly sliced carrots
1½ cups reduced-sodium fat-free chicken broth
¾ teaspoon ground turmeric

Per Serving:
Calories: 250
% of calories from fat: 11
Fat (gm): 3.1
Saturated fat (gm): 0.7
Cholesterol (mg): 51.7
Sodium (mg): 203
Protein (gm): 28.4
Carbohydrate (gm): 29

Exchanges:
Milk: 0.0
Vegetable: 2.0
Fruit: 0.0
Bread: 1.0
Meat: 2.0
Fat: 0.0

¼ teaspoon each: dry mustard, ground cumin, ground coriander
1–2 tablespoons lemon juice
Salt and cayenne pepper, to taste

1. Sauté chicken, onion, and garlic in lightly greased large saucepan until chicken is browned, 5 to 6 minutes; stir in flour and cook 1 minute. Add vegetables, broth, and herbs; heat to boiling. Reduce heat and simmer, covered, until chicken and vegetables are tender, 10 to 15 minutes. Season to taste with lemon juice, salt, and cayenne pepper.

THAI-SPICED CHICKEN AND CARROTS

45 *Peanut sauce, gingerroot, and sesame oil give this easy dish plenty of Asian-style pizzazz!*

4 servings

1 pound boneless, skinless chicken breast, cubed (½-inch)
4 carrots, diagonally sliced
1 tablespoon each: minced gingerroot, garlic, reduced-sodium soy sauce
1 can (14½ ounces) reduced-sodium fat-free chicken broth
¾ cup sliced green onions
1 tablespoon Thai peanut sauce
1 teaspoon sugar
½ - 1 teaspoon Asian sesame oil
3 cups cooked rice, warm

Per Serving:
Calories: 250
% of calories from fat: 11
Fat (gm): 3.1
Saturated fat (gm): 0.7
Cholesterol (mg): 51.7
Sodium (mg): 203
Protein (gm): 28.4
Carbohydrate (gm): 29

Exchanges:
Milk: 0.0
Vegetable: 2.0
Fruit: 0.0
Bread: 1.0
Meat: 2.0
Fat: 0.0

1. Combine chicken, carrots, gingerroot, garlic, soy sauce, and broth in large saucepan. Heat to boiling; reduce heat and simmer, covered, until chicken is cooked and carrots are tender, about 15 minutes. Stir in green onions, peanut sauce, sugar, and sesame oil; simmer 5 minutes. Serve over rice.

NOTE: 1 tablespoon peanut butter and ¼–½ teaspoon crushed red pepper can be substituted for the Thai peanut sauce.

45-MINUTE PREPARATION TIP: Begin cooking rice before preparing the rest of the recipe.

SESAME CHICKEN AND ASPARAGUS STIR-FRY

45 *Check the Asian section of your supermarket for the interesting selection of sauces available for noodles and rice.*

6 servings (about ⅔ cup each)

1 pound boneless, skinless chicken breast, cubed

1 can (15 ounces) black beans, rinsed, drained

8 ounces asparagus, sliced (1-inch)

½ jar (14-ounce size) Mandarin sesame sauce for noodles and rice

1 small tomato, coarsely chopped

¼ teaspoon crushed red pepper

1 package (8 ounces) Chinese egg noodles, cooked, warm

Per Serving:
Calories: 285
% of calories from fat: 8
Fat (gm): 2.9
Saturated fat (gm): 0.6
Cholesterol (mg): 46
Sodium (mg): 295
Protein (gm): 24
Carbohydrate (gm): 45.7

Exchanges:
Milk: 0.0
Vegetable: 1.5
Fruit: 0.5
Bread: 1.5
Meat: 2.0
Fat: 0.0

1. Stir-fry chicken in lightly greased wok or large skillet until browned, about 5 minutes. Add remaining ingredients, except noodles; stir-fry until asparagus is tender, 3 to 4 minutes. Serve over noodles.

45-MINUTE PREPARATION TIP: Begin cooking noodles before preparing the rest of the recipe.

CHICKEN STIR-FRY WITH CHINESE NOODLES

45 *Fresh Chinese noodles and Asian flavors make this pasta dish special.*

4 servings

1 pound boneless, skinless chicken breast, cut into strips

2 cups peeled, cubed, sweet potatoes

¾ cup diagonally sliced green onions

2–3 teaspoons each: minced garlic, gingerroot

3 cups diagonally halved snow peas

½ cup chopped red bell pepper

¾ cup canned, reduced-sodium fat-free chicken broth

1–2 teaspoons reduced-sodium tamari soy sauce

1½ teaspoons cornstarch

Per Serving:
Calories: 237
% of calories from fat: 7
Fat (gm): 1.8
Saturated fat (gm): 0.5
Cholesterol (mg): 35
Sodium (mg): 95
Protein (gm): 17.6
Carbohydrate (gm): 36.9

Exchanges:
Milk: 0.0
Vegetable: 1.0
Fruit: 0.0
Bread: 2.0
Meat: 1.5
Fat: 0.0

1 teaspoon toasted sesame seeds

Salt and pepper, to taste

1 package (12 ounces) Chinese egg noodles, cooked, warm

1. Stir-fry chicken in lightly greased wok or large skillet until browned, about 5 minutes; remove from wok. Add sweet potatoes, green onions, garlic, and gingerroot to wok; stir-fry 2 to 3 minutes. Cook, covered, over low heat until potatoes are crisp-tender, about 10 minutes. Add snow peas and bell pepper; stir-fry until peas are crisp-tender, about 5 minutes. Stir in combined broth, soy sauce, cornstarch, and chicken; heat to boiling, stirring until thickened, about 1 minute. Stir in sesame seeds; season to taste with salt and pepper. Serve with noodles.

45-MINUTE PREPARATION TIP: Begin cooking noodles before preparing the rest of the recipe.

ORIENTAL SATAY

45 *Skewered chicken and vegetables are roasted and served with a chunky Peanut Sauce.*

4 servings

½ medium acorn squash, peeled, seeded, cubed (1-inch)

8 ounces each: broccoli florets, fresh or frozen whole okra

2 medium summer yellow squash, thickly sliced

4 ounces pearl onions, peeled

1 pound chicken tenders, cut into pieces (1-inch)

3 tablespoons reduced-sodium soy sauce

1 tablespoon Asian sesame oil

3 cups cooked rice, warm

Peanut Sauce (recipe follows)

Per Serving:
Calories: 586
% of calories from fat: 18
Fat (gm): 12.2
Saturated fat (gm): 2.5
Cholesterol (mg): 69
Sodium (mg): 760
Protein (gm): 39.8
Carbohydrate (gm): 83.7

Exchanges:
Milk: 0.0
Vegetable: 1.0
Fruit: 0.0
Bread: 5.0
Meat: 3.0
Fat: 0.5

1. Cook acorn squash in 2 inches simmering water in medium saucepan until beginning to soften, 3 to 4 minutes; drain. Place squash, remaining vegetables, and chicken on skewers and arrange on greased aluminum foil-lined jelly roll pan. Roast at 425 degrees until chicken is cooked and vegetables are tender, 15 to 20 minutes, turning after 10 minutes and basting several times with combined soy sauce and oil. Serve with rice and Peanut Sauce.

Peanut Sauce
Makes about ½ cup

2 tablespoons each: reduced-sodium soy sauce, sugar
3 tablespoons reduced-fat chunky peanut butter
¼ cup thinly sliced green onions and tops
1 tablespoon grated gingerroot

1. Combine all ingredients.

CHICKEN MOLE

Mole, the most popular and traditional of all the Mexican sauces, is usually served with turkey or chicken. Picante with chilies and fragrant with sweet spices, the sauce is also flavored with unsweetened chocolate or cocoa. Even this simplified version of the delicious mole is somewhat time consuming to make, so double the recipe and freeze half!

6 servings

6 skinless chicken breast halves (6 ounces each)
Mole Sauce (recipe follows)
3 tablespoons finely chopped cilantro

1. Cook chicken in lightly greased large skillet over medium heat until browned, 8 to 10 minutes; arrange in large baking pan. Spoon Mole Sauce over chicken; bake, loosely covered, until chicken is tender and no longer pink in the center, about 30 minutes. Sprinkle with cilantro.

Per Serving:
Calories: 192
% of calories from fat: 25
Fat (gm): 5.1
Saturated fat (gm): 1
Cholesterol (mg): 68.6
Sodium (mg): 82
Protein (gm): 27.7
Carbohydrate (gm): 6.8

Exchanges:
Milk: 0.0
Vegetable: 1.0
Fruit: 0.0
Bread: 0.0
Meat: 3.0
Fat: 0.0

Mole Sauce
Makes about 1½ cups

2 each: mulato, ancho, pasilla chilies
1 tablespoon sesame seeds
2 each: whole peppercorns, cloves
¼ teaspoon coriander seeds
1½-inch piece cinnamon stick
1 tablespoon each: raisins, slivered almonds, pumpkin seeds
¼ cup chopped onion
2 cloves garlic, finely chopped
½ corn tortilla (6-inch)
Vegetable cooking spray
½ small tomato, chopped
¾ cup reduced-sodium fat-free chicken broth
1 tablespoon unsweetened cocoa
Salt, to taste

1. Cook chilies in lightly greased medium skillet over medium heat until softened; remove and discard stems, seeds, and veins. (If chilies are already soft, omit the cooking step). Pour boiling water over chilies to cover in bowl; let stand until softened, about 15 minutes. Drain, reserving ¾ cup liquid.

2. Cook sesame seeds and spices in lightly greased small skillet over medium heat until toasted, 1 to 2 minutes; remove from skillet. Add raisins, almonds, and pumpkin seeds and cook over medium heat until toasted, 1 to 2 minutes; remove from skillet. Add onion and garlic to skillet and sauté until tender, 2 to 3 minutes; remove from skillet. Spray tortilla lightly with cooking spray; cook in skillet until browned, about 1 minute on each side. Cool; cut into 1-inch pieces.

3. Process all ingredients, except salt, in blender until smooth. Heat mixture to boiling in medium skillet; reduce heat and simmer, uncovered 5 minutes; season to taste with salt.

CHICKEN FAJITAS

45

Fajitas are an American interpretation of a soft taco. If you are grilling fajita ingredients, leave chicken breasts whole and cut peppers in half, then slice before serving.

4 servings (2 each)

1 pound boneless, skinless chicken breast, cut into strips (1½ x ½-inch)
Fajita Marinade (recipe follows)
1 cup each: sliced medium red bell pepper, onion
1 can (15 ounces) black beans, rinsed, drained
1 teaspoon ground cumin
Salt and pepper, to taste
8 flour or corn tortillas (6-inch), warm
¼ cup packed cilantro leaves
1 cup Red Tomato Salsa (½ recipe) (see p. 18)
½ cup fat-free sour cream

Per Serving:
Calories: 424
% of calories from fat: 14
Fat (gm): 7.3
Saturated fat (gm): 1.2
Cholesterol (mg): 51.7
Sodium (mg): 645
Protein (gm): 35.9
Carbohydrate (gm): 61.7

Exchanges:
Milk: 0.0
Vegetable: 2.0
Fruit: 0.0
Bread: 3.0
Meat: 2.0
Fat: 0.0

1. Drizzle chicken with Fajita Marinade and toss; refrigerate, covered, 1 to 2 hours.

2. Cook chicken in lightly greased large skillet over medium heat until browned, about 5 minutes; move chicken to side of pan. Add bell pepper and onion; cook over medium heat until vegetables are tender and chicken is cooked, about 5 minutes. Stir in black beans and cumin; cook until hot, 2 to 3 minutes. Season to taste with salt and pepper. Spoon mixture into tortillas; top with cilantro, salsa, and sour cream, and roll up.

Fajita Marinade
Makes about ¼ cup

¼ cup lime juice
3 cloves garlic, minced
1½ teaspoons dried oregano leaves
½ teaspoon black pepper

1. Mix all ingredients.

CHICKEN ENCHILADAS MOLE

For variation, the enchiladas can also be baked with Tomatillo Sauce (see p. 184). Serve with Jicama Salad (see p. 469) for fresh flavor contrast.

4 servings (2 each)

8 corn or flour tortillas (6-inch)
1 cup mild or medium salsa
1 pound boneless, skinless chicken breast, cooked, shredded
½ cup each: shredded fat-free Cheddar cheese (2 ounces), sliced green onions
4–8 tablespoons fat-free sour cream
¼ cup chopped cilantro
Mole Sauce (see p. 181)

Per Serving:
Calories: 333
% of calories from fat: 15
Fat (gm): 5.9
Saturated fat (gm): 1.1
Cholesterol (mg): 69
Sodium (mg): 752
Protein (gm): 39.1
Carbohydrate (gm): 33.1

Exchanges:
Milk: 0.0
Vegetable: 1.0
Fruit: 0.0
Bread: 2.0
Meat: 3.0
Fat: 0.0

1. Dip tortillas in salsa to coat lightly. Spoon chicken along centers of tortillas; top with cheese, green onions, sour cream, and cilantro. Roll up and place, seam sides down, in baking pan; spoon Mole Sauce over. Bake, loosely covered, at 350 degrees until enchiladas are hot, 20 to 30 minutes.

CHICKEN FLAUTAS WITH TOMATILLO SAUCE

Flautas are usually deep-fried; these are sautéed to achieve the same crispness.

4 servings (2 each)

1 cup chopped tomato
¼ cup each: chopped onion, poblano chili
½ teaspoon each: ground cumin, dried thyme leaves
1 pound boneless, skinless chicken breast, cooked, shredded
¼ cup chopped cilantro
Salt and pepper, to taste
8 flour or corn tortillas (6-inch), warm
Vegetable cooking spray
1 cup Tomatillo Sauce (recipe follows)
4 tablespoons crumbled Mexican white or feta cheese
¼ cup fat-free sour cream

Per Serving:
Calories: 388
% of calories from fat: 23
Fat (gm): 9.8
Saturated fat (gm): 1.4
Cholesterol (mg): 75.7
Sodium (mg): 361
Protein (gm): 34
Carbohydrate (gm): 40.6

Exchanges:
Milk: 0.0
Vegetable: 2.0
Fruit: 0.0
Bread: 2.0
Meat: 3.5
Fat: 0.0

1. Sauté tomato, onion, poblano chili, cumin, and thyme in lightly greased large skillet until onion is tender, about 5 minutes. Add chicken and cilantro; cook 2 to 3 minutes. Season to taste with salt and pepper. Spoon about ⅓ cup mixture on each tortilla; roll up and secure with toothpicks. Spray flautas lightly with cooking spray; cook over medium heat in large skillet until browned on all sides, 5 to 8 minutes. Serve with Tomatillo Sauce, cheese, and sour cream.

Tomatillo Sauce
Makes about 2 cups

1½ pounds tomatillos, husked
½ cup chopped onion
1 teaspoon each: chopped garlic, serrano chili
3 tablespoons chopped cilantro
2–3 teaspoons sugar
Salt and white pepper, to taste

1. Cook tomatillos in 2-inches simmering water in large saucepan until tender, 5 to 8 minutes; drain and cool. Process tomatillos, onion, garlic, chili, and cilantro in food processor or blender until almost smooth. Heat sauce to boiling in lightly greased large skillet; reduce heat and simmer until slightly thickened, about 5 minutes. Season to taste with sugar, salt, and pepper.

CHICKEN BURRITOS WITH POBLANO CHILI SAUCE

Brushed with Poblano Chili Sauce for extra flavor, these burritos are a beautiful adobe red color.

4 servings

12–16 ounces boneless, skinless chicken breast
Salt and pepper, to taste
3 arbol or New Mexico chilies, stems, seeds, and veins discarded
1 small onion, finely chopped
3 cloves garlic, minced
2 tablespoons finely chopped cilantro
1 teaspoon each: dried marjoram and oregano leaves

1 can (15 ounces) pinto beans, rinsed, drained

Cayenne pepper, to taste

4 large flour tortillas (10-inch)

Poblano Chili Sauce (recipe follows)

½ cup fat-free sour cream

Medium or hot salsa (not included in nutritional data)

Per Serving:
Calories: 385
% of calories from fat: 14
Fat (gm): 6.1
Saturated fat (gm): 1.1
Cholesterol (mg): 51.7
Sodium (mg): 661
Protein (gm): 33.1
Carbohydrate (gm): 52.6

Exchanges:
Milk: 0.0
Vegetable: 2.0
Fruit: 0.0
Bread: 3.0
Meat: 2.0
Fat: 0.0

1. Simmer chicken in water to cover in medium saucepan until chicken is tender and cooked, 8 to 10 minutes. Drain, reserving ¼ cup cooking liquid. Shred chicken into small pieces; season to taste with salt and pepper. Cover arbol chilies with hot water in small bowl; let stand until softened, 10 to 15 minutes. Drain; chop finely.

2. Sauté onion, garlic, and herbs in lightly greased medium skillet until onion is tender, 3 to 4 minutes. Add beans, ¼ cup reserved cooking liquid, and arbol chilies; mash coarsely. Cook over medium heat until hot; season to taste with salt and cayenne pepper.

3. Spoon bean mixture and chicken along centers of tortillas; top each with ¼ cup Poblano Chili Sauce. Fold sides of tortillas in, overlapping filling; fold ends in, overlapping to make a square "package"; secure with toothpicks. Cook burritos in lightly greased large skillet until browned on all sides, brushing with remaining Poblano Chili Sauce. Serve with sour cream and salsa.

Poblano Chili Sauce
Makes about 2 cups

2 medium tomatoes, chopped

⅓ cup each: chopped onion, poblano chili

1–2 tablespoons each: minced garlic, chili powder

Salt and pepper, to taste

1. Cook all ingredients, except salt and pepper, in greased medium skillet until tender, 8 to 10 minutes; process in food processor or blender until smooth. Season to taste with salt and pepper.

CHICKEN AND POBLANO TAMALES

Tamales can be tied in "envelopes" as in Beef Pinto Bean Tamales (see p. 140), or in "bundles", as in this recipe.

6 servings (2 each)

½ cup each: chopped onion, poblano chili
3 cloves garlic, minced
½ teaspoon minced jalapeño chili
¾ teaspoon each: dried oregano leaves, ground cumin
12 ounces boneless, skinless chicken breast, cooked, shredded
2 tablespoons finely chopped cilantro
Tamale Dough (see p. 140)
½ cup reduced-sodium chicken broth or water
Salt, to taste
12 corn husks, softened in boiling water, drained

Per Serving:
Calories: 190
% of calories from fat: 24
Fat (gm): 5.2
Saturated fat (gm): 1.0
Cholesterol (mg): 34.4
Sodium (mg): 214
Protein (gm): 16.3
Carbohydrate (gm): 20.0

Exchanges:
Milk: 0.0
Vegetable: 1.0
Fruit: 0.0
Bread: 1.0
Meat: 1.5
Fat: 0.5

1. Sauté onion, poblano chili, garlic, jalapeño chili, oregano, and cumin in lightly greased medium skillet until vegetables are tender, about 5 minutes. Add chicken and cilantro; mix in Tamale Dough and chicken broth. Season to taste with salt.

2. Spoon about ¼ cup tamale mixture onto center of each corn husk; tie ends of tamales, making "bundles". Place tamales on steamer rack in saucepan with 2 inches of water. Steam, covered, 2 hours, adding more water to saucepan if necessary.

CHICKEN AND CHEESE RELLENOS

Our healthy version of chili rellenos eliminates the customary egg coating and frying in oil.

6 servings

6 large poblano chilies
1 each: chopped medium onion, carrot, garlic clove
1 pound boneless, skinless chicken breast, cooked, shredded
½ cup whole kernel corn
½ teaspoon each: ground cumin, dried thyme leaves

½ cup (2 ounces) each: shredded reduced-fat
Monterey Jack, fat-free Cheddar cheese

Salt and pepper, to taste

1 tablespoon vegetable oil

Chili Tomato Sauce (recipe follows)

Per Serving:
Calories: 215
% of calories from fat: 26
Fat (gm): 6.4
Saturated fat (gm): 1.9
Cholesterol (mg): 54.4
Sodium (mg): 213
Protein (gm): 25.2
Carbohydrate (gm): 15.1

Exchanges:
Milk: 0.0
Vegetable: 2.0
Fruit: 0.0
Bread: 0.5
Meat: 3.0
Fat: 0.0

1. Cut stems from tops of chilies; remove and discard seeds and veins. Simmer peppers in water to cover until slightly softened, 2 to 3 minutes; drain and cool.

2. Sauté onion, carrot, and garlic in lightly greased large skillet until tender, 3 to 5 minutes. Add chicken, corn, and herbs; cook over medium heat 1 to 2 minutes. Remove from heat and stir in cheeses; season to taste with salt and pepper. Spoon mixture into peppers; sauté in oil in large skillet until tender and browned on all sides, 6 to 8 minutes. Serve with Chili Tomato Sauce.

Chili Tomato Sauce

Makes 1 cup

1 cup reduced-sodium tomato sauce

2 tablespoons water

1–1½ tablespoons chili powder

1 clove garlic

Salt and pepper, to taste

1. Heat all ingredients, except salt and peppcr, to boiling in small saucepan; reduce heat and simmer, uncovered, 2 to 3 minutes. Season to taste with salt and pepper.

TURKEY CUTLETS WITH SAGE

45 *Sage adds a robust flavor and aroma to this dish.*

4 servings

1 pound turkey breast cutlets

2 tablespoons red wine vinegar

2 teaspoons each: minced garlic, dried sage leaves

¼ teaspoon each: salt, pepper

Flour

2 teaspoons olive oil

1 cup reduced-sodium fat-free chicken broth

1 tablespoon lemon juice

1 tablespoon flour

Per Serving:
Calories: 158
% of calories from fat: 26
Fat (gm): 4.5
Saturated fat (gm): 1
Cholesterol (mg): 44.7
Sodium (mg): 63
Protein (gm): 21.1
Carbohydrate (gm): 7

Exchanges:
Milk: 0.0
Vegetable: 0.0
Fruit: 0.0
Bread: 0.5
Meat: 3.0
Fat: 0.0

1. Pound turkey cutlets with flat side of meat mallet to ¼ inch thickness; brush with combined vinegar, garlic, sage, salt, and pepper. Let stand 5 minutes. Coat both sides of cutlets lightly with flour; sauté in oil in large skillet until browned and cooked, 2 to 3 minutes on each side. Remove cutlets to platter and keep warm. Heat combined broth, lemon juice, and flour to boiling in skillet, stirring until slightly thickened, about 1 minute. Spoon over cutlets.

RIGATONI WITH TURKEY SAUSAGE AND FENNEL PESTO

Fennel Pesto and fresh fennel add a unique twist to a traditional favorite.

6 servings

1 pound Italian-style turkey sausage

1½ cups thinly sliced fennel bulb or celery

1 cup chopped onion

2 cloves garlic, minced

1 can (8 ounces) low-sodium diced tomatoes, undrained

Fennel Pesto (recipe follows)

12 ounces rigatoni or other tube pasta, cooked, warm

Per Serving:
Calories: 406
% of calories from fat: 29
Fat (gm): 13
Saturated fat (gm): 2.9
Cholesterol (mg): 48.2
Sodium (mg): 711
Protein (gm): 24.6
Carbohydrate (gm): 48.3

Exchanges:
Milk: 0.0
Vegetable: 1.0
Fruit: 0.0
Bread: 2.5
Meat: 2.0
Fat: 2.0

1. Cook sausage in lightly greased large skillet over medium heat until browned, about 5 minutes. Remove sausage and slice; return to skillet. Add fennel, onion, and garlic; sauté until onion is tender, about 8 minutes. Stir in tomatoes with liquid and Fennel Pesto. Heat to boiling; reduce heat and simmer, covered, about 15 minutes. Spoon over pasta and toss.

Fennel Pesto

Makes about 1⅓ cups

3 tablespoons hot water
1 tablespoon fennel seeds
1 cup chopped fennel bulb
½ cup loosely packed parsley
2 cloves garlic
14 walnut halves
1 tablespoon olive oil
¼ cup (1 ounce) grated Parmesan cheese

1. Pour hot water over fennel seeds in bowl to cover. Let stand 10 minutes. Process fennel seeds and remaining ingredients in food processor or blender until very finely chopped.

ROASTED VEGETABLES, TURKEY SAUSAGE, AND MUSHROOM TORTELLINI

45

Substitute ravioli or a shaped pasta for the tortellini if you wish.

4 servings

1 cup each: cubed plum tomatoes, halved mushrooms, sliced zucchini, yellow summer squash, broccoli florets

12 ounces low-fat smoked turkey sausage, sliced (½-inch)

Vegetable cooking spray

1½ teaspoons dried Italian seasoning

Salt and pepper, to taste

1 package (9 ounces) fresh mushroom or herb tortellini, cooked, warm

1–2 tablespoons olive oil

Per Serving:
Calories: 386
% of calories from fat: 30
Fat (gm): 13.5
Saturated fat (gm): 4.1
Cholesterol (mg): 89.1
Sodium (mg): 959
Protein (gm): 28.7
Carbohydrate (gm): 42.2

Exchanges:
Milk: 0.0
Vegetable: 3.0
Fruit: 0.0
Bread: 2.0
Meat: 2.0
Fat: 1.0

1. Arrange vegetables and sausage in single layer on greased foil-lined jelly roll pan; spray generously with cooking spray. Sprinkle with Italian seasoning, salt, and pepper. Roast at 425 degrees until vegetables are browned, about 40 minutes, removing broccoli and sausage after about 20 minutes. Combine vegetables, sausage, and tortellini; drizzle with olive oil and toss.

FIVE

Fish
and
Seafood

CRAB CAKES WITH POBLANO CHILI SAUCE

45 *Peeled, cooked shrimp or imitation crabmeat can easily be substituted for all or part of the crab.*

4 servings

12 ounces Alaskan king, lump or claw crabmeat,
   finely chopped
½ each: finely chopped small onion, medium tomato
½ small jalapeño chili, minced
1 egg white
2–4 tablespoons unseasoned dry bread crumbs
½ teaspoon each: dried oregano leaves, salt
Flour or unseasoned dry bread crumbs
1 cup Poblano Chili Sauce (½ recipe) (see p. 185)

Per Serving:
Calories: 133
% of calories from fat: 10
Fat (gm): 1.4
Saturated fat (gm): 0.2
Cholesterol (mg): 35.7
Sodium (mg): 793
Protein (gm): 18.6
Carbohydrate (gm): 12.1

Exchanges:
Milk: 0.0
Vegetable: 2.0
Fruit: 0.0
Bread: 0.0
Meat: 2.0
Fat: 0.0

1. Combine crabmeat, onion, tomato, jalapeño chili, and egg white in small bowl; mix in bread crumbs, oregano, and salt. Shape into 4 patties about ½ inch thick; coat lightly with flour. Cook patties in lightly greased large skillet over medium heat until cooked and lightly browned, 3 to 4 minutes on each side. Serve with Poblano Chili Sauce.

SCALLOPS WITH APPLES AND PEA PODS

45 *This colorful dish with an apple accent is delicious served over steamed rice, rice noodles, or Chinese egg noodles.*

4 servings

3 small apples, unpeeled, thinly sliced
1 each: chopped medium onion, red bell pepper
3 ounces snow peas, trimmed
2 tablespoons vegetable oil, divided
12 ounces scallops
¼ cup apple cider
2 teaspoons cornstarch
1 tablespoon reduced-sodium soy sauce
Salt and pepper, to taste

Per Serving:
Calories: 238
% of calories from fat: 30
Fat (gm): 8.3
Saturated fat (gm): 1
Cholesterol (mg): 36.2
Sodium (mg): 315
Protein (gm): 17.5
Carbohydrate (gm): 26

Exchanges:
Milk: 0.0
Vegetable: 0.0
Fruit: 1.5
Bread: 0.0
Meat: 2.0
Fat: 1.0

1. Stir-fry apples, onion, bell pepper, and snow peas in 1 tablespoon oil in wok or large skillet over medium-high heat until crisp-tender, about 3 minutes. Remove from wok. Add scallops and stir-fry in remaining 1 tablespoon oil until cooked and opaque, about 4 minutes. Stir in combined cider, cornstarch, and soy sauce, and cook until mixture boils and thickens, about 1 minute. Stir in apple mixture; cook 2 minutes. Season to taste with salt and pepper.

SHRIMP WITH ARTICHOKES AND PEPPERS

45 *This skillet supper is quick, easy, and brimming with flavor.*

6 servings

1 cup each: sliced onion, red or green bell pepper
1 teaspoon minced garlic
1 tablespoon olive oil
1 can (15 ounces) reduced-sodium chunky
   tomato sauce
1 can (14 ounces) artichoke hearts, drained, quartered
3 tablespoons dry sherry (optional)
2 teaspoons dried Italian seasoning
12 ounces medium shrimp, peeled, deveined
Salt and pepper, to taste
8 ounces penne, cooked, warm

Per Serving:
Calories: 277
% of calories from fat: 11
Fat (gm): 3.4
Saturated fat (gm): 0.5
Cholesterol (mg): 87
Sodium (mg): 292
Protein (gm): 17.4
Carbohydrate (gm): 40.5

Exchanges:
Milk: 0.0
Vegetable: 2.0
Fruit: 0.0
Bread: 2.0
Meat: 1.5
Fat: 0.0

1. Sauté onion, bell pepper, and garlic in oil in large skillet until tender, about 5 minutes; add tomato sauce, artichoke hearts, and sherry. Heat to boiling; reduce heat and simmer, covered, 5 minutes. Add Italian seasoning and shrimp; simmer until shrimp are cooked, about 5 minutes. Season to taste with salt and pepper; serve over penne.

SHRIMP DIANE

45 *Serve this flavorful shrimp dish over basmati rice, couscous, or angel hair pasta.*

4 servings

½ cup sliced mushrooms

2 tablespoons minced shallots

1 tablespoon margarine or butter

1 can (15½ ounces) quartered artichoke hearts, drained

¼ cup each: dry white wine or reduced-sodium chicken broth, chopped chives, pimiento

12–16 ounces peeled, deveined shrimp

Salt and pepper, to taste

Chopped parsley, as garnish

Per Serving:
Calories: 149
% of calories from fat: 23
Fat (gm): 3.6
Saturated fat (gm): 0.8
Cholesterol (mg): 130
Sodium (mg): 460
Protein (gm): 17.2
Carbohydrate (gm): 8.2

Exchanges:
Milk: 0.0
Vegetable: 1.0
Fruit: 0.0
Bread: 0.0
Meat: 2.0
Fat: 0.0

1. Sauté mushrooms and shallots in margarine in large skillet until tender, about 5 minutes; add artichoke hearts, wine, chives, and pimiento and cook, covered, over medium heat 2 minutes. Add shrimp and cook until shrimp are cooked, 3 to 5 minutes. Season to taste with salt and pepper. Sprinkle with parsley.

SHRIMP WITH GARLIC

45 *The garlic is cooked very slowly, until golden and tender, giving the dish it's special flavor.*

4 servings

1 large head garlic

2 tablespoons olive or vegetable oil

1 pound peeled, deveined shrimp

½ lime

2 tablespoons finely chopped cilantro

Salt and pepper, to taste

Yellow Salsa Rice (see p. 351)

4 corn or flour tortillas (6-inch)

Per Serving:
Calories: 388
% of calories from fat: 20
Fat (gm): 8.5
Saturated fat (gm): 1.3
Cholesterol (mg): 131.6
Sodium (mg): 340
Protein (gm): 21.7
Carbohydrate (gm): 55.1

Exchanges:
Milk: 0.0
Vegetable: 0.0
Fruit: 0.0
Bread: 3.5
Meat: 2.5
Fat: 0.0

1. Peel garlic cloves and cut into halves; cook in oil in medium skillet over low heat until garlic is soft and golden, 15 to 20 minutes; add shrimp and cook over medium heat until shrimp are cooked, about 5 minutes. Squeeze lime juice over and sprinkle with cilantro; season to taste with salt and pepper. Serve with Yellow Salsa Rice and tortillas.

45-MINUTE PREPARATION TIP: Begin cooking the rice before preparing the rest of the recipe.

SPRING VEGETABLE AND SHRIMP STIR-FRY

45 *The best of spring's bounty, seasoned with fresh ginger, sesame oil, and tamari soy sauce.*

4 servings

1 pound asparagus, sliced (1½-inch)

1 cup each: sliced small red potatoes, mushrooms

½ cup each: chopped onion, red bell pepper

2–4 teaspoons minced garlic, gingerroot

½ cup reduced-sodium fat-free chicken broth

12–16 ounces peeled, deveined shrimp

4 teaspoons cornstarch

¼ cup cold water

1–2 tablespoons reduced-sodium tamari soy sauce

1–2 teaspoons Asian sesame oil

Salt and pepper, to taste

3 cups cooked brown and wild rice

Per Serving:
Calories: 310
% of calories from fat: 10
Fat (gm): 3.5
Saturated fat (gm): 0.5
Cholesterol (mg): 130
Sodium (mg): 537
Protein (gm): 23
Carbohydrate (gm): 48.9

Exchanges:
Milk: 0.0
Vegetable: 3.0
Fruit: 0.0
Bread: 2.0
Meat: 2.0
Fat: 0.0

1. Stir-fry vegetables, garlic, and gingerroot in lightly greased wok or large skillet until almost tender, about 10 minutes. Add broth and shrimp and heat to boiling; reduce heat and simmer, covered, until vegetables are crisp-tender and shrimp are cooked, 3 to 5 minutes. Heat to boiling; stir in combined cornstarch and water, stirring until thickened, about 1 minute. Stir in soy sauce and sesame oil; season to taste with salt and pepper. Serve with rice.

SHRIMP AND CHEESE ROTOLO
WITH MANY-CLOVES GARLIC SAUCE

Some people prefer cutting the lasagne noodles into halves before filling, as they are easier to handle when eating. If cut, spread each noodle half with ½ to 2 tablespoons of the cheese mixture.

6 servings

1 pound peeled, deveined cooked shrimp, chopped

1¼ cups reduced-fat ricotta cheese

3–4 cloves garlic, minced

½ teaspoon each: dried marjoram and thyme leaves, salt

¼ teaspoon pepper

12 lasagne noodles (10 ounces), cooked, room temperature

Many-Cloves Garlic Sauce (see p. 377)

Per Serving:
Calories: 323
% of calories from fat: 16
Fat (gm): 5.9
Saturated fat (gm): 1.7
Cholesterol (mg): 128.1
Sodium (mg): 403
Protein (gm): 25
Carbohydrate (gm): 40

Exchanges:
Milk: 0.0
Vegetable: 0.0
Fruit: 0.0
Bread: 2.0
Meat: 3.0
Fat: 0.0

1. Mix shrimp, cheese, garlic, herbs, salt, and pepper. Spread 3 to 4 tablespoons of mixture evenly on each noodle; roll up and place, seam sides down in baking dish. Spoon Many-Cloves Garlic Sauce over rotolo; bake, loosely covered, at 350 degrees until hot, 20 to 30 minutes.

SHRIMP TOSTADAS

Serve these great tostadas with Zucchini from Puebla, Yellow Salsa Rice or Refried Beans (see pp. 446, 351, 335).

4 servings

12–16 ounces peeled, deveined medium shrimp

1 small onion, chopped

½ serrano chili, finely chopped

1 cup Chili Tomato Sauce (see p. 187), warm

4 corn tortillas (6-inch)

2 cups chopped romaine lettuce

1 medium tomato, chopped

¼ cup crumbled Mexican white or fat-free feta cheese

Guacamole (recipe follows)

Per Serving:
Calories: 283
% of calories from fat: 29
Fat (gm): 9.3
Saturated fat (gm): 1.4
Cholesterol (mg): 129
Sodium (mg): 299
Protein (gm): 23.0
Carbohydrate (gm): 28.9

Exchanges:
Milk: 0.0
Vegetable: 0.0
Fruit: 0.0
Bread: 2.0
Meat: 2.0
Fat: 0.5

1. Reserve 4 shrimp for garnish; coarsely chop remaining shrimp. Cook whole and chopped shrimp, onion, and serrano chili in lightly greased medium saucepan until shrimp are cooked, 3 to 5 minutes. Remove whole shrimp and reserve. Stir Chili Tomato Sauce into shrimp mixture.

2. Cook tortillas in lightly greased medium skillet until crisp and browned, about 1 minute on each side. Top tortillas with lettuce and tomato; spoon shrimp mixture over. Sprinkle with crumbled cheese; top each tostada with Guacamole and reserved whole shrimp.

Guacamole

Makes about ⅔ cup

1 medium avocado
½ small onion, finely chopped
1–2 tablespoons finely chopped jalapeño chili, cilantro
Salt and white pepper, to taste

1. Coarsely mash avocado in small bowl; mix in onion, jalapeño chili, and cilantro. Season to taste with salt and pepper.

SHRIMP AND ROASTED VEGETABLE FAJITAS

The vegetables can also be grilled over mesquite chips for a smoky accent; cut vegetables in large enough pieces so they don't fall through the grill rack!

4 servings

1 cup each: thickly sliced red bell peppers, poblano chilies or green bell peppers, carrots, zucchini, chayote squash
2 each: medium tomatoes and onions, cut into wedges
8 ounces large mushrooms, halved
Vegetable cooking spray
2 teaspoons each: ground cumin, dried oregano leaves
12 ounces peeled deveined shrimp, cooked, warm
Fajita Dressing (recipe follows)
Salt and pepper, to taste
8 flour or corn tortillas (6-inch), warm

Per Serving:
Calories: 467
% of calories from fat: 27
Fat (gm): 14.4
Saturated fat (gm): 2.6
Cholesterol (mg): 129
Sodium (mg): 573
Protein (gm): 28.5
Carbohydrate (gm): 58.5

Exchanges:
Milk: 0.0
Vegetable: 0.0
Fruit: 0.0
Bread: 4.0
Meat: 2.0
Fat: 1.5

1. Arrange vegetables in single layer in greased aluminum foil-lined pan; spray generously with cooking spray and sprinkle with herbs. Bake vegetables at 425 degrees until tender and browned, 40 to 45 minutes. Toss shrimp and Fajita Dressing; toss with vegetables and season to taste with salt and pepper. Spoon mixture onto tortillas and roll up.

Fajita Dressing
Makes about ¼ cup

2 tablespoons olive oil
1 tablespoon lime juice
2–3 teaspoons cider vinegar
2–3 cloves garlic, minced

1. Mix all ingredients.

SHRIMP AND CRAB ENCHILADAS WITH PASILLA CHILI SAUCE

The rich Pasilla Chili Sauce is creamy in texture, slightly smoky in flavor; it is also excellent served with grilled chicken breast or lean pork.

4 servings

8 ounces peeled, deveined cooked shrimp, coarsely chopped
4 ounces chopped Alaskan King or lump crabmeat or peeled, deveined shrimp
Pasilla Chili Sauce (recipe follows)
8 flour tortillas (6-inch)
½ cup (2 ounces) shredded fat-free Cheddar cheese
¼ cup finely chopped cilantro

Per Serving:
Calories: 318
% of calories from fat: 13
Fat (gm): 4.5
Saturated fat (gm): 0.7
Cholesterol (mg): 101.9
Sodium (mg): 722
Protein (gm): 28.3
Carbohydrate (gm): 41.2

Exchanges:
Milk: 0.0
Vegetable: 0.5
Fruit: 0.0
Bread: 2.0
Meat: 3.0
Fat: 0.0

1. Combine shrimp, crabmeat, and ¾ cup Pasilla Chili Sauce; divide mixture on tortillas and roll up. Place tortillas, seam sides down, in greased 11 x 7 inch baking dish. Spoon remaining Pasilla Chili Sauce over enchiladas; sprinkle with cheese. Bake, uncovered, at 350 degrees until hot, about 20 minutes. Sprinkle with cilantro.

Pasilla Chili Sauce

Makes about 2 cups

3 pasilla chilies
2 medium tomatoes, coarsely chopped
1 small onion, coarsely chopped
½ teaspoon sugar
1 cup fat-free sour cream
Salt and pepper, to taste

1. Cook chilies in small lightly greased small skillet over medium heat until soft; remove and discard stems, seeds, and veins. Process chilies, tomatoes, onion, and sugar in blender until smooth. Cook mixture in lightly greased medium skillet over medium heat until thickened, about 5 minutes. Reduce heat to low; stir in sour cream and cook until hot, about 2 minutes. Season to taste with salt and pepper.

ROASTED VEGETABLES AND SHRIMP, MOO-SHU STYLE

45 *For simplicity, we've substituted flour tortillas for the Mandarin Pancakes (see p. 154) traditionally served with moo-shu dishes.*

6 servings

8 ounces each: green beans or snow peas, sliced mushrooms
3 medium zucchini, halved lengthwise, sliced
1 medium onion, thinly sliced
Vegetable cooking spray
1¼ teaspoons 5-spice powder, divided
Salt and pepper, to taste
12 ounces peeled, deveined small shrimp
2 teaspoons canola oil
Plum Sauce (see p. 24)
12 flour tortillas (6-inch)
2 cups fresh bean sprouts
2 medium carrots, coarsely shredded
½ cup loosely packed cilantro

Per Serving:
Calories: 407
% of calories from fat: 14
Fat (gm): 6.7
Saturated fat (gm): 1.5
Cholesterol (mg): 86
Sodium (mg): 709
Protein (gm): 24.5
Carbohydrate (gm): 66.5

Exchanges:
Milk: 0.0
Vegetable: 1.0
Fruit: 0.0
Bread: 4.0
Meat: 2.0
Fat: 0.0

1. Arrange green beans, mushrooms, zucchini, and onion in single layer on greased foil-lined jelly roll pan. Spray vegetables with cooking spray and sprinkle with ¾ teaspoon 5-spice powder. Roast at 425 degrees until vegetables are crisp-tender, about 25 minutes; season to taste with salt and pepper.

2. Sauté shrimp in oil in medium skillet until cooked, 3 to 4 minutes; sprinkle with remaining ½ teaspoon 5-spice powder and toss with vegetables. Spread generous tablespoon Plum Sauce in center of each tortilla. Spoon roasted vegetables on tortillas; top with bean sprouts, carrots, and cilantro. Roll up, tucking up one end to hold and eat.

SEAFOOD NEWBURG

45 *Any shellfish or lean white fish can be used in this classic Newburg.*

4 servings

8 ounces each: peeled deveined shrimp, bay scallops

½ cup water

¼ cup finely chopped shallots or onion

2 tablespoons margarine or butter

¼ cup all-purpose flour

1½ cups fat-free half-and-half or fat-free milk

1 egg yolk

1–2 tablespoons dry sherry (optional)

Pinch each: ground nutmeg, cayenne pepper

Salt, to taste

4 slices toast, cut diagonally into halves

Chopped parsley, as garnish

Per Serving:
Calories: 326
% of calories from fat: 26
Fat (gm): 9.1
Saturated fat (gm): 1.8
Cholesterol (mg): 164.8
Sodium (mg): 495
Protein (gm): 26.7
Carbohydrate (gm): 29.9

Exchanges:
Milk: 0.8
Vegetable: 0.0
Fruit: 0.0
Bread: 2.0
Meat: 3.0
Fat: 0.5

1. Simmer shrimp and scallops in water in medium saucepan, covered, until cooked, 3 to 5 minutes. Drain, reserving liquid.

2. Sauté shallots in margarine in medium saucepan until tender, 2 to 3 minutes; mix in flour and cook 1 minute. Whisk in half-and-half and reserved cooking liquid; heat to boiling, whisking until thickened, about 1 minute. Whisk about half the mixture into egg yolk in small bowl; whisk egg mixture into saucepan. Whisk over low heat 30 seconds. Stir in shrimp, scallops, sherry, nutmeg, and cayenne pepper; cook 2 to 3 minutes. Season to taste with salt. Serve on toast; sprinkle with parsley.

CIOPPINO PASTA

Serve in bowls to accommodate the generous serving of sauce.

8 servings

1 cup each: chopped green bell pepper, onion, mushrooms

4 cloves garlic, minced

1 tablespoon olive oil

3 cups chopped tomatoes

½ cup dry white wine or clam juice

1 tablespoon tomato paste

2 tablespoons chopped parsley

2 teaspoons each: dried oregano and basil leaves

1 teaspoon ground turmeric

8 ounces each: sea scallops, cubed crabmeat (½-inch)

4 ounces halibut or haddock, cubed (1-inch)

12 mussels in the shell, scrubbed

½ teaspoon each: salt, pepper

12 ounces fettuccine, cooked, warm

Per Serving:
Calories: 387
% of calories from fat: 24
Fat (gm): 10.2
Saturated fat (gm): 2.1
Cholesterol (mg): 80.9
Sodium (mg): 514
Protein (gm): 24.5
Carbohydrate (gm): 47

Exchanges:
Milk: 0.0
Vegetable: 2.0
Fruit: 0.0
Bread: 2.0
Meat: 2.0
Fat: 0.75

1. Sauté bell pepper, onion, mushrooms, and garlic in oil in large saucepan until onion is tender, about 5 minutes. Stir in tomatoes, wine, tomato paste, and herbs; heat to boiling. Reduce heat and simmer, covered, 5 minutes; simmer, uncovered, until mixture is thickened to desired consistency, about 20 minutes, adding seafood during last 10 minutes of cooking time. Discard any mussels that have not opened. Stir in salt and pepper. Toss with fettuccine.

FLOUNDER EN PAPILLOTE

Traditionally made with a lean white fish, this recipe is also very delicious with salmon or tuna.

6 servings

6 flounder, sole or other lean white fish fillets
  (4 ounces each)
Salt and pepper, to taste
1 cup each: sliced mushrooms, julienned carrots
¼ cup finely chopped shallots or onion
2 cloves garlic, minced
½ teaspoon dried tarragon leaves
2 teaspoons margarine or butter
½ cup dry white wine or water
¼ cup finely chopped parsley
6 lemon wedges

Per Serving:
Calories: 149
% of calories from fat: 17
Fat (gm): 2.8
Saturated fat (gm): 0.6
Cholesterol (mg): 59.8
Sodium (mg): 118
Protein (gm): 22.3
Carbohydrate (gm): 5.7

Exchanges:
Milk: 0.0
Vegetable: 1.0
Fruit: 0.0
Bread: 0.0
Meat: 2.5
Fat: 0.0

1. Cut six 12-inch squares of parchment paper; fold in half, and cut each into a large heart shape. Open hearts and place 1 fish fillet on each; sprinkle lightly with salt and pepper.

2. Sauté mushrooms, carrots, shallots, garlic, and tarragon in margarine in large skillet until carrots are crisp-tender, about 5 minutes. Stir in wine and parsley; season to taste with salt and pepper. Spoon mixture over fish. Fold packets in half, bringing edges together; crimp edges tightly to seal. Bake on jelly roll pan at 425 degrees until packets puff, 10 to 12 minutes. Serve with lemon wedges.

NOTE: Aluminum foil can be used in place of parchment paper; bake fish 15 minutes.

FLORENTINE FISH DINNER

45 *Pasta, spinach, and fish fillets combine to make this quick, flavorful dinner.*

4 servings

1 can (14 ounces) reduced-sodium diced
  tomatoes, undrained
2 cups frozen chopped spinach, thawed
1 tablespoon olive oil
½ teaspoon minced garlic
Salt and pepper, to taste
3 tablespoons grated Parmesan cheese
8 ounces linguine, cooked, warm
1 pound skinless flounder fillets

Per Serving:
Calories: 353
% of calories from fat: 18
Fat (gm): 7.5
Saturated fat (gm): 1.6
Cholesterol (mg): 63.1
Sodium (mg): 355
Protein (gm): 32.6
Carbohydrate (gm): 41.7

Exchanges:
Milk: 0.0
Vegetable: 2.0
Fruit: 0.0
Bread: 2.0
Meat: 3.0
Fat: 0.0

1. Combine tomatoes with liquid, spinach, olive oil, and garlic in medium saucepan; heat to boiling. Reduce heat and simmer until thickened to desired consistency, about 10 minutes; season to taste with salt and pepper. Toss sauce and Parmesan cheese with linguine and keep warm.

2. Cook flounder in lightly greased large skillet over medium heat until flounder is tender and flakes with a fork, 3 to 4 minutes on each side. Sprinkle lightly with salt and pepper. Serve with linguine.

45-MINUTE PREPARATION TIP: Begin cooking pasta before preparing the rest of the recipe.

CARIBBEAN-STYLE FLOUNDER

45 *Annatto seeds can be found in the ethnic section of the supermarket; they give the oil a bright yellow color and subtle flavor.*

4 servings

1 tablespoon annatto seeds (optional)

2 teaspoons peanut oil

1 each: sliced medium onion, cubed sweet potato

2 cups reduced-sodium fat-free chicken broth

1 can (14 ounces) reduced-sodium diced
   tomatoes, undrained

1 teaspoon dried thyme leaves

1 cup frozen peas

1 pound flounder fillets, cubed (¾-inch)

3–4 teaspoons lemon juice

Salt and pepper, to taste

Per Serving:
Calories: 240
% of calories from fat: 16
Fat (gm): 4.2
Saturated fat (gm): 0.8
Cholesterol (mg): 60.1
Sodium (mg): 227
Protein (gm): 28.5
Carbohydrate (gm): 21.4

Exchanges:
Milk: 0.0
Vegetable: 0.0
Fruit: 0.0
Bread: 1.0
Meat: 3.0
Fat: 0.0

1. Cook annatto seeds in oil in large saucepan over medium-high heat 3 minutes; remove and discard annatto seeds. Add onion to saucepan; sauté 2 minutes. Add sweet potato, broth, tomatoes with liquid, and thyme. Heat to boiling; reduce heat and simmer, covered, until potato is tender, about 10 minutes. Using potato masher, coarsely mash mixture in pan. Add peas and flounder; simmer until fish is tender and flakes with a fork, about 5 minutes. Season to taste with lemon juice, salt and pepper.

BRAISED FISH WITH SUN-DRIED TOMATO SAUCE

45 *The combination of tomato sauce and sun-dried tomatoes gives this dish rich tomato flavor. Red snapper or other firm fish can be substituted for the halibut.*

4 servings

1 large onion, chopped

1 teaspoon minced garlic

1 tablespoon olive oil

1 cup clam juice or reduced-fat chicken broth

3 tablespoons chopped sun-dried tomatoes

¾ teaspoon each: dried marjoram and oregano leaves

1 can (8 ounces) reduced-sodium tomato sauce

4 halibut steaks (about 4 ounces each)

Salt and pepper, to taste

Per Serving:
Calories: 204
% of calories from fat: 30
Fat (gm): 6.8
Saturated fat (gm): 0.9
Cholesterol (mg): 36.1
Sodium (mg): 232
Protein (gm): 25.4
Carbohydrate (gm): 9.6

Exchanges:
Milk: 0.0
Vegetable: 2.0
Fruit: 0.0
Bread: 0.0
Meat: 3.0
Fat: 0.0

1. Sauté onion and garlic in oil in large skillet until browned, about 5 minutes. Stir in clam juice, sun-dried tomatoes, and herbs. Heat to boiling; boil, uncovered, stirring frequently until liquid is almost evaporated, about 5 minutes. Add tomato sauce and fish; simmer until fish is tender and flakes with a fork, about 5 minutes. Season to taste with salt and pepper.

HALIBUT WITH SOUR CREAM AND POBLANO SAUCE

45 *The picante Sour Cream and Poblano Sauce is also excellent served with shredded chicken breast or lean pork in soft tacos, or over favorite enchiladas.*

4 servings

4 halibut steaks (4 ounces each)

3 tablespoons lime juice

1 clove garlic, minced

Salt and pepper, to taste

Sour Cream and Poblano Sauce (recipe follows)

4 lime wedges

Per Serving:
Calories: 184
% of calories from fat: 13
Fat (gm): 2.7
Saturated fat (gm): 0.4
Cholesterol (mg): 36.4
Sodium (mg): 101
Protein (gm): 28.2
Carbohydrate (gm): 11.9

Exchanges:
Milk: 0.0
Vegetable: 1.0
Fruit: 0.0
Bread: 0.0
Meat: 3.0
Fat: 0.0

1. Brush halibut with combined lime juice and garlic; let stand 15 minutes. Cook halibut in lightly greased large skillet over medium heat until halibut is tender and flakes with a fork, 4 to 5 minutes on each side. Sprinkle lightly with salt and pepper. Serve with Sour Cream and Poblano Sauce and lime wedges.

Sour Cream and Poblano Sauce

Makes about 1 cup

1 each: thinly sliced large poblano chili, finely chopped small onion
2 cloves garlic, minced
1 cup fat-free sour cream
¼ teaspoon ground cumin
Salt and pepper, to taste

1. Sauté poblano chili, onion, and garlic in lightly greased small saucepan until very tender, about 5 minutes. Stir in sour cream and cumin; cook over low heat 2 to 3 minutes. Season to taste with salt and pepper.

ASPARAGUS-ROUGHY AU GRATIN

Orange roughy is a light-flavored fish with a nice, firm texture—delicious baked with asparagus.

6 servings

4 cups cooked rice
1 pound fresh asparagus, sliced (1-inch)
6 orange roughy fillets (4 ounces each)
1 medium onion, finely chopped
3 tablespoons margarine or butter
⅓ cup all-purpose flour
1 cup each: fat-free milk, shredded reduced-fat
  Cheddar cheese (4 ounces)
¼ teaspoon each: salt, pepper
1 cup unseasoned dry bread crumbs

Per Serving:
Calories: 468
% of calories from fat: 22
Fat (gm): 11.2
Saturated fat (gm): 2.8
Cholesterol (mg): 44
Sodium (mg): 712
Protein (gm): 37.2
Carbohydrate (gm): 51.3

Exchanges:
Milk: 0.0
Vegetable: 1.0
Fruit: 0.0
Bread: 3.0
Meat: 4.0
Fat: 0.0

1. Spoon rice into 13 x 9-inch baking dish; arrange asparagus over rice and top with fish fillets, overlapping if necessary.

2. Sauté onion in margarine in medium saucepan until tender, about 5 minutes. Stir in flour and cook 1 minute. Whisk in milk and heat to boiling, whisking until thickened, about 1 minute. Whisk in cheese, salt, and pepper. Spoon sauce over fish; sprinkle with bread crumbs. Bake, covered, at 350 degrees until sauce is bubbly, about 20 minutes. Bake, uncovered, until browned, about 10 minutes.

RED SNAPPER BAKED WITH CILANTRO

45

Tuna, salmon, cod, or any firm white fish can be used in this recipe.

6 servings

⅓ cup lime juice

1½ tablespoons pickled jalapeño chili juice

1 teaspoon ground cumin

1½ pounds red snapper fillets or steaks

1 medium onion, thinly sliced

2 pickled jalapeño chilies, minced

2 cloves garlic, minced

1 cup coarsely chopped cilantro

Salt and pepper, to taste

Thinly sliced green onions, as garnish

6 lime wedges

Per Serving:
Calories: 135
% of calories from fat: 12
Fat (gm): 1.7
Saturated fat (gm): 0.3
Cholesterol (mg): 41.6
Sodium (mg): 169
Protein (gm): 24
Carbohydrate (gm): 5

Exchanges:
Milk: 0.0
Vegetable: 0.0
Fruit: 0.0
Bread: 0.0
Meat: 3.0
Fat: 0.0

1. Pour combined lime juice, jalapeño juice, and cumin over fish in glass baking dish; top with onion, jalapeño chilies, garlic, and cilantro. Refrigerate, covered, 2 hours, turning fish once.

2. Bake uncovered, at 400 degrees until red snapper is tender and flakes with a fork, about 10 minutes. Sprinkle fish lightly with salt and pepper; sprinkle with green onions and serve with lime wedges.

RED SNAPPER VERACRUZ

45

In this famous dish from Veracruz, Mexico, red snapper is baked in a full-flavored tomato sauce with olives and capers. The fish can also be grilled, then topped with the sauce.

6 servings

1 whole red snapper, dressed (about 2 pounds)

2 tablespoons lime juice

2 cloves garlic, minced

Veracruz Sauce (recipe follows)

6 lime wedges

1. Pierce surfaces of fish with long-tined fork; rub with lime juice and garlic. Refrigerate, covered, in large glass baking dish 2 hours.

2. Spoon Veracruz Sauce over fish. Bake, uncovered, at 400 degrees until fish is tender and flakes with a fork, 25 to 35 minutes. Serve with lime wedges.

Per Serving:
Calories: 198
% of calories from fat: 15
Fat (gm): 3.3
Saturated fat (gm): 0.6
Cholesterol (mg): 55.5
Sodium (mg): 311
Protein (gm): 32.6
Carbohydrate (gm): 9.2

Exchanges:
Milk: 0.0
Vegetable: 2.0
Fruit: 0.0
Bread: 0.0
Meat: 3.0
Fat: 0.0

Veracruz Sauce

Makes about 2 cups

1 cup chopped onion
3 cloves garlic, minced
1 pickled jalapeño chili, minced
2-inch piece cinnamon stick
1 bay leaf
½ teaspoon each: dried oregano and thyme leaves,
   ground cumin
3 cups chopped tomatoes
¼ cup sliced pitted green olives
1–2 tablespoons capers
Salt and pepper, to taste

1. Sauté onion, garlic, jalapeño chili, cinnamon, and herbs in large lightly greased skillet until onion is tender, 5 to 8 minutes. Add tomatoes, olives, and capers; simmer, uncovered, until sauce is a medium consistency, about 10 minutes. Discard bay leaf; season to taste with salt and pepper.

GRILLED RED SNAPPER WITH TROPICAL SALSA

Trendy salsas are making the scene—you'll enjoy our fruit and black bean version.

6 servings

1 whole red snapper, dressed (about 2 pounds)
3 tablespoons lime juice
2 cloves garlic, minced
Tropical Salsa (recipe follows)
Lime wedges, as garnish
Cilantro or parsley sprigs, as garnish

Per Serving:
Calories: 189
% of calories from fat: 11
Fat (gm): 2.2
Saturated fat (gm): 0.5
Cholesterol (mg): 55.5
Sodium (mg): 75
Protein (gm): 32.1
Carbohydrate (gm): 9

Exchanges:
Milk: 0.0
Vegetable: 0.0
Fruit: 0.0
Bread: 0.0
Meat: 3.0
Fat: 0.0

1. Pierce surfaces of fish with long-tined fork; rub with lime juice and garlic. Refrigerate, covered, in large glass baking dish 2 hours.

2. Grill fish over medium-hot coals, or bake, uncovered, at 400 degrees, until fish is tender and flakes with a fork, 20 to 25 minutes. Serve with Tropical Salsa; garnish with lime wedges and cilantro.

Tropical Salsa

Makes about 1½ cups

½ cup each: chopped papaya or mango, pineapple, tomato
¼ cup each: chopped, seeded cucumber, rinsed, drained
   canned black beans, orange juice
½ teaspoon minced jalapeño chili
2 tablespoons finely chopped cilantro
1 tablespoon lime juice
2 teaspoons sugar

1. Combine all ingredients.

POACHED SALMON WITH MOCK HOLLANDAISE SAUCE

45 *Poached salmon can be served warm or cold depending upon the occasion and the season of the year.*

6 servings

¾ cup dry white wine or clam juice
½ cup water
2 thin slices onion
4 dill or parsley sprigs
¼ teaspoon each: dried thyme and tarragon leaves
1 bay leaf
4 peppercorns
½ teaspoon salt
4 small salmon steaks (4 ounces each)
Mock Hollandaise Sauce (see p. 170)
Chopped parsley, as garnish
4 lemon wedges

Per Serving:
Calories: 195
% of calories from fat: 30
Fat (gm): 6.2
Saturated fat (gm): 0.9
Cholesterol (mg): 53.3
Sodium (mg): 351
Protein (gm): 26.9
Carbohydrate (gm): 4.2

Exchanges:
Milk: 0.5
Vegetable: 0.0
Fruit: 0.0
Bread: 0.0
Meat: 3.0
Fat: 0.0

1. Heat wine, water, onion, herbs, peppercorns, and salt to boiling in medium skillet. Reduce heat and simmer, covered, 5 minutes. Add salmon to skillet; simmer, covered, until salmon is cooked and flakes with a fork, 6 to 8 minutes. Spoon Mock Hollandaise Sauce over salmon; sprinkle with parsley. Garnish with lemon wedges.

SALMON WITH CILANTRO PESTO FETTUCCINE

45 *Tuna or halibut can substitute nicely for the salmon.*

6 servings

6 salmon steaks (4 ounces each)
2–3 teaspoons Dijon mustard
12 ounces spinach fettuccine, cooked, warm
Cilantro Pesto (recipe follows)

1. Brush salmon with mustard; broil 6 inches from heat source until salmon is tender and flakes with fork, 10 to 12 minutes, turning once. Toss fettuccine with Cilantro Pesto; serve with salmon.

Cilantro Pesto

Makes about ¾ cup

1½ cups packed cilantro leaves

½ cup packed parsley

1 clove garlic, minced

¼ cup (1 ounce) grated Parmesan cheese

3 tablespoons pine nuts or walnuts

1 tablespoon each: olive oil, lemon juice

¼ teaspoon each: salt, pepper

Per Serving:
Calories: 372
% of calories from fat: 30
Fat (gm): 12.3
Saturated fat (gm): 2.6
Cholesterol (mg): 126.7
Sodium (mg): 319
Protein (gm): 32.7
Carbohydrate (gm): 31.1

Exchanges:
Milk: 0.0
Vegetable: 0.0
Fruit: 0.0
Bread: 2.0
Meat: 3.0
Fat: 1.0

1. Process all ingredients in food processor or blender until finely chopped.

CARIBBEAN SWEET-AND-SOUR SALMON

Sweet-and-sour flavors team with salmon, pineapple, and beans for this island-inspired dish.

6 servings

1 cup each: coarsely chopped onions, sliced red and green bell peppers

4 cloves garlic, minced

2 teaspoons minced gingerroot

1–2 jalapeño chilies, finely chopped

1 can (20 ounces) pineapple chunks in juice, drained, juice reserved

2 tablespoons each: light brown sugar, cider vinegar

2–3 teaspoons curry powder

1½ tablespoons cornstarch

¼ cup cold water

12–16 ounces salmon steaks, cubed (1½-inch)

1 can (15 ounces) black beans, rinsed, drained

4 cups cooked rice, warm

3 small green onions and tops, sliced

Per Serving:
Calories: 350
% of calories from fat: 6
Fat (gm): 2.5
Saturated fat (gm): 0.4
Cholesterol (mg): 28.6
Sodium (mg): 334
Protein (gm): 17.9
Carbohydrate (gm): 67.1

Exchanges:
Milk: 0.0
Vegetable: 0.0
Fruit: 1.0
Bread: 3.0
Meat: 1.5
Fat: 0.0

1. Sauté onions, bell peppers, garlic, gingerroot, and jalapeño chilies in lightly greased large skillet until onions are tender, about 5 minutes. Add enough water to pineapple juice to make 1½ cups.

Add pineapple and juice, brown sugar, vinegar, and curry powder to skillet; heat to boiling. Stir in combined cornstarch and water, stirring thickened, about 1 minute. Stir in salmon and beans; cook over medium heat until salmon is tender and flakes with a fork, about 5 minutes. Serve over rice; sprinkle with green onions.

SALMON RISOTTO

45 *The salmon and sauce are prepared while the risotto is cooking in the microwave oven—a real time-saver!*

6 servings

Microwave Risotto (see pg. 360)
12–16 ounces salmon steaks
¾ cup sliced green onions
¼ cup dry sherry or water
1 cup reduced-fat sour cream
½ cup 1% low-fat milk
1 tablespoon chopped fresh or 2 teaspoons dried dill weed
Salt and pepper, to taste

Per Serving:
Calories: 291
% of calories from fat: 23
Fat (gm): 7.1
Saturated fat (gm): 3.4
Cholesterol (mg): 42.7
Sodium (mg): 175
Protein (gm): 20
Carbohydrate (gm): 31.2

Exchanges:
Milk: 0.0
Vegetable: 0.0
Fruit: 0.0
Bread: 2.0
Meat: 2.0
Fat: 0.5

1. Make Microwave Risotto. While risotto is cooking, cook salmon in lightly greased large skillet over medium heat until salmon is tender and flakes with fork, about 10 minutes. Remove from skillet and discard skin; cut salmon into large pieces. Add green onions and sherry to skillet; cook over medium heat until green onions are tender, 2 to 3 minutes. Stir in sour cream, milk, and dill weed; add salmon and stir into risotto. Season to taste with salt and pepper.

SOLE MEDITERRANEAN-STYLE

45 *This fast and flavorful fish dinner features sole, but any mild-flavored white fish, such as flounder, halibut, or turbot, can be substituted.*

4 servings

½ cup sun-dried tomatoes (not in oil), softened

2 cups each: sliced onions, red or green bell peppers

½ cup reduced-sodium fat-free chicken broth

2 teaspoons olive oil

1 teaspoon each: minced garlic, dried basil leaves

Salt and pepper, to taste

8 ounces penne or mostaccioli, cooked, warm

¼ cup (1 ounce) grated Parmesan cheese

12–16 ounces skinless sole fillets

Chopped parsley, as garnish

Per Serving:
Calories: 387
% of calories from fat: 14
Fat (gm): 6
Saturated fat (gm): 1.7
Cholesterol (mg): 49
Sodium (mg): 347
Protein (gm): 28.3
Carbohydrate (gm): 53.3

Exchanges:
Milk: 0.0
Vegetable: 2.0
Fruit: 0.0
Bread: 3.0
Meat: 2.0
Fat: 0.0

1. Combine tomatoes, onions, bell peppers, broth, olive oil, garlic, and basil in large skillet; heat to boiling. Reduce heat and simmer, uncovered, until vegetables are very tender, about 5 minutes; season to taste with salt and pepper. Toss with penne and Parmesan cheese in large bowl; keep warm.

2. Cook sole in lightly greased large skillet over medium heat until browned on the bottom, 3 to 4 minutes; turn and cook until fish is tender and flakes with fork, 3 to 4 minutes. Sprinkle lightly with salt and pepper. Serve over pasta mixture; sprinkle with parsley.

45-MINUTE PREPARATION TIP: Begin cooking pasta before preparing the rest of the recipe.

TUNA STEAKS WITH GARLIC PASTA

45 *Slow cooking gives the garlic a sweet, mellow flavor.*

4 servings

⅓ cup thinly sliced garlic

2–3 teaspoons olive oil

1 cup frozen peas

1 tablespoon minced fresh or 1 teaspoon dried
rosemary leaves

Salt and pepper, to taste

4 tuna steaks (4 ounces each)

2 cups (8 ounces) orecchiette (little ears) pasta,
cooked, warm

¼–⅓ cup (1 ounce) freshly grated Parmesan cheese

Per Serving:
Calories: 430
% of calories from fat: 13
Fat (gm): 6
Saturated fat (gm): 1.7
Cholesterol (mg): 53.4
Sodium (mg): 173
Protein (gm): 37.9
Carbohydrate (gm): 54.1

Exchanges:
Milk: 0.0
Vegetable: 2.0
Fruit: 0.0
Bread: 3.0
Meat: 3.0
Fat: 0.0

1. Cook garlic in oil in small skillet over medium heat 2 minutes;
reduce heat to medium-low and cook, uncovered, until garlic is
golden, about 10 minutes. Stir in peas and rosemary and cook until
hot, 1 to 2 minutes; season to taste with salt and pepper.

2. While garlic is cooking, broil tuna 6 inches from heat source
until fish is tender and flakes with a fork, 4 to 5 minutes on each
side; season to taste with salt and pepper. Toss garlic mixture with
orecchiette and Parmesan cheese; top with tuna.

GRILLED FISH WITH CHILI PASTE

*Dried ancho and pasilla chilies and vinegar combine to create a piquant
seasoning for the fish.*

4 servings

1 pound fish fillets (red snapper, tuna, or any firm fish)

Chili Paste (recipe follows)

4 lime wedges

1. Spread top of fillets with Chili Paste. Grill over medium-hot
coals or broil 6 inches from heat source until fish is tender and
flakes with a fork, 10 to 15 minutes. Serve with lime wedges.

Chili Paste

Makes about ¼ cup

1 each: ancho and pasilla chili
2 cloves garlic
½ teaspoon salt
1 tablespoon white wine vinegar
Water

1. Cook chilies in lightly greased medium skillet over medium heat until softened, 1 to 2 minutes. Remove and discard stems, seeds, and veins. Process chilies, garlic, salt, and vinegar in food processor or blender, adding small amount of water, if necessary, to make smooth paste.

Per Serving:
Calories: 133
% of calories from fat: 11
Fat (gm): 1.5
Saturated fat (gm): 0.3
Cholesterol (mg): 41.6
Sodium (mg): 377
Protein (gm): 23.4
Carbohydrate (gm): 4.6

Exchanges:
Milk: 0.0
Vegetable: 0.5
Fruit: 0.0
Bread: 0.0
Meat: 2.5
Fat: 0.0

TUNA STEAKS WITH SWEET-SOUR TOMATO-BASIL RELISH

45 *Spicy tomato relish nicely complements grilled tuna in this easy but elegant recipe.*

4 servings

2 teaspoons olive oil
1 teaspoon each: minced garlic, lemon juice
½ teaspoon each: dried basil and thyme leaves
4 tuna steaks (4 ounces each)
Salt and pepper, to taste
Sweet-Sour Tomato-Basil Relish (recipe follows)

1. Combine olive oil, garlic, lemon juice, and herbs in small bowl; brush on tuna. Let stand 15 minutes. Broil tuna 6 inches from heat source until fish is tender and flakes with a fork, 6 to 8 minutes on each side. Sprinkle lightly with salt and pepper; serve with Sweet-Sour Tomato-Basil Relish.

Per Serving:
Calories: 182
% of calories from fat: 23
Fat (gm): 4.6
Saturated fat (gm): 0.7
Cholesterol (mg): 49.4
Sodium (mg): 108
Protein (gm): 26.2
Carbohydrate (gm): 8.4

Exchanges:
Milk: 0.0
Vegetable: 1.0
Fruit: 0.0
Bread: 0.0
Meat: 3.0
Fat: 0.0

Sweet-Sour Tomato-Basil Relish

Makes about 1 cup

1 large tomato, seeded, cubed
2 tablespoons tomato paste
½ tablespoon water
1½ tablespoons each: red wine vinegar, sugar
1 teaspoon olive oil
¼ teaspoon each: dried basil and thyme leaves

1. Sauté tomato in lightly greased small skillet until softened, 3 to 4 minutes; combine with remaining ingredients.

45-MINUTE PREPARATION TIP: Make Sweet-Sour Tomato-Basil Relish before preparing the rest of the recipe.

FISH BAKED WITH STUFFING

Fish fillets are cooked on a bed of seasoned bread stuffing—add a salad and vegetable, and dinner is served!

4 servings

1 cup each: chopped onion, sliced mushrooms
½ teaspoon minced garlic
1½ cups crumb-type seasoned stuffing mix
3 tablespoons grated Parmesan cheese
1 pound lean white fish fillets
¼ teaspoon dried basil leaves
Salt and pepper, to taste
¼ cup dry white wine or chicken broth

Per Serving:
Calories: 241
% of calories from fat: 13
Fat (gm): 3.5
Saturated fat (gm): 1.1
Cholesterol (mg): 63.1
Sodium (mg): 584
Protein (gm): 27.5
Carbohydrate (gm): 22.4

Exchanges:
Milk: 0.0
Vegetable: 0.0
Fruit: 0.0
Bread: 1.5
Meat: 3.0
Fat: 0.0

1. Sauté onion, mushrooms, and garlic in lightly greased large skillet until onion is tender, 5 to 8 minutes. Stir in stuffing mix and Parmesan cheese; spoon into baking dish. Arrange fish on stuffing, overlapping if necessary; sprinkle with basil, salt, and pepper. Pour wine over fish. Bake, covered, at 375 degrees until fish is tender and flakes with a fork, about 20 minutes.

WHITEFISH AND LINGUINE WITH LEMON-CAPER SAUCE

45

Any white-fleshed fish, such as cod, halibut, haddock, or orange roughy, can be used.

6 servings

6 whitefish fillets (about 3 ounces each)

1 tablespoon Dijon mustard

2 cloves garlic, minced

1 teaspoon dried tarragon leaves

2–3 tablespoons margarine or butter

3 tablespoons flour

1 can (14½ ounces) reduced-sodium fat-free chicken broth

2–3 teaspoons lemon juice

3 tablespoons capers

¼ teaspoon salt

⅛ teaspoon white pepper

12 ounces linguine, cooked, warm

Per Serving:
Calories: 326
% of calories from fat: 28
Fat (gm): 10
Saturated fat (gm): 1.5
Cholesterol (mg): 49.3
Sodium (mg): 505
Protein (gm): 23.7
Carbohydrate (gm): 35.4

Exchanges:
Milk: 0.0
Vegetable: 0.0
Fruit: 0.0
Bread: 2.5
Meat: 2.0
Fat: 1.0

1. Brush fish fillets with combined mustard, garlic, and tarragon. Bake at 350 degrees until fish is tender and flakes with fork, 10 to 12 minutes.

2. Melt margarine in small saucepan; stir in flour and cook over medium heat 1 minute. Whisk in chicken broth and lemon juice; heat to boiling, whisking until thickened, about 1 minute. Stir in capers, salt, and pepper. Serve fish on linguine; spoon sauce over.

SIX

Stews

PAPRIKA-SIRLOIN STEW WITH SOUR CREAM

45 *Tender beef and vegetables in a paprika-spiked sour cream sauce are ready to eat in less than 45 minutes.*

4 servings

1 pound boneless beef sirloin steak, fat trimmed,
    cut into strips (1 x ½-inch)

1 cup pearl onions, peeled

1 cup reduced-sodium fat-free beef broth

2 cups Italian green beans

¾ pound red potatoes, cubed

1 can (15 ounces) diced tomatoes, undrained

2 bay leaves

1 tablespoon paprika

½ cup fat-free sour cream

Salt and pepper, to taste

Per Serving:
Calories: 286
% of calories from fat: 17
Fat (gm): 5.4
Saturated fat (gm): 2
Cholesterol (mg): 59.5
Sodium (mg): 768
Protein (gm): 27.4
Carbohydrate (gm): 32.9

Exchanges:
Milk: 0.0
Vegetable: 0.0
Fruit: 0.0
Bread: 2.0
Meat: 3.0
Fat: 0.0

1. Sauté beef and onions in lightly greased large skillet until lightly browned, 8 to 10 minutes; add remaining ingredients, except sour cream, salt and pepper and heat to boiling. Reduce heat and simmer until beef and vegetables are tender, about 15 minutes. Stir in sour cream; season to taste with salt and pepper.

BEEF TENDERLOIN STROGANOFF

45 *A creamy mushroom sauce makes these steaks very special.*

4 servings

4 beef tenderloin steaks (4 ounces each), fat trimmed

Salt and pepper, to taste

Mushrooms Stroganoff (recipe follows)

3 cups cooked rice, warm

Per Serving:
Calories: 398
% of calories from fat: 22
Fat (gm): 9.5
Saturated fat (gm): 3.5
Cholesterol (mg): 73.7
Sodium (mg): 157
Protein (gm): 32.6
Carbohydrate (gm): 43.5

Exchanges:
Milk: 0.0
Vegetable: 3.0
Fruit: 0.0
Bread: 2.0
Meat: 3.0
Fat: 0.0

1. Sauté steaks in lightly greased medium skillet to desired degree of doneness, 3 to 4 minutes on each side for medium. Season to taste with salt and pepper; spoon Mushrooms Stroganoff over. Serve with rice.

Mushrooms Stroganoff
Makes about 1½ cups

3 cups sliced mushrooms
¾ cup chopped red bell pepper
2 ounces fat-free cream cheese
½ teaspoon each: dried marjoram and thyme leaves
⅓ cup reduced-fat sour cream
Salt and pepper, to taste

1. Sauté mushrooms and bell pepper in lightly greased skillet until tender, 5 to 8 minutes. Add cream cheese and herbs, stirring until cream cheese is melted; stir in sour cream and cook 2 to 3 minutes. Season to taste with salt and pepper.

45-MINUTE PREPARATION TIP: Begin cooking rice and make Mushrooms Stroganoff before cooking the steaks.

BEEF STROGANOFF

A favorite for buffet entertaining, this dish enjoys well-deserved popularity.

4 servings

1 pound beef eye of round or sirloin steak, fat
   trimmed, cut into strips (1½ x ½-inch)
1 tablespoon margarine or butter
3 cups sliced mushrooms
½ cup sliced onion
2 cloves garlic, minced
2 tablespoons flour
1½ cups reduced-sodium beef broth
1 teaspoon Dijon mustard
½ teaspoon dried thyme leaves
½ cup fat-free sour cream
Salt and pepper, to taste
3 cups cooked noodles, warm

Per Serving:
Calories: 423
% of calories from fat: 21
Fat (gm): 10
Saturated fat (gm): 2.2
Cholesterol (mg): 64
Sodium (mg): 167
Protein (gm): 39
Carbohydrate (gm): 45.1

Exchanges:
Milk: 0.0
Vegetable: 1.0
Fruit: 0.0
Bread: 2.5
Meat: 4.0
Fat: 0.0

1. Sauté beef in margarine in large saucepan until browned, about 5 minutes; remove from pan. Add mushrooms, onion, and garlic to pan; cook until tender, 5 to 8 minutes. Stir in flour and cook 1 minute. Add beef, beef broth, mustard, and thyme and heat to boiling; reduce heat and simmer, covered, until beef is tender, 45 to 60 minutes. Reduce heat to low; stir in sour cream and cook 2 to 3 minutes. Season to taste with salt and pepper and serve over noodles.

BEEF BOURGUIGNON

This French-inspired stew is perfect for special occasions, when ordinary beef stew is not quite elegant enough!

6 servings

1½ pounds beef eye of round, fat trimmed, cubed (1½-inch)

1 tablespoon olive oil

¼ cup all purpose flour

1 cup each: reduced-sodium beef broth, Burgundy wine or water

1½ cups peeled pearl onions

3 cups sliced carrots

8 ounces small whole mushrooms

1 teaspoon each: dried marjoram and thyme leaves

2 bay leaves

½ teaspoon each: salt and pepper

12 ounces egg noodles, cooked, warm

Per Serving:
Calories: 522
% of calories from fat: 25
Fat (gm): 14.3
Saturated fat (gm): 4.6
Cholesterol (mg): 96.5
Sodium (mg): 309
Protein (gm): 35.3
Carbohydrate (gm): 55

Exchanges:
Milk: 0.0
Vegetable: 1.0
Fruit: 0.0
Bread: 3.0
Meat: 4.0
Fat: 1.0

1. Sauté beef in oil in Dutch oven until browned, about 10 minutes; stir in flour and cook 1 minute. Add broth and wine; heat to boiling. Transfer to oven and bake, covered, at 350 degrees until beef is very tender, 1 to 1½ hours, adding vegetables, herbs, salt, and pepper during last 30 minutes. Discard bay leaves. Serve over noodles.

GREEK BEEF AND LENTIL STEW

45 *Lentils and fresh vegetables partner deliciously in this easy stew.*

6 servings (about 1½ cups each)

1 cup each: chopped onion, green bell pepper,
  cubed zucchini
2 teaspoons minced garlic
2 cups each: cubed Idaho potatoes, cut green beans
1 cup lentils
1 can (15 ounces) reduced-sodium diced
  tomatoes, undrained
3 cups reduced-sodium fat-free beef broth
1 teaspoon each: dried oregano and mint leaves
½ teaspoon each: ground turmeric, coriander
12 ounces cooked, cubed beef eye of round
Salt and pepper, to taste

Per Serving:
Calories: 302
% of calories from fat: 7
Fat (gm): 2.6
Saturated fat (gm): 0.8
Cholesterol (mg): 27.5
Sodium (mg): 122
Protein (gm): 25.5
Carbohydrate (gm): 46.7

Exchanges:
Milk: 0.0
Vegetable: 3.0
Fruit: 0.0
Bread: 2.0
Meat: 1.5
Fat: 0.0

1. Sauté onion, bell pepper, zucchini, and garlic in lightly greased large saucepan until tender, about 5 minutes. Add remaining ingredients, except salt and pepper; heat to boiling. Reduce heat and simmer, covered, until lentils are just tender and stew is thickened, 20 to 30 minutes. Season to taste with salt and pepper.

BEEF AND ANCHO CHILI STEW

This stew has lots of delicious sauce, so serve with crusty warm rolls or tortillas.

8 servings

3 cups boiling water

4–6 ancho chilies, stems, seeds, and veins discarded

4 medium tomatoes, cut into wedges

2 pounds beef eye of round, fat trimmed, cubed (¾-inch)

1 large onion, chopped

2 cloves garlic, minced

1 teaspoon each: minced jalapeño chili, dried oregano leaves, crushed cumin seeds

2 tablespoons flour

Salt and pepper, to taste

Black Beans and Rice (see p. 334)

Per Serving:
Calories: 393
% of calories from fat: 31
Fat (gm): 13.8
Saturated fat (gm): 5.0
Cholesterol (mg): 67.8
Sodium (mg): 406
Protein (gm): 29.7
Carbohydrate (gm): 38.5

Exchanges:
Milk: 0.0
Vegetable: 2.0
Fruit: 0.0
Bread: 2.0
Meat: 3.0
Fat: 1.0

1. Pour boiling water over chilies in bowl; let stand until softened, about 10 minutes. Process chilies, water, and tomatoes in blender or food processor until smooth.

2. Sauté beef in lightly greased Dutch oven until browned, about 5 minutes. Add onion, garlic, jalapeño chili, and herbs; cook until onion is tender, about 5 minutes. Stir in flour; cook over medium heat 1 minute. Add ancho chili mixture; heat to boiling. Reduce heat and simmer, covered, until beef is tender, 45 to 60 minutes. Season to taste with salt and pepper; serve over rice

QUICK BEEF GOULASH

45 *In Hungary, this paprika seasoned stew is called "gulyas" and it's often served with dollops of sour cream.*

4 servings

12 ounces boneless beef round steak, fat trimmed, cubed (¾-inch)

1 teaspoon olive oil

3 large onions, cut into thin wedges

1 cup chopped portobello mushrooms

1 can (15 ounces) diced tomatoes, undrained

1 tablespoon paprika

1 teaspoon unsweetened cocoa

2 cups coarsely sliced cabbage

1 tablespoon caraway seeds

Salt and pepper, to taste

8 ounces medium egg noodles, cooked, warm

Per Serving:
Calories: 407
% of calories from fat: 17
Fat (gm): 7.7
Saturated fat (gm): 2
Cholesterol (mg): 90.9
Sodium (mg): 473
Protein (gm): 29.9
Carbohydrate (gm): 55.2

Exchanges:
Milk: 0.0
Vegetable: 2.0
Fruit: 0.0
Bread: 3.0
Meat: 2.0
Fat: 0.5

1. Sauté beef in oil in large saucepan until browned, about 5 minutes; add onions and mushrooms and sauté 5 minutes. Add tomatoes with liquid, paprika, and cocoa and heat to boiling; reduce heat and simmer, covered, until beef is tender, 45 to 60 minutes, adding cabbage and caraway seeds during last 10 minutes. Season to taste with salt and pepper; serve over noodles.

HUNGARIAN GOULASH

45

Hungarian goulash is oven-baked to tender goodness.

6 servings

2 pounds boneless beef round steak,
    fat trimmed, cubed

1 medium onion, finely chopped

1 teaspoon minced garlic

2 tablespoons flour

1½ teaspoons paprika

¼ teaspoon dried thyme leaves

1 bay leaf

1 can (14½ ounces) diced tomatoes, undrained

1 container (8 ounces) fat-free sour cream

Salt and pepper, to taste

12 ounces egg noodles, cooked, warm

Per Serving:
Calories: 471
% of calories from fat: 17
Fat (gm): 8.7
Saturated fat (gm): 2.9
Cholesterol (mg): 123.5
Sodium (mg): 367
Protein (gm): 44.6
Carbohydrate (gm): 50.5

Exchanges:
Milk: 0.0
Vegetable: 1.0
Fruit: 0.0
Bread: 3.0
Meat: 4.0
Fat: 0.0

1. Sauté beef, onion, and garlic in lightly greased Dutch oven; sprinkle with flour, paprika, and thyme and cook 1 minute. Stir in bay leaf and tomatoes with liquid; transfer to oven and bake, covered, at 325 degrees, until beef is tender, 1 to 1½ hours, stirring in sour cream during last 10 minutes. Season to taste with salt and pepper. Serve over noodles.

VARIATION

Three-Meat Goulash — Make recipe as above, using ¾ pound each cubed lean beef, pork, and veal in place of the beef round steak. Add 8 ounces sliced mushrooms, 1 teaspoon caraway seeds, and ½ teaspoon dried dill weed with the tomatoes.

BEEF BRAISED IN RED WINE

45

A good-quality Chianti works well in this traditional Italian recipe.

6 servings

1½ pounds boneless beef round steak, fat trimmed, cubed (1-inch)
1 tablespoon olive oil
1 cup each: sliced mushrooms, chopped onion, celery
1 large clove garlic, minced
2 tablespoons flour
1 cup each: reduced-sodium fat-free beef broth, dry red wine or water
1 can (15 ounces) reduced-sodium tomato sauce
12 baby carrots
6 medium potatoes, halved
1 teaspoon dried thyme leaves
2 large bay leaves
½ teaspoon dry mustard
Salt and pepper, to taste

Per Serving:
Calories: 366
% of calories from fat: 18
Fat (gm): 7.4
Saturated fat (gm): 2.2
Cholesterol (mg): 55.9
Sodium (mg): 115
Protein (gm): 31.2
Carbohydrate (gm): 36.9

Exchanges:
Milk: 0.0
Vegetable: 2.0
Fruit: 0.0
Bread: 2.0
Meat: 3.0
Fat: 0.0

1. Sauté beef in oil in Dutch oven until browned, about 5 minutes; remove from pan. Add mushrooms, onion, celery, and garlic to pan; cook 5 minutes. Stir in flour and cook 1 minute. Add beef, broth and remaining ingredients, except salt and pepper, and heat

to boiling; transfer to oven and bake, covered, at 350 degrees until beef is tender, about 1 hour. Season to taste with salt and pepper; discard bay leaves.

BEEF AND SWEET POTATO STEW

Apples give this hearty stew a touch of sweetness. Enjoy it in fall when apples are at their peak.

4 servings

1 pound boneless beef round steak, fat trimmed, cubed (¾-inch)

¼ cup all-purpose flour

1 large onion, cut into thin wedges

1 teaspoon olive oil

1¾ cups reduced-sodium fat-free beef broth

1¼ pounds sweet potatoes, peeled, cubed (½-inch)

1 teaspoon dried savory leaves

2 medium McIntosh apples, unpeeled, thickly sliced

½ cup frozen peas

Salt and pepper, to taste

Per Serving:
Calories: 442
% of calories from fat: 13
Fat (gm): 6.7
Saturated fat (gm): 2.1
Cholesterol (mg): 55.9
Sodium (mg): 197
Protein (gm): 34.2
Carbohydrate (gm): 62.3

Exchanges:
Milk: 0.0
Vegetable: 0.0
Fruit: 1.0
Bread: 3.0
Meat: 3.0
Fat: 0.0

1. Toss beef with flour; sauté beef and onion in oil in large saucepan until browned, 5 to 8 minutes. Add broth and heat to boiling; reduce heat and simmer, covered, 30 minutes. Add sweet potatoes and savory; simmer, covered, until potatoes are tender, 15 to 20 minutes, adding apples and peas during last 5 minutes. Season to taste with salt and pepper.

COUNTRY BEEF STEW

Serve this delicious long simmered stew over noodles or rice.

4 servings

2 pounds cubed lean beef for stew, fat trimmed

1 cup each: chopped onion, celery

3 cloves garlic, minced

2½ cups reduced-sodium beef broth

½ cup dry red wine or reduced-sodium beef broth

2 tablespoons tomato paste

½ teaspoon each: dried thyme and rosemary leaves

1 large bay leaf

2 cups each: cubed unpeeled potato, sliced carrots (1-inch)

1 cup cubed parsnip or turnip

½ cup frozen peas

¼ cup all-purpose flour

½ cup cold water

Salt and pepper, to taste

Per Serving:
Calories: 326
% of calories from fat: 16
Fat (gm): 5.8
Saturated fat (gm): 2
Cholesterol (mg): 70.9
Sodium (mg): 171
Protein (gm): 33.5
Carbohydrate (gm): 29.6

Exchanges:
Milk: 0.0
Vegetable: 2.0
Fruit: 0.0
Bread: 1.5
Meat: 3.0
Fat: 0.0

1. Sauté beef in lightly greased large saucepan until browned, 5 to 8 minutes. Add onion, celery, and garlic; sauté until tender, about 5 minutes. Add broth, wine, tomato paste, and herbs; heat to boiling. Reduce heat and simmer, covered, until beef is tender, 1½ to 2 hours, adding remaining vegetables during last 30 minutes. Heat stew to boiling; stir in combined flour and water, stirring until thickened, about 1 minute. Discard bay leaf; season to taste with salt and pepper.

CHILI STEW

A squeeze of lime adds a fresh flavor to this spicy favorite.

6 servings

1 pound lean ground beef

1 cup coarsely chopped onion

½ cup coarsely chopped red bell pepper

½ jalapeño chili, finely chopped

2 cloves garlic, minced

1 can (15 ounces) each: reduced-sodium chunky tomato sauce, rinsed, drained red kidney beans

3 cups reduced-sodium tomato juice

2 cups each: chopped celery, cubed butternut squash

1 cup each: cubed zucchini, sliced mushrooms

1½ teaspoons each: chili powder, ground cumin

Salt and pepper, to taste

6 lime wedges

Per Serving:
Calories: 317
% of calories from fat: 30
Fat (gm): 10.8
Saturated fat (gm): 4
Cholesterol (mg): 46.6
Sodium (mg): 357
Protein (gm): 21.2
Carbohydrate (gm): 36.1

Exchanges:
Milk: 0.0
Vegetable: 1.0
Fruit: 0.0
Bread: 2.0
Meat: 2.0
Fat: 1.0

1. Cook ground beef in lightly greased Dutch oven until browned, about 8 minutes; add onion, bell pepper, jalapeño chili, and garlic. Sauté until tender, 8 to 10 minutes. Add remaining ingredients, except salt, pepper, and lime wedges; heat to boiling. Reduce heat and simmer, covered, until vegetables are tender, about 15 minutes; cook, uncovered, until stew is desired consistency, 15 to 20 minutes. Season to taste with salt and pepper; squeeze lime wedge into each bowl of stew.

GROUND BEEF AND VEGETABLE STROGANOFF

45

Fat-free half-and-half and sour cream contribute rich flavor and creamy texture to this favorite.

8 servings

1½ pounds lean ground beef

2 medium onions, thinly sliced

2 cloves garlic, minced

12 ounces each: sliced mixed wild mushrooms (shiitake, oyster, enoki, or cremini), broccoli florets

¼ cup dry red wine or beef broth

1 cup fat-free half-and-half or fat-free milk

2 tablespoons flour

1½ teaspoons Dijon mustard

1 cup fat-free sour cream

½ teaspoon dried dill weed

Salt and pepper, to taste

16 ounces noodles, cooked, warm

Per Serving:
Calories: 467
% of calories from fat: 22
Fat (gm): 11.3
Saturated fat (gm): 4.1
Cholesterol (mg): 52.9
Sodium (mg): 468
Protein (gm): 27.7
Carbohydrate (gm): 61.5

Exchanges:
Milk: 0.0
Vegetable: 3.0
Fruit: 0.0
Bread: 3.0
Meat: 2.0
Fat: 1.0

1. Cook ground beef in large skillet until browned, about 10 minutes; remove from skillet. Add onions, garlic, and mushrooms to skillet and sauté until tender, about 5 minutes. Return ground beef to skillet; add broccoli and wine and heat to boiling. Reduce heat and simmer, covered, until broccoli is tender, 8 to 10 minutes. Heat to boiling; stir in combined half-and-half, flour, and mustard, stirring until thickened, about 1 minute. Reduce heat to low; stir in sour cream and dill weed and cook 1 to 2 minutes. Season to taste with salt and pepper; serve over noodles.

VEAL STEW SAUVIGNON

45 *This fragrant stew is also delicious served over an aromatic rice, such as basmati or jasmine.*

4 servings

1 pound boneless veal cutlets, cut into strips
   (2 x ½-inch)
2 teaspoons olive oil
1 medium onion, thinly sliced
1 teaspoon minced garlic
1 cup fat-free chicken broth
½ cup sauvignon blanc or other dry white wine
1 tablespoon tomato paste
2 cups small cauliflower florets
1 teaspoon dried marjoram leaves
2 cups torn Swiss chard leaves
Salt and pepper, to taste
8 ounces fettuccine, cooked, warm

Per Serving:
Calories: 427
% of calories from fat: 15
Fat (gm): 6.9
Saturated fat (gm): 1.6
Cholesterol (mg): 90.5
Sodium (mg): 318
Protein (gm): 33.4
Carbohydrate (gm): 51

Exchanges:
Milk: 0.0
Vegetable: 1.0
Fruit: 0.0
Bread: 3.0
Meat: 3.0
Fat: 0.0

1. Sauté veal in oil in large saucepan until lightly browned, 2 to 3 minutes; add onion and garlic and sauté 2 to 3 minutes. Add chicken broth, wine, tomato paste, cauliflower, and marjoram and heat to boiling; reduce heat and simmer, covered, until veal and cauliflower are tender, about 10 minutes. Stir in Swiss chard; cook until wilted, 1 to 2 minutes. Season to taste with salt and pepper. Serve over fettuccine.

VEAL AND VEGETABLE PAPRIKASH

45 *Your preference of hot or sweet paprika can be used in this recipe.*

6 servings

1½ pounds veal scallopine, cut into strips (1-inch)

1 tablespoon olive oil

2 cups thinly sliced cabbage

1 cup each: sliced onion, zucchini, carrots,
    green bell peppers, chopped tomato

1½ cups sliced mushrooms

3 tablespoons flour

1 tablespoon paprika

¾ cup reduced-sodium chicken broth

½ cup fat-free sour cream

Salt and pepper, to taste

12 ounces noodles, cooked, warm

Per Serving:
Calories: 419
% of calories from fat: 20
Fat (gm): 9.1
Saturated fat (gm): 3.2
Cholesterol (mg): 138.5
Sodium (mg): 264
Protein (gm): 33.5
Carbohydrate (gm): 49.8

Exchanges:
Milk: 0.0
Vegetable: 2.0
Fruit: 0.0
Bread: 3.0
Meat: 3.0
Fat: 0.0

1. Sauté veal in oil in large skillet until browned, about 5 minutes; remove from skillet. Add vegetables to skillet and sauté until tender, 8 to 10 minutes. Stir in flour and paprika; cook 1 minute. Stir in veal and broth and heat to boiling; boil, stirring until thickened, about 1 minute. Stir in sour cream; season to taste with salt and pepper. Serve over noodles.

CARIBBEAN GINGER BEAN AND PORK STEW

Fresh gingerroot accents the flavor contrasts in this colorful stew.

6 servings

12 ounces boneless pork loin, fat trimmed, cubed
    (¾-inch)
1 tablespoon olive oil, chopped gingerroot
1 cup each: chopped onion, red bell pepper
2 teaspoons each: minced garlic, jalapeño chili
1 can (15 ounces) each: black beans, black-eyed peas,
    rinsed, drained
¾ cup fresh or frozen cut okra
1 cup each: orange juice, jalapeño chili jelly or
    orange marmalade
½ teaspoon dried thyme leaves
1 can (11 ounces) Mandarin orange segments, drained
Salt and pepper, to taste
3 cups cooked brown or white rice

Per Serving:
Calories: 369
% of calories from fat: 15
Fat (gm): 6.8
Saturated fat (gm): 1.6
Cholesterol (mg): 24.6
Sodium (mg): 704
Protein (gm): 18.9
Carbohydrate (gm): 66.3

Exchanges:
Milk: 0.0
Vegetable: 0.0
Fruit: 1.0
Bread: 3.0
Meat: 2.0
Fat: 0.0

1. Sauté pork in oil in large skillet until browned, 5 to 8 minutes.
Add gingerroot, onion, bell pepper, garlic, and jalapeño chili and
sauté until tender, about 5 minutes. Add black beans, black-eyed
peas, okra, orange juice, jelly, and thyme; heat to boiling. Reduce
heat and simmer, covered, until okra is tender, about 10 minutes.
Add orange segments; cook 1 to 2 minutes. Season to taste with
salt and pepper; serve over rice.

MEDITERRANEAN CURRIED STEW

*Taste buds will be tantalized by the melding of cinnamon-spice and curry
flavors this stew offers. Brightly colored Yellow Salsa Rice completes the
dish perfectly.*

6 servings

1 pound pork tenderloin or beef eye of round, cubed (¾-inch)
2 tablespoons olive oil
1 small eggplant, unpeeled, cubed (1-inch)

3 small onions, quartered

½ cup each: chopped green bell pepper, celery

2 cloves garlic, minced

1 tablespoon flour

½ teaspoon each: ground cinnamon, nutmeg,
curry powder, cumin

⅛ teaspoon cayenne pepper

2 cans (14½ ounces, each) reduced-sodium diced
tomatoes, undrained

½ cup reduced-sodium vegetable broth

1 cup each: cubed zucchini, butternut squash

1 can (15 ounces) garbanzo beans, rinsed, drained

Salt and pepper, to taste

Yellow Salsa Rice (see p. 351)

3 tablespoons each: raisins, toasted slivered almonds

Per Serving:
Calories: 446
% of calories from fat: 22
Fat (gm): 11.1
Saturated fat (gm): 2
Cholesterol (mg): 43.8
Sodium (mg): 427
Protein (gm): 25.3
Carbohydrate (gm): 61.3

Exchanges:
Milk: 0.0
Vegetable: 3.0
Fruit: 0.0
Bread: 3.0
Meat: 2.0
Fat: 1.0

1. Sauté pork in oil in large saucepan until browned, about 5 minutes. Add eggplant, onions, bell pepper, celery, and garlic to saucepan and cook for 10 minutes, or until eggplant is beginning to brown. Stir in flour, spices, and cayenne pepper; cook 1 minute. Add tomatoes with liquid, broth, squash, and beans; heat to boiling. Reduce heat and simmer, covered, until vegetables are tender, 10 to 15 minutes. Season to taste with salt and pepper. Serve over Turmeric Rice and sprinkle with raisins and almonds.

PORK TENDERLOIN WITH GREMOLATA

45 *Gremolata, a refreshing blend of garlic, lemon peel, and parsley, is often used to flavor stews and soups.*

4 servings

1 pound pork tenderloin, cubed (1-inch)

1 teaspoon olive oil

4 shallots, thinly sliced

1 cup reduced-sodium fat-free beef broth

2 medium potatoes, cubed

1 can (15 ounces) diced tomatoes, undrained

Salt and pepper, to taste

Gremolata (recipe follows)

1. Sauté pork in oil in large saucepan until lightly browned; add shallots and sauté 3 to 4 minutes. Stir in broth and heat to boiling; reduce heat and simmer, covered, 10 minutes. Add potatoes and tomatoes with liquid; simmer, covered, until potatoes are tender, about 15 minutes. Season to taste with salt and pepper. Pass Gremolata to stir into stew.

Gremolata

Makes about ½ cup

1 cup packed parsley sprigs
1–2 tablespoons grated lemon zest
4 large cloves garlic, minced

1. Process all ingredients in food processor until finely minced.

Per Serving:
Calories: 289
% of calories from fat: 17
Fat (gm): 5.5
Saturated fat (gm): 1.6
Cholesterol (mg): 65.7
Sodium (mg): 523
Protein (gm): 28.6
Carbohydrate (gm): 31.2

Exchanges:
Milk: 0.0
Vegetable: 0.0
Fruit: 0.0
Bread: 2.0
Meat: 3.0
Fat: 0.0

PORK AND SQUASH RAGOUT

45 *Stews don't have to be long-cooked to be good—this delicious stew is ready to eat in less than 45 minutes. Serve with Garlic Bread (see p. 497).*

4 servings

1 pound pork tenderloin, cubed
1½ cups each: chopped onions, green bell peppers
2 teaspoons minced roasted garlic
1 tablespoon flour
2 cups cubed, peeled, butternut or acorn squash
2 cans (14½ ounces each) reduced-sodium diced tomatoes, undrained
1 can (15 ounces) red kidney beans, rinsed, drained
¾ teaspoon dried Italian seasoning
Salt and pepper, to taste

Per Serving:
Calories: 344
% of calories from fat: 10
Fat (gm): 3.8
Saturated fat (gm): 1.3
Cholesterol (mg): 73.1
Sodium (mg): 504
Protein (gm): 33.2
Carbohydrate (gm): 46.2

Exchanges:
Milk: 0.0
Vegetable: 0.0
Fruit: 0.0
Bread: 3.0
Meat: 3.0
Fat: 0.0

1. Sauté pork in lightly greased large saucepan until browned, 8 to 10 minutes; remove from skillet. Add onions, bell peppers, and garlic and sauté until tender, about 8 minutes. Stir in flour; cook 1 minute. Add pork and remaining ingredients, except salt and pepper. Heat to boiling; reduce heat and simmer until pork is cooked, 15 to 20 minutes. Season to taste with salt and pepper.

SAVORY STEWED PORK AND CHORIZO

This versatile dish is often served rolled in a tortilla or used as a topping for tostadas.

6 servings

12 ounces pork tenderloin, cubed (1-inch)

Chorizo (see p. 154)

1 small onion, sliced

1 clove garlic, minced

2 large tomatoes, chopped

¼ teaspoon each: dried oregano and thyme leaves

1 bay leaf

2–3 pickled jalapeño chilies, finely chopped

1 tablespoon pickled jalapeño chili juice

Salt and pepper, to taste

4 cups cooked rice, warm

Per Serving:
Calories: 298
% of calories from fat: 15
Fat (gm): 4.7
Saturated fat (gm): 1.5
Cholesterol (mg): 65.7
Sodium (mg): 313
Protein (gm): 27.2
Carbohydrate (gm): 35

Exchanges:
Milk: 0.0
Vegetable: 0.0
Fruit: 0.0
Bread: 2.0
Meat: 3.0
Fat: 0.0

1. Simmer pork in 2 inches water in medium saucepan, covered, until tender, 20 to 30 minutes. Cool; drain, reserving ½ cup broth. Finely shred pork.

2. Make Chorizo, but do not make patties. Cook Chorizo in lightly greased large skillet over medium heat until browned, crumbling with a fork. Add onion and garlic; sauté 2 to 3 minutes. Add tomatoes and herbs and cook over medium heat 5 minutes, stirring occasionally. Add pork, reserved broth, jalapeño chilies, and jalapeño juice to skillet. Cook, uncovered, over medium heat, about 10 minutes, stirring occasionally (mixture should be moist). Discard bay leaf; season to taste with salt and pepper. Serve over rice.

ROSEMARY LAMB STEW WITH SWEET POTATOES

The pairing of rosemary and lamb is classic, distinctive, and delightful.

4 servings

1 pound boneless lamb shoulder, fat trimmed, cubed (¾-inch)

1 teaspoon olive oil

1 large onion, cut into thin wedges

2 tablespoons chopped fresh or 1 teaspoon dried rosemary leaves

3 cups reduced-sodium fat-free beef broth

2 bay leaves

1¼ pounds sweet potatoes, peeled, cubed (¾-inch)

1½ cups cut green beans

Salt and pepper, to taste

Per Serving:
Calories: 285
% of calories from fat: 23
Fat (gm): 7.4
Saturated fat (gm): 2.5
Cholesterol (mg): 47.2
Sodium (mg): 171
Protein (gm): 20.6
Carbohydrate (gm): 34.7

Exchanges:
Milk: 0.0
Vegetable: 1.0
Fruit: 0.0
Bread: 2.0
Meat: 2.0
Fat: 0.0

1. Sauté lamb in oil in large saucepan until lightly browned, about 8 minutes. Add onion and rosemary; sauté 5 minutes. Add broth and bay leaves; heat to boiling. Reduce heat and simmer, covered, until lamb is tender, 1 to 1½ hours, adding sweet potatoes and green beans during last 15 minutes. Discard bay leaves; season to taste with salt and pepper.

LAMB AND TURNIP STEW WITH CILANTRO

This homestyle lamb dish has been updated with fresh sage and cilantro.

4 servings

1 pound boneless lamb shoulder, fat trimmed, cubed (1-inch)

1 medium onion, chopped

1 tablespoon minced garlic

1 teaspoon olive oil

¼ cup all-purpose flour

2½ cups reduced-sodium tomato juice

½ cup dry red wine or beef broth

1 tablespoon fresh or 1 teaspoon dried sage leaves

2 cups cubed potatoes

1½ cups cubed turnips

Salt and pepper, to taste

½ cup chopped cilantro

1. Sauté lamb, onion, and garlic in oil in large saucepan until browned, about 8 minutes; stir in flour and cook 1 minute. Add tomato juice, wine, and sage and heat to boiling; reduce heat and simmer, covered, until lamb is tender 1 to 1½ hours, adding vegetables during last 20 minutes. Season to taste with salt and pepper; stir in cilantro.

Per Serving:
Calories: 269
% of calories from fat: 24
Fat (gm): 7.3
Saturated fat (gm): 2.4
Cholesterol (mg): 47.2
Sodium (mg): 81
Protein (gm): 17.4
Carbohydrate (gm): 30

Exchanges:
Milk: 0.0
Vegetable: 0.0
Fruit: 0.0
Bread: 2.0
Meat: 2.0
Fat: 0.0

LAMB AND VEGETABLE TAJINE

A staple of Moroccan cuisine, tajines are traditionally cooked in earthenware pots. Serve with Pita Bread (see p. 499).

6 servings

½ cup each: chopped onion, sliced celery

1–2 teaspoons each: minced gingerroot, garlic

1 cinnamon stick

2 teaspoons each: paprika, ground cumin, coriander

12–16 ounces cooked lean lamb or beef, cubed

2 cans (14½ ounces each) reduced-sodium diced tomatoes, undrained

½ cup reduced-sodium vegetable broth

1 can (16 ounces) garbanzo beans, rinsed, drained

1 cup each: chopped butternut squash, turnip

1 large carrot, sliced

1½ cups whole green beans, halved

1 cup pitted prunes

¼ cup pitted small black olives

Salt and pepper, to taste

4½ cups cooked couscous, warm

Per Serving:
Calories: 466
% of calories from fat: 15
Fat (gm): 8.4
Saturated fat (gm): 2
Cholesterol (mg): 38.9
Sodium (mg): 580
Protein (gm): 24.8
Carbohydrate (gm): 76.9

Exchanges:
Milk: 0.0
Vegetable: 3.0
Fruit: 0.0
Bread: 4.0
Meat: 2.0
Fat: 0.0

1. Sauté onion, celery, gingerroot, and garlic in lightly greased Dutch oven until onion is tender. Stir in spices; cook 1 minute. Add remaining ingredients, except salt, pepper, and couscous. Bake, covered, at 350 degrees, until vegetables are tender, 20 to 30 minutes. Season to taste with salt and pepper; serve over couscous.

CHICKEN STEW WITH PARSLEY DUMPLINGS

For variation, omit the dumplings and serve this savory stew over noodles or Real Mashed Potatoes (see p. 628).

6 servings

1 cup chopped onion

3 carrots, thickly sliced (¾-inch)

½ cup sliced celery

3 cups reduced-sodium chicken broth, divided

1½ cups cubed boneless, skinless chicken breast

¾ teaspoon dried sage leaves

½ cup frozen peas

¼ cup all-purpose flour

Salt and pepper, to taste

Parsley Dumplings (recipe follows)

Per Serving:
Calories: 233
% of calories from fat: 20
Fat (gm): 5.1
Saturated fat (gm): 1.4
Cholesterol (mg): 35.5
Sodium (mg): 383
Protein (gm): 19.2
Carbohydrate (gm): 26.7

Exchanges:
Milk: 0.0
Vegetable: 2.0
Fruit: 0.0
Bread: 1.0
Meat: 1.5
Fat: 0.5

1. Sauté onion, carrots, and celery in lightly greased large saucepan 5 minutes. Add 2½ cups chicken broth, chicken, and sage; heat to boiling. Reduce heat and simmer, covered, until chicken is cooked and vegetables are tender, 10 to 15 minutes; stir in peas. Heat to boiling; stir in combined flour and remaining ½ cup chicken broth, stirring until thickened, about 1 minute. Season to taste with salt and pepper.

2. Spoon dumpling dough into 6 mounds on top of boiling stew; reduce heat and simmer, covered, 10 minutes. Simmer, uncovered, 10 minutes.

Parsley Dumplings
Makes 6

¾ cup all-purpose flour
1 teaspoon baking powder
¼ teaspoon salt
1½ tablespoons vegetable shortening
⅓ cup 2% reduced-fat milk
2 tablespoons finely chopped parsley

1. Combine flour, baking powder, and salt in small bowl. Cut in shortening with pastry blender until mixture resembles coarse crumbs. Stir in milk to make a soft dough; stir in parsley.

CHICKEN AND PORK STEW WITH FRUIT

Enjoy flavor accents of tropical fruit, sweet cinnamon, and piquant ancho chili in this stew; serve over rice or couscous.

6 servings

2 tablespoons slivered almonds
1 tablespoon sesame seeds
1 -inch piece cinnamon stick
3 ancho chilies, seeds, and veins discarded, coarsely chopped
2 medium tomatoes, coarsely chopped
1 can (14½ ounces) reduced-sodium fat-free chicken broth, divided
12 ounces each: pork tenderloin and boneless skinless chicken breast, cubed (1½-inch)
1 cup each: fresh or canned pineapple chunks, sliced ripe plantain, cubed peeled jicama
Salt and pepper, to taste

Per Serving:
Calories: 239
% of calories from fat: 22
Fat (gm): 5.9
Saturated fat (gm): 1.4
Cholesterol (mg): 67.2
Sodium (mg): 81
Protein (gm): 28.1
Carbohydrate (gm): 19.6

Exchanges:
Milk: 0.0
Vegetable: 1.0
Fruit: 1.0
Bread: 0.0
Meat: 3.0
Fat: 0.0

1. Cook almonds, sesame seeds, and cinnamon in lightly greased medium skillet over medium heat until browned, 3 to 4 minutes; remove from skillet. Add chilies and tomatoes to skillet and cook over medium heat until chilies are soft, 3 to 4 minutes. Process almond and chili mixtures and 1 cup broth in blender or food processor until smooth.

2. Sauté pork and chicken in lightly greased large saucepan until browned, about 5 minutes. Add chili mixture and remaining broth and heat to boiling. Reduce heat and simmer, covered, until meats are tender, about 30 minutes, adding fruit and jicama during last 10 minutes. Season to taste with salt and pepper.

CHICKEN VERONIQUE

45 | *No one will guess this elegant entrée is so easy to prepare!*

4 servings

1 cup sliced mushrooms

2 tablespoons each: sliced green onions, vegetable oil

1 pound boneless, skinless chicken breast, cubed

1 tablespoon flour

¼ cup dry white wine or reduced-sodium chicken broth

1 cup each: reduced-sodium fat-free chicken broth, halved seedless green grapes

1 tablespoon drained capers

Salt and pepper, to taste

2 cups cooked rice, warm

Per Serving:
Calories: 341
% of calories from fat: 27
Fat (gm): 10.1
Saturated fat (gm): 1.8
Cholesterol (mg): 69
Sodium (mg): 184
Protein (gm): 29.6
Carbohydrate (gm): 28.8

Exchanges:
Milk: 0.0
Vegetable: 0.0
Fruit: 0.5
Bread: 1.5
Meat: 3.0
Fat: 0.5

1. Sauté mushrooms and green onions in oil in large skillet until tender, about 5 minutes; add chicken and sauté until browned, about 5 minutes. Sprinkle with flour and cook 1 minute. Stir in white wine and broth; heat to boiling. Reduce heat and simmer, covered, until chicken is cooked, 5 to 8 minutes. Stir in grapes and capers; season to taste with salt and pepper. Serve over rice.

45-MINUTE PREPARATION TIP: Begin cooking rice before preparing the rest of the recipe.

CHICKEN ATHENOS

45 *Cinnamon, lemon, and feta cheese give this tomato-based stew the signature flavors of Greece.*

4 servings

1 pound boneless, skinless chicken breast, cubed (¾-inch)

1 teaspoon olive oil

1 can (14 ounces) reduced-sodium stewed tomatoes, undrained

1 tablespoon lemon juice

2 teaspoons minced garlic

1 each: cinnamon stick, bay leaf

¼ cup dry sherry or reduced-sodium chicken broth

Salt and pepper, to taste

8 ounces egg noodles, cooked, warm

¼ cup (1 ounce) crumbled feta cheese

Per Serving:
Calories: 412
% of calories from fat: 17
Fat (gm): 7.9
Saturated fat (gm): 2.5
Cholesterol (mg): 124.2
Sodium (mg): 370
Protein (gm): 34.4
Carbohydrate (gm): 46

Exchanges:
Milk: 0.0
Vegetable: 2.0
Fruit: 0.0
Bread: 2.0
Meat: 4.0
Fat: 0.0

1. Sauté chicken in oil in large saucepan until lightly browned. Add tomatoes with liquid, lemon juice, garlic, cinnamon stick, bay leaf, and sherry. Heat to boiling; reduce heat and simmer, covered, until chicken is cooked, about 15 minutes. Season to taste with salt and pepper; discard bay leaf and cinnamon stick. Serve over noodles; sprinkle with cheese.

GINGER-ORANGE CHICKEN AND SQUASH STEW

Any winter squash, such as acorn, butternut, or Hubbard, is appropriate for this orange and ginger accented stew; sweet potatoes can be used too.

6 servings

1 pound boneless, skinless chicken breast, cubed

1 cup each: coarsely chopped onions, green bell peppers

2 cloves garlic, minced

1 tablespoon olive oil

3 cups cubed, peeled winter yellow squash

2 medium Idaho potatoes, peeled, cubed

1 can (14½ ounces) reduced-sodium diced tomatoes, undrained

2 cups reduced-sodium fat-free chicken broth

½ cup orange juice

1 tablespoon grated orange zest

½ teaspoon ground ginger

½ cup fat-free sour cream

Salt and pepper, to taste

4 cups cooked noodles or brown basmati rice, warm

Per Serving:
Calories: 425
% of calories from fat: 13
Fat (gm): 6.1
Saturated fat (gm): 1.2
Cholesterol (mg): 81.2
Sodium (mg): 162
Protein (gm): 30
Carbohydrate (gm): 60.4

Exchanges:
Milk: 0.0
Vegetable: 3.0
Fruit: 0.0
Bread: 3.0
Meat: 2.0
Fat: 0.0

1. Sauté chicken, onions, bell peppers, and garlic in oil in large saucepan until chicken is browned and vegetables are tender, 8 to 10 minutes. Add squash, potatoes, tomatoes with liquid, broth, orange juice and zest, and ginger; heat to boiling. Reduce heat and simmer, uncovered, 30 minutes. Reduce heat to low and stir in sour cream; season to taste with salt and pepper. Serve over noodles.

SWEET-SOUR CHICKEN AND VEGETABLE STEW

Chicken and vegetables are simmered in cider and seasoned with honey and vinegar for a refreshing sweet-sour flavor.

6 servings

1 pound boneless, skinless chicken breast, cubed

½ cup each: chopped shallots, red bell pepper

2 cloves garlic, minced

1 can (14½ ounces) reduced-sodium diced
tomatoes, undrained

1 cup apple cider or apple juice

1½ tablespoons each: honey, cider vinegar

1 bay leaf

¼ teaspoon ground nutmeg

2 cups cubed peeled winter yellow squash
(butternut or acorn)

1 cup each: cubed peeled Idaho and sweet potatoes,
peeled tart apples, and whole kernel corn

Salt and pepper, to taste

4 cups cooked basmati rice, warm

Per Serving:
Calories: 373
% of calories from fat: 4
Fat (gm): 1.8
Saturated fat (gm): 0.3
Cholesterol (mg): 43.8
Sodium (mg): 85
Protein (gm): 23.3
Carbohydrate (gm): 64.1

Exchanges:
Milk: 0.0
Vegetable: 0.0
Fruit: 0.0
Bread: 4.0
Meat: 2.0
Fat: 0.0

1. Sauté chicken, shallots, bell pepper, and garlic in lightly greased large saucepan until chicken is browned, 6 to 8 minutes. Add remaining ingredients, except corn, salt, pepper, and rice; heat to boiling. Reduce heat and simmer, covered, until vegetables are tender, about 15 minutes, adding apples and corn during last 5 minutes. Discard bay leaf and season to taste with salt and pepper; serve over rice.

GARDEN VEGETABLE AND CHICKEN STEW

45 *Take advantage of your garden's bounty with this quick and easy stew.*

8 servings

2 pounds skinless chicken breast halves, cubed
(1½-inch)

2 medium onions, chopped

4 ounces each: sliced shiitake, cremini mushrooms

1 small jalapeño chili, finely chopped

1 tablespoon flour

2 cups each: reduced-sodium fat-free chicken broth,
chopped tomatoes

1½ cups each: cubed turnips or parsnips, sliced
zucchini, baby carrots

1 bay leaf

½ cup loosely packed cilantro leaves

Salt and pepper, to taste

4 cups cooked couscous, warm

Per Serving:
Calories: 472
% of calories from fat: 5
Fat (gm): 2.8
Saturated fat (gm): 0.6
Cholesterol (mg): 88
Sodium (mg): 294
Protein (gm): 45.4
Carbohydrate (gm): 65.0

Exchanges:
Milk: 0.0
Vegetable: 0.0
Fruit: 0.0
Bread: 4.0
Meat: 4.0
Fat: 0.0

1. Sauté chicken in lightly greased large skillet until browned, about 5 minutes; remove from skillet. Add onions, mushrooms, and jalapeño chili to skillet; sauté until tender, about 5 minutes. Stir in flour; cook 1 minute. Return chicken to skillet; add broth, remaining vegetables, and bay leaf. Heat to boiling; reduce heat and simmer, covered, until vegetables are tender, about 15 minutes. Stir in cilantro; discard bay leaf and season to taste with salt and pepper. Serve with couscous.

45-MINUTE PREPARATION TIP: Cook couscous while the stew is simmering.

SWEET-AND-SOUR ISLAND STEW

45 *Sweet-and-sour flavors team with chicken, pineapple, and beans for this island-inspired dish—delicious with jasmine rice or couscous.*

6 servings

1½ pounds chicken tenders, halved

1 tablespoon vegetable oil

3 cups frozen stir-fry pepper blend

2 teaspoons each: minced garlic, gingerroot, jalapeño chili

3 cups reduced-sodium fat-free chicken broth

1 can (20 ounces) unsweetened pineapple chunks, drained, juice reserved

1 can (15 ounces) black beans, rinsed, drained

2 tablespoons each: light brown sugar, apple cider vinegar

2–3 teaspoons curry powder

2 tablespoons cornstarch

Salt and pepper, to taste

Per Serving:
Calories: 288
% of calories from fat: 12
Fat (gm): 3.9
Saturated fat (gm): 0.3
Cholesterol (mg): 48.2
Sodium (mg): 537
Protein (gm): 29.7
Carbohydrate (gm): 34.7

Exchanges:
Milk: 0.0
Vegetable: 1.0
Fruit: 0.5
Bread: 1.0
Meat: 3.0
Fat: 0.0

1. Cook chicken in oil in large skillet over medium heat until browned, about 8 minutes; remove from skillet. Add pepper blend, garlic, gingerroot, and jalapeño chili to skillet; sauté 5 minutes. Stir in chicken and remaining ingredients, except reserved pineapple juice, cornstarch, salt, and pepper; heat to boiling. Stir in combined cornstarch and reserved pineapple juice, stirring until thickened, about 1 minute. Season to taste with salt and pepper.

CHICKEN FRICASSEE

Cloves and bay leaf add a flavor update to this dish; traditional herbs, rosemary and thyme can be substituted.

6 servings

6 skinless chicken breast halves (6 ounces each)

1 cup each: onion wedges, sliced carrots, celery

2 cloves garlic, minced

3 tablespoons flour

2 cans (14½ ounces each) reduced-sodium fat-free chicken broth

16 whole cloves, tied in cheesecloth

2 bay leaves

1 teaspoon lemon juice

½ teaspoon each: sugar, salt

¼ teaspoon pepper

12 ounces fettuccine, cooked, warm

Per Serving:
Calories: 361
% of calories from fat: 13
Fat (gm): 5.1
Saturated fat (gm): 0.9
Cholesterol (mg): 78.6
Sodium (mg): 401
Protein (gm): 35.9
Carbohydrate (gm): 41.5

Exchanges:
Milk: 0.0
Vegetable: 2.0
Fruit: 0.0
Bread: 2.0
Meat: 3.0
Fat: 0.0

1. Cook chicken in lightly greased large skillet over medium heat until browned, about 8 minutes. Remove from skillet. Add vegetables and garlic to skillet; sauté 5 minutes. Stir in flour and cook 1 minute. Return chicken to skillet. Add remaining ingredients, except pasta; heat to boiling. Reduce heat and simmer, covered, until chicken is tender, about 20 minutes; simmer, uncovered, until sauce is thickened to medium consistency, about 10 minutes. Discard cloves and bay leaves. Serve with fettuccine.

CHICKEN PAPRIKASH

Lean veal can be substituted for the chicken in this recipe.

4 servings

1 pound boneless, skinless chicken breast, cubed (¾-inch)

1 tablespoon margarine or butter

1 cup chopped onion

4 cloves garlic, minced

2 tablespoons flour

½ cup reduced-sodium chicken broth

¼ cup dry white wine or chicken broth

1 cup chopped tomato

1 teaspoon paprika

½ cup fat-free sour cream

Salt and white pepper, to taste

3 cups cooked noodles, warm

Per Serving:
Calories: 416
% of calories from fat: 18
Fat (gm): 8.4
Saturated fat (gm): 1.4
Cholesterol (mg): 69
Sodium (mg): 139
Protein (gm): 35.9
Carbohydrate (gm): 47.9

Exchanges:
Milk: 0.0
Vegetable: 1.0
Fruit: 0.0
Bread: 3.0
Meat: 3.0
Fat: 0.0

1. Sauté chicken in margarine in large saucepan until browned, 8 to 10 minutes; add onion and garlic and sauté 5 minutes. Stir in flour and cook 1 minute. Add chicken broth, wine, tomato, and paprika and heat to boiling; reduce heat and simmer, covered, until chicken is tender, 15 to 20 minutes. Stir in sour cream and cook, uncovered, 2 to 3 minutes. Season to taste with salt and white pepper; serve over noodles.

CHICKEN CACCIATORE

This "Hunter's Stew," of Italian origin, was made from any game brought back from the day's hunting and would vary slightly from kitchen to kitchen.

4 servings

8 ounces each: boneless, skinless chicken
   breast, thighs

2 teaspoons dried oregano leaves

½ teaspoon each: garlic powder, salt, pepper

3 cups quartered mushrooms

1 cup each: chopped onion, green bell pepper

6 cloves garlic, minced

2 cans (14½ ounces each) reduced-sodium tomatoes,
   undrained, coarsely chopped

½ cup dry red wine or water

1 bay leaf

4 teaspoons cornstarch

¼ cup water

Salt and pepper, to taste

3 cups cooked noodles, warm

Per Serving:
Calories: 411
% of calories from fat: 15
Fat (gm): 7.2
Saturated fat (gm): 1.7
Cholesterol (mg): 65.5
Sodium (mg): 199
Protein (gm): 30.9
Carbohydrate (gm): 53.7

Exchanges:
Milk: 0.0
Vegetable: 4.0
Fruit: 0.0
Bread: 2.0
Meat: 3.0
Fat: 0.0

1. Cut chicken breast into large pieces; sprinkle chicken with combined seasonings. Sauté chicken in lightly greased large Dutch oven until browned, 5 to 8 minutes; remove from pan. Add mushrooms, onion, bell pepper, and garlic to pan; sauté 3 to 4 minutes. Add chicken, tomatoes with liquid, wine, and bay leaf; heat to boiling. Reduce heat and simmer, covered, until chicken is tender, about 30 minutes. Heat to boiling; stir in combined cornstarch and water, stirring until thickened, about 1 minute. Discard bay leaf; season to taste with salt and pepper and serve over noodles.

HOMESTYLE TURKEY STEW

45   *A great family meal that's very fast to prepare!*

4 servings

12 ounces boneless, skinless turkey breast, cubed
   (¾-inch)
2 medium onions, cut into thin wedges
4 ounces mushrooms, halved
2 teaspoons olive oil
1 cup each: sliced carrots, cubed unpeeled potatoes
1 can (14½ ounces) reduced-sodium fat-free
   chicken broth
1 teaspoon each: dried thyme leaves, celery seeds
1 cup frozen peas
Salt and pepper, to taste

Per Serving:
Calories: 158
% of calories from fat: 26
Fat (gm): 4.5
Saturated fat (gm): 1
Cholesterol (mg): 44.7
Sodium (mg): 63
Protein (gm): 21.1
Carbohydrate (gm): 7

Exchanges:
Milk: 0.0
Vegetable: 0.0
Fruit: 0.0
Bread: 0.5
Meat: 3.0
Fat: 0.0

1. Sauté turkey, onions, and mushrooms in oil in large saucepan until lightly browned, about 8 minutes. Add remaining ingredients, except peas, salt, and pepper; heat to boiling. Reduce heat and simmer, covered, until turkey and vegetables are tender, about 20 minutes, adding peas during last 5 minutes. Season to taste with salt and pepper.

TURKEY SANCOCHE

45 *Sancoche is a hearty stew of meats, fish, vegetables, and seasonings that hails from Latin America.*

4 servings

1 pound boneless, skinless turkey breast, cubed
(¾-inch)

2 cups cubed, peeled butternut squash (¾-inch)

1 cup each: cubed peeled sweet and white potato,
chopped onion

1 can (15 ounces) black beans, rinsed, drained

1 can (14½ ounces) reduced-sodium fat-free
chicken broth

1 jalapeño chili, minced

1 teaspoon toasted cumin seeds

Salt and pepper, to taste

¼ cup coarsely chopped cashews

Per Serving:
Calories: 324
% of calories from fat: 18
Fat (gm): 7.2
Saturated fat (gm): 1.5
Cholesterol (mg): 44.7
Sodium (mg): 652
Protein (gm): 29.6
Carbohydrate (gm): 43.7

Exchanges:
Milk: 0.0
Vegetable: 0.0
Fruit: 0.0
Bread: 2.5
Meat: 2.0
Fat: 0.0

1. Combine all ingredients, except salt, pepper, and cashews, in large saucepan. Heat to boiling; reduce heat and simmer, covered, until turkey and vegetables are tender, about 20 minutes. Season to taste with salt and pepper. Sprinkle each bowl of stew with cashews.

TURKEY-WILD RICE STEW

Turkey, vegetables, and wild rice combine to create a delicious supper stew.

4 servings

1 pound boneless, skinless turkey breast, cubed

½ cup each: chopped onion, sliced carrot

1 teaspoon olive oil

3 cups reduced-sodium fat-free chicken broth

½ cup wild rice

2 cups small broccoli florets

1 tablespoon chopped fresh or 1 teaspoon dried
sage leaves

Salt and pepper, to taste

Per Serving:
Calories: 250
% of calories from fat: 13
Fat (gm): 3.8
Saturated fat (gm): 0.9
Cholesterol (mg): 44.7
Sodium (mg): 196
Protein (gm): 29
Carbohydrate (gm): 24.6

Exchanges:
Milk: 0.0
Vegetable: 1.0
Fruit: 0.0
Bread: 1.0
Meat: 3.0
Fat: 0.0

1. Sauté turkey, onion, and carrot in oil in large saucepan until lightly browned, about 5 minutes. Add broth and wild rice; heat to boiling. Reduce heat and simmer, covered, until rice is tender, about 50 minutes, adding broccoli and sage during last 10 minutes. Season to taste with salt and pepper.

ITALIAN-STYLE TURKEY SAUSAGE AND FENNEL STEW

Use your preference of sweet or hot Italian sausage in this harvest garden stew.

4 servings

12 ounces Italian turkey sausage

1 medium onion, cut into thin wedges

1 can (15 ounces) reduced-sodium diced
   tomatoes, undrained

1 cup reduced-sodium fat-free chicken broth

1 pound butternut squash, peeled, cubed (¾-inch)

12 Brussels sprouts, halved

2 parsnips, sliced

1 small fennel bulb, sliced

⅛ teaspoon crushed red pepper

1 teaspoon dried Italian seasoning

Salt and pepper, to taste

Per Serving:
Calories: 310
% of calories from fat: 26
Fat (gm): 9.7
Saturated fat (gm): 2.6
Cholesterol (mg): 45.6
Sodium (mg): 780
Protein (gm): 21.8
Carbohydrate (gm): 39.4

Exchanges:
Milk: 0.0
Vegetable: 2.0
Fruit: 0.0
Bread: 2.0
Meat: 2.0
Fat: 0.0

1. Cook sausage and onion in lightly greased large saucepan until sausage is browned, about 10 minutes; remove sausage and slice. Return sausage to saucepan; add remaining ingredients, except salt and pepper and heat to boiling. Reduce heat and simmer, covered, until vegetables are tender, about 20 minutes. Season to taste with salt and pepper.

FISH STEW MARSALA

45 *Marsala wine adds a distinctive, appealing note to this simple Italian fish stew. Substitute any lean white fish you prefer.*

4 servings

1 cup each: chopped onion, red and green bell peppers

½ cup chopped celery

1 teaspoon minced garlic

1½ tablespoons olive oil

2½ cups reduced-sodium fat-free chicken broth

⅓ cup dry Marsala wine or fat-free chicken broth

1 teaspoon dried thyme leaves

¼ cup reduced-sodium tomato paste

2 tablespoons lemon juice

1 pound haddock steaks, cubed (2-inch)

2 cups medium pasta shells, cooked, warm

Salt and pepper, to taste

Per Serving:
Calories: 409
% of calories from fat: 15
Fat (gm): 7
Saturated fat (gm): 1
Cholesterol (mg): 65.2
Sodium (mg): 206
Protein (gm): 33
Carbohydrate (gm): 49

Exchanges:
Milk: 0.0
Vegetable: 1.0
Fruit: 0.0
Bread: 3.0
Meat: 3.0
Fat: 0.0

1. Sauté onion, bell peppers, celery, and garlic in oil in large skillet until tender and lightly browned, about 5 minutes. Add broth, wine, and thyme; heat to boiling. Reduce heat and simmer, uncovered, 10 minutes. Stir in tomato paste, lemon juice, and haddock; simmer, covered, until fish flakes with a fork, about 5 minutes. Stir in pasta; season to taste with salt and pepper.

45-MINUTE PREPARATION TIP: Begin cooking pasta before preparing the rest of the recipe.

VIETNAMESE CURRIED COCONUT STEW

V *Rice stick noodles, made with rice flour, can be round or flat. They must be softened in water before cooking. Cooked angel hair pasta can be substituted.*

6 servings

1 cup each: chopped onion, red bell peppers

2 tablespoons minced gingerroot

1 tablespoon minced garlic

3–4 tablespoons curry powder

3 cups each: vegetable broth, coconut milk

1 cup each: broccoli florets, cubed, peeled, seeded butternut squash

1 tablespoon grated lime zest

1–2 teaspoons Oriental chili paste

½ package (8-ounce size) rice stick noodles

¼ cup each: all-purpose flour, cold water, lime juice

Salt, to taste

Chopped cilantro, as garnish

Per Serving:
Calories: 218
% of calories from fat: 28
Fat (gm): 7.2
Saturated fat (gm): 0.1
Cholesterol (mg): 0
Sodium (mg): 627
Protein (gm): 4.1
Carbohydrate (gm): 37.1

Exchanges:
Milk: 0.0
Vegetable: 1.0
Fruit: 0.0
Bread: 2.0
Meat: 0.0
Fat: 1.0

1. Sauté onion, bell peppers, gingerroot, and garlic in lightly greased large skillet until tender, about 5 minutes. Stir in curry powder; cook 1 minute. Add broth, coconut milk, vegetables, lime zest, and chili paste; heat to boiling. Reduce heat and simmer, covered, until vegetables are tender, about 15 minutes.

2. While stew is cooking, pour cold water over noodles in large bowl; let stand until noodles are separate and soft, about 5 minutes. Stir noodles into 4 quarts boiling water in large saucepan; reduce heat and simmer, uncovered, until tender, about 5 minutes. Drain.

3. Heat stew to boiling; stir in combined flour, cold water, and lime juice. Boil, stirring until thickened, about 1 minute. Season to taste with salt. Serve over noodles in shallow bowls; sprinkle generously with cilantro.

CABBAGE RAGOUT WITH REAL MASHED POTATOES

L *Fresh fennel, gingerroot, and apple lend aromatic highlights to this cabbage stew. If fresh fennel is not available, substitute celery and increase the amount of fennel seeds to 1½ teaspoons.*

6 servings (about 1⅓ cups each)

1 medium eggplant (about 1¼ pounds), unpeeled, sliced (1-inch)

Vegetable cooking spray

1 cup chopped onion

½ cup thinly sliced fennel bulb

1 tablespoon each: minced garlic, gingerroot

1 teaspoon fennel seeds, crushed

8 cups thinly sliced cabbage

2 cups reduced-sodium vegetable broth

2 medium apples, cored, cubed

1 cup fat-free sour cream

Salt and pepper, to taste

Real Mashed Potatoes (see p. 628) or 4 cups cooked whole wheat noodles

Per Serving:
Calories: 249
% of calories from fat: 10
Fat (gm): 3
Saturated fat (gm): 0.5
Cholesterol (mg): 8.8
Sodium (mg): 255
Protein (gm): 8.5
Carbohydrate (gm): 50

Exchanges:
Milk: 0.0
Vegetable: 0.0
Fruit: 0.0
Bread: 3.0
Meat: 0.0
Fat: 0.5

1. Cook 5 or 6 eggplant slices over medium heat in lightly greased large skillet until browned on the bottom, 3 to 5 minutes. Spray tops of slices with cooking spray and turn; cook until browned, 3 to 5 minutes. Repeat with remaining eggplant. Cut eggplant into 1-inch cubes and reserve.

2. Sauté onion, fennel, garlic, gingerroot, and fennel seeds in lightly greased large saucepan until onion is tender, 3 to 5 minutes. Add cabbage and broth and heat to boiling; reduce heat and simmer, covered, until cabbage is wilted and crisp-tender, about 5 minutes. Stir in apples and cook, covered, until apples are tender, about 5 minutes. Stir in reserved eggplant and sour cream; cook over medium heat until hot, 3 to 4 minutes. Season to taste with salt and pepper; serve over potatoes or noodles.

VEGGIE STEW WITH CHILI-CHEESE DUMPLINGS

L

One green bell pepper and one jalapeño chili can be substituted for the poblano chili.

6 servings

2 cups chopped onions

1 cup each: coarsely chopped poblano chili, red and yellow bell peppers

3 cloves garlic, minced

2–3 tablespoons chili powder

1½–2 teaspoons ground cumin

¾ teaspoon each: dried oregano and marjoram leaves

2 tablespoons olive oil

2 cans (15 ounces each) reduced-sodium diced tomatoes, undrained

1 can (15 ounces) each: black-eyed peas and red beans, rinsed, drained

1½ cups cubed, peeled butternut or acorn squash

1 cup fresh or frozen, thawed, okra

Salt and pepper, to taste

Chili-Cheese Dumplings (recipe follows)

Per Serving:
Calories: 433
% of calories from fat: 29
Fat (gm): 14.9
Saturated fat (gm): 2.7
Cholesterol (mg): 3.7
Sodium (mg): 713
Protein (gm): 17.4
Carbohydrate (gm): 65.9

Exchanges:
Milk: 0.0
Vegetable: 3.0
Fruit: 0.0
Bread: 3.0
Meat: 1.0
Fat: 2.0

1. Sauté onions, poblano chili, bell peppers, garlic, and herbs in oil in large saucepan until tender, about 10 minutes. Stir in remaining ingredients, except salt, pepper, and Chili-Cheese Dumplings; heat to boiling. Reduce heat and simmer, covered, until okra and squash are tender, 8 to 10 minutes. Season to taste with salt and pepper.

2. Spoon dumpling dough into 6 mounds on top of stew. Cook, uncovered, 10 minutes. Cook, covered, until dumplings are dry, 5 to 10 minutes longer.

Chili-Cheese Dumplings
Makes 6 dumplings

⅔ cup all-purpose flour

⅓ cup yellow cornmeal

1½ teaspoons baking powder

1 teaspoon chili powder

½ teaspoon salt

2 tablespoons vegetable shortening

¼ cup (1 ounce) shredded reduced-fat Monterey Jack cheese

½ cup fat-free milk

1. Combine flour, cornmeal, baking powder, chili powder, and salt in medium bowl; cut in shortening with pastry blender until mixture resembles coarse crumbs. Mix in cheese; stir in milk, forming a soft dough.

SOUTHERN STEWED BLACK EYES, CHICKPEAS, AND HAM

45 *A hearty stew that can be made in less than 45 minutes with pantry staples. Serve with warm biscuits or corn bread.*

6 servings

12 ounces reduced-sodium ham, cubed

½ cup chopped onion

2 cloves garlic, minced

1 tablespoon olive oil

2 cups halved small okra

1 can (16 ounces) reduced-sodium stewed
    tomatoes, undrained

1 can (15 ounces) each: chickpeas and black-eyed
    peas, rinsed, drained

½ package (10-ounce size) frozen spinach
    partially thawed

1 teaspoon each: dried marjoram and thyme leaves

¼ teaspoon hot pepper sauce

Salt and pepper, to taste

Per Serving:
Calories: 320
% of calories from fat: 23
Fat (gm): 8.2
Saturated fat (gm): 2
Cholesterol (mg): 32.3
Sodium (mg): 841
Protein (gm): 21.8
Carbohydrate (gm): 41.6

Exchanges:
Milk: 0.0
Vegetable: 2.0
Fruit: 0.0
Bread: 2.0
Meat: 0.5
Fat: 0.0

1. Sauté ham, onion, and garlic in oil in large saucepan until onion is tender, 5 to 8 minutes. Stir in remaining ingredients, except salt and pepper; heat to boiling. Reduce heat and simmer, covered, until okra is tender, about 10 minutes. Season to taste with salt and pepper.

ITALIAN-STYLE BEANS AND VEGETABLES WITH POLENTA

This colorful mélange can also be served over pasta, rice, or squares of warm corn bread.

6 servings

12 ounces Italian-style turkey sausage, casing removed

1½ cups each: chopped onions, portobello mushrooms

4 cloves garlic, minced

2 tablespoons olive oil

2 cups broccoli florets

1 cup sliced yellow summer squash

1 can (15 ounces) each: garbanzo and red kidney
   beans, rinsed, drained

1 can (14½ ounces) reduced-sodium diced
   tomatoes, undrained,

2 teaspoons dried Italian seasoning

⅛–¼ teaspoon crushed red pepper

Salt and pepper, to taste

Herbed Polenta (see p. 364)

Per Serving:
Calories: 304
% of calories from fat: 21
Fat (gm): 7.7
Saturated fat (gm): 1
Cholesterol (mg): 0
Sodium (mg): 641
Protein (gm): 13.3
Carbohydrate (gm): 50.2

Exchanges:
Milk: 0.0
Vegetable: 2.0
Fruit: 0.0
Bread: 2.5
Meat: 0.5
Fat: 1.0

1. Sauté sausage, onions, mushrooms, and garlic in oil in large saucepan until browned, about 10 minutes. Stir in remaining ingredients, except salt, pepper, and Polenta; heat to boiling. Reduce heat and simmer, covered, until broccoli is tender, about 10 minutes; season to taste with salt and pepper. Serve over Herbed Polenta.

THREE-BEAN STEW WITH POLENTA

L

Use any kind of canned or cooked dried beans; one 15-ounce can of drained beans yields 1½ cups.

4 servings

1 cup chopped onion

½ cup chopped red bell pepper

1 teaspoon minced roasted garlic

1 tablespoon flour

1 can (15 ounces) each: black-eyed peas, black beans and red beans, rinsed, drained

1 can (16 ounces) reduced-sodium diced tomatoes, undrained

1½ teaspoons dried Italian seasoning

¾ cup reduced-sodium vegetable broth

Salt and pepper, to taste

Polenta (see p. 363)

Per Serving:
Calories: 299
% of calories from fat: 14
Fat (gm): 5.3
Saturated fat (gm): 0.6
Cholesterol (mg): 0
Sodium (mg): 587
Protein (gm): 17.5
Carbohydrate (gm): 56

Exchanges:
Milk: 0.0
Vegetable: 2.0
Fruit: 0.0
Bread: 3.0
Meat: 0.5
Fat: 0.0

1. Sauté onion, bell pepper, and garlic in lightly greased large saucepan until tender, about 5 minutes; stir in flour and cook 1 minute. Add remaining ingredients, except salt, pepper and Polenta to saucepan; heat to boiling. Reduce heat and simmer, covered, 10 minutes. Season to taste with salt and pepper. Serve stew over Polenta.

WINTER BEAN AND VEGETABLE STEW

V *Serve this satisfying stew with Multigrain Batter Bread (see p. 522).*

6 servings

1 cup each: chopped onion, cubed peeled Idaho and sweet potato

½ cup each: sliced carrot, parsnip, chopped green bell pepper

2 cloves garlic, minced

2 tablespoons olive oil

1 tablespoon flour

1½ cups reduced-sodium vegetable broth

1 can (15 ounces) black beans, rinsed, drained

1 can (13¼ ounces) baby lima beans, rinsed, drained

1 large tomato, cut into wedges

¾ teaspoon dried sage leaves

Salt and pepper, to taste

Per Serving:
Calories: 238
% of calories from fat: 20
Fat (gm): 5.7
Saturated fat (gm): 0.7
Cholesterol (mg): 0
Sodium (mg): 399
Protein (gm): 10.8
Carbohydrate (gm): 42.4

Exchanges:
Milk: 0.0
Vegetable: 2.0
Fruit: 0.0
Bread: 2.0
Meat: 0.0
Fat: 1.0

1. Sauté vegetables and garlic in oil in large saucepan 5 minutes; stir in flour and cook 1 minute. Add remaining ingredients, except salt and pepper, and heat to boiling. Reduce heat and simmer, covered, until vegetables are tender, 15 to 20 minutes; season to taste with salt and pepper.

WHEAT BERRY AND LENTIL STEW WITH DUMPLINGS

L *Use vegetable shortening that is trans-fat free for the dumplings.*

8 servings

1 cup wheat berries

2 medium onions, chopped

½ cup each: chopped celery, sliced carrots

4 cloves garlic, minced

1 teaspoon dried savory leaves

3 cups reduced-sodium vegetable broth

2 pounds russet potatoes, unpeeled, cubed

1½ cups cooked lentils

Salt and pepper, to taste

Herb Dumplings (recipe follows)

Per Serving:
Calories: 414
% of calories from fat: 10
Fat (gm): 4.7
Saturated fat (gm): 0.6
Cholesterol (mg): 0.3
Sodium (mg): 259
Protein (gm): 16.8
Carbohydrate (gm): 78.6

Exchanges:
Milk: 0.0
Vegetable: 1.0
Fruit: 0.0
Bread: 5.0
Meat: 0.0
Fat: 0.5

1. Soak wheat berries overnight in 2 to 3 inches water in saucepan. Heat to boiling; reduce heat and simmer, covered, until wheat berries are tender, 45 to 55 minutes. Drain.

2. Sauté onions, celery, carrots, garlic, and savory in lightly greased large saucepan until onions are tender, about 5 minutes. Add broth and potatoes and heat to boiling; reduce heat and simmer, covered, until vegetables are tender, 10 to 15 minutes. Stir in wheat berries and lentils; cook until hot, about 5 minutes. Season to taste with salt and pepper.

3. Spoon dumpling dough in 8 mounds on top of stew; cook, uncovered, 10 minutes. Cook, covered, until dumplings are dry, 5 to 10 minutes.

Herb Dumplings

½ cup each: all-purpose flour, yellow cornmeal
1½ teaspoons baking powder
½ teaspoon each: dried sage and thyme leaves, salt
2 tablespoons vegetable shortening
½ cup fat-free milk

1. Combine flour, cornmeal, baking powder, herbs, and salt in bowl. Cut in shortening with pastry blender until mixture resembles coarse crumbs. Stir in milk to make a soft dough.

SEVEN

Eggs
and
Cheese

CHEESE FONDUE

45

LO

Flavored with wine and a hint of garlic, this creamy fondue is made with fat-free cheese!

8 servings (about ¼ cup each)

1½ cups dry white wine or fat-free milk
2–3 large cloves garlic, peeled
6 ounces fat-free cream cheese
2 cups (8 ounces) shredded fat-free Swiss cheese
1 tablespoon flour
Salt and cayenne pepper, to taste
French bread, cubed, for dipping (not included
 in nutritional data)

Per Serving:
Calories: 100
% of calories from fat: 0
Fat (gm): 0
Saturated fat (gm): 0
Cholesterol (mg): 0
Sodium (mg): 547
Protein (gm): 10.8
Carbohydrate (gm): 5

Exchanges:
Milk: 0.0
Vegetable: 0.0
Fruit: 0.0
Bread: 0.0
Meat: 1.5
Fat: 0.0

1. Heat wine and garlic to boiling in medium saucepan; reduce heat and simmer rapidly, uncovered, until reduced to ¾ cup, about 15 minutes; discard garlic. Add cream cheese and stir over low heat until melted. Toss Swiss cheese with flour; add to saucepan and stir until melted. Season to taste with salt and cayenne pepper. Serve in fondue pot or bowl with bread cubes for dipping.

NOTE: If fondue becomes too thick, it can be thinned with wine or milk.

WELSH RAREBIT

45

L

Rarebit is also delicious served over sliced ham or chicken breast and asparagus spears on toast.

6 servings

¼ cup finely chopped onion
2 tablespoons margarine or butter
¼ cup all-purpose flour
2 cups fat-free milk
½ cup white wine or fat-free milk
2 ounces light pasteurized processed cheese, cubed
½ cup (2 ounces) reduced-fat sharp Cheddar cheese, cubed

¼–½ teaspoon dry mustard

White and cayenne pepper, to taste

6 slices sourdough or multigrain bread

Butter-flavored vegetable cooking spray

6 thick slices tomato

Paprika, as garnish

Per Serving:
Calories: 219
% of calories from fat: 31
Fat (gm): 7.6
Saturated fat (gm): 3.4
Cholesterol (mg): 11.5
Sodium (mg): 502
Protein (gm): 9.9
Carbohydrate (gm): 24.1

Exchanges:
Milk: 0.0
Vegetable: 0.0
Fruit: 0.0
Bread: 1.5
Meat: 1.0
Fat: 1.0

1. Sauté onion in margarine in medium saucepan until tender, 2 to 3 minutes. Stir in flour and cook 1 minute. Whisk in milk and wine; heat to boiling, whisking until thickened, about 1 minute. Stir in cheeses and dry mustard; whisk over low heat until cheeses are melted. Season to taste with white and cayenne pepper.

2. Spray both sides of bread with cooking spray; cook over medium heat in large skillet until browned, 2 to 3 minutes on each side. Sauté tomato slices in lightly greased medium skillet until hot, 2 to 3 minutes. Top bread with tomato slices and spoon cheese sauce over. Sprinkle with paprika.

VARIATION

Cheese and Vegetable Rarebit — Make recipe as above, stirring ½ cup each sautéed chopped portobello mushrooms, yellow summer squash, and broccoli florets into the cheese sauce in step 1; delete tomato in step 2.

TROPICAL TOAST

O

45

❂

Perfect for Sunday breakfast! Serve with warm maple syrup for a finishing touch.

4 servings

6 egg whites or ¾ cup no-cholesterol real egg product

¾ cup orange juice

3 tablespoons lime juice

¼ cup powdered sugar

½ teaspoon coconut extract

8 slices Hawaiian bread (½-inch)

¾ cup unsweetened flaked coconut, divided

Sliced kiwi, as garnish

Pineapple chunks, as garnish

Per Serving:
Calories: 272
% of calories from fat: 21
Fat (gm): 6.7
Saturated fat (gm): 4.5
Cholesterol (mg): 0
Sodium (mg): 333
Protein (gm): 10.6
Carbohydrate (gm): 44.4

Exchanges:
Milk: 0.0
Vegetable: 0.0
Fruit: 0.0
Bread: 3.0
Meat: 1.0
Fat: 0.0

1. Beat egg whites, orange juice, lime juice, powdered sugar, and coconut extract in pie plate until well blended. Dip each bread slice in egg mixture, turning to coat both sides. Arrange bread in single layer on lightly greased cookie sheet. Sprinkle with half the coconut; lightly press coconut onto bread. Bake at 400 degrees until lightly browned, about 10 minutes. Turn slices; sprinkle with remaining coconut. Bake until slices are puffed and browned, or about 10 minutes. Garnish with kiwi and pineapple.

EGGS BENEDICT

45

Six slices of English Muffin Bread (see p. 506) can be substituted for the English muffins.

6 servings

6 ounces sliced lean Canadian bacon

3 English muffins, halved, toasted

Spinach leaves

6 each: tomato slices, poached eggs

Mock Hollandaise Sauce (see p. 170)

Paprika and chopped parsley, as garnish

1. Heat Canadian bacon in lightly greased small skillet until lightly browned, 3 to 4 minutes. Arrange Canadian bacon on muffin halves; top with spinach leaves, tomato slices, and poached eggs. Spoon Mock Hollandaise Sauce over eggs; sprinkle with paprika and parsley.

45-MINUTE PREPARATION TIP: Make Mock Hollandaise Sauce before preparing the rest of the recipe.

Per Serving:
Calories: 204
% of calories from fat: 27
Fat (gm): 5.6
Saturated fat (gm): 1.7
Cholesterol (mg): 228.3
Sodium (mg): 786
Protein (gm): 19
Carbohydrate (gm): 17

Exchanges:
Milk: 0.0
Vegetable: 0.0
Fruit: 0.0
Bread: 1.0
Meat: 2.5
Fat: 0.0

EGGS IN A CUMULUS CLOUD

45

Delicious flavors in a unique presentation.

LO

4 servings

2 pumpernickel bagels, split, toasted
8 tablespoons fat-free cream cheese
4 eggs, separated
Salt and pepper, to taste
Paprika, as garnish

1. Spread bagel halves with cream cheese. Beat egg whites to stiff, but not dry peaks in large bowl; spoon over bagel halves. Make a depression in center of egg whites with a spoon and place 1 yolk in each. Broil 6 inches from heat source until egg whites are lightly browned and yolks are set on top, 2 to 3 minutes. Sprinkle lightly with salt, pepper, and paprika.

Per Serving:
Calories: 188
% of calories from fat: 26
Fat (gm): 6.4
Saturated fat (gm): 1.8
Cholesterol (mg): 214.4
Sodium (mg): 332
Protein (gm): 15.1
Carbohydrate (gm): 26.4

Exchanges:
Milk: 0.0
Vegetable: 0.0
Fruit: 0.0
Bread: 1.5
Meat: 1.0
Fat: 0.5

OMELET PUFF WITH VEGETABLE MÉLANGE

o

Beaten egg whites make this oven-baked omelet soar to new heights.

45

◊

2 servings

2 eggs
¼ teaspoon each: dried tarragon leaves, salt, pepper
5 egg whites
¼ cup water
Vegetable Mélange (recipe follows)

Per Serving:
Calories: 130
% of calories from fat: 4
Fat (gm): 0.5
Saturated fat (gm): 0.1
Cholesterol (mg): 0
Sodium (mg): 553
Protein (gm): 16.2
Carbohydrate (gm): 16.3

Exchanges:
Milk: 0.0
Vegetable: 0.0
Fruit: 0.0
Bread: 2.0
Meat: 2.0
Fat: 0.0

1. Beat eggs, tarragon, salt, and pepper at high speed in small bowl until thick and lemon colored, about 5 minutes. Beat egg whites and water in large bowl with clean beaters until stiff, but not dry, peaks form; fold into beaten eggs.

2. Spread egg mixture evenly in lightly greased ovenproof 10-inch skillet; cook over medium heat until bottom of omelet is lightly browned, about 5 minutes. Bake at 325 degrees, uncovered, until puffed and lightly browned, about 15 minutes. Loosen edge of omelet with spatula; slide onto serving plate, carefully folding omelet in half. Spoon Vegetable Mélange over omelet.

Vegetable Mélange

Makes about 3 cups

1 cup each: small whole okra, tomato wedges, sliced zucchini, onion
½ cup sliced green bell pepper
1 teaspoon dried Italian seasoning
Salt and pepper, to taste

1. Sauté vegetables and Italian seasoning in lightly greased large skillet until tender, 5 to 7 minutes. Season to taste with salt and pepper.

45-MINUTE PREPARATION TIP: Slice vegetables for Vegetable Mélange before preparing the rest of the recipe.

VEGETABLE PUFF

Perfect for brunch or lunch, sautéed vegetables are baked with eggs in a casserole.

6 servings

2 cups each: sliced mushrooms, coarsely chopped broccoli florets

1 cup shredded carrots

½ cup each: chopped red bell pepper, green onions

¼ cup whole kernel corn

2 cloves garlic, minced

2 teaspoons lemon juice

¾ teaspoon dried thyme leaves

Salt and pepper, to taste

1 cup fat-free half-and-half or fat-free milk

2 tablespoons flour

4 eggs, lightly beaten

4 large egg whites, beaten to stiff peaks

Per Serving:
Calories: 139
% of calories from fat: 27
Fat (gm): 4.3
Saturated fat (gm): 1.4
Cholesterol (mg): 143
Sodium (mg): 169
Protein (gm): 10
Carbohydrate (gm): 16

Exchanges:
Milk: 0.0
Vegetable: 3.0
Fruit: 0.0
Bread: 0.0
Meat: 1.0
Fat: 5.0

1. Sauté vegetables and garlic in lightly greased large skillet until tender, about 8 minutes. Stir in lemon juice, and thyme; season to taste with salt and pepper. Remove from heat.

2. Whisk half-and-half and flour in small saucepan; heat to boiling, whisking until thickened, about 1 minute. Whisk mixture into beaten eggs; stir into vegetable mixture. Fold beaten egg whites into vegetable mixture and spoon into greased 1½-quart casserole. Place casserole in a large roasting pan on center oven rack; add 2 inches hot water to pan. Bake, uncovered, at 375 degrees until puffed and browned, about 35 minutes. Serve immediately.

EASY CHEESE PUFF

A delicious casserole that tastes like cheese blintzes, but requires much less time and effort to prepare.

8 servings

4 eggs

1¼ cups fat-free milk

2 tablespoons each: fat-free sour cream, melted margarine or butter

1 teaspoon vanilla

1⅓ cups all-purpose flour

1 tablespoon each: sugar, baking powder

Sweet Cheese Filling (recipe follows)

Powdered sugar, as garnish

2 cups sliced strawberries

Per Serving:
Calories: 299
% of calories from fat: 31
Fat (gm): 10.8
Saturated fat (gm): 4.8
Cholesterol (mg): 141.4
Sodium (mg): 556
Protein (gm): 20.9
Carbohydrate (gm): 32

Exchanges:
Milk: 0.0
Vegetable: 0.0
Fruit: 0.0
Bread: 2.0
Meat: 2.0
Fat: 1.0

1. Combine all ingredients, except Sweet Cheese Filling, powdered sugar, and strawberries in large bowl; beat with mixer until very smooth. Pour 1½ cups batter into lightly greased 13 x 9-inch baking dish. Bake at 350 degrees until set, about 10 minutes.

2. Spread Sweet Cheese Filling over baked layer. Whisk remaining batter to combine; pour over cheese, covering completely. Bake at 350 degrees until top is puffed and browned, about 45 minutes; sprinkle with powdered sugar. Cut into squares and top with strawberries.

Sweet Cheese Filling

Makes about 3½ cups

2 containers (15 ounces each) reduced-fat ricotta cheese

2 eggs

2 tablespoons each: sugar, lemon juice

1. Mix all ingredients.

CHEDDAR CHEESE SOUFFLÉ

LO

This spectacular soufflé soars above the soufflé dish!

45

4 servings

1–2 tablespoons grated fat-free Parmesan cheese

1 cup fat-free milk

3 tablespoons flour

½ teaspoon each: dry mustard, dried marjoram leaves

¼ teaspoon cayenne pepper

2 pinches ground nutmeg

3 egg yolks

¼ cup (1 ounce) shredded fat-free Cheddar cheese

Salt and white pepper, to taste

3 egg whites

¼ teaspoon cream of tartar

Per Serving:
Calories: 162
% of calories from fat: 23
Fat (gm): 4.1
Saturated fat (gm): 1.3
Cholesterol (mg): 160.8
Sodium (mg): 340
Protein (gm): 19.3
Carbohydrate (gm): 11.2

Exchanges:
Milk: 0.0
Vegetable: 0.0
Fruit: 0.0
Bread: 0.5
Meat: 2.5
Fat: 0.0

1. Coat greased 1-quart soufflé dish with Parmesan cheese. Attach a foil collar, extending foil 3 inches above top of dish; lightly grease inside of collar.

2. Whisk milk, flour, and seasonings until blended in small saucepan. Heat to boiling, whisking until thickened, about 1 minute. Whisk about ½ cup mixture into egg yolks; whisk mixture back into saucepan. Add cheese and whisk over low heat until melted; season to taste with salt and white pepper.

3. Beat egg whites and cream of tartar in medium bowl to stiff, but not dry, peaks. Stir about ⅓ the egg whites into cheese mixture; fold cheese mixture into remaining whites. Spoon into prepared soufflé dish. Bake at 350 degrees until soufflé is puffed, browned, and just set in the center, 35 to 40 minutes. Serve immediately.

SPINACH SOUFFLÉ

45

Any cooked vegetable can be substituted for the spinach in this recipe.

4 servings

1 small onion, minced

1 teaspoon margarine or butter

3 tablespoons flour

½ teaspoon ground nutmeg

½ cup each: fat-free milk, reduced-sodium fat-free
chicken or vegetable broth

2 egg yolks, lightly beaten

1 package (10 ounces) frozen chopped spinach,
thawed, well drained

⅛ teaspoon white pepper

4 egg whites

Pinch cream of tartar

Per Serving:
Calories: 118
% of calories from fat: 28
Fat (gm): 3.9
Saturated fat (gm): 1.1
Cholesterol (mg): 107.1
Sodium (mg): 167
Protein (gm): 9.7
Carbohydrate (gm): 12.1

Exchanges:
Milk: 0.0
Vegetable: 1.0
Fruit: 0.0
Bread: 0.5
Meat: 1.0
Fat: 0.0

1. Sauté onion in margarine in medium saucepan until tender, 3 to
4 minutes; stir in flour and nutmeg and cook 1 minute. Whisk in
milk and broth and heat to boiling, whisking until thickened, about
1 minute. Whisk about half the sauce into egg yolks; whisk yolk
mixture back into saucepan. Mix in spinach and white pepper.

2. Beat egg whites and cream of tartar in large bowl to stiff, but
not dry, peaks; fold into spinach mixture and spoon into greased
1-quart soufflé dish. Bake, uncovered, at 350 degrees until puffed
and browned, about 40 minutes. Serve immediately.

PANCAKE PUFF WITH EGGS PIPERADE

LO

45

*A puffed Dutch Pancake makes a tasty serving bowl for chili-inspired
scrambled eggs.*

4 servings

1 cup each: sliced onion, red or green bell pepper

½–1 jalapeño chili, minced

1 teaspoon minced garlic

1 small tomato, chopped

6 eggs
4 egg whites or 1 cup no-cholesterol real egg product
2 tablespoons fat-free milk
Salt and pepper, to taste
Dutch Pancake (recipe follows)
Minced chives or parsley, as garnish

Per Serving:
Calories: 315
% of calories from fat: 30
Fat (gm): 10.3
Saturated fat (gm): 3.2
Cholesterol (mg): 424
Sodium (mg): 430
Protein (gm): 24.1
Carbohydrate (gm): 29.3

Exchanges:
Milk: 0.0
Vegetable: 0.0
Fruit: 0.0
Bread: 2.0
Meat: 3.0
Fat: 0.0

1. Sauté onion, bell pepper, jalapeño chili, and garlic in lightly greased large skillet until tender, 5 to 8 minutes; stir in tomato. Whisk eggs, egg whites, and milk until well blended; add to skillet and cook over medium heat until set, about 5 minutes, stirring frequently. Sprinkle lightly with salt and pepper. Spoon into hot Dutch Pancake; sprinkle with chives.

Dutch Pancake

Makes 1 pancake

2 eggs
4 egg whites or ½ cup no-cholesterol real egg product
¾ cup each: fat-free milk, all-purpose flour
1 tablespoon sugar
¼ teaspoon salt
Vegetable cooking spray

1. Whisk all ingredients, except cooking spray, in large bowl until almost smooth (batter will be slightly lumpy). Spray large oven-proof skillet with cooking spray and heat over medium heat until hot; pour in batter. Bake, uncovered, at 425 degrees until pancake is puffed and browned, 20 to 25 minutes (do not open door during first 15 minutes).

45-MINUTE PREPARATION TIP: Begin cooking vegetable-egg mixture when Dutch Pancake goes into the oven.

SPINACH CHEESE CREPES

LO *For variation, add ½ cup sautéed chopped portobello mushrooms to the cottage cheese mixture.*

4 entrée servings (2 crepes each)

¼ cup chopped onion

1 package (10 ounces) frozen chopped spinach, thawed, well drained

1 cup fat-free cottage cheese

½ teaspoon dried thyme leaves

2–3 pinches ground nutmeg

Salt and pepper, to taste

8 slices (4 ounces) fat-free mozzarella or Swiss cheese

8 Crepes (see p. 170), warm

1½ cups Fresh Tomato and Herb Sauce (½ recipe) (see p. 171)

Per Serving:
Calories: 342
% of calories from fat: 28
Fat (gm): 11
Saturated fat (gm): 2.6
Cholesterol (mg): 123
Sodium (mg): 905
Protein (gm): 36
Carbohydrate (gm): 27

Exchanges:
Milk: 0.0
Vegetable: 0.0
Fruit: 0.0
Bread: 1.5
Meat: 4.0
Fat: 0.0

1. Sauté onion in lightly greased medium skillet until tender, 3 to 4 minutes. Add spinach and cook until very dry, about 5 minutes. Mix with cottage cheese, thyme, and nutmeg; season to taste with salt and pepper.

2. Place cheese slices on crepes; top with spinach-cheese mixture. Roll up crepes and place, seam sides down, in greased baking dish. Bake, loosely covered, at 325 degrees until hot, about 10 minutes. Serve with Fresh Tomato and Herb Sauce.

VEGETABLE STRUDEL WITH CHEESE

L *A meatless entrée that is sure to please—smaller portions can be served as an elegant side dish.*

4 entrée servings

2 packages (1.25 ounces each) cheese sauce mix

1 cup each: sliced shiitake or cremini mushrooms, red bell peppers

¼ cup chopped shallots

1 teaspoon minced garlic

1 tablespoon margarine or butter

1½ cups each: small broccoli florets, cubed
   butternut or acorn squash, cooked crisp-tender
¾ cup (3 ounces) shredded reduced-fat brick or
   Swiss cheese
Salt and pepper, to taste
5 sheets frozen fillo pastry, thawed
Vegetable cooking spray

Per Serving:
Calories: 245
% of calories from fat: 25
Fat (gm): 7.7
Saturated fat (gm): 3.3
Cholesterol (mg): 11.1
Sodium (mg): 724
Protein (gm): 12.1
Carbohydrate (gm): 38.6

Exchanges:
Milk: 0.0
Vegetable: 1.0
Fruit: 0.0
Bread: 2.0
Meat: 1.0
Fat: 0.5

1. Make cheese sauce according to package directions. Sauté mushrooms, bell peppers, shallots, and garlic in margarine in large skillet 5 minutes. Stir in broccoli, squash, and half the cheese sauce; remove from heat. Stir in shredded cheese; season to taste with salt and pepper.

2. Lay 1 sheet fillo on clean kitchen towel; cover remaining fillo with a damp towel to prevent drying out. Spray fillo lightly with cooking spray. Cover with second sheet fillo and spray with cooking spray; repeat with remaining fillo. Spoon vegetable mixture along long side of fillo, 3 to 4 inches from the edge. Fold edge of fillo over filling and roll up, using towel to help lift and roll; place seam side down on greased cookie sheet. Spray top of fillo lightly with cooking spray.

3. Bake at 400 degrees until golden, about 20 minutes. Let stand 5 minutes before cutting. Trim ends; cut strudel into 4 pieces and arrange on plates. Serve with remaining cheese sauce.

PASTA FRITTATA

45   *A pasta frittata is a delicious way to use leftover pasta and vegetables.*

LO   **4 servings**

2 cups cooked thin spaghetti

2 eggs, lightly beaten

2 tablespoons grated Parmesan cheese

½ teaspoon salt

¼ teaspoon pepper

1 cup cauliflower florets

¾ cup each: sliced carrots, red bell peppers

½ cup each: sliced zucchini, chopped tomato

¼ cup sliced green onions

1 tablespoon minced garlic

1½ teaspoons dried Italian seasoning

1 tablespoon olive oil

Salt and pepper, to taste

Per Serving:
Calories: 228
% of calories from fat: 26
Fat (gm): 7
Saturated fat (gm): 1.4
Cholesterol (mg): 106
Sodium (mg): 83
Protein (gm): 10
Carbohydrate (gm): 34

Exchanges:
Milk: 0.0
Vegetable: 1.0
Fruit: 0.0
Bread: 2.0
Meat: 0.0
Fat: 1.0

1. Mix spaghetti, eggs, cheese, salt, and pepper; spread evenly in lightly greased medium skillet. Cook, uncovered, over medium heat until browned on bottom, about 5 minutes. Slide frittata onto plate; invert into skillet and cook until browned on other side, about 5 minutes; keep warm on low heat.

2. Sauté vegetables, garlic, and Italian seasoning in oil in large skillet until tender, 8 to 10 minutes; season to taste with salt and pepper. Serve vegetables over frittata.

45-MINUTE PREPARATION TIP: Prepare recipe ingredients while spaghetti is cooking.

VEGETABLE FRITTATA WITH PARMESAN TOAST

45   *This Italian-style omelet is quick and easy to prepare, and delicious to eat!*

LO   **4 servings**

2 cups sliced mushrooms

½ cup each: sliced poblano chili, onion

2 cloves garlic, minced

6 eggs, lightly beaten

¼ cup fat-free milk

½ cup each: cooked brown rice, shredded fat-free
Cheddar cheese (2 ounces)

¼ teaspoon salt

⅛ teaspoon pepper

4 slices Italian or French bread

4 teaspoons grated Parmesan cheese

Per Serving:
Calories: 285
% of calories from fat: 30
Fat (gm): 9.5
Saturated fat (gm): 3
Cholesterol (mg): 319
Sodium (mg): 732
Protein (gm): 19
Carbohydrate (gm): 30

Exchanges:
Milk: 0.0
Vegetable: 0.0
Fruit: 0.0
Bread: 2.0
Meat: 2.0
Fat: 1.0

1. Sauté vegetables and garlic in lightly greased medium ovenproof skillet until tender, about 8 minutes. Pour combined eggs, milk, rice, cheese, salt, and pepper over vegetables; cook, without stirring, over medium-low heat until eggs are set and lightly browned on bottom, about 10 minutes.

2. Sprinkle bread with Parmesan cheese. Broil bread and frittata 6 inches from heat source until bread is browned and frittata is cooked on top, 2 to 4 minutes. Serve frittata with Parmesan bread.

QUICHE LORRAINE

Enjoy the rich texture and flavor of this classic quiche, modified to low-fat goodness.

6 servings

Basic Pie Crust (see p. 570)

¼ cup finely chopped onion

¾ cup each: fat-free milk

½ can (12-ounce size) evaporated fat-free milk

2 eggs, lightly beaten

¼ cup fat-free sour cream

2 slices bacon, cooked crisp, crumbled

¼ teaspoon salt

⅛ teaspoon each: ground nutmeg, cayenne pepper

1 cup (4 ounces) shredded fat-free Swiss cheese

1 tablespoon flour

Per Serving:
Calories: 276
% of calories from fat: 26
Fat (gm): 7.9
Saturated fat (gm): 2.1
Cholesterol (mg): 38.7
Sodium (mg): 562
Protein (gm): 14.4
Carbohydrate (gm): 34.7

Exchanges:
Milk: 0.0
Vegetable: 0.0
Fruit: 0.0
Bread: 2.0
Meat: 2.0
Fat: 0.5

1. Make Basic Pie Crust in 8-inch pie pan and bake.

2. Sauté onion in lightly greased small skillet until tender, 3 to 5 minutes. Mix onion and remaining ingredients, except cheese and flour, in medium bowl until smooth. Toss cheese with flour; stir into milk mixture and pour into pie crust. Bake at 350 degrees until quiche is set and a sharp knife inserted near center comes out clean, about 40 minutes. Cover edge of pie crust with aluminum foil if becoming too brown. Cool on wire rack 5 minutes.

VARIATION

Spinach Quiche — Make recipe as above, adding ½ package (10-ounce size) frozen, thawed, well drained chopped spinach to sautéed onion; cook over medium heat until mixture is quite dry, 3 to 4 minutes.

HASH AND EGGS

45 *You'll enjoy the variety of vegetables in this hearty hash.*

0 4 servings

1 cup chopped onion
4 medium Idaho potatoes, unpeeled, cooked, cubed
Vegetable cooking spray
1 cup each: frozen peas, whole kernel corn
½ teaspoon dried thyme leaves
Salt and pepper, to taste
4 eggs

Per Serving:
Calories: 180
% of calories from fat: 29
Fat (gm): 5.6
Saturated fat (gm): 1.6
Cholesterol (mg): 212.1
Sodium (mg): 461
Protein (gm): 13.7
Carbohydrate (gm): 17.1

Exchanges:
Milk: 0.0
Vegetable: 0.0
Fruit: 0.0
Bread: 1.5
Meat: 1.0
Fat: 0.5

1. Sauté onion and potatoes in lightly greased large skillet 2 to 3 minutes; spray with cooking spray and cook until potatoes are browned, about 5 minutes. Add peas, corn, and thyme; cook until hot, 2 to 3 minutes. Season to taste with salt and pepper. Move hash to side of skillet; add eggs and cook, covered, over medium-low heat until set, 3 to 4 minutes. Season to taste with salt and pepper.

VARIATION

Herbed Bean and Sweet Potato Hash — Make recipe as above, substituting sweet potatoes for the Idaho potatoes, 1 can (15 ounces) drained dark kidney beans for the peas and corn, and adding ¾ teaspoon crushed dried rosemary leaves.

SWEET POTATO HASH WITH POACHED EGGS

45 *A colorful hash dish that's perfect for a breakfast, brunch, or light supper.*

0

4 servings

2 cups each: cubed, peeled cooked sweet potatoes, Idaho potatoes
½ cup each: chopped onion, red bell pepper
¾ teaspoon each: dried rosemary and thyme leaves
Vegetable cooking spray
Salt and pepper, to taste
4 poached or fried eggs

Per Serving:
Calories: 393
% of calories from fat: 13
Fat (gm): 5.8
Saturated fat (gm): 1.7
Cholesterol (mg): 212
Sodium (mg): 171
Protein (gm): 12.3
Carbohydrate (gm): 74.4

Exchanges:
Milk: 0.0
Vegetable: 0.5
Fruit: 0.0
Bread: 4.5
Meat: 1.0
Fat: 0.0

1. Sauté vegetables and herbs in lightly greased large skillet 5 minutes; spray with cooking spray and cook until potatoes are browned, about 5 minutes. Season to taste with salt and pepper. Top each serving of hash with an egg.

HUEVOS RANCHEROS

0 *Everyone loves Mexican "country-style eggs" for a hearty breakfast! To speed preparation, canned refried beans can be used.*

6 servings

6 corn tortillas (6-inch)
Vegetable cooking spray
6 eggs, fried
Serrano Tomato Sauce (recipe follows)
Refried Beans (see p. 335)

1. Spray tortillas lightly on both sides with cooking spray; cook in large skillet over medium heat until browned, about 1 minute on each side. Top tortillas with eggs; spoon Serrano Tomato Sauce over eggs. Serve with Refried Beans.

Per Serving:
Calories: 252
% of calories from fat: 22
Fat (gm): 6.2
Saturated fat (gm): 1.7
Cholesterol (mg): 213
Sodium (mg): 109
Protein (gm): 14.3
Carbohydrate (gm): 35.6

Exchanges:
Milk: 0.0
Vegetable: 1.0
Fruit: 0.0
Bread: 2.0
Meat: 1.5
Fat: 0.0

Serrano Tomato Sauce

Makes about 2 cups

1 each: finely chopped small onion, clove garlic, serrano chili
2 large tomatoes, pureed
Salt, to taste

1. Sauté onion, garlic, and serrano chili in lightly greased medium skillet until tender, 3 to 4 minutes. Add tomatoes and heat to boiling; cook over medium to medium-high heat until mixture thickens to a medium sauce consistency, 5 to 8 minutes. Season to taste with salt.

MEXICAN SCRAMBLED EGGS WITH CHORIZO

45

In this recipe, the homemade Chorizo is crumbled, rather than being made into patties. Of course, purchased chorizo can also be used.

6 servings

1 large tomato, chopped
½ cup sliced green onions
2–3 teaspoons finely chopped serrano or jalapeño chilies
2 small cloves garlic, minced
Chorizo (see p. 154)
9 eggs, lightly beaten
¼ cup fat-free milk
Salt and pepper, to taste
Tomatillo Sauce, warm (see p. 184)
6 corn or flour tortillas (6-inch), warm

Per Serving:
Calories: 347
% of calories from fat: 31
Fat (gm): 12
Saturated fat (gm): 3
Cholesterol (mg): 388
Sodium (mg): 724
Protein (gm): 28
Carbohydrate (gm): 34

Exchanges:
Milk: 0.0
Vegetable: 0.0
Fruit: 0.0
Bread: 2.0
Meat: 3.0
Fat: 0.5

1. Sauté tomato, green onions, chilies, and garlic in lightly greased large skillet until tender, about 5 minutes. Add Chorizo and cook until browned, 3 to 4 minutes, crumbling with a fork. Add combined eggs and milk and cook over medium heat until eggs are set, stirring occasionally; season to taste with salt and pepper. Serve with Tomatillo Sauce and tortillas.

MEXICAN SCRAMBLED EGGS WITH SHRIMP

45 *Crabmeat can be substituted for the shrimp in this recipe if you prefer.*

4 servings

1 medium tomato, chopped

¼ cup sliced green onions

1–2 teaspoons finely chopped serrano or jalapeño chili

1 small clove garlic, minced

8 ounces peeled deveined shrimp

6 eggs, lightly beaten

2 tablespoons fat-free milk

Salt and pepper, to taste

1 cup Tomatillo Sauce, warm (see p. 184)

Per Serving:
Calories: 217
% of calories from fat: 39
Fat (gm): 9.4
Saturated fat (gm): 2.7
Cholesterol (mg): 404
Sodium (mg): 196
Protein (gm): 22.6
Carbohydrate (gm): 10.2

Exchanges:
Milk: 0.0
Vegetable: 2.0
Fruit: 0.0
Bread: 0.0
Meat: 3.0
Fat: 0.0

1. Sauté tomato, green onions, serrano chili, and garlic in lightly greased skillet until tender, about 5 minutes. Add shrimp and cook over medium heat until shrimp are pink and cooked, 3 to 4 minutes. Add combined eggs and milk; cook over medium to medium-low heat until eggs are cooked, stirring occasionally. Season to taste with salt and pepper. Serve with Tomatillo Sauce.

EGGS SCRAMBLED WITH CRISP TORTILLA STRIPS

LO *This is a good recipe to use with stale tortillas. Complement this hearty egg dish with Chorizo (see p. 154).*

6 servings

6 corn tortillas (6-inch), cut into strips (2 x ½-inch)
Vegetable cooking spray
9 eggs, lightly beaten
3 tablespoons fat-free milk
Salt and pepper, to taste
3 tablespoons each: crumbled Mexican white cheese
  or farmer's cheese, chopped cilantro
Poblano Chili Sauce, warm (see p. 185)
Black Beans and Rice, warm (see p. 334)

Per Serving:
Calories: 367
% of calories from fat: 18
Fat (gm): 7.7
Saturated fat (gm): 2.2
Cholesterol (mg): 215.7
Sodium (mg): 480
Protein (gm): 22.9
Carbohydrate (gm): 55.9

Exchanges:
Milk: 0.0
Vegetable: 1.0
Fruit: 0.0
Bread: 3.0
Meat: 2.5
Fat: 0.0

1. Spray tortilla strips lightly with cooking spray and toss; cook in large skillet over medium to medium-high heat until browned and crisp, 3 to 4 minutes. Pour combined eggs and milk over tortilla strips; cook over medium to medium-low heat until eggs are cooked, stirring occasionally. Season to taste with salt and pepper; sprinkle with cheese and cilantro. Serve with Poblano Chili Sauce and Black Beans and Rice.

EGGS SCRAMBLED WITH CACTUS

45
LO *Cactus paddles, or "nopales," are available canned as well as fresh; the canned cactus does not have to be cooked. Poblano chilies or sweet bell peppers can be substituted, if preferred.*

4 servings

1 quart water
8 ounces cactus paddles, sliced
1 teaspoon salt
¼ teaspoon baking soda
¾ cup each: chopped onion, tomato
1 teaspoon finely chopped jalapeño chili
6 eggs, lightly beaten

2 tablespoons fat-free milk

Salt and pepper, to taste

4 corn or flour tortillas (6-inch), warm

Per Serving:
Calories: 182
% of calories from fat: 29
Fat (gm): 6
Saturated fat (gm): 2
Cholesterol (mg): 212
Sodium (mg): 292
Protein (gm): 13
Carbohydrate (gm): 20

Exchanges:
Milk: 0.0
Vegetable: 0.0
Fruit: 0.0
Bread: 1.0
Meat: 2.0
Fat: 0.0

1. Heat water to boiling in medium saucepan; add cactus, salt, and baking soda. Reduce heat and simmer, uncovered, until cactus is crisp-tender, about 20 minutes. Rinse and drain. Sauté cactus, onion, tomato, and jalapeño chili in lightly greased large skillet until onion is tender, 3 to 4 minutes. Add combined eggs and milk; cook over medium heat until set, stirring occasionally. Season to taste with salt and pepper. Serve with tortillas.

CHIPOTLE POTATO AND EGG BAKE

For convenience, this recipe uses frozen vegetable products. For a serving variation, potato mixture can be spooned onto serving plates and topped with poached or fried eggs.

4 servings

2 cups frozen stir-fry pepper blend

1–2 teaspoons minced garlic

¼–½ small canned chipotle chili in adobo sauce, chopped

1⅓ cups fat-free milk

2⅔ cups frozen mashed potatoes

Salt, to taste

4 eggs

½–¾ cup (2–3 ounces) shredded reduced-fat Cheddar cheese

Per Serving:
Calories: 242
% of calories from fat: 27
Fat (gm): 7.2
Saturated fat (gm): 2.2
Cholesterol (mg): 213.6
Sodium (mg): 452
Protein (gm): 16.5
Carbohydrate (gm): 27.1

Exchanges:
Milk: 0.0
Vegetable: 2.0
Fruit: 0.0
Bread: 1.0
Meat: 2.0
Fat: 0.5

1. Sauté pepper blend and garlic in lightly greased skillet until peppers begin to brown, about 5 minutes. Add chipotle chili and milk; heat until milk is steaming. Stir in potatoes; cook over medium heat, stirring frequently, until potatoes are thickened, 4 to 5 minutes. Season to taste with salt.

2. Spread potato mixture in greased 8-inch square or round baking pan, or 4 individual gratin dishes. Make 4 indentations in potatoes with back of spoon; break eggs into indentations. Sprinkle cheese over potatoes and eggs. Bake at 350 degrees until eggs are desired doneness, 13 to 15 minutes.

BEAN AND CHEESE CHILI RELLENOS

45

L

Chili rellenos are normally coated with a beaten egg white mixture and fried in deep oil; our healthy version omits this fat-laden step.

6 servings

6 medium poblano chilies or green bell peppers

2–3 quarts water

1 tablespoon each: jalapeño chili, minced garlic

1 teaspoon dried oregano leaves

16 ounces fat-free cream cheese, room temperature

½ cup (2 ounces) Mexican white cheese or farmer's cheese, crumbled

1½ cups cooked pinto beans or 1 can (15 ounces) pinto beans, rinsed, drained

1 tablespoon vegetable oil

Per Serving:
Calories: 204
% of calories from fat: 25
Fat (gm): 5.5
Saturated fat (gm): 0.4
Cholesterol (mg): 22.3
Sodium (mg): 520
Protein (gm): 17.2
Carbohydrate (gm): 19.4

Exchanges:
Milk: 0.0
Vegetable: 1.0
Fruit: 0.0
Bread: 1.0
Meat: 1.5
Fat: 0.5

1. Cut stems from tops of poblano chilies; remove and discard seeds and veins. Cook chilies in simmering water to cover, until chilies are slightly softened, 2 to 3 minutes. Drain.

2. Sauté jalapeño chili, garlic, and oregano in lightly greased skillet until chili is tender, 2 to 3 minutes. Mix chili mixture, cheeses, and beans; stuff poblano chilies with mixture. Sauté chilies in oil in large skillet over medium to medium-high heat until tender and browned on all sides, 6 to 8 minutes.

BREAKFAST BURRITOS

A delicious alternative to standard breakfast fare!

6 servings

3 cups cubed, cooked, unpeeled Idaho potatoes

1 cup each: chopped red or green bell peppers,
   green onions

1½ cups cubed zucchini

¼ cup whole kernel corn

4 cloves garlic, minced

8 eggs, lightly beaten

¼ cup finely chopped cilantro

¾ teaspoon dried oregano leaves

1 cup (4 ounces) shredded reduced-fat mozzarella
   or Cheddar cheese

Salt and pepper, to taste

6 large flour tortillas (10-inch)

1–1½ cups mild or hot salsa

Per Serving:
Calories: 478
% of calories from fat: 28
Fat (gm): 14.5
Saturated fat (gm): 5
Cholesterol (mg): 292
Sodium (mg): 785
Protein (gm): 20
Carbohydrate (gm): 65

Exchanges:
Milk: 0.0
Vegetable: 1.0
Fruit: 0.0
Bread: 4.0
Meat: 2.0
Fat: 1.0

1. Sauté vegetables and garlic in lightly greased large skillet until potatoes are browned, about 10 minutes. Add combined eggs, cilantro, and oregano; cook over medium heat until set, stirring occasionally. Remove from heat and stir in cheese; season to taste with salt and pepper. Spoon mixture onto tortillas; fold 2 sides of each tortilla in about 2 inches, then fold in other sides to enclose filling. Serve with salsa.

TOMATO, SPINACH, AND CHEESE BURRITOS

L

A Neapolitan burrito!

45

4 servings

1 cup each: fat-free and reduced-fat ricotta cheese
1 teaspoon grated Parmesan cheese
¾ teaspoon chili powder
½ teaspoon each: crushed red pepper, ground cumin
4 large flour tortillas (10-inch)
4 ounces spinach leaves, thinly sliced
1 large tomato, chopped
Olive oil cooking spray
½ cup each: prepared salsa, fat-free sour cream

Per Serving:
Calories: 285
% of calories from fat: 16
Fat (gm): 5.3
Saturated fat (gm): 1.9
Cholesterol (mg): 16.9
Sodium (mg): 712
Protein (gm): 26.6
Carbohydrate (gm): 34.7

Exchanges:
Milk: 0.0
Vegetable: 2.0
Fruit: 0.0
Bread: 1.0
Meat: 3.0
Fat: 0.0

1. Combine cheeses and seasonings in medium bowl. Spread ½ cup cheese mixture in center of each tortilla; sprinkle with spinach and tomato. Fold 2 sides of each tortilla in about 2 inches, then fold in other sides to enclose filling. Arrange burritos, seam sides down, in greased baking pan; spray lightly with cooking spray. Bake at 400 degrees until browned, about 25 minutes. Serve with salsa and sour cream.

NEW MEXICO EGG TOSTADAS

45

These easy tostadas are baked and served with a simple chili sauce.

4 servings

4 whole wheat tortillas (6-inch)
2 cups fat-free refried beans
2 green onions, thinly sliced
4 eggs
Red Sauce (recipe follows)
4 tablespoons fat-free sour cream
Chopped cilantro, as garnish

Per Serving:
Calories: 251
% of calories from fat: 18
Fat (gm): 5.1
Saturated fat (gm): 1.6
Cholesterol (mg): 212
Sodium (mg): 715
Protein (gm): 15.2
Carbohydrate (gm): 35.1

Exchanges:
Milk: 0.0
Vegetable: 0.0
Fruit: 0.0
Bread: 2.5
Meat: 1.0
Fat: 0.5

1. Quickly immerse tortillas in cold water and drain; bake on greased cookie sheet at 450 degrees until lightly browned, 2 to 3 minutes. Spoon refried beans around outer edge of each tortilla; sprinkle with green onions. Break an egg into center of each tortilla. Bake at 350 degrees until eggs are set, 15 to 20 minutes. Serve with Red Sauce and sour cream; garnish with cilantro.

Red Sauce

Makes about ¾ cup

¼ cup chopped onion
½ cup reduced-sodium fat-free beef broth
¼ cup crushed New Mexico chilies, seeds and stems discarded

1. Heat all ingredients to boiling in small saucepan; reduce heat and simmer, covered, until onion and chilies are soft, about 5 minutes. Process in blender or food processor until smooth.

BLACK BEAN CHEESECAKE WITH SALSA

LO

45

This unusual entrée can also be served in smaller pieces as an appetizer or first course. It can be served at room temperature, or heated as the recipe directs. Make it a day in advance, as overnight chilling is essential.

8 servings

4 flour tortillas (6-inch)
24 ounces fat-free cream cheese, room temperature
6 eggs
1 can (15 ounces) black beans, rinsed, drained
2 tablespoons finely chopped onion
1 tablespoon each: minced garlic, jalapeño chili
2 teaspoons dried cumin
½ teaspoon each: dried oregano leaves, chili powder, salt, cayenne pepper
1 cup hot or mild salsa

Per Serving:
Calories: 249
% of calories from fat: 25
Fat (gm): 7
Saturated fat (gm): 2
Cholesterol (mg): 165
Sodium (mg): 797
Protein (gm): 21.5
Carbohydrate (gm): 25

Exchanges:
Milk: 0.0
Vegetable: 0.0
Fruit: 0.0
Bread: 1.5
Meat: 2.5
Fat: 0.0

1. Line greased 9-inch springform pan with overlapping tortillas.

2. Beat cream cheese in large bowl until smooth; beat in eggs. Mix in remaining ingredients, except salsa; pour into prepared springform pan. Bake, uncovered, at 300 degrees until center is set and sharp knife inserted halfway between center and edge of cheese-cake comes out almost clean, 1¾ to 2 hours. Cool on wire rack; refrigerate 8 hours or overnight.

3. Cook wedges of cheesecake in lightly greased large skillet over medium-low heat until browned on both sides. Serve with salsa.

EIGHT

Pasta

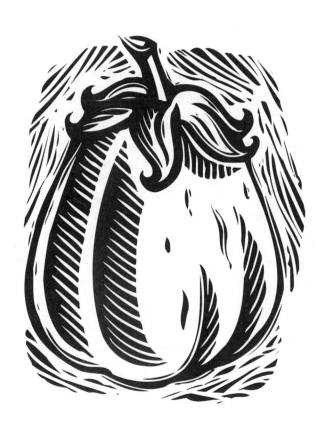

HOMEMADE PASTA

o *Fresh pasta dough is not difficult to make. A pasta machine is a very simple way of kneading, rolling, and cutting the dough, and it produces a high-quality pasta. Rolling and cutting the dough by hand is somewhat more difficult; it requires practice to make thin, delicate pasta. Be sure to follow cooking directions in step 4 carefully. Fresh pasta cooks very quickly—much more quickly than purchased fresh or dried pasta.*

4 entrée servings

1½ cups all-purpose flour

2 large eggs

Additional flour for rolling

Per Serving:
Calories: 208
% of calories from fat: 13
Fat (gm): 3
Saturated fat (gm): 0.8
Cholesterol (mg): 106.5
Sodium (mg): 32
Protein (gm): 8
Carbohydrate (gm): 36.1

Exchanges:
Milk: 0.0
Vegetable: 0.0
Fruit: 0.0
Bread: 2.5
Meat: 0.0
Fat: 0.5

1. Mound flour on cutting board, making a well in center. Drop eggs into center of well. Mix eggs with a fork. While mixing eggs, gradually start to incorporate flour into the eggs. As flour is incorporated, it will be necessary to move the mound of flour toward the center, using your hands. Continue mixing until all or almost all flour has been incorporated, forming a soft, but not sticky, ball of dough.

2. To knead dough with a pasta machine, set machine rollers on the widest setting. Cut dough into 2 equal pieces. Lightly flour outside of 1 piece, and pass it through the machine. Fold piece of dough into thirds; pass it through the machine again, inserting open edges (not the fold) of dough first. Repeat folding and rolling 8 to 12 times or until dough feels smooth and satiny; lightly flour dough only if it begins to feel sticky.

Move machine rollers to next narrower setting. Pass dough, without folding, through the machine, beginning to roll out and stretch dough. Move machine rollers to next narrower setting; pass dough through the machine. Continue process until pasta is as thin as desired. (Often the narrowest setting on machine makes pasta too thin; 1 or 2 settings from the end is usually best.) Lightly flour dough if it begins to feel even slightly sticky at any time. Repeat above procedures with second piece of dough.

To cut pasta with the machine, set cutting rollers for width of pasta desired; pass dough through cutters. Arrange cut pasta in single layer on lightly floured surface.

3. To knead dough by hand, knead on lightly floured surface until smooth and satiny, about 10 minutes. Cover dough lightly with damp towel and let rest 10 minutes.

Place dough on lightly floured surface. Starting in center of dough, roll with rolling pin from center to edge. Continue rolling, always from center to edge, keeping dough as round as possible, until dough is about 1/16 inch thick. Lightly flour dough if it begins to feel even slightly sticky at any time.

To cut pasta by hand, flour top of dough lightly and roll up. Cut into desired widths with sharp knife. Immediately unroll cut pasta and arrange in single layer on lightly floured surface.

4. To cook fresh or dried pasta, heat 4 to 5 quarts lightly salted water to boiling. Add pasta and begin testing for doneness as soon as water returns to boil. Cooking time will vary from 0 to 2 minutes once water has returned to boil.

NOTES: Pasta can be cooked fresh, or it can be dried and frozen or stored in an airtight container to be cooked later. To dry pasta, let stand on floured surface (or hang over rack) until completely dried. (Be sure pasta is completely dried or it will turn moldy in storage.) Store at room temperature in airtight container, or freeze.

Fresh homemade pasta can be used with any recipe, but it will result in a higher cholesterol count than stated with the recipe.

PASTA BOLOGNESE

45 *Bolognese is no doubt the favorite of pasta sauces—enjoy this savory healthful version!*

6 servings

1 pound ground beef eye of round

¼ cup each: chopped onion, carrot, celery

3 cloves garlic, minced

1½ teaspoons dried Italian seasoning

⅛ teaspoon ground nutmeg

1 can (8 ounces) each: reduced-sodium tomato sauce, reduced-sodium whole tomatoes, undrained, chopped

¼ cup dry red wine or tomato juice

½ teaspoon salt

¼ teaspoon pepper

12 ounces spaghetti, cooked, warm

Per Serving:
Calories: 361
% of calories from fat: 16
Fat (gm): 6.2
Saturated fat (gm): 2.2
Cholesterol (mg): 28.2
Sodium (mg): 287
Protein (gm): 24.6
Carbohydrate (gm): 50.2

Exchanges:
Milk: 0.0
Vegetable: 1.0
Fruit: 0.0
Bread: 3.0
Meat: 2.0
Fat: 0.0

1. Cook ground beef in lightly greased medium saucepan over medium heat until browned, 5 to 8 minutes; drain well and crumble. Add onion, carrot, celery, garlic, Italian seasoning, and nutmeg to saucepan; sauté until lightly browned, about 5 minutes. Add tomato sauce, tomatoes with liquid, and wine; heat to boiling. Reduce heat and simmer, uncovered, until thick sauce consistency, about 15 minutes; stir in salt and pepper. Serve over spaghetti.

45-MINUTE PREPARATION TIP: Cook pasta while sauce is simmering.

PASTA WITH TOMATO AND MEATBALL SAUCE

Herb-Seasoned Meatballs can be made up to two days in advance, making the sauce very easy to complete.

8 servings

1 cup chopped onion

1 tablespoon each: minced garlic, olive oil

1 can (16 ounces) reduced-sodium whole tomatoes, undrained, chopped

1 can (8 ounces) reduced-sodium tomato sauce
2 teaspoons dried Italian seasoning
⅛ teaspoon crushed red pepper
Herb-Seasoned Meatballs (recipe follows)
Salt, to taste
12 ounces spaghetti, cooked, warm

Per Serving:
Calories: 355
% of calories from fat: 21
Fat (gm): 8.4
Saturated fat (gm): 1.9
Cholesterol (mg): 42.3
Sodium (mg): 405
Protein (gm): 20.2
Carbohydrate (gm): 48.8

Exchanges:
Milk: 0.0
Vegetable: 3.0
Fruit: 0.0
Bread: 2.0
Meat: 1.5
Fat: 1.0

1. Sauté onion and garlic in oil in large saucepan 2 to 3 minutes. Stir in tomatoes with liquid, tomato sauce, Italian seasoning, and crushed red pepper; heat to boiling. Reduce heat and simmer, uncovered, 10 minutes. Add Herb-Seasoned Meatballs; simmer, uncovered, until medium sauce consistency, 10 to 15 minutes. Season to taste with salt. Serve over spaghetti.

Herb-Seasoned Meatballs

Makes 18 meatballs

1 pound ground turkey or lean beef
⅓ cup unseasoned dry bread crumbs
1 egg white
3 cloves garlic, minced
1 teaspoon dried Italian seasoning
½ teaspoon salt
¼ teaspoon pepper

1. Mix all ingredients; shape into 18 meatballs. Cook meatballs over medium heat in lightly greased skillet until cooked and browned on all sides, 8 to 10 minutes. Drain well.

PASTA PUTTANESCA

45 *Ham, olives, and red pepper flakes add distinctive flavor to this popular sauce.*

8 servings

3 large onions, chopped

2 teaspoons minced garlic

2½ tablespoons olive oil

1 cup diced lean ham or Canadian bacon

2 cans (28 ounces each) reduced-sodium tomatoes,
   undrained, chopped

¼ cup sliced green olives

2 teaspoons dried basil leaves

⅛–¼ teaspoon crushed red pepper

Salt, to taste

16 ounces spaghetti, cooked, warm

Per Serving:
Calories: 330
% of calories from fat: 18
Fat (gm): 6.5
Saturated fat (gm): 1
Cholesterol (mg): 8.4
Sodium (mg): 278
Protein (gm): 12.8
Carbohydrate (gm): 56

Exchanges:
Milk: 0.0
Vegetable: 2.0
Fruit: 0.0
Bread: 3.0
Meat: 1.0
Fat: 0.5

1. Sauté onions and garlic in olive oil in large saucepan until tender and lightly browned, about 10 minutes. Add remaining ingredients, except salt and spaghetti and heat to boiling. Reduce heat and simmer, uncovered, until thickened to medium sauce consistency, about 15 minutes; season to taste with salt and pepper. Serve over spaghetti.

45-MINUTE PREPARATION TIP: Cook pasta while sauce is simmering.

PASTA PEPERONATA

45

The Peperonata mixture is a great addition to Italian sausage or bratwurst sandwiches.

4 servings

1½ cups each: sliced red, green, yellow bell peppers

1 cup each: sliced yellow and red onion

8 cloves garlic, minced

2 tablespoons each: olive oil, water

½ teaspoon dried thyme leaves

1 teaspoon sugar

Salt and pepper, to taste

8 ounces spaghetti, cooked, warm

¼ cup (1 ounce) grated Parmesan cheese

Per Serving:
Calories: 426
% of calories from fat: 25
Fat (gm): 11.8
Saturated fat (gm): 1.6
Cholesterol (mg): 0
Sodium (mg): 8
Protein (gm): 11.1
Carbohydrate (gm): 70.3

Exchanges:
Milk: 0.0
Vegetable: 3.0
Fruit: 0.0
Bread: 3.5
Meat: 0.0
Fat: 2.5

1. Sauté peppers, onions, and garlic in oil in large skillet 2 to 3 minutes. Add water; cook, covered, over medium to medium-high heat until vegetables are softened, about 5 minutes. Stir in thyme and sugar; cook, uncovered, over medium-low heat until mixture is very soft and browned, about 20 minutes. Season to taste with salt and pepper. Toss with spaghetti; sprinkle with cheese.

VARIATION

Roasted Peperonata with Italian Sausage — Make recipe above, omitting olive oil, water, thyme, sugar, and pasta. Arrange vegetables in single layer on greased foil-lined jelly roll pan; spray with olive oil cooking spray and sprinkle with 1½ teaspoons dried Italian seasoning. Roast at 425 degrees until browned and very soft, about 45 minutes; toss with cheese in bowl. While vegetables are roasting, cook 1½ pounds Italian-style turkey sausage in greased large skillet until cooked and browned, about 10 minutes; cut into serving pieces and serve with peperonata.

45-MINUTE PREPARATION TIP: Begin cooking the spaghetti before preparing the rest of the recipe.

PASTA WITH GREENS, RAISINS, AND PINE NUTS

45

V

Radicchio, escarole, curly endive, kale, or mustard greens can be substituted for the brightly colored Oriental kale in this sweet-and-bitter Italian favorite.

4 servings

4 medium onions, sliced

1 tablespoon each: minced garlic, olive oil

1 teaspoon sugar

12 ounces Oriental kale leaves, torn

⅓ cup dark raisins

½ cup reduced-sodium vegetable broth

Salt and pepper, to taste

8 ounces whole wheat spaghetti or linguine, cooked, warm

2 tablespoons pine nuts or slivered almonds

Per Serving:
Calories: 391
% of calories from fat: 17
Fat (gm): 8
Saturated fat (gm): 0.9
Cholesterol (mg): 0.0
Sodium (mg): 127
Protein (gm): 13
Carbohydrate (gm): 75

Exchanges:
Milk: 0.0
Vegetable: 0.0
Fruit: 0.0
Bread: 4.0
Meat: 0.0
Fat: 1.0

1. Sauté onions and garlic in oil in large skillet until tender, 3 to 5 minutes. Stir in sugar; cook over low heat until onions are golden, 10 to 15 minutes, stirring occasionally. Stir in kale, raisins, and broth; cook, covered, over low heat until kale is wilted, about 10 minutes. Season to taste with salt and pepper. Toss with spaghetti and sprinkle with pine nuts.

45-MINUTE PREPARATION TIP: Begin cooking the spaghetti before preparing the rest of the recipe.

PASTA WITH GOAT CHEESE AND ONION CONFIT

45

L

Try this dish with flavored specialty pastas such as dried mushroom, herb, or black pepper.

4 servings

4 cups thinly sliced onions

1 teaspoon each: minced garlic, sugar

½ teaspoon each: dried sage and rosemary leaves

½ cup dry white wine or fat-free milk

2 ounces each: fat-free cream cheese, goat cheese

Salt and pepper, to taste

8 ounces whole wheat thin spaghetti, cooked, warm

2–3 tablespoons coarsely chopped walnuts

Per Serving:
Calories: 395
% of calories from fat: 15
Fat (gm): 6.7
Saturated fat (gm): 2.4
Cholesterol (mg): 6.5
Sodium (mg): 144
Protein (gm): 16
Carbohydrate (gm): 66.9

Exchanges:
Milk: 0.0
Vegetable: 2.0
Fruit: 0.0
Bread: 4.0
Meat: 0.5
Fat: 0.5

1. Sauté onions in lightly greased large skillet 3 to 4 minutes; stir in garlic, sugar, and herbs and cook, uncovered, over medium-low heat until onions are golden, 15 to 20 minutes. Stir in wine; simmer 2 to 3 minutes. Add cream cheese and goat cheese, stirring until melted; season to taste with salt and pepper. Toss with pasta; sprinkle with walnuts.

45-MINUTE PREPARATION TIP: Cook spaghetti while onions are cooking.

WARM ANGEL HAIR AND GOAT CHEESE SALAD

45

L

Goat cheese adds a creamy texture and piquant accent to this flavorful pasta dish.

6 servings

2 cups each: halved snow peas, sliced mushrooms

3 medium carrots, julienned

4 large plum tomatoes, sliced

2 teaspoons dried oregano leaves

1 teaspoon dried tarragon leaves

½ cup each: reduced-sodium vegetable broth, fat-free milk

2 teaspoons tomato paste

¼ teaspoon each: salt, pepper

12 ounces capellini (angel hair) or thin spaghetti cooked, warm

3 ounces goat cheese or reduced-fat cream cheese

Per Serving:
Calories: 328
% of calories from fat: 13
Fat (gm): 4.7
Saturated fat (gm): 2.3
Cholesterol (mg): 6.8
Sodium (mg): 197
Protein (gm): 13.9
Carbohydrate (gm): 58.5

Exchanges:
Milk: 0.0
Vegetable: 2.0
Fruit: 0.0
Bread: 3.0
Meat: 0.0
Fat: 1.0

1. Sauté vegetables and herbs in lightly greased large skillet until snow peas are crisp-tender, 6 to 8 minutes. Stir in broth, milk, and tomato paste; heat to boiling. Reduce heat and simmer, uncovered, until thickened to sauce consistency, about 10 minutes, stirring occasionally. Stir in salt and pepper. Toss with pasta and goat cheese.

45-MINUTE PREPARATION TIP: Begin cooking the capellini before pre–paring the rest of the recipe.

MOLDED CAPELLINI CARBONARA

Thin spaghetti or linguine can be substituted for the angel hair pasta. The center of the mold can be filled with a mixture of vegetables.

4 servings

¼ cup minced shallots

1 teaspoon minced garlic

1 cup seeded chopped Italian plum tomatoes

½ teaspoon dried oregano leaves

¼ teaspoon crushed red pepper

2 slices bacon, fried crisp, crumbled

Salt, to taste

8 ounces capellini (angel hair pasta), cooked

3 eggs, lightly beaten

Per Serving:
Calories: 249
% of calories from fat: 24
Fat (gm): 6.9
Saturated fat (gm): 2.2
Cholesterol (mg): 224.1
Sodium (mg): 99
Protein (gm): 12.8
Carbohydrate (gm): 34.1

Exchanges:
Milk: 0.0
Vegetable: 1.0
Fruit: 0.0
Bread: 2.0
Meat: 1.0
Fat: 0.5

1. Sauté shallots and garlic in lightly greased skillet until tender, 3 to 4 minutes. Add tomatoes, oregano, and crushed red pepper. Cook, covered, over medium heat until tomatoes soften, about 5 minutes; stir in bacon and season to taste with salt. Combine with pasta and eggs and spoon into greased 6-cup ring mold. Bake, uncovered, at 350 degrees until set, about 20 minutes. Invert onto serving plate.

45-MINUTE PREPARATION TIP: Begin cooking the capellini before preparing the rest of the recipe.

STIR-FRIED RICE NOODLES WITH VEGETABLES

Rice noodles are also called cellophane noodles, or "bihon." The dried noodles are soaked in cold water to soften, then drained before using.

4 servings

1 package (8 ounces) rice noodles

1 cup each: cut green beans, cubed yellow
   summer squash

½ cup each: thinly sliced celery, red bell pepper

4 green onions, thinly sliced

1 tablespoon finely chopped gingerroot

1 tablespoon canola oil

2 cups shredded napa cabbage

1 cup reduced-sodium vegetable broth

2 tablespoons dry sherry (optional)

2–3 teaspoons light soy sauce

½–1 teaspoon Szechuan chili sauce

Per Serving:
Calories: 161
% of calories from fat: 20
Fat (gm): 3.8
Saturated fat (gm): 0.5
Cholesterol (mg): 0
Sodium (mg): 137
Protein (gm): 4.2
Carbohydrate (gm): 29.4

Exchanges:
Milk: 0.0
Vegetable: 1.0
Fruit: 0.0
Bread: 1.5
Meat: 0.0
Fat: 0.5

1. Place noodles in large bowl; pour cold water over to cover. Let stand until noodles separate and are soft, about 15 minutes; drain.

2. Stir-fry green beans, squash, celery, bell pepper, green onions, and gingerroot in oil in large wok or skillet until tender, 8 to 10 minutes. Add cabbage and stir-fry 1 minute. Stir in noodles and remaining ingredients. Heat to boiling; reduce heat and simmer, uncovered, until noodles have absorbed all liquid, about 5 minutes.

STIR-FRIED RICE NOODLES WITH SHRIMP

45 *Sea or bay scallops can be substituted for the shrimp.*

4 servings

1 package (8 ounces) rice noodles
8 ounces peeled, deveined shrimp
2 cups shredded napa cabbage
4 green onions, thinly sliced
1 tablespoon finely chopped gingerroot
1 tablespoon vegetable oil
1 cup reduced-sodium chicken broth
2 tablespoons dry sherry (optional)
2–3 teaspoons light soy sauce
½–1 teaspoon Szechuan chili sauce

Per Serving:
Calories: 292
% of calories from fat: 13
Fat (gm): 4.2
Saturated fat (gm): 0.6
Cholesterol (mg): 87.1
Sodium (mg): 223
Protein (gm): 17.1
Carbohydrate (gm): 46.6

Exchanges:
Milk: 0.0
Vegetable: 1.0
Fruit: 0.0
Bread: 3.0
Meat: 1.0
Fat: 0.0

1. Place noodles in large bowl; pour cold water over to cover. Let stand until noodles separate and are soft, about 15 minutes; drain.

2. Stir-fry shrimp in oil in wok or large skillet until cooked, about 5 minutes; remove from wok. Add cabbage, green onions, and gingerroot to wok and stir-fry 3 to 4 minutes. Add remaining ingredients, except shrimp, and heat to boiling; reduce heat and simmer, uncovered, until noodles have absorbed all liquid, about 5 minutes. Return shrimp to wok; stir-fry until hot, 2 to 3 minutes.

45-MINUTE PREPARATION TIP: Cut vegetables while noodles are soaking.

LINGUINE WITH MIXED HERB PESTO

45 *A ½-ounce package of fresh herbs yields about ¼ cup packed herb leaves. Serve pesto sauce at room temperature, mixing with hot pasta.*

4 servings

½ cup each: packed basil and parsley leaves
¼ cup packed oregano leaves
3–4 tablespoons grated fat-free Parmesan cheese
1 ounce walnuts (about 14 medium)
1 tablespoon olive oil, minced garlic

2 teaspoons lemon juice

2–4 tablespoons reduced-sodium fat-free chicken broth or water

½ teaspoon salt

¼ teaspoon pepper

8 ounces linguine, cooked, warm

Per Serving:
Calories: 253
% of calories from fat: 30
Fat (gm): 8.8
Saturated fat (gm): 0.7
Cholesterol (mg): 0
Sodium (mg): 447
Protein (gm): 9.7
Carbohydrate (gm): 36

Exchanges:
Milk: 0.0
Vegetable: 1.0
Fruit: 0.0
Bread: 2.0
Meat: 0.0
Fat: 1.5

1. Process all ingredients, except linguine, in food processor until mixture is a smooth, spoonable paste; toss with linguine.

45-MINUTE PREPARATION TIP: Make pesto while linguine is cooking.

ROASTED SUMMER VEGETABLES WITH PASTA

For attractive serving, the pasta can be shaped into small nests to contain the medley of roasted vegetables.

8 servings

1 medium eggplant, peeled, cubed (1-inch)

1 cup each: sliced zucchini, red or green bell pepper, red onion wedges

Olive oil cooking spray

2 teaspoons crushed caraway seeds

3 tablespoons olive oil

2 tablespoons balsamic or red wine vinegar

1 teaspoon lemon juice

3 cloves garlic, minced

¼ teaspoon each: salt, pepper

16 ounces linguine, cooked, warm

Per Serving:
Calories: 275
% of calories from fat: 21
Fat (gm): 6
Saturated fat (gm): 0.7
Cholesterol (mg): 0.0
Sodium (mg): 258
Protein (gm): 17
Carbohydrate (gm): 38

Exchanges:
Milk: 0.0
Vegetable: 1.0
Fruit: 0.0
Bread: 2.0
Meat: 2.0
Fat: 0.0

1. Arrange vegetables in single layer on greased foil-lined jelly roll pan; spray with cooking spray and sprinkle with caraway seeds. Roast at 425 degrees until vegetables are browned and tender, 30 to 40 minutes. Combine remaining ingredients, except pasta; drizzle over vegetables and toss. Serve with pasta.

45-MINUTE PREPARATION TIP: Cook pasta while vegetables are roasting.

LINGUINE WITH WHITE CLAM SAUCE

45 *One of Italy's most treasured dishes!*

4 servings

1 tablespoon each: minced garlic, olive oil

2 cups bottled clam juice

1 tablespoons cornstarch

½ cup dry white wine or clam juice

1 pound shucked clams or 2 cans (7½ ounces each)
baby clams, undrained

1 tablespoon lemon juice

1 teaspoon dried basil leaves

⅛ teaspoon ground white pepper

8 ounces linguine, cooked, warm

Per Serving:
Calories: 319
% of calories from fat: 18
Fat (gm): 6.5
Saturated fat (gm): 0.6
Cholesterol (mg): 38.6
Sodium (mg): 305
Protein (gm): 23.5
Carbohydrate (gm): 39.1

Exchanges:
Milk: 0.0
Vegetable: 0.5
Fruit: 0.0
Bread: 2.5
Meat: 2.0
Fat: 0.5

1. Sauté garlic in oil in medium saucepan, 1 to 2 minutes. Stir in clam juice and heat to boiling; whisk in combined cornstarch and wine, whisking until thickened, about 1 minute. Add remaining ingredients, except linguine; simmer, covered, until clams are cooked, 5 to 7 minutes. Serve over linguine.

45-MINUTE PREPARATION TIP: Begin cooking pasta before preparing the rest of the recipe.

LINGUINE WITH RED CLAM SAUCE

45 *This light tomato sauce is rich with succulent clams.*

4 servings

1 tablespoon each: minced garlic, olive oil

1 can (28 ounces) Italian tomatoes, undrained, coarsely chopped

¼ cup dry red wine, clam juice, or water

2 teaspoons dried oregano leaves

1 tablespoon lemon juice

⅛–¼ teaspoon cayenne pepper

¼ teaspoon black pepper

1 pound shucked baby clams or 2 cans

(7½ ounces each) baby clams, undrained
8 ounces linguine, cooked, warm

Per Serving:
Calories: 332
% of calories from fat: 16
Fat (gm): 5.8
Saturated fat (gm): 0.6
Cholesterol (mg): 38.1
Sodium (mg): 590
Protein (gm): 22.3
Carbohydrate (gm): 43.8

Exchanges:
Milk: 0.0
Vegetable: 2.0
Fruit: 0.0
Bread: 2.0
Meat: 2.0
Fat: 0.5

1. Sauté garlic in oil in medium saucepan until tender, about 2 minutes. Stir in remaining ingredients, except clams and linguine; heat to boiling. Reduce heat and simmer, uncovered, until mixture is medium sauce consistency, about 10 minutes. Stir in clams; simmer, covered, until clams are cooked, 5 to 7 minutes. Discard any unopened clams. Serve over linguine.

45-MINUTE PREPARATION TIP: Cook pasta while sauce is simmering.

JERK CHICKEN AND SHRIMP WITH LINGUINE

Enjoy the highly seasoned flavors of the Caribbean in this pasta dish!

4 servings

Jerk Sauce (recipe follows)
8 ounces chicken tenders
4 ounces peeled, deveined shrimp
1 can (14½ ounces) reduced-sodium chicken broth
2 teaspoons lime juice
1 pound broccoli florets, cooked crisp-tender
8 ounces linguine, cooked, warm

Per Serving:
Calories: 332
% of calories from fat: 13
Fat (gm): 4.9
Saturated fat (gm): 0.6
Cholesterol (mg): 73
Sodium (mg): 232
Protein (gm): 28
Carbohydrate (gm): 47

Exchanges:
Milk: 0.0
Vegetable: 2.0
Fruit: 0.0
Bread: 2.5
Meat: 2.0
Fat: 0.0

1. Combine Jerk Sauce with chicken and shrimp in glass bowl and toss. Refrigerate, covered, 30 minutes.

2. Cook chicken and shrimp in lightly greased large skillet over medium-high heat until chicken and shrimp are browned, about 5 minutes. Stir in chicken broth and lime juice; heat to boiling. Reduce heat and simmer, uncovered, until liquid is thin sauce consistency, about 5 minutes; add broccoli and cook 2 to 3 minutes. Serve over linguine.

Jerk Sauce
Makes about ⅓ cup

3 tablespoons water
2 tablespoons each: chopped cilantro, gingerroot, light brown sugar
1 tablespoon ground allspice
2 teaspoons each: chopped garlic, black peppercorns
¼ teaspoon each: ground coriander, mace, crushed red pepper

1. Process all ingredients in food processor until coarse paste is formed.

45-MINUTE PREPARATION TIP: Begin cooking linguine before preparing step 2 of recipe.

FETTUCCINE WITH FENNEL, SPROUTS, AND HAM

45 *If fennel is not available, substitute ½ cup thinly sliced celery, and add ½ teaspoon crushed fennel seeds to the sautéed vegetables.*

4 servings

4 ounces sliced reduced-sodium ham, cut into thin strips
1 cup each: thinly sliced fennel bulb, onion
8 ounces small Brussels sprouts, halved
¼ cup water
1 tablespoon lemon juice
Salt and pepper, to taste
8 ounces spinach fettuccine, cooked, warm
½ cup (2 ounces) shredded Parmesan cheese
¼ cup toasted pine nuts or slivered almonds

Per Serving:
Calories: 307
% of calories from fat: 24
Fat (gm): 8.4
Saturated fat (gm): 2.7
Cholesterol (mg): 85.6
Sodium (mg): 474
Protein (gm): 18.7
Carbohydrate (gm): 41.2

Exchanges:
Milk: 0.0
Vegetable: 2.0
Fruit: 0.0
Bread: 2.0
Meat: 1.0
Fat: 1.0

1. Sauté ham, fennel, and onion in lightly greased large skillet until onion is tender and browned, about 5 minutes. Add Brussels sprouts and water and heat to boiling; reduce heat and simmer, covered, until sprouts are crisp-tender, 5 to 8 minutes. Stir in lemon juice; season to taste with salt and pepper. Serve over pasta; sprinkle with Parmesan cheese and pine nuts.

45-MINUTE PREPARATION TIP: Begin cooking the fettuccine before preparing the rest of the recipe.

CREAMY FETTUCCINE PRIMAVERA

45

L

The sauce for this dish should be somewhat thin, as it thickens once removed from the heat. If reheating, the sauce will require additional milk.

4 servings

2 cups each: sliced mushrooms, broccoli florets

½ cup each: chopped red bell pepper, water

8 ounces fat-free cream cheese

1 cup fat-free milk, divided

¼ cup sliced green onions

½ teaspoon dried Italian seasoning

2 tablespoons grated fat-free Parmesan cheese

Salt and white pepper, to taste

8 ounces fettuccine, cooked, warm

Per Serving:
Calories: 273
% of calories from fat: 8
Fat (gm): 2.5
Saturated fat (gm): 0.1
Cholesterol (mg): 0.7
Sodium (mg): 491
Protein (gm): 20.4
Carbohydrate (gm): 43.2

Exchanges:
Milk: 0.5
Vegetable: 2.0
Fruit: 0.0
Bread: 2.0
Meat: 0.5
Fat: 0.0

1. Sauté mushrooms, broccoli, and bell pepper in lightly greased large skillet 3 to 4 minutes. Add water and heat to boiling; reduce heat and simmer, covered, until broccoli is tender, about 8 minutes; drain.

2. Heat cream cheese, ⅔ cup milk, green onions, and Italian seasoning in small saucepan over low heat until cream cheese is melted, stirring frequently. Stir in Parmesan cheese and enough remaining ⅓ cup milk to make a thin consistency. Season to taste with salt and pepper. Toss with fettuccine and vegetables.

45-MINUTE PREPARATION TIP: Begin cooking the fettuccine before preparing the rest of the recipe.

PASTA WITH OYSTER MUSHROOMS

45

L

Although this recipe specifies oyster mushrooms, feel free to substitute any other type.

6 servings

16 ounces oyster mushrooms, separated into pieces

1–2 tablespoons minced garlic

4 tablespoons margarine or butter

2 tablespoons flour

2 cups fat-free milk

½ cup reduced-sodium vegetable broth

2 teaspoons lemon juice

1 cup chopped, seeded tomato

½ teaspoon each: salt, pepper

12 ounces fettuccine, cooked, warm

2 tablespoons grated Parmesan cheese

Per Serving:
Calories: 328
% of calories from fat: 30
Fat (gm): 11.0
Saturated fat (gm): 2
Cholesterol (mg): 3.0
Sodium (mg): 454
Protein (gm): 15.0
Carbohydrate (gm): 44.4

Exchanges:
Milk: 0.0
Vegetable: 3.0
Fruit: 0.0
Bread: 2.0
Meat: 0.0
Fat: 2.0

1. Sauté mushrooms and garlic in margarine in large skillet until soft, about 5 minutes. Stir in flour; cook 1 minute. Add milk, broth, and lemon juice; heat to boiling. Reduce heat and simmer, uncovered, until liquid is reduced to about 1¼ cups, about 10 minutes. Stir in tomato, salt, and pepper. Toss sauce with pasta; sprinkle with Parmesan cheese.

45-MINUTE PREPARATION TIP: Begin cooking pasta while sauce is simmering.

FETTUCCINE PAPRIKASH

45

Use your preference of hot or sweet paprika in this recipe.

6 servings

1 cup each: sliced red and green bell pepper, onion

1 tablespoon margarine or butter

2 tablespoons flour

1 tablespoon sweet Hungarian paprika

½ teaspoon salt

¼ teaspoon pepper

1 can (8 ounces) reduced-sodium tomato sauce

½ cup each: reduced-sodium fat-free chicken broth, dry white wine or chicken broth, reduced-fat sour cream

12 ounces fettuccine, cooked, warm

Per Serving:
Calories: 264
% of calories from fat: 20
Fat (gm): 5.8
Saturated fat (gm): 1.7
Cholesterol (mg): 16.7
Sodium (mg): 267
Protein (gm): 9.5
Carbohydrate (gm): 41

Exchanges:
Milk: 0.0
Vegetable: 2.0
Fruit: 0.0
Bread: 2.0
Meat: 0.0
Fat: 1.5

1. Sauté bell peppers and onion in margarine in large skillet until peppers are very soft, 10 to 15 minutes. Stir in flour, paprika, salt, and pepper; cook 1 minute. Stir in tomato sauce, broth, and wine; heat to boiling. Reduce heat and simmer, uncovered, until sauce is thickened, 5 to 7 minutes; stir in sour cream. Serve over fettuccine.

45-MINUTE PREPARATION TIP: Cook pasta while sauce is simmering.

FETTUCCINE WITH CHILI-MUSHROOM STROGANOFF SAUCE

45

L

Shiitake mushrooms and dried ancho chilies are unique flavor additions to this pasta sauce. The chilies can be quite hot, so adjust amount according to your taste.

8 servings

3 cups boiling water, divided

1–2 dried ancho chilies

1 package (1¾ ounces) dried shiitake mushrooms

2 cups vegetable broth, divided

1 cup chopped onion

8 ounces white mushrooms, halved or quartered

2 tablespoons margarine or butter

¼ cup all-purpose flour

½ teaspoon dried thyme leaves

1 cup reduced-fat sour cream

1 teaspoon Dijon mustard

Salt and pepper, to taste

16 ounces fettuccine, cooked, warm

Per Serving:
Calories: 333
% of calories from fat: 18
Fat (gm): 6.7
Saturated fat (gm): 2.1
Cholesterol (mg): 10
Sodium (mg): 306
Protein (gm): 11.3
Carbohydrate (gm): 56.5

Exchanges:
Milk: 0.0
Vegetable: 2.0
Fruit: 0.0
Bread: 3.0
Meat: 0.0
Fat: 1.5

1. Pour boiling water over ancho chilies and shiitake mushrooms in bowl. Let stand until softened, about 10 minutes. Drain, reserving liquid. Slice mushrooms, discarding tough centers. Process chilies and 1 cup vegetable broth in blender or food processor until smooth.

2. Sauté onion, white and shiitake mushrooms in margarine in large skillet until wilted, about 5 minutes. Stir in flour; cook 1 minute. Stir in reserved liquid, chili mixture, remaining 1 cup broth, and thyme. Heat to boiling; reduce heat and simmer, covered, until shiitake mushrooms are tender, 10 to 15 minutes. Simmer, uncovered, to desired sauce consistency, about 5 minutes. Stir in sour cream and mustard; cook over low heat until hot, 2 to 3 minutes. Season to taste with salt and pepper. Serve with pasta.

45-MINUTE PREPARATION TIP: Begin cooking pasta while sauce is simmering.

FETTUCCINE WITH GORGONZOLA SAUCE

45

Gorgonzola lends rich flavor to this creamy sauce.

L

6 servings

2 cups fat-free milk

¼ cup each: dry white wine or milk, all-purpose flour

3 ounces Gorgonzola cheese, crumbled

2 tablespoons margarine or butter

¼ teaspoon pepper

12 ounces fettuccine, cooked, warm

Per Serving:
Calories: 298
% of calories from fat: 23
Fat (gm): 10
Saturated fat (gm): 3.5
Cholesterol (mg): 22.1
Sodium (mg): 295
Protein (gm): 12.4
Carbohydrate (gm): 38.4

Exchanges:
Milk: 0.0
Vegetable: 2.0
Fruit: 0.0
Bread: 2.0
Meat: 0.0
Fat: 2.0

1. Whisk milk, wine, and flour in medium saucepan until smooth; heat to boiling, whisking until thickened, 1 to 2 minutes. Reduce heat to low and whisk in cheese, margarine, and pepper; cook until cheese is melted, 1 to 2 minutes. Serve over fettuccine.

45-MINUTE PREPARATION TIP: Begin cooking pasta before preparing the rest of the recipe.

MIXED VEGETABLE FETTUCCINE

Roasting is an effortless way to cook many vegetables at the same time!

6 servings

2 sweet potatoes, peeled, thickly sliced

1 each: thickly sliced yellow summer squash, green bell pepper, medium tomato

4 green onions, very thinly sliced

Vegetable cooking spray

¼ cup cider vinegar

2 tablespoons olive oil

1 teaspoon lemon juice

1 tablespoon each: chopped fresh or 1 teaspoon dried oregano leaves and tarragon leaves

8 ounces fettuccine, cooked, warm

1 tablespoon grated Parmesan cheese

Per Serving:
Calories: 267
% of calories from fat: 26
Fat (gm): 8.5
Saturated fat (gm): 1.1
Cholesterol (mg): 1.1
Sodium (mg): 119
Protein (gm): 9.1
Carbohydrate (gm): 46.4

Exchanges:
Milk: 0.0
Vegetable: 1.5
Fruit: 0.0
Bread: 2.5
Meat: 0.0
Fat: 1.5

1. Arrange vegetables in single layer on greased foil-lined jelly roll pan; spray with cooking spray. Roast at 425 degrees until vegetables are browned and tender, about 30 minutes. Toss with combined vinegar, olive oil, lemon juice, and herbs; toss with pasta. Sprinkle with Parmesan cheese.

MEAN BEAN PASTA

45

L

Chock full of beans and highly seasoned with herbs, this hearty dish packs a high-protein nutritional punch.

6 servings

2 medium green bell peppers, chopped

¾ cup chopped onion

4 teaspoons minced garlic

2 tablespoons olive oil

4 cups (16 ounces) thinly sliced cabbage

2 medium yellow summer squash, cubed

1 teaspoon each: dried rosemary, sage, and savory leaves

1 can (15 ounces) each: black and garbanzo beans, rinsed, drained

Salt and pepper, to taste

12 ounces whole wheat fettuccine, cooked, warm

¼ cup (1 ounce) grated fat-free Parmesan cheese

Per Serving:
Calories: 391
% of calories from fat: 19
Fat (gm): 8.9
Saturated fat (gm): 0.8
Cholesterol (mg): 0
Sodium (mg): 644
Protein (gm): 19.7
Carbohydrate (gm): 67.3

Exchanges:
Milk: 0.0
Vegetable: 1.5
Fruit: 0.0
Bread: 4.0
Meat: 0.5
Fat: 1.0

1. Sauté bell peppers, onion, and garlic in oil in large saucepan until tender, about 5 minutes. Add cabbage, squash, and herbs; cook, covered, over medium heat until cabbage is wilted, about 5 minutes. Stir in beans; cook until squash is tender, 5 to 8 minutes, stirring occasionally. Season to taste with salt and pepper. Serve bean mixture over fettuccine; sprinkle with Parmesan cheese.

45-MINUTE PREPARATION TIP: Begin cooking fettuccine before preparing the rest of the recipe.

PASTA WITH THREE-ONION SAUCE

45

The vegetables for this sauce are cooked very slowly until the onions are caramelized.

6 servings

1½ cups each: sliced leeks (white parts only), chopped red onions

6 shallots, sliced

3 tablespoons olive oil

¼ cup all-purpose flour

1 can (14½ ounces) reduced-sodium fat-free chicken broth

¼ teaspoon each: dried thyme leaves, salt, pepper

12 ounces mafalde or other flat pasta, cooked, warm

1. Sauté leeks, onions, and shallots in oil in medium saucepan 2 to 3 minutes. Reduce heat to medium-low and cook slowly until mixture is golden, about 15 minutes. Stir in flour; cook over medium heat 1 to 2 minutes. Add broth, thyme, salt, and pepper; heat to boiling, stirring until thickened, about 1 minute. Serve over mafalde.

45-MINUTE PREPARATION TIP: Cook mafalde while leek mixture is cooking.

Per Serving:
Calories: 327
% of calories from fat: 21
Fat (gm): 7.8
Saturated fat (gm): 1.1
Cholesterol (mg): 0
Sodium (mg): 360
Protein (gm): 9.7
Carbohydrate (gm): 54.4

Exchanges:
Milk: 0.0
Vegetable: 2.0
Fruit: 0.0
Bread: 3.0
Meat: 0.0
Fat: 1.5

MAFALDE WITH SWEET POTATOES AND KALE

Sweet potatoes and kale add peak nutrition to this pasta dish. For an added nutritional boost, use whole wheat pasta.

4 servings

2 medium onions, coarsely chopped

3 cloves garlic, minced

2 medium sweet potatoes, peeled, cubed (¾-inch)

4 cups sliced kale or Swiss chard

½ cup water

8 ounces mafalde, cooked, warm

2 tablespoons grated fat-free Parmesan cheese

1. Sauté onions and garlic in lightly greased large skillet 2 to 3 minutes. Add potatoes, kale, and water; heat to boiling. Reduce heat and simmer, covered, until kale and potatoes are tender and water absorbed, 10 to 12 minutes. Toss with pasta and cheese.

45-MINUTE PREPARATION TIP: Begin cooking the mafalde before preparing the rest of the recipe.

Per Serving:
Calories: 338
% of calories from fat: 4
Fat (gm): 1.5
Saturated fat (gm): 0.2
Cholesterol (mg): 0
Sodium (mg): 51
Protein (gm): 11.8
Carbohydrate (gm): 69.5

Exchanges:
Milk: 0.0
Vegetable: 2.0
Fruit: 0.0
Bread: 4.0
Meat: 0.0
Fat: 0.0

WARM PAPPARDELLE WITH CAJUN SHRIMP

45 *Any of the wide, flat pastas, such as mafalde or trenette, are also appropriate for this highly spiced dish.*

4 servings

⅓ cup each: sliced red bell pepper, onion

12 ounces peeled, deveined shrimp

2 teaspoons each: dried oregano, basil, and thyme leaves

½ teaspoon each: garlic powder, paprika

¼ teaspoon each: cayenne and black pepper, salt

1 cup reduced-sodium chicken broth

¼ cup dry white wine or water

1 tablespoon tomato paste

8 ounces pappardelle, cooked, warm

Per Serving:
Calories: 292
% of calories from fat: 7
Fat (gm): 2.2
Saturated fat (gm): 0.5
Cholesterol (mg): 130.6
Sodium (mg): 329
Protein (gm): 22.7
Carbohydrate (gm): 41.4

Exchanges:
Milk: 0.0
Vegetable: 0.5
Fruit: 0.0
Bread: 3.0
Meat: 1.0
Fat: 0.0

1. Sauté bell pepper and onion in lightly greased large skillet until tender, 3 to 4 minutes. Stir in shrimp and seasonings; cook over medium heat until shrimp just begin to turn pink, about 2 minutes. Stir in broth, wine, and tomato paste; heat to boiling. Reduce heat and simmer, uncovered, until shrimp are cooked, 3 to 4 minutes. Serve over pasta.

45-MINUTE PREPARATION TIP: Begin cooking pappardelle before preparing the rest of the recipe.

PASTA WITH CABBAGE AND POTATOES

45 *Add sautéed cubed ham or sliced smoked turkey sausage to this dish for a heartier entrée.*

8 servings

6 cups thinly sliced cabbage

4 cloves garlic, minced

⅓ cup reduced-sodium chicken broth

4 medium Idaho potatoes, peeled, cubed

1 teaspoon each: dried rosemary and sage leaves

½ teaspoon salt

¼ teaspoon pepper

16 ounces pappardelle or other flat pasta,
  cooked, warm

¼ cup (1 ounce) grated Parmesan cheese

Per Serving:
Calories: 297
% of calories from fat: 6
Fat (gm): 1.8
Saturated fat (gm): 0.7
Cholesterol (mg): 3.2
Sodium (mg): 215
Protein (gm): 10.5
Carbohydrate (gm): 59.6

Exchanges:
Milk: 0.0
Vegetable: 0.0
Fruit: 0.0
Bread: 4.0
Meat: 0.0
Fat: 0.5

1. Combine cabbage, garlic, and broth in large skillet; heat to boiling; reduce heat and simmer, covered, until cabbage is wilted, about 5 minutes. Add potatoes, herbs, salt, and pepper; cook, covered, over medium heat until potatoes are tender and broth is almost evaporated, about 10 minutes. Toss with pasta; sprinkle with Parmesan cheese.

45-MINUTE PREPARATION TIP: Begin cooking pasta before preparing the rest of the recipe.

FUSILLI WITH ARTICHOKE SAUCE

45 *Minced jalapeño chilis add a hint of piquancy to this sauce.*

4 servings

1 cup sliced onion

2 cloves garlic, minced

½–1 teaspoon minced jalapeño chili

1 tablespoon olive oil

2 tablespoons flour

1 can (14 ounces) artichoke hearts, drained, sliced

1 cup reduced-sodium fat-free chicken broth

¼ cup (1 ounce) grated Parmesan cheese

¼ teaspoon each: salt, pepper

8 ounces fusilli (spirals), cooked, warm

Per Serving:
Calories: 339
% of calories from fat: 16
Fat (gm): 6
Saturated fat (gm): 1.6
Cholesterol (mg): 3.9
Sodium (mg): 533
Protein (gm): 14.2
Carbohydrate (gm): 55.6

Exchanges:
Milk: 0.0
Vegetable: 2.0
Fruit: 0.0
Bread: 3.0
Meat: 0.0
Fat: 1.5

1. Sauté onion, garlic, and jalapeño chili in oil in medium saucepan until tender, about 5 minutes; stir in flour and cook 1 minute. Add artichoke hearts and broth; heat to boiling, stirring until thickened, about 1 minute. Stir in Parmesan cheese, salt, and pepper; cook 1 to 2 minutes. Serve over fusilli.

45-MINUTE PREPARATION TIP: Begin cooking fusilli before preparing the rest of the recipe.

BUCATINI WITH BRUSSELS SPROUTS AND WALNUTS

45 | *Bucatini is a spaghetti-type pasta with a hole in the center.*

L | **4 servings**

	Per Serving:
12 ounces Brussels sprouts, halved, cooked crisp-tender	Calories: 367
	% of calories from fat: 16
	Fat (gm): 6.7
2 teaspoons minced garlic	Saturated fat (gm): 0.7
8 ounces bucatini or spaghetti, cooked, warm	Cholesterol (mg): 0
	Sodium (mg): 118
2 cups seeded, chopped Italian plum tomatoes	Protein (gm): 14.9
⅔ cup minced parsley	Carbohydrate (gm): 65.4

12 ounces Brussels sprouts, halved, cooked
   crisp-tender
2 teaspoons minced garlic
8 ounces bucatini or spaghetti, cooked, warm
2 cups seeded, chopped Italian plum tomatoes
⅔ cup minced parsley
¼ cup each: toasted unseasoned dry bread crumbs,
   chopped walnuts
2–4 tablespoons grated fat-free Parmesan cheese
Salt and pepper, to taste

Per Serving:
Calories: 367
% of calories from fat: 16
Fat (gm): 6.7
Saturated fat (gm): 0.7
Cholesterol (mg): 0
Sodium (mg): 118
Protein (gm): 14.9
Carbohydrate (gm): 65.4

Exchanges:
Milk: 0.0
Vegetable: 3.0
Fruit: 0.0
Bread: 3.0
Meat: 0.5
Fat: 1.0

1. Sauté Brussels sprouts and garlic in lightly greased skillet until hot, 3 to 4 minutes. Toss with remaining ingredients, except salt and pepper. Season to taste with salt and pepper.

45-MINUTE PREPARATION TIP: Begin cooking the bucatini before preparing the rest of the recipe.

CREAMY TOMATO-PEPPER SAUCE WITH PENNE

45 | *This sauce is so creamy you'd swear it's high in fat, but it's not!*

L | **6 servings**

1 medium onion, chopped
½ teaspoon minced garlic
1 tablespoon olive oil
2 tablespoons dry sherry or water
1 can (15 ounces) Italian-seasoned tomato sauce
⅓ cup chopped roasted red peppers
2 teaspoons sugar
¼ cup reduced-fat sour cream
Salt and pepper, to taste
12 ounces penne, cooked, warm

Per Serving:
Calories: 276
% of calories from fat: 13
Fat (gm): 4
Saturated fat (gm): 1
Cholesterol (mg): 3.3
Sodium (mg): 406
Protein (gm): 8.5
Carbohydrate (gm): 51.8

Exchanges:
Milk: 0.0
Vegetable: 1.0
Fruit: 0.0
Bread: 3.0
Meat: 0.0
Fat: 1.0

1. Sauté onion and garlic in oil in large saucepan until softened, about 5 minutes. Stir in sherry, tomato sauce, roasted peppers, and sugar. Heat to boiling; reduce heat and simmer, uncovered, until slightly thickened, 10 to 15 minutes. Stir in sour cream; season to taste with salt and pepper. Serve over penne.

45-MINUTE PREPARATION TIP: Cook pasta while sauce is simmering.

ROTINI AND BEANS NIÇOISE

45

L

Garbanzo or kidney beans can be substituted for any of the beans used in this dish.

6 servings

½ cup chopped shallots or red onion

2 cups chopped Italian plum tomatoes

1 teaspoon minced garlic

2 teaspoons margarine or butter

2 cups diagonally sliced green beans, cooked

1 can (13¼ ounces), baby lima beans, rinsed, drained

1 can (15 ounces) cannellini beans, rinsed, drained

2 tablespoons drained capers

½ teaspoon dried tarragon leaves

6 cups cooked rotini or other shaped pasta, warm

Salt and pepper, to taste

Grated Parmesan cheese, as garnish

Per Serving:
Calories: 263
% of calories from fat: 8
Fat (gm): 2.3
Saturated fat (gm): 0.4
Cholesterol (mg): 0
Sodium (mg): 369
Protein (gm): 11.8
Carbohydrate (gm): 50.3

Exchanges:
Milk: 0.0
Vegetable: 0.0
Fruit: 0.0
Bread: 3.0
Meat: 1.0
Fat: 0.0

1. Sauté shallots, tomatoes, and garlic in margarine in large skillet 2 to 3 minutes; cook, covered, over medium heat until tomatoes are wilted, 3 to 5 minutes. Stir in fresh and canned beans, capers, and tarragon; cook, covered, over medium heat until hot, about 5 minutes. Stir in rotini and season to taste with salt and pepper; sprinkle with Parmesan cheese.

45-MINUTE PREPARATION TIP: Begin cooking pasta and green beans before preparing the rest of the recipe.

"LITTLE EARS" WITH GARLIC AND ARTICHOKES

L

The flavors of the garlic and artichokes become sweet and mellow when roasted.

4 servings

2 cans (15½ ounces each) artichoke hearts, rinsed, drained, halved
Olive oil cooking spray
4 bulbs garlic
4 teaspoons olive oil
8 ounces orecchietti ("little ears"), cooked, warm
4 teaspoons grated Romano cheese
½ teaspoon each: salt, pepper
½ cup (2 ounces) crumbled feta cheese

Per Serving:
Calories: 406
% of calories from fat: 23
Fat (gm): 10.6
Saturated fat (gm): 3.8
Cholesterol (mg): 17.4
Sodium (mg): 526
Protein (gm): 19.0
Carbohydrate (gm): 63.6

Exchanges:
Milk: 0.0
Vegetable: 4.0
Fruit: 0.0
Bread: 3.0
Meat: 0.0
Fat: 2.0

1. Place artichokes, cut sides down, in baking pan; spray with cooking spray. Cut a scant ½ inch off tops of garlic bulbs, exposing ends of cloves. Wrap bulbs loosely in aluminum foil and add to pan. Roast at 425 degrees until garlic is very soft, about 40 minutes. Cool garlic slightly; squeeze pulp into small bowl. Mix garlic with olive oil and toss with pasta and remaining ingredients, except feta cheese. Sprinkle with feta cheese.

PASTA FROM PESCIA

45

L

A hearty dish from the Tuscany region of Italy—any root vegetable you enjoy can be used in place of the potatoes.

4 entrée servings

3 cups thinly sliced cabbage
8 small new potatoes, cooked, halved
1½ cups halved Brussels sprouts
2 medium carrots, diagonally sliced
2 cloves garlic, minced
½ teaspoon dried sage leaves
⅓ cup reduced-sodium vegetable broth

2 tablespoons grated Parmesan cheese

Salt and pepper, to taste

8 ounces rigatoni or ziti, cooked, warm

1. Heat cabbage, potatoes, Brussels sprouts, carrots, garlic, sage, and broth to boiling in large skillet. Reduce heat and simmer, covered, until cabbage is wilted, about 5 minutes. Cook, uncovered, until liquid is gone and cabbage is lightly browned, about 5 minutes. Stir in cheese; season to taste with salt and pepper. Toss with pasta.

45-MINUTE PREPARATION TIP: Begin cooking the rigatoni before preparing the rest of the recipe.

Per Serving:
Calories: 486
% of calories from fat: 5
Fat (gm): 2.5
Saturated fat (gm): 0.9
Cholesterol (mg): 2.5
Sodium (mg): 144
Protein (gm): 16.9
Carbohydrate (gm): 102.3

Exchanges:
Milk: 0.0
Vegetable: 3.0
Fruit: 0.0
Bread: 6.0
Meat: 0.0
Fat: 0.0

CREOLE PASTA

45 *Creole flavors accent this substantial sauce. If you enjoy okra, it would be an excellent addition.*

8 servings

1½ cups sliced green bell peppers

⅔ cup each: sliced carrots, onion, celery

3 cloves garlic, minced

2 tablespoons olive oil

1 can (14½ ounces) reduced-sodium chicken broth

1 can (8 ounces) reduced-sodium tomato sauce

1 medium tomato, chopped

1 teaspoon each: dried basil and oregano
  leaves, paprika

½ teaspoon each: dried thyme leaves, gumbo file
  powder, salt

1 bay leaf

¼ teaspoon cayenne pepper

16 ounces rigatoni, cooked, warm

Per Serving:
Calories: 285
% of calories from fat: 14
Fat (gm): 4.6
Saturated fat (gm): 0.6
Cholesterol (mg): 0
Sodium (mg): 204
Protein (gm): 9.8
Carbohydrate (gm): 50.9

Exchanges:
Milk: 0.0
Vegetable: 1.0
Fruit: 0.0
Bread: 3.0
Meat: 0.0
Fat: 1.0

1. Sauté bell peppers, carrots, onion, celery, and garlic in oil until peppers are tender, 8 to 10 minutes. Stir in remaining ingredients,

except rigatoni; heat to boiling. Reduce heat and simmer, uncovered, until vegetables are tender and sauce is thickened to desired consistency, about 20 minutes; discard bay leaf. Serve with rigatoni.

45-MINUTE PREPARATION TIP: Cook pasta while sauce is simmering.

PEASANT-STYLE PASTA WITH BEANS, TOMATOES, AND SAGE

45 *Hearty and chunky, with 2 types of beans, this meal is so easy to make!*

8 servings

1 can (15 ounces) each: red kidney beans, Great
    Northern or cannellini beans, rinsed, drained
½ cup each: chopped onion, celery
2 cloves garlic, minced
1 can (16 ounces) plum tomatoes, drained, chopped
2 cups reduced-sodium chicken broth
1 teaspoon dried sage leaves
¼ teaspoon salt
⅛ teaspoon pepper
16 ounces mostaccioli, cooked, warm

Per Serving:
Calories: 317
% of calories from fat: 4
Fat (gm): 1.5
Saturated fat (gm): 0.1
Cholesterol (mg): 0
Sodium (mg): 495
Protein (gm): 13.3
Carbohydrate (gm): 61.9

Exchanges:
Milk: 0.0
Vegetable: 0.0
Fruit: 0.0
Bread: 4.0
Meat: 0.0
Fat: 0.0

1. Heat all ingredients, except mostaccioli, to boiling in large saucepan. Reduce heat and simmer, covered, 5 minutes; simmer, uncovered, until mixture is desired sauce consistency, about 20 minutes. Serve over pasta.

45-MINUTE PREPARATION TIP: Cook pasta while sauce is simmering.

ROASTED EGGPLANT AND SAUSAGE WITH ZITI

45 *Enjoy with any favorite pasta or Polenta (see p. 363).*

V **6 servings**

1 medium eggplant, unpeeled, sliced (½-inch)

3 medium onions, cut into wedges

Vegetable cooking spray

1½ teaspoons dried Italian seasoning

Salt and pepper, to taste

12 ounces Italian-style turkey sausage,
   cooked, crumbled

1 can (14½ ounces) reduced-sodium diced
   tomatoes, undrained

1 tablespoon roasted garlic

8 ounces ziti, cooked, warm

Per Serving:
Calories: 425
% of calories from fat: 18
Fat (gm): 8.9
Saturated fat (gm): 2.2
Cholesterol (mg): 42.3
Sodium (mg): 702
Protein (gm): 23.6
Carbohydrate (gm): 65.9

Exchanges:
Milk: 0.0
Vegetable: 1.0
Fruit: 0.0
Bread: 4.0
Meat: 2.0
Fat: 0.0

1. Cut eggplant slices into fourths; arrange eggplant and onions in single layer on foil-lined greased jelly roll pan. Spray vegetables with cooking spray; sprinkle with Italian seasoning, salt, and pepper. Roast at 425 degrees 25 minutes; spoon combined sausage, tomatoes with liquid, and roasted garlic over vegetables; roast until eggplant and onions are tender, about 15 minutes. Serve over ziti.

PASTA SANTA FE

45

Picante flavors of the Southwest merge with pasta in this entrée.

V

4 servings

1 medium onion, sliced

3 cloves garlic, minced

2 tablespoons canola oil

2 each: sliced medium zucchini, poblano
    chilies, tomatoes

1 cup whole-kernel corn

2 tablespoons chili powder

1 teaspoon dried oregano leaves

½ teaspoon ground cumin

2 tablespoons chopped cilantro

Salt and pepper, to taste

8 ounces trio maliano (combination of corkscrews,
    shells, and rigatoni) pasta, cooked, warm

Per Serving:
Calories: 350
% of calories from fat: 24
Fat (gm): 9.6
Saturated fat (gm): 1.2
Cholesterol (mg): 0
Sodium (mg): 327
Protein (gm): 11.6
Carbohydrate (gm): 58

Exchanges:
Milk: 0.0
Vegetable: 2.0
Fruit: 0.0
Bread: 3.0
Meat: 0.0
Fat: 2.0

1. Sauté onion and garlic in oil in large skillet until tender, about 5 minutes. Add remaining vegetables, chili powder, oregano, and cumin. Cook, covered, over medium heat until vegetables are crisp-tender, about 10 minutes. Stir in cilantro; season to taste with salt and pepper. Toss with pasta.

45-MINUTE PREPARATION TIP: Begin cooking the pasta before preparing the rest of the recipe.

CHICKEN TORTELLINI WITH SHERRIED VEGETABLE SAUCE

45 *Dry sherry and thyme accent the richly textured and seasoned sauce.*

6 servings

1 cup each: thinly sliced leeks (white parts only), chopped mushrooms

⅓ cup each: chopped onion, shallots

½ cup dry sherry or reduced-sodium chicken broth

2 cups reduced-sodium chicken broth

1 cup chopped tomatoes

1 teaspoon dried thyme leaves

2 bay leaves

Salt and pepper, to taste

2 packages (9 ounces each) fresh chicken tortellini, cooked, warm

4 tablespoons capers, optional

Per Serving:
Calories: 334
% of calories from fat: 16
Fat (gm): 6.2
Saturated fat (gm): 3.0
Cholesterol (mg): 40.4
Sodium (mg): 438
Protein (gm): 17.4
Carbohydrate (gm): 51.6

Exchanges:
Milk: 0.0
Vegetable: 2.0
Fruit: 0.0
Bread: 3.0
Meat: 0.0
Fat: 1.0

1. Sauté leeks, mushrooms, onion, and shallots in lightly greased medium saucepan until very soft, 7 to 10 minutes. Add sherry; cook over high heat until almost absorbed, 2 to 3 minutes. Add broth, tomatoes, and herbs; heat to boiling. Reduce heat and simmer, uncovered, until tomato is very soft, about 15 minutes; discard bay leaves.

2. Process mixture in food processor or blender until smooth. Return to saucepan; cook over medium heat until hot, 2 to 3 minutes. Season to taste with salt and pepper. Spoon over tortellini; sprinkle with capers.

45-MINUTE PREPARATION TIP: Begin cooking tortellini while sauce is simmering.

CURRIED TORTELLINI WITH BEANS AND SQUASH

45 *Coconut milk adds a subtle Asian flavor to this colorful pasta combination.*

V **6 servings**

1⅓ cups coarsely chopped onions
⅔ cup red bell pepper
2 teaspoons minced garlic
1 teaspoon curry powder
1 tablespoon olive oil
2 cups each: diagonally sliced green beans,
  cubed butternut or acorn squash
¼ cup water
1 cup reduced-fat coconut milk
2 packages (9 ounces each) fresh mushroom or
  herb tortellini, cooked, warm
Salt and pepper, to taste
3 tablespoons chopped cilantro

Per Serving:
Calories: 269
% of calories from fat: 25
Fat (gm): 8.3
Saturated fat (gm): 3
Cholesterol (mg): 30
Sodium (mg): 220
Protein (gm): 11.4
Carbohydrate (gm): 44.1

Exchanges:
Milk: 0.0
Vegetable: 2.0
Fruit: 0.0
Bread: 2.0
Meat: 0.0
Fat: 1.5

1. Sauté onions, bell pepper, garlic, and curry powder in oil in large skillet until onions are tender, 3 to 4 minutes. Add green beans, squash, and water; heat to boiling. Reduce heat and simmer, covered, until vegetables are tender, 6 to 8 minutes. Stir in coconut milk and tortellini; cook until hot, 2 to 3 minutes. Season to taste with salt and pepper; sprinkle with cilantro.

45-MINUTE PREPARATION TIP: Begin cooking the tortellini before preparing the rest of the recipe.

CHEESE RAVIOLI WITH VEGETABLES

45 *This pasta dish is packed with fresh vegetables!*

L **6 servings**

1 quart reduced-sodium vegetable broth
1½ cups chopped yellow summer squash
2 carrots, sliced
2 cups torn kale or escarole

4 plum tomatoes, coarsely chopped

2 packages (9 ounces each) fresh cheese
ravioli, cooked

1 teaspoon dried basil leaves

⅛ teaspoon crushed red pepper

Salt, to taste

Per Serving:
Calories: 229
% of calories from fat: 21
Fat (gm): 5.3
Saturated fat (gm): 3
Cholesterol (mg): 29
Sodium (mg): 580
Protein (gm): 11.7
Carbohydrate (gm): 34.1

Exchanges:
Milk: 0.0
Vegetable: 1.0
Fruit: 0.0
Bread: 2.0
Meat: 1.0
Fat: 0.0

1. Heat broth to boiling in large saucepan; add
squash and carrots. Reduce heat and simmer,
covered, until vegetables are tender, about 10
minutes. Add remaining ingredients, except salt;
simmer 5 minutes. Season to taste with salt.

45-MINUTE PREPARATION TIP: Begin cooking
the ravioli before preparing the rest of the recipe.

FETA CHEESE AND SUN-DRIED TOMATO RAVIOLI

LO *Enjoy Mediterranean flavors in these feta-filled ravioli. The herbs and spices
of the sauce add an intriguing accent.*

4 servings

4 ounces fat-free cream cheese

¼–½ cup (2–4 ounces) crumbled reduced-fat
feta cheese

1 ounce sun-dried tomatoes (not in oil),
softened, chopped

1 teaspoon each: grated lemon zest, dried
oregano leaves

32 wonton wrappers

Mediterranean Tomato-Caper Sauce (recipe follows)

Chopped oregano or parsley, as garnish

Per Serving:
Calories: 327
% of calories from fat: 6
Fat (gm): 2.2
Saturated fat (gm): 0.9
Cholesterol (mg): 10.5
Sodium (mg): 728
Protein (gm): 15.3
Carbohydrate (gm): 61.4

Exchanges:
Milk: 0.0
Vegetable: 2.0
Fruit: 0.5
Bread: 3.0
Meat: 0.5
Fat: 0.0

1. Mix cheeses, tomatoes, lemon zest, and oregano. Spoon about 1
tablespoon cheese mixture on wonton wrapper; brush edges of
wrapper with water. Top with second wonton wrapper and press
edges together to seal. Repeat with remaining wonton wrappers
and cheese mixture.

2. Add 4 to 6 ravioli to 2 quarts boiling water in large saucepan; reduce heat and simmer, uncovered, until ravioli float to the surface and are al dente, 3 to 4 minutes. Remove ravioli with slotted spoon; repeat with remaining ravioli. Serve with Mediterranean Tomato-Caper Sauce and sprinkle with oregano.

Mediterranean Tomato-Caper Sauce
Makes about 2 cups

2 cans (8 ounces each) reduced-sodium tomato sauce
2 teaspoons minced garlic
1 teaspoon each: dried oregano leaves, ground cumin, and paprika
¼ teaspoon ground cinnamon
2 teaspoons lime juice
¼ cup raisins
2–3 teaspoons drained capers

1. Heat all ingredients in medium saucepan to simmering; simmer, covered, 5 minutes.

SHRIMP AND ARTICHOKE RAVIOLI WITH TARRAGON SAUCE

Fresh Tomato and Herb Sauce (see p. 171) would also be a great sauce selection for these ravioli.

4 servings

8 ounces finely chopped, peeled, deveined shrimp
1 can (14 ounces) artichoke hearts, drained, finely chopped
1 clove garlic, minced
¼ teaspoon ground nutmeg
3 tablespoons water
32 wonton wrappers
Tarragon Sauce (recipe follows)

Per Serving:
Calories: 289
% of calories from fat: 5
Fat (gm): 1.5
Saturated fat (gm): 0.3
Cholesterol (mg): 92.4
Sodium (mg): 923
Protein (gm): 20.6
Carbohydrate (gm): 45.2

Exchanges:
Milk: 0.0
Vegetable: 0.0
Fruit: 0.0
Bread: 3.0
Meat: 1.0
Fat: 0.0

1. Cook shrimp, artichoke hearts, garlic, nutmeg, and water in lightly greased large skillet over medium heat until shrimp are cooked, about 5 minutes. Spoon about 2 teaspoons shrimp mixture on wonton wrapper; brush edges of wrapper with water. Top with second wonton wrapper and press edges together to seal. Repeat with remaining wonton wrappers and shrimp mixture.

2. Add 6 ravioli to 2 quarts boiling water in large saucepan; reduce heat and simmer, uncovered, until ravioli float to the surface and are al dente, 3 to 4 minutes. Remove with slotted spoon. Repeat with remaining ravioli. Serve with Tarragon Sauce.

Tarragon Sauce
Makes about 1 cup

2 medium shallots or green onions, finely chopped
1 tablespoon finely chopped fresh or ½ teaspoon dried tarragon leaves
1½ cups reduced-sodium chicken broth, divided
1 tablespoon flour
¼ teaspoon salt
⅛ teaspoon white pepper

1. Heat shallots, tarragon, and ½ cup chicken broth to boiling in small saucepan; reduce heat and simmer, uncovered, until mixture is reduced to ¼ cup. Whisk in combined remaining ingredients; heat to boiling, whisking until thickened, about 1 minute (sauce will be thin).

SPEEDY CHICKEN AND RAVIOLI

45 *Use any favorite flavor of ravioli with this quick and nutritious bean sauce.*

4 servings

1 pound chicken tenders, halved crosswise

2 teaspoons minced garlic

¾ cup each: chopped onion, rinsed, drained, canned kidney beans

1 package (9 ounces) fresh sun-dried tomato ravioli, cooked, warm

1 large tomato, cubed

½ teaspoon dried thyme leaves

Salt and pepper, to taste

Per Serving:
Calories: 262
% of calories from fat: 17
Fat (gm): 5.1
Saturated fat (gm): 2.3
Cholesterol (mg): 63.5
Sodium (mg): 626
Protein (gm): 29.8
Carbohydrate (gm): 25.2

Exchanges:
Milk: 0.0
Vegetable: 0.0
Fruit: 0.0
Bread: 1.5
Meat: 3.0
Fat: 0.0

1. Cook chicken, garlic, and onion in large lightly greased skillet until chicken is browned, 5 to 8 minutes. Stir in beans, ravioli, tomato, and thyme; cook over medium heat until hot, about 5 minutes. Season to taste with salt and pepper.

45-MINUTE PREPARATION TIP: Begin cooking ravioli before preparing the rest of the recipe.

CHICKEN AND SWEET POTATO RAVIOLI WITH CURRY SAUCE

A light curry-flavored sauce makes a delicate accompaniment to this unusual ravioli.

4 servings

8 ounces boneless, skinless chicken breast, cooked, finely shredded
1 cup mashed, cooked, sweet potatoes
2 small cloves garlic, minced
½–¾ teaspoon ground ginger
Salt and pepper, to taste
32 wonton wrappers
Curry Sauce (recipe follows)

Per Serving:
Calories: 383
% of calories from fat: 13
Fat (gm): 5.5
Saturated fat (gm): 1.1
Cholesterol (mg): 37.2
Sodium (mg): 587
Protein (gm): 19.8
Carbohydrate (gm): 62.4

Exchanges:
Milk: 0.0
Vegetable: 0.5
Fruit: 0.0
Bread: 4.0
Meat: 1.5
Fat: 0.0

1. Mix chicken, sweet potatoes, garlic, and ginger; season to taste with salt and pepper. Spoon about 1 tablespoon mixture onto wonton wrapper; brush edges of wrapper with water. Top with second wonton wrapper and press edges together to seal. Repeat with remaining wonton wrappers and potato mixture.

2. Add 6 ravioli to 2 quarts boiling water in large saucepan; reduce heat and simmer, uncovered, until ravioli float to the surface and are al dente, 3 to 4 minutes. Remove with slotted spoon. Repeat with remaining ravioli. Serve with Curry Sauce.

Curry Sauce

Makes about 2 cups

¼ cup finely chopped onion
4 cloves garlic, minced
2 tablespoons flour
2 teaspoons curry powder
¼ teaspoon cayenne pepper
2 cups reduced-sodium chicken broth
1 tablespoon cornstarch
¼ cup dry white wine or water
Salt and pepper, to taste

1. Sauté onion and garlic in lightly greased medium saucepan 2 to 3 minutes; stir in flour, curry powder, and cayenne pepper and cook 1 minute. Mix in broth and heat to boiling; stir in combined cornstarch and wine, stirring until thickened, about 1 minute. Season to taste with salt and pepper.

WINE-GLAZED CHICKEN WITH RAVIOLI AND ASPARAGUS

45 *A reduction of broth, white wine, and orange juice creates an elegant and fragrant sauce for chicken and flavorful pasta.*

4 servings

4 boneless, skinless chicken breast halves
  (4 ounces each)
Salt and pepper, to taste
2 cups reduced-sodium fat-free chicken broth
1 cup orange juice
½ cup dry white wine
¼ teaspoon crushed red pepper
1 pound asparagus, sliced (1-inch)
2 tablespoons margarine or butter
1 package (9 ounces) fresh mushroom ravioli,
  cooked, warm

Per Serving:
Calories: 340
% of calories from fat: 34
Fat (gm): 12.5
Saturated fat (gm): 2
Cholesterol (mg): 76.9
Sodium (mg): 454
Protein (gm): 33
Carbohydrate (gm): 11.7

Exchanges:
Milk: 0.0
Vegetable: 1.0
Fruit: 0.0
Bread: 2.0
Meat: 3.0
Fat: 0.5

1. Cook chicken over medium heat in lightly greased large skillet until cooked, about 10 minutes on each side. Sprinkle lightly with salt and pepper; remove from skillet. Add broth, orange juice, white wine, and crushed red pepper and heat to boiling; boil, uncovered, until liquid is reduced to ½ cup, about 10 minutes. Add asparagus; simmer, covered, until crisp-tender, 3 to 4 minutes. Add chicken, margarine, and ravioli; cook until hot, 2 to 3 minutes. Season to taste with salt and pepper.

TURKEY AND HERBED CHEESE RAVIOLI WITH WILD MUSHROOM SAUCE

Italian-style turkey sausage can be substituted nicely in these ravioli.

4 servings

8 ounces ground turkey

1 small onion, minced

2 cloves garlic, minced

1 cup reduced-fat ricotta cheese

1 teaspoon dried rosemary leaves

32 wonton wrappers

Wild Mushroom Sauce (see p. 327)

Per Serving:
Calories: 360
% of calories from fat: 18
Fat (gm): 7.2
Saturated fat (gm): 1.4
Cholesterol (mg): 37
Sodium (mg): 593
Protein (gm): 22
Carbohydrate (gm): 53

Exchanges:
Milk: 0.0
Vegetable: 1.5
Fruit: 0.0
Bread: 3.0
Meat: 1.5
Fat: 0.5

1. Cook turkey in lightly greased small skillet over medium heat until browned, about 5 minutes. Add onion and garlic to skillet and sauté until onion is tender, about 5 minutes. Remove from heat; mix in ricotta cheese and rosemary. Spoon about 1 tablespoon cheese mixture on wonton wrapper; brush edges of wrapper with water. Top with a second wonton wrapper and press edges together to seal. Repeat with remaining wonton wrappers and cheese mixture.

2. Add 6 ravioli to 2 quarts boiling water in large saucepan; reduce heat and simmer, uncovered, until ravioli float to the surface and are al dente, 3 to 4 minutes. Remove with slotted spoon. Repeat with remaining ravioli. Serve with Wild Mushroom Sauce.

Wild Mushroom Sauce

Makes about 2½ cups

2 cups chopped or sliced wild mushrooms (portobello,
  shiitake, cremini, etc.)
¼ cup finely chopped shallots or green onions
2 cloves garlic, minced
⅓ cup dry sherry or water
2–3 tablespoons lemon juice
½ teaspoon dried thyme leaves
2 cups reduced-sodium vegetable broth
2 tablespoons cornstarch
Salt and pepper, to taste

1. Sauté mushrooms, shallots, and garlic in lightly greased medium saucepan until tender, 5 to 8 minutes. Stir in sherry, lemon juice, and thyme; heat to boiling. Reduce heat and simmer, uncovered, until mushrooms are tender and liquid is gone, about 5 minutes. Stir in combined broth and cornstarch; heat to boiling, stirring, until thickened, about 1 minute. Season to taste with salt and pepper.

MUSHROOM RAVIOLI WITH RED PEPPER SALSA

Colorful Red Pepper Salsa is a perfect complement to the mushroom-filled pasta.

4 servings

2 cups finely chopped mushrooms
¼ cup chopped shallots or green onions
2 cloves garlic, minced
¼ teaspoon each: salt, pepper
48 wonton wrappers
Red Pepper Salsa (recipe follows)

Per Serving:
Calories: 364
% of calories from fat: 20
Fat (gm): 8
Saturated fat (gm): 1.4
Cholesterol (mg): 67.6
Sodium (mg): 430
Protein (gm): 12
Carbohydrate (gm): 62

Exchanges:
Milk: 0.0
Vegetable: 2.0
Fruit: 0.0
Bread: 3.0
Meat: 0.0
Fat: 2.0

1. Sauté mushrooms, shallots, and garlic in lightly greased skillet until tender and liquid is evaporated, about 8 minutes; stir in salt and pepper. Spoon about 2 teaspoons mushroom mixture in center of 1 wonton wrapper; brush edges of wrapper with water. Top with a second wonton wrapper, and press edges together to seal. Repeat with remaining wonton wrappers and mushroom mixture.

2. Add 6 ravioli to 2 quarts boiling water in large saucepan; reduce heat and simmer, uncovered, until ravioli float to the surface and are al dente, 3 to 4 minutes. Remove with slotted spoon. Repeat with remaining ravioli. Serve with Red Pepper Salsa.

Red Pepper Salsa

Makes about 2 cups

2 each: finely chopped medium tomatoes, large red bell peppers
2 tablespoons each: finely chopped or 1 tablespoon dried basil
    and cilantro leaves
4 teaspoons each: olive oil, red wine vinegar, minced garlic
½–1 teaspoon minced jalapeño chili
½ teaspoon each: salt, pepper

1. Mix all ingredients; refrigerate 3 to 4 hours for flavors to blend.

POTATO GNOCCHI WITH SAGE CREAM

45   *Fat-free half-and-half is the secret to the rich creaminess of the sauce.*

L   **6 servings**

2 cups fat-free half-and-half or fat-free milk
16–20 thinly sliced fresh or 1 teaspoon dried
    sage leaves
2 tablespoons flour
½ teaspoon ground nutmeg
¼ cup water
1 cup chopped onion
2 teaspoons margarine or butter
4 cups small broccoli florets, cooked crisp-tender
1 package (16 ounces) potato gnocchi, cooked, warm
Salt and pepper, to taste
Shredded Parmesan cheese, as garnish

Per Serving:
Calories: 263
% of calories from fat: 2
Fat (gm): 0.6
Saturated fat (gm): 0.2
Cholesterol (mg): 0.9
Sodium (mg): 150
Protein (gm): 13.4
Carbohydrate (gm): 52.4

Exchanges:
Milk: 0.0
Vegetable: 2.0
Fruit: 0.0
Bread: 2.5
Meat: 0.0
Fat: 0.0

1. Heat half-and-half and sage (if using dried sage, tie leaves in small cheesecloth bag) to boiling in medium saucepan; reduce heat and simmer, covered, 10 minutes. Strain, discarding sage. Return half-and-half to saucepan and heat to boiling; whisk in combined flour, nutmeg, and water, whisking until thickened, about 1 minute.

2. Sauté onion in margarine in large skillet 2 to 3 minutes; add onion, broccoli, and gnocchi to sauce and cook over medium heat until hot, 2 to 3 minutes; season to taste with salt and pepper. Sprinkle with cheese.

45-MINUTE PREPARATION TIP: Begin cooking the gnocchi before preparing the rest of the recipe.

SPINACH GNOCCHI AND CHICKEN PRIMAVERA

Gnocchi, Italian for dumplings, are often made from potatoes. This spinach version is delicious.

6 servings

½ cup chopped onion

2 cloves garlic, minced

3 packages (10 ounces each) frozen chopped spinach, thawed, well drained

⅔ cup plus ¼ cup all-purpose flour, divided

1 cup reduced-fat ricotta cheese

½ cup (2 ounces) grated Parmesan cheese

1 egg

¼ teaspoon ground nutmeg

½ teaspoon each: salt, pepper

1¼ pounds boneless, skinless chicken breasts, baked, sliced, warm

Primavera Sauce (recipe follows)

Per Serving:
Calories: 464
% of calories from fat: 30
Fat (gm): 15.8
Saturated fat (gm): 5.5
Cholesterol (mg): 105.2
Sodium (mg): 664
Protein (gm): 40
Carbohydrate (gm): 41.6

Exchanges:
Milk: 0.0
Vegetable: 4.0
Fruit: 0.0
Bread: 1.5
Meat: 4.0
Fat: 1.0

1. Sauté onion and garlic in lightly greased skillet until tender, about 5 minutes. Stir in spinach; cook over medium heat until mixture is quite dry, about 8 minutes, stirring frequently. Stir in ⅔ cup flour, cheeses, egg, nutmeg, salt, and pepper; cool. Roll mixture into 18 balls, using about 2 tablespoons for each; roll lightly in remaining ¼ cup flour.

2. Add gnocchi to 3 quarts boiling water in large saucepan; reduce heat and simmer, uncovered, until gnocchi float to the surface, about 10 minutes. Arrange on serving platter with chicken; spoon Primavera Sauce over.

Primavera Sauce
Makes about 3 cups

3 tablespoons margarine or butter
¼ cup all-purpose flour
2 cups 2% reduced-fat milk
¼ cup dry white wine or reduced-sodium chicken broth
2 cups each: small broccoli and cauliflower florets, cooked crisp-tender
1 cup diagonally sliced carrots, cooked crisp-tender
1 medium green bell pepper, sliced
¼ cup (1 ounce) grated Parmesan cheese
¼ teaspoon each: ground nutmeg, salt, pepper

1. Melt margarine in large saucepan; add flour and stir over medium heat 1 minute. Stir in milk and wine; heat to boiling. Boil, stirring until thickened, about 1 minute. Stir in vegetables and cook over medium heat until hot, 2 to 3 minutes. Remove from heat stir in remaining ingredients.

RICOTTA-STUFFED SHELLS WITH SPINACH PESTO

L *Spinach Pesto can be made up to 1 week in advance and refrigerated; serve at room temperature.*

4 servings

½ cup finely chopped onion
4–6 cloves garlic, minced
1 teaspoon dried basil leaves
1 cup chopped fresh spinach
1½ cups low-fat ricotta cheese
½ teaspoon each: ground nutmeg, salt, pepper
24 jumbo pasta shells, cooked
Spinach Pesto (recipe follows)

Per Serving:
Calories: 356
% of calories from fat: 24
Fat (gm): 9.4
Saturated fat (gm): 1.6
Cholesterol (mg): 14.4
Sodium (mg): 432
Protein (gm): 19
Carbohydrate (gm): 49.2

Exchanges:
Milk: 0.0
Vegetable: 2.0
Fruit: 0.0
Bread: 3.0
Meat: 1.0
Fat: 1.0

1. Sauté onion, garlic, and basil in lightly greased skillet until onions are tender, 3 to 4 minutes. Add spinach and cook over medium heat until wilted, about 5 minutes. Stir in cheese, nutmeg, salt, and pepper. Stuff mixture into shells; place in baking pan. Bake, covered, at 350 degrees until hot through, about 20 minutes. Serve with Spinach Pesto.

Spinach Pesto
Makes about ½ cup

2 cups loosely packed spinach
⅓ cup loosely packed basil leaves
2–3 cloves garlic
¼ cup (1 ounce) grated Parmesan cheese
4 teaspoons olive oil
2–4 teaspoons lemon juice
Salt and pepper, to taste

1. Process all ingredients, except lemon juice, salt, and pepper, in food processor until almost smooth. Season to taste with lemon juice, salt, and pepper. Serve at room temperature.

45-MINUTE PREPARATION TIP: Begin cooking the pasta shells before preparing the rest of the recipe.

ROASTED EGGPLANT WITH PASTA

Cook the eggplant on a charcoal grill for a wonderful smoky flavor. The eggplant can be roasted or grilled up to 2 days in advance.

6 servings

1 pound eggplant
1 cup coarsely chopped tomato
3 green onions, sliced
12 ounces whole wheat spaghetti, cooked, room temperature
½ cup (2 ounces) shredded Parmesan cheese
2 tablespoons balsamic or red wine vinegar
1 tablespoon olive oil
1–2 teaspoons lemon juice
Salt and pepper, to taste

Per Serving:
Calories: 219
% of calories from fat: 15
Fat (gm): 3.6
Saturated fat (gm): 0.7
Cholesterol (mg): 2.0
Sodium (mg): 137
Protein (gm): 12
Carbohydrate (gm): 36.3

Exchanges:
Milk: 0.0
Vegetable: 1.0
Fruit: 0.0
Bread: 2.0
Meat: 1.0
Fat: 0.0

1. Pierce eggplant 6 to 8 times with fork; place in baking pan. Bake at 425 degrees until tender, about 30 minutes; cool. Cut eggplant in half; scoop out pulp and cut into ¾-inch pieces. Toss eggplant, tomato, onions, pasta, and cheese; drizzle with combined vinegar, oil, and lemon juice and toss. Season to taste with salt and pepper.

PIEROGI WITH MUSHROOM SOUR CREAM SAUCE

45

L

The secret to the delicious sauce is cooking the mushrooms very slowly until deeply browned, intensifying their flavor.

4 servings

12 ounces mushrooms, sliced
¼ cup finely chopped onion
1 teaspoon minced garlic
¼ cup dry white wine or vegetable broth
¼–½ teaspoon dried thyme leaves
¾ cup reduced-fat or fat-free sour cream
Salt and pepper, to taste
2 packages (16 ounces each) fresh or frozen
   potato-and-onion pierogi
1 tablespoon margarine or butter
1 tablespoon olive or vegetable oil

Per Serving:
Calories: 80
% of calories from fat: 2
Fat (gm): 0.2
Saturated fat (gm): 0.1
Cholesterol (mg): 0
Sodium (mg): 24
Protein (gm): 3.5
Carbohydrate (gm): 16.5

Exchanges:
Milk: 0.0
Vegetable: 2.0
Fruit: 0.0
Bread: 0.5
Meat: 0.0
Fat: 0.0

1. Sauté mushrooms, onion, and garlic in lightly greased large skillet 1 to 2 minutes. Add wine and thyme; cook, covered, over medium heat until mushrooms are very tender, about 5 minutes. Cook, uncovered, until mushrooms are dry and well browned, about 15 minutes. Stir in sour cream; cook 1 to 2 minutes. Season to taste with salt and pepper.

2. While mushrooms are cooking, cook pierogi in boiling water to cover in large saucepan until they float to the top, 3 to 5 minutes. Drain. Heat margarine and olive oil in large skillet; cook pierogi over medium heat until browned, 2 to 3 minutes on each side. Serve with mushroom sauce.

NINE

Grains, Beans,
and
Legumes

BLACK BEANS AND RICE

45 *If fresh epazote is available, add a sprig or two while the rice is cooking.*

V **6 side-dish servings**

¼ cup each: chopped onion, sliced green onions
4 cloves garlic, minced
1 cup long-grain rice
2½ cups reduced-sodium vegetable broth
1 can (15 ounces) black beans, rinsed, drained
2 tablespoons finely chopped cilantro
Salt and pepper, to taste

Per Serving:
Calories: 171
% of calories from fat: 2
Fat (gm): 0.4
Saturated fat (gm): 0.1
Cholesterol (mg): 0.0
Sodium (mg): 462
Protein (gm): 6
Carbohydrate (gm): 38

Exchanges:
Milk: 0.0
Vegetable: 0.0
Fruit: 0.0
Bread: 2.5
Meat: 0.0
Fat: 0.0

1. Sauté onion, green onions, and garlic in lightly greased medium saucepan until tender, about 5 minutes. Add rice and stir over medium heat until lightly browned, 2 to 3 minutes, stirring frequently. Add broth and heat to boiling; reduce heat and simmer, covered, until rice is tender, 20 to 25 minutes, adding beans during last 5 minutes. Stir in cilantro; season to taste with salt and pepper.

SEASONED MASHED BLACK BEANS

45 *Black beans at their flavorful best—quick and easy too!*

V **6 side-dish servings**

2 medium onions, chopped
4 cloves garlic, minced
1–2 small jalapeño chilies, minced
2 cans (15 ounces each) black beans, rinsed, drained
2 cups reduced-sodium vegetable broth
¾–1 teaspoon dried cumin
⅓ cup chopped cilantro
Salt and pepper, to taste

Per Serving:
Calories: 109
% of calories from fat: 2
Fat (gm): 0.3
Saturated fat (gm): 0.0
Cholesterol (mg): 0.0
Sodium (mg): 691
Protein (gm): 6.5
Carbohydrate (gm): 25

Exchanges:
Milk: 0.0
Vegetable: 0.0;
Fruit: 0.0
Bread: 1.5
Meat: 0.0
Fat: 0.0

1. Sauté onions, garlic, and jalapeño chili in lightly greased large skillet until tender, about 5 minutes. Add beans and broth and cook over medium heat, coarsely mashing beans with fork. Stir in cumin and cilantro. Season to taste with salt and pepper.

REFRIED BEANS

V *Two cans (15 ounces each) pinto beans, rinsed and drained, can be substituted for the dried beans. Omit step 1 in recipe, and use 2 cups reduced-sodium vegetable broth in place of the cooking liquid.*

6 side-dish servings

1¼ cups dried pinto beans

Water

1 medium onion, coarsely chopped

Salt and pepper, to taste

Per Serving:
Calories: 106
% of calories from fat: 3
Fat (gm): 0.4
Saturated fat (gm): 0.1
Cholesterol (mg): 0
Sodium (mg): 2
Protein (gm): 6.1
Carbohydrate (gm): 20

Exchanges:
Milk: 0.0
Vegetable: 0.0
Fruit: 0.0
Bread: 1.5
Meat: 0.0
Fat: 0.0

1. Cover beans with 2 inches of water in a large saucepan; heat to boiling and boil, uncovered, 2 minutes. Remove from heat; let stand, covered, 1 hour. Drain beans; cover with 2 inches water and heat to boiling. Reduce heat and simmer, covered, until beans are tender, 1½ to 2 hours. Drain, reserving 2 cups liquid.

2. Sauté onion in lightly greased large skillet until tender, 3 to 5 minutes. Add 1 cup beans and 1 cup reserved liquid to skillet. Cook over high heat, mashing beans with end of meat mallet or potato masher until almost smooth. Add half the remaining beans and liquid; continue cooking and mashing beans. Repeat with remaining beans and liquid. Season to taste with salt and pepper.

MEXI-BEANS AND GREENS

V *Four cans (15 ounces each) pinto beans, rinsed and drained, can be substituted for the dried beans; omit step 1 in recipe.*

8 entrée servings

2 cups dried pinto beans

1 each: chopped onion, poblano chili, red bell pepper

2 teaspoons each: minced garlic, serrano chilies, finely chopped gingerroot

2 tablespoons olive oil

3 cups water

2–3 teaspoons each: chili powder, dried oregano leaves

1 teaspoon ground cumin

¼–½ teaspoon cayenne pepper

1 can (15 ounces) diced tomatoes, undrained

2 cups coarsely chopped turnip or mustard greens

Salt, to taste

¼ cup chopped cilantro

Per Serving:
Calories: 361
% of calories from fat: 12
Fat (gm): 4.7
Saturated fat (gm): 0.7
Cholesterol (mg): 0
Sodium (mg): 103
Protein (gm): 14.4
Carbohydrate (gm): 66.7

Exchanges:
Milk: 0.0
Vegetable: 2.0
Fruit: 0.0
Bread: 3.5
Meat: 0.5
Fat: 0.5

1. Cover beans with 2 inches water in large saucepan; heat to boiling and boil, uncovered, 2 minutes. Remove from heat and let stand, covered, 1 hour; drain.

2. Sauté onion, poblano chili, bell pepper, garlic, serrano chilies, and gingerroot in oil in large saucepan until tender, 8 to 10 minutes. Add beans, water, and seasonings; heat to boiling. Reduce heat and simmer, covered, until beans are tender, 1 to 1¼ hours. Stir in tomatoes with liquid and greens; simmer, uncovered, 15 minutes. Season to taste with salt; stir in cilantro.

PINTOS, GREENS, AND RICE

45

V

The chilies and cayenne pepper in this heartily spiced dish can be decreased if less hotness is desired.

8 entrée servings

1 cup each: chopped onion, poblano chili

1 tablespoon each: finely chopped garlic, gingerroot, serrano chili

2 tablespoons olive oil

2 teaspoons each: chili powder, dried oregano leaves

1 teaspoon ground cumin

4 cans (15 ounces each) pinto beans, rinsed, drained

1 can (15 ounces) diced tomatoes, undrained

2 cups coarsely chopped turnip or mustard greens

Salt, to taste

4 cups cooked rice, warm

Per Serving:
Calories: 353
% of calories from fat: 14
Fat (gm): 5.7
Saturated fat (gm): 0.9
Cholesterol (mg): 0
Sodium (mg): 676
Protein (gm): 14
Carbohydrate (gm): 63.3

Exchanges:
Milk: 0.0
Vegetable: 1.0
Fruit: 0.0
Bread: 4.0
Meat: 0.0
Fat: 1.0

1. Sauté onion, poblano chili, garlic, gingerroot, and serrano chilies in oil in large saucepan 8 minutes. Stir in chili powder and herbs; cook 1 to 2 minutes. Stir in beans, tomatoes with liquid, and turnip greens and heat to boiling. Reduce heat and simmer, covered, 10 minutes; uncover and cook until mixture is desired thickness, about 5 minutes. Season to taste with salt. Spoon rice into bowls; top with bean mixture.

HOPPING JOHN

V *Be sure to eat your portion of Hopping John before noon on January 1 to guarantee a new year of good luck!*

6 entrée servings

1½ cups chopped onions

½ cup chopped celery

3 cloves garlic, minced

1 cup long-grain white rice

3 cups reduced-sodium vegetable broth

1 teaspoon dried oregano leaves

1 bay leaf

2 cans (15 ounces each) black-eyed peas, rinsed, drained

2–3 dashes each: red pepper sauce, liquid smoke (optional)

Salt and pepper, to taste

Per Serving:
Calories: 306
% of calories from fat: 21
Fat (gm): 7
Saturated fat (gm): 1
Cholesterol (mg): 0
Sodium (mg): 447
Protein (gm): 9.6
Carbohydrate (gm): 50.7

Exchanges:
Milk: 0.0
Vegetable: 1.0
Fruit: 0.0
Bread: 3.0
Meat: 0.5
Fat: 1.0

1. Sauté onions, celery, and garlic in lightly greased large saucepan until tender, 5 to 8 minutes. Add rice, broth, oregano, and bay leaf; heat to boiling. Reduce heat and simmer, covered, until rice is tender, about 25 minutes, stirring in black-eyed peas, red pepper sauce, and liquid smoke during last 5 minutes. Discard bay leaf; season to taste with salt and pepper.

BOURBON STREET RED BEANS AND RICE

45 *The New Orleans favorite, at its healthy, low-fat best!*

6 entrée servings

5 ounces reduced-fat smoked sausage, sliced

1 cup each: chopped onion, green bell peppers, celery

½–1 jalapeño chili, finely chopped

1 tablespoon olive oil

2 cans (15 ounces each) red beans, rinsed, drained

¾ cup reduced-sodium vegetable or chicken broth

1 teaspoon each: dried thyme and oregano leaves

½ teaspoon each: dried sage leaves, ground cumin

¼ teaspoon each: red pepper sauce, cayenne pepper

4–6 drops liquid smoke (optional)

Salt, to taste

4 cups cooked rice, warm

Per Serving:
Calories: 305
% of calories from fat: 12
Fat (gm): 4.1
Saturated fat (gm): 0.8
Cholesterol (mg): 11
Sodium (mg): 521
Protein (gm): 14
Carbohydrate (gm): 60

Exchanges:
Milk: 0.0
Vegetable: 2.0
Fruit: 0.0
Bread: 2.5
Meat: 0.5
Fat: 0.5

1. Sauté sausage, onion, bell peppers, celery, and jalapeno chili in oil in large saucepan 8 minutes. Add remaining ingredients, except liquid smoke, salt, and rice; cook, covered, over medium heat 10 minutes. Cook, uncovered, until thickened, 5 to 10 minutes. Season to taste with liquid smoke, salt, and rice; serve over rice in shallow bowls.

SANTA FE BAKED BEANS

L

These baked beans boast flavors of the great Southwest.

45

4 entrée servings

1 cup chopped onion

½ cup chopped poblano chili or green bell pepper

½–1 serrano or jalapeño chili, finely chopped

1 tablespoon olive oil

2 cans (15 ounces each) pinto beans, rinsed, drained

2 cups whole kernel corn

6 sun-dried tomatoes (not in oil), softened, sliced

2–3 tablespoons honey

½ teaspoon each: ground cumin, dried thyme leaves

3 bay leaves

Salt and pepper, to taste

½ cup (2 ounces) crumbled Mexican white or
    farmer's cheese

¼ cup finely chopped cilantro

Per Serving:
Calories: 167
% of calories from fat: 21
Fat (gm): 4.1
Saturated fat (gm): 1.4
Cholesterol (mg): 5.4
Sodium (mg): 432
Protein (gm): 7.4
Carbohydrate (gm): 27.9

Exchanges:
Milk: 0.0
Vegetable: 1.0
Fruit: 0.0
Bread: 1.5
Meat: 0.0
Fat: 1.0

1. Sauté onion and chilies in oil in small skillet until tender, about 5 minutes. Combine with remaining ingredients, except salt, pepper, cheese, and cilantro, in 1½-quart casserole; season to taste with salt and pepper. Bake, covered, at 350 degrees until hot, about 30 minutes; sprinkle with cheese and bake, uncovered, until cheese is melted, about 15 minutes. Discard bay leaves. Sprinkle with cilantro.

TUSCAN BEAN BAKE

Easy to make, these beans are lemon-scented and seasoned with sun-dried tomatoes, garlic, and herbs.

4 entrée servings

1 cup dried cannellini or Great Northern beans
1 cup reduced-sodium vegetable broth
½ cup each: chopped onion, red bell pepper
2 teaspoons minced garlic
1 teaspoon each: dried sage and rosemary leaves
2–3 teaspoons grated lemon zest
6 sun-dried tomatoes (not in oil), softened, sliced
Salt and pepper, to taste
1 cup fresh whole wheat bread crumbs
¼ cup minced parsley

Per Serving:
Calories: 250
% of calories from fat: 6
Fat (gm): 1.7
Saturated fat (gm): 0.3
Cholesterol (mg): 0
Sodium (mg): 220
Protein (gm): 14.3
Carbohydrate (gm): 45.4

Exchanges:
Milk: 0.0
Vegetable: 1.5
Fruit: 0.0
Bread: 2.5
Meat: 0.5
Fat: 0.0

1. Cover beans with 2 inches water in large saucepan; heat to boiling and boil, uncovered, 2 minutes. Remove from heat and let stand, covered, 1 hour; drain.

2. Combine beans and remaining ingredients, except bread crumbs and parsley, in 1½-quart casserole. Bake, covered, at 350 degrees, until beans are tender, about 1 hour; season to taste with salt and pepper. Sprinkle combined bread crumbs and parsley over top, pressing lightly onto beans to moisten. Bake, uncovered, until thickened, about 20 minutes.

GINGER BAKED BEANS

Slow baking adds goodness to this special ginger and sweet-spiced bean dish.

12 servings

1½ cups chopped onions
¼ cup finely chopped gingerroot
4 cloves garlic, minced
1–2 tablespoons vegetable oil

6 cups cooked dried Great Northern beans or
   4 cans (15 ounces each) rinsed, drained
   Great Northern beans

½ cup packed light brown sugar

1 can (8 ounces) reduced-sodium tomato sauce

½ cup light molasses

1 teaspoon each: dry mustard, ground ginger

½ teaspoon dried thyme leaves

¼ teaspoon each: ground cinnamon and allspice

2 bay leaves

½ cup coarsely ground gingersnap crumbs

Per Serving:
Calories: 216
% of calories from fat: 8
Fat (gm): 2.1
Saturated fat (gm): 0.4
Cholesterol (mg): 0
Sodium (mg): 52
Protein (gm): 8.3
Carbohydrate (gm): 42.4

Exchanges:
Milk: 0.0
Vegetable: 0.0
Fruit: 0.0
Bread: 3.0
Meat: 0.0
Fat: 0.0

1. Sauté onions, gingerroot, and garlic in oil in medium skillet until tender, 5 to 8 minutes. Mix all ingredients, except gingersnap crumbs, in 2-quart casserole. Bake, covered, at 300 degrees 2 hours. Sprinkle top of beans with gingersnap crumbs; bake, uncovered, until beans are thickened to desired consistency, about 30 minutes. Discard bay leaves.

JUST PEACHY BEAN POT

Peaches and nectar, dried fruit, and mango chutney add special flavor to this bean combo.

6 entrée servings

1 cup chopped onion

1 clove garlic, minced

1–1½ teaspoons curry powder

½ teaspoon ground allspice

⅛–¼ teaspoon crushed red pepper

1 tablespoon margarine

2 cans (15 ounces each) red kidney beans,
   rinsed, drained

1 can (15 ounces) navy beans, rinsed, drained

1½ cups diced peaches

½ cup each: coarsely chopped mixed dried fruit,
   mango chutney, peach nectar

2 tablespoons cider vinegar

Salt and pepper, to taste

Per Serving:
Calories: 332
% of calories from fat: 8
Fat (gm): 3.4
Saturated fat (gm): 0.5
Cholesterol (mg): 0
Sodium (mg): 621
Protein (gm): 17.5
Carbohydrate (gm): 68.8

Exchanges:
Milk: 0.0
Vegetable: 0.0
Fruit: 1.5
Bread: 3.0
Meat: 0.5
Fat: 0.0

1. Sauté onion, garlic, herbs, and red pepper in margarine in small skillet until tender, about 5 minutes. Mix with remaining ingredients, except salt and pepper, in 2½-quart casserole; season to taste with salt and pepper. Bake, covered, at 350 degrees 30 minutes; bake, uncovered, if thicker consistency is desired, about 15 minutes.

FRIED LENTILS

V *Fried lentils, or "dal," are a staple of Indian cooking. Normally cooked in a large quantity of browned clarified butter, or "ghee," we've substituted a small amount of olive oil to keep the dish low in fat.*

8 side-dish servings

1½ cups dried red lentils

1 cup chopped onion

1 teaspoon each: ground turmeric, crushed cumin seeds

¼ teaspoon crushed red pepper

2 tablespoons olive oil

½ cup chopped cilantro

Salt, to taste

2 teaspoons grated lemon zest

Per Serving:
Calories: 171
% of calories from fat: 20
Fat (gm): 4
Saturated fat (gm): 0.5
Cholesterol (mg): 0
Sodium (mg): 4.4
Protein (gm): 10.5
Carbohydrate (gm): 24.6

Exchanges:
Milk: 0.0
Vegetable: 1.0
Fruit: 0.0
Bread: 1.5
Meat: 0.0
Fat: 1.0

1. Cook lentils in 2 inches simmering water, covered, until very soft, 30 to 40 minutes; drain. Sauté onion and seasonings in oil in large skillet until onion is tender, 5 to 8 minutes; reserve ¼ cup mixture. Add lentils to skillet; cook over low heat, stirring frequently, until mixture is thickened, about 10 minutes. Stir in cilantro; season to taste with salt. Sprinkle with reserved ¼ cup onion mixture and lemon zest.

SWEET BULGUR PILAF

45 *A pilaf with sweet accents of yellow squash, raisins, and pie spice.*

V **4 entrée servings**

⅔ cup each: chopped onion, sliced green onions

1 large clove garlic, minced

1 cup bulgur

2¼ cups reduced-sodium vegetable broth

½–¾ teaspoon ground cinnamon

2 cups cubed, peeled butternut or acorn squash

¼ cup each: currants or raisins, toasted pine nuts

Salt and pepper, to taste

Per Serving:
Calories: 263
% of calories from fat: 19
Fat (gm): 6.2
Saturated fat (gm): 1
Cholesterol (mg): 0
Sodium (mg): 44
Protein (gm): 8.7
Carbohydrate (gm): 46.1

Exchanges:
Milk: 0.0
Vegetable: 0.0
Fruit: 0.0
Bread: 3.0
Meat: 0.0
Fat: 1.0

1. Sauté onion, green onions, garlic, and bulgur in lightly greased large saucepan until onions are tender, 5 to 6 minutes. Stir in broth and cinnamon and heat to boiling; reduce heat and simmer, covered, 10 minutes. Stir in squash and currants; simmer, covered, until squash is tender, about 15 minutes. Stir in pine nuts; season to taste with salt and pepper.

BULGUR AND BARLEY WITH LEMON GREENS

V *Grains and greens are cooked together, then combined with tomatoes and toasted nuts.*

8 side-dish servings

¾ cup barley

Vegetable cooking spray

2½ cups reduced-sodium vegetable broth

¼ cup bulgur

½ teaspoon dried thyme leaves

6 ounces thinly sliced turnip greens, kale, or spinach

½ cup thinly sliced green onions

1 large tomato, coarsely chopped

¼–½ cup coarsely chopped walnuts, toasted

1–2 tablespoons lemon juice

Salt and pepper, to taste

1. Add barley to lightly greased large saucepan; spray lightly with cooking spray. Cook over medium heat, stirring occasionally, until barley is golden, 5 to 8 minutes. Add broth and heat to boiling; reduce heat and simmer, covered, 40 minutes. Stir in bulgur and thyme; simmer, covered, until barley and bulgur are tender, about 15 minutes. Stir in greens and green onions; cook, covered, until liquid is absorbed, about 10 minutes. Stir in tomato and walnuts; cook 5 minutes longer. Season to taste with lemon juice, salt, and pepper.

Per Serving:
Calories: 129
% of calories from fat: 20
Fat (gm): 3
Saturated fat (gm): 0.3
Cholesterol (mg): 0
Sodium (mg): 33
Protein (gm): 4.3
Carbohydrate (gm): 20.9

Exchanges:
Milk: 0.0
Vegetable: 0.5
Fruit: 0.0
Bread: 1.0
Meat: 0.0
Fat: 0.5

BARLEY WITH PEPPERS AND POTATOES

V *Enjoy this delicious variation of the Mexican "rajas con papas." If poblano chilies are not available, substitute green bell peppers and 1 to 2 teaspoons minced jalapeño chilies.*

6 side-dish servings

3 large poblano chilies, sliced
1 medium onion, chopped
1 tablespoon olive or canola oil
3 cups cooked cubed unpeeled potatoes
2 cups cooked barley
2 tablespoons finely chopped cilantro leaves
½ teaspoon dried cumin
Salt and cayenne pepper, to taste

Per Serving:
Calories: 313
% of calories from fat: 13
Fat (gm): 5
Saturated fat (gm): 0.6
Cholesterol (mg): 0.0
Sodium (mg): 20
Protein (gm): 8
Carbohydrate (gm): 64

Exchanges:
Milk: 0.0
Vegetable: 0.0
Fruit: 0.0
Bread: 4.0
Meat: 0.0
Fat: 1.0

1. Sauté chilies and onion in oil in large skillet until crisp-tender, about 5 minutes. Add potatoes; sauté until browned, 5 to 8 minutes. Add barley and cook over medium heat until hot, 3 to 4 minutes. Stir in cilantro and cumin; season to taste with salt and cayenne pepper.

TABBOULEH

Always a favorite—this version includes finely chopped mint as well as parsley.

8 side-dish servings

¾ cup bulgur

1½ cups coarsely chopped seeded tomatoes

¾ cup each: thinly sliced green onions, chopped
   parsley

¼ cup finely chopped mint

⅓–⅔ cup fat-free plain yogurt

¼–⅓ cup lemon juice

1½–2 tablespoons olive oil

Salt and pepper, to taste

Per Serving:
Calories: 176
% of calories from fat: 28
Fat (gm): 5.9
Saturated fat (gm): 0.8
Cholesterol (mg): 0.3
Sodium (mg): 34
Protein (gm): 5.7
Carbohydrate (gm): 28.2

Exchanges:
Milk: 0.0
Vegetable: 1.0
Fruit: 0.0
Bread: 1.5
Meat: 0.0
Fat: 1.0

1. Pour boiling water over bulgur to cover; let stand 15 minutes or until bulgur is tender but slightly chewy; drain. Mix bulgur and remaining ingredients, except salt and pepper; season to taste with salt and pepper. Refrigerate 1 to 2 hours for flavors to blend.

MUSHROOM AND ASPARAGUS PILAF

The dried Chinese black mushrooms impart a hearty, woodsy flavor to the pilaf.

8 entrée servings

3⅓ cups reduced-sodium vegetable broth

1 cup dried Chinese mushrooms

1½ cups chopped onions

2 teaspoons each: minced garlic, bouquet garni

1½ pounds cut asparagus (1½-inch)

¼ cup dry sherry or water

2 packages (6 ounces each) tabbouleh wheat
   salad mix (discard seasoning packet)

¼ teaspoon hot pepper sauce

Salt and pepper, to taste

4 green onions, thinly sliced

¼ cup toasted pecan halves

Per Serving:
Calories: 248
% of calories from fat: 12
Fat (gm): 3.4
Saturated fat (gm): 0.3
Cholesterol (mg): 0
Sodium (mg): 537
Protein (gm): 7.5
Carbohydrate (gm): 45.8

Exchanges:
Milk: 0.0
Vegetable: 3.0
Fruit: 0.0
Bread: 2.0
Meat: 0.0
Fat: 0.5

1. Heat broth to boiling; pour over mushrooms in bowl and let stand until mushrooms are softened, about 10 minutes. Drain, reserving broth. Slice mushrooms, discarding tough stems.

2. Sauté mushrooms, onions, garlic, and bouquet garni in lightly greased large skillet until onions are tender, about 5 minutes. Add asparagus; sauté 5 minutes. Add sherry and reserved broth; heat to boiling. Stir in wheat salad mix; reduce heat and simmer, covered, until broth is absorbed and pilaf is tender, 3 to 5 minutes. Stir in hot pepper sauce; season to taste with salt and pepper. Sprinkle with green onions and pecans.

FALAFEL PATTIES

45

L

For appetizers, shape falafel mixture into 1-inch balls; cook and serve as below.

4 entrée servings

1 package (6 ounces) falafel mix
½ cup shredded carrots
¼ cup sunflower kernels
1 tablespoon thinly sliced green onions
Yogurt Cucumber Sauce (recipe follows)

1. Prepare falafel mix with water according to package directions; mix in carrots, sunflower kernels, and green onions. Shape mixture into 8 patties about ½ inch thick; sauté in lightly greased skillet until browned, 4 to 5 minutes on each side. Serve with Yogurt Cucumber Sauce.

Per Serving:
Calories: 255
% of calories from fat: 30
Fat (gm): 7.7
Saturated fat (gm): 0.5
Cholesterol (mg): 1
Sodium (mg): 586
Protein (gm): 11.7
Carbohydrate (gm): 28.6

Exchanges:
Milk: 0.0
Vegetable: 0.0
Fruit: 0.0
Bread: 2.0
Meat: 1.0
Fat: 1.0

Yogurt Cucumber Sauce

Makes about 1⅔ cups

1 cup each: plain fat-free yogurt, finely chopped cucumber
½ teaspoon each: dried dill weed, mint leaves
Salt and white pepper, to taste

1. Mix yogurt, cucumber, and herbs. Season to taste with salt and white pepper.

45-MINUTE PREPARATION TIP: Make Yogurt Cucumber Sauce while patties are cooking.

FALAFEL LOAF

45

LO

Dried fruit provides a sweet accent to this easy-to-make meatless loaf. Serve with fried or poached eggs for heartier fare.

4 entrée servings

1 package (6 ounces) falafel mix
½ cup each: shredded zucchini, chopped mixed dried fruit
3 tablespoons each: coarsely chopped toasted pecans, thinly sliced green onion
2 eggs
¾ cup plain fat-free yogurt

Per Serving:
Calories: 311
% of calories from fat: 29
Fat (gm): 9.5
Saturated fat (gm): 1.1
Cholesterol (mg): 106.8
Sodium (mg): 603
Protein (gm): 12.9
Carbohydrate (gm): 38.3

Exchanges:
Milk: 0.0
Vegetable: 0.0
Fruit: 0.5
Bread: 2.0
Meat: 0.0
Fat: 2.0

1. Prepare falafel mix with water according to package directions; mix in remaining ingredients, except yogurt. Pack mixture into greased 7 x 4-inch loaf pan. Bake, uncovered, at 350 degrees until set, about 30 minutes. Invert loaf onto serving plate; serve with yogurt.

CURRIED COUSCOUS WITH VEGETABLES

45

L

Couscous, a staple in Mediterranean countries, is fast and easy to cook. Serve with a selection of condiments so the dish can be enjoyed with a variety of flavor accents.

4 entrée servings

8 ounces fresh or thawed, frozen whole okra

1 medium onion, chopped

2 cloves garlic, chopped

1 cup each: whole kernel corn, sliced
   mushrooms, carrots

1½ teaspoons curry powder

1 cup reduced-sodium vegetable broth

⅔ cup couscous

1 medium tomato, chopped

Salt and pepper, to taste

Condiments: chopped cucumber, peanuts, raisins, plain
   reduced-fat yogurt (not included in nutritional data)

Per Serving:
Calories: 304
% of calories from fat: 11
Fat (gm): 3.9
Saturated fat (gm): 0.6
Cholesterol (mg): 0.5
Sodium (mg): 55
Protein (gm): 9.5
Carbohydrate (gm): 60.1

Exchanges:
Milk: 0.0
Vegetable: 3.0
Fruit: 1.0
Bread: 2.0
Meat: 0.0
Fat: 0.5

1. Sauté okra, onion, and garlic in lightly greased large saucepan until onion is tender, about 5 minutes. Stir in corn, mushrooms, carrots, curry powder, and broth; heat to boiling. Reduce heat and simmer, covered, until vegetables are tender, 8 to 10 minutes. Stir in couscous and tomato; remove from heat and let stand, covered, until couscous is tender and broth absorbed, about 5 minutes. Season to taste with salt and pepper. Serve with condiments.

FRUIT PILAF

45

V

An easy pilaf, with dried fruit and nuts, that is simply good.

4 entrée servings

½ cup sliced green onions

¼ cup thinly sliced celery

1 tablespoon margarine

⅔ cup brown rice

⅓ cup wild rice

2½ cups reduced-sodium vegetable broth

½ teaspoon each: dried marjoram and thyme leaves
1 large apple, peeled, cubed
⅓ cup each: chopped dried apricots, dried pears
4–6 tablespoons pecan or walnut halves, toasted
Salt and pepper, to taste

Per Serving:
Calories: 353
% of calories from fat: 23
Fat (gm): 9.2
Saturated fat (gm): 1.2
Cholesterol (mg): 0
Sodium (mg): 80
Protein (gm): 6.4
Carbohydrate (gm): 60.9

1. Sauté green onions and celery in margarine in large saucepan until celery is tender, about 5 minutes. Add rices and cook 2 minutes. Stir in broth and herbs and heat to boiling; reduce heat and simmer, covered, 45 minutes. Stir in fruit; simmer, covered, until rice is tender and broth absorbed, about 10 minutes. Stir in pecans; season to taste with salt and pepper.

Exchanges:
Milk: 0.0
Vegetable: 0.0
Fruit: 1.5
Bread: 2.5
Meat: 0.0
Fat: 2.0

ASIAN PILAF

V *A combination of brown rice, millet, and Asian ingredients make this pilaf a favorite.*

4 entrée servings

⅓ cup each: chopped onion, celery
2–3 teaspoons finely chopped gingerroot, garlic
1 tablespoon Asian sesame oil
½ cup each: brown rice, millet
2½ cups reduced-sodium vegetable broth
1½ cups halved snow peas
½ can (6-ounce size) water chestnuts, drained, sliced
½ cup thinly sliced green onions
2–3 tablespoons reduced-sodium tamari soy sauce
Salt and pepper, to taste

Per Serving:
Calories: 273
% of calories from fat: 18
Fat (gm): 5.4
Saturated fat (gm): 0.8
Cholesterol (mg): 0
Sodium (mg): 387
Protein (gm): 8.2
Carbohydrate (gm): 47.9

Exchanges:
Milk: 0.0
Vegetable: 1.0
Fruit: 0.0
Bread: 3.0
Meat: 0.0
Fat: 0.5

1. Sauté onion, celery, gingerroot, and garlic in sesame oil in large saucepan until onion is tender, about 10 minutes. Add rice and millet and cook 2 minutes longer; add broth and heat to boiling. Reduce heat and simmer, covered, 15 minutes. Stir in snow peas, water chestnuts, and green onions; simmer, covered, until grains and snow peas are tender and broth absorbed, about 10 minutes. Season to taste with soy sauce, salt, and pepper.

ASIAN FRIED RICE

45

O

The combination of wild and white rice adds a new dimension to an Asian favorite.

6 side-dish servings

2 cups broccoli florets and sliced stalks

1 cup halved snow peas

¾ cup each: bean sprouts, sliced carrots, shiitake
   mushrooms, chopped celery, green bell pepper

1 teaspoon each: minced garlic, gingerroot

½ cup reduced-sodium vegetable broth

2 tablespoons reduced-sodium soy sauce

1½ cups each: cooked white and wild rice

1 egg, lightly scrambled, crumbled

Salt and pepper, to taste

Per Serving:
Calories: 198
% of calories from fat: 26
Fat (gm): 5.9
Saturated fat (gm): 0.9
Cholesterol (mg): 35.3
Sodium (mg): 709
Protein (gm): 6.3
Carbohydrate (gm): 32.3

Exchanges:
Milk: 0.0
Vegetable: 1.0
Fruit: 0.0
Bread: 2.0
Meat: 0.0
Fat: 1.0

1. Stir-fry vegetables, garlic, and gingerroot in lightly greased large wok or skillet until crisp-tender, 5 to 8 minutes. Add broth and soy sauce; stir in rice and scrambled egg and stir-fry 2 to 3 minutes longer. Season to taste with salt and pepper.

SPICY RICE

L

An aromatic dish of east Indian origins that will complement many meals.

8 side-dish servings

1 medium onion, sliced

1 clove garlic, minced

1 tablespoon olive oil

1 cup basmati rice

½ cup reduced-fat plain yogurt

1–2 cardamom pods, crushed

¼ teaspoon each: ground turmeric, ginger

⅛ teaspoon crushed red pepper

2 cups reduced-sodium vegetable broth

Salt and pepper, to taste

1 small tomato, cut into 8 wedges

1 tablespoon finely chopped cilantro

Per Serving:
Calories: 166
% of calories from fat: 19
Fat (gm): 3.6
Saturated fat (gm): 0.5
Cholesterol (mg): 1.2
Sodium (mg): 54
Protein (gm): 4.4
Carbohydrate (gm): 27.9

Exchanges:
Milk: 0.0
Vegetable: 1.0
Fruit: 0.0
Bread: 1.5
Meat: 0.0
Fat: 0.5

1. Sauté onion and garlic in oil in large saucepan until tender, about 8 minutes. Add rice; stir over medium heat 2 to 3 minutes. Stir in yogurt, spices, and crushed red pepper; cook over medium heat 5 minutes, stirring frequently. Add broth and heat to boiling; reduce heat and simmer, covered, until rice is tender, about 25 minutes. Season to taste with salt and pepper. Garnish with tomato wedges; sprinkle with cilantro.

YELLOW SALSA RICE

45

V

Ground turmeric contributes subtle flavor and an attractive yellow color to the rice.

6 side-dish servings

1 can (14½ ounces) reduced-sodium vegetable broth
½ teaspoon ground turmeric
1 cup long-grain rice
¼ cup medium or hot salsa
1 medium tomato, chopped
Salt and pepper, to taste
Chopped cilantro, as garnish

Per Serving:
Calories: 130
% of calories from fat: 2
Fat (gm): 0.3
Saturated fat (gm): 0.1
Cholesterol (mg): 0
Sodium (mg): 103
Protein (gm): 2.7
Carbohydrate (gm): 28.4

Exchanges:
Milk: 0.0
Vegetable: 1.0
Fruit: 0.0
Bread: 1.5
Meat: 0.0
Fat: 0.0

1. Heat broth and turmeric to boiling in medium saucepan; stir in rice and salsa. Reduce heat and simmer, covered, until rice is tender and liquid absorbed, 20 to 25 minutes, stirring in tomato during last 5 minutes. Season to taste with salt and pepper; sprinkle with cilantro.

ORANGE CILANTRO RICE

45 *A perfect accompaniment to grilled or roasted meats, poultry, or fish.*

V   **6 side-dish servings**

½ cup sliced green onions

1 cup long-grain rice

Grated zest of 1 small orange

2¼ cups water

2 tablespoons finely chopped cilantro

Salt and pepper, to taste

Per Serving:
Calories: 118
% of calories from fat: 1
Fat (gm): 0.2
Saturated fat (gm): 0
Cholesterol (mg): 0
Sodium (mg): 2
Protein (gm): 2.3
Carbohydrate (gm): 26

Exchanges:
Milk: 0.0
Vegetable: 0.0
Fruit: 0.0
Bread: 1.5
Meat: 0.0
Fat: 0.0

1. Sauté onions in lightly greased medium saucepan until tender, 3 to 5 minutes. Add rice and orange zest; stir over medium heat until rice is lightly browned, 2 to 3 minutes. Add water and heat to boiling; reduce heat and simmer, covered, until rice is tender, 20 to 25 minutes. Stir in cilantro; season to taste with salt and pepper.

MEXICAN RED RICE

45 *The tomatoes are pureed in the traditional version of this recipe. We've chosen to chop the tomato for more appealing texture and appearance.*

V

6 side-dish servings

1 large tomato, chopped

½ cup chopped onion, carrot

1 clove garlic, minced

½ teaspoon each: dried oregano leaves, ground cumin

1 cup long-grain rice

1 can (14½ ounces) reduced-sodium vegetable broth

⅓ cup water

½ cup frozen peas

Salt and pepper, to taste

Per Serving:
Calories: 149
% of calories from fat: 2
Fat (gm): 0.4
Saturated fat (gm): 0.1
Cholesterol (mg): 0
Sodium (mg): 45
Protein (gm): 3.7
Carbohydrate (gm): 32.5

Exchanges:
Milk: 0.0
Vegetable: 0.0
Fruit: 0.0
Bread: 2.0
Meat: 0.0
Fat: 0.0

1. Sauté tomato, onion, carrot, garlic, and herbs in lightly greased large saucepan until onion is tender, 3 to 5 minutes. Add rice; stir over medium heat 2 to 3 minutes, stirring frequently. Add broth and water and heat to boiling; reduce heat and simmer, covered, until rice is tender, about 25 minutes, adding peas during last 5 minutes. Season to taste with salt and pepper.

GINGER COCONUT RICE WITH SWEET POTATOES

45

V

Jasmine rice, scented with lemon grass and coconut, enhances this Asian-inspired offering.

6 side-dish servings

½ cup finely chopped onion

1½–2 tablespoons each: minced gingerroot, lemon grass

1 teaspoon minced garlic

1¼ cups each: water, reduced-fat coconut milk

1 cup jasmine or long-grain rice

1 sweet potato, peeled, quartered, sliced (¼-inch)

2 cups frozen stir-fry vegetable blend with asparagus

¼ cup finely chopped cilantro

1–2 tablespoons lime juice

Salt and pepper, to taste

Per Serving:
Calories: 187
% of calories from fat: 13
Fat (gm): 2.6
Saturated fat (gm): 1.7
Cholesterol (mg): 0
Sodium (mg): 32
Protein (gm): 3.9
Carbohydrate (gm): 36.7

Exchanges:
Milk: 0.0
Vegetable: 1.0
Fruit: 0.0
Bread: 2.0
Meat: 0.0
Fat: 0.5

1. Sauté onion, gingerroot, lemon grass, and garlic in lightly greased medium skillet until onion is tender, about 5 minutes. Stir in water, coconut milk, rice, and sweet potato; heat to boiling. Reduce heat and simmer, covered, until sweet potato is almost tender, about 10 minutes. Mix in stir-fry blend; simmer, covered, until vegetables are tender and liquid absorbed, 8 to 10 minutes. Stir in cilantro; season to taste with lime juice, salt, and pepper.

WILD RICE SOUFFLÉ

LO *When you're in the mood for something new and different, try this great soufflé!*

4 entrée servings

1 cup fat-free milk

¼ cup all-purpose flour

½ cup (2 ounces) shredded reduced-fat
   Cheddar cheese

¼ cup thinly sliced green onions

¼–½ teaspoon each: paprika, dried savory, and
   thyme leaves

White pepper, to taste

3 egg yolks

3 egg whites, beaten to stiff peaks

⅓ cup wild rice, cooked

Per Serving:
Calories: 210
% of calories from fat: 28
Fat (gm): 6.5
Saturated fat (gm): 2.4
Cholesterol (mg): 168.3
Sodium (mg): 288
Protein (gm): 13
Carbohydrate (gm): 23

Exchanges:
Milk: 0.0
Vegetable: 0.0
Fruit: 0.0
Bread: 1.5
Meat: 1.5
Fat: 0.5

1. Mix milk and flour in medium saucepan; heat to boiling, whisking until thickened, about 1 minute. Remove from heat; add cheese and stir until melted (sauce will be very thick). Stir in green onions, paprika, and herbs. Season to taste with white pepper.

2. Beat egg yolks in small bowl until thick and lemon colored, about 5 minutes; mix into cheese mixture. Fold in egg whites; fold in rice. Spoon into greased 1-quart soufflé dish. Bake at 350 degrees until knife inserted halfway between center and edge comes out clean, 45 to 55 minutes.

ALL-SEASON RISOTTO

L *A blending of summer and winter squash provides color and flavor to this creamy risotto dish.*

6 entrée servings

2 cups each: peeled, cubed acorn or butternut squash

1 cup each: sliced zucchini, cremini mushrooms, chopped red bell pepper, quartered plum tomatoes

2 teaspoons dried oregano leaves

2 tablespoons olive oil

1 cup chopped onion

2 cloves garlic, minced

1½ cups arborio rice

1½ quarts reduced-sodium vegetable broth

2 cups water

¼ cup (1 ounce) grated fat-free Parmesan cheese

1 can (15½ ounces) black beans, rinsed, drained

½ cup frozen peas, thawed

Salt and pepper, to taste

Per Serving:
Calories: 391
% of calories from fat: 13
Fat (gm): 6.2
Saturated fat (gm): 0.8
Cholesterol (mg): 0
Sodium (mg): 328
Protein (gm): 14.7
Carbohydrate (gm): 75.9

Exchanges:
Milk: 0.0
Vegetable: 2.0
Fruit: 0.0
Bread: 4.0
Meat: 0.0
Fat: 1.0

1. Sauté squash, zucchini, mushrooms, bell pepper, tomatoes, and oregano in oil in large saucepan until tender, about 8 minutes; remove from saucepan. Add onion and garlic to saucepan and sauté until tender, 3 to 4 minutes. Add rice; stir over medium heat 2 to 3 minutes.

2. Heat broth and water to simmering in medium saucepan; reduce heat to low to keep broth hot. Add broth to rice mixture, ½ cup at a time, stirring over medium heat until broth is absorbed before adding next ½ cup. Continue process until rice is al dente and mixture is creamy, 20 to 25 minutes. Stir in cheese, beans, peas, and sautéed vegetables; cook 2 to 3 minutes. Season to taste with salt and pepper.

SUMMER SQUASH RISOTTO

A perfect risotto for summer, when squash and tomatoes are fresh from the garden.

4 entrée servings

1 cup each: sliced zucchini, summer yellow
  squash, chopped onion
3 cloves garlic, minced
1 tablespoon olive oil
8 Italian plum tomatoes, quartered
1½ teaspoons dried oregano leaves
1½ cups arborio rice
1½ quarts reduced-sodium vegetable broth
¼ cup (1 ounce) grated Romano cheese
Salt and pepper, to taste

Per Serving:
Calories: 423
% of calories from fat: 15
Fat (gm): 7.4
Saturated fat (gm): 2
Cholesterol (mg): 7.2
Sodium (mg): 128
Protein (gm): 11.1
Carbohydrate (gm): 79.5

Exchanges:
Milk: 0.0
Vegetable: 3.0
Fruit: 0.0
Bread: 4.0
Meat: 0.0
Fat: 1.5

1. Sauté zucchini, yellow squash, onion, and garlic in oil in lightly greased large saucepan until vegetables are crisp-tender, 6 to 8 minutes; remove from saucepan. Add tomatoes and oregano to saucepan; cook until tomatoes are soft, about 3 minutes. Add rice; stir over medium heat 2 to 3 minutes.

2. Heat broth to boiling in small saucepan; reduce heat to low to keep broth hot. Add broth to rice mixture, ½ cup at a time, stirring over medium heat until broth is absorbed before adding another ½ cup. Continue process until rice is al dente and mixture is creamy, 20 to 25 minutes, adding sautéed vegetables during last 5 minutes. Stir in cheese; season to taste with salt and pepper.

WINTER VEGETABLE RISOTTO

Arborio rice is a short-grain rice grown in the Arborio region of Italy. It's especially suited for making risotto, as it cooks to a wonderful creaminess.

4 entrée servings

1 small onion, chopped
3 cloves garlic, minced
1 cup sliced cremini or white mushrooms

1 teaspoon each: dried rosemary and thyme leaves

1½ cups arborio rice

6 cups reduced-sodium vegetable broth

1 cup each: halved Brussels sprouts, cubed, peeled sweet potato, cooked until crisp-tender

¼ cup (1 ounce) grated Parmesan cheese

Salt and pepper, to taste

Per Serving:
Calories: 384
% of calories from fat: 8
Fat (gm): 3.3
Saturated fat (gm): 1.4
Cholesterol (mg): 4.9
Sodium (mg): 153
Protein (gm): 11
Carbohydrate (gm): 77.3

Exchanges:
Milk: 0.0
Vegetable: 3.0
Fruit: 0.0
Bread: 4.0
Meat: 0.0
Fat: 0.5

1. Sauté onion and garlic in lightly greased large saucepan until tender, about 5 minutes. Add mushrooms and herbs; cook until mushrooms are tender, 5 to 7 minutes. Add rice; stir over medium heat 2 to 3 minutes.

2. Heat broth just to boiling in medium saucepan; reduce heat to low to keep broth hot. Add broth to rice mixture, ½ cup at a time, stirring over medium heat until broth is absorbed before adding next ½ cup. Continue process until rice is al dente and mixture is creamy, 20 to 25 minutes, adding Brussels sprouts and sweet potato during last 10 minutes. Stir in cheese; season to taste with salt and pepper.

PORCINI RISOTTO

L *Use dried shiitake (Chinese black mushrooms) if porcini are not available.*

4 entrée servings

1 cup boiling water

¼–½ ounce dried porcini mushrooms

1 small onion, chopped

3 cloves garlic, minced

1 small tomato, seeded, chopped

1 teaspoon dried sage leaves

1½ cups arborio rice

1½ quarts reduced-sodium vegetable broth

¼ cup (1 ounce) grated Parmesan cheese, toasted pine nuts

Salt and pepper, to taste

Per Serving:
Calories: 389
% of calories from fat: 14
Fat (gm): 6.1
Saturated fat (gm): 1.9
Cholesterol (mg): 4.9
Sodium (mg): 135
Protein (gm): 10.2
Carbohydrate (gm): 68

Exchanges:
Milk: 0.0
Vegetable: 2.0
Fruit: 0.0
Bread: 4.0
Meat: 0.0
Fat: 1.0

1. Pour boiling water over mushrooms in bowl; let stand until mushrooms are soft, about 15 minutes; drain, reserving liquid. Slice mushrooms, discarding tough stems.

2. Sauté mushrooms, onion, and garlic in lightly greased large saucepan until tender, about 5 minutes; add tomato and sage and cook 2 minutes. Add rice; stir over medium heat 2 to 3 minutes.

3. Heat broth and reserved porcini liquid to boiling in medium saucepan; reduce heat to low to keep broth hot. Add broth to rice mixture, ½ cup at a time, stirring over medium heat until broth is absorbed before adding another ½ cup. Continue process until rice is al dente and mixture is creamy, 20 to 25 minutes; stir in cheese and pine nuts. Season to taste with salt and pepper.

SHRIMP AND MUSHROOM RISOTTO

White wine can be substituted for ½ cup of the broth in the recipe.

6 entrée servings

2 cups sliced mushrooms

1 small onion, chopped

3 cloves garlic, minced

1 teaspoon dried thyme leaves

1½ cups arborio rice

1½ quarts reduced-sodium chicken broth

8 ounces peeled, deveined shrimp

2 tablespoons grated Parmesan cheese

Salt and pepper, to taste

Per Serving:
Calories: 252
% of calories from fat: 8
Fat (gm): 2.1
Saturated fat (gm): 0.6
Cholesterol (mg): 59.6
Sodium (mg): 172
Protein (gm): 13.4
Carbohydrate (gm): 43.4

Exchanges:
Milk: 0.0
Vegetable: 0.5
Fruit: 0.0
Bread: 2.5
Meat: 0.5
Fat: 0.0

1. Sauté mushrooms, onion, garlic, and thyme in lightly greased large saucepan until tender, about 10 minutes. Add rice; stir over medium heat 2 to 3 minutes.

2. Heat chicken broth just to boiling in medium saucepan; reduce heat to low to keep broth hot. Add broth to rice mixture, ½ cup at a time, stirring until broth is absorbed before adding next ½ cup. Continue process until rice is al dente and mixture is creamy, 20 to 25 minutes, adding shrimp during last 10 minutes. Stir in cheese; season to taste with salt and pepper.

RISI BISI

L

Opinions vary as to whether Risi Bisi is a risotto or a thick soup. If you agree with the latter definition, use an additional ½ to 1 cup of broth to make the mixture a thick-soup consistency.

4 entrée servings

1 small onion, chopped

3 cloves garlic, minced

1½ cups arborio rice

2 teaspoons dried basil leaves

1½ quarts reduced-sodium vegetable broth

8 ounces frozen tiny peas

¼ cup (1 ounce) grated Parmesan cheese

Salt and pepper, to taste

Per Serving:
Calories: 407
% of calories from fat: 6
Fat (gm): 2.5
Saturated fat (gm): 1.3
Cholesterol (mg): 4.9
Sodium (mg): 291
Protein (gm): 12.2
Carbohydrate (gm): 82.1

Exchanges:
Milk: 0.0
Vegetable: 1.0
Fruit: 0.0
Bread: 5.0
Meat: 0.0
Fat: 0.5

1. Sauté onion and garlic in lightly greased large saucepan until tender, about 5 minutes. Add rice and basil; stir over medium heat 2 to 3 minutes.

2. Heat broth to boiling in medium saucepan; reduce heat to low to keep broth hot. Add broth to rice mixture, ½ cup at a time, stirring over medium heat until broth is absorbed before adding another ½ cup. Continue process until rice is al dente and mixture is creamy, 20 to 25 minutes, stirring in peas during last 10 minutes. Stir in Parmesan cheese; season to taste with salt and pepper.

TWO-CHEESE RISOTTO

45

L

This two-cheese risotto is quickly prepared with a simplified method that requires little stirring.

4 entrée servings

½ cup finely chopped onion

1 cup arborio rice

2½ cups vegetable broth

½ cup dry white wine or vegetable broth

1 cup (4 ounces) shredded Parmesan cheese

¼–½ cup (1 to 2 ounces) crumbled blue cheese

2–3 tablespoons chopped chives or parsley

Salt and pepper, to taste

Per Serving:
Calories: 345
% of calories from fat: 22
Fat (gm): 8.3
Saturated fat (gm): 5.2
Cholesterol (mg): 21.1
Sodium (mg): 525
Protein (gm): 13.9
Carbohydrate (gm): 47.3

Exchanges:
Milk: 0.0
Vegetable: 0.0
Fruit: 0.0
Bread: 3.0
Meat: 1.0
Fat: 1.5

1. Sauté onion and rice in lightly greased large saucepan 1 to 2 minutes. Add vegetable broth and wine and heat to boiling. Reduce heat and simmer, covered, until rice is al dente and liquid absorbed, 20 to 25 minutes, stirring occasionally. Stir in cheeses and chives. Season to taste with salt and pepper.

MICROWAVE RISOTTO

45

This is the easiest possible way to make risotto. Use of the microwave eliminates the constant stirring usually required for this dish.

4 entrée servings

1 cup arborio rice

3¼ cups reduced-sodium fat-free chicken broth, divided

½ cup (2 ounces) grated Parmesan cheese

Salt and pepper, to taste

Per Serving:
Calories: 235
% of calories from fat: 9
Fat (gm): 2.3
Saturated fat (gm): 1.3
Cholesterol (mg): 2.5
Sodium (mg): 266
Protein (gm): 11
Carbohydrate (gm): 39.9

Exchanges:
Milk: 0.0
Vegetable: 0.0
Fruit: 0.0
Bread: 2.5
Meat: 1.0
Fat: 0.0

1. Combine rice and ¼ cup broth in 3-quart glass casserole. Microwave, uncovered, on high power 60 seconds; stir. Add remaining broth; microwave on high power, covered, until rice is al dente, 20 to 25 minutes, stirring every 10 minutes. Let stand 2 to 3 minutes; stir in cheese and season to taste with salt and pepper.

CHEESE AND ARTICHOKE RISOTTO PANCAKES

L *Top each serving with a poached or fried egg for a hearty brunch or light supper.*

4 entrée servings

½ cup chopped onion

1 cup arborio rice

2½ cups reduced-sodium vegetable broth

½ cup dry white wine or vegetable broth

¾ cup (3 ounces) shredded Parmesan cheese

¼–½ cup (1–2 ounces) crumbled blue cheese

2 eggs, lightly beaten

6 canned artichoke hearts, coarsely chopped

¼ cup coarsely chopped roasted red pepper

Salt and pepper, to taste

Chopped parsley, as garnish

Per Serving:
Calories: 372
% of calories from fat: 31
Fat (gm): 12.4
Saturated fat (gm): 5.2
Cholesterol (mg): 122.8
Sodium (mg): 731
Protein (gm): 13.6
Carbohydrate (gm): 45.5

Exchanges:
Milk: 0.0
Vegetable: 0.0
Fruit: 0.0
Bread: 3.0
Meat: 1.0
Fat: 2.0

1. Sauté onion in lightly greased large saucepan 2 minutes; add rice and stir over medium heat 2 to 3 minutes. Add vegetable broth and wine; heat to boiling. Reduce heat and simmer, covered, until rice is tender and liquid absorbed, 20 to 25 minutes, stirring occasionally. Remove from heat and let stand 5 minutes; stir in cheeses, eggs, artichoke hearts, and red pepper. Season to taste with salt and pepper.

2. Heat two lightly greased 10-inch skillets over medium heat until hot. Spoon half the risotto mixture into each skillet, shaping into large pancakes. Cook over medium heat until lightly browned on the bottoms, 5 to 8 minutes. Invert pancakes onto plates; slide back into skillets and cook until lightly browned on the bottoms, 5 to 8 minutes. Cut pancakes in half; slide onto serving plates and sprinkle with parsley.

RISOTTO-VEGETABLE CAKES

L *A great way to use leftover risotto!*

4 entrée servings

1 medium onion, finely chopped

2 cloves garlic, minced

1 teaspoon dried oregano leaves

1 cup arborio rice

3 cups reduced-sodium vegetable broth

¼ cup (1 ounce) each: shredded reduced-fat Cheddar cheese, grated fat-free Parmesan cheese

Salt and pepper, to taste

½ cup each: chopped zucchini, carrots, red bell pepper, celery

1 egg, lightly beaten

⅔ cup seasoned dry bread crumbs

8 large tomatoes, thickly sliced

Per Serving:
Calories: 409
% of calories from fat: 12
Fat (gm): 5
Saturated fat (gm): 2
Cholesterol (mg): 59
Sodium (mg): 1142
Protein (gm): 16
Carbohydrate (gm): 77

Exchanges:
Milk: 0.0
Vegetable: 3.0
Fruit: 0.0
Bread: 4.0
Meat: 0.0
Fat: 1.0

1. Sauté onion, garlic, and oregano in lightly greased large saucepan until tender, about 3 minutes. Add rice; stir over medium heat 2 to 3 minutes.

2. Heat broth to simmering in medium saucepan; reduce heat to low to keep broth warm. Add broth to rice mixture, ½ cup at a time, stirring over medium heat until broth is absorbed before adding next ½ cup. Continue process until rice is al dente and mixture is creamy, 20 to 25 minutes; remove from heat and stir in cheeses. Season to taste with salt and pepper; cool.

3. Sauté vegetables in lightly greased large skillet until tender, 5 to 8 minutes. Stir into rice mixture; stir in egg and bread crumbs. Form mixture into 8 patties, about ¾-inch thick. Broil 6 inches from heat source until browned, 2 to 4 minutes on each side. Top each patty with tomato slice and sprinkle lightly with salt and pepper; broil until tomatoes are browned, 2 to 3 minutes.

POLENTA

45 *This basic recipe can be modified to your taste—note the variations below.*

V 6 side-dish servings

3 cups water
¾ cup yellow cornmeal
Salt and pepper, to taste

Per Serving:
Calories: 63
% of calories from fat: 4
Fat (gm): 0.3
Saturated fat (gm): 0.0
Cholesterol (mg): 0.0
Sodium (mg): 0.5
Protein (gm): 1.5
Carbohydrate (gm): 13

Exchanges:
Milk: 0.0;
Vegetable: 0.0
Fruit: 0.0
Bread: 1.0
Meat: 0.0
Fat: 0.0

1. Heat water to boiling in large saucepan; gradually stir in cornmeal. Cook over medium to medium-low heat, stirring until polenta thickens enough to hold its shape but is still soft, 5 to 8 minutes.

VARIATIONS

Blue Cheese Polenta — Make recipe above, stirring ½ cup (2 ounces) crumbled blue cheese, or other blue veined cheese, into the cooked polenta.

Goat Cheese Polenta — Make recipe above, stirring ¼ to ½ cup (1 to 2 ounces) crumbled goat cheese into the cooked polenta.

Garlic Polenta — Sauté ¼ cup finely chopped onion and 4 to 6 cloves minced garlic in 1 tablespoon olive oil in large saucepan; add water, as above, and complete recipe.

EGGPLANT POLENTA STACK

LO *Packaged polenta comes in several flavors; choose your favorite for this dish.*

45 **6 side-dish servings**

6 slices eggplant (¾-inch)

1 egg, lightly beaten

½ cup seasoned dry bread crumbs

¼ cup (1 ounce) grated Parmesan cheese

6 slices tomato (½-inch)

Salt and pepper, to taste

1 package (16 ounces) Italian-herb polenta, cut into
  6 slices

½ cup (2 ounces) crumbled reduced-fat feta cheese

Per Serving:
Calories: 167
% of calories from fat: 16
Fat (gm): 2.9
Saturated fat (gm): 1.4
Cholesterol (mg): 6
Sodium (mg): 693
Protein (gm): 7.9
Carbohydrate (gm): 27.2

Exchanges:
Milk: 0.0
Vegetable: 0.0
Fruit: 0.0
Bread: 2.0
Meat: 0.0
Fat: 0.5

1. Dip eggplant slices in egg and coat with combined bread crumbs
and Parmesan cheese. Cook in lightly greased large skillet until
browned, 6 to 8 minutes on each side. Arrange eggplant in baking
pan; top with tomato slices and sprinkle lightly with salt and pepper.
Top tomato slices with polenta and sprinkle with feta cheese. Bake
at 500 degrees, loosely covered, until polenta is warm and cheese
softened, about 5 minutes.

HERBED POLENTA

V *Gently seasoned with onions, garlic, and basil, the polenta can also be
served immediately after cooking.*

45

4 to 6 side-dish servings

2 green onions, sliced

1 clove garlic, minced

1 teaspoon dried basil leaves

2½ cups reduced-sodium vegetable broth

¾ cup yellow cornmeal

½ teaspoon salt

Per Serving:
Calories: 124
% of calories from fat: 9
Fat (gm): 1.3
Saturated fat (gm): 0.2
Cholesterol (mg): 0
Sodium (mg): 309
Protein (gm): 2.5
Carbohydrate (gm): 22.4

Exchanges:
Milk: 0.0
Vegetable: 0.0
Fruit: 0.0
Bread: 1.5
Meat: 0.0
Fat: 0.5

1. Sauté onions, garlic, and basil in lightly greased
large saucepan until tender, about 5 minutes.

Add broth and heat to boiling; gradually stir in cornmeal and salt. Cook over low heat, stirring until thickened, about 10 minutes. Pour polenta into greased 8-inch cake pan; cool. Refrigerate, lightly covered, until polenta is firm, 3 to 4 hours.

2. Cut polenta into wedges; cook in lightly greased large skillet over medium heat until browned, 3 to 4 minutes on each side.

CORNMEAL AND MILLET MUSH

A breakfast favorite! Other grains, such as kasha, millet, or wheat berries, can be combined with the cornmeal too.

45

8 entrée servings

4 cups water

1 cup yellow or white cornmeal

1 teaspoon salt

2 cups cooked millet

6 tablespoons brown sugar

Per Serving:
Calories: 283
% of calories from fat: 8
Fat (gm): 2.7
Saturated fat (gm): 0.4
Cholesterol (mg): 0
Sodium (mg): 278
Protein (gm): 6.7
Carbohydrate (gm): 58.3

Exchanges:
Milk: 0.0
Vegetable: 0.0
Fruit: 0.0
Bread: 4.0
Meat: 0.0
Fat: 0.0

1. Heat water to boiling in large saucepan; gradually stir in cornmeal and salt. Reduce heat to medium-low and cook 5 minutes, stirring constantly. Stir in millet and cook until mixture is thick, 3 to 5 minutes longer, stirring constantly. Sprinkle each bowl with brown sugar.

VARIATION

Fried Mush — Make cornmeal mixture as above, deleting brown sugar; pour into greased 8½ x 4½ inch loaf pan and cool. Refrigerate until firm, several hours or overnight. Loosen sides of cornmeal mixture with sharp knife; invert onto cutting board. Cut into slices and fry in lightly greased large skillet over medium heat until browned, 3 to 4 minutes on each side. Serve with warm maple syrup.

BEST BREAKFAST CEREAL

45 *Delicious and nutritious!*

L **6 entrée servings**

3 cups water

Pinch salt

1½ cups each: quick-cooking oats, cooked
    wheat berries

¼ cup chopped toasted pecans or walnuts

½ cup dried fruit bits or raisins

¼ cup packed dark brown sugar

1 cup fat-free milk

Per Serving:
Calories: 313
% of calories from fat: 13
Fat (gm): 4.9
Saturated fat (gm): 0.6
Cholesterol (mg): 0.7
Sodium (mg): 55
Protein (gm): 9.7
Carbohydrate (gm): 61.4

Exchanges:
Milk: 0.0
Vegetable: 0.0
Fruit: 0.5
Bread: 3.5
Meat: 0.0
Fat: 0.5

1. Heat water and salt to boiling in medium saucepan; stir in oats, wheat berries, pecans, and dried fruit. Reduce heat and simmer, uncovered, to soft, spoonable consistency, about 5 minutes. Serve with brown sugar and milk.

TEN

Casseroles

CHICKEN DIVAN

45

Mayonnaise adds the "tang" to this flavorful sauce!

6 entrée servings

4 cups cooked rice
1 pound broccoli florets, cooked crisp-tender
Tangy Cheese Sauce (recipe follows)
1 pound boneless, skinless chicken breasts, cooked, sliced (½-inch)
½ cup (2 ounces) grated fat-free Parmesan cheese

Per Serving:
Calories: 483
% of calories from fat: 26
Fat (gm): 13.7
Saturated fat (gm): 4.4
Cholesterol (mg): 87.4
Sodium (mg): 493
Protein (gm): 40.6
Carbohydrate (gm): 48.4

Exchanges:
Milk: 0.0
Vegetable: 1.0
Fruit: 0.0
Bread: 3.0
Meat: 4.0
Fat: 0.0

1. Spoon rice into greased 13 x 9-inch baking pan; arrange broccoli over rice and top with half the Tangy Cheese Sauce. Top with chicken and remaining sauce; sprinkle with Parmesan cheese. Bake, loosely covered, at 375 degrees until hot and bubbly, about 30 minutes.

Tangy Cheese Sauce

Makes about 3½ cups

½ cup reduced-fat mayonnaise
¼ cup all-purpose flour
1½ cups fat-free milk
1 cup (4 ounces) shredded reduced-fat Cheddar cheese
Salt and pepper, to taste

1. Whisk mayonnaise and flour in medium saucepan; whisk in milk. Heat to boiling; whisk until thickened, about 1 minute. Add cheese, whisking until melted. Season to taste with salt and pepper.

DIJON CHICKEN CASSEROLE

45

Dinner in a dish—what could be easier?

6 entrée servings

1 cup uncooked rice

6 boneless, skinless chicken breast halves
   (4 ounces each)

1 cup each: thickly sliced zucchini, red bell pepper,

½ cup each: dry white wine, reduced-sodium
   chicken broth

¼ cup Dijon mustard

Salt and pepper, to taste

1 cup unseasoned dry bread crumbs

½ cup (2 ounces) grated Parmesan cheese

2 tablespoons dried tarragon leaves

Per Serving:
Calories: 378
% of calories from fat: 12
Fat (gm): 4.6
Saturated fat (gm): 1.8
Cholesterol (mg): 71.6
Sodium (mg): 530
Protein (gm): 34.3
Carbohydrate (gm): 41.5

Exchanges:
Milk: 0.0
Vegetable: 0.0
Fruit: 0.0
Bread: 3.0
Meat: 3.0
Fat: 0.0

1. Spread rice in greased 12 x 8-inch baking dish. Arrange chicken over rice and top with vegetables. Pour combined wine, broth, and mustard over vegetables and chicken. Sprinkle lightly with salt and pepper. Combine remaining ingredients; sprinkle over vegetables. Bake, covered, at 350 degrees 40 minutes; uncover and bake until rice and chicken are tender and liquid is absorbed, about 10 minutes longer.

ORANGE CHICKEN AND VEGETABLES

Both orange juice and zest are used to accent this flavorful dish.

6 entrée servings

6 boneless, skinless chicken breast halves
(4 ounces each)
1 cup each: cubed potatoes, sliced carrots, onion
2 cloves garlic, chopped
½ teaspoon each: dried marjoram and thyme leaves
1-inch piece cinnamon stick
1 tablespoon flour
3 medium tomatoes, chopped
1½ cups orange juice
2 teaspoons grated orange zest
Salt and pepper, to taste

Per Serving:
Calories: 318
% of calories from fat: 10
Fat (gm): 3.5
Saturated fat (gm): 0.9
Cholesterol (mg): 69
Sodium (mg): 87
Protein (gm): 29.4
Carbohydrate (gm): 42.4

Exchanges:
Milk: 0.0
Vegetable: 2.0
Fruit: 0.5
Bread: 1.5
Meat: 2.5
Fat: 0.0

1. Sauté chicken in lightly greased large skillet until browned, about 5 minutes on each side; arrange in 12 x 8-inch baking dish with potatoes and carrots. Add onion, garlic, herbs and cinnamon stick to skillet; sauté until onion is tender, about 5 minutes; add flour and cook 1 minute. Add tomatoes, orange juice, and zest; heat to boiling. Reduce heat and simmer, uncovered, 5 minutes; season to taste with salt and pepper. Pour over chicken and vegetables in baking dish. Bake, covered, at 350 degrees until chicken is tender, about 30 minutes.

CHICKEN, VEGETABLE, AND GOAT CHEESE CASSEROLE

Delicious, with a generous amount of melted cheese.

4 entrée servings

1½ cups cut asparagus (1½-inch)
1 package (9 ounces) frozen artichoke hearts
1 package (6¼ ounces) fast-cooking long-grain and wild rice
12 ounces cooked chicken breast, cubed

3 ounces each: fat-free cream cheese, shredded reduced-fat mozzarella cheese, crumbled reduced-fat goat cheese

Salt and pepper, to taste

1. Cook asparagus and artichoke hearts in boiling water to cover, 4 minutes. Drain. Cook rice according to package directions, using ½ the spice packet. Combine all ingredients, except salt and pepper in 1½-quart casserole; season to taste with salt and pepper. Bake, covered, at 375 degrees until casserole is hot and cheese melted, 20 to 30 minutes.

CHILIQUILES

Leftovers, Mexican style! Chiliquiles is a family-style casserole dish usually made with stale tortillas and leftover cooked meats. Vary this casserole with ingredients you have on hand!

6 entrée servings

8 corn or flour tortillas (6-inch)

Vegetable cooking spray

1 medium green bell pepper, thinly sliced

½–1 teaspoon minced jalapeno chili

Tomatillo Sauce (see p. 184)

1 can (15 ounces) black beans, rinsed, drained

½ cup whole-kernel corn

16 ounces cooked chicken breast, shredded

1 large tomato, thinly sliced

1–1½ cups (4–6 ounces) shredded reduced-fat Cheddar cheese

Medium or hot salsa

1. Spray both sides of tortillas lightly with cooking spray; cook in small skillet over medium-high heat until lightly browned, 30 to 60 seconds per side. Cool slightly; cut into ½-inch strips. Sauté bell pepper and jalapeno chili in lightly greased medium skillet 2 to 3 minutes; stir in Tomatillo Sauce and cook until hot.

2. Arrange ⅓ of the tortilla strips in bottom of 2-quart casserole; top with ⅓ each of the black beans, corn, chicken, tomato slices, cheese, and Tomatillo Sauce mixture. Repeat layers 2 times. Bake, uncovered, at 350 degrees until hot, about 30 minutes, sprinkling with cheese during last 10 minute of baking time. Serve hot with salsa.

ONE-DISH CHICKEN AND RICE

45

Just mix and bake—perfect for a quick dinner.

4 entrée servings

1 can (10½ ounces) reduced-fat cream of
   mushroom soup
¾ cup each: fat-free milk, long-grain rice
1 package (10 ounces) frozen cut green beans
½ teaspoon dried tarragon leaves
Salt and pepper, to taste
2 boneless, skinless chicken breast halves
   (4 ounces each)
Paprika

Per Serving:
Calories: 342
% of calories from fat: 14
Fat (gm): 5.5
Saturated fat (gm): 1.3
Cholesterol (mg): 72.9
Sodium (mg): 675
Protein (gm): 31
Carbohydrate (gm): 41

Exchanges:
Milk: 0.0
Vegetable: 2.0
Fruit: 0.0
Bread: 2.0
Meat: 3.0
Fat: 0.0

1. Combine soup, milk, rice, beans, and tarragon in 2-quart baking dish; season to taste with salt and pepper. Arrange chicken over rice; sprinkle with salt, pepper, and paprika. Bake, covered, at 375 degrees until chicken is cooked, about 45 minutes.

CHICKEN AND NOODLE CASSEROLE

45

A comfort food you may remember from your childhood. It's still delicious!

4 entrée servings

3 tablespoons margarine or butter
¼ cup all-purpose flour
¼ teaspoon each: dried sage and marjoram leaves
2 cups reduced-sodium chicken broth
1 package (10 ounces) frozen mixed vegetables

1 pound boneless, skinless chicken breast, cubed

8 ounces thin egg noodles, cooked

3 tablespoons diced pimientos

¼ teaspoon black pepper

¼ cup unseasoned dry bread crumbs

Per Serving:
Calories: 507
% of calories from fat: 25
Fat (gm): 13.9
Saturated fat (gm): 3
Cholesterol (mg): 118.2
Sodium (mg): 273
Protein (gm): 38.6
Carbohydrate (gm): 55.5

1. Melt margarine in large saucepan over medium heat; whisk in flour and herbs; cook 1 minute. Whisk in broth and heat to boiling, whisking until thickened, about 1 minute. Combine with remaining ingredients, except bread crumbs, in 2-quart casserole; sprinkle with bread crumbs. Bake, uncovered, at 350 degrees until hot and browned, about 30 minutes.

Exchanges:
Milk: 0.0
Vegetable: 3.0
Fruit: 0.0
Bread: 3.0
Meat: 3.0
Fat: 1.0

CAPER CHICKEN WITH TOMATO-BASIL LINGUINE

45

You might try one of the flavored pastas, such as tomato-basil or lemon-pepper, in this dish.

4 entrée servings

8 ounces uncooked linguine

1 pound boneless, skinless chicken breast, cut into strips (1 x ½-inch)

8 ounces mushrooms, sliced

1 package (10 ounces) frozen cut broccoli, thawed

1 can (8 ounces) sliced water chestnuts, drained

1 can (13¾ ounces) reduced-sodium fat-free chicken broth

2 tablespoons cornstarch

3 tablespoons lemon juice

¼ cup diced pimientos

2 tablespoons drained capers

Salt and pepper, to taste

Per Serving:
Calories: 382
% of calories from fat: 11
Fat (gm): 4.7
Saturated fat (gm): 0.9
Cholesterol (mg): 69
Sodium (mg): 415
Protein (gm): 37.3
Carbohydrate (gm): 49.8

Exchanges:
Milk: 0.0
Vegetable: 1.0
Fruit: 0.0
Bread: 3.0
Meat: 3.0
Fat: 0.0

1. Arrange linguine in greased 12 x 8-inch baking dish; top with chicken and combined vegetables. Combine broth and cornstarch in medium saucepan; heat to boiling, whisking until thickened, about 1 minute. Stir in lemon juice, pimientos, and capers; season to taste with salt and pepper and pour over casserole. Bake, covered, at 350 degrees until linguine and chicken are cooked, about 40 minutes.

SUN-DRIED TOMATO COUSCOUS WITH CHICKEN AND MUSHROOMS

45

Packaged couscous is available in many flavor varieties.

4 entrée servings

1 package (6 ounces) sun-dried tomato couscous
4 boneless, skinless chicken breast halves
1 pound mushrooms, halved
1 tablespoon olive oil
1½ cups reduced-sodium fat-free chicken broth

1. Combine couscous and seasoning packet in 11 x 7-inch baking dish. Arrange chicken on couscous and top with mushrooms. Drizzle with olive oil; pour broth over. Bake, covered, at 350 degrees until chicken is cooked, about 35 minutes.

Per Serving:
Calories: 362
% of calories from fat: 20
Fat (gm): 8.3
Saturated fat (gm): 1.3
Cholesterol (mg): 71.5
Sodium (mg): 525
Protein (gm): 34.6
Carbohydrate (gm): 39.3

Exchanges:
Milk: 0.0
Vegetable: 2.0
Fruit: 0.0
Bread: 2.0
Meat: 3.0
Fat: 0.0

CHICKEN-STUFFED SHELLS WITH WHITE SAUCE

Fennel, rosemary, and nutmeg are delicious flavor accents in the filling.

6 entrée servings

1 pound boneless, skinless chicken breast, cubed (1-inch)
1 cup fat-free milk
1 egg white
3 cloves garlic, minced
1½–2 tablespoons fennel seeds, crushed
1 teaspoon dried rosemary leaves
¼ teaspoon each: ground nutmeg, salt, pepper
3–4 dashes hot pepper sauce

Per Serving:
Calories: 321
% of calories from fat: 18
Fat (gm): 6.5
Saturated fat (gm): 2
Cholesterol (mg): 43.8
Sodium (mg): 302
Protein (gm): 27
Carbohydrate (gm): 37.4

Exchanges:
Milk: 0.5
Vegetable: 0.0
Fruit: 0.0
Bread: 2.0
Meat: 2.5
Fat: 0.0

30 jumbo shells (9 ounces), cooked al dente
White Sauce (recipe follows)

1. Process chicken breast in the food processor until very finely chopped. Add remaining ingredients, except pasta and White Sauce; process just until blended. Spoon mixture into shells and arrange in greased baking dish; spoon White Sauce over shells. Bake, loosely covered, at 350 degrees until chicken filling is cooked, 30 to 35 minutes.

White Sauce
Makes about 2 cups

1 tablespoon margarine or butter
2 tablespoons flour
2 cups fat-free milk
¼ cup (1 ounce) grated Parmesan cheese
⅛ teaspoon ground white pepper

1. Melt margarine in medium saucepan; stir in flour. Cook over medium heat, stirring constantly, 1 to 2 minutes. Whisk in milk and heat to boiling; boil, whisking until thickened, about 1 minute (sauce will be very thin). Remove from heat; stir in cheese and pepper.

CHICKEN-VEGETABLE MANICOTTI WITH CREAMED SPINACH SAUCE

Tomato Sauce with Mushrooms and Sherry (see p. 398) is also an excellent accompaniment for the manicotti.

6 entrée servings

½ cup chopped onion

3 cloves garlic, minced

2 cups loosely packed chopped spinach leaves

½ cup each: chopped zucchini, yellow summer squash

1 teaspoon each: dried basil and oregano leaves

8 ounces boneless, skinless chicken, cooked, shredded

¾ cup fat-free ricotta cheese

Salt and pepper, to taste

1 package (8 ounces) manicotti shells, cooked al dente

Creamed Spinach Sauce (recipe follows)

Per Serving:
Calories: 340
% of calories from fat: 24
Fat (gm): 2.7
Saturated fat (gm): 2.5
Cholesterol (mg): 31
Sodium (mg): 427
Protein (gm): 23
Carbohydrate (gm): 435

Exchanges:
Milk: 0.5
Vegetable: 2.0
Fruit: 0.0
Bread: 2.0
Meat: 1.0
Fat: 1.5

1. Sauté onion and garlic in lightly greased large skillet until tender, about 3 minutes. Add vegetables and herbs; sauté until tender, 5 to 8 minutes. Stir in chicken and cheese; season to taste with salt and pepper. Spoon about 3 tablespoons mixture into each manicotti; arrange in baking pan and spoon Creamed Spinach Sauce over. Bake at 350 degrees, loosely covered, until manicotti are hot and sauce is bubbly, 35 to 40 minutes.

Creamed Spinach Sauce

Makes about 3 cups

2 cloves garlic, minced

2 tablespoons margarine or butter

¼ cup all-purpose flour

3 cups 2% reduced-fat milk

1½ pounds fresh spinach, chopped

2 teaspoons dried basil leaves

¼ teaspoon ground nutmeg

4–6 dashes hot pepper sauce

Salt, to taste

1. Sauté garlic in margarine in large saucepan 1 to 2 minutes. Stir in flour and cook over medium heat 1 minute. Whisk in milk;

heat to boiling, whisking until thickened, about 1 minute. Stir in remaining ingredients, except salt; cook over medium heat until spinach is cooked, about 5 minutes. Season to taste with salt.

CHICKEN AND CHEESE ROTOLO WITH MANY-CLOVES GARLIC SAUCE

Some people prefer cutting lasagne noodles into halves before filling, as they are easier to handle in eating. If cut, spread each noodle half with 1½ to 2 tablespoons cheese mixture.

6 entrée servings

1 pound boneless, skinless chicken breast, cooked, shredded

1¼ cups reduced-fat ricotta cheese

3–4 cloves garlic, minced

½ teaspoon each: dried marjoram and thyme leaves, salt

¼ teaspoon pepper

12 lasagne noodles (10 ounces), cooked, room temperature

Many-Cloves Garlic Sauce (recipe follows)

Per Serving:
Calories: 295
% of calories from fat: 28
Fat (gm): 9.4
Saturated fat (gm): 1.1
Cholesterol (mg): 45.1
Sodium (mg): 315
Protein (gm): 23.3
Carbohydrate (gm): 28.1

Exchanges:
Milk: 0.0
Vegetable: 1.0
Fruit: 0.0
Bread: 1.5
Meat: 2.5
Fat: 0.5

1. Mix chicken, cheese, garlic, herbs, salt, and pepper. Spread 3 to 4 tablespoons mixture on each noodle; roll up and place, seam sides down, in 13 x 9-inch baking dish. Spoon Many-Cloves Garlic Sauce over rotolo. Bake, loosely covered, at 350 degrees until rotolo are hot and sauce bubbly, 20 to 30 minutes.

Many-Cloves Garlic Sauce
Makes about 3 cups

25 cloves garlic, peeled

1 tablespoon olive oil

1¾ cups fat-free reduced-sodium chicken broth, divided

¾ cup dry white wine or chicken broth

2 tablespoons each: flour, finely chopped parsley

Salt and white pepper, to taste

1. Cook garlic in oil in medium skillet, covered, over medium-low heat until tender, about 10 minutes. Mash cloves slightly with a fork.

2. Add 1 ½ cups broth and wine to skillet and heat to boiling. Mix flour, parsley, and remaining ¼ cup broth and stir into boiling mixture. Boil until thickened, about 1 minute. Season to taste with salt and pepper.

SAUSAGE LASAGNE

A low-fat version of the traditional lasagne we all love.

8 entrée servings

2 cups fat-free ricotta cheese

¼ cup (1 ounce) grated Parmesan cheese

3 cups (12 ounces) shredded reduced-fat
   mozzarella cheese

Tomato Sauce with Italian Sausage (recipe follows)

12 lasagne noodles (10 ounces), cooked

Per Serving:
Calories: 375
% of calories from fat: 30
Fat (gm): 12.9
Saturated fat (gm): 6
Cholesterol (mg): 47.3
Sodium (mg): 679
Protein (gm): 31.3
Carbohydrate (gm): 33.9

Exchanges:
Milk: 0.0
Vegetable: 2.5
Fruit: 0.0
Bread: 1.5
Meat: 3.5
Fat: 0.5

1. Combine cheeses in bowl. Spread 1 cup sauce on bottom of 13 x 9-inch baking pan; top with 4 lasagne noodles, overlapping slightly. Spoon ⅓ of cheese mixture over noodles, spreading lightly with rubber spatula. Repeat layers 2 times, ending with remaining 1 cup sauce. Bake, loosely covered, at 350 degrees until sauce is bubbly, about 1 hour. Let stand 10 minutes before cutting.

Tomato Sauce with Italian Sausage
Makes about 4 cups

8 ounces Italian-style turkey sausage, casing removed, crumbled

2 cups chopped onions

3 cloves garlic, minced

1 teaspoon each: dried basil, tarragon, and thyme leaves

2 cans (16 ounces each) reduced-sodium whole tomatoes,
   undrained, coarsely chopped

2 cans (8 ounces each) reduced-sodium tomato sauce

1 cup water

1–2 teaspoons sugar

¼ teaspoon each: salt, pepper

1. Sauté sausage, onions, garlic, and herbs in lightly greased large saucepan until lightly browned, about 5 minutes; add remaining ingredients; heat to boiling. Reduce heat and simmer, uncovered, until sauce is reduced to about 4 cups, 15 to 20 minutes.

TURKEY DIVAN

45

For real convenience, assemble this casserole in advance and refrigerate up to 24 hours; sprinkle with bread crumbs and bake until bubbly, about 40 minutes.

4 entrée servings

½ cup chopped onion

1 tablespoon margarine or butter

¼ cup all-purpose flour

¾ cup each: reduced-sodium chicken broth, fat-free half-and-half or milk

¼ cup dry white wine (optional)

½ teaspoon each: dried savory and marjoram leaves

2–3 pinches ground nutmeg

1 cup (4 ounces) shredded fat-free Swiss cheese

Salt, pepper, to taste

1½ cups cubed cooked turkey or chicken breast

2 cups broccoli florets, cooked crisp-tender

3–4 tablespoons unseasoned dry bread crumbs

Per Serving:
Calories: 300
% of calories from fat: 13
Fat (gm): 4.2
Saturated fat (gm): 0.9
Cholesterol (mg): 70.9
Sodium (mg): 566
Protein (gm): 37.4
Carbohydrate (gm): 22.9

Exchanges:
Milk: 0.5
Vegetable: 1.0
Fruit: 0.0
Bread: 1.0
Meat: 3.0
Fat: 0.0

1. Sauté onion in margarine in medium sauce–pan until tender, 2 to 3 minutes. Mix flour and chicken broth until smooth; whisk into saucepan with half-and-half and wine. Heat to boiling, whisking until thickened, 1 minute. Add seasonings and cheese, whisking until cheese is melted. Season to taste with salt and pepper.

2. Arrange turkey and broccoli in 10 x 7-inch baking dish; pour sauce over and sprinkle with bread crumbs. Bake at 350 degrees until bubbly, about 25 minutes.

TURKEY POT PIE

Leftovers from Thanksgiving dinner are welcome ingredients in this delectable pot pie.

6 entrée servings

1 cup chopped onion

½ cup chopped green bell pepper

2½ cups reduced-sodium chicken broth

1 cup each: cubed potato, parsnip, sliced carrots, broccoli florets

½ cup each: small mushrooms, whole-kernel corn, peas

1 pound cooked turkey breast, cubed

½ teaspoon each: dried rosemary and thyme leaves

⅓ cup all-purpose flour

⅔ cup fat-free half-and-half or fat-free milk

Salt and pepper, to taste

Pot Pie Pastry (recipe follows)

Fat-free milk

1 tablespoon grated Parmesan cheese

Per Serving:
Calories: 380
% of calories from fat: 17
Fat (gm): 7.1
Saturated fat (gm): 2.1
Cholesterol (mg): 65.5
Sodium (mg): 284
Protein (gm): 32.8
Carbohydrate (gm): 45.1

Exchanges:
Milk: 0.0
Vegetable: 0.0
Fruit: 0.0
Bread: 3.0
Meat: 3.0
Fat: 0.0

1. Sauté onion and bell pepper in lightly greased large saucepan until lightly browned, about 5 minutes. Add chicken broth, remaining vegetables, turkey, and herbs. Heat to boiling; reduce heat and simmer, covered, until vegetables are tender, about 10 minutes. Heat mixture to boiling. Stir in combined flour and fat-free half-and-half, stirring until thickened, 1 to 2 minutes. Season to taste with salt and pepper. Pour into 2-quart casserole or soufflé dish.

2. Roll pastry on floured surface to fit top of casserole; place on casserole, trim, and flute. Cut steam vents in top of pastry. Bake at 425 degrees 20 minutes; brush with milk and sprinkle with cheese. Bake until browned, 5 to 10 minutes. Cool 10 minutes before serving.

Pot Pie Pastry

1 cup all-purpose flour
2 tablespoons grated Parmesan cheese
2½–3 tablespoons vegetable shortening
3–4 tablespoons ice water

1. Combine flour and Parmesan cheese in medium bowl. Cut in shortening with pastry blender until mixture resembles coarse crumbs. Add water, one tablespoon at a time, mixing with fork just until dough holds together. Refrigerate until ready to use.

TORTA RUSTICA

45

An Italian pizza in a deep-dish pie.

8 entrée servings

1½ cups chopped onions
1½ teaspoons minced roasted garlic
8 ounces Italian-style turkey sausage, casing removed
1 can (16 ounces) reduced-sodium diced tomatoes, undrained
3 cups each: sliced zucchini, mushrooms
Salt and pepper, to taste
1 package (16 ounces) hot roll mix
1 cup very hot water (120 degrees)
1 egg
1–1½ cups (4–6 ounces) shredded reduced-fat mozzarella cheese
2 tablespoons fat-free milk

Per Serving:
Calories: 457
% of calories from fat: 23
Fat (gm): 11.5
Saturated fat (gm): 4.2
Cholesterol (mg): 65.8
Sodium (mg): 760
Protein (gm): 23.5
Carbohydrate (gm): 63.7

Exchanges:
Milk: 0.0
Vegetable: 1.0
Fruit: 0.0
Bread: 4.0
Meat: 2.0
Fat: 1.0

1. Sauté onions, garlic, and sausage in lightly greased large skillet until sausage is browned, about 5 minutes; stir in tomatoes with liquid, zucchini, and mushrooms; heat to boiling. Reduce heat and simmer, covered, 5 minutes. Simmer, uncovered, until sauce is thickened, about 10 minutes. Season to taste with salt and pepper.

2. Make hot roll mix according to package directions, using hot water and egg. Roll ⅔ of the dough on floured surface to fit 2-quart casserole or soufflé dish. Ease dough into casserole, allowing dough to extend 1 inch over edge. Spoon half the vegetable mixture into casserole; sprinkle with half the cheese. Top with remaining vegetable mixture and cheese.

3. Roll remaining dough into circle to fit top of casserole. Bring outside edges of dough together and crimp. Cut 1 or 2 slits in top of dough with sharp knife. Brush top of dough with milk. Bake at 400 degrees until crust is browned, about 30 minutes. Let stand 10 minutes before serving.

TURKEY BOW-TIE PASTA AU GRATIN

The flavors of a favorite pasta salad are recreated in this cold-weather casserole.

8 entrée servings

16 ounces bow-tie pasta (farfalle), cooked

1 pound cooked turkey breast, cubed

1 package (10 ounces) frozen cut broccoli, thawed, well drained

1 rib celery, chopped

½ cup each: reduced-sodium fat-free chicken broth, fat-free sour cream

1 tablespoon dried dill weed

¼ teaspoon pepper

1 cup (4 ounces) shredded reduced-fat mozzarella cheese

¼ cup unseasoned dry bread crumbs

Per Serving:
Calories: 396
% of calories from fat: 18
Fat (gm): 7.6
Saturated fat (gm): 2.6
Cholesterol (mg): 111.8
Sodium (mg): 217
Protein (gm): 32.6
Carbohydrate (gm): 46.4

Exchanges:
Milk: 0.0
Vegetable: 2.0
Fruit: 0.0
Bread: 2.0
Meat: 3.0
Fat: 0.0

1. Toss pasta, turkey, broccoli, and celery in 2½-quart casserole; mix in combined broth, sour cream, dill, and pepper. Sprinkle with cheese and bread crumbs. Bake, covered, at 350 degrees 20 minutes; uncover and bake until hot and browned, about 15 minutes longer.

TURKEY TETRAZZINI

This dish was named for the famous Italian opera singer, Lucia Tetrazzini, who claimed it as her favorite.

8 entrée servings

8 ounces mushrooms, sliced

2 tablespoons each: margarine or butter, flour

1 can (14½ ounces) reduced-sodium chicken broth

1½ cups fat-free milk

16 ounces thin spaghetti, cooked

12 ounces cooked boneless, skinless turkey or chicken breast, cubed

¼ cup (1 ounce) grated Parmesan cheese

¼ teaspoon each: ground nutmeg, salt, pepper

Per Serving:
Calories: 370
% of calories from fat: 16
Fat (gm): 6.5
Saturated fat (gm): 1.7
Cholesterol (mg): 35.7
Sodium (mg): 218
Protein (gm): 23.6
Carbohydrate (gm): 50.3

Exchanges:
Milk: 0.0
Vegetable: 1.0
Fruit: 0.0
Bread: 3.0
Meat: 2.0
Fat: 0.5

1. Sauté mushrooms in margarine in large saucepan until tender, about 5 minutes. Stir in flour; cook 1 minute. Stir in chicken broth and milk and heat to boiling, stirring until thickened, about 1 minute (sauce will be very thin). Combine with remaining ingredients in 2-quart casserole or baking dish; bake, uncovered, at 350 degrees until hot and lightly browned, about 30 minutes.

BEEF STROGANOFF CASSEROLE

Add the sour cream to this casserole near the end of baking time to avoid curdling.

6 entrée servings

12 ounces uncooked wide egg noodles

1½ pounds boneless beef round or sirloin steak, cut into strips (1-inch)

½ cup all-purpose flour

1 pound mushrooms, coarsely chopped

2 tablespoons finely chopped onion

1 tablespoon paprika

½ teaspoon ground nutmeg

1 can (13¾ ounces) reduced-sodium fat-free beef broth

1 container (8 ounces) fat-free sour cream

Salt and pepper, to taste

1. Place uncooked noodles in 2½-quart casserole. Coat beef with flour; arrange on top of noodles. Top with combined mushrooms, onion, paprika, and nutmeg. Pour beef broth over. Bake, covered, at 325 degrees 1 hour; stir in sour cream and bake, uncovered, 15 minutes. Season to taste with salt and pepper.

Per Serving:
Calories: 409
% of calories from fat: 14
Fat (gm): 6.4
Saturated fat (gm): 1.9
Cholesterol (mg): 103.6
Sodium (mg): 132
Protein (gm): 33.7
Carbohydrate (gm): 52.4

Exchanges:
Milk: 0.0
Vegetable: 1.0
Fruit: 0.0
Bread: 3.0
Meat: 3.0
Fat: 0.0

GOULASH CASSEROLE

45

This sauerkraut dish, creamy with sour cream and seasoned with caraway, is excellent served with Real Mashed Potatoes (see p. 628).

4 entrée servings

1 pound ground beef eye of round
2 medium onions, chopped
1½ cups chopped red and green bell pepper
2 cloves garlic, minced
1 tablespoon flour
2 teaspoons paprika
1 teaspoon crushed caraway seeds
1 can (14 ounces) sauerkraut, rinsed, drained
1 large tomato, coarsely chopped
1 cup fat-free sour cream
Salt and pepper, to taste

Per Serving:
Calories: 318
% of calories from fat: 26
Fat (gm): 9.2
Saturated fat (gm): 3.5
Cholesterol (mg): 53.1
Sodium (mg): 782
Protein (gm): 31.0
Carbohydrate (gm): 27.6

Exchanges:
Milk: 0.0
Vegetable: 3.0
Fruit: 0.0
Bread: 1.0
Meat: 3.0
Fat: 0.0

1. Cook ground beef in lightly greased large skillet until browned, about 8 minutes; add onions, bell peppers, and garlic and cook until tender, 8 to 10 minutes. Stir in flour, paprika, and caraway seeds; cook 1 minute. Spoon into greased 2-quart casserole. Stir in sauerkraut, tomato, and sour cream; season to taste with salt and pepper. Bake, covered, at 350 degrees until hot, about 30 minutes.

SPICY BEEF AND ASPARAGUS WITH RICE NOODLES

45

Using frozen stir-fry vegetables saves kitchen prep time!

4 entrée servings

8 ounces rice noodles

1 pound boneless beef round steak, cut into strips
(1½ x ½-inch)

12 ounces fresh asparagus, sliced (1-inch)

1 package (16 ounces) frozen stir-fry vegetables,
thawed, drained

¾ cup reduced-sodium beef broth

2 tablespoons flour

1 tablespoon each: reduced-sodium soy sauce, catsup

1 teaspoon minced garlic

¼ teaspoon pepper

3–4 drops hot pepper sauce

Per Serving:
Calories: 418
% of calories from fat: 7
Fat (gm): 3.3
Saturated fat (gm): 0.9
Cholesterol (mg): 64.4
Sodium (mg): 617
Protein (gm): 31.0
Carbohydrate (gm): 63

Exchanges:
Milk: 0.0
Vegetable: 0.0
Fruit: 0.0
Bread: 4.0
Meat: 3.0
Fat: 0.0

1. Soak rice noodles in cold water to cover in bowl 10 minutes;
drain. Combine noodles, beef, asparagus, and stir-fry vegetables in
2½-quart casserole. Whisk beef broth and remaining ingredients
and pour over casserole. Bake, covered, at 350 degrees until beef
is tender, 45 to 60 minutes.

TAMALE PIE

Enjoy the flavor and goodness of tamales the easy way with this delicious casserole.

4 entrée servings

1 pound lean ground beef

1 medium onion, chopped

1 clove garlic, minced

1 can (15 ounces) reduced-sodium tomato sauce

1 can (4 ounces) diced green chilies, drained

1 cup each: whole kernel corn, shredded fat-free
   Cheddar cheese (4 ounces)

2 teaspoons each: chili powder, ground cumin

2 cups water

1 cup yellow cornmeal

3–4 drops hot pepper sauce

Per Serving:
Calories: 493
% of calories from fat: 28
Fat (gm): 15.5
Saturated fat (gm): 5.7
Cholesterol (mg): 70.4
Sodium (mg): 423
Protein (gm): 37.3
Carbohydrate (gm): 52.6

Exchanges:
Milk: 0.0
Vegetable: 3.0
Fruit: 0.0
Bread: 3.0
Meat: 3.0
Fat: 1.0

1. Sauté ground beef, onion, and garlic in large skillet until beef is browned, about 8 minutes; stir in remaining ingredients, except water, cornmeal, and hot pepper sauce. Spread mixture on bottom of greased 2-quart baking dish.

2. Heat water to boiling in large saucepan; gradually stir in cornmeal; Reduce heat and simmer until thickened, about 5 minutes, stirring frequently. Stir in hot pepper sauce; pour over meat mixture in casserole. Bake, uncovered, at 375 degrees until hot and browned, about 20 minutes.

AUTUMN POT PIE

Choose ingredients from your garden or produce market for this savory pie.

6 entrée servings

16 ounces pork tenderloin, cubed

½ cup each: chopped onion, sliced celery, red bell pepper

2 cloves garlic, minced

½ teaspoon each: dried sage and thyme leaves

3 tablespoons flour

2 cups reduced-sodium vegetable broth

1 cup each: cubed peeled sweet potato and turnip, unpeeled russet potato, halved Brussels sprouts

½ cup each: lima beans, halved small mushrooms

Salt and pepper, to taste

9-inch purchased pie pastry

Per Serving:
Calories: 362
% of calories from fat: 30
Fat (gm): 11.7
Saturated fat (gm): 4.8
Cholesterol (mg): 55.4
Sodium (mg): 265
Protein (gm): 20
Carbohydrate (gm): 42.5

Exchanges:
Milk: 0.0
Vegetable: 0.0
Fruit: 0.0
Bread: 3.0
Meat: 2.0
Fat: 1.0

1. Sauté pork in lightly greased large saucepan until browned, about 5 minutes; add onion, celery, bell pepper, garlic, and herbs to saucepan and sauté until vegetables are tender, about 5 minutes. Stir in flour; cook 1 minute. Add broth and remaining vegetables; heat to boiling. Reduce heat and simmer, covered, until vegetables are tender, about 10 minutes; season to taste with salt and pepper. Spoon into 1½-quart casserole.

2. Roll pastry on floured surface into circle 1 inch larger than top of casserole; place on top of casserole and flute edge. Bake at 425 degrees until pastry is browned, about 20 minutes.

HAM AND POTATO CASSEROLE AU GRATIN

45

This old-fashioned casserole has been modified to meet today's healthy nutritional standards.

6 entrée servings

6 large red potatoes, peeled, thinly sliced, divided

12–16 ounces reduced-sodium ham, fat trimmed, cubed (¾-inch)

1 small green bell pepper, finely chopped

3 green onions, sliced

½–1 cup (2–4 ounces) shredded reduced-fat Cheddar cheese

White Sauce with Mustard (recipe follows)

¼–½ cup unseasoned dry bread crumbs

Per Serving:
Calories: 301
% of calories from fat: 30
Fat (gm): 10.4
Saturated fat (gm): 3.6
Cholesterol (mg): 40.5
Sodium (mg): 796
Protein (gm): 20.9
Carbohydrate (gm): 32.9

Exchanges:
Milk: 0.0
Vegetable: 0.0
Fruit: 0.0
Bread: 2.0
Meat: 2.0
Fat: 1.0

1. Arrange half the potatoes in greased 2-quart casserole, overlapping slightly; sprinkle with ham, bell pepper, and green onions. Top with remaining potatoes and sprinkle with cheese. Pour White Sauce with Mustard over. Bake, covered, at 375 degrees for 45 minutes. Sprinkle with bread crumbs and bake, uncovered, until potatoes are tender and casserole is golden brown, 15 to 20 minutes.

White Sauce with Mustard

Makes about 2 cups

2 tablespoons margarine or butter
3 tablespoons flour
¾ teaspoon dry mustard
2 cups fat-free milk
¼ teaspoon paprika
Salt and pepper, to taste

1. Melt margarine in small saucepan; add flour and dry mustard, stirring over medium heat 1 minute. Whisk in milk and paprika and heat to boiling, whisking until thickened, about 1 minute. Season to taste with salt and pepper.

SHEPHERD'S PIE

Usually the recipient of the week's leftovers, this hearty dish may be different each time it is made.

6 entrée servings

1½ pounds boneless leg of lamb, fat trimmed, cubed (½-inch)
1 tablespoon margarine or butter
¾ cup each: chopped onion, green bell pepper, sliced celery
3 cloves garlic, minced
3 tablespoons flour
2½ cups reduced-sodium beef broth
1½ cups sliced carrots
1 tablespoon tomato paste

Per Serving:
Calories: 274
% of calories from fat: 27
Fat (gm): 8.4
Saturated fat (gm): 2.3
Cholesterol (mg): 48.5
Sodium (mg): 179
Protein (gm): 21.7
Carbohydrate (gm): 28.5

Exchanges:
Milk: 0.0
Vegetable: 2.0
Fruit: 0.0
Bread: 1.0
Meat: 2.5
Fat: 0.5

½ teaspoon each: dried rosemary and thyme leaves
1 bay leaf
¾ cup frozen peas
Salt and pepper, to taste
2 cups Real Mashed Potatoes (½ recipe) (see p. 628)

1. Sauté lamb in margarine or butter in large saucepan until browned, 5 to 8 minutes; remove from pan. Add onion, bell pepper, celery, and garlic; sauté until lightly browned, 5 to 8 minutes. Stir in flour; cook 1 minute. Return lamb to saucepan; add broth, carrots, tomato paste, and herbs. Heat to boiling; reduce heat and simmer, covered, until lamb is tender, about 1 hour. Discard bay leaf and stir in peas; season to taste with salt and pepper.

2. Pour stew into 1½-quart casserole. Spoon Real Mashed Potatoes around edge of casserole. Bake, uncovered, at 400 degrees until potatoes are browned, about 10 minutes.

PASTITSIO

45

Sweet cinnamon and nutmeg season this Greek favorite.

6 entrée servings

1 pound lean ground lamb or beef
1 cup chopped onion
1 can (8 ounces) reduced-sodium tomato paste
⅓ cup water
Salt and pepper, to taste
2 cups elbow macaroni, cooked
⅓ cup (1½ ounces) grated fat-free Parmesan cheese
¼ teaspoon each: ground cinnamon and nutmeg
2⅓ cups fat-free milk
2 tablespoons margarine or butter
2 eggs, lightly beaten

Per Serving:
Calories: 361
% of calories from fat: 23
Fat (gm): 9.3
Saturated fat (gm): 2.5
Cholesterol (mg): 104.7
Sodium (mg): 266
Protein (gm): 25.6
Carbohydrate (gm): 42.8

Exchanges:
Milk: 0.0
Vegetable: 0.0
Fruit: 0.0
Bread: 3.0
Meat: 3.0
Fat: 0.0

1. Cook lamb and onion in lightly greased large skillet over medium heat until lamb is browned, about 5 minutes. Stir in tomato paste and water; cook 2 to 3 minutes longer. Season to taste with salt and pepper. Spoon ½ of the macaroni into greased 13 x 9-inch baking pan; spoon meat mixture over macaroni. Sprinkle combined cheese and spices over lamb; spoon remaining macaroni over the top.

2. Heat milk and margarine in medium saucepan, stirring until margarine is melted. Gradually whisk milk mixture into eggs; pour over macaroni. Bake, uncovered, at 350 degrees until casserole is bubbly, 50 to 60 minutes.

45-MINUTE PREPARATION TIP: Begin cooking macaroni before preparing the rest of the recipe.

VEGETABLE MOUSSAKA

Vegetables and barley are added to traditional moussaka to make this delicious casserole.

8 entrée servings

1 large eggplant, unpeeled, sliced
Olive oil cooking spray
1 pound potatoes, unpeeled, sliced
3 cups chopped onions
2 cups sliced carrots
3 cloves garlic, minced
1 teaspoon each: ground cinnamon, dried oregano
  and thyme leaves
¾ cup reduced-sodium fat-free beef broth
2 cups each: chopped tomatoes, sliced mushrooms,
  cooked barley
1 pound ground lean lamb or beef, cooked, drained
1 small zucchini, sliced
Salt and pepper, to taste
Custard Topping (recipe follows)
Ground nutmeg, to taste

Per Serving:
Calories: 381
% of calories from fat: 26
Fat (gm): 11.3
Saturated fat (gm): 2.7
Cholesterol (mg): 64.2
Sodium (mg): 246
Protein (gm): 22
Carbohydrate (gm): 49.8

Exchanges:
Milk: 0.0
Vegetable: 1.0
Fruit: 0.0
Bread: 3.0
Meat: 2.0
Fat: 1.0

1. Arrange eggplant in single layer on greased foil-lined jelly roll pan and spray with cooking spray. Bake at 350 degrees until eggplant is tender but still firm, about 20 minutes. Arrange eggplant on bottom of 13 x 9-inch baking pan.

2. Heat potatoes, onions, carrots, garlic, seasonings, and broth to boiling in large skillet; reduce heat and simmer, covered, 5 minutes.

Add tomatoes and mushrooms; simmer, covered, until tomatoes are soft, 2 to 3 minutes. Add barley, lamb, and zucchini; cook, uncovered, until mixture is thick, about 5 minutes. Season to taste with salt and pepper. Spoon mixture over eggplant.

3. Pour Custard Topping over casserole and sprinkle with nutmeg. Bake at 350 degrees until lightly browned on the top, about 45 minutes. Cool 5 to 10 minutes before cutting.

Custard Topping

⅓ cup margarine or butter
½ cup all-purpose flour
3 cups fat-free milk
2 eggs, lightly beaten
Salt and white pepper, to taste

1. Melt margarine in medium saucepan; whisk in flour and cook over medium heat 2 minutes. Whisk in milk and heat to boiling, whisking until thickened, about 1 minute. Whisk about 1 cup milk mixture into eggs; whisk egg mixture back into saucepan. Cook over low heat, whisking until thickened, 2 to 3 minutes. Season to taste with salt and white pepper.

TUNA CASSEROLE

Just like Mom used to make, but a healthier version!

8 entrée servings

12 ounces thin egg noodles, cooked
2 cans (12 ounces each) solid white tuna in water, drained, flaked
1 jar (2½ ounces) diced pimientos, drained
8 ounces mushrooms, sliced
1 can (10½ ounces) each: reduced-fat cream of mushroom soup, reduced-fat cream of celery soup
1 cup water
½ cup dry bread crumbs

Per Serving:
Calories: 364
% of calories from fat: 15
Fat (gm): 5.6
Saturated fat (gm): 1.3
Cholesterol (mg): 77.7
Sodium (mg): 684
Protein (gm): 28.5
Carbohydrate (gm): 44.2

Exchanges:
Milk: 0.0
Vegetable: 0.0
Fruit: 0.0
Bread: 3.0
Meat: 2.0
Fat: 0.0

1. Place half the noodles in 2½-quart casserole. Layer half the tuna, pimientos, and mushrooms on noodles. Repeat layers. Pour combined soups and water over casserole; top with bread crumbs. Bake, covered, at 375 degrees for 20 minutes; bake uncovered until browned and bubbly, about 15 minutes.

SALMON CASSEROLE

This light and flavorful casserole is great for brunch, lunch, or dinner.

6 entrée servings

2 cans (14¾ ounces each) salmon, drained, flaked

1 pound mushrooms, coarsely chopped

¼ teaspoon each: ground nutmeg, pepper

¼ cup finely chopped onion

1–2 tablespoons margarine or butter

2 tablespoons flour

1½ cups fat-free milk

½ cup unseasoned dry bread crumbs

Per Serving:
Calories: 371
% of calories from fat: 23
Fat (gm): 9.7
Saturated fat (gm): 1.9
Cholesterol (mg): 115.5
Sodium (mg): 679
Protein (gm): 39.7
Carbohydrate (gm): 32.9

Exchanges:
Milk: 0.0
Vegetable: 2.0
Fruit: 0.0
Bread: 0.0
Meat: 4.0
Fat: 0.0

1. Combine salmon, mushrooms, nutmeg, and pepper in 12 x 8-inch baking dish. Sauté onion in margarine in medium saucepan 1 minute; stir in flour and cook 1 minute. Whisk in milk; heat to boiling, whisking until thickened, about 1 minute. Pour over salmon and sprinkle with bread crumbs. Bake, uncovered, at 375 degrees until lightly browned, about 35 minutes.

SALMON SOUFFLÉ

This casserole requires some care in preparation, but the results are well worth it.

4 entrée servings

⅔ cup each: chopped green and red bell pepper

1 tablespoon margarine or butter

¼ cup all-purpose flour

1½ cups fat-free milk

¾ teaspoon dried dill weed

¼ teaspoon salt
⅛ teaspoon white pepper
2–3 egg yolks, lightly beaten
1 can (6½ ounces) salmon, drained, flaked
1 cup whole kernel corn
5 egg whites
Pinch cream of tartar

Per Serving:
Calories: 268
% of calories from fat: 30
Fat (gm): 9.3
Saturated fat (gm): 2.3
Cholesterol (mg): 114.9
Sodium (mg): 509
Protein (gm): 19.7
Carbohydrate (gm): 28.2

Exchanges:
Milk: 0.0
Vegetable: 0.0
Fruit: 0.0
Bread: 2.0
Meat: 2.0
Fat: 0.5

1. Sauté bell peppers in margarine in large saucepan until tender, about 5 minutes. Stir in flour and cook 1 minute. Whisk in milk, dill weed, salt, and pepper; heat to boiling. Whisk about half the mixture into egg yolks in bowl; whisk mixture back into saucepan. Mix in salmon and corn.

2. Beat egg whites and cream of tartar in large bowl to stiff but not dry peaks; fold into salmon mixture. Pour into lightly greased 2-quart soufflé dish. Bake, uncovered, at 350 degrees until golden brown and knife inserted near center comes out clean, about 45 minutes. Serve immediately.

MEDITERRANEAN TORTA

L *Hot roll mix makes this recipe no-fail and easy. Enjoy Mediterranean flavors in the colorful filling.*

6 entrée servings

1 package (16 ounces) hot roll mix
1 cup hot water
1 egg
1 medium zucchini, thinly sliced
⅓ cup chopped onion
1 can (14½ ounces) reduced-sodium diced tomatoes, undrained
1 can (15 ounces) garbanzo beans, rinsed, drained
⅓ cup raisins
1½ teaspoons minced roasted garlic
½ teaspoon each: ground cinnamon, cumin, and dried mint leaves
½–1 cup (2–4 ounces) each: shredded low-sodium mozzarella cheese, crumbled feta cheese

1. Make hot roll mix according to package directions, using hot water and egg and omitting margarine; let rise 10 to 15 minutes. Roll ¾ of the dough on floured surface into 14-inch circle; ease dough into greased 8-inch springform pan, allowing edge to come to top of pan.

2. Sauté zucchini and onion in lightly greased large skillet until tender, about 5 minutes. Stir in remaining ingredients and spoon into prepared pan.

3. Fold edge of dough over vegetables. Roll remaining dough on floured surface to fit top of springform pan; place over vegetables and crimp edges. Cut 1 or 2 slits in crust with sharp knife. Bake at 400 degrees until browned, 25 to 30 minutes; cool on wire rack 5 to 10 minutes. Remove side of pan and cut into wedges.

Per Serving:
Calories: 480
% of calories from fat: 15
Fat (gm): 8
Saturated fat (gm): 2.8
Cholesterol (mg): 48.8
Sodium (mg): 780
Protein (gm): 17.7
Carbohydrate (gm): 82.9

Exchanges:
Milk: 0.0
Vegetable: 2.0
Fruit: 0.0
Bread: 5.0
Meat: 0.0
Fat: 1.5

SPAGHETTI AND EGGPLANT PARMESAN

L

Baked in a springform pan, the presentation of this dish is unusual and very attractive.

8 entrée servings

1 large eggplant (about 3 pounds), unpeeled, sliced (¼ inch)
1 tablespoon olive oil
1 small onion, finely chopped
3 cloves garlic, minced
2 cans (8 ounces each) reduced-sodium tomato sauce
8 medium plum tomatoes, chopped
⅛ teaspoon crushed red pepper
3 tablespoons finely chopped fresh or 2 teaspoons dried basil leaves
Salt, to taste
12 ounces spaghetti, cooked
¼ cup each: grated Parmesan cheese (1 ounce), unseasoned dry bread crumbs

Per Serving:
Calories: 279
% of calories from fat: 13
Fat (gm): 4.1
Saturated fat (gm): 1.1
Cholesterol (mg): 2.5
Sodium (mg): 104
Protein (gm): 10.1
Carbohydrate (gm): 52.5

Exchanges:
Milk: 0.0
Vegetable: 2.0
Fruit: 0.0
Bread: 2.5
Meat: 0.0
Fat: 1.0

1. Cook eggplant slices in oil large skillet until browned, 3 to 4 minutes on each side; remove from skillet. Add onion and garlic to skillet; sauté until tender, 3 to 5 minutes. Add tomato sauce, tomatoes, red pepper, and basil; heat to boiling. Reduce heat and simmer, uncovered, until mixture is medium sauce consistency, about 15 minutes. Season to taste with salt. Toss sauce with spaghetti and Parmesan cheese.

2. Coat greased 9-inch springform pan with bread crumbs. Line bottom and side of pan with ¾ of the eggplant slices, overlapping slices and allowing those on sides to extend 1 to 1½ inches above top of pan. Spoon spaghetti mixture into pan, pressing firmly. Fold eggplant slices at top of pan over spaghetti mixture. Overlap remaining eggplant slices on top, pressing firmly into place. Bake, uncovered, until hot, about 30 minutes. Let stand 10 minutes; loosen side of pan with sharp knife and remove side of pan. Cut into wedges.

VEGETARIAN TETRAZZINI

L

Any combination of vegetables or pasta can be used in this versatile dish.

45

8 entrée servings

8 ounces mushrooms, sliced

1 cup each: sliced zucchini, red bell pepper, broccoli florets

½ cup chopped onion

1–2 tablespoons margarine or butter

1¾ cups reduced-sodium vegetable broth

1 cup fat-free milk

½ cup dry white wine or fat-free milk

2 tablespoons flour

1 pound thin or regular spaghetti, cooked

¼ cup (1 ounce) grated Parmesan cheese

¼ teaspoon each ground nutmeg, salt and pepper

Per Serving:
Calories: 344
% of calories from fat: 11
Fat (gm): 4.1
Saturated fat (gm): 1.2
Cholesterol (mg): 3
Sodium (mg): 176
Protein (gm): 12.9
Carbohydrate (gm): 60.3

Exchanges:
Milk: 0.0
Vegetable: 2.0
Fruit: 0.0
Bread: 3.5
Meat: 0.0
Fat: 1.0

1. Sauté vegetables in margarine in large saucepan until tender, 8 to 10 minutes. Add broth and milk and heat to boiling. Stir in combined wine and flour, stirring until thickened, about 1 minute (sauce will be very thin). Mix with remaining ingredients in 2-quart casserole or baking dish. Bake, uncovered, at 350 degrees until hot and lightly browned, 30 to 40 minutes.

BAKED FUSILLI AND CHEESE PRIMAVERA

L

45

Asparagus spears, broccoli florets, sliced zucchini, carrots, and mushrooms are other vegetable choices for this cheesy casserole.

6 entrée servings

1 cup sliced cremini or white mushrooms

¾ cup each: chopped onion, red or green bell pepper

1 teaspoon minced garlic

2 tablespoons margarine or butter

3 cups fat-free milk

⅓ cup all-purpose flour

3 ounces light pasteurized processed cheese, cubed

½ cup (2 ounces) shredded reduced-fat sharp Cheddar cheese

1 teaspoon Dijon mustard

10 ounces fusilli or rotini, cooked

¾ cup frozen peas

Salt and pepper, to taste

2 tablespoons unseasoned dry bread crumbs

Per Serving:
Calories: 369
% of calories from fat: 19
Fat (gm): 7.9
Saturated fat (gm): 2.9
Cholesterol (mg): 14
Sodium (mg): 231
Protein (gm): 19.6
Carbohydrate (gm): 54.1

Exchanges:
Milk: 0.0
Vegetable: 2.0
Fruit: 0.0
Bread: 3.0
Meat: 1.0
Fat: 1.0

1. Sauté mushrooms, onion, bell pepper, and garlic in margarine in large saucepan until tender, 5 to 8 minutes. Stir in combined milk and flour and heat to boiling, stirring until thickened, about 1 minute. Reduce heat to low; add cheeses and mustard, stirring until melted. Combine sauce, fusilli, and peas in 2-quart casserole; season to taste with salt and pepper and sprinkle with bread crumbs. Bake, uncovered, at 375 degrees until hot, 20 to 25 minutes.

ARTICHOKE TORTELLINI BAKE

LO

45

Refrigerated fresh tortellini and ravioli are convenient to have on hand for speedy meals—use any favorite in this dish.

4 entrée servings

2 cups sliced mushrooms

1 small onion, sliced

1 teaspoon minced garlic

2 tablespoons flour

1 cup fat-free milk

Salt and cayenne pepper, to taste

1 can (14 ounces) artichoke hearts, drained

1 package (9 ounces) fresh cheese tortellini, cooked, warm

½ cup (2 ounces) shredded reduced-fat Italian 6-cheese blend

1–2 tablespoons seasoned dry bread crumbs

Per Serving:
Calories: 267
% of calories from fat: 21
Fat (gm): 6.4
Saturated fat (gm): 3.4
Cholesterol (mg): 29.1
Sodium (mg): 523
Protein (gm): 16.9
Carbohydrate (gm): 37.4

Exchanges:
Milk: 0.0
Vegetable: 1.0
Fruit: 0.0
Bread: 2.0
Meat: 1.0
Fat: 0.5

1. Sauté mushrooms, onion, and garlic in lightly greased large saucepan until tender, about 5 minutes. Stir in flour; cook 1 to 2 minutes. Stir in milk and heat to boiling, stirring until thickened, 1 to 2 minutes. Season to taste with salt and cayenne pepper. Stir in artichokes, tortellini, and cheese. Spoon into greased 1½-quart casserole; sprinkle with bread crumbs. Bake, uncovered, at 375 degrees until bubbly, about 15 minutes.

45-MINUTE PREPARATION TIP: Begin cooking the tortellini before preparing the rest of the recipe.

MUSHROOM-BROCCOLI MANICOTTI

L

Any pasta that's going to be filled and baked should be cooked just until al dente *so the baked pasta is not overcooked.*

4 entrée servings

4 shallots or green onions, chopped

2 cloves garlic, minced

1½ teaspoons each: dried basil and marjoram leaves

2 cups each: sliced mushrooms, chopped
   cooked broccoli

1 cup reduced-fat ricotta cheese

¼ teaspoon each: salt, pepper

1 package (8 ounces) manicotti, cooked al dente

Tomato Sauce with Mushrooms and Sherry
   (recipe follows)

Per Serving:
Calories: 444
% of calories from fat: 16
Fat (gm): 8.3
Saturated fat (gm): 2.1
Cholesterol (mg): 15.0
Sodium (mg): 908
Protein (gm): 21.5
Carbohydrate (gm): 71.5

Exchanges:
Milk: 0.0
Vegetable: 2.0
Fruit: 0.0
Bread: 4.0
Meat: 2.0
Fat: 0.0

1. Cook shallots, garlic, herbs, and mushrooms in lightly greased large skillet over medium heat, covered, until mushrooms release juices, 3 to 5 minutes. Cook, uncovered, over medium heat until liquid is gone, 5 to 10 minutes. Stir in broccoli, cheese, salt, and pepper. Spoon about 3 tablespoons vegetable-cheese mixture into each manicotti; arrange in baking pan and spoon Tomato Sauce with Mushrooms and Sherry over. Bake at 350 degrees, loosely covered, until manicotti are hot and sauce is bubbly, 30 to 35 minutes.

Tomato Sauce with Mushrooms and Sherry

Makes about 3 cups

1 small onion, finely chopped

2 cloves garlic, minced

1 tablespoon olive oil

4 cups sliced mushrooms

3 tablespoons dry sherry or water

1 can (28 ounces) crushed tomatoes, undrained

½ teaspoon each: dried rosemary and oregano leaves

1 teaspoon sugar

¼ teaspoon each: salt, pepper

1. Sauté onion and garlic in oil in medium saucepan 2 to 3 minutes. Add mushrooms and sherry; cook, covered, over medium-high heat until mushrooms are wilted and release liquid, about 5 minutes. Cook, uncovered, over medium heat, stirring occasionally, until mushrooms are browned, 10 to 15 minutes. Stir in remaining ingredients; heat to boiling. Reduce heat and simmer, covered, 10 to 15 minutes.

EASY EGGPLANT ROTOLO

L

Incredibly simple to prepare, thanks to no-boil lasagne noodles!

45

4 entrée servings

8 no-boil lasagne noodles
4 cups frozen stir-fry pepper blend
2 teaspoons minced garlic
1 tablespoon olive oil
1 small eggplant (about 1 pound), unpeeled, cubed
1–2 teaspoons dried Italian seasoning
2 cups fat-free ricotta cheese
Salt and pepper, to taste
2 cans (16 ounces each) reduced-sodium
  spaghetti sauce
¼ cup (1 ounce) grated Parmesan cheese

Per Serving:
Calories: 512
% of calories from fat: 29
Fat (gm): 16.3
Saturated fat (gm): 3.8
Cholesterol (mg): 11.4
Sodium (mg): 370
Protein (gm): 28.8
Carbohydrate (gm): 60.8

Exchanges:
Milk: 0.0
Vegetable: 3.0
Fruit: 0.0
Bread: 3.0
Meat: 2.0
Fat: 2.0

1. Arrange noodles in shallow baking dish or pan and cover with warm water; let stand until noodles are softened, about 8 minutes. Drain well.

2. Sauté pepper blend and garlic in oil in large skillet 3 to 4 minutes. Add eggplant and Italian seasoning and cook, covered, until eggplant is tender, about 10 minutes, stirring occasionally. Remove from heat and stir in ricotta cheese; season to taste with salt and pepper.

3. Spread ½ cup cheese mixture on each noodle and roll up and place, seam sides down, in 13 x 9-inch baking pan. Spoon spaghetti sauce over and sprinkle with Parmesan cheese. Bake, loosely covered at 350 degrees until rotolo are hot and sauce bubbly, about 20 minutes.

SPINACH-MUSHROOM ROTOLO WITH MARINARA SAUCE

L

No-boil lasagne noodles can be used in this recipe. Soak them in warm water until softened, about 8 minutes, before using.

6 entrée servings

2 cups sliced mushrooms

1 package (10 ounces) fresh spinach, chopped

2 cloves garlic, minced

1 teaspoon each: dried basil and tarragon leaves

4 ounces reduced-fat cream cheese, room temperature

½ cup fat-free ricotta cheese

¼ teaspoon each: salt, pepper

12 lasagne noodles, cooked, room temperature

Marinara Sauce (recipe follows)

Per Serving:
Calories: 286
% of calories from fat: 30
Fat (gm): 10.3
Saturated fat (gm): 2.7
Cholesterol (mg): 8.7
Sodium (mg): 686
Protein (gm): 12.5
Carbohydrate (gm): 38

Exchanges:
Milk: 0.0
Vegetable: 3.0
Fruit: 0.0
Bread: 1.5
Meat: 0.0
Fat: 2.0

1. Cook mushrooms, spinach, garlic, and herbs in lightly greased large skillet, covered, over medium heat until mushrooms release juices, about 5 minutes. Cook, uncovered, over medium-high heat until liquid is gone, about 5 minutes; cool. Remove from heat; stir in cheeses, salt, and pepper.

2. Spread 3 to 4 tablespoons mixture on each noodle; roll up and place, seam sides down, in baking dish. Spoon Marinara Sauce over rotolo. Bake, loosely covered, at 350 degrees until rotolo are hot and sauce bubbly, 20 to 30 minutes.

Marinara Sauce

Makes about 4 cups

2 medium onions, chopped

6–8 cloves garlic, minced

2 tablespoons olive oil

2 cans (16 ounces each) plum tomatoes, drained, chopped

½ cup dry white wine or tomato juice

¼ cup tomato paste

2–3 tablespoons lemon juice

½ teaspoon salt

¼ teaspoon pepper

1. Sauté onions and garlic in oil in large saucepan until tender, about 5 minutes. Stir in tomatoes, wine, and tomato paste; heat to boiling. Reduce heat and simmer, uncovered, until a medium sauce consistency, about 20 minutes. Stir in lemon juice, salt, and pepper.

ARTICHOKE LASAGNE

L

The lasagne can be assembled up to a day in advance and refrigerated, covered. Increase baking time by 15 to 20 minutes.

8 entrée servings

1½ cups each: sliced shiitake mushrooms, chopped onions

1 cup chopped red bell pepper

2 teaspoons minced garlic

8 cups loosely packed baby spinach

2 packages (9 ounces each) frozen, thawed, artichoke hearts, quartered

Salt and pepper, to taste

3 cups fat-free milk, divided

¼ cup plus 2 tablespoons flour

1 cup (4 ounces) grated fat-free Parmesan cheese

4 ounces fat-free cream cheese, cubed

⅔ cup finely chopped parsley

1 teaspoon each: dried thyme leaves, lemon juice

12 lasagne noodles (10 ounces), cooked

1 cup (4 ounces) shredded reduced-fat mozzarella cheese

Per Serving:
Calories: 278
% of calories from fat: 7
Fat (gm): 2.1
Saturated fat (gm): 0.2
Cholesterol (mg): 1.5
Sodium (mg): 438
Protein (gm): 22.5
Carbohydrate (gm): 46.4

Exchanges:
Milk: 0.0
Vegetable: 3.0
Fruit: 0.0
Bread: 2.0
Meat: 1.0
Fat: 0.0

1. Sauté mushrooms, onions, bell pepper, and garlic in lightly greased large skillet 3 minutes; add spinach and artichoke hearts. Cook, covered, over medium heat until spinach is wilted, about 5 minutes; cook, uncovered, until mixture is dry. Remove from heat; season to taste with salt and pepper.

2. Heat 2 cups milk to boiling in large saucepan. Whisk in combined remaining 1 cup milk and flour and heat to boiling, whisking, until thickened, about 1 minute. Remove from heat; mix in Parmesan and cream cheese, parsley, thyme, and lemon juice, stirring until cream cheese is melted. Season to taste with salt and pepper.

3. Spread 1 cup sauce in bottom of 13 x 9-inch baking pan; arrange 4 noodles in pan, overlapping edges. Spoon ½ of the artichoke mixture over noodles and spread with 1 cup sauce. Repeat layers; top with remaining 4 noodles and spread with 1 cup sauce. Sprinkle with mozzarella cheese. Bake at 350 degrees, loosely covered, until noodles are al dente, 50 to 60 minutes. Let stand 10 minutes before cutting.

SQUASH AND MUSHROOM LASAGNE

L *A white sauce and tomato sauce are combined in this delicate lasagne.*

8 entree servings

1 cup sliced onion

1 tablespoon minced garlic

1 pound portobello or cremini mushrooms, sliced

½ cup dry white wine or vegetable broth

Salt and pepper, to taste

¼ cup finely chopped shallots or green onions

¾ teaspoon each: dried rosemary and thyme leaves

2 teaspoons margarine or butter

¼ cup all-purpose flour

2 cups each: fat-free milk, prepared reduced-sodium
   spaghetti sauce

4 ounces fat-free cream cheese, cubed

¾ cup (3 ounces) grated fat-free Parmesan cheese, divided

12 lasagne noodles (10 ounces), cooked

1 pound acorn or butternut squash, peeled, thinly sliced

Per Serving:
Calories: 306
% of calories from fat: 14
Fat (gm): 4.8
Saturated fat (gm): 1
Cholesterol (mg): 4
Sodium (mg): 226
Protein (gm): 15
Carbohydrate (gm): 49.6

Exchanges:
Milk: 0.0
Vegetable: 1.0
Fruit: 0.0
Bread: 3.0
Meat: 1.0
Fat: 0.5

1. Sauté onion and garlic in lightly greased large skillet 3 to 4 minutes; add mushrooms and sauté 5 minutes. Add wine and heat to boiling; reduce heat to medium and cook until mixture is dry, about 5 minutes. Season to taste with salt and pepper.

2. Sauté shallots and herbs in margarine in medium saucepan until tender, 2 to 3 minutes. Whisk in combined flour and milk and heat to boiling, whisking until thickened, about 1 minute. Mix in spaghetti sauce, cream cheese, and ½ cup Parmesan cheese; cook, stirring until sauce is hot and cream cheese melted, about 5 minutes. Season to taste with salt and pepper.

3. Stir 1 cup sauce into mushroom mixture. Spread about ¾ cup remaining sauce in bottom of 13 x 9-inch baking pan; arrange 4 noodles in pan, overlapping edges. Spoon ½ of mushroom mixture and squash slices over noodles and spread with ¾ cup sauce. Repeat layers; top with remaining 4 noodles and ¾ cup sauce. Sprinkle with remaining ¼ cup Parmesan cheese. Bake at 350 degrees, loosely covered, until noodles and squash are tender, 50 to 60 minutes. Let stand 10 minutes before serving.

VEGGIE LASAGNE WITH EGGPLANT SAUCE

L *The hearty Eggplant Sauce is also delicious served over shaped pasta or tortellini.*

8 entrée servings

1 cup each: sliced onion, zucchini, red bell pepper, mushrooms

3 cloves garlic, minced

2 cups fat-free ricotta cheese

¼ cup (1 ounce) grated Parmesan cheese

Eggplant Sauce (recipe follows)

12 lasagne noodles (10 ounces), cooked

2 medium sweet potatoes, cooked, sliced

2 cups (8 ounces) shredded reduced-fat mozzarella cheese, divided

Per Serving:
Calories: 375
% of calories from fat: 24
Fat (gm): 10.4
Saturated fat (gm): 4.2
Cholesterol (mg): 2.3
Sodium (mg): 685
Protein (gm): 2.4
Carbohydrate (gm): 47

Exchanges:
Milk: 0.0
Vegetable: 3.0
Fruit: 0.0
Bread: 2.0
Meat: 2.5
Fat: 0.5

1. Sauté onion, zucchini, bell pepper, mushrooms, and garlic in lightly greased large skillet until tender, about 10 minutes. Mix ricotta and Parmesan cheese. Spread 1½ cups Eggplant Sauce in bottom of 13 x 9-inch baking pan; top with 4 lasagne noodles, overlapping slightly. Top with ⅓ each ricotta cheese mixture, sweet potatoes, sautéed vegetables, and 1½ cups Eggplant Sauce; sprinkle with ⅔ cup mozzarella cheese. Repeat layers 2 times. Bake, loosely covered, at 350 degrees until sauce is bubbly, about 1 hour. Let stand 10 minutes before cutting.

Eggplant Sauce
Makes about 6 cups

1 pound eggplant, unpeeled, cubed (1-inch)
1 cup chopped onion
½ cup chopped green bell pepper
6 cloves garlic, minced
2 tablespoons olive oil
3 cups chopped tomatoes
1 can (28 ounces) crushed tomatoes, undrained
½ cup dry red wine or water
2 tablespoons drained capers
1 teaspoon each: dried tarragon and thyme leaves
2 teaspoons sugar
½ teaspoon each: salt, pepper

1. Sauté eggplant, onion, bell pepper, and garlic in oil in large saucepan until onion is tender, about 5 minutes. Add remaining ingredients and heat to boiling. Reduce heat and simmer, covered, until eggplant is tender, about 15 minutes. Simmer, uncovered, until desired sauce consistency, about 10 minutes more.

ROASTED RED PEPPER AND SPINACH LASAGNE

L

For convenience, the recipe uses jarred roasted red peppers, but you can roast your own using the method in Roasted Red Pepper Sauce (see p. 59).

8 entrée servings

1 cup chopped onion
2 teaspoons minced garlic
¾ teaspoon each: dried marjoram and oregano leaves
3 cups fat-free milk, divided
⅓ cup all-purpose flour
1 cup (4 ounces) grated fat-free Parmesan cheese
4 ounces fat-free cream cheese, cubed
⅔ cup finely chopped parsley
Salt and pepper, to taste
2 packages (10 ounces each) frozen, thawed, chopped spinach, very well drained
⅔ cup fat-free ricotta cheese

Per Serving:
Calories: 261
% of calories from fat: 13
Fat (gm): 3.8
Saturated fat (gm): 1.7
Cholesterol (mg): 9.1
Sodium (mg): 386
Protein (gm): 21.4
Carbohydrate (gm): 36.8

Exchanges:
Milk: 0.5
Vegetable: 2.0
Fruit: 0.0
Bread: 1.5
Meat: 1.0
Fat: 0.0

12 lasagne noodles (10 ounces), cooked
1 jar (15 ounces) roasted red peppers, drained, cut into 1-inch slices
1 cup (4 ounces) reduced-fat mozzarella cheese

1. Sauté onion, garlic, and herbs in lightly greased large saucepan until tender, 5 to 8 minutes; add 2 cups milk and heat to boiling. Whisk in combined remaining 1 cup milk and flour and heat to boiling, whisking until thickened, about 1 minute. Remove from heat; mix in cheeses and parsley, stirring until cream cheese is melted. Season with salt and pepper. Mix spinach and ricotta cheese; season to taste with salt and pepper.

2. Spread ¾ cup sauce in bottom of 13 x 9-inch baking pan. Arrange 4 noodles in pan, overlapping edges. Top with ½ of the spinach mixture and red pepper slices; spread with generous 1 cup sauce. Repeat layers; top with remaining 4 noodles and spread with remaining 1¼ cups sauce. Sprinkle with mozzarella cheese. Bake at 350 degrees, loosely covered, until noodles are tender, 50 to 60 minutes. Let stand 10 minutes before serving.

MEXICAN-STYLE LASAGNE

A lasagne with a difference!

8 entrée servings

Chili-Tomato Sauce (recipe follows)
12 lasagne noodles (10 ounces), cooked
2 cups (8 ounces) each: fat-free ricotta cheese, shredded reduced-fat Monterey Jack cheese
1 can (15 ounces) each: pinto beans, black beans, rinsed, drained

Per Serving:
Calories: 360
% of calories from fat: 18
Fat (gm): 8
Saturated fat (gm): 3.1
Cholesterol (mg): 26.3
Sodium (mg): 748
Protein (gm): 30.7
Carbohydrate (gm): 51

Exchanges:
Milk: 0.0
Vegetable: 3.0
Fruit: 0.0
Bread: 2.0
Meat: 2.5
Fat: 0.5

1. Spread 1 cup sauce on bottom of a 13 x 9-inch baking pan; top with 4 lasagne noodles, over-lapping slightly. Spoon ⅓ of the combined cheeses over noodles, spreading lightly with rubber spatula; top with ⅓ of the combined beans and 1⅓ cups Chili-Tomato Sauce. Repeat layers 2 times. Bake at 350 degrees, loosely covered, until hot and bubbly, about 1 hour. Let stand 10 minutes before cutting.

Chili-Tomato Sauce
Makes about 5 cups

2 cups chopped onions
2–3 teaspoons each: minced garlic, jalapeño chili
2 cans (14½ ounces each) low-sodium stewed tomatoes
2 cans (8 ounces each) low-sodium tomato sauce
2 tablespoons chili powder
2 teaspoons ground cumin
1 teaspoon dried oregano leaves
Salt, to taste

1. Sauté onions, garlic, and jalapeño chili in lightly greased large skillet until onions are tender, 5 to 8 minutes. Stir in remaining ingredients, except salt; heat to boiling. Reduce heat and simmer, uncovered, until sauce is reduced to 5 cups, about 20 minutes. Season to taste with salt.

MEXI-CAN LASAGNE

This simple South-of-the-Border lasagne is one you'll say "ole" to!

4 entrée servings

6 no-boil lasagne noodles
1 can (15 ounces) low-fat refried beans
1 can (11 ounces) nacho cheese soup
⅓ cup fat-free milk
1 tablespoon minced jalapeño chili
1 teaspoon ground cumin
1 cup frozen or canned, drained, whole-kernel corn
1 can (14½ ounces) reduced-sodium stewed tomatoes
2 teaspoons chili powder
½ teaspoon dried oregano leaves
½–¾ cup (2–3 ounces) shredded reduced-fat
  Monterey Jack or Cheddar cheese

Per Serving:
Calories: 393
% of calories from fat: 24
Fat (gm): 11.3
Saturated fat (gm): 4.5
Cholesterol (mg): 20.2
Sodium (mg): 686
Protein (gm): 20.8
Carbohydrate (gm): 58.6

Exchanges:
Milk: 0.0
Vegetable: 2.0
Fruit: 0.0
Bread: 3.0
Meat: 2.0
Fat: 0.5

1. Place 2 lasagne noodles in lightly greased 8-inch square baking pan; top with ½ the refried beans. Mix cheese soup, milk, jalapeño chili, and cumin; spoon ½ the mixture over the beans and sprinkle with ½ the corn. Repeat layers, ending with 2 noodles. Combine tomatoes, chili powder, and oregano in small bowl; spoon over the top. Bake, covered, at 375 degrees until noodles are tender, about 30 minutes. Uncover and sprinkle with shredded cheese; let stand 5 to 10 minutes before serving.

ASPARAGUS POLENTA BAKE

This dish can be prepared a day in advance and refrigerated; increase baking time 5 to 10 minutes.

6 side-dish servings

6 ounces portobello mushrooms, thinly sliced

8 ounces asparagus, sliced (1-inch)

1–2 teaspoons olive oil

1 package (16 ounces) prepared Italian-herb polenta

1 cup water

1 ounce sun-dried tomatoes (not in oil),
   softened, sliced

¼–½ cup (1–2 ounces) shredded Parmesan cheese

Per Serving:
Calories: 110
% of calories from fat: 18
Fat (gm): 2.2
Saturated fat (gm): 1
Cholesterol (mg): 4.2
Sodium (mg): 94
Protein (gm): 5.4
Carbohydrate (gm): 16.7

Exchanges:
Milk: 0.0
Vegetable: 2.0
Fruit: 0.0
Bread: 0.5
Meat: 0.0
Fat: 0.5

1. Sauté mushrooms and asparagus in oil in large skillet until asparagus is crisp-tender, about 5 minutes. Mash polenta with water in medium saucepan; cook over medium heat, whisking until smooth and hot, about 5 minutes. Stir in mushroom mixture and sun-dried tomatoes. Spoon into 4 ramekins or a shallow casserole or quiche dish; sprinkle with Parmesan cheese. Bake at 425 degrees until cheese is browned, about 20 minutes.

VEGGIE CASSEROLE

L

A perfect pot-luck dish!

45

6 side-dish servings

1 cup each: sliced leek (white part only), red or
  green bell pepper
2 teaspoons minced garlic
3 tablespoons flour
1½ teaspoons bouquet garni
2 cups reduced-sodium vegetable broth
1 cup each: cubed, peeled potatoes, sliced yellow
  summer squash, halved green beans
½ cup each: cauliflower florets, frozen peas
Salt and pepper, to taste
¾ cup fresh bread crumbs
2 tablespoons margarine or butter, melted

Per Serving:
Calories: 158
% of calories from fat: 24
Fat (gm): 4.3
Saturated fat (gm): 0.9
Cholesterol (mg): 0
Sodium (mg): 129
Protein (gm): 4.3
Carbohydrate (gm): 26.4

Exchanges:
Milk: 0.0
Vegetable: 2.0
Fruit: 0.0
Bread: 1.0
Meat: 0.0
Fat: 1.0

1. Sauté leek, bell pepper, and garlic in lightly greased large saucepan 5 minutes; stir in flour and bouquet garni and cook 1 minute.
Add broth and remaining vegetables; heat to boiling. Reduce heat
and simmer, covered, until vegetables are tender, about 10 minutes.
Season to taste with salt and pepper. Pour mixture into 1½-quart
casserole; top with combined bread crumbs and margarine. Bake
at 350 degrees until crumbs are browned, about 10 minutes.

MEXICAN-STYLE VEGETABLES AND RICE

L

Rice combines with vegetables and south-of-the-border flavors.

45

8 side-dish servings

⅔ cup each: chopped red bell pepper, onion
3 cloves garlic, minced
1 jalapeño chili, finely chopped
2 cups each: cubed peeled chayote squash, halved small
  cremini mushrooms
1 cup whole kernel corn
½ teaspoon each: dried oregano leaves, ground cumin, chili powder

Salt and pepper, to taste

4 cups cooked white or brown rice

1 cup fat-free sour cream

¾ cup (3 ounces) shredded reduced-fat
Monterey Jack cheese

2 green onions, sliced

Per Serving:
Calories: 208
% of calories from fat: 28
Fat (gm): 6.6
Saturated fat (gm): 2.7
Cholesterol (mg): 11.4
Sodium (mg): 106
Protein (gm): 8
Carbohydrate (gm): 30.9

Exchanges:
Milk: 0.0
Vegetable: 0.0
Fruit: 0.0
Bread: 2.0
Meat: 0.0
Fat: 1.0

1. Sauté bell pepper, onion, garlic, and jalapeño chili in lightly greased large skillet 5 minutes; add squash, mushrooms, corn, and herbs. Cook, covered, over medium heat until squash and mushrooms are tender, about 8 minutes, stirring occasionally. Season to taste with salt and pepper.

2. Spoon half of the rice into greased 2-quart casserole. Top with vegetable mixture and sour cream; spoon remaining rice on top. Bake, loosely covered, at 300 degrees until hot, 30 to 40 minutes. Sprinkle with cheese, and bake, uncovered, until cheese is melted, 5 to 10 minutes; sprinkle with green onions.

45-MINUTE PREPARATION TIP: Begin cooking rice before preparing the rest of the recipe.

VEGETABLE AND MIXED RICE CASSEROLE

L

Vary the vegetables according to season or preference.

45

8 side-dish servings (about ¾ cup each)

1½ cups sliced shiitake or cremini mushrooms

1 cup sliced zucchini

½ cup each: chopped onion, green and red
bell pepper

1 teaspoon dried thyme leaves

1 package (6 ounces) brown and wild rice mix,
cooked with spice packet

1 can (15 ounces) pinto beans, rinsed, drained

1 cup each: whole kernel corn, fat-free sour
cream, shredded reduced-fat Cheddar cheese
(4 ounces), divided

Salt and pepper, to taste

Per Serving:
Calories: 203
% of calories from fat: 15
Fat (gm): 3.5
Saturated fat (gm): 1.9
Cholesterol (mg): 10.1
Sodium (mg): 141
Protein (gm): 10.5
Carbohydrate (gm): 33.7

Exchanges:
Milk: 0.0
Vegetable: 1.0
Fruit: 0.0
Bread: 2.0
Meat: 0.0
Fat: 0.5

1. Sauté mushrooms, zucchini, onion, bell peppers, and thyme in lightly greased medium skillet until vegetables are tender, 8 to 10 minutes. Combine vegetables with rice, beans, corn, sour cream, and ½ cup cheese in 2-quart casserole. Season to taste with salt and pepper; sprinkle with remaining ½ cup cheese. Bake, uncovered, at 350 degrees until hot, 30 to 40 minutes.

EGG AND BROCCOLI CASSEROLE

 LO *A new side-dish recipe your family will love!*

 45 **4 side-dish servings**

2 packages (10 ounces each) frozen chopped broccoli, cooked, well drained

4 hard-cooked eggs, thinly sliced

1 cup fat-free sour cream

½ cup fat-free mayonnaise

2 tablespoons white wine vinegar

1½ teaspoons dried tarragon leaves

Paprika, as garnish

Per Serving:
Calories: 205
% of calories from fat: 23
Fat (gm): 5.2
Saturated fat (gm): 1.6
Cholesterol (mg): 212
Sodium (mg): 357
Protein (gm): 14.7
Carbohydrate (gm): 24.3

Exchanges:
Milk: 0.0
Vegetable: 2.0
Fruit: 0.0
Bread: 1.0
Meat: 1.0
Fat: 0.5

1. Arrange broccoli in lightly greased 13 x 9-inch baking dish; top with egg slices. Heat combined sour cream, mayonnaise, vinegar, and tarragon in small saucepan over low heat, stirring until warm, about 4 minutes. Pour over broccoli and eggs; sprinkle with paprika. Bake, uncovered, at 325 degrees 15 to 20 minutes.

VEGGIE KUGEL

LO *This kugel, with lots of veggies, is high in protein and low in fat.*

 45 **6 servings**

¾ cup each: chopped red bell pepper, onion

2 tablespoons margarine or butter

2 cups each: halved Brussels sprouts, cubed peeled sweet potatoes, cooked

¾ teaspoon each: dried thyme, marjoram leaves

1 can (12 ounces) evaporated fat-free milk

2 tablespoons flour

1 package (10 ounces each) frozen chopped spinach, thawed, well drained

12 ounces no-yolk noodles, cooked

3 eggs, lightly beaten

½ teaspoon each: salt, pepper

Per Serving:
Calories: 205
% of calories from fat: 11
Fat (gm): 2.3
Saturated fat (gm): 0.4
Cholesterol (mg): 127
Sodium (mg): 290
Protein (gm): 10.8
Carbohydrate (gm): 33.8

Exchanges:
Milk: 0.0
Vegetable: 0.0
Fruit: 0.0
Bread: 2.0
Meat: 1.0
Fat: 0.0

1. Sauté bell pepper and onion in margarine in large skillet until tender, about 5 minutes; add Brussels sprouts, sweet potatoes, and herbs. Stir in combined evaporated milk and flour; heat to boiling, stirring until thickened, about 1 minute. Cool; mix in remaining ingredients. Spoon into greased 13 x 9-inch baking dish. Bake, uncovered, at 350 degrees 35 minutes, or until sharp knife inserted near center comes out clean. Cool on wire rack 5 minutes.

45-MINUTE PREPARATION TIP: Begin cooking noodles before preparing the rest of the recipe.

NOODLES FLORENTINE

This recipe will serve 4 as a vegetarian entrée; serve with a salad and multigrain bread.

8 side-dish servings

¾ cup each: finely chopped red onion, red bell pepper

2 cloves garlic, minced

1 package (10 ounces each) frozen chopped spinach, thawed, drained

2 cups cooked spinach noodles

3 eggs, lightly beaten

1 cup fresh whole wheat bread crumbs

2 teaspoons sugar

½ teaspoon each: ground nutmeg, salt, pepper

½ cup (2 ounces) shredded reduced-fat Swiss cheese

Per Serving:
Calories: 184
% of calories from fat: 9
Fat (gm): 1.8
Saturated fat (gm): 0.6
Cholesterol (mg): 15.7
Sodium (mg): 377
Protein (gm): 12.6
Carbohydrate (gm): 27.2

Exchanges:
Milk: 0.0
Vegetable: 0.0
Fruit: 0.0
Bread: 2.0
Meat: 1.0
Fat: 0.0

1. Sauté onion, bell pepper, and garlic in lightly greased medium skillet until tender, about 4 minutes; stir in spinach and remove from heat. Mix in remaining ingredients, except cheese, and spoon into greased 11 x 7-inch baking dish. Bake, uncovered, at 325 degrees 30 minutes. Sprinkle with cheese; bake until cheese is melted and sharp knife inserted near center comes out clean, about 10 minutes. Cool on wire rack 5 minutes.

45-MINUTE PREPARATION TIP: Begin cooking noodles before preparing the rest of the recipe.

FETTUCCINE FLORENTINE TIMBALE

L

45

◊

An impressive side dish for entertaining or special family meals. The casserole can be assembled several hours in advance and refrigerated; increase baking time by 10 minutes.

10 side-dish servings

3 tablespoons unseasoned dry bread crumbs

1 package (1.8 ounces) white sauce mix

2¼ cups fat-free milk

1½ cups (6 ounces) shredded reduced-fat Italian 6-cheese blend, divided

12 ounces spinach fettuccine, cooked

1 package (10 ounces) frozen chopped spinach, thawed, well drained

1 cup fat-free cottage cheese

½ cup roasted red peppers, drained

Per Serving:
Calories: 190
% of calories from fat: 14
Fat (gm): 2.9
Saturated fat (gm): 1.2
Cholesterol (mg): 43.1
Sodium (mg): 399
Protein (gm): 14.4
Carbohydrate (gm): 26.4

Exchanges:
Milk: 0.0
Vegetable: 1.0
Fruit: 0.0
Bread: 1.5
Meat: 1.0
Fat: 0.0

1. Coat side and bottom of greased 9-inch springform pan with bread crumbs. Make white sauce mix in large saucepan according to package directions, using milk; stir in ½ cup shredded cheese and fettuccine; spoon ½ the mixture into prepared pan. Top with combined spinach, ½ cup shredded cheese and cottage cheese; top with roasted peppers and remaining pasta mixture.

2. Bake, uncovered, at 350 degrees until golden, 55 to 60 minutes, sprinkling with remaining ½ cup shredded cheese during last 10 minutes of baking time. Let stand 10 minutes; loosen side of pan with sharp knife and remove. Cut into wedges.

FRENCH TOAST CASSEROLE

LO

45

Your favorite fruit, such as bananas, blueberries, strawberries, or golden raisins, can be used instead of raspberries.

6 entrée servings

2 cups fat-free milk

3 eggs, lightly beaten

12 slices whole-grain or sourdough bread, halved, divided

3 tablespoons melted margarine or butter, divided

9 tablespoons powdered sugar, divided

2 cups fresh or frozen, thawed, drained, raspberries, divided

1 tablespoon ground cinnamon

Lite Pancake Syrup, warm (optional)

Per Serving:
Calories: 328
% of calories from fat: 29
Fat (gm): 11.3
Saturated fat (gm): 2
Cholesterol (mg): 107.4
Sodium (mg): 316
Protein (gm): 14.4
Carbohydrate (gm): 47.4

Exchanges:
Milk: 0.0
Vegetable: 0.0
Fruit: 0.0
Bread: 3.0
Meat: 1.0
Fat: 1.0

1. Beat milk and eggs in 11 x 7-inch baking dish. Dip bread halves into egg mixture, coating both sides well. Arrange 8 bread halves in lightly greased 9-inch square baking dish. Drizzle with 1 tablespoon margarine; sprinkle with 3 tablespoons sugar and 1 cup raspberries. Repeat layers 1 more time, arranging bread halves in opposite direction from bottom layer. Top with remaining 8 bread halves, margarine, and sugar. Sprinkle with cinnamon.

2. Bake, covered, 25 minutes at 400 degrees; uncover and bake until browned, about 10 minutes longer. Serve with syrup, if desired.

ELEVEN

Vegetable
Side Dishes

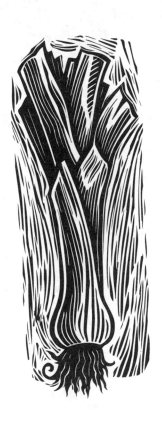

ARTICHOKES WITH MOCK HOLLANDAISE SAUCE

L

45

The Mock Hollandaise Sauce is excellent served over steamed asparagus spears, broccoli, or cauliflower. Also see p. 264 for delicious Eggs Benedict.

4–6 servings

4–6 whole artichokes, stems removed
Mock Hollandaise Sauce (see p. 170)

Per Serving:
Calories: 114
% of calories from fat: 2
Fat (gm): 0.3
Saturated fat (gm): 0.1
Cholesterol (mg): 0.2
Sodium (mg): 396
Protein (gm): 11.9
Carbohydrate (gm): 17.5

Exchanges:
Milk: 0.5
Vegetable: 2.0
Fruit: 0.0
Bread: 0.0
Meat: 0.5
Fat: 0.0

1. Cut 1 inch from tops of artichokes and discard. Place artichokes in medium saucepan and sprinkle lightly with salt; add 1 inch water to pan. Heat to boiling; reduce heat and simmer, covered, until artichokes are tender, about 30 minutes (bottom leaves will pull out easily). Serve with Mock Hollandaise Sauce.

45-MINUTE PREPARATION TIP: Make Mock Hollandaise Sauce while artichokes are cooking.

ASPARAGUS WITH PEANUT SAUCE

V

45

Asian flavors are the perfect complement to spring's freshest asparagus—serve warm or chilled.

6 servings

2 tablespoons reduced-fat peanut butter
¼ cup sugar
2–3 tablespoons reduced-sodium tamari soy sauce
3–4 teaspoons rice wine (sake), dry sherry, or water
1 teaspoon grated gingerroot
1½ pounds asparagus spears, cooked crisp-tender

Per Serving:
Calories: 95
% of calories from fat: 21
Fat (gm): 2.3
Saturated fat (gm): 0.5
Cholesterol (mg): 0
Sodium (mg): 246
Protein (gm): 4.8
Carbohydrate (gm): 15

Exchanges:
Milk: 0.0
Vegetable: 3.0
Fruit: 0.0
Bread: 0.0
Meat: 0.0
Fat: 0.5

1. Mix peanut butter, sugar, soy sauce, rice wine, and gingerroot until smooth. Serve with asparagus.

ASPARAGUS AND WHITE BEANS, ITALIAN-STYLE

45

L

A lovely accompaniment to grilled or roasted meat, this dish will also serve 4 as a meatless entrée.

8 servings

1 pound asparagus, cut (2-inch pieces)

2 teaspoons each: minced garlic, olive oil

2 cups chopped Italian plum tomatoes

1 can (15 ounces) cannellini or Great Northern, beans, rinsed, drained

¾ cup reduced-sodium vegetable broth

1 teaspoon dried rosemary leaves

Salt and pepper, to taste

8 ounces linguine or thin spaghetti, cooked, warm

¼–½ cup (1–2 ounces) shredded Parmesan cheese

Per Serving:
Calories: 169
% of calories from fat: 16
Fat (gm): 3.1
Saturated fat (gm): 0.7
Cholesterol (mg): 2
Sodium (mg): 229
Protein (gm): 7.9
Carbohydrate (gm): 29.4

Exchanges:
Milk: 0.0
Vegetable: 1.0
Fruit: 0.0
Bread: 1.0
Meat: 0.0
Fat: 0.5

1. Sauté asparagus and garlic in oil in large skillet until crisp-tender, 3 to 4 minutes. Stir in tomatoes, beans, broth, and rosemary; cook over medium heat until hot, 2 to 3 minutes. Season to taste with salt and pepper; toss with linguine and cheese.

GREEN BEAN CASSEROLE

L

45

Reduced-fat cream of mushroom soup and fat-free sour cream make this old favorite possible in a healthy, low-fat form. We've used fresh green beans, but canned or frozen may be used.

6 servings

1 can (10¾ ounces) reduced-fat cream of mushroom soup

½ cup fat-free sour cream

¼ cup fat-free milk

1¼ pounds green beans, halved, cooked crisp-tender

½ cup canned French-fried onions

Per Serving:
Calories: 81
% of calories from fat: 31
Fat (gm): 2.9
Saturated fat (gm): 0.8
Cholesterol (mg): 1.3
Sodium (mg): 172
Protein (gm): 3
Carbohydrate (gm): 11.6

Exchanges:
Milk: 0.0
Vegetable: 2.0
Fruit: 0.0
Bread: 0.0
Meat: 0.0
Fat: 0.5

1. Mix soup, sour cream, milk, and beans in 2-quart casserole. Bake, uncovered, at 350 degrees until mixture is hot, 30 to 40 minutes; sprinkling with onions during last 10 minutes.

GREEK-STYLE GREEN BEANS

45

V

Fresh green beans are long-simmered with tomatoes, herbs, and garlic in traditional Greek style.

4–6 servings

½ cup chopped onion

4 cloves garlic, minced

¾ teaspoon each: dried oregano and basil leaves

1 tablespoon olive oil

1 can (28 ounces) reduced-sodium tomatoes, undrained, coarsely chopped

1 pound green beans

Salt and pepper, to taste

Per Serving:
Calories: 123
% of calories from fat: 28
Fat (gm): 4.3
Saturated fat (gm): 0.6
Cholesterol (mg): 0
Sodium (mg): 30
Protein (gm): 4.5
Carbohydrate (gm): 20.5

Exchanges:
Milk: 0.0
Vegetable: 4.0
Fruit: 0.0
Bread: 0.0
Meat: 0.0
Fat: 0.5

1. Sauté onion, garlic, and herbs in oil in large skillet until onion is tender, 3 to 4 minutes. Add tomatoes with liquid and green beans and heat to boiling; reduce heat and simmer, covered, until beans are very tender, about 30 minutes. Season to taste with salt and pepper.

ORIENTAL GREEN BEANS

45

V

This dish complements any grilled or roasted meat or poultry.

4 servings

¼ cup each: chopped onion, red bell pepper

2 teaspoons each: finely chopped gingerroot, garlic

2 cups halved green beans

1 cup rinsed, drained canned adzuki or black beans

½ cup sliced water chestnuts

1 tablespoon rice wine vinegar

1–2 teaspoons reduced-sodium tamari soy sauce

Salt and pepper, to taste

Per Serving:
Calories: 109
% of calories from fat: 2
Fat (gm): 0.2
Saturated fat (gm): 0
Cholesterol (mg): 0
Sodium (mg): 64
Protein (gm): 5.8
Carbohydrate (gm): 22.5

Exchanges:
Milk: 0.0
Vegetable: 1.5
Fruit: 0.0
Bread: 1.0
Meat: 0.0
Fat: 0.0

1. Stir-fry onion, bell pepper, gingerroot, and garlic in lightly greased wok or large skillet 2

minutes; add green beans and stir-fry until beans are crisp-tender, 5 to 8 minutes. Add adzuki beans, water chestnuts, vinegar, and soy sauce; stir-fry until hot, about 2 minutes. Season to taste with salt and pepper.

HONEY GLAZED ROASTED BEETS

Roasting maximizes the sweet flavor of beets.

6 servings

1½ pounds medium beets

2 medium red onions, cut into wedges

Vegetable cooking spray

¼ cup currants or raisins

¼ cup each: toasted walnuts, honey

2–3 tablespoons red wine vinegar

1 tablespoon canola oil

4 cloves garlic, minced

Salt and pepper, to taste

Per Serving:
Calories: 94
% of calories from fat: 18
Fat (gm): 1.9
Saturated fat (gm): 0.4
Cholesterol (mg): 0
Sodium (mg): 70
Protein (gm): 1.1
Carbohydrate (gm): 19.3

Exchanges:
Milk: 0.0
Vegetable: 2.0
Fruit: 0.0
Bread: 0.5
Meat: 0.0
Fat: 0.0

1. Arrange beets and onions in single layer on greased foil-lined jelly roll pan; spray with cooking spray. Roast at 425 degrees until beets are tender, about 40 minutes. Peel beets and cut into 1-inch pieces. Combine beets, onions, currants, and walnuts in bowl; heat combined remaining ingredients, except salt and pepper, pour over vegetables and toss. Season to taste with salt and pepper.

BEETS DIJON

45

L

The easiest way to peel beets is to cook them with the skins on; after cooking, the skins slip off easily!

4 servings

⅓ cup finely chopped onion
2 cloves garlic, minced
⅓ cup fat-free sour cream
2 tablespoons Dijon mustard
2–3 teaspoons lemon juice
Salt and white pepper, to taste
1½ pounds medium beets, cooked, cubed or
   sliced, warm

Per Serving:
Calories: 71
% of calories from fat: 7
Fat (gm): 0.6
Saturated fat (gm): 0.1
Cholesterol (mg): 0
Sodium (mg): 185
Protein (gm): 3.5
Carbohydrate (gm): 13.8

Exchanges:
Milk: 0.0
Vegetable: 3.0
Fruit: 0.0
Bread: 0.0
Meat: 0.0
Fat: 0.0

1. Sauté onion and garlic in lightly greased small saucepan until tender, 3 to 4 minutes. Stir in sour cream, mustard, and lemon juice; heat over low heat until hot, 2 to 3 minutes. Season to taste with salt and pepper; spoon over beets.

45-MINUTE PREPARATION TIP: Cook beets before making sour cream sauce.

BROCCOLI RABE SAUTÉED WITH GARLIC

45

V

This simple flavorful vegetable recipe can also be made with broccoli, green beans, or asparagus.

4–6 servings

1 pound broccoli rabe, cooked crisp-tender
4 cloves garlic, minced
Salt and pepper, to taste

Per Serving:
Calories: 32
% of calories from fat: 8
Fat (gm): 0.4
Saturated fat (gm): 0.1
Cholesterol (mg): 0
Sodium (mg): 25
Protein (gm): 3.1
Carbohydrate (gm): 5.9

Exchanges:
Milk: 0.0
Vegetable: 1.0
Fruit: 0.0
Bread: 0.0
Meat: 0.0
Fat: 0.0

1. Sauté broccoli rabe and garlic in lightly greased large skillet until broccoli rabe is beginning to brown, 4 to 5 minutes. Season to taste with salt and pepper.

BROCCOLI TERRINE WITH LEMON HERB MAYONNAISE

LO

45

◊

❄

The terrine can also be served with Roasted Red Pepper Sauce or Fresh Tomato-Basil Sauce (see pp. 59, 171).

8 servings

1 pound broccoli, cut into large pieces, cooked
½ cup fat-free sour cream
¼ cup (1 ounce) grated fat-free Parmesan cheese
2–3 teaspoons lemon juice
½ teaspoon each: dried tarragon, thyme, and basil leaves
Salt and pepper, to taste
4 eggs
Lemon-Herb Mayonnaise (recipe follows)

Per Serving:
Calories: 103
% of calories from fat: 28
Fat (gm): 3
Saturated fat (gm): 1
Cholesterol (mg): 111
Sodium (mg): 227
Protein (gm): 7
Carbohydrate (gm): 11.5

Exchanges:
Milk: 0.0
Vegetable: 2.0
Fruit: 0.0
Bread: 0.0
Meat: 0.0
Fat: 1.0

1. Process broccoli in food processor until mixture is almost smooth; mix in sour cream, cheese, lemon juice, and herbs. Season to taste with salt and pepper. Mix in eggs.

2. Pour mixture into greased loaf pan, 7½ x 3½ inches. Place pan in large roasting pan on middle oven rack; add 2 inches hot water to roasting pan. Bake, covered with foil, at 350 degrees until set, about 1 hour. Remove loaf pan from roasting pan and uncover. Let stand 10 minutes. Loosen sides of loaf with sharp knife and invert onto serving plate, smoothing edges with knife, if necessary. Slice and serve warm or chilled with Lemon Herb Mayonnaise.

Lemon-Herb Mayonnaise

Makes about ¾ cup

½ cup fat-free mayonnaise
¼ cup fat-free sour cream
1–2 teaspoons each: lemon juice and zest
½ teaspoon dried tarragon leaves
¼ teaspoon dried thyme leaves

1. Mix all ingredients.

SUGAR-GLAZED BRUSSELS SPROUTS AND PEARL ONIONS

45

V

Large Brussels sprouts can be halved for faster cooking. The pearl onions can be fresh, frozen, or canned.

4–6 servings

1 tablespoon margarine

¼ cup sugar

8 ounces each: small Brussels sprouts, pearl onions, cooked until crisp-tender, warm

Salt and white pepper, to taste

Per Serving:
Calories: 107
% of calories from fat: 25
Fat (gm): 3.2
Saturated fat (gm): 0.6
Cholesterol (mg): 0
Sodium (mg): 48
Protein (gm): 2.3
Carbohydrate (gm): 19.7

Exchanges:
Milk: 0.0
Vegetable: 2.0
Fruit: 0.0
Bread: 0.5
Meat: 0.0
Fat: 0.5

1. Heat margarine in medium skillet until melted; stir in sugar and cook over medium heat until mixture is bubbly. Add vegetables and toss to coat. Season to taste with salt and white pepper.

WINE-BRAISED CABBAGE

45

You'll enjoy the combination of aromatic anise and caraway seeds in this cabbage dish.

4–6 servings

¾ cup chopped onion

½ cup chopped green bell pepper

3 cloves garlic, minced

½ teaspoon each: crushed caraway and anise seeds

1 medium head cabbage, thinly sliced

½ cup each: canned reduced-sodium vegetable broth, dry white wine

2 slices diced bacon, cooked crisp, drained

Salt and pepper, to taste

Per Serving:
Calories: 118
% of calories from fat: 10
Fat (gm): 1.5
Saturated fat (gm): 0.1
Cholesterol (mg): 0
Sodium (mg): 148
Protein (gm): 6.4
Carbohydrate (gm): 19.3

Exchanges:
Milk: 0.0
Vegetable: 3.0
Fruit: 0.0
Bread: 0.5
Meat: 0.0
Fat: 0.0

1. Sauté onion, bell pepper, garlic, caraway, and anise seeds in lightly greased large saucepan 3 to 4 minutes. Add cabbage, vegetable broth, and wine; heat to boiling. Reduce heat and simmer, covered, until cabbage is wilted, about 5 minutes. Simmer, uncovered, until cabbage is tender and liquid is gone, 10 to 15 minutes. Stir in bacon; season to taste with salt and pepper.

GINGERED CARROT PUREE

L

This intensely flavored puree has a velvety texture.

6 servings

2 pounds carrots, sliced, cooked
2 cups cubed, peeled Idaho potato, cooked
1–2 tablespoons margarine or butter
¼–½ cup fat-free half-and-half or fat-free milk, warm
½ teaspoon ground ginger
Salt and pepper, to taste

Per Serving:
Calories: 122
% of calories from fat: 16
Fat (gm): 2.2
Saturated fat (gm): 0.4
Cholesterol (mg): 0
Sodium (mg): 132
Protein (gm): 2.4
Carbohydrate (gm): 24.1

Exchanges:
Milk: 0.0
Vegetable: 2.5
Fruit: 0.0
Bread: 0.5
Meat: 0.0
Fat: 0.5

1. Process carrots and potato in food processor until smooth; transfer to large skillet and cook over medium to medium-low heat, stirring until mixture is the consistency of thick mashed potatoes (do not brown), about 15 minutes. Beat margarine and enough half-and-half into mixture to make a creamy consistency. Stir in ground ginger; season to taste with salt and pepper.

VARIATIONS

Cauliflower-Fennel Puree — Make recipe as above, substituting cauliflower for the carrots, deleting the ground nutmeg, and adding 1–1½ teaspoons crushed fennel or caraway seeds.

Celery Root Puree — Make recipe as above substituting celery root for the carrots.

Fennel Puree — Make recipe as above, substituting fennel bulbs for the carrots and deleting the nutmeg. Add ½ cup cooked onion to the fennel and potatoes when pureeing.

Herbed Broccoli Puree — Make recipe as above, substituting broccoli for the carrots, and adding ½ teaspoon each dried marjoram and savory leaves.

ORANGE-GLAZED BABY CARROTS

45

L

The sweet-spiced orange glaze is also delicious over sweet potatoes or beets.

4 servings

¾ cup orange juice
½ cup packed light brown sugar
2 tablespoons cornstarch
½ teaspoon ground cinnamon
¼ teaspoon each: ground allspice, mace
1 tablespoon margarine or butter
Salt and white pepper, to taste
1 pound baby carrots, cooked crisp-tender, warm

Per Serving:
Calories: 191
% of calories from fat: 13
Fat (gm): 3
Saturated fat (gm): 0.6
Cholesterol (mg): 0
Sodium (mg): 145
Protein (gm): 1.8
Carbohydrate (gm): 42.4

Exchanges:
Milk: 0.0
Vegetable: 2.0
Fruit: 2.0
Bread: 0.0
Meat: 0.0
Fat: 0.5

1. Mix orange juice, brown sugar, cornstarch, and spices in small saucepan; heat to boiling. Boil, stirring until thickened, about 1 minute. Stir in margarine; season to taste with salt and pepper. Stir into carrots.

45-MINUTE PREPARATION TIP: Begin cooking carrots before preparing the rest of the recipe.

CARROT PUDDING

This recipe is served as a dessert in Mexico—we think it makes an excellent side dish!

8 servings

2 pounds carrots, cooked, mashed
½ cup sugar
1½ tablespoons margarine or butter, melted
½ cup all-purpose flour
1½ teaspoons baking powder
½ teaspoon each: ground cinnamon, salt
½ cup each: raisins, shredded fat-free Cheddar cheese
4 egg whites, beaten to stiff peaks
¼ cup sliced almonds

Per Serving:
Calories: 191
% of calories from fat: 11
Fat (gm): 2.5
Saturated fat (gm): 0.5
Cholesterol (mg): 1.3
Sodium (mg): 339
Protein (gm): 6.3
Carbohydrate (gm): 37.9

Exchanges:
Milk: 0.0
Vegetable: 1.5
Fruit: 0.5
Bread: 1.5
Meat: 0.0
Fat: 0.5

1. Mix carrots, sugar, and margarine in bowl; mix in combined flour, baking powder, cinnamon, and salt. Mix in raisins and cheese; fold in beaten egg whites. Spoon mixture into greased 8-inch-square baking pan; sprinkle with almonds. Bake at 475 degrees 10 minutes; reduce temperature to 350 degrees and bake until browned and set, 50 to 60 minutes. Cut into squares; serve warm.

CAULIFLOWER WITH CREAMY CHEESE SAUCE

45

L

For flavor variations, make the cheese sauce with other reduced-fat cheeses, such as Havarti, Gruyère, American, or blue.

6 servings

1 large head cauliflower (about 2 pounds), sliced
Creamy Cheese Sauce (recipe follows)
Paprika, as garnish

Per Serving:
Calories: 102
% of calories from fat: 31
Fat (gm): 3.6
Saturated fat (gm): 1.5
Cholesterol (mg): 5.7
Sodium (mg): 194
Protein (gm): 6.5
Carbohydrate (gm): 11.7

Exchanges:
Milk: 0.0
Vegetable: 2.0
Fruit: 0.0
Bread: 0.0
Meat: 0.5
Fat: 0.5

1. Cook cauliflower in 2 inches simmering water in medium saucepan, covered, until tender, 20 to 25 minutes; drain. Spoon Creamy Cheese Sauce over and sprinkle with paprika.

Creamy Cheese Sauce

Makes about 1¼ cups

2 tablespoons minced onion
1 tablespoon margarine or butter
2 tablespoons flour
1 cup fat-free milk
½ cup (2 ounces) cubed reduced-fat pasteurized processed cheese
¼ teaspoon dry mustard
2–3 drops red pepper sauce
Salt and white pepper, to taste

1. Sauté onion in margarine in small saucepan 2 to 3 minutes. Stir in flour; cook 1 minute. Whisk in milk and heat to boiling, stirring until thickened, about 1 minute. Reduce heat to low; add cheese, dry mustard, and pepper sauce, whisking until cheese is melted. Season to taste with salt and white pepper.

FRIED CORN

45 *Use fresh corn, if you can!*

V **6 servings**

3 cups whole-kernel corn
¾ cup each: sliced green and red bell pepper
3 cloves garlic, minced
¼ cup water
Salt and pepper, to taste

Per Serving:
Calories: 85
% of calories from fat: 2
Fat (gm): 0.2
Saturated fat (gm): 0
Cholesterol (mg): 0
Sodium (mg): 5
Protein (gm): 3.3
Carbohydrate (gm): 21

Exchanges:
Milk: 0.0
Vegetable: 1.0
Fruit: 0.0
Bread: 1.0
Meat: 0.0
Fat: 0.0

1. Combine corn, bell peppers, and garlic in lightly greased large skillet; cook, covered, over medium heat until vegetables are tender and browned, about 25 minutes, stirring occasionally. Add water and cook, covered, over low heat until water is absorbed, about 15 minutes. Season to taste with salt and pepper.

TEX-MEX SWEET CORN

45 *Flavors of the Southwest make corn-on-the-cob better than ever!*

V **6 servings**

2–3 tablespoons margarine
½ teaspoon each: chili and garlic powder, ground cumin, dried oregano leaves
⅛ teaspoon cayenne pepper
6 ears corn, cooked, warm
Salt, to taste
Chopped cilantro, as garnish

Per Serving:
Calories: 153
% of calories from fat: 25
Fat (gm): 4.8
Saturated fat (gm): 0.9
Cholesterol (mg): 0
Sodium (mg): 52
Protein (gm): 4.1
Carbohydrate (gm): 28.5

Exchanges:
Milk: 0.0
Vegetable: 0.0
Fruit: 0.0
Bread: 1.5
Meat: 0.0
Fat: 1.0

1. Heat margarine, herbs, and cayenne pepper in small saucepan over medium heat until butter is melted. Brush on corn; sprinkle lightly with salt and cilantro.

SEASONED EGGPLANT SAUTÉ

45

Simply delicious and easy to make!

V

4 servings

1½ pounds eggplant, unpeeled, cubed
1 cup chopped onion
½ cup chopped red bell pepper
6 cloves garlic, minced
¾ teaspoon each: dried oregano and thyme leaves
⅛ teaspoon crushed red pepper
½ cup reduced-sodium vegetable broth
Salt and pepper, to taste

Per Serving:
Calories: 83
% of calories from fat: 6
Fat (gm): 0.6
Saturated fat (gm): 0.1
Cholesterol (mg): 0
Sodium (mg): 18
Protein (gm): 2.8
Carbohydrate (gm): 19.3

Exchanges:
Milk: 0.0
Vegetable: 3.0
Fruit: 0.0
Bread: 0.0
Meat: 0.0
Fat: 0.0

1. Sauté vegetables, garlic, herbs, and red pepper in lightly greased large skillet 5 minutes. Add broth and heat to boiling; reduce heat and simmer, covered, until vegetables are tender and broth absorbed, 15 to 20 minutes. Season to taste with salt and pepper.

EGGPLANT AND VEGETABLE SAUTÉ

45

Minced roasted garlic is available in jars in your produce section; substitute fresh minced garlic if desired.

V

6 servings

1 large eggplant (about 1¼ pounds), unpeeled, cubed
1½ cups each: sliced red or green bell peppers, onions
4 teaspoons minced roasted garlic
½ teaspoon each: dried rosemary and thyme leaves
2 teaspoons olive oil
1 can (15 ounces) cannellini or Great Northern
  beans, rinsed, drained
Salt and pepper, to taste

Per Serving:
Calories: 109
% of calories from fat: 16
Fat (gm): 2
Saturated fat (gm): 0.3
Cholesterol (mg): 0
Sodium (mg): 114
Protein (gm): 4.1
Carbohydrate (gm): 19.1

Exchanges:
Milk: 0.0
Vegetable: 2.0
Fruit: 0.0
Bread: 1.0
Meat: 0.0
Fat: 0.5

1. Cook eggplant, bell pepper, onions garlic, and herbs in oil in large saucepan over medium heat, covered, until vegetables are tender, 8 to 10 minutes; stir in beans and cook until hot, about 2 minutes. Season to taste with salt and pepper.

EGGPLANT AND TOMATO CASSEROLE

L

45

Assemble the casserole up to a day in advance, then bake before serving—perfect potluck fare!

8 servings

1 large eggplant (about 1½ pounds), peeled, cubed (1-inch)

½ cup each: seasoned dry bread crumbs, chopped onion

3 cloves garlic, minced

2 teaspoons dried Italian seasoning

Salt and pepper, to taste

2 eggs, lightly beaten

3 medium tomatoes, sliced

¼ cup grated fat-free Parmesan cheese

Per Serving:
Calories: 98
% of calories from fat: 16
Fat (gm): 1.9
Saturated fat (gm): 0.5
Cholesterol (mg): 53.3
Sodium (mg): 245
Protein (gm): 5.1
Carbohydrate (gm): 16.9

Exchanges:
Milk: 0.0
Vegetable: 2.0
Fruit: 0.0
Bread: 0.5
Meat: 0.0
Fat: 0.5

1. Cook eggplant in 2 inches simmering water in medium saucepan, covered, until tender, 5 to 8 minutes; drain. Mash eggplant with fork; mix in bread crumbs, onion, garlic, and Italian seasoning. Season to taste with salt and pepper; mix in eggs. Spoon into greased 11 x 7-inch baking dish; arrange tomatoes over top and sprinkle with cheese. Bake, uncovered, at 350 degrees until hot, about 20 minutes.

LEMON-SPIKED GARLIC GREENS

45

0

Kale, collard, turnip, or beet greens make excellent choices for this quick and easy healthful dish.

4 servings

¼ cup each: finely chopped onion, red bell pepper

4 cloves garlic, minced

1½ pounds greens, coarsely chopped

½ cup water

1–2 tablespoons lemon juice

Salt and pepper, to taste

1 hard-cooked egg, chopped

1. Sauté onion, bell pepper, and garlic in lightly greased large saucepan until tender, 3 to 4 minutes. Add greens and water; heat to boiling. Reduce heat and simmer, covered, until greens are wilted, 4 to 5 minutes; drain. Season to taste with lemon juice, salt, and pepper; sprinkle with egg.

Per Serving:
Calories: 58
% of calories from fat: 23
Fat (gm): 1.7
Saturated fat (gm): 0.4
Cholesterol (mg): 53.3
Sodium (mg): 43
Protein (gm): 5.9
Carbohydrate (gm): 7

Exchanges:
Milk: 0.0
Vegetable: 2.0
Fruit: 0.0
Bread: 0.0
Meat: 0.0
Fat: 0.0

BRAISED KALE

45 *Packed with vitamins and minerals, kale and other dark leafy greens offer great nutrition. Try other greens such as beet, turnip, or mustard with this recipe too.*

4 servings

1 medium leek (white part only), sliced
2–3 teaspoons olive oil
1 pound kale, torn into pieces
½ cup reduced-sodium chicken broth
½ cup fat-free sour cream
1 teaspoon Dijon mustard
1–2 tablespoons crumbled cooked bacon
Salt and pepper, to taste

Per Serving:
Calories: 109
% of calories from fat: 27
Fat (gm): 3.5
Saturated fat (gm): 0.5
Cholesterol (mg): 0
Sodium (mg): 232
Protein (gm): 5.7
Carbohydrate (gm): 15.8

Exchanges:
Milk: 0.0
Vegetable: 3.0
Fruit: 0.0
Bread: 0.0
Meat: 0.0
Fat: 0.5

1. Sauté leek in oil in large saucepan until tender, 3 to 4 minutes. Add kale and chicken broth; heat to boiling. Reduce heat and simmer, covered, until kale is wilted, about 5 minutes; cook uncovered until greens are almost dry. Stir in sour cream, mustard, and bacon; cook over low heat 2 to 3 minutes. Season to taste with salt and pepper.

SAUTÉED LEEKS AND PEPPERS

45   *A colorful side dish that will brighten any meal!*

V   **6 servings**

3 medium leeks (white parts only), sliced (½-inch)
½ cup each: sliced yellow, red, and green bell pepper
½ teaspoon dried bouquet garni
Salt and pepper, to taste

1. Cook vegetables and bouquet garni in lightly greased large skillet, covered, over medium heat until softened, 2 to 3 minutes. Cook, uncovered, until vegetables are tender and beginning to brown, about 5 minutes. Season to taste with salt and pepper.

Per Serving:
Calories: 63
% of calories from fat: 5
Fat (gm): 0.4
Saturated fat (gm): 0
Cholesterol (mg): 0
Sodium (mg): 13
Protein (gm): 2
Carbohydrate (gm): 14.6

Exchanges:
Milk: 0.0
Vegetable: 2.5
Fruit: 0.0
Bread: 0.0
Meat: 0.0
Fat: 0.0

GULFPORT OKRA

45   *Select small okra for best flavor and tenderness.*

V   **6 servings**

1½ pounds fresh or frozen thawed, okra
Garlic powder, to taste
Salt and pepper, to taste

1. Cook okra in boiling water 1 to 2 minutes; drain. Cook okra in lightly greased large skillet over medium heat until well browned, about 10 minutes, stirring occasionally. Sprinkle generously with garlic powder; season to taste with salt and pepper.

Per Serving:
Calories: 37
% of calories from fat: 4
Fat (gm): 0.2
Saturated fat (gm): 0.1
Cholesterol (mg): 0
Sodium (mg): 6
Protein (gm): 2.1
Carbohydrate (gm): 8.2

Exchanges:
Milk: 0.0
Vegetable: 1.5
Fruit: 0.0
Bread: 0.0
Meat: 0.0
Fat: 0.0

QUARTET OF ONIONS

45

V

Cooked slowly until caramelized, the onion mixture is scented with mint and sage.

6 servings

2 pounds sweet onions, sliced

1 small leek (white part only), thinly sliced

½ cup each: chopped shallots, sliced green onions, reduced sodium vegetable broth

1–1½ teaspoons dried mint leaves

½ teaspoon dried sage leaves

Salt and white pepper, to taste

Per Serving:
Calories: 90
% of calories from fat: 4
Fat (gm): 0.4
Saturated fat (gm): 0.1
Cholesterol (mg): 0
Sodium (mg): 16
Protein (gm): 2.7
Carbohydrate (gm): 20.1

Exchanges:
Milk: 0.0
Vegetable: 4.0
Fruit: 0.0
Bread: 0.0
Meat: 0.0
Fat: 0.0

1. Sauté onions, leek, shallots, and green onions in lightly greased large skillet 3 to 4 minutes. Stir in broth and herbs and heat to boiling; reduce heat and simmer, covered, 5 minutes. Cook, uncovered, over medium-low heat until onion mixture is golden, about 15 minutes. Season to taste with salt and white pepper.

FRUIT-STUFFED VIDALIA ONIONS

V

The onions can be poached and filled with fruit up to 1 day in advance; increase baking time 10 to 15 minutes.

4 servings

2 large Vidalia onions, cut crosswise into halves

½ cup each: water, dry white wine

4 each: whole peppercorns, allspice

1 teaspoon mustard seeds

2 bay leaves

Salt, to taste

1 small apple, unpeeled, finely chopped

¼ cup each: chopped dried fruit, golden raisins

2–3 teaspoons sugar

Per Serving:
Calories: 142
% of calories from fat: 4
Fat (gm): 0.6
Saturated fat (gm): 0.1
Cholesterol (mg): 0
Sodium (mg): 7
Protein (gm): 1.9
Carbohydrate (gm): 30.5

Exchanges:
Milk: 0.0
Vegetable: 2.0
Fruit: 1.5
Bread: 0.0
Meat: 0.0
Fat: 0.0

1. Cut small slices off bottoms of onion halves so onions can stand securely. Remove centers of onions, leaving scant ¾-inch shells;

chop onion centers and reserve. Stand onions in medium skillet; add water, wine, and seasonings; heat to boiling. Reduce heat and simmer, covered, until crisp-tender, about 10 minutes. Remove onions with slotted spoon and transfer to baking pan; sprinkle lightly with salt. Reserve ¼ cup cooking liquid.

2. Sauté reserved onion centers and apple in lightly greased small skillet until tender, about 5 minutes. Stir in reserved ¼ cup cooking liquid, dried fruit, raisins, and sugar; cook over medium-low heat until liquid is absorbed. Spoon into onion halves. Bake, covered, at 375 degrees until onions are tender, 20 to 30 minutes.

BRAISED PARSNIPS AND WINTER VEGETABLES

45

V

Idaho or sweet potatoes, winter squash, or Brussels sprouts would be flavorful additions to this colorful vegetable dish.

6 servings

1 cup each: sliced parsnips, carrots, cubed celery root or celery, shredded red or green cabbage

¼ cup minced onion

2 teaspoons minced garlic

½ cup dry red wine or vegetable broth

2 tablespoons light brown sugar

1 teaspoon balsamic or red wine vinegar

¾ teaspoon each: dried sage and thyme leaves

Salt and pepper, to taste

Per Serving:
Calories: 92
% of calories from fat: 3
Fat (gm): 0.3
Saturated fat (gm): 0.1
Cholesterol (mg): 0
Sodium (mg): 47
Protein (gm): 1.5
Carbohydrate (gm): 19.3

Exchanges:
Milk: 0.0
Vegetable: 2.0
Fruit: 0.0
Bread: 0.5
Meat: 0.0
Fat: 0.0

1. Sauté vegetables and garlic in lightly greased large skillet until beginning to brown, 8 to 10 minutes; add remaining ingredients, except salt and pepper, and heat to boiling; reduce heat and simmer, covered, until vegetables are tender, 8 to 10 minutes. Season to taste with salt and pepper.

PEPERONATA

45

V

Sweet bell peppers and onions are slowly cooked until tender and creamy in this Italian-inspired dish.

8 servings

2 cups sliced onions
1 cup each: sliced green and red bell pepper
6 cloves garlic, minced
¼ cup water
Salt and pepper, to taste

Per Serving:
Calories: 29
% of calories from fat: 4
Fat (gm): 0.1
Saturated fat (gm): 0.0
Cholesterol (mg): 0.0
Sodium (mg): 2.5
Protein (gm): 1
Carbohydrate (gm): 7

Exchanges:
Milk: 0.0
Vegetable: 1.0
Fruit: 0.0
Bread: 0.0
Meat: 0.0
Fat: 0.0

1. Sauté vegetables and garlic in lightly greased medium skillet over medium heat 5 minutes, stirring occasionally. Add water and cook, covered, over medium-low heat until vegetables are very tender, 20 to 25 minutes, stirring occasionally. Season to taste with salt and pepper.

GREENS AND SMASHED POTATOES

45

The potatoes are not peeled, giving this dish a rustic character.

4 servings

¼ cup finely chopped onion
3 cloves garlic, minced
1½ cups thinly sliced greens (kale, mustard, or
   turnip greens)
¼ cup water
3 medium Idaho potatoes, cubed, cooked
¼ cup fat-free sour cream
2–4 tablespoons fat-free milk
1–2 tablespoons margarine or butter
Salt and pepper, to taste

Per Serving:
Calories: 141
% of calories from fat: 19
Fat (gm): 3.1
Saturated fat (gm): 0.6
Cholesterol (mg): 0.1
Sodium (mg): 60
Protein (gm): 3.8
Carbohydrate (gm): 25.4

Exchanges:
Milk: 0.0
Vegetable: 2.0
Fruit: 0.0
Bread: 1.0
Meat: 0.0
Fat: 0.5

1. Sauté onion and garlic in lightly greased medium skillet until tender, 3 to 4 minutes. Add greens and water; heat to boiling. Reduce heat and simmer, covered, until greens are tender about

5 minutes; cook, uncovered until water has evaporated and greens are almost dry.

2. Mash potatoes with potato masher or electric mixer, adding sour cream, milk, and margarine; stir into greens and cook over low heat until hot, about 5 minutes. Season to taste with salt and pepper.

45-MINUTE PREPARATION TIP: Begin cooking potatoes before preparing the rest of the recipe.

CREAMY POTATO AND BEAN MASHERS

45   *Beans boost flavor and nutrition in this great dish!*

L   6 servings

1 pound Idaho potatoes, unpeeled, quartered, cooked

1 can (15½ ounces) Great Northern or navy beans, rinsed, drained

1–2 teaspoon minced roasted garlic

2 tablespoons margarine or butter

¼–½ cup fat-free milk, hot

Salt and pepper, to taste

Per Serving:
Calories: 187
% of calories from fat: 20
Fat (gm): 4
Saturated fat (gm): 0.9
Cholesterol (mg): 0.2
Sodium (mg): 55
Protein (gm): 7
Carbohydrate (gm): 31

Exchanges:
Milk: 0.0
Vegetable: 0.0
Fruit: 0.0
Bread: 2.0
Meat: 0.0
Fat: 1.0

1. Mash potatoes, beans, garlic, and margarine in medium bowl, adding enough milk for desired consistency; season to taste with salt and pepper. Heat in saucepan over medium heat until hot, about 5 minutes.

VARIATIONS

Cheesy Bean and Onion Mashers — Sauté 1 cup chopped onion in 1 tablespoon margarine in small skillet until tender, about 5 minutes. Make recipe as above, adding onion and remaining 1 tablespoon margarine.

Lima Bean and Mushroom Mashers — Sauté 1 cup quartered cremini mushrooms in 2 tablespoons margarine in small skillet until tender, about 5 minutes. Make recipe as above, substituting lima beans for the Great Northern beans and deleting margarine; stir in mushrooms.

Mashed Potato and Bean Colcannon — Make recipe as above; keep warm. Sauté 3 cups thinly sliced cabbage and ½ teaspoon crushed caraway seeds in 1 tablespoon margarine 3 to 4 minutes; add ¼ cup water and cook, covered, until tender, about 5 minutes. Cook uncovered until liquid is gone, 3 to 4 minutes; season to taste with salt and pepper. Mix into potato-bean mixture.

ROOT VEGGIES AND MASHED POTATOES

L

45

A selection of winter root vegetables, roasted to perfection and served with garlic-spiked mashed potatoes.

8 servings

3 each: peeled, cubed medium beets, turnips
2 cups halved Brussels sprouts
1 cup baby carrots
1 leek (white part only), thickly sliced
Vegetable cooking spray
1 tablespoon caraway seeds
Salt and pepper, to taste
1½ pounds Idaho potatoes, unpeeled, cubed
4 cloves garlic, peeled
¼ cup fat-free milk, hot
2 tablespoons margarine or butter, cut into pieces

Per Serving:
Calories: 194
% of calories from fat: 15
Fat (gm): 3.5
Saturated fat (gm): 0.7
Cholesterol (mg): 0.1
Sodium (mg): 164
Protein (gm): 6.2
Carbohydrate (gm): 37.8

Exchanges:
Milk: 0.0
Vegetable: 1.0
Fruit: 0.0
Bread: 2.0
Meat: 0.0
Fat: 0.5

1. Arrange beets, turnips, Brussels sprouts, carrots, and leek in single layer on greased foil-lined jelly roll pan; spray with cooking spray and sprinkle with caraway seeds, salt and pepper. Bake at 450 degrees until vegetables are tender and lightly browned, about 25 minutes.

2. Cook potatoes and garlic in simmering water in covered saucepan until tender, 10 to 15 minutes; drain. Mash potatoes and garlic with potato masher or electric mixer, adding milk and margarine. Season to taste with salt and pepper. Heat in saucepan over medium heat until hot, about 5 minutes. Spoon roasted vegetables over potatoes.

VEGGIE-STUFFED BAKERS

The potatoes are greased and baked for a crispy skin; for a softer skin, wrap in aluminum foil.

6 servings

2 large Idaho potatoes (8–10 ounces each)

⅓ cup fat-free sour cream or plain yogurt

¾ cup (3 ounces) shredded fat-free Cheddar cheese, divided

1 cup each: chopped onion, green bell pepper

½ cup whole-kernel corn

4 cloves garlic, minced

Salt and pepper, to taste

1 cup broccoli florets, cooked crisp-tender

Per Serving:
Calories: 160
% of calories from fat: 2
Fat (gm): 0.3
Saturated fat (gm): 0
Cholesterol (mg): 0
Sodium (mg): 119
Protein (gm): 9
Carbohydrate (gm): 32.4

Exchanges:
Milk: 0.0
Vegetable: 1.0
Fruit: 0.0
Bread: 1.5
Meat: 0.5
Fat: 0.0

1. Pierce potatoes with a fork; grease lightly and bake at 400 degrees until tender, about 1 hour. Cut lengthwise into halves; let stand until cool enough to handle. Scoop out potatoes, being careful to leave shells intact. Mash potatoes in medium bowl, adding sour cream and half the Cheddar cheese.

2. Sauté onion, bell pepper, corn, and garlic in lightly greased medium skillet until tender, about 5 minutes. Mix into potatoes; season to taste with salt and pepper. Spoon into potato shells; arrange broccoli on top and sprinkle with remaining cheese. Bake, uncovered, at 350 degrees until hot, 20 to 30 minutes.

POTATOES WITH POBLANO CHILIES

In this recipe, roasted poblano chilies are combined with potatoes for a hearty side dish. Serve with fried eggs and salsa for a brunch entrée.

4 servings

4 medium poblano chilies, halved

1 medium onion, sliced

1 pound Idaho potatoes, unpeeled, cooked, cubed

Salt and pepper, to taste

1. Broil chilies, skin sides up, 6 inches from heat source until skin is blackened and blistered. Wrap chilies in plastic bag or paper toweling 5 minutes; peel off skin and discard. Cut chilies into strips. Sauté chilies, onion, and potatoes in lightly greased large skillet over medium heat until onion is tender and potatoes browned, about 8 minutes. Season to taste with salt and pepper.

Per Serving:
Calories: 147
% of calories from fat: 2
Fat (gm): 0.3
Saturated fat (gm): 0.1
Cholesterol (mg): 0
Sodium (mg): 11
Protein (gm): 3.7
Carbohydrate (gm): 34

Exchanges:
Milk: 0.0
Vegetable: 1.0
Fruit: 0.0
Bread: 1.5
Meat: 0.0
Fat: 0.0

POTATOES GRATIN

These potatoes taste so rich and creamy you'll never imagine they were made without heavy cream!

8 servings

2 tablespoons margarine or butter

3 tablespoons flour

1¾ cups fat-free milk

2 ounces light pasteurized processed cheese, cubed

½ cup (2 ounces) shredded reduced-fat
   Cheddar cheese

Salt and pepper, to taste

2 pounds Idaho potatoes, peeled, sliced (¼-inch)

¼ cup thinly sliced onion

Ground nutmeg, to taste

Per Serving:
Calories: 202
% of calories from fat: 23
Fat (gm): 5.1
Saturated fat (gm): 1.7
Cholesterol (mg): 8.5
Sodium (mg): 259
Protein (gm): 7.6
Carbohydrate (gm): 31.7

Exchanges:
Milk: 0.0
Vegetable: 0.0
Fruit: 0.0
Bread: 2.0
Meat: 0.5
Fat: 0.5

1. Melt margarine in medium saucepan; stir in flour and stir over medium heat 2 minutes. Whisk in milk and heat to boiling; boil, whisking until thickened, about 1 minute. Remove from heat; add cheeses, stirring until melted. Season to taste with salt and pepper.

2. Layer ⅓ of the potatoes and onion in greased 2-quart casserole; sprinkle lightly with salt, pepper, and nutmeg. Spoon ⅔ cup sauce over. Repeat layers 2 times. Bake, covered, at 350 degrees 45 minutes; uncover and bake until potatoes are tender and browned, 20 to 30 minutes.

VARIATIONS

Scalloped Potatoes — Make sauce as above, increasing margarine to 3 tablespoons, flour to ¼ cup, and milk to 2¼ cups; delete cheeses. Assemble and bake as directed.

Scalloped Potatoes and Ham — Make Scalloped Potatoes as above, layering 12 ounces cubed lean smoked ham between potatoes.

POTATOES AND WILD MUSHROOMS AU GRATIN

L

45

This time-savvy casserole utilizes a variety of convenience foods to speed preparation.

6 servings

½ cup each: chopped red or green bell pepper, onion, frozen tiny peas

1½ cups frozen broccoli florets

1½ ounces dried shiitake mushrooms, broken into small pieces (about 6 mushrooms)

2 cups water

1 package (4½ ounces) dried julienned potatoes

¾ cup fat-free milk

1–1½ cups (4–6 ounces) shredded reduced-fat Swiss or Cheddar cheese

Per Serving:
Calories: 199
% of calories from fat: 20
Fat (gm): 4.5
Saturated fat (gm): 2.1
Cholesterol (mg): 14.1
Sodium (mg): 572
Protein (gm): 12.5
Carbohydrate (gm): 28.7

Exchanges:
Milk: 0.0
Vegetable: 3.0
Fruit: 0.0
Bread: 1.0
Meat: 0.0
Fat: 1.0

1. Sauté bell pepper and onion in lightly greased medium saucepan until tender, about 5 minutes. Add peas, broccoli, dried mushrooms, and water; heat to boiling. Pour mixture over potato and sauce mix in 2-quart casserole; stir in milk and cheese. Bake, uncovered, at 400 degrees until golden, 20 to 30 minutes.

COUNTRY-STYLE POTATO KUGEL

O

This hash brown kugel owes its light texture to beaten sauce (see Index).

45

6 servings

2 packages (5½ ounces each) hash brown potato mix with onions

3 cups boiling water

6 egg yolks, lightly beaten

1½ cups cold water

1 teaspoon each: baking powder, dried basil and oregano leaves, salt

2 tablespoons snipped chives

½ teaspoon pepper

6 egg whites, beaten to stiff peaks

Per Serving:
Calories: 123
% of calories from fat: 28
Fat (gm): 3.9
Saturated fat (gm): 1.2
Cholesterol (mg): 159.8
Sodium (mg): 559
Protein (gm): 6.3
Carbohydrate (gm): 15.8

Exchanges:
Milk: 0.0
Vegetable: 0.0
Fruit: 0.0
Bread: 1.0
Meat: 1.0
Fat: 0.0

1. Place potato mix in large bowl; pour boiling water over. Let stand 20 to 25 minutes, stirring occasionally. Mix combined remaining ingredients, except egg whites, into potatoes. Fold potato mixture into egg whites. Spoon mixture into lightly greased 11 x 7-inch baking dish; bake at 300 degrees until browned and set, about 1 hour.

CRISPY FRENCH "FRIES"

V

Golden brown, delicious, and crisp, these potatoes look and taste like they've been deep-fried: salting the raw potatoes is the secret!

45

4–6 servings

1 pound Idaho potatoes, unpeeled

2 teaspoons salt

Vegetable cooking spray

Salt and pepper, to taste

Per Serving:
Calories: 166
% of calories from fat: 1
Fat (gm): 0.2
Saturated fat (gm): 0
Cholesterol (mg): 0
Sodium (mg): 12
Protein (gm): 3.5
Carbohydrate (gm): 38.6

Exchanges:
Milk: 0.0
Vegetable: 0.0
Fruit: 0.0
Bread: 2.5
Meat: 0.0
Fat: 0.0

1. Cut potatoes into sticks 3 to 4 inches long and a scant ½ inch wide. Sprinkle lightly with 2 teaspoons salt and let stand 10 minutes. Rinse in cold water and dry on paper toweling. Arrange potatoes in single layer on greased foil-lined jelly roll pan; spray with cooking spray, tossing to coat all sides. Sprinkle lightly with salt and pepper. Bake at 350 degrees until golden brown and crisp, 40 to 45 minutes, turning halfway through cooking time.

NOTE: Potatoes can be kept warm in a 200-degree oven for up to 1 hour.

VARIATIONS

Parmesan "Fries" — Make recipe as above, sprinkling potatoes lightly with grated fat-free Parmesan cheese before baking.

Steak Fries — Make recipe as above, cutting potatoes into wedges 4 inches long and 1 inch wide, and increasing baking time to 1 to 1¼ hours.

ORANGE-LIME SWEET POTATOES

45

V

Sweet potatoes are gently sauced with citrus juices; use freshly squeezed juices for best flavor.

6 servings

1 cup chopped onion
1 teaspoon minced garlic
1 pound sweet potatoes, peeled, cubed (1-inch)
1 cup orange juice
¼ cup lime juice
Salt and pepper, to taste

Per Serving:
Calories: 95
% of calories from fat: 3
Fat (gm): 0.3
Saturated fat (gm): 0.1
Cholesterol (mg): 0
Sodium (mg): 9
Protein (gm): 1.7
Carbohydrate (gm): 22.3

Exchanges:
Milk: 0.0
Vegetable: 0.0
Fruit: 0.5
Bread: 1.0
Meat: 0.0
Fat: 0.0

1. Sauté onion and garlic in lightly greased medium skillet 3 to 4 minutes. Add sweet potatoes and juices; heat to boiling. Reduce heat and simmer, covered, until potatoes are tender, about 10 minutes. Cook, uncovered, until juices are thickened, 8 to 10 minutes. Season to taste with salt and pepper.

SWEET POTATO PONE

LO

45

More of a country-style pudding than a soufflé, this comfort food will become a favorite. Drizzle with warm maple syrup, if you like.

4 servings

1 small onion, finely chopped

1 tablespoon margarine or butter

3 tablespoons flour

1 cup fat-free milk

2 eggs

2 cups cubed sweet potatoes, cooked, coarsely mashed

2 tablespoons packed light brown sugar

¼ teaspoon each: ground cinnamon, cloves, salt

2–3 dashes white pepper

4 egg whites, beaten to stiff peaks

Per Serving:
Calories: 179
% of calories from fat: 16
Fat (gm): 3.1
Saturated fat (gm): 0.7
Cholesterol (mg): 1.0
Sodium (mg): 303
Protein (gm): 5.5
Carbohydrate (gm): 27.7

Exchanges:
Milk: 0.0
Vegetable: 0.5
Fruit: 0.0
Bread: 1.0
Meat: 0.5
Fat: 0.0

1. Sauté onion in margarine in small saucepan until tender, 3 to 5 minutes. Stir in flour; cook 1 to 2 minutes. Stir in milk and heat to boiling, stirring, until thickened, about 1 minute. Remove from heat.

2. Beat eggs in medium bowl until thick and lemon colored, 3 to 4 minutes. Slowly whisk milk mixture into eggs; mix in remaining ingredients, except egg whites. Fold in egg whites. Spoon into greased 1-quart soufflé dish or casserole. Bake, uncovered, at 375 degrees until puffed and golden and a sharp knife inserted halfway between center and edge comes out almost clean, 30 to 35 minutes.

45-MINUTE PREPARATION TIP: Begin cooking sweet potatoes before preparing the rest of the recipe.

CANDIED YAMS

V

45

Whether they are called yams or sweet potatoes in your family, the sweet goodness of this dish is the same! If marshmallows are a must, add them 10 minutes before the end of baking time.

8–10 servings

⅓ cup packed light brown sugar

2 tablespoons light corn syrup

1 tablespoon each: flour, margarine

1 can (40 ounces) cut sweet potatoes in syrup, drained, sliced

Per Serving:
Calories: 176
% of calories from fat: 8
Fat (gm): 1.5
Saturated fat (gm): 0.3
Cholesterol (mg): 0
Sodium (mg): 63
Protein (gm): 1.5
Carbohydrate (gm): 39.5

Exchanges:
Milk: 0.0
Vegetable: 0.0
Fruit: 0.0
Bread: 2.5
Meat: 0.0
Fat: 0.0

1. Combine brown sugar, corn syrup, flour, and margarine in small saucepan; heat just to boiling, stirring. Layer sweet potatoes in 10 x 6-inch baking dish, spooning sugar mixture between each layer and over the top. Bake, uncovered, at 350 degrees until hot, 25 to 30 minutes.

NOTE: Two pounds fresh sweet potatoes can be substituted for the canned. Peel and slice potatoes. Cook, covered, in medium saucepan in 2 to 3 inches of simmering water until fork-tender, about 10 minutes. Drain well, cool slightly, and proceed with recipe.

HOLIDAY SWEET POTATO LOAF WITH APPLE-CRANBERRY RELISH

0

Perfect for the winter holidays—but this loaf is so delicious and easy to make, you'll want to serve it year-round.

12 servings

2½ cups coarsely grated, peeled sweet potatoes

1 each: finely chopped onion, tart cooking apple

½ cup raisins

1 teaspoon dried thyme leaves

½ teaspoon ground cinnamon

¼ teaspoon ground nutmeg

½ cup all-purpose flour

¼ cup orange juice

Salt and pepper, to taste

2 eggs

1 egg white

Apple-Cranberry Relish (recipe follows)

Per Serving:
Calories: 421
% of calories from fat: 12
Fat (gm): 5.6
Saturated fat (gm): 1
Cholesterol (mg): 71
Sodium (mg): 63.6
Protein (gm): 7.3
Carbohydrate (gm): 88.9

1. Mix sweet potatoes, onion, apple, raisins, seasonings, flour, and orange juice in bowl; season to taste with salt and pepper. Mix in eggs and egg white. Pack mixture in greased 7½ x 3¾-inch loaf pan. Bake, covered, at 350 degrees until loaf is set, about 1 hour. Let stand 10 minutes before serving. Loosen sides of loaf with sharp knife; unmold onto serving plate. Slice loaf and serve with Apple-Cranberry Relish.

Exchanges:
Milk: 0.0
Vegetable: 0.0
Fruit: 3.0
Bread: 3.0
Meat: 0.0
Fat: 0.5

Apple-Cranberry Relish
Makes about 1½ cups

1 cup whole berry cranberry sauce
½ cup each: coarsely chopped tart apple, segmented orange
¼ cup each: chopped pecans or walnuts, sugar
1 tablespoon grated lemon zest

1. Heat all ingredients in small saucepan over medium heat until sugar is dissolved and apple is tender, 3 to 5 minutes. Cool.

CREAMED SPINACH

45

Try this recipe with other dark leafy greens, such as Swiss chard or kale.

L

4 servings

¼ cup finely chopped onion

2 teaspoons margarine or butter

2 tablespoons flour

1 cup fat-free milk or fat-free half-and-half

2 packages (10 ounces each) fresh spinach,
    cooked, drained

¼ cup fat-free sour cream

Ground nutmeg, to taste

Salt and pepper, to taste

Per Serving:
Calories: 92
% of calories from fat: 20
Fat (gm): 2.2
Saturated fat (gm): 0.5
Cholesterol (mg): 1
Sodium (mg): 145
Protein (gm): 6.6
Carbohydrate (gm): 13.3

Exchanges:
Milk: 0.0
Vegetable: 2.5
Fruit: 0.0
Bread: 0.0
Meat: 0.0
Fat: 0.5

1. Sauté onion in margarine in small saucepan until tender, 3 to 5 minutes. Stir in flour; cook 1 minute. Whisk in milk and heat to boiling; boil, whisking until thickened, about 1 minute. Reduce heat to medium; stir in spinach and sour cream. Cook until hot, 2 to 3 minutes; season to taste with nutmeg, salt, and pepper.

VARIATION

Spinach au Gratin — Prepare recipe as directed above, reserving ⅓ cup sauce; mix spinach and remaining sauce and spoon into a small casserole. Spread reserved sauce over spinach; sprinkle with ¼ cup (1 ounce) grated Parmesan or Cheddar cheese. Bake, uncovered, at 375 degrees until cheese is melted, 5 to 8 minutes.

APPLE-PECAN ACORN SQUASH

V

Fruit and maple flavors complement sweet, baked winter squash.

45

4 servings

1 large acorn squash, quartered, seeded

½ cup coarsely chopped mixed dried fruit

1 small sweet apple, cored, coarsely chopped

¼–½ cup coarsely chopped, toasted pecans

½ teaspoon ground cinnamon

⅛ teaspoon each: ground nutmeg, mace

¼–½ cup maple syrup

1. Place squash quarters, cut sides up, in baking pan; add ½ inch hot water. Bake, covered, at 400 degrees until squash is fork-tender, about 30 minutes. Spoon combined fruit, pecans, and spices into squash; drizzle with maple syrup. Bake, loosely covered, at 350 degrees until apples are tender, about 10 minutes.

Per Serving:
Calories: 187
% of calories from fat: 1
Fat (gm): 0.3
Saturated fat (gm): 0.1
Cholesterol (mg): 0
Sodium (mg): 39
Protein (gm): 1.7
Carbohydrate (gm): 47

Exchanges:
Milk: 0.0
Vegetable: 0.0
Fruit: 2.0
Bread: 1.0
Meat: 0.0
Fat: 0.0

CHAYOTE WITH PEPITAS

45

V

To toast the pepitas (Mexican pumpkin seeds), cook over medium heat in a lightly greased skillet. They will begin to pop and jump in the skillet, signaling that they are toasted!

4 servings

½ cup finely chopped onion

2 cloves garlic, minced

1 chayote squash, peeled, pitted, cubed

4 teaspoons pepitas, toasted

Salt and pepper, to taste

1. Sauté onion and garlic in lightly greased large skillet until tender, 3 to 5 minutes. Add squash and cook over medium heat until squash is crisp-tender, about 20 minutes, stirring occasionally. Stir in pepitas; season to taste with salt and pepper.

Per Serving:
Calories: 35
% of calories from fat: 16
Fat (gm): 0.7
Saturated fat (gm): 0.1
Cholesterol (mg): 0
Sodium (mg): 2
Protein (gm): 1.1
Carbohydrate (gm): 7

Exchanges:
Milk: 0.0
Vegetable: 1.5
Fruit: 0.0
Bread: 0.0
Meat: 0.0
Fat: 0.0

PARMESAN-HERB SPAGHETTI SQUASH

Italian seasoning and Parmesan cheese compliment the delicate flavor of the squash.

4 servings

1 spaghetti squash (2½–3 pounds), halved lengthwise, seeded
2 tablespoons sliced green onions
1 teaspoon each: minced garlic, dried Italian seasoning
1–2 tablespoons margarine or butter
¼ cup reduced-sodium vegetable broth or water
½ cup (2 ounces) fat-free Parmesan cheese
Salt and pepper, to taste

Per Serving:
Calories: 99
% of calories from fat: 29
Fat (gm): 3.6
Saturated fat (gm): 0.7
Cholesterol (mg): 0
Sodium (mg): 102
Protein (gm): 5.1
Carbohydrate (gm): 14.3

Exchanges:
Milk: 0.0
Vegetable: 2.0
Fruit: 0.0
Bread: 0.0
Meat: 0.5
Fat: 0.5

1. Place squash, cut sides down, in baking pan; add ½ inch hot water. Bake, covered, at 450 degrees until tender, about 30 minutes. Fluff strands of squash with tines of fork, leaving squash in shells.

2. Sauté green onions, garlic, and Italian seasoning in margarine in small saucepan until tender, 3 to 4 minutes. Stir in broth; cook until hot, about 2 minutes. Spoon half the mixture into each squash half and toss; sprinkle with Parmesan cheese and toss. Season to taste with salt and pepper.

ZUCCHINI FROM PUEBLA

If the Mexican white cheese queso blanco is not available, farmer's cheese or feta cheese can be easily substituted.

6 servings

1 cup chopped onion
2 pounds zucchini, diagonally sliced (¼-inch)
4 roasted red bell peppers, sliced
½ cup reduced-sodium vegetable broth
½–1 teaspoon ground cumin
Salt and pepper, to taste
2 tablespoons crumbled Mexican white cheese

1. Sauté onion in lightly greased large skillet until tender, 5 to 8 minutes. Add zucchini, roasted peppers, broth, and cumin. Heat to boiling. Reduce heat and simmer, covered, until zucchini is crisp-tender, 5 to 8 minutes. Season to taste with salt and pepper; sprinkle with cheese.

Per Serving:
Calories: 62
% of calories from fat: 14
Fat (gm): 1
Saturated fat (gm): 0.1
Cholesterol (mg): 2.6
Sodium (mg): 32
Protein (gm): 2.9
Carbohydrate (gm): 11.8

Exchanges:
Milk: 0.0
Vegetable: 2.0
Fruit: 0.0
Bread: 0.0
Meat: 0.0
Fat: 0.0

ZUCCHINI FANS PROVENÇAL

| V |

Zucchini are thinly sliced, then spread out to form "fans."

| 45 |

4 servings

2 medium sweet onions, thinly sliced

6 cloves garlic, minced

4 small zucchini, halved lengthwise

3 medium tomatoes, thinly sliced

½ cup dry white wine or reduced-sodium vegetable broth

Salt and pepper, to taste

1½ teaspoons dried Italian seasoning

Per Serving:
Calories: 89
% of calories from fat: 6
Fat (gm): 0.6
Saturated fat (gm): 0.1
Cholesterol (mg): 0
Sodium (mg): 16
Protein (gm): 3.4
Carbohydrate (gm): 15.3

Exchanges:
Milk: 0.0
Vegetable: 3.0
Fruit: 0.0
Bread: 0.0
Meat: 0.0
Fat: 0.0

1. Separate onions into rings; arrange half the onions and garlic in bottom of 11 x 7-inch baking pan. Cut zucchini halves lengthwise into scant ¼-inch slices, cutting to, but not through, small ends. Alternate zucchini and tomato slices in rows over onions, spreading zucchini slices into "fans." Arrange remaining onions and garlic on top; pour wine over. Sprinkle lightly with salt, pepper and Italian seasoning. Bake, covered, at 350 degrees until zucchini is tender, about 25 minutes.

FRIED TOMATOES

45

Either green or red tomatoes can be used in this recipe—try both!

V

4 servings

4 medium green or red tomatoes, sliced (¼-inch)
¼ cup all-purpose flour
Salt and pepper, to taste

Per Serving:
Calories: 58
% of calories from fat: 5
Fat (gm): 0.3
Saturated fat (gm): 0
Cholesterol (mg): 0
Sodium (mg): 16
Protein (gm): 2.3
Carbohydrate (gm): 12.2

1. Coat tomato slices lightly with flour; cook over medium heat in lightly greased large skillet until browned, 2 to 3 minutes on each side. Sprinkle lightly with salt and pepper.

Exchanges:
Milk: 0.0
Vegetable: 1.0
Fruit: 0.0
Bread: 0.5
Meat: 0.0
Fat: 0.0

VARIATIONS

Sugar-Glazed Fried Tomatoes — Make recipe as above, but do not coat with flour. After tomatoes are browned, sprinkle lightly with sugar and cook until caramelized, about 1 minute on each side. Do not season with salt and pepper.

Cornmeal-Fried Tomatoes — Make recipe as above, substituting yellow cornmeal for the flour.

GREENS-STUFFED BAKED TOMATOES

L

45

We've used turnip greens, but any other flavorful greens, such as kale, mustard greens, or spinach, may be substituted.

6 servings

6 medium tomatoes
10 ounces fresh or frozen turnip greens, cooked, coarsely chopped
½ teaspoon each: dried chervil and marjoram leaves
Salt and pepper, to taste
1 tablespoon each: grated fat-free Parmesan cheese, unseasoned dry bread crumbs

Per Serving:
Calories: 42
% of calories from fat: 11
Fat (gm): 0.6
Saturated fat (gm): 0.1
Cholesterol (mg): 0
Sodium (mg): 42
Protein (gm): 2.1
Carbohydrate (gm): 9

Exchanges:
Milk: 0.0
Vegetable: 2.0
Fruit: 0.0
Bread: 0.0
Meat: 0.0
Fat: 0.0

1. Cut thin slice from tops of tomatoes; scoop pulp from tomatoes, discarding seeds. Chop pulp and mix with turnip greens and herbs; season to taste with salt and pepper. Spoon into tomatoes and sprinkle with combined cheese and bread crumbs. Place in baking pan and bake at 350 degrees until tender, about 20 minutes.

TOMATO PUDDING

Dry stuffing cubes can be substituted for the croutons. Two cups coarsely chopped fresh tomatoes can be substituted for the canned tomatoes; simmer until tomatoes wilt and release juices, 5 to 8 minutes.

4 servings

½ cup each: thinly sliced celery, chopped onion, green bell pepper

1 can (16 ounces) reduced-sodium diced tomatoes, undrained

½ teaspoon each: celery seeds, dried marjoram leaves

1 tablespoon light brown sugar

Salt and pepper, to taste

1½ cups (½ recipe) Sourdough Croutons (see p. 498)

Per Serving:
Calories: 85
% of calories from fat: 9
Fat (gm): 0.9
Saturated fat (gm): 0.1
Cholesterol (mg): 0
Sodium (mg): 88
Protein (gm): 2.6
Carbohydrate (gm): 17.9

Exchanges:
Milk: 0.0
Vegetable: 2.0
Fruit: 0.0
Bread: 0.5
Meat: 0.0
Fat: 0.0

1. Sauté celery, onion, and bell pepper in lightly greased medium skillet until tender, about 8 minutes. Add tomatoes with liquid, celery seeds, marjoram, and brown sugar; season to taste with salt and pepper. Spoon into 1-quart soufflé dish or casserole. Stir in Sourdough Croutons, leaving some of the croutons on top. Bake, uncovered, at 375 degrees until hot, about 20 minutes.

45-MINUTE PREPARATION TIP: Make Sourdough Croutons before preparing the rest of the recipe.

TWELVE

Salads

and

Dressings

SMOKED CHICKEN BREAST AND LINGUINE SALAD

No time to grill? Smoked chicken or turkey breast from the deli can be used in this salad.

4 entrée servings

1 pound boneless, skinless chicken breast
8 ounces linguine, cooked, room temperature
2 cups sliced carrots, cooked crisp-tender
½ can (15-ounce size) quartered artichoke hearts, drained, rinsed
12 cherry tomatoes, halved
¼ cup sliced green onions
Sour Cream Dressing (recipe follows)

Per Serving:
Calories: 404
% of calories from fat: 11
Fat (gm): 5.2
Saturated fat (gm): 0.8
Cholesterol (mg): 58
Sodium (mg): 800
Protein (gm): 34.9
Carbohydrate (gm): 58.5

Exchanges:
Milk: 0.0
Vegetable: 4.0
Fruit: 0.0
Bread: 2.5
Meat: 2.0
Fat: 0.0

1. Smoke chicken in smoker or on grill, using manufacturer's directions. Cool; refrigerate several hours or overnight to allow flavor to mellow. Shred or cube chicken; combine with remaining ingredients and toss.

Sour Cream Dressing

Makes about ⅔ cup

⅓ cup each: fat-free sour cream, mayonnaise
1 tablespoon red wine vinegar
1 clove garlic, minced
½ teaspoon each: crushed dried rosemary leaves, salt
¼ teaspoon pepper

1. Mix all ingredients.

BLACK BEAN AND SMOKED CHICKEN SALAD

The smoky flavor of the chicken is a pleasant contrast to the picante chili, fresh cilantro, and Mustard-Honey Dressing.

4 entree servings

2 cans (15 ounces each) black beans, rinsed, drained

12 ounces smoked chicken breast, cubed

1 cup each: chopped tomato, red bell pepper

½ cup sliced red onion

¼ cup each: finely chopped cilantro, parsley

2 teaspoons each: finely chopped jalapeno chili, roasted garlic

Mustard-Honey Dressing (recipe follows)

Per Serving:
Calories: 383
% of calories from fat: 28
Fat (gm): 12.9
Saturated fat (gm): 2.2
Cholesterol (mg): 65.5
Sodium (mg): 953
Protein (gm): 35
Carbohydrate (gm): 40

Exchanges:
Milk: 0.0
Vegetable: 0.0
Fruit: 0.0
Bread: 2.5
Meat: 2.5
Fat: 0.0

1. Combine all ingredients in salad bowl and toss.

Mustard-Honey Dressing

Makes about ½ cup

3 tablespoons each: olive oil, cider vinegar

1 tablespoon Dijon mustard

1–2 tablespoons honey

½ teaspoon dried oregano leaves

1–2 dashes red pepper sauce

1. Mix all ingredients.

ORANGE-MARINATED CHICKEN AND BEAN SALAD

45 *A medley of beans is enhanced with chicken and a freshly flavored Orange Dressing.*

6 entrée servings

12 ounces cooked chicken breast, cubed or shredded

1 can (15 ounces) each: Great Northern and red kidney beans, rinsed, drained

1 cup thinly sliced cabbage

⅓ cup each: thinly sliced green onions, yellow bell pepper, celery, carrot

Orange Dressing (recipe follows)

Salt and white pepper, to taste

3 large red bell peppers, halved

Shredded lettuce, as garnish

Per Serving:
Calories: 192
% of calories from fat: 20
Fat (gm): 4.3
Saturated fat (gm): 0.8
Cholesterol (mg): 26
Sodium (mg): 268
Protein (gm): 16
Carbohydrate (gm): 22.5

Exchanges:
Milk: 0.0
Vegetable: 1.0
Fruit: 0.0
Bread: 1.0
Meat: 2.0
Fat: 0.0

1. Combine chicken, beans, and vegetables; pour Orange Dressing over and toss; season to taste with salt and white pepper. Spoon salad into bell pepper halves; serve on lettuce-lined plates.

Orange Dressing
Makes about ½ cup

⅓ cup orange juice

¼ cup white wine vinegar

2 tablespoons olive oil

2 cloves garlic, minced

1 tablespoon finely chopped cilantro

2 teaspoons grated orange zest

1. Mix all ingredients.

ITALIAN RICE AND SAUSAGE SALAD

45 *This light salad entree is also excellent made with brown rice, or a wild and white rice combination.*

4 entrée servings

1 cup each: cooked long-grain rice, shredded cabbage, cubed red or yellow bell pepper

4 ounces Italian-style turkey sausage, cooked, crumbled

8–12 large black olives, pitted, sliced

¼ cup minced chives or thinly sliced green onions

½–¾ cup fat-free Italian salad dressing

Salt and pepper, to taste

Per Serving:
Calories: 250
% of calories from fat: 16
Fat (gm): 4.6
Saturated fat (gm): 1.1
Cholesterol (mg): 15.2
Sodium (mg): 675
Protein (gm): 9
Carbohydrate (gm): 42.9

Exchanges:
Milk: 0.0
Vegetable: 0.0
Fruit: 0.0
Bread: 2.5
Meat: 1.0
Fat: 0.5

1. Combine all ingredients, except salt and pepper, in bowl; season to taste with salt and pepper.

BEEF AND PASTA SALAD VINAIGRETTE

45 *Any lean beef or pork can be substituted for the flank steak.*

4 entrée servings

12 ounces beef flank steak, broiled or grilled to medium doneness

2 medium tomatoes, cut into wedges

¾ cup each: sliced zucchini, green bell pepper

½ cup each: sliced carrot, red onion

3 cups rotini (corkscrews), cooked, room temperature

Mixed Herb Vinaigrette (recipe follows)

Lettuce leaves, as garnish

Per Serving:
Calories: 469
% of calories from fat: 27
Fat (gm): 14
Saturated fat (gm): 4.5
Cholesterol (mg): 57
Sodium (mg): 391
Protein (gm): 32.9
Carbohydrate (gm): 52.1

Exchanges:
Milk: 0.0
Vegetable: 2.0
Fruit: 0.0
Bread: 2.5
Meat: 0.0
Fat: 1.5

1. Slice flank steak into very thin slices, cutting diagonally across the grain. Combine flank steak and remaining ingredients, except lettuce, and toss. Serve on lettuce-lined plates.

Mixed Herb Vinaigrette
Makes about ⅔ cup

⅓ cup each: red wine vinegar, reduced-sodium beef broth or water
1 tablespoon olive oil
2 teaspoons each: sugar, Dijon mustard, minced garlic
1 teaspoon crushed mustard seeds
1 tablespoon each: finely chopped fresh or½ teaspoon each: dried
    marjoram, tarragon, and thyme leaves
½ teaspoon each: salt, pepper

1. Mix all ingredients.

ROAST PORK AND APPLE SALAD WITH PASTA

*Roast pork tenderloin can be warm or at room temperature when tossed
with the salad; apples can be sweet or tart, as preferred.*

4 entrée servings

1 pork tenderloin (about 12 ounces), fat trimmed
Honey-Mustard Dressing (recipe follows)
2 cups thinly sliced green or red cabbage
1 large apple, cored, sliced
½ cup each: sliced celery, raisins
¼ cup thinly sliced green onions
8 ounces mini-lasagne or mafalde, broken into
    1½-inch pieces, cooked, room temperature

Per Serving:
Calories: 472
% of calories from fat: 15
Fat (gm): 7.9
Saturated fat (gm): 1.7
Cholesterol (mg): 49.3
Sodium (mg): 219
Protein (gm): 26.1
Carbohydrate (gm): 75.7

Exchanges:
Milk: 0.0
Vegetable: 0.0
Fruit: 0.0
Bread: 5.0
Meat: 2.0
Fat: 0.0

1. Place pork in 13 x 9-inch baking pan; brush with 2 tablespoons
Honey-Mustard Dressing. Roast pork at 425 degrees until no longer
pink in center, 30 to 35 minutes. Remove pork to cutting board; let
stand, loosely covered with aluminum foil, 5 minutes.

2. Combine cabbage, apple, celery, raisins, green onions, and pasta
in salad bowl. Slice pork into ¼-inch slices; add to pasta mixture.
Pour remaining Honey-Mustard Dressing over and toss.

Honey-Mustard Dressing

Makes about ½ cup

3 tablespoons each: apple juice, cider vinegar
2 tablespoons honey
1 tablespoon vegetable oil
2 teaspoons Dijon mustard
1 clove garlic, minced
⅛ teaspoon ground allspice
¼ teaspoon each: salt, pepper

1. Mix all ingredients.

PASTA, PORK, AND PORTOBELLO MUSHROOM SALAD

45 *Strips of warm sautéed pork and mushrooms tossed with vegetables and pasta make a refreshing summer supper.*

4 entrée servings

12 ounces pork tenderloin, sliced (½-inch)
1 tablespoon olive oil
12 ounces portobello mushrooms, sliced
2 medium tomatoes, cut into wedges
1 each: medium sliced yellow summer squash
 or zucchini
⅓ cup each: sliced green bell pepper, carrot, red onion
8 ounces rotini, cooked, room temperature
½–¾ cup reduced-fat Italian dressing

Per Serving:
Calories: 312
% of calories from fat: 29
Fat (gm): 10
Saturated fat (gm): 1.9
Cholesterol (mg): 51.1
Sodium (mg): 300
Protein (gm): 24.8
Carbohydrate (gm): 29.9

Exchanges:
Milk: 0.0
Vegetable: 3.0
Fruit: 0.0
Bread: 1.0
Meat: 3.0
Fat: 0.0

1. Cut pork slices into ¼-inch strips; cook in oil in large skillet 2 to 3 minutes. Add mushrooms and cook until tender, about 5 minutes. Combine pork mixture, vegetables, and pasta in bowl; toss with Italian dressing.

45-MINUTE PREPARATION TIP: Begin cooking rotini before preparing the rest of the recipe.

PASTA AND CRABMEAT SALAD
WITH FRUIT VINAIGRETTE

45 *Any firm-textured fish, such as halibut or haddock, can be substituted for the crabmeat; surimi (imitation crabmeat) can also be used.*

4 entrée servings

6 ounces lump crabmeat

½ cup each: chopped seeded cucumber, medium tomato

1 cup cooked peas

8 ounces farfalle (bow tie) pasta, cooked, room temperature

Fruit Vinaigrette (recipe follows)

1. Combine all ingredients and toss.

Per Serving:
Calories: 330
% of calories from fat: 16
Fat (gm): 6.1
Saturated fat (gm): 0.9
Cholesterol (mg): 42.5
Sodium (mg): 267
Protein (gm): 19.4
Carbohydrate (gm): 50.1

Exchanges:
Milk: 0.0
Vegetable: 1.0
Fruit: 0.0
Bread: 3.0
Meat: 1.0
Fat: 0.5

Fruit Vinaigrette

Makes about ⅔ cup

¼ cup orange juice

3 tablespoons raspberry red wine vinegar

2 tablespoons each: lime juice, chopped cilantro

1 tablespoon olive oil

1 teaspoon grated lime zest, minced garlic

¼ teaspoon each: ground nutmeg, salt

⅛ teaspoon pepper

1. Mix all ingredients.

45-MINUTE PREPARATION TIP: Begin cooking farfalle before preparing the rest of the recipe.

"LITTLE EARS" WITH SHRIMP AND VEGETABLES

45 *For variety, substitute cooked cubed chicken breast, lean beef, or lean pork for the shrimp in this salad.*

4 entrée servings

12 ounces peeled, deveined cooked shrimp
3 cups broccoli florets, cooked crisp-tender, cooled
1 medium yellow or green bell pepper sliced
12 cherry tomatoes, halved
2 cups (8 ounces) orecchiette (little ears) or small
    pasta shells, cooked, room temperature
Mustard Seed Vinaigrette (recipe follows)

Per Serving:
Calories: 367
% of calories from fat: 23
Fat (gm): 9.6
Saturated fat (gm): 1.4
Cholesterol (mg): 130.6
Sodium (mg): 451
Protein (gm): 24.7
Carbohydrate (gm): 47.3

Exchanges:
Milk: 0.0
Vegetable: 2.0
Fruit: 0.0
Bread: 2.5
Meat: 2.0
Fat: 0.5

1. Combine all ingredients in salad bowl and toss.

Mustard Seed Vinaigrette

Makes about ⅓ cup

2 tablespoons each: olive oil, white wine vinegar,
    lemon juice, chopped cilantro
2 each: cloves garlic, medium shallots, finely chopped
¼ teaspoon each: salt, pepper

1. Mix all ingredients.

45-MINUTE PREPARATION TIP: Begin cooking pasta and broccoli before preparing the rest of the recipe; rinse in cold water to cool.

TUNA AND VEGETABLE PLATTER

This tuna and vegetable medley is drizzled with vinaigrette and served with garlic-spiked aioli.

6 entrée servings

12 small red potatoes, cooked, quartered

12 ounces green beans, cooked

2 large beets, cooked, cubed

4 Braised Whole Artichokes (see p. 647)

3 hard-cooked eggs, halved

2 medium tomatoes, cut into wedges

2 cans (6⅛ ounces each) white tuna in water, drained, flaked

3 cups mixed salad greens

2 tablespoons sliced ripe olives

1 tablespoon capers

½ cup fat-free Italian dressing

Salt and pepper, to taste

Aioli (recipe follows)

Per Serving:
Calories: 451
% of calories from fat: 19
Fat (gm): 10.0
Saturated fat (gm): 2.3
Cholesterol (mg): 204.5
Sodium (mg): 1389
Protein (gm): 35.6
Carbohydrate (gm): 59.6

Exchanges:
Milk: 0.0
Vegetable: 0.0
Fruit: 0.0
Bread: 4.0
Meat: 3.0
Fat: 0.0

1. Arrange cooked vegetables, Braised Whole Artichokes, eggs, tomatoes, and tuna on greens-lined plates; sprinkle with olives and capers. Drizzle with Italian dressing; sprinkle lightly with salt and pepper. Serve with Aioli.

Aioli

Makes about ¾ cup

¾ cup fat-free mayonnaise

1 teaspoon each: tarragon vinegar, lemon juice, Dijon mustard

3 cloves garlic, minced

Salt and white pepper, to taste

1. Mix all ingredients, except salt and pepper; season to taste with salt and pepper.

TUNA PASTA SALAD

45 *A tuna salad with a difference! Purchased low-fat dressing may be substituted for the homemade Italian Dressing.*

6 entrée servings

12 ounces penne or mostaccioli, cooked,
   room temperature
1 can (15 ounces) quartered artichoke hearts, drained
4 plum tomatoes, coarsely chopped
1½ cups cubed zucchini
¼ cup each: sliced green onion tops, black olives
Italian Dressing (recipe follows)
2 cans (6⅛ ounces each) white tuna in water,
   drained, flaked
Salt and pepper, to taste

Per Serving:
Calories: 435
% of calories from fat: 29
Fat (gm): 14.1
Saturated fat (gm): 2.1
Cholesterol (mg): 24.3
Sodium (mg): 590
Protein (gm): 23.9
Carbohydrate (gm): 52.7

Exchanges:
Milk: 0.0
Vegetable: 3.0
Fruit: 0.0
Bread: 2.0
Meat: 2.0
Fat: 2.0

1. Combine all ingredients, except salt and pepper, in large bowl and toss; season to taste with salt and pepper.

Italian Dressing

Makes about ½ cup

¼ cup olive oil
1 tablespoon each: lemon juice, red wine vinegar, water
½ teaspoon each: minced garlic, dry mustard, sugar,
   dried oregano and thyme leaves

1. Combine all ingredients.

45-MINUTE PREPARATION TIP: Begin cooking penne before preparing the rest of the recipe.

TUNA, FENNEL, AND PASTA SALAD WITH ORANGE VINAIGRETTE

Haddock, halibut, or salmon are tasty alternatives to the tuna in this orange and fennel accented dish.

6 entrée servings

1 pound tuna steaks, grilled or broiled, warm
1½ cups (6 ounces) pasta shells, cooked, room temperature
3 cups torn leaf lettuce, Belgium endive
2 medium oranges, peeled, cut into segments
½ cup very thinly sliced fennel bulb or celery
1 small red bell pepper, sliced
Orange Vinaigrette (recipe follows)

Per Serving:
Calories: 296
% of calories from fat: 26
Fat (gm): 8.6
Saturated fat (gm): 1.2
Cholesterol (mg): 33.9
Sodium (mg): 140
Protein (gm): 23.4
Carbohydrate (gm): 31.6

Exchanges:
Milk: 0.0
Vegetable: 1.0
Fruit: 0.5
Bread: 1.5
Meat: 2.0
Fat: 0.5

1. Remove skin and any bones from tuna; break tuna into large chunks. Combine tuna and remaining ingredients and toss.

Orange Vinaigrette

Makes about ⅔ cup

¼ cup orange juice
3 tablespoons each: olive oil, balsamic or red wine vinegar
2 tablespoons finely chopped shallots or green onion
2 cloves garlic, minced
1 teaspoon dried rosemary leaves
½ teaspoon fennel seeds, crushed
¼ teaspoon salt
⅛ teaspoon white pepper

1. Mix all ingredients.

CHILI-DRESSED TUNA SALAD WITH RADIATORE

45 *A fun pasta, radiatore look like the tiny radiators for which they are named! Other shaped pastas can be also be used.*

4 entrée servings

Chili Dressing (recipe follows)

3 cups (8 ounces) radiatore, cooked, room temperature

1 can (9¼ ounces) white tuna in water, drained, flaked

2 medium tomatoes, cut into wedges

½ medium avocado, cubed

2 tablespoons finely chopped cilantro

4 cups torn salad greens

Per Serving:
Calories: 388
% of calories from fat: 30
Fat (gm): 12.9
Saturated fat (gm): 1.9
Cholesterol (mg): 18.7
Sodium (mg): 238
Protein (gm): 25.5
Carbohydrate (gm): 43.2

Exchanges:
Milk: 0.0
Vegetable: 2.0
Fruit: 0.0
Bread: 2.5
Meat: 2.0
Fat: 1.0

1. Pour dressing over pasta in medium bowl and toss. Add remaining ingredients, except salad greens and toss; serve over greens.

Chili Dressing

Makes about ¼ cup

3 tablespoons lemon juice
2 tablespoons olive oil
½ teaspoon chili powder
¼ teaspoon crushed red pepper

1. Mix all ingredients.

45-MINUTE PREPARATION TIP: Begin cooking radiatore before preparing the rest of the recipe. Rinse in cold water to cool.

PASTA SALAD NIÇOISE

A pasta salad with the flavors of the traditional salad Niçoise. The salad can be made several hours in advance and refrigerated.

4 entrée servings

3 cups cooked small pasta shells, room temperature
12–16 Greek olives, pitted, sliced
2 cups green beans, cooked
¼ cup sliced green onions
1 tomato, chopped
1 can (6 ounces) solid white tuna in water, drained
Niçoise Dressing (recipe follows)
Salt and pepper, to taste

Per Serving:
Calories: 251
% of calories from fat: 25
Fat (gm): 7.2
Saturated fat (gm): 1.1
Cholesterol (mg): 17.9
Sodium (mg): 289
Protein (gm): 15.8
Carbohydrate (gm): 32.4

Exchanges:
Milk: 0.0
Vegetable: 0.0
Fruit: 0.0
Bread: 2.0
Meat: 1.0
Fat: 1.0

1. Toss all ingredients, except salt and pepper, in salad bowl; season to taste with salt and pepper.

Niçoise Dressing
Makes about ¾ cup

½ cup loosely packed parsley
¼ cup each: tarragon wine vinegar, water
1 large clove garlic
1–2 tablespoons olive oil
½ teaspoon Dijon mustard
1 teaspoon dried oregano leaves

1. Process all ingredients in blender until smooth.

45-MINUTE PREPARATION TIP: Begin cooking pasta and green beans before preparing the rest of the recipe. Rinse in cold water.

TORTELLINI AND TUNA SALAD

45 *A great "carry dish" for that next picnic or family reunion!*

6 entrée servings

12 ounces cheese tortellini, cooked,
　room temperature
1 cup fresh or frozen, thawed peas
½ cup each: sliced green onions, chopped
　green bell pepper
1 can (14 ounces) artichoke hearts, drained, quartered
1 can (6 ounces) solid white tuna in water, drained
¼ cup chopped fresh or 2 teaspoons dried basil
　leaves, parsley
Tomato Vinaigrette (recipe follows)
Salt and pepper, to taste

Per Serving:
Calories: 277
% of calories from fat: 28
Fat (gm): 8.4
Saturated fat (gm): 2.6
Cholesterol (mg): 28.6
Sodium (mg): 540
Protein (gm): 17.8
Carbohydrate (gm): 31.6

Exchanges:
Milk: 0.0
Vegetable: 0.0
Fruit: 0.0
Bread: 2.0
Meat: 2.0
Fat: 0.5

1. Toss all ingredients, except salt and pepper, in salad bowl; season to taste with salt and pepper.

Tomato Vinaigrette

Makes about 1 cup

2 small tomatoes, quartered
2 tablespoons each: white wine vinegar, extra-virgin olive oil
2 teaspoons Dijon mustard
1 teaspoon each: chopped garlic, dried oregano and basil leaves
¼ cup (1 ounce) grated fat-free Parmesan cheese

1. Process all ingredients in blender until smooth.

45-MINUTE PREPARATION TIP: Cook tortellini and rinse in cold water before preparing the rest of the recipe.

MAFALDE WITH GARBANZO BEANS, TOMATOES, AND CROUTONS

45

L

Serve with this vegetarian entrée with Italian-style vegetarian sausage, if you like.

8 entrée servings

½ cup each: chopped onion, poblano chili or green bell pepper

1 teaspoon minced garlic

1 can (15 ounces) garbanzo beans, rinsed, drained

2 cups seeded, chopped Italian plum tomatoes

¼ cup each: chopped basil leaves, fat-free Italian salad dressing

8 ounces mafalde or other flat pasta, cooked, warm

1½ cups (½ recipe) Herb or Parmesan Croutons (see p. 498)

Grated Parmesan cheese, as garnish

Per Serving:
Calories: 393
% of calories from fat: 18
Fat (gm): 7.7
Saturated fat (gm): 1.0
Cholesterol (mg): 0.0
Sodium (mg): 531
Protein (gm): 12.3
Carbohydrate (gm): 69

Exchanges:
Milk: 0.0
Vegetable: 0.0
Fruit: 0.0
Bread: 4.0
Meat: 1.0
Fat: 1.0

1. Sauté onion, poblano chili, and garlic in lightly greased medium skillet until tender, 5 to 8 minutes. Add beans, tomatoes, and basil; cook, covered, over medium heat until hot, 3 to 4 minutes. Toss with salad dressing, pasta and croutons; sprinkle with Parmesan cheese.

45-MINUTE PREPARATION TIP: Begin cooking the mafalde before preparing the rest of the recipe.

FROZEN FRUIT SALAD

L

An old-fashioned favorite—simple, tasty, and refreshing!

45

8 side-dish servings

8 ounces fat-free cream cheese, room temperature

1 cup fat-free sour cream

⅓ cup sugar

1 tablespoon grated lemon zest

Pinch salt

5 cups assorted fresh, frozen, or drained, canned fruit

Lettuce leaves

1. Beat cream cheese, sour cream, sugar, lemon zest, and salt in large bowl until smooth. Mix in fruit. Spread in 11 x 7-inch baking dish and freeze until firm, 8 hours or overnight. Before serving, let stand at room temperature until soft enough to cut, 10 to 15 minutes. Cut into squares; serve on lettuce-lined plates.

Per Serving:
Calories: 77
% of calories from fat: 1
Fat (gm): 0.1
Saturated fat (gm): 0
Cholesterol (mg): 0
Sodium (mg): 5
Protein (gm): 1.4
Carbohydrate (gm): 18.7

Exchanges:
Milk: 0.0
Vegetable: 0.0
Fruit: 1.0
Bread: 0.0
Meat: 0.0
Fat: 0.0

WALDORF SALAD

45

LO

This colorful version of waldorf uses both red and green apples. Add miniature marshmallows, if your family insists!

4 side-dish servings

2 cups unpeeled, cubed red and green apples
1 cup sliced celery
¼ cup each: chopped, toasted walnuts, raisins, fat-free mayonnaise, sour cream
2–3 teaspoons lemon juice
1–2 tablespoons honey

1. Combine apples, celery, walnuts, and raisins in bowl. Mix in combined remaining ingredients.

Per Serving:
Calories: 149
% of calories from fat: 26
Fat (gm): 4.7
Saturated fat (gm): 0.3
Cholesterol (mg): 0
Sodium (mg): 227
Protein (gm): 3.5
Carbohydrate (gm): 26.5

Exchanges:
Milk: 0.0
Vegetable: 0.5
Fruit: 1.5
Bread: 0.0
Meat: 0.0
Fat: 1.0

SPINACH AND MELON SALAD

45

A colorful salad, accented with sweet Honey Dressing.

V

8 side-dish servings

8 cups torn spinach

1½ cups each: watermelon, honeydew, and
   cantaloupe balls

⅓ cup each: thinly sliced cucumber, red onion

Honey Dressing (recipe follows)

1. Combine all ingredients in salad bowl and toss.

Per Serving:
Calories: 85
% of calories from fat: 36
Fat (gm): 3.6
Saturated fat (gm): 0.5
Cholesterol (mg): 0
Sodium (mg): 50
Protein (gm): 1.7
Carbohydrate (gm): 13.2

Exchanges:
Milk: 0.0
Vegetable: 0.0
Fruit: 1.0
Bread: 0.0
Meat: 0.0
Fat: 0.5

Honey Dressing

Makes about ½ cup

2–3 tablespoons honey

1–2 tablespoons each: red wine vinegar, olive oil

2–3 tablespoons each: orange and lime juice

1 teaspoon dried tarragon leaves

⅛ teaspoon salt

1. Mix all ingredients.

BROCCOLI SALAD WITH SOUR CREAM-MAYONNAISE DRESSING

45

Serve this nutrient-packed salad on a bed of salad greens or in scooped-out tomato halves.

6 side-dish servings

4 cups broccoli florets and sliced stalks

1½ cups each: sliced zucchini, mushrooms, chopped green bell peppers

12 cherry tomatoes, halved

3 green onions, sliced

⅓ cup dark raisins

¼ cup chopped walnuts

Sour Cream-Mayonnaise Dressing (recipe follows)

1. Combine all ingredients in bowl and toss.

Sour Cream-Mayonnaise Dressing
Makes about 1¼ cups

⅓ cup each: fat-free sour cream, fat-free mayonnaise
3 cloves garlic, minced
3 tablespoons each: fat-free milk, crumbled
   blue cheese

1. Mix all ingredients.

Per Serving:
Calories: 118
% of calories from fat: 29
Fat (gm): 4.2
Saturated fat (gm): 1.1
Cholesterol (mg): 5.5
Sodium (mg): 202
Protein (gm): 6.1
Carbohydrate (gm): 16.6

Exchanges:
Milk: 0.0
Vegetable: 0.0
Fruit: 0.0
Bread: 1.0
Meat: 0.0
Fat: 1.0

JICAMA SALAD

45

V

Jicama adds a marvelous crispness to salads, complementing both fruits and vegetables.

6 side-dish servings

12 ounces jicama, peeled, cut into strips (1½- x
   ½-inch)
½ cup sliced zucchini
1 small orange, peeled, cut into segments
2–3 thin slices red onion
Cilantro Lime Dressing (recipe follows)
Salt and pepper, to taste

1. Combine all ingredients, except salt and
pepper, in salad bowl and toss. Season to taste
with salt and pepper.

Per Serving:
Calories: 77
% of calories from fat: 27
Fat (gm): 2.4
Saturated fat (gm): 0.3
Cholesterol (mg): 0
Sodium (mg): 1
Protein (gm): 1.3
Carbohydrate (gm): 13.5

Exchanges:
Milk: 0.0
Vegetable: 1.0
Fruit: 0.5
Bread: 0.0
Meat: 0.0
Fat: 0.5

Cilantro Lime Dressing
Makes about ⅓ cup

3 tablespoons each: lime juice, chopped cilantro
2 tablespoons orange juice
1–2 tablespoons olive or canola oil
2 teaspoons sugar

1. Combine all ingredients.

10-LAYER SALAD

LO *Or make this salad as many layers as you want! Add a layer of cubed chicken breast or lean smoked ham for an entrée salad, using 3 ounces cooked meat per person.*

8 side-dish servings

2 cups thinly sliced romaine lettuce

1 cup each: sliced red cabbage, mushrooms, carrots, green bell pepper, halved cherry tomatoes, small broccoli or cauliflower florets

½ cup each: sliced cucumber, red onion

Herbed Sour Cream Dressing (recipe follows)

Finely chopped parsley, as garnish

Per Serving:
Calories: 68
% of calories from fat: 4
Fat (gm): 0.4
Saturated fat (gm): 0.1
Cholesterol (mg): 0
Sodium (mg): 380
Protein (gm): 3.3
Carbohydrate (gm): 14.8

Exchanges:
Milk: 0.0
Vegetable: 1.5
Fruit: 0.0
Bread: 0.0
Meat: 0.0
Fat: 0.0

1. Arrange lettuce in bottom of 1½-quart glass bowl; arrange remaining vegetables in layers over lettuce. Spread Herbed Sour Cream Dressing over top of salad and sprinkle with parsley. Refrigerate, loosely covered, 8 hours or overnight. Toss before serving.

Herbed Sour Cream Dressing
Makes about 1½ cups

¾ cup each: fat-free mayonnaise and sour cream

2–3 cloves garlic, minced

½ teaspoon each: dried basil and tarragon leaves

¼ teaspoon each: salt, pepper

1. Mix all ingredients.

CREAMY POTATO SALAD

For the creamiest salad, toss the potatoes with the dressing while they're still slightly warm.

8 side-dish servings

1½ pounds russet potatoes, peeled, cooked, cubed, warm

1 cup sliced celery

½ cup sliced green onions

¼ cup each: chopped green and red bell pepper, sweet pickle relish

2 hard-cooked eggs, chopped

4 slices bacon, fried, well drained, crumbled

1 cup fat-free mayonnaise

½ cup fat-free sour cream

2 tablespoons cider vinegar

1 tablespoon yellow mustard

½ teaspoon celery seeds

Salt and pepper, to taste

Per Serving:
Calories: 169
% of calories from fat: 16
Fat (gm): 3.0
Saturated fat (gm): 0.7
Cholesterol (mg): 58.3
Sodium (mg): 470
Protein (gm): 4.8
Carbohydrate (gm): 31.7

Exchanges:
Milk: 0.0
Vegetable: 0.0
Fruit: 0.0
Bread: 2.0
Meat: 0.0
Fat: 0.5

1. Combine vegetables, pickle relish, eggs, and bacon in bowl. Mix in combined remaining ingredients, except salt and pepper; season to taste with salt and pepper.

GERMAN POTATO SALAD

45 *Tart and tangy in flavor, this salad is best served warm from the skillet.*

6 side-dish servings

1 cup chopped onion

1 tablespoon flour

½ cup reduced-sodium beef broth

1¼ cups cider vinegar

1 tablespoon sugar

½ teaspoon celery seeds

1½ pounds peeled potatoes, cooked, sliced, warm

Salt and pepper, to taste

2 slices bacon, cooked, crumbled

1. Sauté onion in lightly greased medium skillet until tender and browned, about 5 minutes. Stir in flour; cook 1 minute. Add broth, vinegar, sugar, and celery seeds and heat to boiling, stirring until thickened, about 1 minute. Add potatoes and toss. Season to taste with salt and pepper; sprinkle with bacon.

45-MINUTE PREPARATION TIP: Begin cooking the potatoes before preparing the rest of the recipe.

Per Serving:
Calories: 125
% of calories from fat: 5
Fat (gm): 0.7
Saturated fat (gm): 0.1
Cholesterol (mg): 0
Sodium (mg): 69.3
Protein (gm): 3
Carbohydrate (gm): 30.7

Exchanges:
Milk: 0.0
Vegetable: 0.0
Fruit: 0.0
Bread: 2.0
Meat: 0.0
Fat: 0.0

CARIBBEAN POTATO SALAD

LO

45

❄

Sweet and white potatoes combine with a creamy cumin and lime mayonnaise dressing; olives provide a pungent accent.

8 side-dish servings

1½ pounds each: sweet and russet potatoes, peeled, cooked, cubed (¾-inch)

¼ cup small pimiento-stuffed olives

¾ cup fat-free mayonnaise

½ cup fat-free milk

2 teaspoons lime juice

2 green onions, sliced

1 teaspoon ground cumin

⅛ teaspoon red cayenne pepper

Salt, to taste

Per Serving:
Calories: 167
% of calories from fat: 5
Fat (gm): 1
Saturated fat (gm): 0.2
Cholesterol (mg): 0.3
Sodium (mg): 416
Protein (gm): 3.1
Carbohydrate (gm): 37.2

Exchanges:
Milk: 0.0
Vegetable: 0.0
Fruit: 0.0
Bread: 2.5
Meat: 0.0
Fat: 0.0

1. Combine potatoes and olives in bowl; mix in combined remaining ingredients, except salt. Season to taste with salt. Refrigerate 2 to 3 hours for flavors to blend.

MANGO AND BLACK BEAN SALAD

45

V

Any tropical fruit, such as pineapple, kiwi, papaya, or star fruit, can be used in this refreshing salad.

8 side-dish servings

4 large ripe mangoes, peeled, pitted, cubed
1 cup cubed pineapple
½ medium cucumber, seeded, sliced
¼ cup each: finely chopped red bell pepper, sliced
  green onions
1 can (15 ounces) black beans, rinsed, drained
Honey-Lime Dressing (recipe follows)

Per Serving:
Calories: 164
% of calories from fat: 20
Fat (gm): 4.3
Saturated fat (gm): 0.6
Cholesterol (mg): 0
Sodium (mg): 169
Protein (gm): 5.2
Carbohydrate (gm): 32.7

Exchanges:
Milk: 0.0
Vegetable: 0.0
Fruit: 1.0
Bread: 1.0
Meat: 0.0
Fat: 1.0

1. Combine all ingredients in salad bowl and toss.

Honey-Lime Dressing

Makes about ⅓ cup

2 tablespoons each: olive oil, water
1 tablespoon each: honey, tarragon wine vinegar,
  grated lime zest
3–4 teaspoons lime juice
½ teaspoon dried mint leaves
Pinch salt

1. Mix all ingredients.

45-MINUTE PREPARATION TIP: Make Honey-Lime Dressing before preparing the rest of the recipe.

VEGETABLE SALAD WITH 2 BEANS

45

V

Enjoy the fresh flavors of cilantro and orange and the accent of jalapeño chili in this great salad.

8 side-dish servings

1 package (10 ounces) frozen baby lima
   beans, cooked
1 can (15 ounces) garbanzo beans, rinsed, drained
1 large Idaho potato, peeled, cooked, cubed
1 cup each: peeled, seeded, chopped cucumber,
   sliced zucchini
½ cup chopped green pepper
¼ cup chopped cilantro
Citrus Vinaigrette (recipe follows)

Per Serving:
Calories: 170
% of calories from fat: 24
Fat (gm): 4.7
Saturated fat (gm): 0.7
Cholesterol (mg): 0
Sodium (mg): 232
Protein (gm): 6.3
Carbohydrate (gm): 27.4

Exchanges:
Milk: 0.0
Vegetable: 1.0
Fruit: 0.0
Bread: 1.5
Meat: 0.0
Fat: 1.0

1. Combine all ingredients in salad bowl and toss.

Citrus Vinaigrette
Makes about ⅔ cup

¼ cup each: orange juice, lime juice
2 tablespoons olive oil
1 teaspoon each: dried cumin, minced jalapeño chili
¼ teaspoon each: paprika, salt, cayenne pepper

1. Mix all ingredients.

BEAN, TOMATO, AND BREAD SALAD

45 *Use summer's ripest tomatoes for best flavor. Any favorite bean can be used.*

L **8 side-dish servings**

3 cups cubed sourdough bread (½-inch)

Olive oil cooking spray

2 large tomatoes, cubed

½ small red onion, thinly sliced

2 cans (15 ounces each) navy or Great Northern,
    beans, rinsed, drained

1 cup chopped roasted red peppers

Parmesan Vinaigrette (recipe follows)

Salt and pepper, to taste

Per Serving:
Calories: 199
% of calories from fat: 19
Fat (gm): 4.2
Saturated fat (gm): 0.7
Cholesterol (mg): 0
Sodium (mg): 454
Protein (gm): 9.8
Carbohydrate (gm): 30.4

Exchanges:
Milk: 0.0
Vegetable: 0.0
Fruit: 0.0
Bread: 2.0
Meat: 0.0
Fat: 1.0

1. Spray bread cubes generously with cooking spray; arrange in single layer on jelly roll pan. Bake at 350 degrees until golden, 10 to 15 minutes, stirring occasionally. Cool.

2. Combine tomatoes, onion, beans, and roasted red peppers in salad bowl; pour Parmesan Vinaigrette over and toss. Season to taste with salt and pepper. Let stand 15 minutes; add bread cubes and toss. Serve immediately.

Parmesan Vinaigrette

Makes about ½ cup

2–4 tablespoons each: olive oil, red wine vinegar

2 tablespoons each: grated fat-free Parmesan cheese,
    chopped fresh or 1½ teaspoons dried basil and oregano leaves

1 teaspoon minced garlic

1. Mix all ingredients.

BEAN AND PASTA SALAD WITH WHITE BEAN DRESSING

L

Pureed beans, fat-free sour cream, and seasonings combine to make a rich, delicious salad dressing—use on green salads too!

10 side-dish servings

4 ounces tri-color rotini, cooked, room temperature

1 can (14¼ ounces) baby lima beans, rinsed, drained

½ can (15-ounce size) Great Northern beans, rinsed, drained

½ package (9-ounce size) frozen artichoke hearts, cooked, halved

2 cups cut green beans, cooked

¼ cup each: sliced red bell pepper, pitted black olives

½ cup (2 ounces) julienned reduced-fat brick cheese

White Bean Dressing (recipe follows)

Per Serving:
Calories: 188
% of calories from fat: 19
Fat (gm): 4.0
Saturated fat (gm): 0.8
Cholesterol (mg): 3.1
Sodium (mg): 313
Protein (gm): 9.7
Carbohydrate (gm): 30.1

Exchanges:
Milk: 0.0
Vegetable: 1.0
Fruit: 0.0
Bread: 1.5
Meat: 0.5
Fat: 0.5

1. Combine all ingredients in bowl and toss.

White Bean Dressing

Makes about 1½ cups

½ can (15-ounce size) Great Northern beans, rinsed, drained

½ cup fat-free sour cream

1 tablespoon olive oil

2–3 tablespoons red wine vinegar

2 cloves garlic

1 teaspoon dried oregano leaves

2 tablespoons sliced green onions

Salt and pepper, to taste

1. Process all ingredients, except green onions, salt, and pepper in food processor or blender until smooth. Stir in green onions; season to taste with salt and pepper. Refrigerate several hours for flavors to blend.

VEGETABLE SALAD WITH MILLET

45

V

Serve this salad in large scooped-out tomato halves, or use it as a filling for warm pita pockets.

6 side-dish servings

1¼ cups millet

3⅓ cups water

½ cup each: sliced celery, red bell pepper

¼ cup each: sliced green onions, carrot, parsley, and basil leaves

½ small head iceberg lettuce, sliced

1 medium tomato, coarsely chopped

Oregano Vinaigrette (recipe follows)

Salt and pepper, to taste

Per Serving:
Calories: 182
% of calories from fat: 32
Fat (gm): 6.6
Saturated fat (gm): 1.0
Cholesterol (mg): 0.0
Sodium (mg): 19
Protein (gm): 4.3
Carbohydrate (gm): 26.6

Exchanges:
Milk: 0.0
Vegetable: 0.0
Fruit: 0.0
Bread: 2.0
Meat: 0.0
Fat: 1.0

1. Cook millet in large saucepan over medium heat until toasted, 2 to 3 minutes, stirring frequently. Add water and heat to boiling; reduce heat and simmer, covered, until millet is tender and liquid absorbed, about 15 minutes. Remove from heat and let stand, covered, 10 minutes; cool.

2. Process celery, bell pepper, green onions, carrot, parsley, and basil in food processor until finely chopped; transfer to large bowl. Process lettuce until finely chopped; add to bowl. Add tomato, millet, and Oregano Vinaigrette; toss. Season to taste with salt and pepper.

Oregano Vinaigrette
Makes about ⅓ cup

3 tablespoons each: olive oil, white wine vinegar

1 teaspoon dried oregano leaves

1. Mix all ingredients.

WHEAT BERRY AND GARDEN TOMATO SALAD

L

The texture of wheat berries is a perfect complement to crisp cucumbers and sun-ripened tomatoes. Kamut is an excellent grain to substitute for the wheat berries.

6 side-dish servings

3 cups cooked wheat berries
4 cups coarsely chopped ripe tomatoes
1½ cups cubed, seeded cucumber
⅓ cup each: sliced green onions, chopped parsley
½ cup (2 ounces) crumbled reduced-fat feta cheese
Roasted Garlic Vinaigrette (recipe follows)
Salt and pepper, to taste

Per Serving:
Calories: 86
% of calories from fat: 31
Fat (gm): 3.2
Saturated fat (gm): 0.8
Cholesterol (mg): 1.6
Sodium (mg): 74
Protein (gm): 3.1
Carbohydrate (gm): 12.7

Exchanges:
Milk: 0.0
Vegetable: 0.0
Fruit: 0.0
Bread: 1.0
Meat: 0.0
Fat: 0.5

1. Combine all ingredients, except salt and pepper, and toss; season to taste with salt and pepper.

Roasted Garlic Vinaigrette

Makes about ⅓ cup

2–4 tablespoons olive oil
¼ cup balsamic vinegar
2 teaspoons minced roasted garlic
1 teaspoon each: dried mint and oregano leaves

1. Mix all ingredients.

WHEAT BERRY WALDORF

O

Enjoy the variety of textures in this salad—substitute any grain that you like.

8 side-dish servings

1¼ cups wheat berries
1 cup each: fresh orange segments, cubed pineapple and unpeeled apple, thinly sliced fennel bulb
½ cup coarsely chopped walnuts

⅓ cup fat-free mayonnaise

2½ teaspoons Dijon mustard

1½ tablespoons lemon juice

2 teaspoons sugar

¾ teaspoon crushed fennel seeds

Per Serving:
Calories: 159.2
% of calories from fat: 12
Fat (gm): 2.3
Saturated fat (gm): 0.2
Cholesterol (mg): 0
Sodium (mg): 155
Protein (gm): 3.9
Carbohydrate (gm): 32.9

1. Cover wheat berries with 2 to 3 inches water in saucepan; let stand overnight. Heat to boiling; reduce heat and simmer, covered, until wheat berries are tender, 50 to 60 minutes. Drain and cool. Combine wheat berries, fruit, fennel, and walnuts in bowl; mix in combined remaining ingredients.

Exchanges:
Milk: 0.0
Vegetable: 0.0
Fruit: 1.0
Bread: 1.5
Meat: 0.0
Fat: 0.0

TABBOULEH AND VEGETABLE SALAD MEDLEY

Two salads—tabbouleh dressed with Lemon-Cinnamon Vinaigrette, and a mixed vegetable salad with chunky Cucumber-Sour Cream Dressing—are lightly combined for a contrast of flavors. Or, the salads can be served side by side if you prefer.

8 side-dish servings

1 package (5¼ ounces) tabbouleh wheat salad mix (spice packet discarded)

1 cup cold water

⅓ cup each: finely chopped celery, sliced green onions

8 pitted prunes, chopped

1 tablespoon finely chopped fresh or 1 teaspoon dried basil leaves

1 clove garlic, minced

Lemon-Cinnamon Vinaigrette (recipe follows)

2 cups cauliflower florets

⅔ cup each: chopped red bell pepper, diagonally sliced carrots, halved cherry tomatoes

Cucumber-Sour Cream Dressing (recipe follows)

Salt and pepper, to taste

¼ cup (1 ounce) crumbled feta cheese

Per Serving:
Calories: 191
% of calories from fat: 28
Fat (gm): 6.3
Saturated fat (gm): 1.3
Cholesterol (mg): 3.3
Sodium (mg): 300
Protein (gm): 5.7
Carbohydrate (gm): 30.8

Exchanges:
Milk: 0.0
Vegetable: 1.5
Fruit: 0.5
Bread: 0.5
Meat: 0.0
Fat: 1.0

1. Mix tabbouleh and cold water in medium bowl; let stand until water is absorbed, about 30 minutes. Toss with celery, green onions, prunes, basil, garlic, and Lemon-Cinnamon Vinaigrette.

2. Combine cauliflower, bell pepper, carrots, and tomatoes in large bowl; spoon Cucumber-Sour Cream Dressing over and toss. Add tabbouleh salad and toss; season to taste with salt and pepper. Sprinkle with feta cheese.

Lemon-Cinnamon Vinaigrette
Makes about ½ cup

⅓ cup lemon juice
3 tablespoons olive or canola oil
¼ teaspoon dried cinnamon

1. Combine all ingredients.

Cucumber-Sour Cream Dressing
Makes about 1 cup

½ cup fat-free sour cream
¼ cup fat-free plain yogurt
1 teaspoon each: white wine vinegar, dried dill weed
½ medium cucumber, peeled, seeded, chopped

1. Combine all ingredients.

LENTIL SALAD WITH FETA CHEESE

L *Don't overcook the lentils—they need to retain their shape for this salad.*

10 side-dish servings

1¼ cups dried lentils
2½ cups reduced-sodium vegetable broth
1½ cups each: coarsely chopped iceberg lettuce, tomatoes
½ cup each: thinly sliced celery, chopped yellow bell pepper, onion, cucumber
¾ cup (2 ounces) crumbled fat-free feta cheese
Balsamic Dressing (recipe follows)
Salt and pepper, to taste

1. Heat lentils and broth to boiling in large saucepan; reduce heat and simmer, covered, until lentils are just tender, about 20 minutes. Drain; cool. Combine lentils and remaining ingredients, except salt and pepper, in bowl and toss; season to taste with salt and pepper.

Per Serving:
Calories: 169
% of calories from fat: 21
Fat (gm): 4.0
Saturated fat (gm): 1.0
Cholesterol (mg): 2.0
Sodium (mg): 110
Protein (gm): 9.8
Carbohydrate (gm): 24.8

Exchanges:
Milk: 0.0
Vegetable: 0.5
Fruit: 0.0
Bread: 1.5
Meat: 0.5
Fat: 0.0

Balsamic Dressing

Makes about ⅓ cup

3 tablespoons balsamic or red wine vinegar

2 tablespoons each: olive oil, lemon juice

2 cloves garlic, minced

½ teaspoon dried thyme leaves

1. Mix all ingredients.

MACARONI SALAD

45

0

The fourth of July signals fried chicken, apple pie, and, of course, homemade macaroni salad! Add halved summer-ripe cherry tomatoes for festive color.

6 side-dish servings

3 cups cooked elbow macaroni, room temperature

½ cup each: frozen, thawed baby peas, chopped onion, celery, shredded carrot, red bell pepper

¼ cup sliced ripe or pimiento-stuffed olives

¾ cup fat-free mayonnaise

2 teaspoons yellow mustard

1 teaspoon sugar

Salt and pepper, to taste

Per Serving:
Calories: 152
% of calories from fat: 12
Fat (gm): 2.1
Saturated fat (gm): 0.3
Cholesterol (mg): 2.8
Sodium (mg): 357
Protein (gm): 4.5
Carbohydrate (gm): 29.8

Exchanges:
Milk: 0.0
Vegetable: 0.0
Fruit: 0.0
Bread: 2.0
Meat: 0.0
Fat: 0.0

1. Combine macaroni, vegetables, and olives in bowl. Mix in combined mayonnaise, mustard, and sugar; season to taste with salt and pepper.

45-MINUTE PREPARATION TIP: Begin cooking the macaroni before preparing the rest of the recipe; rinse macaroni in cold water to cool it quickly.

MACARONI-BLUE CHEESE SALAD

45

A not-so-traditional macaroni salad with blue cheese pizzazz!

LO

6 side-dish servings

4 ounces elbow macaroni, cooked, room temperature
⅔ cup each: chopped red bell pepper, cucumber,
   shredded carrots
¼ cup sliced green onions
Blue Cheese Dressing (recipe follows)

Per Serving:
Calories: 110
% of calories from fat: 15
Fat (gm): 1.9
Saturated fat (gm): 0.7
Cholesterol (mg): 4.0
Sodium (mg): 216
Protein (gm): 3.6
Carbohydrate (gm): 20.3

Exchanges:
Milk: 0.0
Vegetable: 0.0
Fruit: 0.0
Bread: 1.5
Meat: 0.0
Fat: 0.5

1. Combine all ingredients in bowl and toss.

Blue Cheese Dressing

Makes about 1 cup

¾ cup fat-free mayonnaise or salad dressing
3 tablespoons crumbled blue cheese
1½ tablespoons red wine vinegar
1 teaspoon celery seeds
½ teaspoon salt
⅛ teaspoon each: cayenne and black pepper

1. Mix all ingredients.

45-MINUTE PREPARATION TIP: Begin cooking the macaroni
before preparing the rest of the recipe. Rinse the macaroni in
cold water to cool it quickly.

PASTA COLESLAW

45

The addition of pasta updates a traditional cabbage slaw.

LO

4 side-dish servings

4 ounces fusilli (spirals) or farfalle (bow ties), cooked,
   room temperature
1 cup thinly sliced green cabbage
⅔ cup each: chopped tomato, green bell pepper

¼ cup sliced celery

Creamy Dressing (recipe follows)

1. Combine all ingredients in bowl and toss.

Creamy Dressing

Makes about ½ cup

¼ cup each: fat-free mayonnaise, low-fat plain yogurt

1 tablespoon lemon juice

2 cloves garlic, minced

½ teaspoon dried tarragon leaves

¼ teaspoon each: salt, pepper

1. Mix all ingredients.

45-MINUTE PREPARATION TIP: Begin cooking the fusilli before preparing the rest of the recipe; rinse fusilli in cold water to cool it quickly.

Per Serving:
Calories: 139
% of calories from fat: 8
Fat (gm): 1.2
Saturated fat (gm): 0.3
Cholesterol (mg): 0.9
Sodium (mg): 156
Protein (gm): 5.4
Carbohydrate (gm): 27.3

Exchanges:
Milk: 0.0
Vegetable: 1.0
Fruit: 0.0
Bread: 1.5
Meat: 0.0
Fat: 0.0

FUSILLI WITH TOMATOES AND CORN

45

V

A perfect salad, especially when homegrown tomatoes, corn, and basil are available!

8 side-dish servings

2 cups chopped plum tomatoes

1 cup cooked whole-kernel corn

½ cup sliced green onions

6 ounces fusilli (spirals), cooked, room temperature

Fresh Basil Dressing (recipe follows)

1. Combine all ingredients and toss.

Per Serving:
Calories: 135
% of calories from fat: 26
Fat (gm): 4
Saturated fat (gm): 0.6
Cholesterol (mg): 0
Sodium (mg): 141
Protein (gm): 4.1
Carbohydrate (gm): 21.8

Exchanges:
Milk: 0.0
Vegetable: 1.0
Fruit: 0.0
Bread: 1.0
Meat: 0.0
Fat: 1.0

Fresh Basil Dressing
Makes about ⅓ cup

⅓ cup red wine vinegar
2 tablespoons olive or canola oil
3 tablespoons chopped fresh or 1½ teaspoons dried basil leaves
2 cloves garlic, minced
½ teaspoon salt
¼ teaspoon pepper

1. Mix all ingredients.

45-MINUTE PREPARATION TIP: Begin cooking the fusilli before preparing the rest of the recipe.

PASTA, WHITE BEAN, AND RED CABBAGE SALAD

45

LO

The salad can be made in advance; stir in the cabbage just before serving for fresh color.

6 side-dish servings

6 ounces rotini (corkscrews), cooked, room temperature
1 cup each: rinsed, drained, canned Great Northern beans, sliced red cabbage
¼ cup each: chopped onion, green bell pepper
Caraway Dressing (recipe follows)

1. Combine all ingredients in salad bowl and toss.

Per Serving:
Calories: 185
% of calories from fat: 5
Fat (gm): 1.1
Saturated fat (gm): 0.2
Cholesterol (mg): 0
Sodium (mg): 268
Protein (gm): 8.7
Carbohydrate (gm): 35.9

Exchanges:
Milk: 0.0
Vegetable: 1.5
Fruit: 0.0
Bread: 2.0
Meat: 0.0
Fat: 0.0

Caraway Dressing

Makes about 1 cup

½ cup each: fat-free mayonnaise, fat-free sour cream
2 teaspoons lemon juice
1 teaspoon each: minced garlic, crushed caraway seeds
¼ teaspoon each: salt, pepper

1. Mix all ingredients.

45-MINUTE PREPARATION TIP: Begin cooking rotini before preparing the rest of the recipe; rinse rotini in cold water to cool quickly.

SESAME PASTA SALAD WITH SUMMER VEGETABLES

45 *The vegetables used in this salad can vary according to seasonal availability.*

6 side-dish servings

1 small eggplant
1 cup each: sliced carrots, yellow summer squash, red bell pepper, cooked broccoli florets
¼ cup sliced green onions
8 ounces thin spaghetti, cooked, room temperature
Sesame Dressing (recipe follows)
2 teaspoons toasted sesame seeds

Per Serving:
Calories: 220
% of calories from fat: 17.7
Fat (gm): 4.3
Saturated fat (gm): 0.6
Cholesterol (mg): 0
Sodium (mg): 136
Protein (gm): 6.7
Carbohydrate (gm): 38.8

Exchanges:
Milk: 0.0
Vegetable: 2.0
Fruit: 0.0
Bread: 2.0
Meat: 0.0
Fat: 1.0

1. Pierce eggplant 6 to 8 times with fork; roast in baking pan at 425 degrees until tender, about 30 minutes; cool. Cut eggplant in half; scoop out pulp and cut into ¾-inch pieces. Combine eggplant, vegetables, and pasta in salad bowl; toss with Sesame Dressing and sprinkle with sesame seeds.

Sesame Dressing
Makes about ⅓ cup

2 tablespoons each: reduced-sodium soy sauce, sesame oil
⅛–¼ teaspoon hot chili oil (optional)
1 tablespoon each: balsamic or red wine vinegar, chopped cilantro
1½ tablespoons sugar
1 clove garlic, minced

1. Mix all ingredients.

45-MINUTE PREPARATION TIP: Cook the spaghetti and cut vegetables while the eggplant is roasting.

LIGHT SUMMER PASTA SALAD

45

L

The fragrant aroma and flavor of fresh herbs accent summer's finest tomatoes in this salad.

8 side-dish servings

8 ounces spaghetti, cooked, room temperature
1 pound plum tomatoes, chopped
¾ cup (3 ounces) cubed reduced-fat mozzarella
  cheese (¼-inch)
¼ cup packed basil leaves, chopped
Garlic Vinaigrette (recipe follows)

Per Serving:
Calories: 150
% of calories from fat: 30
Fat (gm): 5.7
Saturated fat (gm): 0.5
Cholesterol (mg): 3.8
Sodium (mg): 176
Protein (gm): 7.4
Carbohydrate (gm): 19.7

Exchanges:
Milk: 0.0
Vegetable: 1.0
Fruit: 0.0
Bread: 1.0
Meat: 0.0
Fat: 1.0

1. Combine all ingredients in salad bowl and toss.

Garlic Vinaigrette
Makes about ⅓ cup

3 tablespoons red wine vinegar
2 tablespoons olive oil
3 cloves garlic, minced
⅛ teaspoon each salt, pepper

1. Mix all ingredients.

45-MINUTE PREPARATION TIP: Cook spaghetti and rinse in cold water before preparing the rest of the recipe.

GARDEN VEGETABLE AND PASTA SALAD

The eggplant can be roasted and refrigerated 1 to 2 days in advance.

6 side-dish servings

1 medium eggplant, unpeeled, cubed (¾-inch)
Vegetable cooking spray
2 cups each: cauliflower and broccoli florets,
   cooked crisp-tender
10 cherry tomatoes, halved
½ medium green bell pepper, sliced
8 ounces fettuccine or linguine, cooked,
   room temperature
Basil Vinaigrette (recipe follows)
Salt and pepper, to taste
2 ounces feta cheese, crumbled

Per Serving:
Calories: 202
% of calories from fat: 25
Fat (gm): 6
Saturated fat (gm): 1.8
Cholesterol (mg): 8.3
Sodium (mg): 282
Protein (gm): 8.5
Carbohydrate (gm): 31.5

Exchanges:
Milk: 0.0
Vegetable: 1.0
Fruit: 0.0
Bread: 1.5
Meat: 0.0
Fat: 1.0

1. Arrange eggplant on greased foil-lined jelly roll pan; spray with cooking spray. Roast at 425 degrees until tender, about 30 minutes; cool. Combine eggplant, remaining vegetables, and pasta in salad bowl; toss with Basil Vinaigrette. Season to taste with salt and pepper; sprinkle with cheese.

Basil Vinaigrette
Makes about ⅓ cup

¼ cup balsamic vinegar
1 tablespoon olive oil
3 tablespoons chopped basil leaves

1. Mix all ingredients.

45-MINUTE PREPARATION TIP: Cook the fettuccine and vegetables while the eggplant is roasting. Rinse the fettuccine in cold water to cool it quickly.

FETTUCCINE SALAD WITH ROASTED GARLIC, ONIONS, AND PEPPERS

Deceptively simple to make, and incredibly delicious to eat!

8 side-dish servings

2 bulbs garlic
Olive oil cooking spray
3 medium onions, cut into wedges
2 large red bell peppers, thickly sliced
2 tablespoons each: olive oil, lemon juice
½ teaspoon salt
¼ teaspoon pepper
8 ounces fettuccine, cooked, warm

Per Serving:
Calories: 151
% of calories from fat: 26
Fat (gm): 4.5
Saturated fat (gm): 0.5
Cholesterol (mg): 0
Sodium (mg): 184
Protein (gm): 5
Carbohydrate (gm): 24.4

Exchanges:
Milk: 0.0
Vegetable: 1.5
Fruit: 0.0
Bread: 1.0
Meat: 0.0
Fat: 1.0

1. Cut a scant ½ inch off tops of garlic bulbs, exposing ends of cloves; spray with cooking spray. Wrap garlic bulbs loosely in aluminum foil. Arrange garlic, onions, and bell peppers in single layer on greased foil-lined jelly roll pan. Roast at 425 degrees until garlic is very soft and vegetables are tender, 30 to 40 minutes. Cool garlic slightly; squeeze pulp into small bowl. Stir in oil, lemon juice, salt, and pepper. Toss with pasta and roasted vegetables.

45-MINUTE PREPARATION TIP: Begin cooking the fettuccine before preparing the rest of the recipe.

MIXED VEGETABLES AND ORZO VINAIGRETTE

45

V

The turmeric gives the salad dressing its unusual yellow color. Curry powder can be used instead to impart the same color and add a delicate curry flavor.

8 side-dish servings

2 cups sliced asparagus (1½-inch), cooked crisp-tender
1½ cups thinly sliced zucchini
1 cup frozen peas, thawed
½ cup sliced carrots, cooked crisp-tender
¾ cup halved cherry tomatoes
¼ cup orzo, cooked, room temperature
Mustard-Turmeric Vinaigrette (recipe follows)

1. Combine all ingredients in salad bowl and toss.

Per Serving:
Calories: 142
% of calories from fat: 27
Fat (gm): 4.2
Saturated fat (gm): 0.6
Cholesterol (mg): 0
Sodium (mg): 112
Protein (gm): 5.5
Carbohydrate (gm): 20.9

Exchanges:
Milk: 0.0
Vegetable: 1.0
Fruit: 0.0
Bread: 1.0
Meat: 0.0
Fat: 1.0

Mustard-Turmeric Vinaigrette

Makes about ½ cup

¼ cup white wine vinegar

¼ teaspoon ground turmeric

2–3 tablespoons lemon juice

2 tablespoons olive or canola oil

2 teaspoons Dijon mustard

2 cloves garlic, minced

¼ teaspoon each: salt, pepper

1. Heat vinegar and turmeric in small saucepan over medium heat, stirring until turmeric is dissolved, 2 to 3 minutes; cool. Combine with remaining ingredients.

45-MINUTE PREPARATION TIP: Begin cooking the orzo, carrots, and asparagus before preparing the rest of the recipe.

ORZO WITH SUN-DRIED TOMATOES AND MUSHROOMS

45 *A simple salad, intensely flavored with sun-dried tomatoes, rosemary, and sherry.*

4 side-dish servings

Per Serving:
Calories: 135
% of calories from fat: 6
Fat (gm): 0.8
Saturated fat (gm): 0.1
Cholesterol (mg): 0
Sodium (mg): 218
Protein (gm): 5.1
Carbohydrate (gm): 27.2

Exchanges:
Milk: 0.0
Vegetable: 0.0
Fruit: 0.0
Bread: 2.0
Meat: 0.0
Fat: 0.0

2 sun-dried tomatoes (not in oil), softened, sliced

1½ cups sliced mushrooms

¼ cup sliced green onions

2 cloves garlic, minced

½ cup vegetable broth

2 tablespoons dry sherry (optional)

½ cup (4 ounces) orzo, cooked, room temperature

2 tablespoons chopped fresh or 1 teaspoon dried
    rosemary leaves

¼ teaspoon each: salt, pepper

1. Sauté sun-dried tomatoes, mushrooms, green onions, and garlic in lightly greased large skillet until mushrooms are tender, 5 to 7 minutes. Add broth and sherry; heat to boiling. Reduce heat and simmer, uncovered, until liquid is reduced to about ¼ cup, about 5 minutes; cool. Toss with orzo, rosemary, salt and pepper in salad bowl.

45-MINUTE PREPARATION TIP: Begin cooking the orzo before preparing the rest of the recipe.

BRUSSELS SPROUTS AND GNOCCHI SALAD

45

Use spinach or potato gnocchi; pasta shells can be substituted, if preferred.

L

8 side-dish servings

8 ounces gnocchi, cooked, room temperature
8 ounces Brussels sprouts, halved, cooked
1 cup each: chopped tomato, sliced green bell pepper
¼ cup thinly sliced red onion
Sun-Dried Tomato and Goat Cheese Dressing
   (recipe follows)

Per Serving:
Calories: 172
% of calories from fat: 27
Fat (gm): 5.4
Saturated fat (gm): 0.9
Cholesterol (mg): 3.5
Sodium (mg): 179
Protein (gm): 6.3
Carbohydrate (gm): 26.3

Exchanges:
Milk: 0.0
Vegetable: 1.0
Fruit: 0.0
Bread: 1.5
Meat: 0.0
Fat: 1.0

1. Combine all ingredients in bowl and toss.

Sun-Dried Tomato and Goat Cheese Dressing

Makes about ⅓ cup

2 tablespoons each: olive oil, white wine vinegar,
   lemon juice, grated Romano cheese
1 tablespoon goat cheese or cream cheese, room temperature
3 sun-dried tomatoes (not in oil), softened, finely chopped
2 cloves garlic, minced
½ teaspoon each: dried marjoram and thyme leaves
¼ teaspoon each: salt, pepper

1. Mix all ingredients.

ORIENTAL NOODLE SALAD

45

V

If you enjoy the flavor of sesame oil, substitute 1 tablespoon each Asian sesame and canola oil for the olive oil.

8 side-dish servings

2 packages (4 ounces each) rice noodles

2 cups each: halved snow peas, cooked crisp-tender, sliced red bell pepper

1 cup each: bean sprouts, sliced mushrooms, orange segments

5-Spice Salad Dressing (recipe follows)

Per Serving:
Calories: 198
% of calories from fat: 16
Fat (gm): 3.7
Saturated fat (gm): 0.5
Cholesterol (mg): 0
Sodium (mg): 72
Protein (gm): 5.9
Carbohydrate (gm): 36.9

Exchanges:
Milk: 0.0
Vegetable: 0.5
Fruit: 0.5
Bread: 2.0
Meat: 0.0
Fat: 0.5

1. Pour boiling water over noodles to cover in large bowl; let stand until noodles separate and are tender, about 10 minutes; drain. Cool. Combine noodles and remaining ingredients in salad bowl and toss.

5-Spice Salad Dressing

Makes about ½ cup

⅓ cup orange juice

1 tablespoons olive oil

2 cloves garlic, minced

½ teaspoon five-spice powder

¼ teaspoon each: salt, pepper

1. Mix all ingredients.

THIRTEEN

Breads
and
Sandwiches

EASY HERB LAVOSH

45 *Quick, easy, delicious, and versatile!*

V **6 servings**

1 Whole Wheat Lavosh (recipe follows) or
    purchased lavosh
Vegetable or olive oil cooking spray
½–¾ teaspoon caraway seeds or other desired herbs

1. Spray top of lavosh lightly with cooking spray
and sprinkle with herbs. Bake on a cookie sheet
at 350 degrees until browned, 4 to 6 minutes
(watch carefully, as lavosh can burn easily).

Per Serving:
Calories: 132
% of calories from fat: 3
Fat (gm): 0.6
Saturated fat (gm): 0.1
Cholesterol (mg): 0
Sodium (mg): 1
Protein (gm): 5
Carbohydrate (gm): 29.9

Exchanges:
Milk: 0.0
Vegetable: 0.0
Fruit: 0.0
Bread: 2.0
Meat: 0.0
Fat: 0.0

VARIATION

Parmesan-Thyme Lavosh — Make recipe as above, substituting
dried thyme leaves for the caraway seeds and sprinkling with ¼
cup grated Parmesan cheese.

WHOLE WHEAT LAVOSH

  *A flat cracker bread that is perfect to serve with dips and spreads, or as an
accompaniment to soups and salads.*

8 lavosh (1 each)

½ cup fat-free milk, warm (110–115 degrees)
1 package active dry yeast
2⅓ cups whole wheat flour
½–1 cup all-purpose flour, divided
½ teaspoon salt
1 egg white, lightly beaten
1 tablespoon water

Per Serving:
Calories: 186
% of calories from fat: 4
Fat (gm): 0.8
Saturated fat (gm): 0.2
Cholesterol (mg): 0.3
Sodium (mg): 150
Protein (gm): 7.7
Carbohydrate (gm): 38.5

Exchanges:
Milk: 0.0
Vegetable: 0.0
Fruit: 0.0
Bread: 2.5
Meat: 0.0
Fat: 0.0

1. Mix milk and yeast in large bowl; let stand 5
minutes. Mix in whole wheat flour, ½ cup all-
purpose flour, and salt; mix in enough remaining

½ cup all-purpose flour to make a smooth dough. Let stand, covered, 15 to 20 minutes.

2. Divide dough into 8 equal pieces. Roll each on lightly floured surface into a 3-inch round; place on greased cookie sheet. Brush combined egg white and water over top of dough. Bake at 425 degrees until crisp and browned, 5 to 8 minutes, turning over halfway through baking time. (Lavosh will become crisper upon cooling, so do not overbake.) Cool on wire rack.

BRUSCHETTA

45

V

These simple-to-make Italian garlic toasts are perfect for serving with any kind of savory appetizer spread.

12 servings (2 each)

1 loaf French bread (8 ounces) (about 15 inches long)
Olive oil cooking spray
2 cloves garlic, halved

Per Serving:
Calories: 53
% of calories from fat: 10
Fat (gm): 0.6
Saturated fat (gm): 0.1
Cholesterol (mg): 0.0
Sodium (mg): 115
Protein (gm): 1.7
Carbohydrate (gm): 10

1. Cut bread into 24 slices; spray both sides of bread lightly with cooking spray. Broil on cookie sheet 4 inches from heat source until browned, 2 to 3 minutes on each side. Rub top sides of bread slices with cut sides of garlic.

Exchanges:
Milk: 0.0
Vegetable: 0.0
Fruit: 0.0
Bread: 0.5
Meat: 0.0
Fat: 0.0

VARIATIONS

Herb Bruschetta — Make recipe as above, sprinkling one side of bread with desired dried herb leaves, such as basil, oregano, or dried Italian seasoning before broiling.

Parmesan Bruschetta — Make recipe as above, sprinkling one side of bread with 1 teaspoon grated Parmesan cheese before broiling; watch carefully so cheese does not burn.

PITA CHIPS

V

Perfect to serve with any dip, or to eat as a snack.

45

6 servings (8 each)

3 whole wheat pocket breads
Butter-flavored cooking spray
3–4 teaspoons dried Italian seasoning or other
desired herbs

1. Open breads and separate each into 2 halves;
cut each half into 8 wedges. Arrange wedges,
soft sides up, in single layer on jelly roll pan.
Spray with cooking spray and sprinkle with
Italian seasoning. Bake at 425 degrees until
browned and crisp, 5 to 10 minutes.

Per Serving:
Calories: 86
% of calories from fat: 8
Fat (gm): 0.9
Saturated fat (gm): 0.1
Cholesterol (mg): 0
Sodium (mg): 171
Protein (gm): 3.2
Carbohydrate (gm): 17.7

Exchanges:
Milk: 0.0
Vegetable: 0.0
Fruit: 0.0
Bread: 1.0
Meat: 0.0
Fat: 0.0

VARIATIONS

Seasoned Pita Chips — Make recipe above, substituting 1 to 2
teaspoons chili powder, ground cumin or garlic powder for the
Italian seasoning.

Parmesan Pita Chips — Make recipe above, substituting 2 to 3
tablespoons grated Parmesan cheese for the Italian Seasoning.

CROUSTADES

V

*These crisp toast cups can be filled with just about any hot or cold, sweet or
savory filling. Bake the Croustades up to a week in advance and store in an
airtight container.*

45

8 servings (2 each)

16 slices soft white or whole wheat bread
Butter-flavored cooking spray

1. Cut 2½-inch rounds out of bread slices with cookie cutter
(remaining bread can be used for croutons or soft or dry bread

crumbs). Press bread rounds firmly into 16 greased mini-muffin cups. Spray bread generously with cooking spray. Bake at 350 degrees until browned and crisp, 10 to 12 minutes.

Per Serving:
Calories: 67
% of calories from fat: 12
Fat (gm): 0.9
Saturated fat (gm): 0.2
Cholesterol (mg): 0
Sodium (mg): 135
Protein (gm): 2.1
Carbohydrate (gm): 12.4

Exchanges:
Milk: 0.0
Vegetable: 0.0
Fruit: 0.0
Bread: 1.0
Meat: 0.0
Fat: 0.0

GARLIC BREAD

Select a good quality French or Italian loaf for this aromatic bread, or use sourdough bread for a flavorful variation.

4 servings

4 thick slices French or Italian bread
Olive oil cooking spray
2 cloves garlic, halved

1. Spray both sides of bread generously with cooking spray. Broil on cookie sheet 4 inches from heat source until browned, about 1 minute on each side. Rub both sides of hot toast with cut sides of garlic.

Per Serving:
Calories: 71
% of calories from fat: 10
Fat (gm): 0.8
Saturated fat (gm): 0.2
Cholesterol (mg): 0
Sodium (mg): 152
Protein (gm): 2.3
Carbohydrate (gm): 13.5

Exchanges:
Milk: 0.0
Vegetable: 0.0
Fruit: 0.0
Bread: 1.0
Meat: 0.0
Fat: 0.0

VARIATION

Parmesan Garlic Bread — Combine 2 tablespoons grated Parmesan cheese and 4 teaspoons minced garlic. Spray bread with cooking spray as above and spread top of each slice with cheese mixture. Broil as above, or wrap loosely in foil and bake at 350 degrees until warm, about 10 minutes.

CROUTONS

Croutons can brighten a soup, add crunch to a salad, and provide a flavor accent for many dishes.

12 servings

3 cups cubed firm or day-old French or Italian bread (½–¾–inch)
Vegetable cooking spray

Per Serving:
Calories: 20
% of calories from fat: 13
Fat (gm): 0.3
Saturated fat (gm): 0.1
Cholesterol (mg): 0
Sodium (mg): 39
Protein (gm): 0.6
Carbohydrate (gm): 3.7

Exchanges:
Milk: 0.0
Vegetable: 0.0
Fruit: 0.0
Bread: 0.0
Meat: 0.0
Fat: 0.0

1. Spray bread cubes with cooking spray; arrange in single layer on jelly roll pan. Bake at 375 degrees until browned, 8 to 10 minutes, stirring occasionally. Cool; store in airtight container up to 2 weeks.

VARIATIONS

Italian-Style Croutons — Spray Italian bread cubes with vegetable cooking spray; sprinkle with combined 1 teaspoon garlic powder and 1 teaspoon dried Italian seasoning and toss. Bake as above.

Sourdough Croutons — Spray sourdough bread cubes with vegetable cooking spray; sprinkle with 2 teaspoons bouquet garni and toss. Bake as above.

Parmesan Croutons — Spray Italian bread cubes with vegetable cooking spray; sprinkle with 1 to 2 tablespoons grated Parmesan cheese and toss. Bake as above.

Rye Caraway Croutons — Spray rye bread cubes with vegetable cooking spray; sprinkle with 2 teaspoons crushed caraway seeds and toss. Bake as above.

Sesame Croutons — Spray bread cubes with vegetable cooking spray; sprinkle with 3 to 4 teaspoons sesame seeds and toss. Bake as above.

Herb Croutons — Spray multigrain or whole wheat bread cubes with vegetable cooking spray; sprinkle with 2 teaspoons dried herbs or herb combinations, and toss. Bake as above.

PITA BREADS

V *Also called Syrian bread or pocket breads, pitas can be eaten plain or split and filled. The breads freeze well, so make lots!*

12 pitas (1 each)

1 package active dry yeast
1⅓ cups warm water (110–115 degrees)
¼ teaspoon sugar
1½ tablespoons olive oil
3–4 cups all-purpose flour, divided
1 teaspoon salt

Per Serving:
Calories: 131
% of calories from fat: 14
Fat (gm): 2
Saturated fat (gm): 0.3
Cholesterol (mg): 0
Sodium (mg): 178
Protein (gm): 3.5
Carbohydrate (gm): 24.2

Exchanges:
Milk: 0.0
Vegetable: 0.0
Fruit: 0.0
Bread: 2.0
Meat: 0.0
Fat: 0.0

1. Combine yeast, warm water, and sugar in large bowl; let stand 5 minutes. Add oil, 3 cups flour, and salt, mixing until smooth. Mix in enough remaining 1 cup flour to make smooth dough.

2. Knead dough on floured surface until smooth and elastic, about 5 minutes. Place in greased bowl; let stand, covered, in warm place until double in size, about 1 hour. Punch dough down.

3. Shape dough into 12 balls; let stand, covered, 30 minutes (dough will not double in size). Roll balls of dough on floured surface into rounds 5 to 6 inches in diameter; place 2 to 3 inches apart on greased cookie sheets; let stand 30 minutes. Bake, 1 pan at a time, at 500 degrees until pitas are puffed and brown, 3 to 5 minutes. Remove to wire racks and cool.

SPINACH-MUSHROOM FLATBREAD

L

This attractive bread is made in a freeform shape and topped with spinach and Parmesan cheese. The bread can be made in advance and reheated at 300 degrees, loosely wrapped in foil, for 15 to 20 minutes.

1 loaf (12–16 servings)

2½–3½ cups all-purpose flour, divided

1½ cups whole wheat flour

2 tablespoons sugar

1½ teaspoons dried rosemary leaves, crushed

½ teaspoon each: dried thyme leaves, salt

1 package fast-rising yeast

2 cups very hot water (125–130 degrees)

¼ cup sliced onion

3 cloves garlic, minced

2 cups torn spinach leaves

1 cup sliced cremini or white mushrooms

¼ cup (2 ounces) shredded reduced-fat mozzarella cheese

2–3 tablespoons grated fat-free Parmesan cheese

Per Serving:
Calories: 190
% of calories from fat: 5
Fat (gm): 1
Saturated fat (gm): 0.4
Cholesterol (mg): 1.3
Sodium (mg): 123
Protein (gm): 7
Carbohydrate (gm): 38.8

Exchanges:
Milk: 0.0
Vegetable: 0.0
Fruit: 0.0
Bread: 2.5
Meat: 0.0
Fat: 0.0

1. Combine 2½ cups all-purpose flour, whole wheat flour, sugar, herbs, salt, and yeast in large bowl; add water, mixing until smooth. Mix in enough remaining 1 cup all-purpose flour to make soft dough.

2. Knead dough on floured surface until smooth and elastic, about 5 minutes. Place in greased bowl; let rise, loosely covered, in warm place until double in size, 30 to 45 minutes. Punch dough down.

3. Pat dough into a round on floured surface. Pull the edges of the dough into a freeform shape, about 10 x 14 inches. Transfer dough to greased cookie sheet and let stand 20 minutes (dough will rise, but will not double in size). Bake at 350 degrees until golden, about 20 minutes.

4. While bread is baking, sauté onion and garlic in lightly greased skillet until tender, 3 to 4 minutes. Add spinach and mushrooms; cook, covered, over medium until spinach is wilted, about 5 minutes. Cook, uncovered, until mushrooms are tender, about 5 minutes. Remove from heat. Arrange spinach mixture over top of baked bread; sprinkle with cheeses. Return to oven until cheese is melted, 5 to 10 minutes. Transfer to wire rack and cool.

FOCACCIA

L *This delicious Italian bread is very versatile—see Leek and Onion Focaccia and Fruit Focaccia (p. 502). Focaccia can be frozen, so bake extra to have on hand.*

2 focaccia (10 servings each)

4–5½ cups bread or all-purpose flour, divided

1 package (¼ ounce) fast-rising yeast

1 teaspoon each: sugar, salt

1¾ cups very hot water (125–130 degrees)

Olive oil cooking spray

¼ cup (1 ounce) grated Parmesan cheese

Per Serving:
Calories: 139
% of calories from fat: 5
Fat (gm): 0.8
Saturated fat (gm): 0.2
Cholesterol (mg): 1
Sodium (mg): 131
Protein (gm): 5.2
Carbohydrate (gm): 28.2

Exchanges:
Milk: 0.0
Vegetable: 0.0
Fruit: 0.0
Bread: 2.0
Meat: 0.0
Fat: 0.0

1. Combine 4 cups flour, yeast, sugar, and salt in large mixing bowl. Add water, mixing until smooth. Mix in enough remaining 1½ cups flour to make soft dough.

2. Knead dough on floured surface until dough is smooth and elastic, about 5 minutes. Place in greased bowl; turn greased side up and let rise, covered, in warm place until double in size, about 1 hour. Punch dough down.

3. Divide dough into halves. Roll 1 piece dough on floured surface to fit jelly roll pan, 15 x 10 inches; ease dough into greased pan. Repeat with remaining dough. Let dough rise until double in size, 45 to 60 minutes. Make ¼-inch-deep indentations with fingers to "dimple" the dough; spray lightly with cooking spray and sprinkle with Parmesan cheese. Bake at 425 degrees until browned, about 30 minutes. Cool in pans on wire racks.

FRUIT FOCACCIA

L *Serve as a dessert or a meal accompaniment.*

8 servings

1 cup boiling water
½ cup each: dried cranberries or cherries,
    dried fruit bits
1 Focaccia (½ recipe) (see p. 501)
2 tablespoons granulated sugar
1 tablespoon melted margarine or butter
⅓ cup packed light brown sugar

Per Serving:
Calories: 253
% of calories from fat: 8
Fat (gm): 2.4
Saturated fat (gm): 0.6
Cholesterol (mg): 1.2
Sodium (mg): 188
Protein (gm): 6.6
Carbohydrate (gm): 52.6

Exchanges:
Milk: 0.0
Vegetable: 0.0
Fruit: 0.5
Bread: 3.0
Meat: 0.0
Fat: 0.0

1. Pour boiling water over combined dried fruit in bowl; let stand until softened, 10 to 15 minutes. Drain.

2. Make Focaccia, adding granulated sugar to the flour mixture. After first rising, spread dough in greased baking dish, 11 x 7 inches. Let rise until double in size, about 30 minutes. Make ¼-inch indentations with fingers to "dimple" dough. Spread margarine over dough; sprinkle with fruit and brown sugar. Bake at 425 degrees until browned, 20 to 25 minutes. Cool in pan on wire rack.

LEEK AND ONION FOCACCIA

L *This bread would make a perfect addition to a soup and salad supper.*

8 servings

1 Focaccia (½ recipe; see p. 501)
½ cup each: thinly sliced leek (white part only),
    yellow and red onion
½ teaspoon crumbled dried sage leaves
1–2 teaspoons olive oil
Salt and pepper, to taste
1–2 tablespoons grated fat-free Parmesan cheese

Per Serving:
Calories: 193
% of calories from fat: 7
Fat (gm): 1.6
Saturated fat (gm): 0.4
Cholesterol (mg): 1.2
Sodium (mg): 171
Protein (gm): 7.1
Carbohydrate (gm): 38.4

Exchanges:
Milk: 0.0
Vegetable: 1.0
Fruit: 0.0
Bread: 2.5
Meat: 0.0
Fat: 0.0

1. Make Focaccia; after first rising, spread dough in greased jelly roll pan, 15 x 10 inches.

Let stand until dough is doubled in size, about 30 minutes. Make ¼-inch indentations with fingers to "dimple" the dough. Toss leek, onion, and sage with oil and spread over dough. Sprinkle with salt, pepper, and Parmesan cheese. Bake at 425 degrees until golden, 20 to 25 minutes. Cool in pan on wire rack.

SOFT PRETZELS

LO *To achieve their typical dense, chewy texture, pretzels are cooked in boiling water before baking.*

12 pretzels (1 each)

1 package active dry yeast
½ cup warm water (110–115 degrees)
1 tablespoon sugar
1 cup fat-free milk, heated to simmering, cooled
2–4 cups all-purpose flour, divided
1 teaspoon salt
2 quarts water
1 tablespoon baking soda
1 egg, lightly beaten
1 tablespoon cold water
Toppings: poppy seeds, sesame seeds, coarse salt, herbs, dried onion flakes, etc.

Per Serving:
Calories: 152
% of calories from fat: 5
Fat (gm): 0.8
Saturated fat (gm): 0.2
Cholesterol (mg): 18.1
Sodium (mg): 509
Protein (gm): 5.2
Carbohydrate (gm): 30.2

Exchanges:
Milk: 0.0
Vegetable: 0.0
Fruit: 0.0
Bread: 2.0
Meat: 0.0
Fat: 0.0

1. Mix yeast, warm water, and sugar in large bowl; let stand 5 minutes. Add milk, 2 cups flour, and salt, beating until smooth. Mix in enough remaining 2 cups flour to make smooth dough. Knead dough on floured surface until smooth and elastic, about 5 minutes. Place in greased bowl; let rise, covered, in warm place until double in size, 45 to 60 minutes. Punch dough down.

2. Roll dough on floured surface to rectangle 16 x 12 inches. Cut dough lengthwise into 12 strips, 1 inch wide. Roll one strip dough with palms of hands into "rope," 18 to 20 inches long. Form loop, holding ends of "rope" and twisting 2 times. Bring ends of "rope" down and fasten at opposite sides of loop to form pretzel shape. Repeat with remaining dough, transferring pretzels to floured surface. Let pretzels stand, lightly covered, 30 minutes (they may not double in size).

3. Heat 2 quarts water to boiling in large saucepan; stir in baking soda. Transfer pretzels, a few at a time, into boiling water; boil until dough feels firm, about 1 minute. Remove pretzels from boiling water with slotted spoon, draining well. Place on generously greased foil-lined cookie sheets. Brush pretzels with combined egg and cold water; sprinkle with desired toppings. Bake at 400 degrees until golden, 18 to 20 minutes. Cool on wire racks.

POTATO BREAD

LO

Breads made with mashed potatoes are very moist and retain freshness well. This dough can be made in advance and refrigerated up to 5 days.

2 loaves (16 servings each)

1 package active dry yeast

1½ cups warm water (110–115 degrees)

2 tablespoons sugar

3 tablespoons margarine or butter, room temperature

2 eggs

1 cup mashed potatoes, lukewarm

5½–6½ cups all-purpose flour, divided

1 cup whole wheat flour

1 teaspoon salt

Fat-free milk

Per Serving:
Calories: 121
% of calories from fat: 13
Fat (gm): 1.7
Saturated fat (gm): 0.4
Cholesterol (mg): 13.4
Sodium (mg): 103
Protein (gm): 3.6
Carbohydrate (gm): 22.7

Exchanges:
Milk: 0.0
Vegetable: 0.0
Fruit: 0.0
Bread: 1.5
Meat: 0.0
Fat: 0.5

1. Mix yeast and warm water in large bowl; let stand 5 minutes. Mix in sugar, margarine, eggs, and mashed potatoes until blended; mix in 5½ cups all-purpose flour, whole wheat flour, and salt. Mix in enough remaining 1 cup all-purpose flour to make smooth dough.

2. Knead dough on floured surface until smooth and elastic, about 5 minutes. Place in greased bowl; let rise, covered, in warm place until double in size, 1 to 1½ hours. Punch dough down.

3. Divide dough into halves; shape into loaves and place in greased 9 x 5-inch loaf pans. Let stand, loosely covered, until double in size, about 45 minutes. Brush tops of loaves with milk. Bake at 375 degrees until loaves are golden and sound hollow when tapped, about 45 minutes. Remove from pans and cool on wire racks.

ROASTED RED PEPPER BREAD

LO *Bake this loaf in a freeform long or round shape, or in a pan. For convenience, use jarred roasted red pepper.*

1 loaf (16 servings)

2¼–2¾ cups all-purpose flour, divided

¾ cup whole wheat flour

¼ cup (1 ounce) grated fat-free Parmesan cheese

1½ teaspoons dried Italian seasoning, divided

½ teaspoon salt

1 package fast-rising active dry yeast

1¼ cups very hot water (125–130 degrees)

1 tablespoon olive oil

4 ounces reduced-fat mozzarella cheese, cubed (½-inch)

½ cup coarsely chopped roasted red pepper

1 egg white, beaten

Per Serving:
Calories: 119
% of calories from fat: 16
Fat (gm): 2.2
Saturated fat (gm): 0.9
Cholesterol (mg): 3.8
Sodium (mg): 133
Protein (gm): 5.6
Carbohydrate (gm): 19

Exchanges:
Milk: 0.0
Vegetable: 0.0
Fruit: 0.0
Bread: 1.5
Meat: 0.0
Fat: 0.5

1. Combine 2¼ cups all-purpose flour, whole wheat flour, Parmesan cheese, 1 teaspoon Italian seasoning, salt, and yeast in large bowl; add hot water and oil, mixing until blended. Mix in mozzarella cheese, red pepper, and enough remaining ½ cup all-purpose flour to make smooth dough.

2. Knead dough on floured surface until smooth and elastic, about 5 minutes. Place in greased bowl; let rise, covered, in warm place until double in size, about 30 minutes. Punch dough down.

3. Shape dough into loaf and place in greased 9 x 5-inch loaf pan. Let stand, covered, until double in size, about 30 minutes. Make 3 or 4 slits in top of loaf with sharp knife. Brush egg white over dough and sprinkle with remaining Italian seasoning. Bake at 375 degrees until loaf is golden and sounds hollow when tapped, 35 to 40 minutes. Remove from pan and cool on wire rack.

ENGLISH MUFFIN BREAD

L *This quick and easy single-rise bread has a coarse texture similar to English muffins. Delicious warm from the oven, or toasted, with Orange-Rosemary Jelly (see p. 547).*

1 loaf (16 servings)

1½–2½ cups all-purpose flour, divided
½ cup quick-cooking oats
1 package active dry yeast
¼ teaspoon baking soda
1 teaspoon salt
1¼ cups warm fat-free milk (110–115 degrees)
1 tablespoon honey
Cornmeal

Per Serving:
Calories: 79
% of calories from fat: 4
Fat (gm): 0.4
Saturated fat (gm): 0.1
Cholesterol (mg): 0.3
Sodium (mg): 163
Protein (gm): 2.9
Carbohydrate (gm): 15.9

Exchanges:
Milk: 0.0
Vegetable: 0.0
Fruit: 0.0
Bread: 1.0
Meat: 0.0
Fat: 0.0

1. Combine 1½ cups flour, oats, yeast, baking soda, and salt in large bowl. Add milk and honey, mixing until smooth. Stir in enough of remaining 1 cup flour to make a thick batter. Pour into greased, cornmeal-coated 8 x 4-inch loaf pan. Let rise, covered, in warm place until double in size, 45 to 60 minutes. Bake at 400 degrees until bread is golden and sounds hollow when tapped, 25 to 30 minutes. Remove from pan and cool on wire rack.

VARIATION

Cinnamon-Raisin Bread — Make recipe as above, adding 1 teaspoon ground cinnamon and ½ cup raisins to the batter; do not coat loaf pan with cornmeal.

SWEET POTATO BRAIDS

LO *Canned pumpkin can be substituted for the sweet potatoes, if desired.*

2 loaves (12 servings each)

2 packages active dry yeast
¼ cup warm fat-free milk (110–115 degrees)
1 cup mashed cooked sweet potatoes

1¾ cups fat-free milk

¼ cup canola oil

1 egg

3–4 cups all-purpose flour, divided

2 cups whole wheat flour

1 teaspoon salt

Per Serving:
Calories: 156
% of calories from fat: 17
Fat (gm): 2.9
Saturated fat (gm): 0.5
Cholesterol (mg): 9.2
Sodium (mg): 105
Protein (gm): 4.9
Carbohydrate (gm): 27.7

Exchanges:
Milk: 0.0
Vegetable: 0.0
Fruit: 0.0
Bread: 2.0
Meat: 0.0
Fat: 0.5

1. Mix yeast and warm milk in large bowl; let stand 5 minutes. Mix in sweet potatoes, 1¾ cups milk, oil, and egg until blended; mix in 3 cups all-purpose flour, whole wheat flour, and salt. Mix in enough remaining 1 cup all-purpose flour to make smooth dough.

2. Knead dough on floured surface until smooth and elastic, about 5 minutes. Place in greased bowl; let rise, covered, in warm place until double in size, about 1 hour. Punch dough down.

3. Divide dough into halves; divide each half into thirds. Roll pieces of dough into strips, 12 inches long. Braid 3 strips; fold ends under and place on greased cookie sheet. Repeat with remaining dough. Let rise, loosely covered, until double in size, 30 to 45 minutes. Bake at 375 degrees until breads are golden and sound hollow when tapped, 45 to 55 minutes. Transfer to wire racks and cool.

BUBBLE LOAF

LO

Also called Bath Buns and Monkey Bread, this pull-apart loaf is easy to make, fun to eat, and perfect for potluck offerings and parties. The recipe can be halved and baked in a 6-cup fluted cake pan.

1 loaf (16 servings)

2 packages active dry yeast

1 cup fat-free milk, warm (110–115 degrees)

6 tablespoons margarine or butter, room temperature

¼ cup sugar

3 eggs

4 cups all-purpose flour

½ teaspoon salt

1. Stir yeast into milk in bowl; let stand 2 to 3 minutes. Beat margarine and sugar until fluffy in large bowl; beat in eggs, 1 at a time. Mix in combined flour and salt alternately with milk mixture, beginning and ending with dry ingredients and beating well after each addition. Let stand, covered, in warm place until dough doubles in size, about 1 hour. Punch dough down.

2. Drop dough by large spoonfuls into greased 10-inch tube pan. Let rise, covered, until dough is double in size, about 30 minutes. Bake at 350 degrees until browned, 25 to 30 minutes. Cool in pan on wire rack 10 minutes; remove from pan. Serve warm.

Per Serving:
Calories: 186
% of calories from fat: 27
Fat (gm): 5.5
Saturated fat (gm): 1.2
Cholesterol (mg): 40.2
Sodium (mg): 137
Protein (gm): 5.3
Carbohydrate (gm): 28.3

Exchanges:
Milk: 0.0
Vegetable: 0.0
Fruit: 0.0
Bread: 2.0
Meat: 0.0
Fat: 1.0

GRANOLA BREAD

L *A wonderful breakfast bread—serve with plenty of Spiced Rhubarb Jam (see p. 546). For convenience, this bread is made with an electric mixer and has only 1 rise.*

2 loaves (16 servings each)

2 packages active dry yeast
¾ cup warm water (110–115 degrees)
2 tablespoons light brown sugar
1¼ cups buttermilk
3 cups all-purpose flour
¾–1½ cups whole wheat flour, divided
2 teaspoons baking powder
1 teaspoon salt
2–3 tablespoons margarine or butter,
   room temperature
1½ cups low-fat granola
Buttermilk

Per Serving:
Calories: 200
% of calories from fat: 17
Fat (gm): 3.8
Saturated fat (gm): 0.6
Cholesterol (mg): 9
Sodium (mg): 131
Protein (gm): 3.1
Carbohydrate (gm): 38.9

Exchanges:
Milk: 0.0
Vegetable: 0.0
Fruit: 0.0
Bread: 2.5
Meat: 0.0
Fat: 0.5

1. Mix yeast, warm water, and brown sugar in large mixer bowl; let stand 5 minutes. Mix in buttermilk, all-purpose flour, ¾ cup whole wheat flour, baking powder, salt, and margarine on low speed until smooth. Mix in granola and enough remaining ¾ cup whole wheat flour to make a smooth dough (dough will be slightly sticky.) Knead dough on floured surface until smooth and elastic, about 5 minutes.

2. Divide dough into halves. Roll each into a rectangle 18 x 10 inches. Roll up, beginning at short ends; press ends to seal. Place loaves, seam sides down, in greased 9 x 5-inch loaf pans. Let rise, covered, in warm place until double in size, about 1 hour; brush with buttermilk. Bake at 375 degrees until loaves are golden and sound hollow when tapped, 40 to 45 minutes. Remove from pans and cool on wire racks.

CRANBERRY-NUT WHEAT LOAF

LO *Dried cranberries and walnuts make this bread a perfect fall and winter offering.*

1 loaf (16 servings)

1 package active dry yeast
¾ cup warm water (110–115 degrees)
3 tablespoons honey
2–3 tablespoons margarine or butter,
  room temperature
1 egg
1–2 cups all-purpose flour, divided
1 cup whole wheat flour
1 teaspoon salt
1 cup dried cranberries
⅔ cup coarsely chopped walnuts
Fat-free milk, for glaze

Per Serving:
Calories: 153
% of calories from fat: 27
Fat (gm): 4.7
Saturated fat (gm): 0.6
Cholesterol (mg): 0
Sodium (mg): 141
Protein (gm): 4.1
Carbohydrate (gm): 24.6

Exchanges:
Milk: 0.0
Vegetable: 0.0
Fruit: 0.5
Bread: 1.0
Meat: 0.0
Fat: 1.0

1. Mix yeast, warm water, and honey in large bowl; let stand 5 minutes. Add margarine, egg, 1 cup all-purpose flour, whole wheat flour, and salt, mixing until blended. Mix in cranberries, walnuts, and enough remaining 1 cup all-purpose flour to make smooth dough.

2. Knead dough on floured surface until smooth and elastic, about 5 minutes. Place in greased bowl; let rise, covered, in warm place until double in size, 1 to 1½ hours. Punch dough down.

3. Shape into loaf and place in greased 9 x 5-inch loaf pan. Let stand, covered, until double in size, about 45 minutes. Brush top of loaf with fat-free milk. Bake at 375 degrees until loaf is golden and sounds hollow when tapped, 35 to 40 minutes. Remove from pan and cool on wire rack.

LIMA BEAN WHEAT BREAD

L   *Any kind of pureed bean can be used in this moist, dense bread.*

3 loaves (10–12 servings each)

2 packages active dry yeast

¼ cup warm water (110–115 degrees)

1 cup each: cooked dried lima beans or rinsed, drained canned lima beans, cold water

2 cups fat-free milk

4–6 tablespoons melted margarine or butter

⅓ cup sugar

4½–5½ cups all-purpose flour, divided

1½ cups whole wheat flour

1½ teaspoons salt

Fat-free milk, for glaze

Per Serving:
Calories: 125
% of calories from fat: 13
Fat (gm): 1.9
Saturated fat (gm): 0.4
Cholesterol (mg): 0.3
Sodium (mg): 133
Protein (gm): 4
Carbohydrate (gm): 23.2

Exchanges:
Milk: 0.0
Vegetable: 0.0
Fruit: 0.0
Bread: 1.5
Meat: 0.0
Fat: 0.5

1. Mix yeast and warm water in small bowl; let stand 5 minutes. Process beans and 1 cup cold water in food processor or blender until smooth. Mix bean puree, 2 cups fat-free milk, margarine, and sugar in large bowl. Mix in yeast mixture, 4½ cups all-purpose flour, whole wheat flour, and salt. Mix in enough remaining 1 cup all-purpose flour to make soft dough.

2. Knead dough on floured surface until smooth and elastic, about 5 minutes. Place in greased bowl and let rise, covered, in warm place until double in size, about 1 hour. Punch dough down.

3. Divide dough into 3 equal pieces. Shape each into oval loaf on greased cookie sheet. Let rise, loosely covered, until double in size, about 45 minutes; brush with milk. Bake at 375 degrees until loaves are golden and sound hollow when tapped, about 1 hour. Transfer to wire racks and cool.

PEASANT BREAD

V

Five grains and ground pecans combine in this hearty dense-textured country-style bread. Wonderful toasted, delicious with honey!

2 small loaves (8–10 servings each)

2 packages active dry yeast

½ cup warm water (110–115 degrees)

1¼ cups whole wheat flour

½ cup each: millet, cracked wheat, yellow cornmeal, bulgur wheat, quick cooking oats, ground pecans

1 teaspoon salt

1¼ cups lukewarm water

¼ cup honey

2 tablespoons canola oil

1–2 cups unbleached all-purpose flour

Per Serving:
Calories: 197
% of calories from fat: 22
Fat (gm): 5
Saturated fat (gm): 0.6
Cholesterol (mg): 0
Sodium (mg): 137
Protein (gm): 5.4
Carbohydrate (gm): 34.2

Exchanges:
Milk: 0.0
Vegetable: 0.0
Fruit: 0.0
Bread: 2.0
Meat: 0.0
Fat: 1.0

1. Mix yeast and ½ cup warm water in large bowl; let stand 5 minutes. Mix in remaining ingredients, except all-purpose flour; mix in enough all-purpose flour to make smooth dough.

2. Knead dough on floured surface until smooth and elastic, about 5 minutes (dough will be heavy and difficult to maneuver). Place in greased bowl; let rise, covered, in warm place until double in size, about 1½ hours. Punch dough down.

3. Divide dough into halves; shape into round loaves on greased baking sheet. Let stand, loosely covered, until double in size, about 1½ hours. Bake at 350 degrees until loaves are deep golden brown and sound hollow when tapped, about 40 minutes. Transfer to wire racks and cool.

HEARTY VEGETABLE-RYE BREAD

L *Cauliflower adds moistness and subtle flavor to this aromatic rye loaf.*

1 loaf (10–12 servings)

1 package active dry yeast

⅓ cup warm water (110–115 degrees)

1 teaspoon sugar

1 cup pureed cooked cauliflower

1 tablespoon each: melted margarine or butter,
    light molasses, spicy brown mustard

2–3 cups all-purpose flour, divided

1 cup rye flour

½ teaspoon salt

1½ teaspoons each: caraway and fennel seeds,
    crushed, divided

1 teaspoon dried dill weed

Melted margarine or butter

Per Serving:
Calories: 177
% of calories from fat: 9
Fat (gm): 1.9
Saturated fat (gm): 0.3
Cholesterol (mg): 0
Sodium (mg): 149
Protein (gm): 5.3
Carbohydrate (gm): 34.8

Exchanges:
Milk: 0.0
Vegetable: 0.0
Fruit: 0.0
Bread: 2.0
Meat: 0.0
Fat: 0.5

1. Mix yeast, warm water, and sugar in large bowl; let stand 5 minutes. Mix in cauliflower, 1 tablespoon margarine, molasses, and mustard until blended. Mix in 2 cups all-purpose flour, rye flour, salt, 1 teaspoon each caraway and fennel seeds, and dill weed. Mix in enough remaining 1 cup all-purpose flour to make smooth dough.

2. Knead dough on floured surface until smooth and elastic, about 5 minutes. Place in greased bowl; let stand, covered, in warm place until double in size, about 1 hour. Punch dough down.

3. Shape dough into long or round loaf on greased cookie sheet. Let rise, loosely covered, until double in size, 45 to 60 minutes. Make 3 or 4 slits in top of loaf with sharp knife; brush with melted margarine and sprinkle with remaining ½ teaspoon each caraway and fennel seeds. Bake at 350 degrees until bread is golden and sounds hollow when tapped, 40 to 50 minutes. Transfer to wire rack and cool.

SQUASH DINNER ROLLS

LO

Use pumpkin, Hubbard, or acorn squash for these rolls; mashed sweet pota-toes can be used also. If a loaf is preferred, bake in a greased 8 x 4-inch loaf pan until loaf is browned and sounds hollow when tapped, about 40 minutes.

24 rolls (1 each)

1½–2½ cups all-purpose flour, divided

1 cup whole wheat flour

2 packages fast-rising yeast

1–2 teaspoons salt

½ cup fat-free milk

¼ cup honey

1–2 tablespoons margarine or butter

¾ cup mashed cooked winter squash

1 egg

Per Serving:
Calories: 70
% of calories from fat: 11
Fat (gm): 0.9
Saturated fat (gm): 0.2
Cholesterol (mg): 9
Sodium (mg): 100
Protein (gm): 2.2
Carbohydrate (gm): 13.5

Exchanges:
Milk: 0.0
Vegetable: 0.0
Fruit: 0.0
Bread: 1.0
Meat: 0.0
Fat: 0.0

1. Combine 1½ cups all-purpose flour, whole wheat flour, yeast, and salt in large bowl. Heat milk, honey, and margarine in small saucepan to 125–130 degrees; add to flour mixture, mixing until smooth. Mix in squash, egg, and enough remaining 1 cup all-purpose flour to make smooth dough.

2. Knead dough on floured surface until smooth and elastic, about 5 minutes. Place in greased bowl; let stand, covered, in warm place until double in size, 30 to 45 minutes. Punch dough down.

3. Divide dough into 24 pieces; shape into round rolls and place in greased muffin cups. Bake at 375 degrees until browned, 20 to 25 minutes. Remove from pans and cool on wire racks.

VARIATION

Raisin-Walnut Pumpkin Bread — Make recipe as above, substituting mashed cooked or canned pumpkin for the squash and adding ½ cup each raisins and chopped walnuts. Shape into loaf in 9 x 5-inch loaf pan and let rise; bake at 375 degrees until loaf is browned and sounds hollow when tapped, about 40 minutes.

APPLE HONEY KUCHEN

LO *Use your favorite baking apple, tart or sweet, for this brunch bread.*

2 kuchens (8–10 servings each)

1 package active dry yeast

¾ cup warm fat-free milk (110–115 degrees)

6 tablespoons granulated sugar, divided

4 tablespoons margarine or butter, divided

1 egg

2–3 cups all-purpose flour

¾ teaspoon salt

1 pound baking apples, peeled, sliced

½ cup raisins

¼ cup packed light brown sugar

2 tablespoons grated orange zest

¼ teaspoon ground cinnamon

⅛ teaspoon ground nutmeg

2–4 tablespoons honey

Fat-free milk

Per Serving:
Calories: 162
% of calories from fat: 19
Fat (gm): 3.4
Saturated fat (gm): 0.7
Cholesterol (mg): 13.5
Sodium (mg): 145
Protein (gm): 2.8
Carbohydrate (gm): 30.9

Exchanges:
Milk: 0.0
Vegetable: 0.0
Fruit: 0.0
Bread: 2.0
Meat: 0.0
Fat: 0.5

1. Mix yeast, milk, and 2 tablespoons granulated sugar in large bowl; let stand 5 minutes. Add 2 tablespoons margarine, egg, 2 cups flour, and salt, mixing until blended. Mix in enough remaining 1 cup flour to make smooth dough.

2. Knead dough on floured surface until smooth and elastic, about 5 minutes. Place in greased bowl; let rise, covered, in warm place until double in size, 1 to 1½ hours. Punch dough down.

3. Heat remaining 2 tablespoons margarine in large skillet until melted; add apples and raisins and cook over medium heat until apples are tender, 5 to 8 minutes. Remove from heat. Sprinkle combined brown sugar, orange zest, cinnamon, and nutmeg over apple mixture and toss.

4. Divide dough into halves. Roll each on floured surface into a 12-inch round. Arrange apple mixture on half of each round; drizzle each with 1 to 2 tablespoons honey. Brush edges of dough with milk; fold dough over filling and press edges with tines of fork to seal. Transfer to greased cookie sheets; sprinkle with remaining 4 tablespoons granulated sugar. Let rise, covered, until impression of finger remains in dough when touched, about 1 hour. Reseal edges, if necessary. Bake at 375 degrees until golden, about 20 minutes. Transfer to wire racks and cool; serve warm.

CRANBERRY COFFEECAKE

LO

45

Quick and easy to make, this sweet-tart coffeecake can be ready to bake in less than 10 minutes.

1 coffeecake (12 servings)

1½ cups fresh or frozen, thawed cranberries

1 cup sugar, divided

1 teaspoon grated orange zest

1½ cups all-purpose flour

2 teaspoons baking powder

½ teaspoon salt

1 egg

¼ cup each: orange juice, fat-free milk

3 tablespoons margarine or butter, room temperature

¼–½ cup chopped pecans

Per Serving:
Calories: 180
% of calories from fat: 25
Fat (gm): 5
Saturated fat (gm): 0.8
Cholesterol (mg): 17.8
Sodium (mg): 185
Protein (gm): 2.6
Carbohydrate (gm): 31.8

Exchanges:
Milk: 0.0
Vegetable: 0.0
Fruit: 0.0
Bread: 2.0
Meat: 0.0
Fat: 1.0

1. Arrange cranberries in greased 8-inch-square baking pan; sprinkle with ½ cup sugar and orange zest. Mix remaining ingredients until just moistened in medium bowl; drop by spoonfuls over cranberries, spreading batter evenly to sides of pan. Bake at 400 degrees until wooden pick inserted in center comes out clean, 25 to 30 minutes. Immediately invert onto serving plate; serve warm.

SOUR CREAM COFFEECAKE
WITH APPLE-DATE FILLING

LO *An irresistible offering, this moist cake is filled with apples, dates, sugar, and spices.*

1 coffeecake (24 servings)

½ cup margarine or butter, room temperature

¼ cup unsweetened applesauce

1 cup granulated sugar

⅓ cup packed light brown sugar

1½ teaspoons vanilla

3 eggs

3 cups all-purpose flour

1½ teaspoons each: baking powder, baking soda

1 teaspoon ground cinnamon

½ teaspoon salt

1½ cups fat-free sour cream

Apple-Date Filling (recipe follows)

Cream Cheese Glaze (recipe follows)

Per Serving:
Calories: 198
% of calories from fat: 21
Fat (gm): 4.6
Saturated fat (gm): 1
Cholesterol (mg): 26.6
Sodium (mg): 235
Protein (gm): 3.8
Carbohydrate (gm): 36.1

Exchanges:
Milk: 0.0
Vegetable: 0.0
Fruit: 0.0
Bread: 2.0
Meat: 0.0
Fat: 1.0

1. Beat margarine, applesauce, sugars, and vanilla in large bowl until smooth. Beat in eggs, 1 at a time; mix in combined flour, baking powder, baking soda, cinnamon, and salt alternately with sour cream, beginning and ending with dry ingredients.

2. Spoon ⅓ of the batter into greased and floured 12-cup fluted cake pan; spoon ½ the Apple-Date Filling over batter. Repeat layers, ending with batter. Bake at 325 degrees until toothpick inserted in center of cake comes out clean, about 1 hour. Cool in pan on wire rack 10 minutes; remove from pan and cool on wire rack. Spoon Cream Cheese Glaze over.

Apple-Date Filling

Makes about 1 cup

½ cup dried apples, coarsely chopped

¼ cup chopped dates

⅔ cup water

⅓ cup packed light brown sugar

1 tablespoon flour

¼ teaspoon ground nutmeg

⅛ teaspoon salt

1. Heat all ingredients to boiling in small saucepan; reduce heat and simmer, uncovered, until apples are tender and mixture is thick, 5 to 8 minutes. Cool.

Cream Cheese Glaze

Makes ½ cup

2 ounces fat-free cream cheese, room temperature

1 cup powdered sugar

1. Beat cream cheese and powdered sugar in bowl until smooth.

STICKY BUNS

LO *Impossible to resist, especially when the buns are fresh from the oven! Finger licking permitted!*

24 buns (1 each)

2–3½ cups all-purpose flour, divided

⅓ cup plus 2 tablespoons sugar, divided

1 package active dry yeast

1 tablespoon plus 1 teaspoon ground cinnamon, divided

1 teaspoon salt

1 cup warm fat-free milk (110–115 degrees)

¼ cup fat-free sour cream

1 egg, beaten

Grated zest from 1 orange

Sticky Bun Topping (recipe follows)

½ cup pecan pieces

Per Serving:
Calories: 199
% of calories from fat: 17.5
Fat (gm): 4.0
Saturated fat (gm): 0.6
Cholesterol (mg): 9.4
Sodium (mg): 138
Protein (gm): 3.1
Carbohydrate (gm): 38.8

Exchanges:
Milk: 0.0
Vegetable: 0.0
Fruit: 0.0
Bread: 2.5
Meat: 0.0
Fat: 0.5

1. Combine 2 cups flour, ⅓ cup sugar, yeast, 1 tablespoon cinnamon, and salt in large bowl. Stir in milk, sour cream, egg, and orange zest until blended. Stir in enough remaining 1½ cups flour to make soft dough.

2. Knead dough on floured surface until smooth and elastic, about 5 minutes. Place in greased bowl and let stand, covered, in warm place until double in size, 30 to 45 minutes. Punch dough down.

3. Divide Sticky Bun Topping among 3 lightly greased 9-inch round cake pans, using about ½ cup topping in each pan; sprinkle with pecans. Combine remaining 2 tablespoons sugar and 1 teaspoon cinnamon in small bowl. Divide dough into halves. Roll one half on floured surface into rectangle 12 x 7 inches; sprinkle with half the sugar mixture. Roll dough up, beginning with long side; cut into 12 equal slices.

4. Repeat with remaining dough and sugar mixture. Place 8 rolls, cut sides up, in each prepared pan, over the topping. Let rise, covered, in warm place, until double in size, about 30 minutes. Bake at 375 degrees until rolls are golden, 15 to 20 minutes. Immediately invert rolls onto serving plates or aluminum foil; serve warm.

Sticky Bun Topping
Makes about 1½ cups

4 tablespoons margarine or butter
1½ cups packed light brown sugar
½ cup light corn syrup
¼ cup all-purpose flour

1. Melt margarine in small saucepan; stir in remaining ingredients and cook until bubbly.

VARIATION

Cinnamon Rolls — Delete Sticky Bun Topping. Make dough as above, mixing in ½ cup raisins. Let dough rise, then roll and shape as above, sprinkling with double the amount of sugar and cinnamon. Place rolls, cut sides up, in greased muffin cups. Bake as above, and invert rolls onto wire racks. Mix 2 cups powdered sugar with enough fat-free milk to make a thick glaze; drizzle over slightly warm rolls.

ORANGE MARMALADE CRESCENTS

L

These fragrant coffeecakes for special occasions are drizzled with a warm honey and orange topping.

2 loaves (12 servings each)

Potato Bread (see p. 504)

¼ cup sugar

2 tablespoons margarine or butter, room temperature

¾ cup orange marmalade

½ cup raisins

¼–½ cup sliced almonds, divided

¼ cup each: light rum or orange juice and
 1 teaspoon rum extract

¼ cup honey

2 tablespoons orange juice

Per Serving:
Calories: 229
% of calories from fat: 13
Fat (gm): 3.2
Saturated fat (gm): 0.7
Cholesterol (mg): 17.9
Sodium (mg): 151
Protein (gm): 4.9
Carbohydrate (gm): 44.7

Exchanges:
Milk: 0.0
Vegetable: 0.0
Fruit: 0.0
Bread: 3.0
Meat: 0.0
Fat: 0.5

1. Make recipe for Potato Bread through step 2, adding ¼ cup sugar. Divide dough into halves; roll each on floured surface into 15 x 6 inch rectangle. Spread each rectangle with 1 tablespoon margarine and place on greased cookie sheets.

2. Make 2-inch cuts at 1-inch intervals along the long sides of rectangles. Mix orange marmalade, raisins, half the almonds, and rum; spread half the mixture down center of each rectangle. Crisscross the cut strips over filling; pinch ends of coffeecakes to seal. Curve each coffeecake into a crescent shape. Let rise, covered, until impression of finger remains in dough, 1 to 1½ hours. Bake at 375 degrees until coffeecakes are golden, about 20 minutes. Transfer coffeecakes to wire racks and cool.

3. Heat honey and orange juice in small saucepan until hot; brush over warm coffeecakes and sprinkle with remaining almonds. Serve warm.

BANANA BREAD

LO

45

Brown sugar gives this banana bread a caramel flavor; the applesauce adds moistness. It's the best!

1 loaf (16 servings)

4 tablespoons margarine or butter, room temperature

¼ cup applesauce

2 eggs

2 tablespoons fat-free milk or water

¾ cup packed light brown sugar

1 cup mashed banana (2–3 medium bananas)

1¾ cups all-purpose flour

2 teaspoons baking powder

½ teaspoon baking soda

¼ teaspoon salt

¼ cup coarsely chopped walnuts or pecans

Per Serving:
Calories: 151
% of calories from fat: 28
Fat (gm): 4.8
Saturated fat (gm): 0.9
Cholesterol (mg): 26.7
Sodium (mg): 160
Protein (gm): 2.9
Carbohydrate (gm): 24.9

Exchanges:
Milk: 0.0
Vegetable: 0.0
Fruit: 0.5
Bread: 1.0
Meat: 0.0
Fat: 1.0

1. Beat margarine, applesauce, eggs, milk, and brown sugar in large mixer bowl until smooth. Add banana and mix at low speed; beat at high speed 1 to 2 minutes. Mix in combined flour, baking powder, baking soda, and salt; mix in walnuts. Pour into greased 8 x 4-inch loaf pan. Bake at 350 degrees until bread is golden and toothpick inserted in center comes out clean, 55 to 60 minutes. Cool in pan 10 minutes; remove from pan and cool on wire rack.

MINT AND CITRUS TEA BREAD

LO

45

Finely textured and lightly scented with mint, orange, and lemon, this bread is a delicious addition to any meal.

1 loaf (12 servings)

½ cup fat-free milk

2 tablespoons each: finely chopped fresh or 2 teaspoons
  dried mint leaves, grated orange zest

1 tablespoon grated lemon zest

5 tablespoons margarine, softened

¾ cup sugar

2 eggs

1½ cups all-purpose flour

½ cup whole wheat flour

1½ teaspoons baking powder

½ teaspoon salt

¼ cup orange juice

½ cup powdered sugar

Fat-free milk

Ground nutmeg, as garnish

Per Serving:
Calories: 153
% of calories from fat: 25
Fat (gm): 4.4
Saturated fat (gm): 0.9
Cholesterol (mg): 26.8
Sodium (mg): 151
Protein (gm): 2.9
Carbohydrate (gm): 26

Exchanges:
Milk: 0.0
Vegetable: 0.0
Fruit: 0.0
Bread: 1.5
Meat: 0.0
Fat: 1.0

1. Heat milk, mint, orange zest, and lemon zest in small saucepan to simmering; strain and cool. Beat margarine and sugar until smooth in medium bowl; beat in eggs. Mix in combined all-purpose and whole wheat flour, baking powder, and salt alternately with cooled milk mixture and orange juice, beginning and ending with dry ingredients. Pour batter into greased 8 x 4-inch loaf pan. Bake at 325 degrees until bread is golden and toothpick inserted in center comes out clean, about 45 minutes. Remove from pan and cool on wire rack.

2. Mix powdered sugar with enough milk to make medium glaze consistency; drizzle glaze over bread and sprinkle lightly with nutmeg.

THREE-GRAIN MOLASSES BREAD

V

Molasses and brown sugar give this hearty quick bread a special flavor.

45 **1 loaf** (16 servings)

1 cup each: all-purpose flour, whole wheat flour, yellow cornmeal

1 teaspoon baking soda

½ teaspoon salt

1¼ cups water

½ cup each: light molasses, packed light brown sugar

3 tablespoons vegetable oil

Per Serving:
Calories: 155
% of calories from fat: 17
Fat (gm): 3
Saturated fat (gm): 0.4
Cholesterol (mg): 0
Sodium (mg): 153
Protein (gm): 2.5
Carbohydrate (gm): 30.5

Exchanges:
Milk: 0.0
Vegetable: 0.0
Fruit: 0.0
Bread: 2.0
Meat: 0.0
Fat: 0.5

1. Mix all ingredients in bowl; pour into greased 9 x 5-inch loaf pan. Bake at 350 degrees until wooden pick comes out clean, about 1 hour. Remove bread from pan and cool on wire rack.

FRUITED BRAN BREAD

LO

45

Use any combination of dried fruit you want in this quick, healthy, no-rise batter bread.

1 loaf (16 servings)

1¼ cups all-purpose flour
½ cup whole wheat flour
2 teaspoons baking powder
½ teaspoon each: baking soda, salt
1½ cups whole bran cereal
1⅓ cups buttermilk
¾ cup packed light brown sugar
3 tablespoons margarine or butter melted
1 egg
1 cup coarsely chopped mixed dried fruit
¼–½ cup chopped walnuts

Per Serving:
Calories: 169
% of calories from fat: 20
Fat (gm): 4.2
Saturated fat (gm): 0.8
Cholesterol (mg): 14.1
Sodium (mg): 261
Protein (gm): 4.1
Carbohydrate (gm): 33.1

Exchanges:
Milk: 0.0
Vegetable: 0.0
Fruit: 0.0
Bread: 2.0
Meat: 0.0
Fat: 0.5

1. Combine flours, baking powder, baking soda, salt, and bran cereal in medium bowl. Add buttermilk, brown sugar, margarine, and egg, mixing just until dry ingredients are moistened. Gently fold in dried fruit and walnuts. Pour into greased and floured 9 x 5-inch loaf pan. Bake at 350 degrees until wooden pick inserted in center comes out clean, about 1 hour. Remove from pan; cool on wire rack before slicing.

MULTIGRAIN BATTER BREAD

LO

Batter bread preparation is quick and easy, requiring no kneading and only one rise.

2 loaves (16 servings each)

3¼ cups all-purpose flour
1 cup whole wheat flour
¼ cup soy flour or quick-cooking oats

¾ cup quick-cooking oats

¼ cup sugar

½ teaspoon salt

2 packages fast-rising yeast

1 cup cooked brown rice

2¼ cups fat-free milk, hot (125–130 degrees)

2 tablespoons vegetable oil

1. Combine flours, oats, sugar, salt, and yeast in large bowl; add rice, milk, and oil, mixing until smooth. Spoon into 2 greased 8 x 4-inch bread pans; let stand, covered, until double in size, about 30 minutes. Bake at 375 degrees until loaves are browned and sound hollow when tapped, 35 to 40 minutes. Remove from pans and cool on wire racks.

Per Serving:
Calories: 97
% of calories from fat: 13
Fat (gm): 1.4
Saturated fat (gm): 0.2
Cholesterol (mg): 0.3
Sodium (mg): 43
Protein (gm): 3.5
Carbohydrate (gm): 17.9

Exchanges:
Milk: 0.0
Vegetable: 0.0
Fruit: 0.0
Bread: 1.0
Meat: 0.0
Fat: 0.5

WILD RICE MUFFINS

LO *Wild rice adds crunchy texture and a nutritional boost to these muffins.*

12 muffins (1 each)

1 cup fat-free milk

4 tablespoons margarine or butter, melted

1 egg

½ cup wild rice, cooked, cooled

1 cup all-purpose flour

½ cup whole wheat flour

3 tablespoons baking powder

1 tablespoon sugar

½ teaspoon salt

Per Serving:
Calories: 136
% of calories from fat: 30
Fat (gm): 4.5
Saturated fat (gm): 0.9
Cholesterol (mg): 18.1
Sodium (mg): 494
Protein (gm): 4.6
Carbohydrate (gm): 19.4

Exchanges:
Milk: 0.0
Vegetable: 0.0
Fruit: 0.0
Bread: 1.5
Meat: 0.0
Fat: 0.5

1. Mix milk, margarine, egg, and rice in large bowl. Add combined flours, baking powder, sugar, salt, mixing just until dry ingredients are moistened.

2. Spoon batter into 12 greased muffin cups. Bake at 400 degrees until browned, 20 to 25 minutes. Remove from pans and cool on wire racks.

CARDAMOM-PEAR MUFFINS

 Any dried fruit can be substituted for the pears, and cinnamon can be substituted for the cardamom.

12 muffins (1 each)

1 cup fat-free milk

4 tablespoons margarine or butter, melted

1 egg

2 cups all-purpose flour

⅓ cup plus 2 tablespoons sugar, divided

3 teaspoons baking powder

½ teaspoon salt

1 cup chopped dried pears

1 teaspoon grated orange or lemon zest

½ teaspoon ground cardamom

Per Serving:
Calories: 193
% of calories from fat: 21
Fat (gm): 4.5
Saturated fat (gm): 1
Cholesterol (mg): 18.1
Sodium (mg): 232
Protein (gm): 3.7
Carbohydrate (gm): 35.4

Exchanges:
Milk: 0.0
Vegetable: 0.0
Fruit: 0.0
Bread: 2.0
Meat: 0.0
Fat: 1.0

1. Mix milk, margarine, and egg in medium bowl. Add combined flour, ⅓ cup sugar, baking powder, and salt, mixing just until dry ingredients are moistened. Gently mix in pears and orange zest.

2. Spoon batter into 12 greased muffin cups; sprinkle with remaining 2 tablespoons sugar and cardamom. Bake at 400 degrees until muffins are browned and toothpick inserted in centers of muffins comes out clean, 20 to 25 minutes. Remove from pans and cool on wire racks.

HIGH-ENERGY MUFFINS

These muffins have a nutritional bonus, thanks to the addition of pureed beans.

24 muffins (1 each)

3 cups cooked, dried red kidney beans or 2 cans
    (15 ounces each) red kidney beans, rinsed, drained

⅓ cup fat-free milk

4 tablespoons margarine or butter, room temperature

¾ cup packed light brown sugar

3 eggs

1 teaspoon vanilla

1 cup all-purpose flour

½ cup whole wheat flour

1 teaspoon each: baking soda, cinnamon

¼ teaspoon each: ground allspice, mace

½ teaspoon salt

¾ cup raisins

Cinnamon Streusel (recipe follows)

Vanilla Glaze (recipe follows)

Per Serving:
Calories: 174
% of calories from fat: 19
Fat (gm): 3.7
Saturated fat (gm): 0.8
Cholesterol (mg): 26.7
Sodium (mg): 146
Protein (gm): 4.1
Carbohydrate (gm): 31.9

Exchanges:
Milk: 0.0
Vegetable: 0.0
Fruit: 0.0
Bread: 2.0
Meat: 0.0
Fat: 0.5

1. Process beans and milk in food processor until smooth. Beat margarine, brown sugar, eggs, and vanilla until smooth in medium bowl; beat in bean mixture. Add combined flours, baking soda, spices, and salt, mixing just until blended. Mix in raisins.

2. Spoon batter into 24 greased muffin cups and sprinkle with Cinnamon Streusel. Bake at 375 degrees until toothpick inserted in centers of muffins comes out clean, 20 to 25 minutes. Cool muffins in pans 5 minutes; remove and cool on wire racks. Drizzle with Vanilla Glaze.

Cinnamon Streusel

Makes about ¾ cup

½ cup packed light brown sugar

2 tablespoons each: quick-cooking oats, flour

¼ teaspoon ground cinnamon

2 tablespoons cold margarine or butter, cut into pieces

1. Combine brown sugar, oats, flour, and cinnamon in small bowl; cut in margarine until mixture resembles coarse crumbs.

Vanilla Glaze

Makes about ⅓ cup

1 cup powdered sugar

1 teaspoon vanilla

2–3 tablespoons fat-free milk

1. Mix powdered sugar, vanilla and enough milk to make medium glaze consistency.

QUICK SELF-RISING BISCUITS

Two cups all-purpose flour, combined with 1 tablespoon baking powder and ½ teaspoon salt, can be substituted for the self-rising flour.

18 biscuits (1 each)

1 tablespoon vegetable shortening
2 cups self-rising flour
¾–1 cup fat-free milk
1 tablespoon margarine or butter melted

1. Cut shortening into flour in medium bowl until mixture resembles coarse crumbs. Stir in enough milk to make a soft dough. Roll dough on floured surface to ½–inch thickness; cut into 18 biscuits with 2-inch cutter. Place in greased 13 x 9-inch baking pan; brush with melted margarine. Bake at 425 degrees until golden, about 15 minutes. Remove from pan; serve warm.

Per Serving:
Calories: 65
% of calories from fat: 21
Fat (gm): 1.4
Saturated fat (gm): 0.3
Cholesterol (mg): 0.2
Sodium (mg): 189
Protein (gm): 1.7
Carbohydrate (gm): 10.8

Exchanges:
Milk: 0.0
Vegetable: 0.0
Fruit: 0.0
Bread: 1.0
Meat: 0.0
Fat: 0.0

VARIATIONS

Chive Biscuits — Make biscuits as above, mixing 3 tablespoons snipped fresh or dried chives into the dough.

Parmesan Biscuits — Make biscuits as above; sprinkle with 2 tablespoons grated fat-free Parmesan cheese before baking.

SWEET POTATO BISCUITS

Sweet potatoes offer moistness and a delicate sweetness to these biscuits. For a nonsweet biscuit, white potatoes can be substituted.

18 biscuits (1 each)

¾ cup mashed, cooked sweet potatoes
3–4 tablespoons margarine or butter, melted
⅔ cup fat-free milk
2 cups all-purpose flour, divided

4 teaspoons baking powder

1 tablespoon brown sugar

½ teaspoon salt

Fat-free milk

Ground nutmeg

Per Serving:
Calories: 82
% of calories from fat: 23
Fat (gm): 2.1
Saturated fat (gm): 0.4
Cholesterol (mg): 0.1
Sodium (mg): 161
Protein (gm): 1.8
Carbohydrate (gm): 14

1. Mix sweet potatoes and margarine in medium bowl; stir in ⅔ cup milk. Mix in 1¾ cups flour, baking powder, brown sugar, and salt. Mix in remaining ¼ cup flour if dough is too sticky to handle easily.

Exchanges:
Milk: 0.0
Vegetable: 0.0
Fruit: 0.0
Bread: 1.0
Meat: 0.0
Fat: 0.5

2. Knead dough on floured surface 5 to 6 times. Roll on floured surface to ½-inch thickness; cut into 18 biscuits with 2-inch biscuit cutter and place close together on greased baking sheet. Brush biscuits lightly with milk and sprinkle with nutmeg. Bake at 425 degrees until golden, 12 to 15 minutes. Remove from pan; serve warm.

VINEGAR BISCUITS

L

45

Vegetable shortening contributes to the fine texture of these biscuits. Vegetable shortening with no trans-fats is now available.

12 biscuits (1 each)

¾ cup fat-free milk

¼ cup cider vinegar

3 tablespoons vegetable shortening, melted

2 cups all-purpose flour

1½ teaspoons baking soda

1 teaspoon cream of tartar

½ teaspoon salt

Per Serving:
Calories: 109
% of calories from fat: 27
Fat (gm): 3.2
Saturated fat (gm): 0.8
Cholesterol (mg): 0.3
Sodium (mg): 255
Protein (gm): 2.7
Carbohydrate (gm): 17.1

Exchanges:
Milk: 0.0
Vegetable: 0.0
Fruit: 0.0
Bread: 1.0
Meat: 0.0
Fat: 0.5

1. Mix milk, vinegar, and shortening; mix into combined flour, baking soda, cream of tartar, and salt in medium bowl. Knead dough on generously floured surface 1 to 2 minutes. Pat dough into ½-inch thickness; cut into 12 biscuits with 3-inch-round cutter. Bake on greased cookie sheet at 425 degrees until golden, 10 to 12 minutes. Remove from pan; serve warm.

BLUEBERRY PANCAKES WITH BLUEBERRY MAPLE SYRUP

45

LO

For special occasions or just for fun, drizzle pancake batter into heart or other shapes in the skillet!

4 servings

¾ cup fat-free milk

1 egg

1 tablespoon margarine or butter, melted

¾ cup all-purpose flour

¼ cup whole wheat flour

1–2 tablespoons sugar

2 teaspoons baking powder

½ teaspoon salt

⅛ teaspoon ground nutmeg

¾ cup fresh or frozen, thawed blueberries

Blueberry Maple Syrup (recipe follows) or light
     pancake syrup, warm

Per Serving:
Calories: 308
% of calories from fat: 14
Fat (gm): 4.7
Saturated fat (gm): 1.1
Cholesterol (mg): 54
Sodium (mg): 511
Protein (gm): 6.9
Carbohydrate (gm): 60.9

Exchanges:
Milk: 0.0
Vegetable: 0.0
Fruit: 2.0
Bread: 2.0
Meat: 0.0
Fat: 1.0

1. Mix milk, egg, and margarine in medium bowl; add combined remaining ingredients, except blueberries and syrup, beating until almost smooth. Gently mix in blueberries.

2. Pour batter into lightly greased large skillet, using about ¼ cup batter for each pancake. Cook over medium heat until bubbles form in pancakes and they are browned on the bottoms, 3 to 5 minutes. Turn pancakes; cook until browned on other side, 3 to 5 minutes. Serve with Blueberry Maple Syrup.

Blueberry Maple Syrup

Makes about 1 cup

½–¾ cup maple syrup

½ cup fresh or frozen blueberries

1 teaspoon each: grated orange and lemon zest

1. Heat all ingredients in small saucepan over medium heat until hot, 3 to 5 minutes.

BUTTERMILK BUCKWHEAT PANCAKES

45

Whole wheat flour can be substituted for the buckwheat flour.

LO

4 servings

1 cup buttermilk

1 egg

1–2 tablespoons vegetable oil

½ cup each: all-purpose flour, buckwheat flour

1 tablespoon sugar

1 teaspoon each: baking powder, orange zest

½ teaspoon each: baking soda, salt

½–1 cup maple syrup, light pancake syrup or
  Blueberry Maple Syrup (see p. 528), warm

Per Serving:
Calories: 291
% of calories from fat: 18
Fat (gm): 5.8
Saturated fat (gm): 1.3
Cholesterol (mg): 55.5
Sodium (mg): 593
Protein (gm): 7.1
Carbohydrate (gm): 54

Exchanges:
Milk: 0.0
Vegetable: 0.0
Fruit: 1.5
Bread: 2.0
Meat: 0.0
Fat: 1.0

1. Mix buttermilk, egg, and oil in medium bowl; add combined remaining ingredients, except syrup, beating until almost smooth.

2. Pour batter into lightly greased large skillet, using about ¼ cup batter for each pancake. Cook over medium heat until bubbles form in pancakes and they are browned on the bottoms, 3 to 5 minutes. Turn pancakes; cook until browned on other side, 3 to 5 minutes. Serve with warm syrup.

SWEET-STUFFED FRENCH TOAST

45

A rich breakfast entrée with a sweet surprise inside! Serve with warm maple syrup or a drizzle of honey.

LO

4 servings

4 thick slices sourdough or Italian bread (1-inch)

4 tablespoons fat-free cream cheese

4 teaspoons strawberry or other flavor fruit preserves

2 eggs

¼ cup fat-free half-and-half or fat-free milk

1 teaspoon ground cinnamon

¼ teaspoon ground nutmeg

1–2 tablespoons margarine or butter

1 cup maple syrup or light pancake syrup, warm

Per Serving:
Calories: 383
% of calories from fat: 16
Fat (gm): 7
Saturated fat (gm): 2
Cholesterol (mg): 108
Sodium (mg): 334
Protein (gm): 8
Carbohydrate (gm): 74

Exchanges:
Milk: 0.0
Vegetable: 0.0
Fruit: 0.0
Bread: 5.0
Meat: 0.0
Fat: 0.5

1. Cut a pocket in the side of each bread slice; fill with each with 1 tablespoon cream cheese and 1 teaspoon preserves. Lightly beat eggs, half-and-half, and spices in shallow bowl. Dip bread in egg mixture, turning to coat both sides. Cook bread slices in margarine in large skillet on medium to medium-low heat until browned, about 5 minutes on each side. Serve with warm syrup.

CRUNCHY FRENCH TOAST SANDWICHES

LO

45

Crushed corn flakes add a crunchy texture to this nouveaux French toast breakfast sandwich.

2 servings

1 egg

¾ cup fat-free milk

1 teaspoon vanilla

1 cup corn flakes, crushed

1 teaspoon ground cinnamon

2 teaspoons granulated sugar

¼ cup fresh or frozen blueberries

⅔ cup fat-free cottage cheese

2 teaspoons grated lemon zest

4 slices day-old sourdough bread

Per Serving:
Calories: 303
% of calories from fat: 11
Fat (gm): 3.8
Saturated fat (gm): 1.1
Cholesterol (mg): 110.9
Sodium (mg): 702
Protein (gm): 20.1
Carbohydrate (gm): 50

Exchanges:
Milk: 0.0
Vegetable: 0.0
Fruit: 0.0
Bread: 3.0
Meat: 2.0
Fat: 0.0

1. Beat egg, milk, and vanilla in pie plate. Combine corn flakes, cinnamon, and granulated sugar on sheet of waxed paper. Combine blueberries, cottage cheese, and lemon zest; spread on 2 slices of bread and top with remaining bread. Dip both sides of sandwiches into egg mixture, then lightly into crumb mixture, coating both sides. Bake on lightly greased cookie sheet at 450 degrees until browned, about 10 minutes on each side.

HOT CHEESE BAVARIAN

45 *A little German mustard would set this Bavarian sandwich off to perfection!*

L **2 servings**

2 slices rye bread

2 teaspoons margarine or butter

¼ cup each: drained sauerkraut, thinly sliced cabbage

2 slices tomato

4 ounces sliced reduced-fat mozzarella cheese

1. Spread bread with margarine; top unbuttered sides with combined sauerkraut and cabbage. Top with tomato slices and cheese; cook, covered, over medium-low heat in medium skillet until bread is browned on the bottom and cheese is melted, 4 to 5 minutes.

Per Serving:
Calories: 218
% of calories from fat: 21
Fat (gm): 5
Saturated fat (gm): 1
Cholesterol (mg): 0
Sodium (mg): 765
Protein (gm): 21.2
Carbohydrate (gm): 21.9

Exchanges:
Milk: 0.0
Vegetable: 1.0
Fruit: 0.0
Bread: 1.0
Meat: 2.0
Fat: 0.0

VARIATION

Hot Ham and Slaw Sandwiches — Make sandwiches as above, topping each unbuttered side of bread with 2 ounces thinly sliced lean ham, and substituting cole slaw for the sauerkraut and cabbage, and Cheddar cheese for the mozzarella cheese.

BEER-CHEESE PUFF

45 *Just a touch of beer flavors the cheese topping on this open-faced sandwich.*

L **2 servings**

¾ cup fat-free cottage cheese

½ cup (2 ounces) shredded reduced-fat
  Cheddar cheese

1 tablespoon grated Parmesan cheese

¼ cup minced green onion

2 tablespoons beer, apple juice, or cider

2–3 dashes each: Worcestershire sauce, hot pepper
  sauce

2 large slices pumpernickel bread, toasted

Per Serving:
Calories: 226
% of calories from fat: 24
Fat (gm): 6.3
Saturated fat (gm): 3.7
Cholesterol (mg): 12.1
Sodium (mg): 782
Protein (gm): 22.6
Carbohydrate (gm): 19.9

Exchanges:
Milk: 0.0
Vegetable: 0.0
Fruit: 0.0
Bread: 1.0
Meat: 3.0
Fat: 0.0

1. Combine all ingredients, except bread, in bowl; spread half the cheese mixture on each bread slice. Broil 6 inches from heat source until bubbly, 3 to 4 minutes.

COUNTRY EGG AND GREEN ONION SANDWICHES

45

0

A simple, unsophisticated sandwich that is super quick to make and remarkably satisfying.

2 servings

4 slices multigrain bread
Vegetable cooking spray
2 tablespoons chili sauce
2 large eggs, fried
Salt and pepper, to taste
2 green onions, sliced

Per Serving:
Calories: 215
% of calories from fat: 29
Fat (gm): 7.1
Saturated fat (gm): 2
Cholesterol (mg): 212
Sodium (mg): 442
Protein (gm): 11.1
Carbohydrate (gm): 26.8

Exchanges:
Milk: 0.0
Vegetable: 0.0
Fruit: 0.0
Bread: 2.0
Meat: 1.0
Fat: 0.5

1. Spray both sides of bread with cooking spray; cook bread in large skillet over medium heat until toasted, 2 to 3 minutes on each side. Spread 2 slices of bread with chili sauce; top with eggs and sprinkle with salt and pepper. Top with green onions, and remaining bread.

TUNA PAN BAGNA

45

The bread absorbs the savory dressing, thus giving this Mediterranean sandwich its name, literally, bathed bread.

4 servings

2 cans (6 ounces each) oil-packed solid white tuna
½ cup chopped roasted red bell peppers
1½ tablespoons drained capers
2 tablespoons each: balsamic or red wine vinegar,
    chopped fresh chives or green onions
1 loaf (12 ounces) French bread, halved horizontally

4 leaves romaine lettuce

1 tomato, sliced

2 slices red onion

2–4 pepperoncini

Per Serving:
Calories: 443
% of calories from fat: 20
Fat (gm): 9.7
Saturated fat (gm): 1.9
Cholesterol (mg): 15.3
Sodium (mg): 802
Protein (gm): 33
Carbohydrate (gm): 52.5

1. Drain tuna, reserving 3 tablespoons oil. Combine tuna, reserved oil, bell peppers, capers, vinegar, and chives in bowl; spread over bottom half of bread. Cover with remaining ingredients and top half of bread. Wrap sandwich tightly in plastic wrap, pressing to compact sandwich. Refrigerate at least 10 minutes, or up to 8 hours.

Exchanges:
Milk: 0.0
Vegetable: 2.0
Fruit: 0.0
Bread: 3.0
Meat: 3.0
Fat: 0.0

EGGPLANT PARMESAN SANDWICHES

45 *Try crumbled feta cheese as a delicious alternative for the mozzarella.*

L   **4 servings**

4 thick slices eggplant (¾-inch)

1 egg, beaten

⅓ cup seasoned dry bread crumbs

2 tablespoons grated fat-free Parmesan cheese

4 ounces sliced fat-free mozzarella cheese

4 French rolls or hoagie buns, toasted

2 roasted small red peppers, halved

Pizza Sauce (recipe follows)

Per Serving:
Calories: 255
% of calories from fat: 13
Fat (gm): 3.6
Saturated fat (gm): 1
Cholesterol (mg): 58
Sodium (mg): 588
Protein (gm): 17
Carbohydrate (gm): 37.6

Exchanges:
Milk: 0.0
Vegetable: 0.0
Fruit: 0.0
Bread: 2.5
Meat: 1.0
Fat: 0.0

1. Dip eggplant slices in egg and coat with combined bread crumbs and Parmesan cheese. Cook in lightly greased large skillet over medium heat until tender and browned, about 5 minutes on each side. Top each eggplant slice with 1 ounce cheese; cook, covered, until cheese is melted, 2 to 3 minutes. Serve in buns with roasted red peppers and Pizza Sauce.

Pizza Sauce

Makes about 1 cup

¼ cup each: chopped onion, green bell pepper
2 cloves garlic, minced
1 can (8 ounces) reduced-sodium tomato sauce
½ teaspoon each: dried basil and oregano leaves
Salt and pepper, to taste

1. Sauté onion, bell pepper, and garlic in lightly greased medium saucepan until tender, about 5 minutes. Stir in tomato sauce and herbs; heat to boiling. Reduce heat and simmer, uncovered, until sauce thickens, about 5 minutes. Season to taste with salt and pepper.

45-MINUTE PREPARATION TIP: Make Pizza Sauce before preparing the rest of the recipe.

HERBED VEGGIE BURGERS

LO   *These fabulous meatless burgers can star in any meal.*

4 servings

¾ cup each: finely chopped broccoli florets, mushrooms
¼ cup finely chopped onion
2 cloves garlic, minced
2 teaspoons each: dried bouquet garni
⅔ cup cooked wild or brown rice
⅓ cup each: quick-cooking oats, coarsely chopped toasted walnuts
½ cup each: shredded fat-free Cheddar cheese (2 ounces), 1% fat cottage cheese
Salt and pepper, to taste
1 egg
3 multigrain or whole wheat buns, toasted
⅓ cup fat-free mayonnaise
Lettuce leaves

Per Serving:
Calories: 313
% of calories from fat: 26
Fat (gm): 9.5
Saturated fat (gm): 1.3
Cholesterol (mg): 1.3
Sodium (mg): 700
Protein (gm): 19.6
Carbohydrate (gm): 40

Exchanges:
Milk: 0.0
Vegetable: 0.0
Fruit: 0.0
Bread: 2.5
Meat: 2.0
Fat: 0.5

1. Sauté broccoli, mushrooms, onion, garlic, and bouquet garni in lightly greased medium skillet until tender, 8 to 10 minutes. Mix in rice, oats, walnuts, and cheeses; season to taste with salt and pepper. Mix in egg.

2. Shape mixture into 4 burgers; cook in lightly greased skillet over medium to medium-low heat until browned, 3 to 4 minutes on each side. Serve in buns with mayonnaise and lettuce.

FALAFEL BURGERS WITH TAHINI DRESSING

Enjoy these healthful meatless burgers with Eggplant Soup with Roasted Red Pepper Sauce (see p. 59).

4 servings

1½ cups cooked dried or drained, canned garbanzo beans, coarsely pureed

¼ cup finely chopped parsley

2 tablespoons chopped onion

2 cloves garlic, minced

1–2 tablespoons lemon juice

¼ cup all-purpose flour

1¼ teaspoons ground cumin

Salt and pepper, to taste

2 pita breads, halved

Tahini Dressing (recipe follows)

¼ cup each: chopped tomato, cucumber, thinly sliced green onions

Per Serving:
Calories: 291
% of calories from fat: 23
Fat (gm): 7.6
Saturated fat (gm): 0.3
Cholesterol (mg): 0.3
Sodium (mg): 194
Protein (gm): 13.2
Carbohydrate (gm): 45.0

Exchanges:
Milk: 0.0
Vegetable: 2.0
Fruit: 0.0
Bread: 2.5
Meat: 0.5
Fat: 1.0

1. Mix garbanzo beans, parsley, onion, garlic, lemon juice, flour, and cumin in bowl; season to taste with salt and pepper.

2. Shape mixture into 4 burgers and cook in lightly greased skillet until browned, 3 to 4 minutes on each side. Arrange burgers in pitas; drizzle 2 tablespoons Tahini Dressing over each burger. Spoon combined tomato, cucumber, and sliced green onions into pitas.

Tahini Dressing
Makes about 1⅓ cups

⅓ cup fat-free yogurt
2–3 tablespoons tahini (sesame seed paste)
1 small clove garlic, minced
½–1 teaspoon lemon juice

1. Mix all ingredients; refrigerate until ready to use.

45-MINUTE PREPARATION TIP: Make Tahini Dressing before preparing the rest of the recipe.

VARIATION

Falafel Pitas — Make recipe as above, but shape mixture into meatballs; coat lightly with unseasoned dry bread crumbs. Spray meatballs with cooking spray and bake at 375 degrees until browned, about 15 minutes. Serve in pitas.

SLOPPY JOES

45 *Toasted buns are a must for this sweet-sour beef filling.*

4 servings

1 pound ground beef eye of round
½ cup each: chopped onion, celery, red or green
  bell pepper
2 cloves garlic, minced
1 cup reduced-sodium catsup
½ cup water
2 tablespoons prepared mustard
1 tablespoon cider vinegar
2 teaspoons packed light brown sugar
Salt and pepper, to taste
4 hamburger buns, toasted

Per Serving:
Calories: 385
% of calories from fat: 17
Fat (gm): 7.4
Saturated fat (gm): 2.2
Cholesterol (mg): 64
Sodium (mg): 423
Protein (gm): 32.5
Carbohydrate (gm): 48.2

Exchanges:
Milk: 0.0
Vegetable: 2.0
Fruit: 0.0
Bread: 2.0
Meat: 3.5
Fat: 0.0

1. Cook ground beef, onion, celery, bell pepper, and garlic in lightly greased medium skillet over medium heat until beef is browned and vegetables tender, about 10 minutes. Stir in remaining ingredients, except salt, pepper, and buns; heat to boiling. Reduce heat and simmer, uncovered, until mixture is thickened, about 5 minutes. Season to taste with salt and pepper. Serve in buns.

VARIATION

Baked Sloppy Potatoes — Make recipe as above, deleting buns. Spoon mixture into 4 large baked potatoes.

CHEESEBURGERS SUPREME

45 *Serve these great burgers with Crispy French Fries (see p. 439). And see Herbed Veggie Burgers (p. 534) for other tasty burger variations.*

4 servings

1 pound very lean ground beef

2–4 tablespoons finely chopped onion

3 tablespoons water

½ teaspoon salt

¼ teaspoon pepper

4 slices (1 ounce each) fat-free or reduced-fat Cheddar or Swiss cheese

4 hamburger buns, toasted

Per Serving:
Calories: 326
% of calories from fat: 19
Fat (gm): 6.7
Saturated fat (gm): 2.2
Cholesterol (mg): 64
Sodium (mg): 768
Protein (gm): 39.5
Carbohydrate (gm): 24.1

Exchanges:
Milk: 0.0
Vegetable: 0.0
Fruit: 0.0
Bread: 1.5
Meat: 4.0
Fat: 0.0

1. Mix ground beef, onion, water, salt, and pepper in medium bowl just until blended. Shape mixture into four 1-inch-thick patties. Cook burgers in lightly greased skillet to desired degree of doneness, 3 to 4 minutes per side for medium. Top each burger with slice of cheese; cover skillet and cook until cheese is beginning to melt, 1 to 2 minutes. Serve in buns.

VARIATIONS

Smothered Onion-Garlic Burgers — Make burgers above, deleting cheese. Thinly slice 1 large onion and 4 large cloves garlic; cook in 1 tablespoon vegetable oil in large skillet over medium heat until very soft, about 15 minutes. Season to taste with salt and pepper; serve over burgers in toasted buns.

Wild Mushroom Burgers — Make burgers above, deleting cheese. Sauté 2 to 3 cups sliced wild mushrooms in 2 tablespoons vegetable oil in large skillet until tender, 5 to 8 minutes; season to taste with dried thyme leaves, salt, and pepper. Serve over burgers in toasted sesame buns.

Mega-Cheese Burgers — Make burgers above, deleting cheese. Top each cooked burger with ½-ounce each reduced-fat Cheddar, Swiss, and Pepper-Jack cheese; cook, covered, over medium heat until cheeses are melted, 3 to 4 minutes. Serve in toasted buns.

Blues Burgers — Make burgers above, deleting cheese. Top each cooked burger with 2 slices crisp vegetarian bacon and 1 ounce crumbled blue cheese; cook, covered, over medium heat until cheese is melted, 2 to 3 minutes. Serve in toasted onion buns.

Swiss-Kraut Burgers — Make burgers above, deleting cheese. Spread 1 tablespoon reduced-fat 1,000 island salad dressing on each cooked burger and top with 1 slice reduced-fat Swiss cheese and 2–3 tablespoons sauerkraut. Cook, covered, over medium heat until cheese is melted, 2 to 3 minutes. Serve in toasted rye bread.

Mediterranean Veggie Burgers — Make burgers above, deleting cheese. Spray both sides of eggplant slices with olive oil cooking spray; saute in skillet until browned, 3 to 4 minutes on each side. Season to taste with salt and pepper. Top each burger with eggplant slice, 2 roasted red pepper strips and 1 ounce crumbled fat-free feta cheese; serve in toasted Italian bread.

Mexi-Veggie Burgers — Make burgers above, deleting cheese. Sauté 1 each small sliced poblano chili and onion in lightly greased skillet until tender, about 5 minutes; season to taste with dried oregano leaves, salt, and pepper. Spoon over burgers and roll in flour tortillas with chopped tomato and cilantro.

Greek Isle Veggie Burgers — Make burgers above, deleting cheese. Sauté ¾ cup each chopped tomato and zucchini in lightly greased skillet until tender, about 5 minutes; season to taste with dried mint and oregano leaves, salt, and pepper. Serve with cooked burgers and crumbled fat-free feta cheese in pita breads.

CALZONES

L *These Italian-style pies filled with cheese and vegetables can also be served for lunch or supper. A packaged mix makes a quick and easy dough.*

16 servings

1 cup each: chopped zucchini, sliced mushrooms

½ cup each: chopped onion, green bell pepper

1 can (14½ ounces) diced tomatoes with roasted garlic, undrained

2 teaspoons dried Italian seasoning

1 cup fat-free ricotta cheese

2 cups (8 ounces) shredded reduced-fat mozzarella cheese

Salt and pepper, to taste

1 package (16 ounces) hot roll mix

1¼ cups hot water

1 tablespoon olive oil

Fat-free milk

Per Serving:
Calories: 185
% of calories from fat: 28
Fat (gm): 5.8
Saturated fat (gm): 1.6
Cholesterol (mg): 7.6
Sodium (mg): 379
Protein (gm): 9.4
Carbohydrate (gm): 23.6

Exchanges:
Milk: 0.0
Vegetable: 1.5
Fruit: 0.0
Bread: 1.0
Meat: 1.0
Fat: 0.5

1. Sauté zucchini, mushrooms, onion, and bell pepper in lightly greased skillet 5 minutes. Add tomatoes with liquid and Italian seasoning; simmer until vegetables are tender and excess liquid is gone, about 10 minutes. Remove from heat; stir in cheeses and season to taste with salt and pepper.

2. Make hot roll mix according to package directions for pizza, using hot water and oil. Divide dough into 8 equal pieces; roll each on floured surface into a 7-inch circle. Spoon about ½ cup vegetable mixture on each; fold in half and flute edges or seal edges with tines of fork. Brush tops of pastries with fat-free milk. Bake on cookie sheet at 375 degrees until browned, about 15 minutes. Cut calzones into halves.

SWEET FENNEL CALZONES

L *Fresh fennel, onion, sour cream, and melted cheese are combined in these golden calzones.*

8 servings

6 cups thinly sliced fennel bulb

1½ cups chopped onion

⅔ cup chopped red bell pepper

2 cloves garlic, minced

1 cup (4 ounces) shredded fat-free mozzarella cheese

½ cup fat-free sour cream

Salt and pepper, to taste

1 package (16 ounces) hot roll mix

1¼ cups very hot water (120 degrees)

1 tablespoon olive oil

2 tablespoons fat-free milk

Per Serving:
Calories: 307
% of calories from fat: 15
Fat (gm): 5.3
Saturated fat (gm): 0.8
Cholesterol (mg): 3.4
Sodium (mg): 378
Protein (gm): 13.8
Carbohydrate (gm): 52

Exchanges:
Milk: 0.0
Vegetable: 1.5
Fruit: 0.0
Bread: 3.0
Meat: 0.5
Fat: 0.5

1. Cook fennel, onion, bell pepper, and garlic in lightly greased large skillet, covered, over medium heat until tender, about 10 minutes, stirring occasionally. Cool; stir in cheese and sour cream. Season to taste with salt and pepper.

2. Make hot roll mix according to package directions for pizza, using hot water and oil. Divide dough into 8 equal pieces; roll each piece of dough on floured surface into a 7-inch circle. Spoon about ⅔ cup fennel mixture on each; fold into halves and flute edges of dough or seal with tines of fork. Brush tops of pastries with milk. Bake on greased cookie sheet at 375 degrees until browned, about 15 minutes. Cut calzones into halves.

MONTE CRISTO

45 *The sourdough bread and egg-batter coating make this grilled sandwich special. Substitute any desired lean meat and cheese for variety.*

4 servings

4 slices (3 ounces) each: lean smoked ham and
   turkey breast
4 slices (4 ounces) fat-free Cheddar cheese
8 slices sourdough or Italian bread
2 eggs, lightly beaten

1. Arrange meats and cheese on 4 slices of bread;
top with remaining bread. Dip sandwiches in
egg, coating both sides of sandwiches; cook
in lightly greased large skillet over medium
to medium-low heat until browned, about 5
minutes on each side.

Per Serving:
Calories: 248
% of calories from fat: 9
Fat (gm): 2.4
Saturated fat (gm): 0.5
Cholesterol (mg): 27.7
Sodium (mg): 756
Protein (gm): 26.8
Carbohydrate (gm): 28.9

Exchanges:
Milk: 0.0
Vegetable: 0.0
Fruit: 0.0
Bread: 2.0
Meat: 2.0
Fat: 0.0

VARIATION

Blue Cheese Cristo —Make recipe as above, substituting sliced
chicken breast for the ham and crumbled blue cheese for the
Cheddar cheese.

SMOKED TURKEY AND GOAT CHEESE HOAGIES

45 *A sandwich full of flavor surprises!*

4 servings

4 cups sliced onions
2 cups sliced green bell peppers
2 teaspoons minced garlic
⅓ cup water
¼ cup raisins
1–1½ tablespoons balsamic vinegar
Salt and pepper, to taste
4 ounces fat-free cream cheese, room temperature
½ cup (2 ounces) goat cheese
4 French rolls or hoagie buns
16 spinach leaves
4 ounces thinly sliced smoked turkey breast

Per Serving:
Calories: 330
% of calories from fat: 18
Fat (gm): 6.7
Saturated fat (gm): 3.5
Cholesterol (mg): 12.3
Sodium (mg): 792
Protein (gm): 18.3
Carbohydrate (gm): 52.1

Exchanges:
Milk: 0.0
Vegetable: 3.0
Fruit: 0.0
Bread: 2.0
Meat: 2.0
Fat: 0.0

1. Cook onions, bell peppers, and garlic in lightly greased large skillet over medium to medium-low heat, covered, until softened and beginning to brown, 15 to 20 minutes. Add water, raisins, and vinegar; heat to boiling. Reduce heat and simmer, covered, until water has evaporated, 5 to 8 minutes. Season to taste with salt and pepper. Spread combined cheeses on tops and bottoms of rolls; fill with spinach, turkey, and vegetable mixture.

TURKEY AND SUN-DRIED TOMATO PESTO GRILL

45 *Basil pesto can also be used. Thin onion slices can be added to the sandwich or substituted for the tomato slices.*

4 servings

8 slices sourdough bread
½ cup prepared sun-dried tomato pesto
8 slices (6 ounces) fat-free mozzarella cheese
4 ounces thinly sliced turkey breast
8 thin slices ripe tomato
Vegetable cooking spray

1. Spread each bread slice with 1 tablespoon pesto. Layer 4 slices bread with cheese, turkey, tomato, and remaining bread slices. Spray both sides of sandwiches with cooking spray; cook in lightly greased large skillet over medium to medium-low heat until browned, about 5 minutes on each side.

Per Serving:
Calories: 366
% of calories from fat: 30
Fat (gm): 12.2
Saturated fat (gm): 1.8
Cholesterol (mg): 23.5
Sodium (mg): 777
Protein (gm): 28.1
Carbohydrate (gm): 35.8

Exchanges:
Milk: 0.0
Vegetable: 1.0
Fruit: 0.0
Bread: 2.0
Meat: 3.0
Fat: 1.0

CRAB MELT

45 *Canned tuna, cooked shrimp, or surimi (imitation crabmeat) can be used in place of the crab.*

2 servings

4 ounces cooked crabmeat, flaked
1 medium green onion, thinly sliced
2 tablespoons each: chopped red bell pepper,
    fat-free mayonnaise, fat-free sour cream
½ teaspoon dried dill weed
1–2 teaspoons lemon juice
Salt and pepper, to taste
2 slices each: white or whole wheat bread, fat-free
    American cheese

Per Serving:
Calories: 182
% of calories from fat: 10
Fat (gm): 2
Saturated fat (gm): 0.3
Cholesterol (mg): 56.7
Sodium (mg): 786
Protein (gm): 19.9
Carbohydrate (gm): 20.4

Exchanges:
Milk: 0.0
Vegetable: 0.0
Fruit: 0.0
Bread: 1.0
Meat: 2.0
Fat: 0.0

1. Mix crabmeat, green onion, red bell pepper, mayonnaise, sour cream, and dill weed in small bowl; season to taste with lemon juice, salt, and pepper. Spread on bread slices and top with cheese. Bake at 400 degrees or broil until sandwiches are hot and cheese melted.

TURKEY AND CRANBERRY CHEESE MELT

45 | *Lots of melted cheese, with cranberry and walnut accents.*

4 servings

2 ounces fat-free cream cheese, room temperature

¼ cup (1 ounce) shredded smoked Gouda or
  Swiss cheese

¼ cup chopped walnuts

8 slices whole wheat bread

8 ounces thinly sliced turkey breast

½ medium onion, thinly sliced

¼ cup whole-berry cranberry sauce

½ cup (2 ounces) shredded fat-free Cheddar cheese

Vegetable cooking spray

Per Serving:
Calories: 336
% of calories from fat: 28
Fat (gm): 10.6
Saturated fat (gm): 2.7
Cholesterol (mg): 32.9
Sodium (mg): 734
Protein (gm): 27.8
Carbohydrate (gm): 34.2

Exchanges:
Milk: 0.0
Vegetable: 0.0
Fruit: 0.5
Bread: 2.0
Meat: 3.0
Fat: 0.0

1. Mix cream and Gouda cheeses and walnuts; spread on 4 slices bread. Top with turkey, onion, cranberry sauce, Cheddar cheese, and remaining bread. Spray both sides of sandwiches lightly with cooking spray; cook in large skillet over medium to medium-low heat until browned, about 5 minutes on each side.

VARIATION

Ham and Marmalade Melt — Make recipe as above, substituting brick cheese for the smoked Gouda and Cheddar cheeses, lean ham for the turkey breast, and orange marmalade for the cranberry sauce.

CUCUMBER, HAM, AND CHEESE MELT

45 | *A great combination of flavors that will keep you coming back for more!*

4 servings

2 ounces fat-free cream cheese, room temperature

2 tablespoons crumbled blue cheese

8 slices multigrain bread

¼ cup apricot jam

16 cucumber slices
2 ounces shaved reduced-sodium ham
4 slices (4 ounces) fat-free Swiss cheese
Vegetable cooking spray

1. Mix cream cheese and blue cheese; spread on 4 slices of bread. Spread each with 1 tablespoon jam and top with 4 cucumber slices, ham, a slice of Swiss cheese, and remaining bread. Spray both sides of sandwiches with cooking spray; cook in large skillet over medium to medium-low heat until browned, about 5 minutes on each side.

Per Serving:
Calories: 237
% of calories from fat: 9
Fat (gm): 2.7
Saturated fat (gm): 0.9
Cholesterol (mg): 10.4
Sodium (mg): 692
Protein (gm): 18.4
Carbohydrate (gm): 39.5

Exchanges:
Milk: 0.0
Vegetable: 0.0
Fruit: 0.5
Bread: 2.0
Meat: 1.0
Fat: 0.0

BLUE CHEESE AND PEAR MELT

45 *Blue cheese and pears are perfect flavor companions, any way they are served.*

4 servings

8 slices honey wheat or light rye bread
4 slices (4 ounces) fat-free Swiss cheese
¼ cup mango chutney
1 medium pear, cored, sliced (¼-inch)
½ cup (2 ounces) crumbled blue cheese
Vegetable cooking spray

Per Serving:
Calories: 284
% of calories from fat: 20
Fat (gm): 6.6
Saturated fat (gm): 3.2
Cholesterol (mg): 10.5
Sodium (mg): 780
Protein (gm): 13.6
Carbohydrate (gm): 44.6

Exchanges:
Milk: 0.0
Vegetable: 0.0
Fruit: 1.0
Bread: 2.0
Meat: 1.0
Fat: 0.5

1. Top 4 slices bread with Swiss cheese and spread each with 1 tablespoon chutney; top with pear slices, blue cheese, and remaining bread. Spray both sides of sandwiches with cooking spray; cook in large skillet over medium to medium-low heat until browned, about 5 minutes on each side.

SPICED PEAR BUTTER

V | *Use ripe pears that are still firm for this gently spiced spread.*

Makes 1½ pints (1 tablespoon per serving)

2½ pounds firm, ripe pears, peeled, cored, chopped
½ cup water
1 tablespoon lemon juice
¾ teaspoon each: ground cinnamon, ginger
⅛ teaspoon ground nutmeg
2 cups sugar

Per Serving:
Calories: 47
% of calories from fat: 2
Fat (gm): 0.1
Saturated fat (gm): 0
Cholesterol (mg): 0
Sodium (mg): 0
Protein (gm): 0.1
Carbohydrate (gm): 12

Exchanges:
Milk: 0.0
Vegetable: 0.0
Fruit: 0.75
Bread: 0.0
Meat: 0.0
Fat: 0.0

1. Heat pears and water to boiling in large saucepan; reduce heat and simmer, covered, until pears are very tender, about 10 minutes. Process pears and liquid in food processor or blender until smooth. Return pear puree to saucepan; stir in remaining ingredients and heat to boiling. Reduce heat and simmer, uncovered, stirring frequently, until mixture thickens to desired consistency, 10 to 20 minutes. Pour pear butter into sterilized jars; cool and cover with lids. Refrigerate up to 2 weeks.

SPICED RHUBARB JAM

V | *Cook this jam to desired consistency, as it's not made with pectin.*

About 2 pints (1 tablespoon per serving)

1½ pounds rhubarb, sliced (1-inch)
2 cups sugar
1 cup water
2 pieces gingerroot (1-inch), halved lengthwise
1 cinnamon stick
¼ teaspoon ground cardamom

Per Serving:
Calories: 27
% of calories from fat: 1
Fat (gm): 0
Saturated fat (gm): 0
Cholesterol (mg): 0
Sodium (mg): 1
Protein (gm): 0.1
Carbohydrate (gm): 6.8

Exchanges:
Milk: 0.0
Vegetable: 0.0
Fruit: 0.5
Bread: 0.0
Meat: 0.0
Fat: 0.0

1. Heat rhubarb, sugar, and water to boiling in large saucepan; reduce heat and simmer, covered, until rhubarb is tender, about 10 minutes.

Strain rhubarb, returning juice to saucepan; reserve rhubarb. Add spices to juice and heat to boiling. Reduce heat and simmer rapidly, stirring occasionally, until very thick, 10 to 15 minutes. Discard cinnamon stick and gingerroot.

2. Stir rhubarb into juice mixture; simmer, if necessary for mixture to be a jam consistency, stirring to prevent sticking. Pour jam into sterilized jars; cool and cover with lids. Refrigerate up to 2 weeks.

ROSE GERANIUM JELLY

45 *Simply delicious, and perfect for gift giving.*

V   **About 2 pints** (1 tablespoon each)

1 cup boiling water

½ cup packed, torn rose geranium leaves

1 can (6 ounces) unsweetened frozen apple
   juice concentrate

1 package (1¾ ounces) powdered fruit pectin

2–3 tablespoons lemon juice

1 tablespoon white distilled vinegar

Pinch salt

3⅓ cups sugar

Per Serving:
Calories: 48
% of calories from fat: 0
Fat (gm): 0
Saturated fat (gm): 0
Cholesterol (mg): 0
Sodium (mg): 2
Protein (gm): 0
Carbohydrate (gm): 12.33

Exchanges:
Milk: 0.0
Vegetable: 0.0
Fruit: 1.0
Bread: 0.0
Meat: 0.0
Fat: 0.0

1. Pour boiling water over rose geranium leaves in small bowl; let stand until cool. Strain; discard rose geranium leaves. Combine rose geranium water and apple juice in 2-cup measure; add water to measure 2 cups. Heat juice mixture and remaining ingredients, except sugar, to boiling in large saucepan; stir in sugar and return to boiling, stirring. Boil hard 1 minute, stirring. Pour into sterilized pint jars; seal and cool. Refrigerate up to 1 month.

VARIATIONS

Apple-Mint Jelly — Make recipe as above, substituting ½ cup packed fresh or 3 tablespoons dried mint leaves for the rose geranium leaves.

Orange-Rosemary Jelly — Make recipe as above, substituting 2 tablespoons crushed fresh or 1 tablespoon dried rosemary leaves for the rose geranium leaves, and orange concentrate for the apple. Increase lemon juice to ¼ cup.

TARRAGON WINE JELLY

V

A delicious jelly for biscuits or scones!

45

Makes 3 pints (1 tablespoon per serving)

4 cups dry white wine
2 tablespoons dried tarragon leaves
6 cups sugar
1 package (6 ounces) liquid pectin

1. Heat wine and tarragon to boiling in medium saucepan; reduce heat and simmer, covered, 10 minutes. Strain; discard tarragon. Return wine to saucepan; add sugar and heat to boiling, stirring occasionally. Stir in pectin and heat to boiling; boil hard 1 minute, stirring constantly. Pour jelly into sterilized jars; seal and cool. Store in refrigerator.

Per Serving:
Calories: 58
% of calories from fat: 0
Fat (gm): 0
Saturated fat (gm): 0
Cholesterol (mg): 0
Sodium (mg): 10
Protein (gm): 0
Carbohydrate (gm): 14.1

Exchanges:
Milk: 0.0
Vegetable: 0.0
Fruit: 1.0
Bread: 0.0
Meat: 0.0
Fat: 0.0

EASY GINGER JELLY

V

For best flavor, refrigerate 3 days before serving. Serve on crackers, home-made bread, or biscuits.

45

Makes 2 half-pints (1 tablespoon per serving)

2 jars (8 ounces each) apple jelly
4–6 quarter-size slices gingerroot (⅛ inch), finely chopped

1. Heat jelly and gingerroot to boiling over medium heat in small saucepan; cool. Pour jelly and ginger into sterilized jars; cool and cover with lids. Store in refrigerator.

Per Serving:
Calories: 39
% of calories from fat: 0
Fat (gm): 0
Saturated fat (gm): 0
Cholesterol (mg): 0
Sodium (mg): 2
Protein (gm): 0
Carbohydrate (gm): 10.1

Exchanges:
Milk: 0.0
Vegetable: 0.0
Fruit: 0.5
Bread: 0.0
Meat: 0.0
Fat: 0.0

GINGERED HONEY

For best flavor, make this aromatic honey 2 weeks in advance of serving. Serve on toast, crackers, biscuits, or pancakes, or spoon over ice cream or fruit!

Makes 1 pint (1 tablespoon per serving)

4 ounces gingerroot, peeled, sliced paper-thin
1⅓ cups honey, clover or other flavor, warm

1. Loosely fill sterilized pint jar with gingerroot; fill to top with warm honey, covering ginger completely. Cool and cover with lid. Store in refrigerator.

Per Serving:
Calories: 46
% of calories from fat: 0
Fat (gm): 0
Saturated fat (gm): 0
Cholesterol (mg): 0
Sodium (mg): 1
Protein (gm): 0
Carbohydrate (gm): 11.9

Exchanges:
Milk: 0.0
Vegetable: 0.0
Fruit: 0.75
Bread: 0.0
Meat: 0.0
Fat: 0.0

FOURTEEN

Desserts

CHOCOLATE BUTTERMILK CAKE WITH MOCHA FROSTING

LO

45

A chocolate dream come true, this cake is 3 layers high and generously covered with creamy mocha frosting!

16 servings

6 tablespoons vegetable shortening

1 cup granulated sugar

½ cup packed light brown sugar

3 eggs

1 teaspoon vanilla

2 cups cake flour

½ cup unsweetened cocoa

2 teaspoons baking powder

½ teaspoon each: baking soda, salt

1 cup buttermilk

Mocha Frosting (recipe follow)

Per Serving:
Calories: 287
% of calories from fat: 17
Fat (gm): 6
Saturated fat (gm): 1
Cholesterol (mg): 32
Sodium (mg): 172
Protein (gm): 3
Carbohydrate (gm): 57

Exchanges:
Milk: 0.0
Vegetable: 0.0
Fruit: 0.0
Bread: 4.0
Meat: 0.0
Fat: 0.5

1. Beat shortening, sugars, eggs, and vanilla in large bowl until smooth. Mix in combined flour, cocoa, baking powder, baking soda, and salt alternately with buttermilk, beginning and ending with dry ingredients. Pour into 3 greased and floured 8-inch round cake pans.

2. Bake at 350 degrees until toothpicks inserted in centers of cakes come out clean, 25 to 30 minutes. Cool in pans on wire racks 10 minutes; invert onto wire racks and cool. Place 1 cake layer on serving plate; frost with about ½ cup frosting. Repeat with second cake layer; top with third layer, frosting top and side.

Mocha Frosting
Makes about 2½ cups

5 cups powdered sugar

½ cup unsweetened cocoa

2–3 teaspoons instant coffee crystals

1 tablespoons margarine or butter, room temperature

1 teaspoon vanilla

4–5 tablespoons fat-free milk

1. Combine powdered sugar, cocoa, coffee crystals, and margarine in large bowl; beat in vanilla and enough milk to make spreadable consistency.

CHOCOLATE SAUERKRAUT CAKE

Aunt Ruby will never reveal the secret ingredient in this chocolatey moist cake—is it the sauerkraut or the beer?

15 servings

1½ cups sugar

½ cup vegetable shortening

2 eggs

1¼ teaspoons vanilla

½ cup unsweetened cocoa

2¼ cups all-purpose flour

1 teaspoon each: baking powder, baking soda

½ teaspoon salt

1 cup beer or water

⅔ cup well drained, rinsed sauerkraut, chopped

Chocolate Cream Cheese Frosting (recipe follows)

Per Serving:
Calories: 308
% of calories from fat: 27
Fat (gm): 9.2
Saturated fat (gm): 2.8
Cholesterol (mg): 32
Sodium (mg): 324
Protein (gm): 4
Carbohydrate (gm): 51

Exchanges:
Milk: 0.0
Vegetable: 0.0
Fruit: 0.0
Bread: 3.0
Meat: 0.0
Fat: 2.0

1. Beat sugar and shortening in large bowl until blended; beat in eggs, vanilla, and cocoa. Mix in combined flour, baking powder, baking soda, and salt alternately with beer, beginning and ending with dry ingredients. Mix in sauerkraut.

2. Spread batter in greased 13 x 9-inch baking pan. Bake at 350 degrees until toothpick inserted in center comes out clean, 40 to 45 minutes. Cool in pan on wire rack; spread with Chocolate Cream Cheese Frosting.

Chocolate Cream Cheese Frosting

Makes about 1½ cups

4 ounces reduced-fat cream cheese, room temperature
1 tablespoon margarine or butter, softened
1¾–2 cups powdered sugar
3 tablespoons unsweetened cocoa

1. Beat cream cheese and margarine in medium bowl until smooth; beat in powdered sugar and cocoa.

RED VELVET CAKE

Also known as Waldorf Astoria Cake, this colorful red dessert is reputed to have originated at the famed New York hotel. The cake can also be frosted with Cream Cheese Frosting (see p. 562).

16 servings

1½ cups sugar
6 tablespoons vegetable shortening
2 eggs
1 teaspoon vanilla
2 bottles (1 ounce each) red food coloring
¼ cup unsweetened cocoa
2¼ cups all-purpose flour
1 teaspoon baking soda
½ teaspoon salt
1 cup buttermilk
1 tablespoon white distilled vinegar
Buttercream Frosting (recipe follows)

Per Serving:
Calories: 361
% of calories from fat: 17
Fat (gm): 6.9
Saturated fat (gm): 1.7
Cholesterol (mg): 27.2
Sodium (mg): 207
Protein (gm): 3.4
Carbohydrate (gm): 71.7

Exchanges:
Milk: 0.0
Vegetable: 0.0
Fruit: 0.0
Bread: 5.0
Meat: 0.0
Fat: 0.0

1. Beat sugar and shortening until well blended in large bowl. Add eggs and vanilla, blending well; beat in food coloring and cocoa until well blended. Mix in combined flour, baking soda, and salt alternately with combined buttermilk and vinegar. Pour batter into 2 greased and floured 9-inch round cake pans.

2. Bake at 350 degrees until toothpick inserted in center of cake comes out clean, 25 to 30 minutes. Cool in pans on wire rack 10 minutes; remove cakes from pans and cool completely. Place 1 cake layer on serving plate; spread with generous ½ cup Buttercream Frosting. Top with remaining layer; frost cake.

Buttercream Frosting
Makes about 3 cups

5 cups powdered sugar
2 tablespoons margarine or butter, room temperature
1 teaspoon vanilla
3–4 tablespoons fat-free milk

1. Mix powdered sugar, margarine, vanilla, and enough milk to make spreading consistency.

RICH LEMON POUND CAKE

LO

Savor the rich flavor of this cake, which is enhanced with the Lemon Syrup.

45

12 servings

¾ cup sugar
⅓ cup margarine or butter, room temperature
1 cup reduced-fat sour cream
3 egg whites
2 teaspoons lemon juice
1 tablespoon grated lemon zest
2½ cups cake flour
1 teaspoon baking soda
¼ teaspoon salt
Lemon Syrup (recipe follows)
Powdered sugar, as garnish

Per Serving:
Calories: 230
% of calories from fat: 26
Fat (gm): 6.5
Saturated fat (gm): 1
Cholesterol (mg): 6.3
Sodium (mg): 235
Protein (gm): 3.5
Carbohydrate (gm): 38.8

Exchanges:
Milk: 0.0
Vegetable: 0.0
Fruit: 0.0
Bread: 2.5
Meat: 0.0
Fat: 1.0

1. Beat sugar and margarine in large bowl until fluffy; beat in sour cream, egg whites, lemon juice, and zest until smooth. Mix in combined flour, baking soda, and salt, beating about 1 minute. Spoon into greased and floured 6-cup fluted cake pan.

2. Bake 40 to 50 minutes or until toothpick inserted in center of cake comes out clean. Cool in pan on wire rack 20 minutes. Pierce cake at 1-inch intervals with skewer or long-tined fork. Spoon warm

Lemon Syrup over and let stand 30 minutes. Invert onto serving plate; sprinkle generously with powdered sugar.

Lemon Syrup
Makes about ⅔ cup

⅔ cup powdered sugar
¼ cup lemon juice
3 tablespoons water

1. Heat all ingredients to boiling in small saucepan, stirring until sugar is dissolved. Cool slightly.

ORANGE POPPY SEED CAKE

LO

This citrus-fresh cake is a perfect addition to any brunch menu.

45

◊

12 servings

½ cup sugar
6 tablespoons margarine or butter, room temperature
2 eggs
¾ cup fat-free sour cream
2 tablespoons frozen orange juice concentrate, thawed
2 cups cake flour
2 tablespoons poppy seeds
1 teaspoon baking powder
½ teaspoon baking soda
¼ teaspoon salt
Citrus Glaze (recipe follows)

Per Serving:
Calories: 278
% of calories from fat: 33
Fat (gm): 10
Saturated fat (gm): 3
Cholesterol (mg): 48
Sodium (mg): 277
Protein (gm): 5
Carbohydrate (gm): 42

Exchanges:
Milk: 0.0
Vegetable: 0.0
Fruit: 0.0
Bread: 2.5
Meat: 0.0
Fat: 2.0

1. Beat sugar and margarine in large bowl until fluffy. Beat in eggs, sour cream, and orange juice; add combined flour, poppy seeds, baking powder, baking soda, and salt, beating on medium-high speed until smooth, 1 to 2 minutes. Pour into greased and floured 6-cup fluted cake pan.

2. Bake at 350 degrees 40 to 55 minutes or until toothpick inserted in center of cake comes out clean. Cool in pan on wire rack 25 to 30 minutes; invert onto wire rack and cool. Spoon Citrus Glaze over cake.

Citrus Glaze

1 cup powdered sugar
3–4 tablespoons orange juice

1. Mix sugar and enough orange juice to make glaze consistency.

GINGERED PEAR CAKE

Serve this cake topped with sweetened sour cream and ginger; a drizzle of Citrus Glaze (see p. 557) is also delicious.

12 servings

1 cup packed light brown sugar
¼ cup margarine or butter, room temperature
1 egg
1½ cups all-purpose flour
1½ teaspoons baking soda
¼ teaspoon each: salt, ground cloves
1 teaspoon ground ginger
2 tablespoons chopped crystallized ginger
2 small pears, peeled, cored, shredded
Gingered Sour Cream Topping (recipe follows)

Per Serving:
Calories: 228
% of calories from fat: 22
Fat (gm): 5.7
Saturated fat (gm): 2.1
Cholesterol (mg): 6.7
Sodium (mg): 287
Protein (gm): 4
Carbohydrate (gm): 40.7

Exchanges:
Milk: 0.0
Vegetable: 0.0
Fruit: 0.0
Bread: 2.5
Meat: 0.0
Fat: 1.0

1. Beat brown sugar, margarine, and egg in large bowl until smooth; mix in combined flour, baking soda, salt, spices, and crystallized ginger. Gently mix in pears. Pour batter into greased and floured 6-cup fluted tube pan.

2. Bake at 350 degrees until toothpick inserted in center of cake comes out clean, 50 to 60 minutes. Cool cake in pan on wire rack 10 minutes; remove from pan and cool. Serve with Gingered Sour Cream Topping.

Gingered Sour Cream Topping

Makes 1 to 1½ cups

1–1½ cups reduced-fat sour cream
2–3 tablespoons sugar
2–4 tablespoons coarsely chopped crystallized ginger

1. Mix all ingredients.

RHUBARB STREUSEL CAKE

A rich and crispy streusel and a light orange glaze top this wonderfully moist cake.

12 servings

½ cup margarine or butter, room temperature
1⅓ cups sugar
1 egg, beaten
1 teaspoon vanilla
2 cups all-purpose flour
1 teaspoon each: baking soda, ground cinnamon
½ teaspoon each: ground nutmeg, salt
1 cup buttermilk
2 cups sliced fresh or frozen thawed rhubarb (1-inch)
⅓ cup raisins
2 teaspoons grated orange zest
Crisp Streusel (recipe follows)
Orange Glaze (recipe follow)

Per Serving:
Calories: 342
% of calories from fat: 27
Fat (gm): 10.4
Saturated fat (gm): 2.2
Cholesterol (mg): 18.5
Sodium (mg): 336
Protein (gm): 4.1
Carbohydrate (gm): 59.3

Exchanges:
Milk: 0.0
Vegetable: 0.0
Fruit: 1.0
Bread: 3.0
Meat: 0.0
Fat: 1.5

1. Beat margarine and sugar until smooth in large bowl; beat in egg and vanilla. Mix in combined flour, baking soda, cinnamon, nutmeg, and salt alternately with buttermilk, beginning and ending with dry ingredients. Mix in rhubarb, raisins, and orange zest. Pour into greased and floured 13 x 9-inch baking pan; sprinkle with Crisp Streusel.

2. Bake at 350 degrees until toothpick inserted in center of cake comes out clean, 35 to 40 minutes. Cool in pan on wire rack 15 minutes; drizzle with Orange Glaze.

Crisp Streusel

½ cup packed light brown sugar
2 tablespoons each: quick-cooking oats, flour,
   cold margarine or butter, cut into pieces

1. Combine brown sugar, oats, and flour in small bowl; cut in margarine to form crumbly mixture.

Orange Glaze

½ cup powdered sugar
1 teaspoon grated orange zest
2–4 teaspoons orange juice

1. Mix powdered sugar and orange zest with enough orange juice to make glaze consistency.

45-MINUTE PREPARATION TIP: Make Crisp Streusel before preparing the rest of the recipe.

SUGARED PECAN AND DATE CAKE

A cake moist and sweet with dates, topped with a warm crunchy pecan glaze. Best served warm!

8 to 10 servings

1 cup sugar
¼ cup margarine or butter, room temperature
1 teaspoon vanilla
1 egg yolk
1 cup all-purpose flour
½ teaspoon baking soda
⅛ teaspoon salt
½ cup buttermilk
⅓ cup chopped dates
3 egg whites, beaten to stiff peaks
Broiled Pecan Frosting (recipe follows)

Per Serving:
Calories: 378
% of calories from fat: 33
Fat (gm): 13.9
Saturated fat (gm): 2.5
Cholesterol (mg): 27.2
Sodium (mg): 277
Protein (gm): 4.8
Carbohydrate (gm): 60.2

Exchanges:
Milk: 0.0
Vegetable: 0.0
Fruit: 0.0
Bread: 4.0
Meat: 0.0
Fat: 2.0

1. Mix sugar, margarine, and vanilla in large bowl; beat in egg yolk. Mix in combined flour, baking soda, and salt alternately with buttermilk, beginning and ending with dry ingredients. Stir in dates; fold in egg whites. Pour batter into greased and floured 9-inch round or square cake pan.

2. Bake at 350 degrees until toothpick inserted in center of cake comes out clean, 20 to 25 minutes. Cool cake in pan on wire rack 10 minutes; remove from pan and cool 10 to 15 minutes. Place cake on ovenproof serving plate or cookie sheet. Spread Broiled Pecan Frosting evenly on cake; broil 4 inches from heat source until mixture is bubbly and pecans browned, about 1 minute. Serve warm.

Boiled Pecan Frosting

½ cup packed light brown sugar

3 tablespoons each: flour, margarine or butter

½ teaspoon ground cinnamon

2 tablespoons fat-free milk

⅓ cup coarsely chopped pecans

1. Heat all ingredients, except pecans, to boiling in small saucepan, stirring frequently; cook over medium heat 2 minutes, stirring constantly. Remove from heat; stir in pecans.

MOM'S APPLE DAPPLE CAKE

Caramel apple flavors in a wonderfully moist cake!

16 to 24 servings

⅓ cup vegetable oil

⅔ cup applesauce

2 cups sugar

3 eggs

2 teaspoons vanilla

3 cups all-purpose flour

1 teaspoon baking soda

½ teaspoon salt

3 cups peeled chopped apples

Per Serving:
Calories: 358
% of calories from fat: 27
Fat (gm): 10.8
Saturated fat (gm): 1.6
Cholesterol (mg): 39.8
Sodium (mg): 205
Protein (gm): 4.8
Carbohydrate (gm): 61.9

Exchanges:
Milk: 0.0
Vegetable: 0.0
Fruit: 0.0
Bread: 4.0
Meat: 0.0
Fat: 1.5

½ cup chopped walnuts
Brown Sugar Syrup (recipe follows)

1. Mix oil, applesauce, sugar, eggs, and vanilla until well blended in large bowl; mix in combined flour, baking soda, and salt. Mix in apples and walnuts. Pour batter into greased and floured 12-cup fluted tube pan.

2. Bake at 350 degrees until toothpick inserted in center of cake comes out clean, about 60 minutes. Remove from oven and cool on wire rack 5 minutes. Pierce top of cake with long-tined fork and pour hot Brown Sugar Syrup over cake. Let cake cool in pan 2 hours. Invert onto serving plate.

Brown Sugar Syrup
Makes about 1 cup

1 cup packed light brown sugar
¼ cup each: fat-free milk, margarine or butter

1. Heat all ingredients to boiling in small saucepan, stirring to melt margarine; boil 3 minutes.

CARROT CAKE WITH CREAM CHEESE FROSTING

Moist and sweetly spiced, this cake is one you'll want to make over and over again.

16 servings

3 cups shredded carrots
½ cup raisins
1 cup packed light brown sugar
⅓ cup vegetable oil
3 eggs
2 cups all-purpose flour
1 teaspoon each: baking powder, baking soda, ground cinnamon
¼ teaspoon each: ground allspice, nutmeg, salt
Cream Cheese Frosting (recipe follows)

Per Serving:
Calories: 346
% of calories from fat: 24
Fat (gm): 9.7
Saturated fat (gm): 2.7
Cholesterol (mg): 44.9
Sodium (mg): 255
Protein (gm): 4.7
Carbohydrate (gm): 62.2

Exchanges:
Milk: 0.0
Vegetable: 1.0
Fruit: 0.0
Bread: 5.0
Meat: 0.0
Fat: 2.0

1. Mix carrots, raisins, brown sugar, oil, and eggs in large bowl. Mix in combined remaining ingredients, except Cream Cheese Frosting. Pour into 2 greased and floured 8-inch-round cake pans.

2. Bake at 350 degrees until toothpicks inserted in cakes come out clean, 25 to 30 minutes. Cool in pans on wire rack 10 minutes; remove from pans and cool. Place 1 cake layer on serving plate and frost. Top with second cake layer, frosting top and side of cake.

Cream Cheese Frosting

Makes about 3 cups

4 ounces reduced-fat cream cheese, room temperature
2 tablespoons margarine or butter, room temperature
1 teaspoon vanilla
4–5 cups powdered sugar

1. Beat cream cheese, margarine, and vanilla in medium bowl until smooth; beat in enough powdered sugar to make spreadable consistency.

BOSTON CREAM CAKE

LO *A comfort food, with chocolatey glaze and a luxurious cream filling. Although sometimes called a "pie," it is, indeed, a cake.*

12 servings

8 tablespoons margarine or butter, room temperature
1¼ cups sugar
2 eggs
1 teaspoon vanilla
2⅔ cups all-purpose flour
3 teaspoons baking powder
½ teaspoon salt
1⅔ cups fat-free milk
Vanilla Cream Filling (recipe follows)
Chocolate Glaze (recipe follows)

Per Serving:
Calories: 353
% of calories from fat: 23
Fat (gm): 9.3
Saturated fat (gm): 2
Cholesterol (mg): 54.2
Sodium (mg): 305
Protein (gm): 6.6
Carbohydrate (gm): 61.3

Exchanges:
Milk: 0.0
Vegetable: 0.0
Fruit: 0.0
Bread: 4.0
Meat: 0.0
Fat: 1.5

1. Beat margarine, sugar, eggs, and vanilla until smooth in medium bowl. Mix in combined flour, baking powder, and salt alternately with milk, beginning and ending with dry ingredients. Pour into 2 greased and floured 8- or 9-inch-round cake pans.

2. Bake at 350 degrees until cakes spring back when touched, about 40 minutes. Cool in pans on wire rack 10 minutes; remove from pans and cool. Place 1 cake layer on serving plate; spread with Vanilla Cream Filling. Top with second cake layer and spoon Chocolate Glaze over.

Vanilla Cream Filling

Makes about 1¼ cups

¼ cup sugar
2 tablespoons cornstarch
1 cup fat-free milk
1 egg, beaten
½ teaspoon vanilla

1. Mix sugar and cornstarch in small saucepan; whisk in milk and heat to boiling. Boil, whisking, until thickened, about 1 minute. Whisk about ½ the milk mixture into beaten egg in small bowl; whisk back into saucepan. Whisk over low heat 30 to 60 seconds. Stir in vanilla and cool.

Chocolate Glaze

1 cup powdered sugar
2 tablespoons unsweetened cocoa
½ teaspoon vanilla
1–2 tablespoons fat-free milk

1. Mix all ingredients, using enough milk to make glaze consistency.

CITRUS POPPYSEED ANGEL FOOD CAKE

A tall, tender cake, bursting with sweet citrus flavor!

16 servings

12 egg whites, room temperature
1 teaspoon cream of tartar
2 teaspoons lemon juice
1½ cups sugar, divided
1 cup cake flour
½ teaspoon salt
1 tablespoon finely grated lemon zest
2 tablespoons each: finely grated orange zest,
    poppy seeds
Citrus Glaze (see p. 557)

Per Serving:
Calories: 149
% of calories from fat: 3
Fat (gm): 0.5
Saturated fat (gm): 0.1
Cholesterol (mg): 0
Sodium (mg): 118
Protein (gm): 3.6
Carbohydrate (gm): 32.8

Exchanges:
Milk: 0.0
Vegetable: 0.0
Fruit: 0.0
Bread: 2.0
Meat: 0.0
Fat: 0.0

1. Beat egg whites and cream of tartar to soft peaks in large bowl. Beat in lemon juice; beat just to stiff peaks, adding ½ cup sugar gradually (do not overbeat). Sprinkle ½ cup sugar over egg whites and fold in. Combine remaining ½ cup sugar, flour, and salt; sift half the flour mixture over egg whites and fold in. Repeat with remaining flour mixture. Fold in citrus zest and poppy seeds. Pour batter into ungreased 12-cup tube pan.

2. Bake at 350 degrees until cake is golden and cracks look dry, about 40 minutes. Invert pan on funnel and cool completely. Loosen side of cake from pan with metal spatula and invert onto serving plate. Drizzle with Citrus Glaze.

CLASSIC SPONGE CAKE

This luscious, very low-fat cake can be combined with different fillings and frostings—or simply sprinkle with powdered sugar and serve with a medley of berries.

12 servings

3 egg yolks

1 cup sugar, divided

2 teaspoons vanilla

¼ cup water

1 cup cake flour

1 teaspoon baking powder

¼ teaspoon salt

5 egg whites

¼ teaspoon cream of tartar

Per Serving:
Calories: 122
% of calories from fat: 10
Fat (gm): 1.4
Saturated fat (gm): 0.4
Cholesterol (mg): 53.2
Sodium (mg): 114
Protein (gm): 2.9
Carbohydrate (gm): 24.3

Exchanges:
Milk: 0.0
Vegetable: 0.0
Fruit: 0.0
Bread: 1.5
Meat: 0.0
Fat: 0.0

1. Beat egg yolks in large mixing bowl, gradually adding ¾ cup sugar; beat at high speed until yolks are thick and lemon colored, about 5 minutes. Mix in vanilla and water; mix in combined flour, baking powder, and salt on low speed just until blended.

2. With clean beaters and large bowl, beat egg whites and cream of tartar to soft peaks. Beat to stiff peaks, gradually adding remaining ¼ cup sugar. Stir ¼ of the egg whites into batter; fold batter into remaining whites. Pour batter into ungreased 12-cup tube pan.

3. Bake at 350 degrees 35 minutes or until cake springs back when touched lightly. Invert pan on funnel and cool to room temperature. Loosen side of cake with small metal spatula and remove from pan.

TIP: Cake can be baked in an ungreased 10-inch springform pan. Invert on wire rack to cool.

LEMON CUSTARD SPONGE CAKE

A beautiful cake that will make any occasion memorable.

12 servings

3 egg yolks

¾ cup sugar, divided

1 teaspoon vanilla

3 egg whites

⅛ teaspoon cream of tartar

⅓ cup each: all-purpose flour, cornstarch

⅛ teaspoon salt

Lemon Custard (recipe follows)

2½ cups light whipped topping, divided

½ cup raspberries

Lemon zest, as garnish

Mint sprigs, as garnish

Per Serving:
Calories: 196
% of calories from fat: 25
Fat (gm): 5.4
Saturated fat (gm): 2.6
Cholesterol (mg): 71.5
Sodium (mg): 126
Protein (gm): 3.2
Carbohydrate (gm): 33

Exchanges:
Milk: 0.0
Vegetable: 0.0
Fruit: 0.0
Bread: 2.0
Meat: 0.0
Fat: 1.0

1. Beat egg yolks, ½ cup sugar, and vanilla in small bowl until thick and lemon colored, 3 to 5 minutes. Using clean beaters and bowl, beat egg whites and cream of tartar to soft peaks; beat to stiff peaks, adding remaining ¼ cup sugar gradually. Fold egg yolk mixture into egg whites. Fold in combined flour, cornstarch, and salt. Spread batter in greased and floured parchment-lined 9-inch round cake pan.

2. Bake at 350 degrees until toothpick inserted in center of cake comes out clean, about 30 minutes. Cool cake in pan 10 minutes; remove from pan and cool completely. Discard parchment.

3. Cut cake horizontally in half. Place bottom of cake on serving plate. Spread 1 cup Lemon Custard on cake and top with second layer. Spread remaining 1 cup Lemon Custard on top of cake. Spread 2 cups whipped topping on side of cake. Using a pastry bag with star tip, pipe remaining ½ cup whipped topping around edge of cake. Garnish with raspberries, lemon zest, and mint. Refrigerate until serving time.

Lemon Custard

Makes about 2 cups

⅓ cup sugar
¼ cup cornstarch
¼ teaspoon salt
1⅓ cups fat-free milk
1 egg yolk
2 tablespoons margarine or butter
2 teaspoons grated lemon zest
⅓ cup lemon juice

1. Combine sugar, cornstarch, and salt in medium saucepan; whisk in milk. Heat to boiling over medium-high heat, whisking constantly; boil, whisking, until thickened, about 1 minute. Whisk about ½ cup milk mixture into egg yolk; whisk yolk mixture back into saucepan. Cook over low heat, whisking 1 to 2 minutes. Remove from heat; stir in margarine, lemon zest, and lemon juice. Cool; refrigerate until chilled.

VARIATION

Sponge Cake with Rosemary Syrup and Blueberries — Make cake as above, omitting Lemon Custard. Cool uncut cake on wire rack 20 minutes; remove from pan and place on serving plate. To make Rosemary Syrup, heat ¾ cup each sugar and water, 2 tablespoons crushed dried rosemary leaves, and 1 tablespoon lemon juice to boiling in small saucepan. Reduce heat and simmer, uncovered, 10 minutes; strain, discarding rosemary. Pierce top of cake with long-tined fork; drizzle ½ cup warm syrup over warm cake. Mix remaining syrup with 1½ quarts blueberries and serve over cake slices.

HOT FUDGE PUDDING CAKE

For the ultimate treat serve warm, topped with scoops of sugar-free ice cream or frozen yogurt.

6 servings

1 cup all-purpose flour

½ cup packed light brown sugar

6 tablespoons Dutch process cocoa, divided

1½ teaspoons baking powder

¼ teaspoon salt

½ cup fat-free milk

2 tablespoons vegetable oil

1 teaspoon vanilla

⅓ cup granulated sugar

1½ cups boiling water

Per Serving:
Calories: 259
% of calories from fat: 18
Fat (gm): 5.2
Saturated fat (gm): 0.9
Cholesterol (mg): 0.4
Sodium (mg): 240
Protein (gm): 4.1
Carbohydrate (gm): 49.1

Exchanges:
Milk: 0.0
Vegetable: 0.0
Fruit: 0.0
Bread: 3.0
Meat: 0.0
Fat: 1.0

1. Combine flour, brown sugar, 3 tablespoons cocoa, baking powder, and salt in medium bowl. Add combined milk, oil, and vanilla to flour mixture, mixing well. Spoon batter into greased 8- or 9-inch square baking pan; sprinkle with combined remaining 3 tablespoons cocoa and granulated sugar. Pour boiling water over batter; do not stir.

2. Bake at 350 degrees until cake springs back when touched, about 30 minutes. Cool on wire rack 5 to 10 minutes; serve warm.

VARIATION

Mocha Latte Pudding Cake — Make cake as above, substituting granulated sugar for the brown sugar and adding 1 tablespoon instant espresso coffee powder and ½ teaspoon ground cinnamon to flour mixture. Serve warm pudding cake with a scoop of sugar-free vanilla or chocolate ice cream and light whipped topping.

LEMON PUDDING CAKE

A luscious combination of moist cake and creamy pudding—for best flavor, use fresh lemon juice.

8 servings

1¼ cups sugar, divided

½ cup all-purpose flour

⅛ teaspoon salt

1 cup reduced-fat 2% milk

⅓ cup lemon juice

2 tablespoons margarine or butter, melted

1 egg

1 tablespoon grated lemon zest

3 egg whites

⅛ teaspoon cream of tartar

Per Serving:
Calories: 208
% of calories from fat: 17
Fat (gm): 4.1
Saturated fat (gm): 1.1
Cholesterol (mg): 28.8
Sodium (mg): 114
Protein (gm): 4
Carbohydrate (gm): 39.9

Exchanges:
Milk: 0.0
Vegetable: 0.0
Fruit: 0.0
Bread: 2.5
Meat: 0.0
Fat: 0.5

1. Combine 1 cup sugar, flour, and salt in large bowl. Mix in combined milk, lemon juice, margarine, egg, and lemon zest.

2. Beat egg whites and cream of tartar to soft peaks in large bowl; beat to stiff peaks, adding remaining ¼ cup sugar gradually. Fold egg whites into cake batter (batter will be slightly lumpy and thin). Pour batter into greased 1½-quart casserole or soufflé dish. Place casserole in roasting pan on oven rack; add 1 to 2 inches boiling water to pan.

3. Bake at 350 degrees until cake is golden and springs back when touched, about 40 minutes. Cool on wire rack 15 minutes; serve warm.

BASIC PIE CRUST

L

45

This pastry contains a minimum of margarine yet is not difficult to handle or roll.

8 servings (one 8- or 9-inch pie crust)

1¼ cups all-purpose flour

2 tablespoons sugar

¼ teaspoon salt

3 tablespoons cold margarine or butter

4–5 tablespoons ice water

Per Serving:
Calories: 121
% of calories from fat: 33
    (will decrease in
    pie servings)
Fat (gm): 4.4
Saturated fat (gm): 0.9
Cholesterol (mg): 0
Sodium (mg): 117
Protein (gm): 2.1
Carbohydrate (gm): 18.1

Exchanges:
Milk: 0.0
Vegetable: 0.0
Fruit: 0.0
Bread: 1.0
Meat: 0.0
Fat: 1.0

1. Combine flour, sugar, and salt in medium bowl. Cut in margarine with pastry blender or 2 knives until mixture resembles coarse crumbs. Sprinkle with water, 1 tablespoon at a time, mixing lightly with a fork after each addition until pastry just holds together. Flatten into a round, wrap in plastic wrap and refrigerate 30 minutes.

2. Roll pastry on lightly floured surface into circle 1½ inches larger than inverted pie pan. Wrap pastry around rolling pin and unroll onto 8- or 9-inch pie or tart pan, easing pastry onto bottom and side of pan. Trim edge, fold under, and flute. Fill and bake as recipe directs. If recipe indicates that the crust is baked before filling, pierce bottom of crust with tines of fork and bake at 425 degrees until browned, about 15 minutes; cool on wire rack.

VARIATION

Double Pie Crust — Make recipe above, using 2 cups flour, 3 tablespoons sugar, ½ teaspoon salt, 5 tablespoons margarine and 6–7 tablespoons ice water. Roll as directed in recipe.

CORNMEAL DOUBLE PIE CRUST

LO

This Italian-Style crust is particularly good with fruit pies.

45
❄

8 servings (one 8- or 9-inch double crust pie crust)

2 cups all-purpose flour
⅓ cup yellow cornmeal
1 teaspoon baking powder
½ teaspoon salt
5 tablespoons cold margarine or butter,
   cut into pieces
2 ounces cold fat-free cream cheese, cut into pieces
3 egg whites

Per Serving:
Calories: 209
% of calories from fat: 33
   (will decrease in
   pie servings)
Fat (gm): 7.6
Saturated fat (gm): 1.5
Cholesterol (mg): 0.6
Sodium (mg): 351
Protein (gm): 6.1
Carbohydrate (gm): 28.4

Exchanges:
Milk: 0.0
Vegetable: 0.0
Fruit: 0.0
Bread: 2.0
Meat: 0.0
Fat: 1.5

1. Combine flour, cornmeal, baking powder, and salt in bowl; cut in margarine and cream cheese until mixture resembles coarse crumbs. Add egg whites, mixing until dough is moist and crumbly. Flatten into a round, wrap in plastic wrap and refrigerate 30 minutes. Roll and bake as pie recipe directs.

GRAHAM CRACKER CRUMB CRUST

L

Mix this crust right in the pie pan—quick and easy, no bowl to clean!

45

8 servings (one 8- or 9-inch pie crust)

1¼ cups graham cracker crumbs
2 tablespoons sugar
3 tablespoons margarine or butter, melted
1–2 tablespoon honey

Per Serving:
Calories: 131
% of calories from fat: 44
   (will decrease in
   pie servings)
Fat (gm): 6.4
Saturated fat (gm): 0.8
Cholesterol (mg): 0
Sodium (mg): 148
Protein (gm): 1.3
Carbohydrate (gm): 17.2

Exchanges:
Milk: 0.0
Vegetable: 0.0
Fruit: 0.0
Bread: 1.0
Meat: 0.0
Fat: 1.0

1. Combine graham crumbs, sugar, and margarine in 8- or 9-inch pie pan, adding enough honey for mixture to hold together; pat mixture evenly on bottom and side of pan. Bake at 350 degrees 8 to 10 minutes or until edge of crust is lightly browned. Cool on wire rack.

VANILLA CRUMB CRUST

L

A perfect recipe when a delicately flavored crust is desired.

45

8 servings (from 8- or 9-inch pie crust)

1 cup vanilla wafer cookie crumbs
2 tablespoons margarine or butter, melted

1. Combine vanilla crumbs and margarine in 8- or 9-inch pie pan; pat mixture evenly on bottom and side of pan. Bake at 350 degrees until lightly browned, 8 to 10 minutes. Cool on wire rack.

VARIATION

Gingersnap Crust – Make crust as above, substituting ½ cup each graham cracker and gingersnap crumbs for the vanilla wafer crumbs.

Per Serving:
Calories: 83
% of calories from fat: 51
 (will decrease in
 pie servings)
Fat (gm): 4.7
Saturated fat (gm): 0.9
Cholesterol (mg): 7.8
Sodium (mg): 64
Protein (gm): 0.6
Carbohydrate (gm): 9.4

Exchanges:
Milk: 0.0
Vegetable: 0.0
Fruit: 0.0
Bread: 0.5
Meat: 0.0
Fat: 1.0

SHORTBREAD CRUST

LO

A tender, sweet pastry that is almost like a cookie.

45

12 servings (one 10- or 12-inch tart crust)

1⅓ cups all-purpose flour
½ cup powdered sugar
Pinch salt
5 tablespoons cold margarine or butter, cut
 into pieces
1 egg, lightly beaten
1 teaspoon vanilla

1. Combine flour, sugar, and salt in medium bowl. Cut in margarine until mixture resembles coarse crumbs. Mix in combined egg and vanilla with fork, stirring just until mixture forms a dough. Form dough into a ball; flatten slightly and wrap in plastic wrap and refrigerate 1 hour. Roll and bake as recipe directs.

Per Serving:
Calories: 209
% of calories from fat: 33
 (will decrease in
 pie servings)
Fat (gm): 7.6
Saturated fat (gm): 1.5
Cholesterol (mg): 0.6
Sodium (mg): 351
Protein (gm): 6.1
Carbohydrate (gm): 28.4

Exchanges:
Milk: 0.0
Vegetable: 0.0
Fruit: 0.0
Bread: 2.0
Meat: 0.0
Fat: 1.5

CHOCOLATE COOKIE CRUMB CRUST

L

45

You can choose chocolate wafer crumbs or chocolate sandwich cookie crumbs.

8 servings (one 8- or 9-inch pie crust)

1¼ cups chocolate cookie crumbs
2 tablespoons sugar
3 tablespoons margarine or butter, melted
1–2 tablespoons honey

Per Serving:
Calories: 158
% of calories from fat: 44
  (will decrease in
  pie servings)
Fat (gm): 8
Saturated fat (gm): 1.5
Cholesterol (mg): 0
Sodium (mg): 225
Protein (gm): 1.3
Carbohydrate (gm): 21.6

Exchanges:
Milk: 0.0
Vegetable: 0.0
Fruit: 0.0
Bread: 1.5
Meat: 0.0
Fat: 1.0

1. Combine cookie crumbs, sugar, and margarine in bottom of 8- or 9-inch pie pan; add enough honey for mixture to stick together. Press evenly on bottom and side of pie pan. Bake at 350 degrees 6 to 8 minutes. Cool on wire rack.

VARIATION

Chocolate Pecan Crumb Crust — Make crust as above, decreasing margarine to 1 tablespoon, increasing honey to 3 tablespoons, and adding ¼ cup ground pecans.

PEACH ALMOND STREUSEL PIE

L

45

The taste of the Deep South, with brown sugar, peaches, and the crunch of almonds.

10 servings

5 cups sliced, peeled peaches

1 cup granulated sugar

¾ cup packed dark brown sugar

¼ cup all-purpose flour

1 teaspoon ground cinnamon

½ teaspoon ground nutmeg

¼ teaspoon salt

2 tablespoons lemon juice

1 tablespoon grated orange zest

1 teaspoon almond extract

Basic Pie Crust (see p. 570)

Almond Streusel (recipe follows)

Per Serving:
Calories: 377
% of calories from fat: 19
Fat (gm): 8.2
Saturated fat (gm): 1.5
Cholesterol (mg): 0
Sodium (mg): 206
Protein (gm): 3.7
Carbohydrate (gm): 72.6

Exchanges:
Milk: 0.0
Vegetable: 0.0
Fruit: 1.0
Bread: 3.5
Meat: 0.0
Fat: 1.5

1. Toss peaches with combined remaining ingredients, except pie crust and Almond Streusel. Arrange fruit in crust; sprinkle with Almond Streusel.

Bake on baking sheet at 400 degrees 40 to 50 minutes, until fruit is tender and bubbly and Almond Streusel is browned. Cool on wire rack.

Almond Streusel

Makes about 1 cup

¼ cup each: all-purpose flour, packed dark brown sugar, quick-cooking oats

2 tablespoons cold margarine, cut into pieces

½ teaspoon almond extract

3 tablespoons sliced almonds

1. Combine flour, brown sugar, and oats in bowl. Cut in margarine until mixture resembles coarse crumbs; stir in almond extract and almonds.

45-MINUTE PREPARATION TIP: Make pie crust before preparing the rest of the recipe.

PEAR TART WITH CRÈME ANGLAISE

LO

45

Select pears that are just ripe, but not soft, for this elegant and delicate tart.

8 servings

2 pounds pears, peeled, cored, sliced (¼ inch)
¼ cup all-purpose flour
3 tablespoons sugar
½ teaspoon ground cinnamon
¼ teaspoon ground nutmeg
Basic Pie Crust (see p. 570), baked in a 9-inch tart pan
Crème Anglaise (recipe follows)

Per Serving:
Calories: 210
% of calories from fat: 14
Fat (gm): 3.5
Saturated fat (gm): 0.6
Cholesterol (mg): 25
Sodium (mg): 66
Protein (gm): 3.6
Carbohydrate (gm): 42

Exchanges:
Milk: 0.0
Vegetable: 0.0
Fruit: 1.0
Bread: 2.0
Meat: 0.0
Fat: 0.5

1. Toss pears with combined flour, sugar, cinnamon, and nutmeg; arrange in overlapping circles in baked crust. Bake at 375 degrees until pears are tender, 20 to 25 minutes. Serve warm with Crème Anglaise.

Crème Anglaise
Makes about 1 cup

1 tablespoon cornstarch
2 teaspoons sugar
1 cup fat-free milk
1 egg yolk
⅛–¼ teaspoon ground nutmeg

1. Mix cornstarch and sugar in small saucepan; whisk in milk. Heat to boiling over medium-high heat, whisking until thickened, about 1 minute. Whisk about ½ cup milk mixture into egg yolk; whisk egg yolk mixture back into saucepan. Whisk over low heat 30 to 60 seconds (mixture will coat back of spoon). Remove from heat; stir in nutmeg. Serve warm or chilled.

45-MINUTE PREPARATION TIP: Make pie pastry before preparing the rest of the recipe.

MIXED BERRY TART

Select as many kinds of berries as you can for beautiful color and texture contrast.

8 servings

Shortbread Crust (see p. 572)
Mock Mascarpone (recipe follows)
3–4 cups mixed berries (raspberries, blackberries, strawberries, blueberries, gooseberries, currants, etc.)
¼ cup currant or apple jelly, melted
Powdered sugar, as garnish

Per Serving:
Calories: 264
% of calories from fat: 31
Fat (gm): 9
Saturated fat (gm): 2.3
Cholesterol (mg): 30.9
Sodium (mg): 255
Protein (gm): 8
Carbohydrate (gm): 37.9

Exchanges:
Milk: 0.0
Vegetable: 0.0
Fruit: 0.5
Bread: 2.0
Meat: 0.0
Fat: 2.0

1. Roll pastry between 2 sheets of waxed paper into 12-inch circle. Ease into 10-inch tart pan and trim; pierce bottom with fork. Bake at 425 degrees until crisp and golden brown, 10 to 15 minutes. Cool on wire rack.

2. Spread Mock Mascarpone evenly on cooled pastry; top with berries and drizzle with jelly. Dust serving plates with powdered sugar; top with tart slices.

Mock Mascarpone

Makes about 1¼ cups

8 ounces fat-free cream cheese, room temperature
3 tablespoons reduced-fat sour cream
2–3 tablespoons 2% reduced-fat milk

1. Beat cream cheese until fluffy; mix in sour cream and milk. Refrigerate several hours or up to several days.

RUSTIC COUNTRY FRUIT TART

LO

45

❄

◊

Perfect for a lazy-day summer picnic, this tumble of garden fruits is lightly glazed and encased in a free-form pastry.

8 servings

Basic Pie Crust (see p. 570)
½ cup all-purpose flour, divided
2 tablespoons cold margarine or butter
2 cups each: raspberries, sliced strawberries
1 cup seedless grapes
4 each: halved peeled medium apricots, peaches
⅓ cup sugar
½ teaspoon ground cinnamon
¼ cup apricot preserves
2 tablespoons water

Per Serving:
Calories: 295
% of calories from fat: 23
Fat (gm): 7.8
Saturated fat (gm): 1.5
Cholesterol (mg): 0
Sodium (mg): 152
Protein (gm): 4
Carbohydrate (gm): 54.4

Exchanges:
Milk: 0.0
Vegetable: 0.0
Fruit: 1.0
Bread: 2.5
Meat: 0.0
Fat: 1.0

1. Make Basic Pie Crust, adding ¼ cup flour and 2 tablespoons margarine to recipe. Roll pastry on lightly floured surface into a 12-inch circle (edges do not need to be even). Transfer pastry to a 12-inch pizza pan.

2. Toss fruits with combined remaining ¼ cup flour, sugar, and cinnamon. Arrange fruits in center of pastry, leaving a 2- to 3-inch border around outer edge. Gently gather and fold outer edge of pastry over fruits (fruits will not be completely enclosed).

3. Bake at 425 degrees 20 to 25 minutes, or until crust is browned and fruit is tender. Heat preserves and water in small saucepan until warm; brush over fruit.

KIWI TART

LO

Add other sliced spring or summer fruit to this tart if you wish.

8 servings

45 ❄ ◊

¼ cup sugar
2 tablespoons cornstarch
1¼ cups 2 % milk
1 tablespoon lemon juice
1 egg, slightly beaten
Basic Pie Crust (see p. 570), baked in 9-inch tart pan
5 medium kiwi, peeled, sliced

Per Serving:
Calories: 168
% of calories from fat: 20
Fat (gm): 3.8
Saturated fat (gm): 1
Cholesterol (mg): 29
Sodium (mg): 78
Protein (gm): 3.7
Carbohydrate (gm): 30.4

Exchanges:
Milk: 0.0
Vegetable: 0.0
Fruit: 1.0
Bread: 1.0
Meat: 0.0
Fat: 1.0

1. Mix sugar and cornstarch in small saucepan; whisk in milk and lemon juice and heat to boiling over medium-high heat, whisking until thickened, about 1 minute. Whisk about ½ cup milk mixture into egg; whisk egg mixture back into saucepan. Whisk over low heat 30 to 60 seconds. Pour into crust, spreading evenly; cool to room temperature. Lightly cover custard with plastic wrap; refrigerate 2 to 4 hours, or until set. Arrange kiwi slices in overlapping circles on custard.

45-MINUTE PREPARATION TIP: Make pie crust before preparing the rest of the recipe.

TARTE TATIN

Caramelized sugar contributes special flavor to this French-style upside-down apple tart.

8 servings

5 cups sliced, peeled Granny Smith apples (about 5 large)
¾ cup sugar, divided
¼ teaspoon ground nutmeg
1 tablespoon lemon juice
2 tablespoons margarine or butter
Basic Pie Crust (see p. 570)

1. Toss apples with combined ½ cup sugar and nutmeg in bowl; sprinkle with lemon juice. Heat remaining ¼ cup sugar in 10-inch oven-proof skillet over medium heat until melted and golden, about 5 minutes, stirring occasionally (watch carefully as the sugar can burn easily). Add apple mixture and margarine; cook until apples are just tender, about 5 minutes, stirring occasionally. Remove from heat; arrange apples in skillet so they are slightly mounded in the center.

2. Roll pastry into 11-inch circle; place on top of skillet, tucking edges around apples. Cut slits in pastry. Bake at 425 degrees 20 to 25 minutes or until pastry is lightly browned. Invert onto serving plate. Serve warm or at room temperature.

Per Serving:
Calories: 279
% of calories from fat: 24
Fat (gm): 7.6
Saturated fat (gm): 1.5
Cholesterol (mg): 0
Sodium (mg): 83.1
Protein (gm): 1.4
Carbohydrate (gm): 53.8

Exchanges:
Milk: 0.0
Vegetable: 0.0
Fruit: 1.5
Bread: 2.0
Meat: 0.0

VARIATIONS

Caramelized Pear and Almond Tarte Tatin — Substitute pears for the apples, tossing with combined ½ cup sugar, ⅓ cup sliced almonds, 1 tablespoon flour, 1 teaspoon grated lemon zest, ½ teaspoon ground cinnamon, and ¼ teaspoon ground nutmeg. Complete recipe as above, beginning with Step 2.

Apple-Cheddar Tarte Tatin — Make recipe as above, adding ⅓ cup raisins to apples in Step 1. Prepare Basic Pie Crust, substituting vegetable shortening for the margarine, and adding ⅓ cup shredded reduced-fat or fat-free Cheddar cheese before sprinkling with water; add additional water if necessary.

SPICED SWEET POTATO PIE

LO

45

A change from traditional pumpkin, this pie will brighten any winter holiday table.

10 servings

1½ cups mashed, cooked, peeled sweet potatoes
¾ cup packed light brown sugar
2 eggs
1½ cup fat-free milk
1 teaspoon each: ground cinnamon, ginger
½ teaspoon ground mace
¼ teaspoon salt
Basic Pie Crust (see p. 570), baked in an 8-inch pie pan
Light whipped topping (optional)

Per Serving:
Calories: 215
% of calories from fat: 24
Fat (gm): 6
Saturated fat (gm): 1
Cholesterol (mg): 43
Sodium (mg): 217
Protein (gm): 5
Carbohydrate (gm): 37

Exchanges:
Milk: 0.0
Vegetable: 0.0
Fruit: 0.0
Bread: 2.5
Meat: 0.0
Fat: 1.0

1. Beat sweet potatoes and remaining ingredients, except pie crust and whipped topping, in bowl; pour into baked crust. Bake at 350 degrees until sharp knife inserted near center of pie comes out clean, about 45 minutes. Serve warm or room temperature with whipped topping.

45-MINUTE PREPARATION TIP: Make pie crust before preparing the rest of the recipe.

PECAN CRUNCH TART

LO

45

We've reduced the calories and fat in this rich-tasting pecan pie.

8 servings

Basic Pie Crust (see p. 570)
2 eggs
1 cup maple syrup or pancake syrup
1 tablespoon vanilla
⅛ teaspoon salt
⅔ cup each: reduced-fat granola, coarsely chopped pecans
⅓ cup wheat and barley cereal (Grape-Nuts)

Per Serving:
Calories: 356
% of calories from fat: 22
Fat (gm): 8.9
Saturated fat (gm): 3.2
Cholesterol (mg): 56.2
Sodium (mg): 279
Protein (gm): 9.6
Carbohydrate (gm): 63.1

Exchanges:
Milk: 0.0
Vegetable: 0.0
Fruit: 0.0
Bread: 4.0
Meat: 0.0
Fat: 1.5

1. Make Basic Pie Crust, using 10-inch tart pan. Beat eggs, syrup, vanilla, and salt until smooth. Stir in remaining ingredients; pour into pastry. Bake at 350 degrees until set, about 35 minutes.

LEMON CLOUD PIE

LO

45

Other flavors of this wonderful dessert are easy to make—just substitute another flavor yogurt, such as strawberry, raspberry, or cherry.

8 servings

1½ cups each: light whipped topping, low-fat custard-style lemon yogurt
2 tablespoons grated lemon zest
Meringue Pie Crust (recipe follows)
Lemon slices, as garnish

1. Combine whipped topping, yogurt, and lemon zest and spoon into Meringue Pie Crust at serving time. Garnish with lemon slices.

Per Serving:
Calories: 170
% of calories from fat: 17
Fat (gm): 3.5
Saturated fat (gm): 0.3
Cholesterol (mg): 2
Sodium (mg): 62
Protein (gm): 3.6
Carbohydrate (gm): 35.5

Exchanges:
Milk: 0.5
Vegetable: 0.0
Fruit: 2.0
Bread: 0.0
Meat: 0.0
Fat: 0.5

Meringue Pie Crust
Makes one 9-inch crust

4 egg whites
½ teaspoon cream of tartar
1 cup sugar

1. Beat egg whites and cream of tartar in medium bowl to soft peaks; beat to stiff, but not dry peaks, adding sugar gradually. Spoon into ungreased 9-inch pie plate, spreading on bottom and side to form a large bowl shape. Bake at 275 degrees until crust is firm to touch and very lightly browned, about 45 minutes. Turn oven off and let crust cool in oven.

45-MINUTE PREPARATION TIP: Make Meringue Pie Crust before preparing the rest of the recipe.

BANANA-STRAWBERRY CREAM PIE

LO

Strawberries add a new twist to this old favorite.

45
❄
🔥

8 servings

Graham Cracker Crumb Crust (see p. 571)

¼ cup graham cracker crumbs

1 tablespoon margarine or butter, melted

⅓ cup sugar

¼ cup cornstarch

2 tablespoons flour

¼ teaspoon salt

2½ cups fat-free milk

3 egg yolks

1 teaspoon vanilla

¼ teaspoon each: ground cinnamon, nutmeg

1 cup sliced strawberries

2 medium bananas

Per Serving:
Calories: 250
% of calories from fat: 30
Fat (gm): 8.5
Saturated fat (gm): 1.7
Cholesterol (mg): 81.1
Sodium (mg): 226
Protein (gm): 5.4
Carbohydrate (gm): 38.9

Exchanges:
Milk: 0.0
Vegetable: 0.0
Fruit: 0.5
Bread: 2.0
Meat: 0.0
Fat: 1.5

1. Make pie crust, adding ¼ cup graham crumbs and 1 tablespoon margarine to recipe and using 9-inch pie pan.

2. Mix sugar, cornstarch, flour, and salt in medium saucepan; whisk in milk. Heat to boiling over medium-high heat, whisking until thickened, about 1 minute. Whisk about ½ cup mixture into egg yolks; whisk egg mixture back into saucepan. Whisk low heat 30 to 60 seconds. Stir in vanilla, cinnamon, and nutmeg; cool, stirring frequently. Refrigerate until chilled, 1 to 2 hours.

3. Reserve 8 strawberry slices. Slice 1½ bananas and arrange in crust with remaining strawberries. Spoon custard over fruit; refrigerate until set, 4 to 6 hours. Slice remaining banana; garnish top of pie with banana and strawberry slices.

GRANDMA'S LEMON MERINGUE PIE

A perfect flavor combination of sweet and tart, topped with a mile-high meringue! Be sure to spread the meringue while filling is hot, sealing to the edge of the crust to prevent weeping.

10 servings

2 cups sugar, divided

½ cup cornstarch

1½ cups water

½ cup lemon juice

1 egg, lightly beaten

2 tablespoons margarine or butter

Basic Pie Crust (see p. 570), baked in 9-inch pie pan

4 egg whites

¼ teaspoon cream of tartar

Per Serving:
Calories: 318
% of calories from fat: 21
Fat (gm): 7
Saturated fat (gm): 2
Cholesterol (mg): 21
Sodium (mg): 168
Protein (gm): 4
Carbohydrate (gm): 60

Exchanges:
Milk: 0.0
Vegetable: 0.0
Fruit: 0.0
Bread: 4.0
Meat: 0.0
Fat: 1.0

1. Combine 1½ cups sugar and cornstarch in medium saucepan; whisk in water and lemon juice. Heat to boiling, whisking until thickened, about 1 minute. Whisk about 1 cup lemon mixture into egg; whisk mixture back into saucepan. Cook over very low heat, whisking, 30 to 60 seconds. Remove from heat; add margarine, stirring until melted. Pour into baked crust.

2. Beat egg whites to soft peaks in large bowl; add cream of tartar and beat to stiff but not dry peaks, adding remaining ½ cup sugar gradually. Spread meringue over hot filling, sealing well to edge of pie crust. Bake at 400 degrees until meringue is browned, about 5 minutes. Cool completely on wire rack before cutting. Refrigerate leftover pie.

45-MINUTE PREPARATION TIP: Make pie crust before preparing the rest of the recipe.

TOASTED COCONUT CREAM TART

LO

45

❄️

🔥

Tucked in a tart pan for a new look, you'll enjoy this updated version of an old favorite.

8 servings

⅓ cup sugar

2 tablespoons cornstarch

1½ cups 2% milk

1 egg, slightly beaten

⅓ cup flaked, toasted, unsweetened coconut

Basic Pie Crust (see p. 570), baked in a 9-inch tart pan

Per Serving:
Calories: 170
% of calories from fat: 26
Fat (gm): 4.9
Saturated fat (gm): 1.1
Cholesterol (mg): 30
Sodium (mg): 85
Protein (gm): 3.8
Carbohydrate (gm): 28

Exchanges:
Milk: 0.0
Vegetable: 0.0
Fruit: 0.0
Bread: 2.0
Meat: 0.0
Fat: 1.0

1. Mix sugar and cornstarch in small saucepan; whisk in milk. Heat to boiling over medium-high heat, whisking until thickened, about 1 minute. Whisk about ½ cup mixture into egg; whisk egg mixture back into saucepan. Whisk over low heat 30 to 60 seconds. Stir in ¼ cup coconut; pour into baked crust, spreading evenly. Sprinkle with remaining 1½ tablespoons coconut; cool. Refrigerate until set, 2 to 4 hours.

45-MINUTE PREPARATION TIP: Make pie crust before preparing the rest of the recipe.

SPRING BERRY CHEESECAKE

LO

45

🔥

❄️

You won't believe how delicious this cheesecake is!

16 servings

Vanilla Crumb Crust or Gingersnap Crust (see p. 572)

1 cup low-fat cottage cheese

8 ounces fat-free cream cheese, room temperature

1 cup fat-free sour cream

⅓ cup plus ¼ cup sugar, divided

3 eggs

½ cup fat-free milk

2 tablespoons lemon juice

3 tablespoons each: finely grated lemon zest,
all-purpose flour

1 teaspoon vanilla

⅛ teaspoon salt

1 quart sliced strawberries or blueberries

Per Serving:
Calories: 122
% of calories from fat: 23
Fat (gm): 3.1
Saturated fat (gm): 0.8
Cholesterol (mg): 42.6
Sodium (mg): 209
Protein (gm): 6.7
Carbohydrate (gm): 16.6

1. Make Vanilla Crumb Crust and press evenly
in bottom of 9-inch springform pan.

Exchanges:
Milk: 0.0
Vegetable: 0.0
Fruit: 0.5
Bread: 0.5
Meat: 0.5
Fat: 0.5

Process cottage cheese in food processor or
blender until smooth. Transfer to large bowl and
beat in cream cheese, sour cream, and ⅓ cup
sugar until fluffy. Add eggs one at a time, beating
well after each addition. Mix in milk, lemon juice
and zest, flour, vanilla, and salt. Pour over crust.

2. Bake at 325 degrees until the cheesecake is set, but still slightly
soft in the center, about 50 minutes. Cool on wire rack; carefully
loosen side of pan. Refrigerate, covered, 8 hours or overnight.
Combine berries and remaining ¼ cup sugar; serve over cheesecake slices.

NEW YORK-STYLE CHEESECAKE

LO

There's only one word for this cheesecake—spectacular!

45

12 servings

Graham Cracker Crumb Crust (see p. 571)

24 ounces fat-free cream cheese, room temperature

¾ cup sugar

2 eggs

2 tablespoons cornstarch

1 teaspoon vanilla

1 cup reduced-fat sour cream

Per Serving:
Calories: 209
% of calories from fat: 28
Fat (gm): 6.2
Saturated fat (gm): 3.2
Cholesterol (mg): 45
Sodium (mg): 452
Protein (gm): 10.4
Carbohydrate (gm): 258

Exchanges:
Milk: 0.0
Vegetable: 0.0
Fruit: 0.0
Bread: 1.5
Meat: 1.0
Fat: 1.0

1. Make Graham Cracker Crumb Crust, patting
mixture on bottom and ½ inch up sides of 9-
inch springform pan. Beat cream cheese and
sugar in large bowl until fluffy; beat in remaining
ingredients; pour into crust.

2. Bake at 325 degrees until cheesecake is set but still slightly soft in the center, 45 to 50 minutes. Turn oven off; let cheesecake cool in oven with door ajar for 2 hours. Carefully loosen side of pan; refrigerate, covered, 8 hours or overnight.

TURTLE CHEESECAKE

LO *A combination of brownie crust, caramel cheesecake, and pecans, smothered with caramel sauce—who can resist such an incredible offering?*

12 servings

Brownie Crust (recipe follows)
¾ package (14-ounce size) caramels (about 35)
¼ cup fat-free milk
16 ounces fat-free cream cheese, room temperature
½ cup granulated sugar
2 eggs
¼ cup fat-free sour cream
Caramel Glaze (recipe follows)
¼–½ cup pecan halves

Per Serving:
Calories: 356
% of calories from fat: 22
Fat (gm): 8.9
Saturated fat (gm): 3.2
Cholesterol (mg): 56.2
Sodium (mg): 279
Protein (gm): 9.6
Carbohydrate (gm): 63.1

Exchanges:
Milk: 0.0
Vegetable: 0.0
Fruit: 0.0
Bread: 4.0
Meat: 0.0
Fat: 1.5

1. Make Brownie Crust. Heat caramels and milk in small saucepan over medium-low heat until melted, stirring occasionally. Pour caramel over Brownie Crust, spreading evenly. Refrigerate until caramel is cold, about 20 minutes. Beat cream cheese and sugar in medium bowl until well blended. Beat in eggs, 1 at a time, beating well after each addition; mix in sour cream. Pour over caramel in crust.

2. Bake on cookie sheet at 350 degrees 45 minutes or until center is almost set. Run sharp knife around side of pan to loosen cheesecake; cool on wire rack. Refrigerate 8 hours or overnight. Remove side of pan; place cheesecake on serving plate. Pour Caramel Glaze over top of cheesecake; garnish with pecan halves.

Brownie Crust

Makes one 9-inch crust

½ cup all-purpose flour

⅓ cup each: packed light brown sugar, reduced-fat
   semisweet chocolate morsels, melted

3 tablespoons margarine or butter, melted

1 egg

1. Mix all ingredients in medium bowl until blended; spread evenly in bottom of greased 9-inch springform pan. Bake at 350 degrees until firm to touch, 13 to 15 minutes; cool on wire rack.

Caramel Glaze

Makes about 1 cup

½ package (14-ounce size) caramels (about 35 caramels)

⅓ cup fat-free milk

1. Heat caramels and milk in small saucepan over medium-low heat until melted, stirring occasionally. Let stand, stirring occasionally, until thickened enough to spread, 5 to 10 minutes.

VARIATIONS

Triple Chocolate Brownie Cheesecake — Make cheesecake as above, omitting the caramels and Caramel Glaze, and adding ¼ cup unsweetened cocoa and ⅓ cup reduced-fat semisweet chocolate morsels to the filling. Bake as above.

Peanut Butter Cup Cheesecake — Make cheesecake as above, omitting caramels and Caramel Glaze, substituting brown sugar for the granulated sugar, and adding ¾ cup reduced-fat peanut butter. Bake and chill as above. Drizzle top of cheesecake with 1 ounce melted semisweet chocolate; garnish with halved peanut butter cup candies.

WHITE CHOCOLATE CHEESECAKE

Rich, creamy, and delicious. Serve with raspberry or chocolate sauce for an extra-special treat.

12 servings

Nut Crunch Crust (recipe follows)
16 ounces fat-free cream cheese, room temperature
1¼ cups sugar
1 cup fat-free sour cream
3 eggs
¼ cup lemon juice
1 tablespoon grated lemon zest
2 teaspoons vanilla extract
¼ teaspoon ground nutmeg
Pinch salt
6–8 ounces white baking chocolate, melted

Per Serving:
Calories: 266
% of calories from fat: 23
Fat (gm): 6.7
Saturated fat (gm): 3.8
Cholesterol (mg): 58.6
Sodium (mg): 266
Protein (gm): 9.8
Carbohydrate (gm): 40.7

Exchanges:
Milk: 0.0
Vegetable: 0.0
Fruit: 0.0
Bread: 3.0
Meat: 0.0
Fat: 1.0

1. Make Nut Crunch Crust; sprinkle over bottom of greased 9-inch springform pan. Beat cream cheese in large bowl until fluffy; beat in remaining ingredients, except chocolate. Mix in chocolate and pour into prepared pan. Bake at 325 degrees until cheesecake is almost set in the center, 1 to 1¼ hours. Cool on wire rack. Refrigerate 8 hours or overnight.

Nut Crunch Crust

Makes one 9-inch crust

¼ cup wheat and barley cereal (Grape-Nuts)
2 tablespoons sugar
1 tablespoon chopped almonds

1. Process all ingredients in food processor or blender until finely ground.

CHOCOLATE CHIP COOKIES

America's favorite cookie—best eaten warm!

45

5 dozen cookies (1 each)

8 tablespoons margarine or butter, room temperature
1 cup packed light brown sugar
½ cup granulated sugar
1 egg
1 teaspoon vanilla
2½ cups all-purpose flour
½ teaspoon each: baking soda, salt
⅓ cup fat-free milk
½ package (12-ounce size) reduced-fat semisweet
  chocolate morsels

Per Serving:
Calories: 66
% of calories from fat: 27
Fat (gm): 2
Saturated fat (gm): 0.7
Cholesterol (mg): 3.6
Sodium (mg): 70
Protein (gm): 0.8
Carbohydrate (gm): 11.2

Exchanges:
Milk: 0.0
Vegetable: 0.0
Fruit: 0.0
Bread: 0.5
Meat: 0.0
Fat: 0.5

1. Beat margarine and sugars in medium bowl until fluffy; beat in egg and vanilla. Mix in combined flour, baking soda, and salt alternately with milk, beginning and ending with dry ingredients. Mix in chocolate morsels. Drop cookies by tablespoonfuls onto greased cookie sheets. Bake at 375 degrees until browned, about 10 minutes. Cool on wire racks.

RAISIN OATMEAL COOKIES

Moist and chewy, just the way they should be!

45

2½ dozen cookies (1 each)

6 tablespoons margarine or butter, room temperature
¼ cup fat-free sour cream
1 egg
1 teaspoon vanilla
1 cup packed light brown sugar
1½ cups quick-cooking oats
1 cup all-purpose flour
½ teaspoon baking soda
¼ teaspoon baking powder
1 teaspoon ground cinnamon
½ cup raisins

Per Serving:
Calories: 90
% of calories from fat: 27
Fat (gm): 2.7
Saturated fat (gm): 0.5
Cholesterol (mg): 7.1
Sodium (mg): 57
Protein (gm): 1.5
Carbohydrate (gm): 15.3

Exchanges:
Milk: 0.0
Vegetable: 0.0
Fruit: 0.0
Bread: 1.0
Meat: 0.0
Fat: 0.5

1. Mix margarine, sour cream, egg, and vanilla in large bowl; beat in brown sugar. Mix in combined remaining ingredients, except raisins; mix in raisins. Drop dough onto greased cookie sheets, using 2 tablespoons for each cookie. Bake at 350 degrees until browned, 12 to 15 minutes. Cool on wire racks.

SOFT MOLASSES COOKIES

Fill your home with the scent of spices when you bake these cookies.

3 dozen cookies (1 each)

¼ cup vegetable shortening

½ cup packed dark brown sugar

1 egg yolk

1¼ cups all-purpose flour

2 teaspoons baking soda

½ teaspoon each: ground cinnamon, ginger

¼ teaspoon each: ground nutmeg, salt

¼ cup light molasses

2 tablespoons water

½ cup currants or chopped raisins

Per Serving:
Calories: 53
% of calories from fat: 25
Fat (gm): 1.5
Saturated fat (gm): 0.4
Cholesterol (mg): 5.9
Sodium (mg): 89
Protein (gm): 0.6
Carbohydrate (gm): 9.3

Exchanges:
Milk: 0.0
Vegetable: 0.0
Fruit: 0.0
Bread: 0.5
Meat: 0.0
Fat: 0.0

1. Beat shortening, brown sugar, and egg yolk in medium bowl until blended. Mix in combined flour, baking soda, spices, and salt alternately with combined molasses and water, beginning and ending with dry ingredients. Mix in currants. Drop mixture by rounded teaspoons onto greased cookie sheets. Bake at 350 until lightly browned (cookies will be soft), 8 to 10 minutes. Cool on wire racks.

CARDAMOM CUT-OUTS

LO

45

Intensely flavored with cardamom, these delicate cookies are also delicious made with cinnamon. Cut into tiny 1-inch rounds for tea cookies.

5 dozen cookies (1 each)

½ cup vegetable shortening
1 cup plus 2 tablespoons sugar, divided
3 tablespoons fat-free milk
1 egg yolk
¾ teaspoon ground cardamom, divided
2 cups all-purpose flour
¼ teaspoon salt

Per Serving:
Calories: 46
% of calories from fat: 34
Fat (gm): 1.7
Saturated fat (gm): 0.4
Cholesterol (mg): 3.6
Sodium (mg): 10
Protein (gm): 0.5
Carbohydrate (gm): 7

Exchanges:
Milk: 0.0
Vegetable: 0.0
Fruit: 0.0
Bread: 0.5
Meat: 0.0
Fat: 0.0

1. Beat shortening, 1 cup sugar, milk, egg yolk, and ½ teaspoon cardamom in medium bowl until well blended; mix in flour and salt. Roll ½ the dough on floured surface to scant ¼ inch thickness; cut into rounds or decorative shapes with 2-inch cutter. Repeat with remaining dough. Bake on greased baking sheets at 375 degrees until browned, 8 to 10 minutes. Combine remaining 2 tablespoons sugar and ¼ teaspoon cardamom; sprinkle over warm cookies. Cool on wire racks.

TART LEMON DAINTIES

LO

45

Enjoy the subtle lemon flavor of these tiny crisp cookies—perfect with coffee or tea.

4 dozen cookies (1 each)

4 tablespoons margarine or butter, room temperature
1 cup granulated sugar
1 egg
3 tablespoons fat-free milk
2 teaspoons lemon juice
1 teaspoon finely grated lemon zest
2 cups all-purpose flour
1 teaspoon baking powder
¼ teaspoon salt

Per Serving:
Calories: 46
% of calories from fat: 22
Fat (gm): 1.1
Saturated fat (gm): 0.2
Cholesterol (mg): 4.4
Sodium (mg): 35
Protein (gm): 0.7
Carbohydrate (gm): 8.2

Exchanges:
Milk: 0.0
Vegetable: 0.0
Fruit: 0.0
Bread: 0.5
Meat: 0.0
Fat: 0.0

1. Beat margarine, sugar, egg, milk, lemon juice, and lemon zest in bowl until blended. Mix in combined flour, baking powder, and salt. Refrigerate until chilled, 2 to 3 hours.

2. Roll ½ the dough on floured surface to ¼ inch thickness; cut into rounds or decorative shapes with 1½-inch cutter. Repeat with remaining dough. Bake on greased cookie sheets at 375 degrees until lightly browned, 7 to 8 minutes. Cool on wire racks.

ALMOND TUILES

L

These lacy crisp cookies can be folded, rolled, or formed into small basket shapes for ice cream or other fillings.

3 dozen cookies (1 each)

½ cup quick-cooking oats

¼ cup finely chopped blanched almonds

4 tablespoons margarine or butter, melted

½ cup light corn syrup

⅓ cup sugar

1 teaspoon almond extract

½ cup all-purpose flour

¼ teaspoon salt

Per Serving:
Calories: 49
% of calories from fat: 33
Fat (gm): 1.7
Saturated fat (gm): 0.3
Cholesterol (mg): 0
Sodium (mg): 36
Protein (gm): 0.5
Carbohydrate (gm): 7.5

Exchanges:
Milk: 0.0
Vegetable: 0.0
Fruit: 0.0
Bread: 0.5
Meat: 0.0
Fat: 0.5

1. Place oats and almonds in separate pie pans. Bake at 350 degrees until toasted, 5 to 8 minutes for the almonds and about 10 minutes for the oats. Cool.

2. Mix margarine, corn syrup, sugar, and almond extract in medium bowl; mix in combined oats, almonds, flour, and salt. Drop batter by well-rounded teaspoons, 3 inches apart, onto parchment-lined cookie sheets (4 to 6 cookies per pan). Bake at 350 degrees until golden and bubbly, 7 to 10 minutes. Let cookies cool just until firm enough to remove from pan, about 1 minute. Working quickly, remove each cookie and roll or fold over the handle of a wooden spoon, or leave flat; cool on wire racks. If cookies have cooled too much to shape, return to warm oven for about 1 minute to soften.

VARIATION

Cream-Filled Tuiles — Remove warm tuiles from cookie sheet 1 at a time and roll loosely around handle of wooden spoon; transfer to wire rack and cool. Mix 3 cups light whipped topping and ⅓ cup powdered sugar. Using pastry bag with medium plain tip, fill cookies with mixture. Drizzle cookies with 1 ounce melted semi-sweet chocolate.

Florentines — Make tuiles, leaving them flat. Make ½ recipe Buttercream Frosting (see p. 555); spread ½ the tuiles with frosting, using about 1 tablespoon for each. Top with remaining tuiles and drizzle with 1 ounce melted semisweet baking chocolate.

GRANOLA LACE COOKIES

LO

45

When the cookies are still warm, they can be rolled or folded over the handle of a wooden spoon, or "pinched" in the center to form bow shapes; see recipe for Almond Tuiles, p. 592, for shaping directions. Bake only 4 to 6 cookies at a time, as they must be handled quickly and carefully before cooling.

4 dozen cookies (1 each)

4 tablespoons margarine or butter, room temperature

¼ cup each: granulated sugar, packed light brown sugar

2 egg whites

1 tablespoon orange juice

¼–½ teaspoon orange extract

½ cup each: finely crushed reduced-fat granola without raisins, all-purpose flour

¼ teaspoon each: baking soda, salt

2 teaspoons finely grated orange zest

Per Serving:
Calories: 27
% of calories from fat: 33
Fat (gm): 1
Saturated fat (gm): 0.2
Cholesterol (mg): 0
Sodium (mg): 35
Protein (gm): 0.4
Carbohydrate (gm): 4.1

Exchanges:
Milk: 0.0
Vegetable: 0.0
Fruit: 0.0
Bread: 0.5
Meat: 0.0
Fat: 0.0

1. Beat all ingredients in large bowl until smooth. Drop rounded ½ teaspoons dough 3 inches apart on parchment-lined cookie sheets, making 4 to 6 cookies per pan. Bake at 400 degrees until lightly browned, about 3 minutes. Let stand until firm enough to remove from pans, about 1 minute. Cool on wire racks.

CHOCOLATE FUDGE MERINGUES

O

Better bake several batches, as these won't last long!

45

24 cookies (1 per serving)

3 egg whites

½ teaspoon cream of tartar

¼ teaspoon salt

2 cups powdered sugar

½ cup unsweetened cocoa

1 ounce semisweet chocolate, finely chopped

Per Serving:
Calories: 43
% of calories from fat: 11
Fat (gm): 0.5
Saturated fat (gm): 0
Cholesterol (mg): 0
Sodium (mg): 29
Protein (gm): 0.8
Carbohydrate (gm): 9.1

Exchanges:
Milk: 0.0
Vegetable: 0.0
Fruit: 0.0
Bread: 0.5
Meat: 0.0
Fat: 0.0

1. Beat egg whites to soft peaks in large bowl; add cream of tartar and salt and beat, adding sugar gradually, until stiff, but not dry, peaks form. Fold in cocoa and chocolate. Drop by tablespoons onto parchment or foil-lined cookie sheets. Bake at 300 degrees until cookies feel crisp when touched, 20 to 25 minutes. Cool on pans on wire racks.

VARIATIONS

Orange-Almond Meringues — Make recipe as above, substituting ¾ cup granulated sugar for the powdered sugar, and adding ½ teaspoon orange extract. Delete cocoa and semisweet chocolate. Fold ½ cup chopped almonds into beaten egg white mixture.

Peppermint Clouds — Make Orange-Almond Meringue, deleting orange extract and substituting crushed peppermint candies for the almonds.

CHOCOLATE CRINKLES

LO

These cookies have crinkled, crisp tops but are soft inside.

45

4½ dozen cookies (1 each)

8 tablespoons margarine or butter, room temperature

1¼ cups packed light brown sugar

⅓ cup reduced-fat sour cream

1 egg

1–2 ounces semisweet baking chocolate, melted

1 teaspoon vanilla

1¾ cups all-purpose flour

¾ cup unsweetened cocoa

1 teaspoon each: baking soda, ground cinnamon

¼ cup granulated sugar

Per Serving:
Calories: 61
% of calories from fat: 31
Fat (gm): 2.1
Saturated fat (gm): 0.6
Cholesterol (mg): 4.5
Sodium (mg): 49
Protein (gm): 0.8
Carbohydrate (gm): 9.8

Exchanges:
Milk: 0.0
Vegetable: 0.0
Fruit: 0.0
Bread: 0.5
Meat: 0.0
Fat: 0.5

1. Beat margarine and brown sugar in large bowl until fluffy. Mix in sour cream, egg, chocolate, and vanilla. Mix in combined flour, cocoa, baking soda, and cinnamon. Refrigerate, covered, 2 to 3 hours.

2. Drop dough by tablespoons into granulated sugar in pie plate; roll into balls (dough will be soft). Place cookies on greased cookie sheets; flatten with fork or bottom of glass. Bake at 350 degrees until firm to touch, 10 to 12 minutes. Cool on wire racks.

HAZELNUT MACAROONS

O

Use any favorite nuts in these moist and crunchy macaroons.

45

30 cookies (1 each)

4 egg whites

⅛ teaspoon cream of tartar

¼ teaspoon salt

1 cup each: sugar, sweetened flaked coconut

¼ cup finely chopped hazelnuts or pecans

Per Serving:
Calories: 44
% of calories from fat: 28
Fat (gm): 1.4
Saturated fat (gm): 0.8
Cholesterol (mg): 0
Sodium (mg): 25.6
Protein (gm): 0.7
Carbohydrate (gm): 7.6

Exchanges:
Milk: 0.0
Vegetable: 0.0
Fruit: 0.0
Bread: 0.5
Meat: 0.0
Fat: 0.5

1. Beat egg whites, cream of tartar, and salt to stiff, but not dry, peaks, adding sugar gradually. Fold in coconut and hazelnuts. Drop mixture by tablespoons onto parchment or foil-lined cookie sheets. Bake at 300 degrees until cookies begin to brown and feel crisp when touched, 20 to 25 minutes. Cool in pans on wire racks.

FROSTED SUGAR COOKIES

LO *Rich, crisp, and generously frosted, these cookies will flatter any holiday or special occasion.*

6 dozen cookies (1 per serving)

10 tablespoons margarine or butter,
    room temperature
2 tablespoons fat-free sour cream
1 egg
1 teaspoon lemon extract
1 cup powdered sugar
2 cups all-purpose flour
1 teaspoon baking powder
¼ teaspoon salt
Sugar Frosting (recipe follows)
Ground cinnamon or nutmeg

Per Serving:
Calories: 48
% of calories from fat: 31
Fat (gm): 1.7
Saturated fat (gm): 0.3
Cholesterol (mg): 3
Sodium (mg): 45
Protein (gm): 0.5
Carbohydrate (gm): 7.7

Exchanges:
Milk: 0.0
Vegetable: 0.0
Fruit: 0.0
Bread: 0.5
Meat: 0.0
Fat: 0.5

1. Beat margarine, sour cream, egg, and lemon extract in medium bowl until smooth; mix in powdered sugar. Mix in combined flour, baking powder, and salt. Refrigerate 4 to 6 hours.

2. Roll dough on floured surface to ¼ inch thickness. Cut out shapes with 2-inch cookie cutters. Bake at 375 degrees on greased cookie sheets until lightly browned, 8 to 10 minutes. Cool on wire racks. Frost with Sugar Frosting; sprinkle lightly with cinnamon.

Sugar Frosting
Makes about ¾ cup

2 cups powdered sugar
½ teaspoon lemon extract or vanilla
2–3 tablespoons fat-free milk

1. Mix powdered sugar, lemon extract, and enough milk to make the spreadable consistency.

ANISE-ALMOND BISCOTTI

LO

45

Crisp because they're baked twice, biscotti are perfect for dunking into coffee, tea, or Vin Santo, the Italian way!

60 bars (1 each)

4 tablespoons margarine or butter, room temperature

¾ cup sugar

3 eggs

2½ cups all-purpose flour

2 teaspoons crushed anise seeds

1½ teaspoons baking powder

½ teaspoon baking soda

¼ teaspoon salt

⅓ cup (1 ounce) whole blanched almonds

Per Serving:
Calories: 41
% of calories from fat: 26
Fat (gm): 1.2
Saturated fat (gm): 0.2
Cholesterol (mg): 7.1
Sodium (mg): 40
Protein (gm): 1
Carbohydrate (gm): 6.7

Exchanges:
Milk: 0.0
Vegetable: 0.0
Fruit: 0.0
Bread: 0.5
Meat: 0.0
Fat: 0.0

1. Beat margarine, sugar, and eggs until smooth. Mix in combined remaining ingredients, except almonds; mix in almonds. Shape dough on greased cookie sheets into 4 slightly flattened rolls, 1½ inches in diameter. Bake at 350 degrees until lightly browned, about 20 minutes. Cool on wire rack 10 to 15 minutes.

2. Cut rolls into ½-inch slices; arrange slices, cut sides down, on ungreased cookie sheets. Bake at 350 degrees until toasted and almost dry, 7 to 10 minutes on each side. Cool on wire racks.

FROSTED COCOA BROWNIES

LO

45

You'll never guess these very chocolatey and slightly chewy brownies are low in fat.

25 brownies (1 per serving)

1 cup each: all-purpose flour, sugar

¼ cup unsweetened cocoa

5 tablespoons margarine or butter, melted

¼ cup fat-free milk

2 eggs

¼ cup honey

1 teaspoon vanilla

Cocoa Frosting (recipe follows)

Per Serving:
Calories: 111
% of calories from fat: 24
Fat (gm): 3.1
Saturated fat (gm): 0.6
Cholesterol (mg): 8.6
Sodium (mg): 42
Protein (gm): 1.5
Carbohydrate (gm): 20.4

Exchanges:
Milk: 0.0
Vegetable: 0.0
Fruit: 1.5
Bread: 0.0
Meat: 0.0
Fat: 0.5

1. Combine flour, sugar, and cocoa in medium bowl; mix in margarine, milk, eggs, honey, and vanilla, blending well. Pour into greased and floured 8-inch square baking pan. Bake at 350 degrees until brownies spring back when touched, about 30 minutes. Cool in pan on wire rack; spread with Cocoa Frosting.

Cocoa Frosting
Makes about ½ cup

1 cup powdered sugar
2–3 tablespoons unsweetened cocoa
1 tablespoon margarine or butter, room temperature
2–3 tablespoons fat-free milk

1. Mix all ingredients, adding enough milk to make spreadable consistency.

MISSISSIPPI MUD BARS

o

45

A favorite with kids of all ages—serve with ice cream and warm chocolate sauce for the ultimate treat.

2 dozen bars (1 per serving)

5 tablespoons margarine, softened
½ cup each: granulated sugar, packed light
  brown sugar
1 teaspoon vanilla
3 eggs
1 cup all-purpose flour
⅓ cup unsweetened cocoa
½ teaspoon baking powder
¼ teaspoon salt
3 cups miniature marshmallows
⅓ cup chopped pecans
½ cup reduced-fat semisweet chocolate
  morsels, melted

Per Serving:
Calories: 140
% of calories from fat: 32
Fat (gm): 5.2
Saturated fat (gm): 1.9
Cholesterol (mg): 26.6
Sodium (mg): 81
Protein (gm): 1.9
Carbohydrate (gm): 22.9

Exchanges:
Milk: 0.0
Vegetable: 0.0
Fruit: 0.0
Bread: 1.5
Meat: 0.0
Fat: 1.0

1. Beat margarine, sugars, and vanilla in medium bowl until blended; beat in eggs, 1 at a time. Mix in combined flour, cocoa, baking powder, and salt. Pour batter into greased 13 x 9-inch baking pan. Bake at 325 degrees until toothpick inserted in center comes out clean, 18 to 20 minutes. Sprinkle top of cake with marshmallows and pecans; bake until marshmallows are lightly browned, 2 to 3 minutes. Cool on wire rack. Drizzle melted chocolate over marshmallows. Cut into bars.

PUTTING ON THE RITZ BARS

V

Never have these rice cereal treats been quite so glamorous!

45

❄

2½ dozen bars (1 each)

1 package (10 ounces) marshmallows
4 tablespoons margarine
3 cups rice cereal (Rice Krispies)
½ cup flaked coconut
1 cup each: dried cranberries or raisins, chopped dried mixed fruit
½–¾ cup coarsely chopped walnuts
2 ounces semisweet baking chocolate, melted

Per Serving:
Calories: 108
% of calories from fat: 30
Fat (gm): 3.7
Saturated fat (gm): 1.1
Cholesterol (mg): 0
Sodium (mg): 59
Protein (gm): 1.2
Carbohydrate (gm): 18.7

Exchanges:
Milk: 0.0
Vegetable: 0.0
Fruit: 0.0
Bread: 1.0
Meat: 0.0
Fat: 1.0

1. Heat marshmallows and margarine in large saucepan over low heat until melted, stirring frequently. Stir in remaining ingredients, except chocolate, mixing well. Press into an even layer in greased 15 x 10-inch jelly roll pan; refrigerate 1 hour. Drizzle top with chocolate; refrigerate until set, about 15 minutes. Cut into bars.

BANANAS FOSTER

L *A real taste of New Orleans!*

45 **4 servings**

¼ cup packed light brown sugar

1½ teaspoons cornstarch

½ cup water

1 tablespoon rum or ½ teaspoon rum extract

1 teaspoon vanilla

2 medium bananas, sliced

¼ cup toasted pecan halves

1⅓ cups frozen low-fat vanilla yogurt

Per Serving:
Calories: 236
% of calories from fat: 20
Fat (gm): 5.5
Saturated fat (gm): 0.5
Cholesterol (mg): 0
Sodium (mg): 5
Protein (gm): 3.4
Carbohydrate (gm): 43

Exchanges:
Milk: 0.0
Vegetable: 0.0
Fruit: 2.0
Bread: 1.0
Meat: 0.0
Fat: 1.0

1. Mix brown sugar and cornstarch in small saucepan; stir in water and heat to boiling. Boil, stirring, until thickened, about 1 minute. Stir in rum and vanilla; add bananas and simmer until warm, 1 to 2 minutes. Stir in pecans; serve warm over frozen yogurt.

PEARS BELLE HÉLÈNE

L *Serve Chocolate Crinkles (see p. 594) to compliment this elegant offering.*

45

4 servings

4 cups water

¼ cup sugar

4 small pears, peeled, with stems intact

1 cup frozen low-fat vanilla yogurt

Bittersweet Chocolate Sauce (recipe follows)

Per Serving:
Calories: 183
% of calories from fat: 5
Fat (gm): 1.1
Saturated fat (gm): 0
Cholesterol (mg): 0
Sodium (mg): 0
Protein (gm): 2.3
Carbohydrate (gm): 43.9

Exchanges:
Milk: 0.0
Vegetable: 0.0
Fruit: 2.0
Bread: 1.0
Meat: 0.0
Fat: 0.0

1. Heat water and sugar to boiling in small saucepan; add pears, reduce heat, and simmer, covered, until pears are tender, 10 to 15 minutes. Cool pears in syrup; refrigerate until chilled, 1 to 2 hours. Drain.

2. Flatten scoops of frozen yogurt in 4 shallow dishes; place pears on top and drizzle with Bittersweet Chocolate Sauce.

Bittersweet Chocolate Sauce

Makes about 1½ cups

¾ cup unsweetened cocoa
½ cup sugar
¾ cup fat-free milk
2 tablespoons margarine or butter
1 teaspoon vanilla
¼–½ teaspoon ground cinnamon

1. Mix cocoa and sugar in small saucepan; stir in milk and margarine. Heat to boiling, stirring; reduce heat and simmer until sauce is smooth and slightly thickened, 3 to 4 minutes. Stir in vanilla and cinnamon. Serve warm or at room temperature.

VARIATION

Pears with Raspberry Sauce — Make recipe as above, deleting Bittersweet Chocolate Sauce. Process 1 pint fresh or frozen thawed raspberries and ⅓ cup sugar in blender or food processor until smooth. Strain, discarding seeds. Makes about 1 cup Raspberry Sauce.

SPICED CUSTARD

LO *Pumpkin pie spice adds an extraordinary flavor to this smooth custard.*

45 **4 servings**

2 cups fat-free milk
¼ cup sugar
⅛ teaspoon salt
2 eggs, beaten
½ teaspoon vanilla
2–3 teaspoons pumpkin pie spice

Per Serving:
Calories: 133
% of calories from fat: 19
Fat (gm): 2.8
Saturated fat (gm): 1
Cholesterol (mg): 108.2
Sodium (mg): 168
Protein (gm): 7.4
Carbohydrate (gm): 19.5

Exchanges:
Milk: 0.5
Vegetable: 0.0
Fruit: 0.0
Bread: 1.0
Meat: 0.5
Fat: 0.0

1. Whisk all ingredients until well blended in medium bowl; strain mixture into 1½-quart casserole. Place casserole in roasting pan on middle oven rack; add 1 inch hot water to pan. Bake, covered, at 325 degrees until knife inserted near center of custard comes out clean, about

1 hour. Remove casserole from pan; cool on wire rack. Serve warm, or refrigerate and serve chilled.

HERBED CUSTARD BRULÉE

LO

45

Scented with herbs, the delicate custard is topped with a sprinkling of caramelized sugar.

6 servings

3 cups fat-free milk

2 tablespoons each: chopped fresh or ½ teaspoon dried basil, cilantro, and tarragon leaves

5 eggs

½ cup granulated sugar

3 tablespoons packed light brown sugar

Per Serving:
Calories: 191
% of calories from fat: 20
Fat (gm): 4
Saturated fat (gm): 1
Cholesterol (mg): 179
Sodium (mg): 113
Protein (gm): 9
Carbohydrate (gm): 29

Exchanges:
Milk: 0.5
Vegetable: 0.0
Fruit: 0.0
Bread: 1.0
Meat: 1.0
Fat: 0.5

1. Heat milk and herbs in medium saucepan to boiling; remove from heat, cover, and let stand 10 minutes. Strain; discard herbs. Beat eggs and granulated sugar in medium bowl until thick and pale yellow, about 5 minutes. Gradually whisk milk mixture into eggs; strain and pour into 8 custard cups.

2. Place cups in 15 x 10-inch roasting pan on center oven rack; pour 2 inches hot water into pan. Bake, uncovered, at 350 degrees until knife inserted halfway between center and edge of custard cups comes out clean, about 20 minutes. Cool custard cups on wire rack. Refrigerate until chilled, 2 to 4 hours.

3. Sprinkle brown sugar evenly over custards in baking pan; broil, 4 inches from heat source, until sugar is melted and caramelized, 2 to 3 minutes. Serve immediately.

FRESH APRICOT CUSTARD

A delicate custard with fresh apricots gently folded in. Serve with cookies (see Index).

6 servings

½ cup sugar

3 tablespoons cornstarch

2 cups fat-free milk

½ cup apricot nectar

2 egg yolks, slightly beaten

2 tablespoons margarine or butter

1½ cups peeled, coarsely chopped fresh apricots

Per Serving:
Calories: 193
% of calories from fat: 26
Fat (gm): 5.8
Saturated fat (gm): 1.4
Cholesterol (mg): 72.3
Sodium (mg): 90
Protein (gm): 4.4
Carbohydrate (gm): 32

Exchanges:
Milk: 0.0
Vegetable: 0.0
Fruit: 0.5
Bread: 1.5
Meat: 0.0
Fat: 1.0

1. Mix sugar and cornstarch in medium saucepan; whisk in milk and apricot nectar. Heat to boiling over medium-high heat, whisking until thickened, about 1 minute. Whisk about ½ cup milk mixture into egg yolks; whisk mixture back into saucepan. Whisk over low heat, 30 to 60 seconds. Stir in margarine; cool. Refrigerate, covered with plastic wrap, until chilled, 1 to 2 hours. Stir custard until fluffy; stir in apricots.

PEACH-ALLSPICE SOUFFLÉS

Fresh or frozen drained peaches can be used for this recipe.

6 servings

1½ cups chopped fresh or canned drained peaches

2 teaspoons lemon juice

1 teaspoon vanilla

¼ cup plus 1 teaspoon sugar, divided

⅛ teaspoon ground allspice

2 egg yolks

4 egg whites

⅛ teaspoon cream of tartar

Powdered sugar, as garnish

Per Serving:
Calories: 85
% of calories from fat: 18
Fat (gm): 1.7
Saturated fat (gm): 0.5
Cholesterol (mg): 71
Sodium (mg): 39
Protein (gm): 3.6
Carbohydrate (gm): 14.1

Exchanges:
Milk: 0.0
Vegetable: 0.0
Fruit: 1.0
Bread: 0.0
Meat: 0.5
Fat: 0.5

1. Process peaches, lemon juice, vanilla, 1 teaspoon sugar, and all-spice in food processor or blender until smooth. Add egg yolks, one at a time, processing until smooth.

2. Beat egg whites and cream of tartar to soft peaks in large bowl; gradually beat in ¼ cup sugar, beating to stiff but not dry peaks. Fold in peach mixture. Spoon into 6 greased 1-cup soufflé dishes; arrange in baking pan.

3. Bake, uncovered, at 450 degrees 7 minutes; reduce heat to 425 degrees and bake until soufflés are lightly browned and a sharp knife inserted halfway between center and edge of dishes comes out clean, about 7 minutes. Sprinkle with powdered sugar; serve immediately.

NOTE: The soufflé can be baked in a 1-quart soufflé dish. Bake at 450 degrees for 10 minutes; reduce heat to 425 degrees and bake until sharp knife inserted halfway between center and edge of dish comes out clean about 10 minutes.

RICH CHOCOLATE PUDDING

LO

45

❄

This pudding is unbelievably rich in flavor and smooth in texture. Use Dutch or European process cocoa for fullest flavor.

4 servings

½ cup sugar
⅓ cup unsweetened cocoa
3 tablespoons cornstarch
⅛ teaspoon salt
2 cups 2% reduced-fat milk
1 egg yolk, slightly beaten
2 teaspoons vanilla

Per Serving:
Calories: 216
% of calories from fat: 17
Fat (gm): 4.3
Saturated fat (gm): 2
Cholesterol (mg): 62.3
Sodium (mg): 135
Protein (gm): 6.2
Carbohydrate (gm): 41.2

Exchanges:
Milk: 0.5
Vegetable: 0.0
Fruit: 0.0
Bread: 2.0
Meat: 0.0
Fat: 0.5

1. Mix sugar, cocoa, cornstarch, and salt in medium saucepan; whisk in milk and heat to boiling, whisking, until thickened, about 1 minute. Whisk about ½ cup milk mixture into egg yolk; whisk egg yolk mixture back into saucepan. Whisk over low heat 30 to 60 seconds. Stir in vanilla; cool. Spoon into dessert bowls. Refrigerate, covered with plastic wrap, 1 to 2 hours.

BAKED CEREAL PUDDING

Eat warm from the oven or refrigerate for a chilled dessert. Either way, this comfort food is delicious.

6 servings

3 eggs

¼ cup each: sugar, packed brown sugar

¾ cup natural wheat and barley cereal (Grape-Nuts)

2 cups fat-free milk

2 tablespoons margarine or butter, melted

1 teaspoon vanilla

⅛ teaspoon salt

Per Serving:
Calories: 214
% of calories from fat: 24
Fat (gm): 5.8
Saturated fat (gm): 1.4
Cholesterol (mg): 72.3
Sodium (mg): 262
Protein (gm): 7.9
Carbohydrate (gm): 33.2

Exchanges:
Milk: 0.0
Vegetable: 0.0
Fruit: 0.0
Bread: 2.0
Meat: 0.5
Fat: 1.0

1. Beat eggs and sugars in medium bowl until blended; mix in remaining ingredients. Pour into greased 1-quart soufflé dish or casserole. Place dish in roasting pan on oven rack; pour 2 inches hot water into pan. Bake, uncovered, at 375 degrees until pudding is set, about 50 minutes, stirring well halfway through baking time. Cool on wire rack; serve warm or chilled.

WARM INDIAN PUDDING

Molasses and sweet spices signal the welcome flavors of fall.

6 servings

3 cups milk, divided

¼ cup yellow cornmeal

¾ cup light molasses

⅓ cup packed light brown sugar

¼ teaspoon salt

3 tablespoons margarine or butter

¼ cup dark raisins

½ teaspoon ground cinnamon

¼ teaspoon ground nutmeg

⅛ teaspoon each: ground cloves, ginger

Per Serving:
Calories: 277
% of calories from fat: 19
Fat (gm): 6.1
Saturated fat (gm): 1.3
Cholesterol (mg): 2
Sodium (mg): 143
Protein (gm): 5.3
Carbohydrate (gm): 35

Exchanges:
Milk: 0.5
Vegetable: 0.0
Fruit: 0.5
Bread: 2.5
Meat: 0.0
Fat: 0.5

1. Heat 2¾ cups milk just to boiling in medium saucepan; reduce heat and gradually stir in cornmeal. Simmer until thickened, about 15 minutes, stirring occasionally. Stir in remaining ingredients, except remaining ¼ cup milk. Pour into greased 1½-quart casserole; pour remaining ¼ cup milk over top. Bake, uncovered, until knife inserted near center comes out clean, about 1¼ hours. Serve warm.

OLD-FASHIONED BAKED RICE PUDDING

L

Delicious served with a sprinkling of fresh raspberries or blueberries!

45

6 servings

½ cup uncooked rice

3 cups fat-free milk

⅓ cup sugar

¼ cup golden raisins

½ teaspoon ground cinnamon

2 dashes ground nutmeg

Per Serving:
Calories: 158
% of calories from fat: 2
Fat (gm): 0.3
Saturated fat (gm): 0.2
Cholesterol (mg): 2
Sodium (mg): 65
Protein (gm): 5.4
Carbohydrate (gm): 34

Exchanges:
Milk: 0.5
Vegetable: 0.0
Fruit: 0.5
Bread: 1.0
Meat: 0.0
Fat: 0.0

1. Combine all ingredients in 2-quart casserole. Bake, uncovered, at 350 degrees until rice is tender and milk is absorbed, about 2½ hours, stirring occasionally. Serve warm or chilled.

BLUEBERRY BREAD PUDDING WITH TART LEMON SAUCE

LO

Warm Rum Sauce (p. 621) is a flavorful sauce choice for this pudding too.

45

8 servings

3 tablespoons margarine or butter, room temperature

6 slices whole wheat bread

1 cup fresh or frozen blueberries

2 cups fat-free milk

2 eggs, lightly beaten

½ cup sugar

¼ teaspoon salt

1 teaspoon vanilla

Tart Lemon Sauce (recipe follows)

1. Spread margarine on one side of each bread slice; cut into 2-inch squares and place in greased 1-quart casserole. Add blueberries and toss. Heat milk in small saucepan until just boiling; whisk in combined eggs, sugar, salt,and vanilla; pour over bread cubes.

2. Place casserole in a roasting pan on middle oven rack; pour 1 inch hot water into pan. Bake, uncovered, at 350 degrees 35 to 40 minutes or until knife inserted near center comes out clean. Serve warm with Tart Lemon Sauce.

Per Serving:
Calories: 302
% of calories from fat: 29
Fat (gm): 10
Saturated fat (gm): 2.2
Cholesterol (mg): 80.9
Sodium (mg): 332
Protein (gm): 7.7
Carbohydrate (gm): 47.7

Exchanges:
Milk: 0.0
Vegetable: 0.0
Fruit: 0.0
Bread: 3.0
Meat: 0.0
Fat: 2.0

Tart Lemon Sauce
Makes 1½ cups

2 tablespoons margarine or butter
⅔–1 cup sugar
1 cup lemon juice
2 eggs, slightly beaten

1. Melt margarine over low heat in small saucepan; stir in sugar and lemon juice. Cook over medium heat until sugar is dissolved. Whisk about ½ cup hot lemon mixture into eggs. Whisk egg mixture back into saucepan; cook over low heat, whisking until thickened, 2 to 3 minutes. Serve warm or room temperature.

VARIATION

Raisin-Pecan Bread Pudding — Make recipe above, substituting ⅓ cup each raisins and toasted pecan halves for the blueberries.

DUTCH PANCAKE WITH SPICED FRUIT MÉLANGE

LO · *A spectacular dessert or brunch entree that will win raves!*

8 servings

Dutch Pancake (recipe follows)
3 medium cooking apples, peeled, cored, sliced
1¼ cups mixed dried fruit
¼ cup each: dried cranberries or cherries, sugar
½ cup orange juice
1 teaspoon ground cinnamon
Maple syrup, warm

Per Serving:
Calories: 225
% of calories from fat: 22
Fat (gm): 6
Saturated fat (gm): 1
Cholesterol (mg): 106
Sodium (mg): 154
Protein (gm): 6
Carbohydrate (gm): 40

Exchanges:
Milk: 0.0
Vegetable: 0.0;
Fruit: 0.5
Bread: 2.0
Meat: 0.0
Fat: 1.0

1. Make Dutch Pancake. While Dutch Pancake is baking, sauté apples in lightly greased large skillet 2 to 3 minutes. Add remaining ingredients, except maple syrup, and cook, covered, over medium heat until apples are crisp-tender, about 5 minutes. Heat to boiling and cook, uncovered, until liquid is syrupy, 2 to 3 minutes. Spoon into warm Dutch Pancake; cut into wedges and serve with maple syrup.

Dutch Pancake

4 eggs
¾ cup each: fat-free milk, all-purpose flour
1 tablespoon sugar
¼ teaspoon salt
2 tablespoons margarine or butter

1. Whisk all ingredients, except margarine, in large bowl until almost smooth (batter will be slightly lumpy). Heat margarine in 12-inch ovenproof skillet until melted and bubbly; pour in batter. Bake, uncovered, at 425 degrees until pancake is puffed and browned, 20 to 25 minutes (do not open door during first 15 minutes).

LEMON ICE

Serve this sweet-and-tart ice as a dessert or as a refreshing palate cleanser between dinner courses.

8 servings

2 cups water
1 cup each: sugar, lemon juice
½ cup grated lemon zest

1. Heat water, sugar, lemon juice and zest to boiling in medium saucepan, stirring until sugar is dissolved. Reduce heat and simmer, uncovered, 5 minutes; cool.

2. Freeze mixture in ice cream maker according to manufacturer's directions. Or pour into 8-inch-square baking pan and freeze until slushy, about 2 hours; spoon into bowl and beat until fluffy, then return to pan and freeze until firm, 6 hours or overnight.

Per Serving:
Calories: 101
% of calories from fat: 0
Fat (gm): 0
Saturated fat (gm): 0
Cholesterol (mg): 0
Sodium (mg): 1.3
Protein (gm): 0.2
Carbohydrate (gm): 27.6

Exchanges:
Milk: 0.0
Vegetable: 0.0
Fruit: 0.0
Bread: 1.5
Meat: 0.0
Fat: 0.0

MIXED FRUIT TORTONI

Traditionally made with heavy cream and candied fruits, our version of this Italian favorite uses fresh seasonal fruits and low-fat topping.

12 servings

1½ cups fresh or frozen thawed raspberries

½ cup pitted, halved sweet cherries, divided

⅓ cup each: cubed peeled apricots, pineapple

¼ cup sugar

3 envelopes (1.3 ounces each) low-fat whipped topping mix

1½ cups 2% milk

¼ cup chopped pistachio nuts or slivered almonds, divided

Per Serving:
Calories: 126
% of calories from fat: 28
Fat (gm): 3.5
Saturated fat (gm): 0.7
Cholesterol (mg): 2
Sodium (mg): 32
Protein (gm): 2.1
Carbohydrate (gm): 18.2

Exchanges:
Milk: 0.0
Vegetable: 0.0
Fruit: 1.5
Bread: 0.0
Meat: 0.0
Fat: 0.5

1. Process raspberries in food processor or blender until smooth; strain and discard seeds. Reserve 12 cherry halves. Combine remaining cherries, apricots, pineapple and sugar in small bowl. Beat whipped topping and milk in large bowl at high speed until topping forms soft peaks, about 4 minutes; fold in raspberry puree, sugared fruits, and 2 tablespoons nuts. Spoon into 12 paper-lined muffin cups; garnish tops of each with reserved cherry halves and remaining nuts. Freeze until firm, 6 hours or overnight.

NOTE: If desired, 1 tablespoon sherry or ½ teaspoon sherry extract can be folded into the whipped topping mixture.

ORANGE BAKED ALASKA PIE

Orange Baked Alaska Pie can be frozen overnight—or, freeze with unbaked meringue and bake just before serving.

45

8 servings

Gingersnap Crust (see p. 572)

½ cup graham cracker crumbs

1 tablespoon margarine or butter, melted

1 quart frozen low-fat vanilla yogurt, slightly softened

2 tablespoons orange-flavored liqueur or orange
   juice concentrate

½ teaspoon ground nutmeg

3 egg whites

⅛ teaspoon cream of tartar

¼ cup sugar

Per Serving:
Calories: 332
% of calories from fat: 25
Fat (gm): 9.2
Saturated fat (gm): 2.5
Cholesterol (mg): 45
Sodium (mg): 245
Protein (gm): 10.7
Carbohydrate (gm): 50

Exchanges:
Milk: 0.0
Vegetable: 0.0
Fruit: 0.0
Bread: 3.5
Meat: 0.0
Fat: 2.0

1. Make crumb crust, adding ½ cup graham cracker crumbs and 1 tablespoon margarine, and using 8-inch pie pan. Spoon combined frozen yogurt, liqueur, and nutmeg into cooled crust. Cover with plastic wrap and freeze until firm, 8 hours or overnight.

2. Beat egg whites and cream of tartar to soft peaks in large bowl; beat to stiff but not dry peaks, adding sugar gradually. Spread meringue over frozen pie, carefully sealing to edge of crust. Bake at 500 degrees 3 to 5 minutes or until meringue is golden. Serve immediately.

VARIATION

Chocolate Baked Alaska — Make recipe above, using Vanilla Crumb Crust (see p. 572), and adding ½ cup vanilla wafer crumbs and 1 tablespoon margarine. Substitute low-fat frozen chocolate yogurt for the vanilla and delete orange liqueur and nutmeg.

FIFTEEN

Memorable Menus

The nine menus in this chapter have been designed for busy people like you, to take the guesswork out of the meal planning and cooking. The menus are perfect for family dining, casual entertaining, and festive occasions too.

Recipes for some of the menu items are not given because these are side dishes, breads, or desserts you already know how to make, can prepare from packaged foods, or may purchase ready-made. Feel free to substitute a favorite recipe in any menu, or to look through other chapters in this book for more ideas.

Nutrional analyses have been given for each recipe as well as for the entire menu. For menu items without recipes, nutritional analyses were based on a per person serving of one-half cup side dish, one bread item with 1 teaspoon of margarine or butter, and one cookie.

SPRING FLING

Herbed Cucumber Soup*

Chicken Cordon Bleu*

Asparagus with Lemon-Wine Sauce*

Parslied Rice

French Bread

Sugared Lemon Squares*

* Recipes included

PREPARATION TIPS

1–2 Days in Advance: Make Cucumber Soup; refrigerate.

Early in the Day: Trim asparagus. Assemble Chicken Cordon Bleu; refrigerate. Make Sugared Lemon Squares.

40 Minutes Before Serving: Cook Chicken Cordon Bleu.

25 Minutes Before Serving: Cook rice. Make Lemon-Wine Sauce for asparagus.

10 Minutes Before Serving: Cook asparagus; spoon Lemon-Wine Sauce over.

HERBED CUCUMBER SOUP

This soup is very delicate in flavor. Use a serrated grapefruit spoon to seed cucumbers quickly and easily.

6 first-course servings

½ cup chopped onion

6 medium cucumbers , peeled, seeded, chopped

3 tablespoons flour

4 cups reduced-sodium fat-free chicken broth

1 teaspoon dried mint or dill weed

½ cup fat-free half-and-half or fat-free milk

Salt and white pepper, to taste

Paprika, sliced cucumber, as garnish

Per Serving:
Calories: 70
% of calories from fat: 8
Fat (gm): 0.6
Saturated fat (gm): 0.1
Cholesterol (mg): 0
Sodium (mg): 33
Protein (gm): 3.1
Carbohydrate (gm): 13.7

Exchanges:
Milk: 0.0
Vegetable: 1.0
Fruit: 0.0
Bread: 0.5
Meat: 0.0
Fat: 0.0

1. Sauté onion in lightly greased skillet until tender, 3 to 5 minutes. Add cucumbers and cook over medium heat 5 minutes; stir in flour and cook 1 minute. Add broth and mint; heat to boiling. Reduce heat and simmer, covered, 10 minutes. Process soup in food processor or blender until smooth; stir in half-and-half and season to taste with salt and pepper. Serve warm or chilled; garnish each bowl of soup with paprika and cucumber slices.

CHICKEN CORDON BLEU

A gourmet favorite, the ham and cheese-stuffed chicken breasts are delicious in their svelte low-fat form!

6 servings

6 boneless, skinless chicken breast halves
   (4 ounces each)

4 ounces sliced fat-free Swiss cheese

3 ounces lean smoked ham

Flour

1 egg, lightly beaten

⅓ cup unseasoned dry bread crumbs

Vegetable cooking spray

Per Serving:
Calories: 210
% of calories from fat: 18
Fat (gm): 3.9
Saturated fat (gm): 1.1
Cholesterol (mg): 73.2
Sodium (mg): 540
Protein (gm): 34.6
Carbohydrate (gm): 6.3

Exchanges:
Milk: 0.0
Vegetable: 0.0
Fruit: 0.0
Bread: 0.0
Meat: 4.0
Fat: 0.0

1. Pound chicken breasts with flat side of meat mallet until very thin and even in thickness. Layer cheese and ham on chicken, cutting to fit; roll up and secure with toothpicks. Coat chicken rolls lightly with flour; dip in egg and coat with bread crumbs. Spray rolls generously with cooking spray and cook in large oven-proof skillet over medium heat until browned on all sides, 8 to 10 minutes. Transfer to oven and bake at 350 degrees, uncovered, until cooked, about 25 minutes.

ASPARAGUS WITH LEMON-WINE SAUCE

45

L

This rich sauce is also delicious served with crisp-tender broccoli, cauliflower, green beans, or Brussels sprouts.

4 servings

2 tablespoons minced shallots or green onions

¼ cup dry white wine or water

¾ cup fat-free half-and-half or milk

1 tablespoon flour

½ teaspoon each: dried thyme and marjoram leaves

1 tablespoon lemon juice

Salt and white pepper, to taste

1 pound asparagus spears, cooked crisp-tender, warm

Per Serving:
Calories: 85
% of calories from fat: 4
Fat (gm): 0.4
Saturated fat (gm): 0.1
Cholesterol (mg): 0
Sodium (mg): 59
Protein (gm): 4.8
Carbohydrate (gm): 13.4

Exchanges:
Milk: 0.0
Vegetable: 2.0
Fruit: 0.0
Bread: 0.5
Meat: 0.0
Fat: 0.0

1. Sauté shallots in lightly greased small saucepan until tender, 2 to 3 minutes. Add wine and heat to boiling; reduce heat and simmer, uncovered, until wine is evaporated, 3 to 4 minutes. Stir in combined half-and-half, flour, and herbs; heat to boiling, stirring until thickened, about 1 minute. Stir in lemon juice; season to taste with salt and pepper. Spoon over asparagus.

SUGARED LEMON SQUARES

LO *Just like the favorites you remember, but with a low-fat bonus!*

45 **25 squares** (1 per serving)

¾ cup all-purpose flour

4 tablespoons margarine or butter, room temperature

2 tablespoons reduced-fat sour cream

1 cup and 2 tablespoons granulated sugar, divided

2 eggs

1 tablespoon grated lemon zest

3 tablespoons lemon juice

½ teaspoon baking powder

¼ teaspoon salt

Powdered sugar

Per Serving:
Calories: 71
% of calories from fat: 27
Fat (gm): 2.1
Saturated fat (gm): 0.4
Cholesterol (mg): 8.9
Sodium (mg): 57
Protein (gm): 1
Carbohydrate (gm): 12.2

Exchanges:
Milk: 0.0
Vegetable: 0.0
Fruit: 0.0
Bread: 1.0
Meat: 0.0
Fat: 0.5

1. Mix flour, margarine, sour cream, and 2 tablespoons granulated sugar in bowl to form soft dough; pat into bottom and ¼ inch up sides of an 8 x 8-inch baking pan. Bake at 350 degrees until lightly browned, about 20 minutes. Cool on wire rack.

2. Mix remaining 1 cup granulated sugar and remaining ingredients, except powdered sugar, in small bowl; pour over baked pastry. Bake at 350 degrees until no indentation remains when touched in the center, 20 to 25 minutes. Cool on wire rack; cut into squares. Sprinkle lightly with powdered sugar.

AUTUMN HARVEST MENU

Ripe Tomato and Leek Soup*

Rosemary Roast Pork Tenderloin*

Baked Corn Pudding*

Brussels Sprouts

Rye or Whole-Grain Bread

Pumpkin-Ginger Cake with Warm Rum Sauce*

* Recipes included

PREPARATION TIPS

1–2 Days in Advance: Make soup; refrigerate. Make Pumpkin-Ginger Cake and Rum Sauce.

Early in the Day: Prepare pork tenderloin for roasting; refrigerate in baking pan. Clean Brussels sprouts.

1 Hour Before Serving: Make Corn Pudding.

30 Minutes Before Serving: Roast the pork tenderloin. Cook Brussels sprouts. Reheat soup.

At Dessert Time: Heat Rum Sauce for cake.

RIPE TOMATO AND LEEK SOUP

Use summer's ripest tomatoes for this soup, cooking only briefly to maintain their sweetness. Peel the tomatoes or not, as you prefer.

6 first-course servings

2 cups sliced leeks
3 cloves garlic, minced
1 tablespoon olive oil
6 large tomatoes (about 2½ pounds)
4 cups reduced-sodium fat-free chicken broth
½–1 teaspoon dried basil leaves
Salt and white pepper, to taste
6 tablespoons fat-free sour cream or plain yogurt
Basil sprigs, as garnish

Per Serving:
Calories: 99
% of calories from fat: 24
Fat (gm): 2.9
Saturated fat (gm): 0.5
Cholesterol (mg): 0
Sodium (mg): 64
Protein (gm): 3.5
Carbohydrate (gm): 17.3

Exchanges:
Milk: 0.0
Vegetable: 3.0
Fruit: 0.0
Bread: 0.0
Meat: 0.0
Fat: 0.5

1. Sauté leeks and garlic in oil in large saucepan until tender, about 8 minutes. Add tomatoes, broth, and basil to saucepan; heat to boiling. Reduce heat and simmer, covered, 10 minutes. Process soup in food processor or blender until smooth; season to taste with salt and white pepper. Serve soup warm or chilled; top each bowl of soup with a tablespoon of sour cream and garnish with basil sprigs.

ROSEMARY ROAST PORK TENDERLOIN

So easy to prepare, you'll make this delicious entrée often.

4 servings

1 pound pork tenderloin, fat trimmed
1 clove garlic, cut into 8 to 10 slivers
Vegetable cooking spray
1 teaspoon crushed dried rosemary leaves
Salt and pepper, to taste

Per Serving:
Calories: 139
% of calories from fat: 28
Fat (gm): 4
Saturated fat (gm): 1.4
Cholesterol (mg): 66
Sodium (mg): 47
Protein (gm): 23.5
Carbohydrate (gm): .44

Exchanges:
Milk: 0.0
Vegetable: 0.0
Fruit: 0.0
Bread: 0.0
Meat: 3.0
Fat: 0.0

1. Cut small slits in pork and insert garlic slivers. Place pork in small roasting pan and spray lightly with cooking spray. Rub surface of pork with rosemary leaves. Sprinkle lightly with salt and pepper. Roast at 425 degrees to desired degree of doneness, 160 degrees (slightly pink), 20 to 30 minutes.

NOTE: Pork can be eaten slightly pink; it is safe to eat after the internal temperature has reached 140 degrees.

BAKED CORN PUDDING

Use fresh corn cut from the cob for best flavor, though frozen or canned can be used for convenience.

6 servings

2 tablespoons unseasoned dry bread crumbs

2 cups whole-kernel corn

½ cup fat-free milk

3 tablespoons flour

1½ tablespoons margarine or butter, melted

2 eggs, lightly beaten

1 teaspoon sugar

½ teaspoon each: dried thyme leaves, salt

⅛ teaspoon pepper

Per Serving:
Calories: 122
% of calories from fat: 28
Fat (gm): 3.9
Saturated fat (gm): 0.9
Cholesterol (mg): 35.8
Sodium (mg): 272
Protein (gm): 5.3
Carbohydrate (gm): 17.9

Exchanges:
Milk: 0.0
Vegetable: 0.0
Fruit: 0.0
Bread: 1.0
Meat: 0.5
Fat: 0.5

1. Coat lightly greased 1-quart casserole or soufflé dish with bread crumbs. Process corn, milk, and flour in food processor or blender until a coarse puree. Stir in combined remaining ingredients and pour into prepared casserole. Bake, uncovered, at 350 degrees until pudding is set and beginning to brown, about 35 minutes.

PUMPKIN-GINGER CAKE WITH WARM RUM SAUCE

Moist with pumpkin and savory with spices, this cake is a perfect choice for fall and winter holidays.

8 servings

½ cup each: canned pumpkin, packed light
  brown sugar
¼ cup each: margarine or butter, room temperature,
  light molasses
1 egg
1½ cups all-purpose flour
½ teaspoon each: baking powder, baking soda,
  ground allspice, cloves, ginger
Warm Rum Sauce (recipe follows)

Per Serving:
Calories: 245
% of calories from fat: 28
Fat (gm): 8
Saturated fat (gm): 2
Cholesterol (mg): 22
Sodium (mg): 196
Protein (gm): 4
Carbohydrate (gm): 39

Exchanges:
Milk: 0.0
Vegetable: 0.0
Fruit: 0.0
Bread: 2.5
Meat: 0.0;
Fat: 1.5

1. Combine pumpkin, brown sugar, margarine, molasses, and egg in large bowl; beat at medium speed until fluffy. Mix in combined flour, baking powder, baking soda, allspice, cloves, and ginger until moistened. Pour into greased and floured 8-inch-square baking pan.

2. Bake 350 degrees until toothpick inserted in center of cake comes out clean, 30 to 40 minutes. Cool in pan on wire rack 10 minutes; remove from pan and cool. Serve with Warm Rum Sauce.

Warm Rum Sauce
Makes 1½ cups

¼ cup sugar
1 tablespoon cornstarch
1¼ cups fat-free milk
2 tablespoons each: rum or ½ teaspoon rum extract, margarine or butter
½ teaspoon vanilla
⅛ teaspoon ground nutmeg

1. Mix sugar and cornstarch in small saucepan; whisk in milk and rum. Heat to boiling, whisking until thickened, about 1 minute. Remove from heat; add margarine, vanilla, and nutmeg, stirring until margarine is melted. Serve warm.

FRIDAY NIGHT SUPPER

Tuna Patties with Creamed Pea Sauce*

Harvard Beets*

Carrot-Raisin Salad*

Warm Buns or Rolls

Rhubarb Crunch*

* Recipes included

PREPARATION TIPS

1 Day in Advance: Make Tuna Patties, but do not cook. Instead, refrigerate. Make Rhubarb Crunch.

Early in the Day: Cook and slice beets. Make Carrot-Raisin Salad.

20 Minutes Before Serving: Cook Tuna Patties and make Creamed Pea Sauce. Complete Harvard Beets.

TUNA PATTIES WITH CREAMED PEA SAUCE

45 *These generous patties can also be served in buns, or the mixture can be baked in a small loaf pan.*

4 servings

2 cans (6⅛ ounces each) light tuna packed in water, drained
¾ cup unseasoned dry bread crumbs, divided
¼ cup each: finely chopped onion, celery
2 tablespoons chopped green bell pepper
3 tablespoons fat-free mayonnaise
2 teaspoons Worcestershire sauce
Salt and cayenne pepper, to taste
1 egg
Creamed Pea Sauce (recipe follows)

Per Serving:
Calories: 325
% of calories from fat: 25
Fat (gm): 8.9
Saturated fat (gm): 2
Cholesterol (mg): 79.2
Sodium (mg): 726
Protein (gm): 30
Carbohydrate (gm): 28.6

Exchanges:
Milk: 0.5
Vegetable: 1.0
Fruit: 0.0
Bread: 1.0
Meat: 3.5
Fat: 0.0

1. Combine tuna, ½ cup bread crumbs, onion, celery, bell pepper, mayonnaise, and Worcestershire sauce in medium bowl; season to taste with salt and cayenne pepper. Mix in egg; shape into 4 patties, about ½ inch thick and coat with remaining ¼ cup bread crumbs. Cook patties in lightly greased medium skillet over medium heat until browned, about 5 minutes on each side. Serve with Creamed Pea Sauce.

Creamed Pea Sauce

Makes about 1 cup

2 tablespoons each: margarine or butter, flour
1 cup each: fat-free half-and-half or fat-free milk, frozen, thawed peas
Salt and pepper, to taste

1. Melt margarine in small saucepan; stir in flour and cook 1 minute. Whisk in half-and-half; heat to boiling, whisking until thickened, about 1 minute. Stir in peas; cook over low heat 2 to 3 minutes. Season to taste with salt and pepper.

45-MINUTE PREPARATION TIP: Make Creamed Pea Sauce and keep warm while preparing Tuna Patties.

HARVARD BEETS

45

L

Sweet and tart, the sauce can also be served over cooked carrots or pearl onions. Vary the amount of vinegar for the right amount of tartness.

4 servings

3 tablespoons sugar
1½ tablespoons cornstarch
¾ cup water
3–4 tablespoons cider vinegar
2 teaspoons margarine or butter
Salt and white pepper, to taste
1 pound medium beets, cooked, sliced, warm

Per Serving:
Calories: 94
% of calories from fat: 18
Fat (gm): 1.9
Saturated fat (gm): 0.4
Cholesterol (mg): 0
Sodium (mg): 70
Protein (gm): 1.1
Carbohydrate (gm): 19.3

Exchanges:
Milk: 0.0
Vegetable: 2.0
Fruit: 0.0
Bread: 0.5
Meat: 0.0
Fat: 0.0

1. Mix sugar and cornstarch in small saucepan; whisk in water and vinegar. Heat to boiling, whisking until thickened, about 1 minute. Whisk in margarine; season to taste with salt and pepper. Pour sauce over beets and toss.

CARROT-RAISIN SALAD

45

O

Always a popular salad—a small can of drained pineapple tidbits can be added.

6 servings

2½ cups shredded carrots
¾ cup chopped celery
⅓ cup each: raisins, coarsely chopped walnuts
¾ cup fat-free mayonnaise
½ teaspoon Dijon mustard
1–2 teaspoons sugar
⅛ teaspoon salt

Per Serving:
Calories: 115
% of calories from fat: 30
Fat (gm): 4.1
Saturated fat (gm): 0.3
Cholesterol (mg): 0
Sodium (mg): 460
Protein (gm): 2.6
Carbohydrate (gm): 19.2

Exchanges:
Milk: 0.0
Vegetable: 2.0
Fruit: 0.5
Bread: 0.0
Meat: 0.0
Fat: 1.0

1. Combine carrots, celery, raisins, and walnuts in bowl; mix in combined remaining ingredients.

RHUBARB CRUNCH

 With a crunchy sweet crust on top and bottom, you'll lick your bowl clean and ask for more! The recipe can be halved and baked in a 9-inch-square baking pan.

16 servings

1 cup each: all-purpose flour, whole wheat flour

1½ cups packed light brown sugar

1 cup quick-cooking oats

½ cup bran or quick-cooking oats

2 teaspoons ground cinnamon

10 tablespoons margarine, melted

2 pounds fresh or frozen, thawed, rhubarb, cut into
   1-inch pieces

2 cups granulated sugar

¼ cup cornstarch

2 cups water

2 teaspoons vanilla

Per Serving:
Calories: 341
% of calories from fat: 10
Fat (gm): 7.9
Saturated fat (gm): 1.5
Cholesterol (mg): 0
Sodium (mg): 94
Protein (gm): 3.8
Carbohydrate (gm): 66.9

Exchanges:
Milk: 0.0
Vegetable: 0.0
Fruit: 1.0
Bread: 3.0
Meat: 0.0
Fat: 1.5

1. Combine flours, brown sugar, oats, bran, and cinnamon in large bowl; stir in margarine to make a crumbly mixture. Press half the mixture evenly on bottom of 13 x 9-inch baking pan. Arrange rhubarb evenly over crust.

2. Combine granulated sugar and cornstarch in medium saucepan; stir in water and heat to boiling, stirring, until thickened, about 1 minute. Stir in vanilla; pour over rhubarb. Sprinkle remaining crumb mixture over rhubarb. Bake at 350 degrees, uncovered, until bubbly around the edges, 55 to 60 minutes.

COUNTRY CHICKEN DINNER

Crisp Oven-Fried Chicken with Cream Gravy*

Real Mashed Potatoes*

Tiny Peas and Pearl Onions*

Biscuits

Double-Crust Apple Pie*

* Recipes included

PREPARATION TIPS

1–2 Days in Advance: Make pie crust and refrigerate.

Early in the Day: Peel potatoes; store in pan of water. Bake pie.

1 Hour Before Serving: Make Oven-Fried Chicken with Cream Gravy. Make Real Mashed Potatoes.

15 Minutes Before Serving: Make Tiny Peas and Onions. Bake biscuits.

CRISP OVEN-FRIED CHICKEN WITH CREAM GRAVY

45

Serve with Real Mashed Potatoes, if you like (see p. 628).

6 servings

6 skinless chicken breast halves (6 ounces each)

Flour

3 egg whites or ⅓ cup no-cholesterol real egg product, lightly beaten

¼ cup 2% reduced-fat milk

1¼ cups finely crushed corn flakes cereal

½ cup unseasoned dry bread crumbs

½ teaspoon each: dried rosemary and thyme leaves, crushed

Vegetable cooking spray

Salt and pepper, to taste

Cream Gravy (see p. 131)

½ teaspoon chicken bouillon crystals

Per Serving:
Calories: 387
% of calories from fat: 13
Fat (gm): 5.4
Saturated fat (gm): 1.5
Cholesterol (mg): 104.2
Sodium (mg): 557
Protein (gm): 44.8
Carbohydrate (gm): 36

Exchanges:
Milk: 0.0
Vegetable: 0.0
Fruit: 0.0
Bread: 2.5
Meat: 4.0
Fat: 0.0

1. Coat chicken breasts lightly with flour; dip in combined egg whites and milk, then coat generously with combined corn flakes, bread crumbs, and herbs. Place meat sides up, in greased baking pan; spray generously with cooking spray and sprinkle lightly with salt and pepper. Bake at 350 degrees until chicken is browned and juices run clear, 45 to 60 minutes.

2. Make Cream Gravy, substituting chicken bouillon crystals for the beef; serve over chicken.

REAL MASHED POTATOES

45

L

Just like grandma used to make! For a country-style variation, leave potatoes unpeeled.

8 servings

2 pounds Idaho potatoes, peeled, quartered, cooked

½ cup fat-free sour cream

¼ cup fat-free milk, hot

2 tablespoons margarine or butter

Salt and pepper, to taste

Per Serving:
Calories: 124
% of calories from fat: 21
Fat (gm): 2.9
Saturated fat (gm): 0.6
Cholesterol (mg): 0.2
Sodium (mg): 53
Protein (gm): 3.1
Carbohydrate (gm): 22.2

Exchanges:
Milk: 0.0
Vegetable: 0.0
Fruit: 0.0
Bread: 1.5
Meat: 0.0
Fat: 0.5

1. Mash potatoes with potato masher or electric mixer, adding sour cream, milk, and margarine. Season to taste with salt and pepper. Heat in saucepan over medium heat until hot, about 5 minutes.

VARIATIONS

Garlic Mashed Potatoes — Make recipe above, cooking 10 peeled cloves of garlic with the potatoes; mash garlic with potatoes.

Horseradish Mashed Potatoes — Make Real or Garlic Mashed Potatoes, beating in 2 teaspoons horseradish.

Potato Pancakes — Make any of the mashed potato recipes above; refrigerate until chilled. Mix in 1 egg, 4 chopped green onions, and ¼ cup (1 ounce) grated fat-free Parmesan cheese. Form mixture into 8 patties, using about ½ cup mixture for each. Coat patties in flour, dip in beaten egg, and coat with plain dry bread crumbs. Cook over medium heat in lightly greased large skillet until browned, 3 to 5 minutes on each side.

TINY PEAS AND PEARL ONIONS

45 *The refreshing flavors of mint and dill give this dish a Mediterranean accent.*

L   **6 servings**

½ package (16-ounce size) frozen pearl onions

½ cup water

1 package (8 ounces) frozen tiny peas

2–3 teaspoons margarine or butter

½ teaspoon each: dried mint leaves, dill weed

Salt and pepper, to taste

1. Heat onions and water to boiling in medium saucepan; reduce heat and simmer until tender, 8 to 10 minutes, adding peas during the last 5 minutes. Drain. Add margarine and herbs, stirring until melted. Season to taste with salt and pepper.

Per Serving:
Calories: 63
% of calories from fat: 20
Fat (gm): 1.4
Saturated fat (gm): 0.3
Cholesterol (mg): 0
Sodium (mg): 57
Protein (gm): 2.5
Carbohydrate (gm): 10.4

Exchanges:
Milk: 0.0
Vegetable: 0.0
Fruit: 0.0
Bread: 1.0
Meat: 0.0
Fat: 0.0

DOUBLE-CRUST APPLE PIE

Nothing is more American than real homemade apple pie. Enjoy it warm with a generous scoop of fat-free frozen yogurt or a slice of reduced-fat Cheddar cheese.

10 servings

Double Pie Crust (see p. 570)

8 cups peeled, cored, sliced tart baking apples

1 cup sugar

4–5 tablespoons all-purpose flour

¾ teaspoon ground cinnamon

¼ teaspoon ground nutmeg

⅛ teaspoon each: ground cloves, salt

2 tablespoons margarine or butter, cut into
   pieces (optional)

Per Serving:
Calories: 297
% of calories from fat: 19
Fat (gm): 6.3
Saturated fat (gm): 1.2
Cholesterol (mg): 0
Sodium (mg): 200
Protein (gm): 3.1
Carbohydrate (gm): 58.9

Exchanges:
Milk: 0.0
Vegetable: 0.0
Fruit: 1.0
Bread: 3.5
Meat: 0.0
Fat: 1.5

1. Roll ⅔ of the pastry on floured surface into circle 2 inches larger than inverted 9-inch pie pan; ease pastry into pan.

2. Toss apples with combined sugar, flour, spices, and salt in bowl; arrange in pastry and dot with margarine, if using. Roll remaining pastry to fit top of pie and place over apples. Trim edges of pastry to within ½ inch of pan; fold top pastry over bottom pastry and flute. Cut vents in top crust.

3. Bake at 425 degrees until apples are tender and pastry browned, 40 to 50 minutes. Cover pastry with foil if becoming too brown. Cool 10 to 15 minutes before cutting.

FAMILY FAVORITES

Creamed Corn Soup*

Salisbury Steaks with Mushroom Gravy*

Twice-Baked Potatoes with Cheese*

Steamed Green Beans

Multigrain Bread

Flourless Chocolate Cake*

* Recipes included

PREPARATION TIPS

2 Days in Advance: Make Chocolate Cake; do not frost. Refrigerate, lightly wrapped.

1 Day in Advance: Make Creamed Corn Soup and assemble Twice-Baked Potatoes; refrigerate.

Early in the Day: Make Salisbury Steaks but do not cook; refrigerate. Clean green beans. Frost cake.

45 Minutes Before Serving: Bake Twice-Baked Potatoes. Cook Salisbury Steaks; make gravy. Cook green beans. Reheat soup.

CREAMED CORN SOUP

45

L

For a flavor accent, garnish bowls of soup generously with finely chopped cilantro or parsley.

4 first-course servings

½ cup chopped onion

1 medium Idaho potato, peeled, cubed

2 cloves garlic, minced

1 can (15½ ounces) whole kernel corn, drained

3 tablespoons flour

½ teaspoon ground coriander

⅛ teaspoon cayenne pepper

2 cans (14½ ounces each) vegetable or chicken broth

1 cup fat-free milk

2 medium tomatoes, seeded, chopped

Salt and pepper, to taste

Per Serving:
Calories: 238
% of calories from fat: 8
Fat (gm): 2.3
Saturated fat (gm): 0.4
Cholesterol (mg): 1
Sodium (mg): 443
Protein (gm): 7.7
Carbohydrate (gm): 45.7

Exchanges:
Milk: 0.0
Vegetable: 3.0
Fruit: 0.0
Bread: 2.0
Meat: 0.0
Fat: 0.5

1. Sauté onion, potato, and garlic in lightly greased saucepan until onion is tender, about 5 minutes. Stir in corn, flour, coriander, and cayenne pepper; cook 1 minute. Stir in broth and heat to boiling; reduce heat and simmer, covered, until potato is tender, about 10 minutes.

2. Process soup in food processor or blender until almost smooth; return to saucepan; stir in milk and tomatoes and heat to boiling. Reduce heat and simmer, uncovered, 5 minutes. Season to taste with salt and pepper.

SALISBURY STEAKS WITH MUSHROOM GRAVY

45

Rich Mushroom Gravy is a flavorful complement to moist Salisbury steaks.

4 servings

1 pound ground beef eye of round

2–4 tablespoons finely chopped onion

3 tablespoons water

½ teaspoon salt

¼ teaspoon pepper

Mushroom Gravy (recipe follows)

1. Mix all ingredients, except Mushroom Gravy; shape into four 1-inch thick oval patties. Cook patties in lightly greased large skillet to desired degree of doneness, 3 to 4 minutes per side for medium. Serve with Mushroom Gravy.

Per Serving:
Calories: 184
% of calories from fat: 24
Fat (gm): 4.6
Saturated fat (gm): 1.7
Cholesterol (mg): 64
Sodium (mg): 341
Protein (gm): 28.7
Carbohydrate (gm): 5.2

Exchanges:
Milk: 0.0
Vegetable: 1.0
Fruit: 0.0
Bread: 0.0
Meat: 3.0
Fat: 0.0

Mushroom Gravy

Makes about 1¼ cups

1 cup sliced mushrooms
¼ cup finely chopped onion
2 tablespoons flour
1 cup reduced-sodium beef broth
Salt and pepper, to taste

1. Sauté mushrooms and onion in lightly greased medium skillet until tender, about 5 minutes; stir in flour and cook 1 minute. Stir in beef broth and heat to boiling, stirring until thickened, about 1 minute. Season to taste with salt and pepper.

45-MINUTE PREPARATION TIP: Prepare ingredients for Mushroom Gravy before beginning the rest of the recipe; make gravy while Salisbury Steaks are cooking.

TWICE-BAKED POTATOES WITH CHEESE

L *These stuffed bakers are always a favorite!*

4 servings

2 large Idaho potatoes (8 ounces each), baked, warm
¼ cup each: fat-free sour cream, fat-free milk
¾ cup (3 ounces) shredded reduced-fat sharp or mild Cheddar cheese, divided
Salt and pepper, to taste
Paprika, as garnish

Per Serving:
Calories: 177
% of calories from fat: 16
Fat (gm): 3.2
Saturated fat (gm): 1.6
Cholesterol (mg): 11.6
Sodium (mg): 314
Protein (gm): 8.4
Carbohydrate (gm): 29.2

Exchanges:
Milk: 0.0
Vegetable: 0.0
Fruit: 0.0
Bread: 2.0
Meat: 0.5
Fat: 0.0

1. Cut potatoes lengthwise into halves; scoop out pulp, being careful to leave shells intact.

Mash potatoes with potato masher or electric mixer, adding sour cream, milk, and ½ cup cheese; season to taste with salt and pepper. Spoon into potato shells; sprinkle with remaining ¼ cup cheese and paprika. Bake, uncovered, at 400 degrees until hot, 15 to 20 minutes.

FLOURLESS CHOCOLATE CAKE

LO

It's hard to believe a cake so sinfully rich and wonderful can actually be low-fat! Although regular cocoa can be used, the Dutch process cocoa lends a special flavor.

8 servings

½ cup Dutch process cocoa

¾ cup packed light brown sugar

3 tablespoons flour

2 teaspoons instant coffee crystals

⅛ teaspoon salt

¾ cup fat-free milk

1 teaspoon vanilla

2 ounces each: chopped unsweetened and semisweet chocolate

1 egg, lightly beaten

3 egg whites

⅛ teaspoon cream of tartar

⅓ cup granulated sugar

Rich Chocolate Frosting (recipe follows)

Per Serving:
Calories: 335
% of calories from fat: 22
Fat (gm): 8.9
Saturated fat (gm): 3.6
Cholesterol (mg): 27.1
Sodium (mg): 107
Protein (gm): 6.3
Carbohydrate (gm): 66.1

Exchanges:
Milk: 0.0
Vegetable: 0.0
Fruit: 0.0
Bread: 4.0
Meat: 0.0
Fat: 1.0

1. Combine cocoa, brown sugar, flour, coffee crystals, and salt in medium saucepan; add milk and vanilla, stirring until smooth. Heat over medium heat, stirring frequently, until mixture is hot and sugar dissolved (do not boil). Remove from heat; add chocolate, stirring until melted. Whisk about ½ cup chocolate mixture into egg; whisk mixture back into saucepan. Cool.

2. Beat egg whites to soft peaks in medium bowl; add cream of tartar and beat, adding sugar gradually, until stiff, but not dry, peaks form. Stir about ¼ of the egg whites into chocolate mixture; fold chocolate mixture back into egg whites. Pour into greased and floured parchment-lined 9-inch round cake pan.

3. Place cake pan in large roasting pan on center oven rack; add 1 inch hot water to pan. Bake cake at 350 degrees until just firm when touched, 25 to 30 minutes (do not test with toothpick as cake will still be soft in the center). Cool in pan on wire rack; refrigerate, covered, 8 hours or overnight.

4. Loosen side of cake from pan with sharp knife. Remove from pan and place on serving plate. Frost with Rich Chocolate Frosting.

Rich Chocolate Frosting
Makes about ¾ cup

1–2 tablespoons margarine or butter, room temperature
1½ cups powdered sugar
¼ cup Dutch process cocoa
½ teaspoon vanilla
3–4 tablespoons fat-free milk

1. Mix all ingredients, except milk, adding enough milk to make the spreadable consistency.

SOUTHWEST SOJOURN

Quesadillas*

Black and White Bean Chili*

Tossed Salad

Green Chili Corn Bread*

Caramel Flan*

* Recipes included

PREPARATION TIPS

Several Days in Advance: Make Chili; refrigerate.

1 Day in Advance: Make Flan and refrigerate; do not unmold. Thaw chili.

Early in the Day: Wash greens for salad. Assemble Quesadillas but do not cook; refrigerate. Make Green Chili Corn bread. Unmold Flan; refrigerate.

30 Minutes Before Serving: Heat Chili. Reheat corn bread. Make salad. Cook Quesadillas.

QUESADILLAS

L

The simplest quesadillas are made only with cheese. Our version adds the Mexican poblano chili, onion, and cilantro; Chorizo (see p. 154) would be a flavorful addition.

6 servings

½ cup each: chopped poblano chili or green bell pepper, finely chopped onion

1 teaspoon ground cumin

3 tablespoons chopped cilantro

1 cup (4 ounces) shredded reduced-fat Cheddar cheese

6 flour tortillas (6-inch)

Vegetable cooking spray

Green Tomato Salsa (recipe follows)

6 tablespoons fat-free sour cream

Per Serving:
Calories: 165
% of calories from fat: 26
Fat (gm): 4.8
Saturated fat (gm): 1.7
Cholesterol (mg): 10.1
Sodium (mg): 393
Protein (gm): 8.3
Carbohydrate (gm): 22.9

Exchanges:
Milk: 0.0
Vegetable: 1.5
Fruit: 0.0
Bread: 1.0
Meat: 0.5
Fat: 0.5

1. Sauté poblano chili, onion, and cumin in lightly greased large skillet until vegetables are tender, 3 to 5 minutes; stir in cilantro. Sprinkle cheese on half of each tortilla; spoon vegetable mixture over. Fold tortillas in half. Cook in lightly greased large skillet over medium to medium-low heat until browned on the bottom, 2 to 3 minutes. Spray tops of quesadillas with cooking spray; turn and cook until browned on other side. Cut into wedges; serve warm with salsa and sour cream.

Green Tomato Salsa

Makes about 1 cup

12 ounces tomatillos, husked

2 tablespoons finely chopped onion

1 clove garlic, minced

¼ small jalapeño chili, finely chopped

2 tablespoons finely chopped cilantro

½ teaspoon ground cumin

¼ teaspoon dried oregano leaves

⅛–¼ teaspoon sugar

Salt, to taste

1. Simmer tomatillos in water to cover in large saucepan until tender, 5 to 8 minutes. Cool; drain, reserving liquid. Process all ingredients, except sugar and salt, in food processor or blender until almost smooth, adding enough reserved liquid to make medium dipping consistency. Season to taste with sugar and salt.

BLACK AND WHITE BEAN CHILI

A colorful soup, rich in flavor.

4 entrée servings (about 1¼ cups each)

12 ounces very lean ground beef

1 cup chopped onion

½ cup chopped green bell pepper

2 teaspoons each: minced jalapeno chili, garlic

2 cans (16 ounces each) reduced-sodium whole tomatoes, undrained, coarsely chopped

1 can (15 ounces) each: Great Northern and black beans, rinsed, drained

¼ cup sun-dried tomatoes (not in oil), softened, chopped

2–3 tablespoons chili powder

1–1½ teaspoons each: ground cumin, dried oregano leaves

1 bay leaf

Salt and pepper, to taste

¼ cup chopped cilantro

Per Serving:
Calories: 305
% of calories from fat: 12
Fat (gm): 4.9
Saturated fat (gm): 1.2
Cholesterol (mg): 41.2
Sodium (mg): 770
Protein (gm): 28.9
Carbohydrate (gm): 52.4

Exchanges:
Milk: 0.0
Vegetable: 2.0
Fruit: 0.0
Bread: 2.0
Meat: 2.0
Fat: 0.0

1. Cook ground beef, onion, bell pepper, jalapeño chili, and garlic in lightly greased large saucepan until beef is browned and vegetables are tender, 8 to 10 minutes. Stir in remaining ingredients, except salt, pepper, and cilantro; heat to boiling. Reduce heat and simmer, covered, 30 minutes. Discard bay leaf; season to taste with salt and pepper. Stir in cilantro.

GREEN CHILI CORN BREAD

LO

45

Corn bread, Southwest-style! If using mild canned chilies, consider adding a teaspoon or two of minced jalapeño chili for a piquant accent.

9 servings

¼ cup chopped red bell pepper

2 cloves garlic, minced

½ teaspoon cumin seeds, crushed

1¼ cups yellow cornmeal

¾ cup all-purpose flour

2 teaspoons baking powder

1 teaspoon sugar

½ teaspoon each: baking soda, salt

1¼ cups buttermilk

½ cup canned cream-style corn

1 can (4 ounces) chopped hot or mild green chilies,
    well drained

2 eggs

3½ tablespoons margarine or butter, melted

Per Serving:
Calories: 184
% of calories from fat: 29
Fat (gm): 6.1
Saturated fat (gm): 1.3
Cholesterol (mg): 24.9
Sodium (mg): 563
Protein (gm): 5.6
Carbohydrate (gm): 27.6

Exchanges:
Milk: 0.0
Vegetable: 0.0
Fruit: 0.0
Bread: 2.0
Meat: 0.0
Fat: 1.0

1. Sauté bell pepper, garlic, and cumin seeds in lightly greased small skillet until pepper is tender, 2 to 3 minutes.

2. Combine cornmeal, flour, baking powder, sugar, baking soda, and salt in large bowl. Mix in bell pepper mixture, buttermilk, and remaining ingredients; spread in greased 8-inch-square baking pan. Bake at 425 degrees until golden, about 30 minutes. Cool in pan on wire rack; serve warm.

CARAMEL FLAN

LO

45

Unbelievably delicate and fine in texture, this flan is one you'll serve over and over again.

8 servings

½ cup sugar, divided
4 cups fat-free milk
5 eggs, lightly beaten
2 teaspoons vanilla

Per Serving:
Calories: 140
% of calories from fat: 14
Fat (gm): 2.1
Saturated fat (gm): 0.7
Cholesterol (mg): 81.9
Sodium (mg): 114
Protein (gm): 8.3
Carbohydrate (gm): 21.3

Exchanges:
Milk: 0.5
Vegetable: 0.0
Fruit: 0.0
Bread: 1.0
Meat: 0.0
Fat: 0.5

1. Heat ¼ cup sugar in small skillet over medium-high heat until sugar melts and turns golden, stirring occasionally (watch carefully as the sugar can burn easily!). Quickly pour caramel into bottom of 2-quart soufflé dish, tilting to spread caramel over bottom. Cool.

2. Mix milk and remaining ¼ cup sugar in medium saucepan; heat until beginning to bubble at the edges. Whisk milk mixture gradually into eggs in bowl; stir in vanilla. Pour mixture through strainer into soufflé dish.

3. Place soufflé dish in roasting pan on middle oven rack. Cover dish with lid or foil. Pour 2 inches hot water into roasting pan. Bake at 350 degrees until sharp knife inserted halfway between center and edge of custard comes out clean, about 1 hour. Cool soufflé dish on wire rack. Refrigerate 8 hours or overnight. To unmold, loosen edge of custard with sharp knife. Place rimmed serving dish over soufflé dish and invert.

VARIATION

Orange Flan — Make recipe above, substituting ¼ cup orange juice concentrate for ¼ cup of the milk, and adding 1 egg and 1 teaspoon orange extract.

WEEKEND DINNER

Mock Chicken Legs*

Warm Rice

Sauteed Squash with Snow Peas*

Herbed Tomato Halves*

French Bread

Praline Sundaes*

* Recipes included

PREPARATION TIPS

Early in the Day: Assemble Mock Chicken Legs on skewers; refrigerate. Slice squash; clean snow peas. Make Herbed Tomato Halves, but do not bake; refrigerate.

45 Minutes Before Serving: Cook Mock Chicken Legs. Cook Squash with Snow Peas. Bake Herbed Tomato Halves. Cook rice.

At Dessert Time: Make Praline Sundaes.

MOCK CHICKEN LEGS

Looking a little like lumpy chicken legs, these kebabs are also known as City Chicken.

6 servings

1 pound pork tenderloin, fat trimmed, cubed (1-inch)
8 ounces boneless beef sirloin steak, fat trimmed, cubed (1-inch)
¼ cup all-purpose flour
Salt and pepper, to taste
Cream Gravy (see p. 131)
4½ cups cooked rice or noodles, warm

Per Serving:
Calories: 397
% of calories from fat: 20
Fat (gm): 8.7
Saturated fat (gm): 2.5
Cholesterol (mg): 66.6
Sodium (mg): 140
Protein (gm): 30.7
Carbohydrate (gm): 46.3

Exchanges:
Milk: 0.5
Vegetable: 0.0
Fruit: 0.0
Bread: 2.5
Meat: 3.0
Fat: 0.0

1. Alternate pork and beef cubes on small wooden skewers; coat with flour and let stand 15 minutes. Cook in lightly greased medium skillet over medium heat until browned on all sides, about 10 minutes. Add ½ inch water to skillet; heat to boiling. Reduce heat and simmer, covered, until meat is fork-tender, 15 to 20 minutes. Remove from skillet; sprinkle lightly with salt and pepper. Serve with Cream Gravy and rice.

SAUTÉED SUMMER SQUASH WITH SNOW PEAS

45

V

The vegetables are best when crisp-tender, so don't overcook! Zucchini or chayote squash may also be used in the recipe.

4 servings

2 each: sliced green onions, minced garlic cloves
1½ cups yellow summer squash
2 ounces snow peas
1 tablespoon finely chopped fresh or 1 teaspoon dried tarragon or basil leaves
Salt and white pepper, to taste

Per Serving:
Calories: 27
% of calories from fat: 10
Fat (gm): 0.3
Saturated fat (gm): 0.1
Cholesterol (mg): 0
Sodium (mg): 2
Protein (gm): 1.4
Carbohydrate (gm): 5.7

Exchanges:
Milk: 0.0
Vegetable: 1.0
Fruit: 0.0
Bread: 0.0
Meat: 0.0
Fat: 0.0

1. Sauté green onions and garlic in lightly greased large skillet 2 to 3 minutes. Add squash, snow peas, and tarragon and cook over medium heat

until vegetables are crisp-tender, about 5 minutes. Season to taste
with salt and pepper.

HERBED TOMATO HALVES

45

L

*Select ripe, yet firm, tomatoes, and vary the herbs to complement the main
dish you're serving.*

4 servings

4 medium tomatoes, halved

¼ cup (1 ounce) grated fat-free Parmesan cheese

1 tablespoon unseasoned dry bread crumbs

½ teaspoon each: dried basil, marjoram, and
  thyme leaves

⅛–¼ teaspoon garlic powder

2–3 pinches pepper

Per Serving:
Calories: 45
% of calories from fat: 9
Fat (gm): 0.5
Saturated fat (gm): 0.1
Cholesterol (mg): 0
Sodium (mg): 60
Protein (gm): 2.8
Carbohydrate (gm): 8.8

Exchanges:
Milk: 0.0
Vegetable: 2.0
Fruit: 0.0
Bread: 0.0
Meat: 0.0
Fat: 0.0

1. Place tomatoes, cut sides up, in baking pan;
sprinkle with combined remaining ingredients.
Bake at 375 degrees until tomatoes are hot and
topping is browned, 15 to 20 minutes.

PRALINE SUNDAES

45

L

Fresh peach slices would make a delicious addition to the sundaes, or serve with one of the cookies from this chapter.

4 servings

¼ cup packed light brown sugar

1½ teaspoons cornstarch

½ cup water

1 tablespoon bourbon or ½ teaspoon brandy extract

1 teaspoon margarine or butter

½ teaspoon vanilla

2 tablespoons chopped pecans

1 pint frozen low-fat vanilla yogurt

Per Serving:
Calories: 256
% of calories from fat: 20
Fat (gm): 5.7
Saturated fat (gm): 1.9
Cholesterol (mg): 45
Sodium (mg): 72
Protein (gm): 8.3
Carbohydrate (gm): 41.1

Exchanges:
Milk: 0.0
Vegetable: 0.0
Fruit: 0.0
Bread: 3.0
Meat: 0.0
Fat: 1.0

1. Mix sugar and cornstarch in small saucepan; stir in water. Heat to boiling over medium heat; boil, stirring, until thickened, about 1 minute. Add bourbon, margarine, vanilla and pecans, stirring until margarine is melted. Serve warm over frozen yogurt.

RISOTTO REPAST

Mushroom Bruschetta*

Italian Sausage and Broccoli Risotto*

Braised Whole Artichokes*

Italian Bread

Spiced Orange Compote with Anise-Almond Biscotti*

* Recipes included

PREPARATION TIPS

1–2 Days in Advance: Make topping for Bruschetta and refrigerate. Make Biscotti; store in airtight container.

Early in the Day: Make turkey mixture for risotto and steam broccoli; refrigerate. Make Spiced Orange Compote.

45 Minutes Before Serving: Complete risotto. Make Braised Artichokes. Assemble Bruschetta and broil.

MUSHROOM BRUSCHETTA

45

L

Use any desired wild mushrooms, such as portobello, shiitake, oyster, or enoki in this recipe.

12 servings (1 each)

½ cup chopped red bell pepper

2 each: thinly sliced green onions, minced garlic cloves

2 cups chopped wild mushrooms

1½ teaspoons dried basil leaves

2 tablespoons grated fat-free Parmesan cheese

Few drops balsamic vinegar

Salt and pepper, to taste

Bruschetta (see p. 495)

¼ cup (2 ounces) shredded reduced-fat
  mozzarella cheese

Per Serving:
Calories: 92
% of calories from fat: 17
Fat (gm): 1.7
Saturated fat (gm): 0.7
Cholesterol (mg): 2.5
Sodium (mg): 194
Protein (gm): 4.4
Carbohydrate (gm): 14.6

Exchanges:
Milk: 0.0
Vegetable: 0.5
Fruit: 0.0
Bread: 1.0
Meat: 0.5
Fat: 0.0

1. Sauté bell pepper, onions, and garlic 2 to 3 minutes in lightly greased skillet. Add mushrooms and basil and cook, covered, over medium heat until wilted, about 5 minutes. Uncover and cook until liquid is gone, 8 to 10 minutes. Stir in Parmesan cheese; season to taste with balsamic vinegar, salt, and pepper.

2. Spoon mushroom mixture on Bruschetta and sprinkle with mozzarella cheese; broil 6 inches from heat source until cheese is melted, 1 to 2 minutes.

ITALIAN SAUSAGE AND BROCCOLI RISOTTO

This risotto is enhanced with the addition of homemade Italian-style sausage, made with ground turkey and abundantly seasoned with spices and herbs.

6 entrée servings

12 ounces ground turkey

1 teaspoon each: crushed fennel seeds, dried sage and thyme leaves

½ teaspoon each: dried oregano leaves

¼ teaspoon each: ground allspice, mace, salt

1 small onion, chopped

2 cloves garlic, minced

1½ cups arborio rice

1½ quarts reduced-sodium chicken broth

2 cups broccoli florets, cooked

½ cup raisins

2 tablespoons grated Parmesan cheese

Salt and pepper, to taste

Per Serving:
Calories: 322
% of calories from fat: 16
Fat (gm): 5.6
Saturated fat (gm): 1.3
Cholesterol (mg): 21.1
Sodium (mg): 101
Protein (gm): 14.6
Carbohydrate (gm): 53.4

Exchanges:
Milk: 0.0
Vegetable: 1.0
Fruit: 0.5
Bread: 2.5
Meat: 1.0
Fat: 0.5

1. Mix ground turkey, herbs, spices, and salt; refrigerate 1 to 2 hours. Cook turkey mixture in lightly greased large saucepan until browned, crumbling with a fork; remove from pan. Add onion and garlic to saucepan; sauté until tender, about 5 minutes. Add rice; stir over medium heat 2 to 3 minutes.

2. Heat chicken broth to boiling in medium saucepan; reduce heat to low to keep broth hot. Add broth to rice mixture, ½ cup at a time, stirring until broth is absorbed before adding another ½ cup. Continue process until rice is al dente, 20 to 25 minutes; add turkey mixture, broccoli, and raisins during last 10 minutes. Stir in cheese; season to taste with salt and pepper.

BRAISED WHOLE ARTICHOKES

45

The artichokes are cooked slowly until the bottoms are browned and crusty—the resulting flavor is marvelous!

4 servings

4 medium artichokes, stems removed

Salt

2–4 teaspoons olive oil

Per Serving:
Calories: 80
% of calories from fat: 24
Fat (gm): 2.4
Saturated fat (gm): 0.3
Cholesterol (mg): 0
Sodium (mg): 114
Protein (gm): 4.2
Carbohydrate (gm): 13.4

Exchanges:
Milk: 0.0
Vegetable: 2.0
Fruit: 0.0
Bread: 0.0
Meat: 0.0
Fat: 0.5

1. Cut 1 inch from tops of artichokes and discard. Place artichokes in medium saucepan and sprinkle lightly with salt; add 1 inch water to pan. Heat to boiling; reduce heat and simmer, covered, until artichokes are tender, about 30 minutes (bottom leaves will pull out easily). Drain. Holding artichokes with a towel, brush bottoms with olive oil; return to saucepan. Cook, uncovered, over medium to medium-low heat until bottoms of artichokes are deeply browned, 10 to 15 minutes.

SPICED ORANGE COMPOTE

45

V

A perfect dessert for winter, when other fresh fruits are not available. Serve with a favorite cookie (see Index).

8 servings

5 oranges, peeled, sliced
⅓ cup orange juice
3 tablespoons packed light brown sugar
2–3 tablespoons orange-flavored liqueur (optional)
4 whole allspice
1 cinnamon stick
Mint sprigs, as garnish

Per Serving:
Calories: 72
% of calories from fat: 1
Fat (gm): 0.1
Saturated fat (gm): 0
Cholesterol (mg): 0
Sodium (mg): 2
Protein (gm): 0.8
Carbohydrate (gm): 16.8

Exchanges:
Milk: 0.0
Vegetable: 0.0
Fruit: 1.0
Bread: 0.0
Meat: 0.0
Fat: 0.0

1. Place oranges in shallow glass bowl. Heat remaining ingredients, except mint, to boiling in small saucepan; pour over orange slices. Refrigerate, covered, 8 hours or overnight for flavors to blend. Garnish with mint.

ELEGANT EVENING

Steak Diane*

Steamed New Potatoes

Mushrooms with Sour Cream*

Warm Spinach Salad*

Sourdough Bread

Raspberry-Glazed Blueberry Tart*

* Recipes included

PREPARATION TIPS

1 Day in Advance: Make and bake pie crust for the tart; store, covered, at room temperature.

Early in the Day: Assemble ingredients for the salad and mushrooms. Complete Raspberry-Glazed Blueberry Tart.

30 Minutes Before Serving: Make Mushrooms with Sour Cream. Make Steak Diane. Complete Spinach Salad. Steam potatoes.

STEAK DIANE

45

4 servings

4 beef eye of round steaks (4 ounces each), visible
   fat trimmed
Salt and pepper, to taste
⅓ cup brandy or beef broth
¼ cup fat-free sour cream
Finely chopped chives or parsley, for garnish

Per Serving:
Calories: 212
% of calories from fat: 20
Fat (gm): 4.5
Saturated fat (gm): 1.6
Cholesterol (mg): 64
Sodium (mg): 68
Protein (gm): 27.7
Carbohydrate (gm): 2.1

Exchanges:
Milk: 0.0
Vegetable: 0.0
Fruit: 0.0
Bread: 0.0
Meat: 3.5
Fat: 0.0

1. Cook steaks in lightly greased medium skillet
over medium heat to desired degree of doneness, 3 to 4 minutes on each side for medium.
Season steaks lightly with salt and pepper;
arrange on serving plates.

2. Add brandy, to skillet heat to boiling. Boil, scraping bottom of
skillet to loosen cooked particles. Boil until reduced to about 2
tablespoons, 2 to 3 minutes; stir in sour cream and cook over low
heat 1 to 2 minutes. Spoon sauce over steaks; sprinkle with chives.

MUSHROOMS WITH SOUR CREAM

*Cooking the mushrooms very slowly until deeply browned intensifies their
flavor. Also delicious served with pierogi, ravioli, or grilled eggplant slices.*

4 servings

12 ounces shiitake or cremini mushrooms, stems
   discarded, sliced
¼ cup finely chopped onion
1 teaspoon minced garlic
¼ cup dry white wine or reduced-sodium
   vegetable broth
¼ teaspoon dried thyme leaves
½ cup fat-free sour cream
Salt and cayenne pepper, to taste

Per Serving:
Calories: 80
% of calories from fat: 2
Fat (gm): 0.2
Saturated fat (gm): 0.1
Cholesterol (mg): 0
Sodium (mg): 24
Protein (gm): 3.5
Carbohydrate (gm): 16.5

Exchanges:
Milk: 0.0
Vegetable: 2.0
Fruit: 0.0
Bread: 0.5
Meat: 0.0
Fat: 0.0

1. Sauté mushrooms, onion, and garlic in lightly greased large skillet 3 to 4 minutes. Add wine and thyme; heat to boiling. Reduce heat and simmer, covered, until mushrooms are tender, 8 to 10 minutes. Cook, uncovered, on low heat until mushrooms are dry and well browned, about 20 to 25 minutes. Stir in sour cream; season to taste with salt and pepper.

WILTED SPINACH SALAD

45 *A healthful variation of this favorite salad that includes crumbled bacon for traditional flavor.*

4 servings

1 package (10 ounces) fresh spinach
4 green onions, sliced
4 slices bacon, fried crisp, well drained, crumbled
1 hard-cooked egg, chopped
1 cup fat-free French or sweet-sour salad dressing
Salt and pepper, to taste

1. Combine spinach, onions, bacon, and egg in salad bowl. Heat French dressing to boiling in small saucepan; pour over salad and toss. Season to taste with salt and pepper.

Per Serving:
Calories: 95
% of calories from fat: 26
Fat (gm): 2.6
Saturated fat (gm): 0.8
Cholesterol (mg): 38.2
Sodium (mg): 418
Protein (gm): 3.4
Carbohydrate (gm): 12.6

Exchanges:
Milk: 0.0
Vegetable: 1.0
Fruit: 0.0
Bread: 0.5
Meat: 0.0
Fat: 0.5

RASPBERRY-GLAZED BLUEBERRY TART

L *Top slices with a small scoop of frozen low-fat vanilla or lemon yogurt.*

45 8 servings

3 cups fresh blueberries

Basic Pie Crust (see p. 570), baked in a 9-inch tart pan

¾ cup raspberry spreadable fruit

1 tablespoon raspberry-flavor liqueur (optional)

2 teaspoons cornstarch

¼ teaspoon each: ground cinnamon, nutmeg

1. Arrange blueberries in baked crust. Heat combined remaining ingredients to boiling in small saucepan, stirring frequently; spoon over blueberries. Refrigerate until glaze is slightly firm, about 30 minutes.

45-MINUTE PREPARATION TIP: Make pie crust before preparing the rest of the recipe.

Per Serving:
Calories: 169
% of calories from fat: 13
Fat (gm): 2.6
Saturated fat (gm): 0.4
Cholesterol (mg): 0
Sodium (mg): 70
Protein (gm): 2
Carbohydrate (gm): 13

Exchanges:
Milk: 0.0
Vegetable: 0.0
Fruit: 1.0
Bread: 1.0
Meat: 0.0
Fat: 0.5

INDEX

mle

METRIC GUIDELINES

With the tables below and a little common sense, you'll have no trouble making these recipes using metric measuring instruments. We have rounded off the liters, milliliters, centimeters and kilos to make conversion as simple as possible.

SOME BENCHMARKS—ALL YOU REALLY NEED TO KNOW

Water boils at 212°F

Water freezes at 32°F

325°F is the oven temperature for roasting

Your 250 mL measure replaces one 8 oz cup

Your 15 mL measure replaces one tablespoon

Your 5 mL measure replaces one teaspoon

a 20 cm x 20 cm baking pan replaces a U.S. 8" x 8"

a 22.5 x 22.5 cm baking pan replaces a U.S. 9" x 9"

a 30 cm x 20 cm baking pan replaces a U.S. 12" x 8"

a 22.5 cm pie pan replaces a 9" pie pan

a 21.25 cm x 11.25 cm loaf pan replaces an 8" x 4" loaf pan

a 1.5 liter casserole, sauce pan or soufflé dish replaces a 1 1/2 qt dish

a 3 liter casserole, sauce pan or soufflé dish replaces a 3 qt dish

5 cm is about 2 inches

1 pound is a little less than 500 gm

2 pounds is a little less than 1 kg

OVEN TEMPERATURES

175°F	80°C	350°F	180°C
200°F	100°C	375°F	190°C
225°F	110°C	400°F	200°C
250°F	120°C	425°F	220°C
275°F	140°C	450°F	240°C
300°F	150°C	500°F	260°C

FAHRENHEIT TO U.K. GAS STOVE MARKS

275°F	mark 1	400°F	mark 6
300°F	mark 2	425°F	mark 7
325°F	mark 3	450°F	mark 8
350°F	mark 4	475°F	mark 9
375°F	mark 5		

VOLUME

1/4 cup	50 mL	4 cups (1 quart)	0.95 L
1/2 cup	125 mL	1.06 quarts	1 L
1/3 cup	75 mL	4 quarts (1 gallon)	3.8 L
3/4 cup	175 mL		
1 cup	250 mL	1 teaspoon	5 mL
1 1/4 cups	300 mL	1/2 teaspoon	2 mL
1 1/2 cups	375 mL	1/4 teaspoon	1 mL
2 cups	500 mL	1 tablespoon	15 mL
2 1/2 cups	625 mL	2 tablespoons	25 mL
3 cups	750 mL	3 tablespoons	50 mL

WEIGHT

1 oz	25 gm	1 pound	500 grams
2 oz	50 gm	2 pounds	1 kg
1/4 pound	125 gm (4 oz.)	5 pounds	2 1/2 kg

LENGTH

1/2 inch	1 cm
1 inch	2.5 cm
4 inches	10 cm

This material was prepared with the assistance of the Canadian Home Economics Association and the American Association of Family and Consumer Services